TROUILLOT
REMIXED

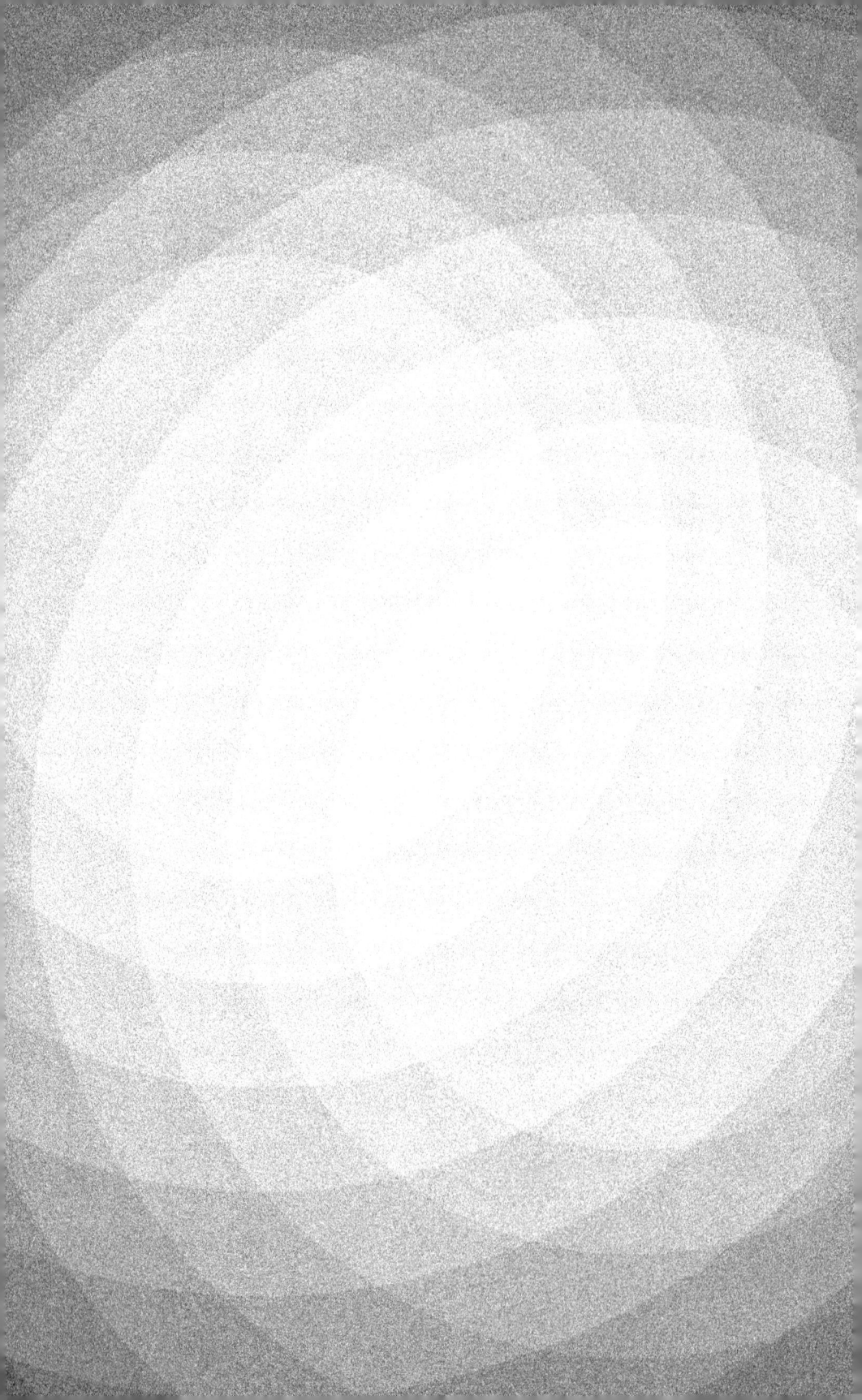

TROUILLOT
REMIXED

THE
MICHEL-ROLPH
TROUILLOT
READER

Michel-Rolph Trouillot

EDITED BY YARIMAR BONILLA, GREG BECKETT,
AND MAYANTHI L. FERNANDO

Duke University Press / Durham and London / 2021

0.1 Michel-Rolph
Trouillot at his home
in Chicago.

Designed by Matthew Tauch
Typeset in Alegreya Regular by Westchester Publishing
Services

Library of Congress Cataloging-in-Publication Data
Names: Trouillot, Michel-Rolph, [date] author. | Bonilla,
Yarimar, [date] editor. | Beckett, Greg, [date] editor. |
Fernando, Mayanthi L., [date] editor.
Title: Trouillot remixed : the Michel-Rolph Trouillot reader /
Michel-Rolph Trouillot ; edited by Yarimar Bonilla,
Greg Beckett, and Mayanthi L. Fernando.
Other titles: Michel-Rolph Trouillot reader
Description: Durham : Duke University Press, 2021. |
Includes bibliographical references and index.
Identifiers: LCCN 2021004433 (print)
LCCN 2021004434 (ebook)
ISBN 9781478013310 (hardcover)
ISBN 9781478014225 (paperback)
ISBN 9781478021537 (ebook)
Subjects: LCSH: Anthropology—Philosophy. | Ethnology—
Philosophy. | Political science—Anthropological aspects. |
Caribbean Area—History. | Caribbean Area—Politics and
government. | Caribbean Area—Civilization. | BISAC:
SOCIAL SCIENCE / Anthropology / Cultural & Social |
HISTORY / Caribbean & West Indies / General Classification:
LCC F2175.T76 2021 (print) | LCC F2175 (ebook) | DDC 972.9—
dc23
LC record available at https://lccn.loc.gov/2021004433
LC ebook record available at https://lccn.loc.gov/2021004434

Cover art: Tomm El-Saieh, *Song and Dance*, 2017–18. Acrylic
on canvas. 96 × 72 in. (243.8 × 182.9 cm). © Tomm El-Saieh;
courtesy of the artist, CENTRAL FINE, Miami Beach, and
Luhring Augustine, New York. Collection of Pilar Crespi
Robert. Photo: Armando Vaquer.

How does one acknowledge a formative presence as though it were external to oneself or somehow in the past, when that presence constitutes the very ground of one's scholarship, past, present, and future? When we were graduate students at the University of Chicago, we came into being as the scholars we are first and foremost through the guidance of Michel-Rolph Trouillot. Rolph was, as he might have said, the condition of possibility for our thinking and our work, not just in this volume but, in ways large and small, in everything we write.

The idea for this volume emerged after Rolph's death in July 2012; from the moment of his passing we have been thinking with and through this project in one way or another. The volume began to take concrete form through a conference we organized in anticipation of the twenty-fifth anniversary of *Silencing the Past* at the University of Chicago, Rolph's last institutional home. We imagined the conference as an occasion to use Rolph's most widely known text to think through his oeuvre as a whole and to consider the import of that oeuvre for anthropologists, historians, philosophers, literary critics, novelists, poets, and so on. We would like to express our deepest gratitude to François Richard, our co-organizer, for all his work to make the conference happen. Vital contributions to the conference and to the evolution of our engagement with Rolph's work were made by the conference panelists—Nadia Abu el-Haj, Gil Anidjar, Madison Smartt Bell, Herman Bennett, Vincent Brown, Hazel Carby, Colin Dayan, Marlene Daut, Marisa Fuentes, Saidiya Hartman, Walter Mignolo, Harvey Neptune, Jemima Pierre, Christina Sharpe, Deborah Thomas, and Rinaldo Walcott—and panel chairs—Hussein Agrama, Ryan Jobson, Natacha Nsabimana, and Stephan Palmié—and we thank all of them, as well as the conference audience. This volume owes a debt to the incredibly generative nature of that event. The conference website (https://silencingthepast25.wordpress.com) includes video recordings of many of the keynotes and panels. The Department of Anthropology at the University of Chicago generously funded and hosted the event; we would especially like to thank department chairs Joseph Masco and William Mazzarella for their support, as well as Kimberly

Schafer, who provided unparalleled logistical help before, during, and after the conference.

Anne-Carine Trouillot was at that conference, and she has been a generous and constant source of encouragement and support, both in this endeavor and in our lives more generally. We came to know her in graduate school long ago when she opened her home to us, and we are grateful that she has remained not only a thoughtful guardian of Rolph's intellectual legacy but also a vibrant, joyful, and caring presence in our lives. We thank her especially for granting us permission to reprint Rolph's work in this volume and for trusting us with this project.

Laura Wagner painstakingly translated and edited Rolph's interview by journalist and poet Richard Brisson from the Radio Haiti Archives at Duke University (interlude 2). We thank her for the care with which she not only translated (with detailed attention to nuance and form) but also carefully annotated the text with rich explanatory footnotes. We also want to thank her for her role as the main archivist for the Radio Haiti project and for the work she did cataloging this priceless collection and promoting its contents. It was through her efforts at dissemination that we first discovered the interview on the archive's SoundCloud page.

Various research assistants also helped bring this project into being. Marie-Pier Cantin provided invaluable assistance on the production of the manuscript and helped turn a wide range of files and formats into a single, well-formatted and proofed document. Isabel Guzzardo assisted in finalizing and formatting the bibliography, and Kimberly Roa assisted in securing permissions. We are grateful to Western University and Hunter College for providing the funding necessary for this support.

We would like to thank our editor, Elizabeth Ault, who has been in many ways our greatest champion. She was a virtual participant in the October 2018 conference and later approached us to discuss the possibility of some kind of subsequent publication. During the entire process she has provided both encouragement and sound advice about content, form, and timeline. In addition, our two anonymous readers gave us excellent suggestions for revising our introductory essay and chapter selections. Lastly, we are grateful to Lisl Hampton, project editor; to Stephanie Attia Evans for copyediting the text; to Derek Gottlieb for proofreading it; and to our colleague (and fellow Trouillot student) Lisa Outar for lovingly crafting our index.

Prelude

Remembering the Songwriter: The Life
and Legacies of Michel-Rolph Trouillot

As a young graduate student, frustrated with the "Indiana Jones" image evoked by the label "anthropologist," I once asked my adviser, Michel-Rolph Trouillot, how he defined himself. For example, if he met a stranger on a plane, would he say he was an anthropologist, a historian, a college professor, a writer, or . . . what? The question seemed relevant given Trouillot's disciplinary promiscuity: he was an anthropologist by training and by professional appointment, but he had written both academic and popular books about Haiti, a book about historiography, and (according to his own claims) kept an unfinished novel stashed away in his desk drawer. When I posed the question, he smirked, took a puff of his cigarette, and replied, "I'd tell them I'm a songwriter." He then crushed out his cigarette, smiled mischievously, and dashed away before I could say anything else, leaving me to ponder (for over a decade) what exactly he meant.

Knowing Rolph, I was sure that this was no mere joke, but given my other preoccupations at the time, I filed away the unsolved riddle in the recesses of my mind along with the many other cryptic aphorisms he offered as an adviser. It was not until the week of his passing that the memory of this playful exchange came flooding back. It happened as I came upon a Facebook post by the Haitian writer and artist Michelle Voltaire Marcelin describing her reaction to the news of Rolph's death.[1] She wrote:

> My brother Buyu Ambroise called me today to commiserate the passing
> of Haitian anthropologist, historian, and political scientist Michel-Rolph

Trouillot who died last night in Chicago. We did not know the eminent scholar who is mourned today. However we both knew Roro Trouillot, the artist, quite well. It was the early 70s. We were young with very little money. We lived in a basement and slept on the floor. The only furnishings were a white mirrored piano, a stereo, and a few hundred LP albums. . . . Most of our friends were struggling artists or musicians. . . . There was music aficionado Sansan Etienne, Joe Charles and his electric bass, Demst Emile and his guitar, Buyu Ambroise, who was skinny then with a huge afro and carried his tenor sax wherever he went[;] and there was Michel-Rolph Trouillot[,] who started Tanbou Libete [Drum of Freedom] rehearsals in that basement. Convinced that theater could be used to instigate social change and alter the course of politics, Roro as he was then affectionately called, founded Tanbou Libete with other activists based in New York in 1971. For the next few years, it would perform, often in non-traditional venues, the texts Roro wrote in Kreyòl to promote resistance. Many vocalists interpreted his songs—the most renowned being "Alyenkat" about undocumented immigrants who lived in the constant fear of harassment, detention[,] and deportation that their precarious status imposed on them. The song questioned the ethics of the USA's immigration policy and the required Alien Registration Card. Popularized by Manno Charlemagne, it became a hymn to the undocumented in Haiti and the diaspora.

Stumbling upon this anecdote about Rolph's time in Brooklyn (poignantly enough, as I began to make Brooklyn my home) brought a rush of memories of the scattered references Rolph had made about this period in his life—memories that I had never been able to string together into a coherent narrative. Much like Michelle, who said she only knew Roro, the artist, I felt like I only knew Trouillot, the scholar. I could easily call forth the memory of him laughing irreverently as he tormented his students at the University of Chicago or picture him pensively touring the ruins of Sans Souci, as he described in the pages of *Silencing the Past*. It was a bit harder, however, to imagine "Roro" the exile, activist, cab driver, and student at Brooklyn College writing Kreyòl songs and plays in Michelle's sparsely furnished basement. It seems easy to dismiss this period in his life as simply a youthful era of heady politics—much like the oft-drawn divide between the young and old Marx. Yet Trouillot himself had taught us to question those spurious divides, often arguing that one could not understand the teachings of *Capital* without a close reading of *The Eighteenth Brumaire*.

With these thoughts in mind, I tracked down the song referenced in Michelle's post and began to think about how it might fit within Trouillot's intellectual biography. Comforted by the beauty of its simple melody and charmed by its wry lyrics, I began to see past Trouillot's ruse. I realized that what I felt as I listened to the grainy recording from the 1970s was not a feeling of estrangement but of *familiarity*. For, indeed, Trouillot the scholar and Roro the songwriter were one and the same: they shared a common voice, a common set of concerns, and a driving set of, in Trouillot's words, "burning questions" to which he would return time and again in various forms and genres.[2]

In what follows, I parse various pieces by Trouillot for what they reveal about his intellectual catalog. Although I trace a somewhat chronological path through his career, my focus is on the connective threads that tie together his numerous works. For, although each of his pieces stands alone as a powerful "single," when viewed as a collection, they reveal the unique constellation of themes, approaches, and preoccupations that defined this particular songwriter's life and work.

COMMUNITIES OF INTEREST

Trouillot's intellectual genealogy is often traced back to his family roots in Haiti. As he states in *Silencing the Past*, for the Trouillot family, "history sat at the dinner table" (Trouillot 1995, xvii). History was both the preferred profession and the favored pastime of many of his relatives. His father, Ernest Trouillot, was a lawyer and professor at a prestigious lycée and also hosted a television show about Haitian history. His uncle, Henock Trouillot, was the director of the Haitian national archives in addition to being a prolific writer and public historian. All his siblings (Evelyne, Jocelyne, and Lyonel) have become important novelists, essayists, scholars, and educators who blur intellectual traditions and genres, suggesting that it was not only history that sat at the family dinner table but also literature, music, art, and politics (Danticat 2005).

This legacy alone might explain Trouillot's academic career. But his life was also profoundly marked by the personal experience of migration and exile. In 1968, Trouillot left Haiti as part of the large wave of student activists fleeing the repression of the Duvalier dictatorship. He joined his aunt in Park Slope, Brooklyn, and completed a bachelor's degree in Caribbean history and culture in 1978 at Brooklyn College, while working as a taxi

P.1 The Trouillot siblings in front of their family home in Port-au-Prince, Haiti, ca. 1958. *From left to right*: Lyonel Trouillot, Evelyne Trouillot, Michel-Rolph Trouillot, and Jocelyne Trouillot. Photograph courtesy of Evelyne Trouillot.

driver and participating in the flourishing political and cultural activism of the Haitian diaspora.

It was during this time that Trouillot, along with other activists, helped found the theater group Tanbou Libete, an outgrowth of the *kilti libete* (freedom culture) movement of the 1970s, which sought to build political consciousness among the Haitian diaspora. The *mizik angaje* (politically engaged music) produced by these groups was shuttled across state borders on inexpensive cassette tapes along with news, speeches, and calls for resistance. At the time, Duvalier had successfully co-opted numerous cultural institutions (including vodou temples, rara bands, and peasant secret societies) into his state apparatus; he had also laid claim to the figure of the *Nèg mawon*, erecting the statue of the Unknown Maroon, Le Marron Inconnu de Saint-Domingue, in front of the presidential palace. The cultural activists of the 1970s sought to give a new valorization to peasant forms and to the politics of *marronage* in order to demonstrate that, contrary to what anti-Duvalier elites might suspect, peasant traditions were not intrinsically linked to the Duvalierist project and could serve as both a site and a vehicle for political reform.

The song that Michelle Voltaire Marcelin mentioned in her post was one of the best-known pieces created by Tanbou Libete, and it was later recorded by the popular Haitian singer Manno Charlemagne on his 1984 album *Konviksyon*. The lyrics make reference to the Alien Registration Card (*alyenkat*) that Haitians were required to carry in the United States under threat of deportation and posed several provocative questions: When Christopher Columbus arrived in the Americas, did the Indigenous people ask him for his alien card? Did Sonthonax (a French civil commissioner during the Haitian Revolution) have an alien card? Were the US troops who murdered the Haitian nationalist hero Charlemagne Peralte during the US occupation *moun alyen-kat* (alien-card people)? In this text, Trouillot historicized, with his usual audacious wit, the politics of surveillance and exclusion faced by contemporary Haitian migrants by embedding these within a longer history of colonial and imperial intervention.[3]

Trouillot referred to his time among the Haitian diaspora as a kind of "apprenticeship" through which he acquired a new appreciation for the lessons acquired amid his extraordinarily learned family in Haiti:

> The Haitian exile community in New York provided a sanctuary where I combined artistic and intellectual pursuits with political activism. That apprenticeship reinforced earlier propensities: a desire to reach an audience not defined by academic membership; a conviction that an intellectual is so much more than a mere academic and the member of multiple overlapping communities. I had absorbed these beliefs growing up within the so-called intellectual elite so closely tied to the state in Haiti. Political activism in New York turned this heredity into conscious choices. (1996; interlude 4, this volume, 341)

Trouillot described this period as both a sanctuary and an apprenticeship: a space in which to develop nascent skills, convictions, and proclivities. In fact, it was from this space that in 1977, as a twenty-eight-year-old activist and undergraduate, he published the first nonfiction book ever written in Haitian Kreyòl, *Ti dife boule sou istwa Ayiti* [A small fire burning on Haitian history] (Trouillot [1977] 2012).[4] The book's title suggests an attempt at shedding new light on, and igniting new interpretations of, Haitian history.

Trouillot described *Ti dife* as a synthesis of the intellectual traditions he inherited from his family in Haiti and the cultural politics he practiced among the Haitian community in Brooklyn: "This was a natural evolution: my father and my uncle both wrote history. In a deeper sense, it was going against class origins and attitudes. *Ti dife* questions the 'great men' tradition of Haitian historiography. More important, it is also the first non-fiction book written in Haitian" (1996; interlude 4, this volume, 341).

Ti dife set the tone for what would become Trouillot's lifelong tasks: to question dominant sources and paradigms of history and the interests they serve, to produce scholarly work that self-reflectively engages with its own conditions of production, and to write in forms and venues that are accessible and compelling to various publics. The book challenged hero-driven narratives of the Haitian Revolution by exploring lesser-known figures who had been buried under the weight of historical silences. Its narrative form defies the conventions of professional history by using the structure of Haitian storytelling, with a raconteur narrator identified as Grenn Pwomennen. The bibliography contains more than fifty references, but none is cited in the text. Instead, the pages are filled with Kreyòl proverbs, wordplay, musical lyrics, and references to vodou cosmology (Past 2004).

Trouillot exhibited, even in this first book, an interest in the distinction between history and historicity, and an awareness of the weak monopoly that professional historians held over the latter. In a later essay on historiography, he wrote that "the field of Haitian historical discourse is not limited to writings explicitly and exclusively deemed historical, nor even to written texts alone. Rather, history enters into any discourse that speaks of and to the society at large. The past is often explicitly present in talk about culture, society or politics. . . . Haitian historical consciousness is also expressed through various activities not specifically constructed as narratives, from religious rituals, to art, to the naming of children" (1999, 452).

The linguistic and stylistic choices that Trouillot made in *Ti dife* evidence the careful attention he paid to questions of form and how he carefully tailored his pieces in relation to his audience. Each of his texts was produced with a particular public in mind, according to which he would carefully calibrate language, style, and "venue." It is telling that he never sought to translate *Ti dife* for non-Kreyòlophone readers. Some of his later reflections on the politics of translation hint at his concerns in this regard. In the preface to *Haiti: State against Nation*, he explained that the original French version, *Les racines historiques de l'État duvaliérien*, "drew from a common pool of images, of historical, social, and political references easily decoded by Haitian urbanites"; the book therefore required more than a mere "linguistic transcription" to become intelligible to an international audience (Trouillot 1990, 10).

Trouillot described the process of creating the English version of *Haiti: State against Nation* as an act of "cultural translation for which the shift from French to English was but a metaphor." He stressed that the original book arose from a particular conversation among a specific "community of interest," and as such it "said as much about its author as it did about its audience." In other words, Trouillot was acutely aware that all texts are produced in dialogue with multiple linguistic—but also political and intellectual—communities. Some might gloss this as simple attention to intertextuality, but for Trouillot, these relationships spanned beyond the text—hence his reference to communities of "interest" rather than simply to communities of readers. For Trouillot, the process of translation required not just linguistic skill but also the social grace of "filling in historical and cultural blanks" and creating "multiple points of entry into the discussion" (1990, 10). Only then could newly arrived interlocutors, unfamiliar with the terms, context, and *stakes* of an ongoing conversation, possibly enter the dialogue.[5]

PEASANTS AND CONCEPTS

In 1978, Trouillot left his apprenticeship in Brooklyn and entered the anthropology doctoral program at Johns Hopkins University. His choice of disciplinary home was not an obvious one. As he once reflected, had he stayed in Haiti or gone on to France, he would have likely studied philosophy or history, given his "penchant—almost esthetic—for theoretical reflection grounded in historical concreteness, regardless of discipline or persuasion" (1996; interlude 4, this volume, 341). However, when Richard Price and Sidney Mintz recruited him for their newly formed program, its "special character"—its close attention to historical process and focus on the Atlantic world as a site of global connection—"tipped the balance towards anthropology."

His doctoral dissertation, later published as *Peasants and Capital*, reflects the combination of those interests at the particular intellectual moment when Trouillot entered anthropology. *Peasants and Capital* bears the marks of the methodological experimentation of the time: the move toward multi-sited ethnography, the increased interest in global processes, the dismantling of bounded notions of culture, the concern with the role of the native voice in the text, and the search for disciplinary relevance in a world where the fictions of remote natives and "pure cultures" no longer held sway. The result is a methodologically innovative text that sought to examine the peasant economy in Dominica through the prism of world-systems theory, historical anthropology, and critical ethnography.[6]

Peasants and Capital thus not only speaks to a particular problem-space in anthropology but also reflects Trouillot's distinctive approach to Caribbean studies. Building on the work of his teacher Sidney Mintz, Trouillot consistently foregrounded how Caribbean societies troubled dominant theories of culture, modernity, globalization, and capitalism. Early on he was concerned with the provincial and prescriptive nature of these categories, which he would later describe as "North Atlantic universals" (2002b; see also chapter 5, this volume).

In *Peasants and Capital*, Trouillot deployed this method by decentering the category of "the peasant." He argued that "within the dominant historical perception of the West, the word peasant evokes a being of another age—indeed, one most typical of the Middle Ages . . . who inexplicably survived the coming of civilization" (1988, 1). He argued that in the Caribbean, however, "tradition" succeeded modernity, and what could be called a "peasant way of life" blossomed on the ruins of industrial sugar production (21). Thus, he concluded, we must question whether the word *peasant* "is anything but a descriptive category within a Euro-American folk view" (2).

For Trouillot, the implications were both analytical and political. He insisted that Caribbean peasants needed to be reimagined not as obstacles to progress but as the richest source of wealth for Caribbean societies: "Not only should we stop thinking of peasants as inherent liabilities, but we should start thinking of them as potential resources. . . . Given their proven resilience, given the fact that they have been able to support the lives and wealth of so many others, local and foreign, for so long, it is time to start developing policies that take that contribution and the potential it reveals into account" (293–94).

The lessons that Trouillot drew from *Peasants and Capital* were not confined to the borders of Dominica. He later argued that the fundamental problem of Haitian society was precisely the alienation of the peasantry, the construction of peasants as *moun andeyò* (people outside of the nation), and the expropriation of their wealth by urban elites, government institutions, and foreign interests (Trouillot 1990).

As I have argued elsewhere, Trouillot firmly believed that Caribbean studies required a regional perspective and repeatedly advocated placing Haiti within a comparative frame (Bonilla 2013b). Always attentive to the politics of "the guild," he was also concerned with the construction of minority anthropologists as "native" anthropologists, and frequently encouraged his students to study societies other than their own.[7] He likened the experience of doing comparative research to that of learning a new dance, insisting that acquiring new moves brought greater appreciation for one's own, more familiar, steps. However, Trouillot's emphasis on the value of the estranging perspective of ethnographic research should not be seen as an uncritical celebration of disciplinary traditions. For, in fact, his signature move was to turn disciplinary methods against themselves.

In *Global Transformations*, Trouillot called upon anthropologists to turn their gaze inward in order to examine their discipline as both the product and the main purveyor of what he termed "the Savage slot." He challenged anthropologists to pay greater attention to their folk concepts and carefully unpacked many of the discipline's master categories, including globalization, culture, the field, and "the native." Turning an oft-cited dictum by Clifford Geertz on its head, Trouillot described his project as an effort to examine the silences (rather than the stories) in "the history the West tells itself about itself" (2003, 1).

In his most celebrated book, *Silencing the Past*, Trouillot carried out a similar move, arguing for the need to historicize the conditions of possibility and epistemic limits of historical production. *Silencing the Past* dismantles the positivist claim to history as an objective account of "what happened" by demonstrating that the raw materials of history itself—factual evidence— are inherently conditioned by the epistemic constraints of their time. Taking the example of the Haitian Revolution, Trouillot examined how events that are unthinkable at the moment they occur become silenced and trivialized in the historical record. How then, he asked, can these events be rendered into history? In his words, "How does one write a history of the impossible?" (1995, 74; see also chapter 4, this volume).

The problem, as Trouillot saw it, was not empirical but ontological. The fact of slave resistance was widely recognized at the time, for indeed slave rebellions were both a constant threat and a feverish preoccupation for the planter class. However, although slaves were recognized as having the capacity to resist the whip, they were not imagined as having the ability—or the right—to establish their own forms of governance. Thus, even though the *fact* of the Haitian Revolution was recognized, its political implications could not be entertained because they brought into question the guiding principles of the prevailing social order. To recognize the Haitian Revolution as a modern national revolution would have required acknowledging that enslaved populations had both the capacity and the *right* to self-determination. Accepting such a principle was unthinkable.

Trouillot's argument pushes us to critically examine the narrative frames we impose upon emerging forms of struggle as well as the interpretive frames we cast in hindsight. For example, he decried the fact that scholars continued to inscribe the Haitian Revolution within the framework of the French Revolution rather than examining the novel political forms forged through its internal processes. This, he insisted, speaks to how the Haitian Revolution remains buried under the history of the West: "The silencing of the Haitian Revolution is only a chapter within a narrative of global domination. It is part of the history of the West and it is likely to persist, even in attenuated form, as long as the history of the West is not retold in ways that bring forward the perspective of the world" (1995, 107).

Trouillot (2002a) leaves us with this challenge or, in his words, this "duty." Ever critical of political naïveté, he urges us not to underestimate, or take lightly, the power embedded in the stories we tell. In fact, he presses us to recast our most well-trodden stories—particularly the master narratives that have propelled and sustained our global order. He calls upon us to take seriously our own "double-sided historicity" and become aware of our dual roles as both historical actors and historical narrators. This is what Trouillot means when he asks us to examine the "conditions of possibility" of our own intellectual production. He does not expect us to step out of our time and place (to stand outside of history, so to speak), but he dares us to think critically about how our own biographies inform the questions we ask and the answers we find comfort in. In other words, he encourages us to come to terms with our own "burning questions," to develop our own authorial voice, and to be mindful of the various publics to which we sing and write.

It is for this reason that I have come to terms with Trouillot's playful riddle and have chosen to remember him as a songwriter. Not because it encapsulates everything he was, for indeed nothing can, but rather because in his songwriting we can see how the different elements that defined him came together into a powerful sum. After all, few others could so artfully combine a strident critique of US anti-immigration practices with a

P.2 Michel-Rolph Trouillot at a party with graduate students from the University of Chicago, ca. 2001. *From left to right*: Mayanthi L. Fernando, Michel-Rolph Trouillot, and Yarimar Bonilla.

charming melody, an incisive Haitian proverb, and a well-timed joke about Christopher Columbus. In his song, we can clearly distinguish the guiding principles that defined his life and work: the attention to history, the concern with the political stakes of the present, the commitment to both home and the world, and the belief that scholarship, art, and politics are all best carried out with a touch of humor, an eye for beauty, and a catchy beat.

NOTES

I would like to thank Michelle Voltaire Marcelin and Buyu Ambroise for generously sharing their recollections of "Roro." I am also grateful to Gustav Michaux-Vignes from La Mediatheque Caraibe in Guadeloupe for his kind assistance in helping me locate a recorded version of "Alyenkat."

Editors' Note: This essay was originally published in *Cultural Dynamics* for a special issue on Michel-Rolph Trouillot; see Yarimar Bonilla, "Remembering the Songwriter: The Life and Legacies of Michel-Rolph Trouillot," *Cultural Dynamics* 26, no. 2 (2014): 163–72. The essay has been lightly edited for this collection.

1. Michele Voltaire Marcelin, Facebook, July 6, 2012, https://www.facebook.com/photo.php?fbid=10151005937804501&set=a.41634809500.

2. For more on Trouillot's "voice," see Scott 2012. For more on the importance of Trouillot's "burning questions," see Bonilla 2013a.

3. *Editors' Note:* For full song lyrics and context, see Tanbou Libète 2020.

4. *Editors' Note:* Trouillot's first book was originally published as *Ti difé boulé sou istoua Ayiti* (see Trouillot 1977), before Haitian Kreyòl orthography was standardized. It was republished in 2012 with a title that reflects standard modern Kreyòl orthography. We use the standardized form of the title throughout this volume.

5. It appears that Trouillot's careful attention to translation centered mostly on the languages in which he was fluent, and the communities of interest to which he belonged. He authorized several translations of his works into Spanish and German, entrusting the translators with the burden of properly introducing his texts to their linguistic communities. Translations to and from French and English were, however, more carefully attended to. Indeed, this is one of the reasons why the French translation of *Silencing the Past* is yet to be completed.

6. *Editors' Note:* For more on the methodological contributions of this text, see the overture to this volume.

7. *Editors' Note:* For more on Trouillot's relationship to "native anthropology," see the overture to this volume.

REFERENCES

Agard-Jones, Vanessa. 2013. "Bodies in the System." *Small Axe: A Caribbean Journal of Criticism* 17, no. 3 (42): 182–92.

Averill, G. 1997. *A Day for the Hunter, a Day for the Prey: Popular Music and Power in Haiti.* Chicago: University of Chicago Press.

Bonilla, Yarimar. 2013a. "Burning Questions: The Life and Work of Michel-Rolph Trouillot, 1949–2012." NACLA *Report on the Americas* 46, no. 1: 82–84.

Bonilla, Yarimar. 2013b. "Ordinary Sovereignty." *Small Axe: A Caribbean Journal of Criticism* 17, no. 3 (42): 152–65.

Bonilla, Yarimar. 2014. "Remembering the Songwriter: The Life and Legacies of Michel-Rolph Trouillot." *Cultural Dynamics* 26, no. 2: 163–72.

Danticat, Edwidge. 2005. "Evelyne Trouillot." *Bomb* 90. http://bombsite.com /issues/90/articles/2708.

Past, Mariana. 2004. "Toussaint on Trial in *Ti difé boulé sou istoua Ayiti*, or the People's Role in the Haitian Revolution." *Journal of Haitian Studies* 10, no. 11: 87–102.

Scott, David. 2012. "The Futures of Michel-Rolph Trouillot: In Memoriam." *Small Axe: A Caribbean Journal of Criticism* 16, no. 3 (39): vii–x.

Tanbou Libeté. "Immigration." In *The Haiti Reader: History, Culture, Politics*, edited by Laurent Dubois, Kaiama Glover, Nadève Ménard, Millery Polyné, and Chantalle F. Verna, 384–85. Durham, NC: Duke University Press.

Trouillot, Michel-Rolph. 1977. *Ti difé boulé sou istoua Ayiti*. Brooklyn, NY: Koleksion Lakensiel.

Trouillot, Michel-Rolph. 1988. *Peasants and Capital: Dominica in the World Economy*. Baltimore, MD: Johns Hopkins University Press.

Trouillot, Michel-Rolph. 1990. *Haiti: State against Nation; The Origins and Legacy of Duvalierism*. New York: Monthly Review Press.

Trouillot, Michel-Rolph. 1995. *Silencing the Past: Power and the Production of History*. Boston: Beacon Press.

Trouillot, Michel-Rolph. 1996. "Theorizing a Global Perspective: A Conversation with Michel-Rolph Trouillot." *Cross Currents: Newsletter of the Institute for Global Studies in Culture, Power, and History* 4, no. 1.

Trouillot, Michel-Rolph. 1999. "Historiography of Haiti." In *General History of the Caribbean*. Vol. 6, *Methodology and Historiography of the Caribbean*, edited by Barry W. Higman, 451–77. London: UNESCO.

Trouillot, Michel-Rolph. 2002a. "Adieu, Culture: A New Duty Arises." In *Anthropology beyond Culture*, edited by Richard G. Fox and Barbara J. King, 37–60. Wenner-Gren International Symposium Series. Oxford: Berg.

Trouillot, Michel-Rolph. 2002b. "North Atlantic Universals: Analytical Fictions, 1492–1945." *South Atlantic Quarterly* 101, no. 4: 839–58.

Trouillot, Michel-Rolph. 2003. *Global Transformations: Anthropology and the Modern World*. New York: Palgrave Macmillan.

Trouillot, Michel-Rolph. (1977) 2012. *Ti dife boule sou istwa Ayiti*. Edited by Lyonel Trouillot. Port-au-Prince: Edisyon KIK, Inivèsite Karayib.

YARIMAR BONILLA, GREG BECKETT,
AND MAYANTHI L. FERNANDO

Overture

Trouillot Remixed

If Michel-Rolph Trouillot preferred to identify himself as a musician and songwriter rather than an academic, as Yarimar Bonilla describes in the prelude to this volume, then this volume is a mixtape of sorts, and we its DJs. The three of us have been thinking with Trouillot and his oeuvre for over two decades; he was our teacher and mentor, and his work a touchstone for our own. That work—despite the variety of topics, languages, methods, and fields of engagement through which Trouillot moved—demonstrates a consistency of themes and preoccupations. Although perhaps best known for his attention to the production of history and the historicization of anthropology, Trouillot's contributions spanned far beyond the two disciplines with which he engaged explicitly or was located in institutionally, and his work continues to resonate in fields like postcolonial studies, Black studies, ethnic studies, and literature.

Indeed, while his thinking and writing continually evolved over the course of his life, there are a series of threads that weave across Trouillot's entire scholarly catalog with remarkable consistency of argument and voice.[1] We have therefore chosen to organize this volume not by periods, but by those thematic threads, cutting together early-, mid-, and late-career work in order to make this mixtape. We included a few classic hits—such as "Anthropology and the Savage Slot" and selections from *Silencing the Past*—as well as a number of lesser-read essays, or deep cuts. Some of the latter are from out-of-print publications, such as "The Odd and the Ordinary: Haiti, the Caribbean, and the World," which has long been passed around as a faded photocopy among colleagues and friends, like a treasured but impossible-to-find B side.

More than a mere compilation, however, this volume is best understood as a *remix*, in the sense that it features new arrangements and pairings that might allow the reader to engage with Trouillot's work in new or unexpected ways. We have chosen to publish some of his best-known pieces in earlier "demo" versions that reveal the progression of his thought. "From Planters' Journals to Academia: The Haitian Revolution as Unthinkable History," for example, is the first published version of the intellectual kernel at the heart of *Silencing the Past*, and "Anthropology and the Savage Slot" is the version from the edited volume *Recapturing Anthropology* (Fox 1991), where it first appeared. We have also sought to demonstrate Trouillot's early academic influences, in order to hear him sample from other scholars' jams, so to speak. In "Caribbean Peasantries and World Capitalism: An Approach to Micro-level Studies," for instance, we see how he was building on—while already beginning to depart from—the intellectual traditions of his mentors, Sidney Mintz and Eric Wolf. Other selections, such as "The Vulgarity of Power," which originally appeared as a response to an article by Achille Mbembe, allows us to see the way in which Trouillot engaged critically with scholars emerging out of other traditions, such as Black and postcolonial studies.

Each section of this volume opens with an interlude in which Trouillot speaks to us in a different voice (our nod to Trouillot's own use of different voices in *Silencing the Past*). The second interlude, for instance, is a 1977 radio interview (translated from Kreyòl and annotated by Laura Wagner) between Trouillot, who at the time had just begun his graduate studies in anthropology, and the radio journalist and poet Richard Brisson. In that interview, Trouillot explains how his family history, his activist commitments in the Haitian diaspora, and his graduate training in anthropology all shaped the intellectual project of his first book, *Ti dife boule sou istwa Ayiti*—the first monograph of Haitian history published entirely in Kreyòl (Trouillot [1977] 2012).[2] The other three interludes are various "Director's Word" segments written by Trouillot between 1993 and 1997 for the quarterly newsletter of the Johns Hopkins Institute for Global Studies in Culture, Power, and History, which he directed during that time. These reflections—more akin to blog posts than academic articles—offer insight into how Trouillot imagined the institutional location of his work, particularly the importance he gave to area studies as a site of interdisciplinarity and as one of the few spaces in which disciplines like political science and economics were forced to question their conceptual and methodological arsenals in order to address the experiences of the non-West in ways that might "unsettle" sociocultural theory.

By remixing these essays, chapters, interviews, and reflections from the long arc of Trouillot's career, we hope not only to provide readers with a sense of what he described as "his burning questions" (Bonilla 2013), but also to open new avenues for thinking both about and with Trouillot. Our aim in this introductory essay is thus to offer an opening—an *overture*—onto the key themes around which we have organized the book's tracks: the relationship between what Trouillot called the West's geography of imagination and its geography of management; the ways in which the Caribbean unsettles disciplinary traditions; the need to reimagine and transform the fields in which we work; and how to envision and embrace the new ethical and political duties before us, in scholarship and beyond.

THE GEOGRAPHY OF IMAGINATION AND
THE GEOGRAPHY OF MANAGEMENT

> The place we most often call the West is best called the North Atlantic—not only for the sake of geographical precision but also because such usage frees us to emphasize that "the West" is always a fiction, an exercise in global legitimation.
>
> MICHEL-ROLPH TROUILLOT, introduction, *Global Transformations*

This volume begins with what is perhaps Trouillot's most read—and misread—essay, "Anthropology and the Savage Slot: The Poetics and Politics of Otherness" (chapter 1).[3] Simultaneously published under the alternative title "Anthropology as Metaphor: The Savage's Legacy and the Postmodern World" (Trouillot 1991), the text critiques the "crisis of representation" within the discipline (this volume, chapter 1, 57) as it began to reckon with its role as "the handmaiden of colonialism" (Gough 1968). In the postwar era, domestic and international movements for decolonization, the rise of women-of-color feminism, and Black Power movements had begun to force transformations in academic thinking across the humanities and social sciences (e.g., Said 1979; Asad 1973; Deloria 1969; Césaire 1972). As marginalized populations entered the halls of academe, the empire was suddenly "writing back" (Ashcroft, Griffiths, and Tiffin 2003), pushing against the foundational Eurocentrism of much disciplinary thinking. This moment of reckoning was perhaps felt most acutely in anthropology, as critics within and outside the discipline began to wonder whether decolonization would mean that "the science of the savages" would disappear altogether (Macquet 1964).[4]

By the 1970s, then, anthropologists were beginning to grapple with the weight of history in the places in which they worked, unable to ignore the effects of colonialism, imperialism, and globalization on communities around the world. Early attempts at a critical appraisal focused on anthropology's structural role in the colonial encounter (Asad 1973; Hymes 1974); by the 1980s, American cultural anthropology had turned to a more inward-focused critique. That turn is now often referred to as the *Writing Culture* moment, named after an eponymous essay collection that prompted a new concern for power and representation within the discipline. *Writing Culture*'s editors framed their critique as an investigation into the "poetics and politics of ethnography," where ethnography meant not research method (i.e., fieldwork) but rather the practice of writing about another culture (Clifford and Marcus 1986). This turn to textuality was intended as a "tectonic shift" in the way anthropologists would represent others (Clifford 1986, 22).

For Trouillot, however, the turn to poetics represented a turn away from the larger field of significance in which anthropology came to study "others" in the first place, and he saw this as both a turn away from structure and (therefore) a turn away from power. Much, of course, depends here on one's definition of power. Those inspired by *Writing Culture* embraced a long-standing tradition in American cultural anthropology that defined the discipline in terms of its capacity for interpretation and cross-cultural translation, although they also self-consciously saw themselves as critiquing the discursive power inherent in modes of representation and genres of writing. For Trouillot, such critiques inadequately attended to material social processes and were thus unable to fully theorize the conditions of possibility of the discipline itself. He argued that the focus on textuality and the autocritique of ethnography treated anthropology as a closed discourse, analytically separable from the world in which it operates. By contrast, Trouillot insisted that the discipline is historically tied to broader Western modes of thinking about otherness, and that "the primary focus on the textual construction of the Other *in* anthropology may turn our attention away from the construction of Otherness upon which anthropology is premised" (this volume, chapter 1, 65). These foundational modes of thought about the West's others, he contended, allowed for and were reproduced by Western forms of political and economic expansion and conquest. European colonialism and the transatlantic slave system provided, then, not only a set of material relationships by which the West and its others were entwined, but also a space of experience in which the concepts and values of all who lived in this world were constituted.

There are two important points to underscore in Trouillot's argument thus far: first, that the self-conception of the West was never sui generis but was instead irreducibly tied to alterity—that is, to a specific relation to otherness in and around which the West continues to think of itself (see also Trouillot 2002a, 2002b, 2003);[5] and second, that anthropology "came to fill the Savage slot of a larger thematic field, performing a role" earlier played by travelogues and literature (this volume, chapter 1, 65). If anthropology emerged in the nineteenth century as the specialized study of the West's others, then the West's self-conception and the particular discursive formations and epistemological foundations that ground it constitute the discipline's conditions of possibility. Any critique of anthropology—including its modes of representation—therefore requires adequately theorizing the relationship between anthropology and what Trouillot called the West's *geography of imagination*, or the concepts and symbols used to think about others, and its *geography of management*, the material relations of domination and subjugation of others by the West. As he argued, "to historicize the West is to historicize anthropology and vice versa" (this volume, chapter 1, 70).

For Trouillot, this meant attending to the dialectical relationship between the West as knowing subject and the Other as object of knowledge, a dialectical relationship that produced both the Savage (as metaphor) and Savage slot (as anthropology). In this relationship, the Savage came to serve as evidence, positive or negative, in a Western debate about universal humanity, reason, and the basis of moral and political order. At times noble, at other times barbarous, the Savage operates—and continues to operate—as a metaphor in arguments within the West about what the latter is and what it could be.[6] The emergence of the Savage as metaphor was accompanied by what Trouillot called the Savage slot, that is, the site of knowledge-production about the Savage that served—and continues to serve—as the evidentiary basis for an argument within the West about itself (via its others). Trouillot stressed the particular nature of the Savage slot, which renders all differences in similar terms; that is, otherness is always determined in relation to the unmarked category of the West. It is through the Savage slot and this particular configuration of alterity that the West made itself as a universal subject, a subject that realized itself precisely through its ability to treat non-Western others as objects of knowledge in the pursuit of order, reason, and universal humanity.

Some have read the Savage not as metaphor but as referring to a real demographic and have therefore misread Trouillot's critique as a simple call for anthropologists to move away from the study of non-Western peoples (e.g., Robbins 2013).[7] Yet, in later essays, Trouillot argued that even as anthropology started to abandon its traditional object of study and to recalibrate its modes of representation, an untheorized and unmarked West would remain and, indeed, be reinforced through the rise of new universals. For example, in "Abortive Rituals: Historical Apologies in the Global Era" (chapter 15), he demonstrated how the rise of collective apologies and recognition schemes rely on the concept of the "international community," which he diagnosed as an emerging North Atlantic universal.[8]

For Trouillot, then, breaking with the Savage slot required not just moving away from the representation of non-Western peoples as savages, but also undertaking what Harvey Neptune describes as "savaging" the West. This entails turning the well-honed methods of the discipline toward the grounds of its own formation. As Neptune argues, Trouillot was riffing on Clifford Geertz's seminal definition of culture by urging scholars to interrogate the tales the West "tells itself about itself" (Neptune 2014, 222). This requires, for starters, interrogating how a particular place with a particular history—the North Atlantic, or even more precisely, the United States and Western Europe—came to constitute itself as a universal and ahistorical subject: the West. Thus, in "Good Day, Columbus: Silences, Power, and Public History (1492–1892)" (chapter 4), Trouillot mapped the historical commemorations—the myths and rituals—through which the North Atlantic came to understand itself as the West, and he underscored the centrality of "The Discovery" to that imagination. He also attended to how the United States—which could have been considered part of the postcolonial world—instead came to refashion itself as part of the West (as a project, not a place).[9]

It is worth noting that for Trouillot, anthropology played a critical role in this historicization of the West for two reasons: first, because the discipline has been key to the emergence, solidification, and reproduction of the Savage slot; and second, because anthropology, more than any other discipline in the social sciences, is best equipped to grapple with the question of alterity, to turn its methods against itself and engage in the work of critique. We might say that anthropology was for Trouillot what political economy had been for Marx: a disciplinary location for an immanent critique of his real object of study, namely, the West.

However, Trouillot did not see this as a task limited to anthropology, since he saw the Savage slot as part of a larger constellation of knowledge-production through which the West understands and projects itself.[10] Disciplines like political science, economics, sociology, philosophy, literature, history, and art continue to take the West as their default subject and object—that is, they continue to operate as sites for knowing "ourselves" and "our" societies in ways that keep the West unmarked as such (while marking the non-West through subcategories like "comparative politics" and "world literature"). This particular-qua-universal ontological order determines who constitutes a people with and without history, what counts as a Great Book, what defines an artistic masterpiece, what is an empire (or a failed state), what represents rational (or aberrant) behavior, what science is and is not, and what constitutes the difference between theory and ideology.

Throughout his career, Trouillot was concerned with how the experiences of the non-West are consistently pathologized, trivialized, or simply silenced when they challenge the ontological order on which academic disciplines were founded. In *Silencing the Past*, he showed how this ontological order rendered the Haitian Revolution "unthinkable." In "The Odd and the Ordinary" (chapter 2), he examined how claims to Haitian exceptionalism—"the poorest country in the Western hemisphere" and a "chronically failed state"—mask the global processes and historical actors that have produced Haiti's material conditions. For these reasons, as demonstrated in "The Vulgarity of Power" (chapter 3), he was equally concerned with claims to African exceptionalism even when they were deployed by postcolonial scholars like Achille Mbembe.

For Trouillot, it is precisely through the creation of the aberrant, the undemocratic, the illiberal, the nonsovereign, and the nonmodern that the West constitutes itself. At the same time, his work consistently destabilized these sedimented categories by underscoring how attending to sociohistorical processes in both Haiti and the Caribbean as a whole challenged the epistemic structures of European thought. In "The Otherwise Modern: Caribbean Lessons from the Savage Slot" (chapter 5), for instance, he examined both how the North Atlantic took shape through the construction of a nonmodern, nonsovereign Other and how the Caribbean simultaneously unmasked modernity's conceits. Rather than seeing Haiti and the Caribbean as either odd or exceptional, then, he showed how both were central to the construction of the West, and therefore pivotal to unsettling its geography of imagination.

> The point is not to insist that the Antilles or other regions of the world
> were as modern as Europe in the eighteenth and nineteenth centuries—
> though a legitimate argument can be made along those lines. . . .
> Rather, if my sketchy narrative about the Caribbean holds true, it sug-
> gests much less the need to rewrite Caribbean history than the neces-
> sity to question the story that the North Atlantic tells about itself.
>
> MICHEL-ROLPH TROUILLOT, "The Otherwise Modern: Caribbean
> Lessons from the Savage Slot"

For Trouillot, then, Haiti, but also the broader Caribbean, were central
points of departure from which to theorize the West. This was because
the Caribbean, more than any other place in the world, has been distinctly
shaped by its long relationship with the West. The region is home to the
oldest and longest-held overseas colonies of Europe. It is, as Sidney Mintz
(2010) put it, "anciently colonial." And, even though the historical importance of the region has often been silenced, we might even say that the West
was born in the Caribbean (Trouillot 1992, 2003).[11]

Scholars of the Caribbean have detailed how institutions and social
forms there predate their modern European equivalents, and how the
transatlantic slave trade and the Caribbean plantation system provided a
crucial economic and caloric boost that helped bolster the early phases of
industrial capitalism (Mintz 1985; Scott 2004). The relationship between
slavery and capitalism, between industrial production and the plantation
system, and between European wealth and Atlantic modes of labor extraction all constitute the West's geography of management. Indeed, the relations of production, disciplinary techniques, modes of consumption, and
forms of self-fashioning that became central to the definition of Western
modernity first emerged in the Caribbean, often before they were evident
in Europe itself (see chapters 5, 6, and 7). But, as Trouillot contended in "The
Otherwise Modern," the Caribbean reveals something more than a curious chronology in which Europe's so-called savage others embody modern
forms of being avant la lettre (chapter 5). As he argued over the course of
his scholarship, the historical experience of the Caribbean is, above all, an
encounter with the first truly planetary project. The geographies of imagination and management through which European contact, conquest, and
colonization took shape explicitly framed the region as a *mundus novus*—a

new and unknown world that became the dominion of Latin Christendom as the latter morphed into the West (this volume, chapter 1, 59).

Europeans imagined this New World as an Elsewhere they could control, a place that they could make in their own image. The so-called Columbian Exchange ushered in a global shift in plant and animal species and set the stage for one of the world's largest demographic transitions in the form of the transatlantic slave system (Crosby 1972).[12] As an Elsewhere for Europe, the New World was imagined as both a utopia full of noble savages to be converted and a dangerous place full of barbarians to be conquered. The West's geography of imagination was thus premised on and reproduced a dual structure of Us and Them, Here and Elsewhere, framing Europe's others within the terms of the Savage slot, and this new imaginary gave shape to concrete forms of control and management. But the very structure of the Savage slot produced the conditions of its undoing or, at the very least, a radical interruption of its terms. The symbolic schema of the Savage slot could never fully capture its object, leaving open a gap between *what was happening* throughout the centuries of Western conquest and colonization and *what was said to have happened* by those endowed with the power to write history—and to write others out of history (see chapter 12; see also Trouillot 1995; Wolf 1982).

That gap is perhaps starkest in the historical formation of Caribbean societies, and this fact—the gap between what happened and what was said to have happened—provided the epistemological anchor for much of Trouillot's work, from "Anthropology and the Savage Slot" to *Silencing the Past*. Moreover, that gap and the possibility of attending to the actors actively silenced by power—for instance, to Haitian slaves who created a revolution, a kingdom, and a democracy, and to Dominican peasants who upend the terms of global capitalism—underpinned Trouillot's ultimate commitment to anthropology, since its disciplinary investment in attending to the small and the marginalized peoples of the non-West enabled these stories to come to the fore (see chapters 7, 10, 12, and 16). Thus, in "Culture on the Edges: Creolization in the Plantation Context," Trouillot pushed back against linguists' conventional attitude toward creolization as a "miracle," arguing that the study of creolization in the Caribbean could serve as a site for re-theorizing how we understand cultural change, broadly speaking (chapter 7). This line of argument continued a critique he had begun in some of this earliest work. For example, in "Motion in the System: Coffee, Color, and Slavery in Eighteenth-Century Saint-Domingue," an essay in which he was clearly thinking with his mentors Sidney Mintz and Eric Wolf as well as with world-systems theorists like Fernand Braudel and Eric Williams, Trouillot contended that colonial peripheries played a greater *conceptual* role in the constitution of imperial centers than previously imagined (Trouillot 1982; see also chapters 7 and 8).

It took anthropology a long time to recognize the Caribbean as a suitable location for study, and the role of the Caribbean as an "open frontier" for anthropology has always been a curious one (chapter 6).[13] As Trouillot showed repeatedly, the Caribbean was central to the construction of the Savage slot and to the development of European conceptions of alterity. It is no accident, then, that the region should be both historically central to the construction of the West's geography of imagination and conceptually difficult to interpret using the terms and the symbolic schema of that imagination.

For anthropology, this was largely because Caribbean societies were *too* historical. That is, as Trouillot argued in "The Otherwise Modern," they could not be understood outside of and apart from the historical processes that produced them, and as such they could not be reconciled with the early mode of ethnographic research and writing in which other societies were encoded in synchronic terms, as if they were isolated wholes with no history (chapter 5; see also Wolf 1982). Concomitantly, in "The Caribbean Region: An Open Frontier in Anthropological Theory," Trouillot argued that this fiction of synchronicity, integral to both American and European anthropology, could never be fully supported in Caribbean societies, which were populated by non-European others whose difference was known to be due to a specific history of European colonization and slavery (chapter 6). In other words, Caribbean societies were not only "anciently colonial" (Mintz 2010) but also "*inherently* colonial," since their basic characteristics and features "cannot be accounted for, or even described, without reference to colonialism," and therefore to the West (this volume, chapter 6, 163–64). And this, in turn, meant that, by the very fact of their existence, Caribbean societies "questioned the West/non-West dichotomy and the category of the native, upon both of which anthropology was premised" (this volume, chapter 6, 162).

Anthropology from a Caribbean point of view was thus, for Trouillot, always something more than an anthropology of the Caribbean; any anthropological account of Caribbean peoples would also have to become an anthropology of the West, because there was simply no way to adequately understand the Caribbean without acknowledging the historical facts of colonialism, slavery, and racism, all of which were foundational to Western projects of conquest and control. Yet, as Trouillot emphasized repeatedly, the converse was also true: there is no way to understand the West without fully engaging with its foundational others, foremost among them, the peoples of the Caribbean.

The region held another important lesson for anthropology. As we just noted, the Caribbean was fundamental to the production of the Savage slot yet resistant to assimilation within its symbolic schema given the region's "inescapable historicity" (this volume, chapter 6).[14] Reckoning with this fact required anthropologists to rethink their discipline-defining concept of culture. The history of the Caribbean showed that culture, like history, is *made* and, importantly, made by sociomaterial processes, by people acting in the world. Indeed, for Trouillot, Caribbean societies offered the best examples of humans making their own history, although not under circumstances of their choosing. Out of some of the harshest conditions ever conceived, these humans created new cultural forms and new social relations, from creole languages to new religions, from peasant horticultural practices to modes of warfare (chapters 6 and 7, this volume; see also Mintz and Price 1992). Caribbean societies have thereby consistently challenged the dominant Euro-American model of history imagined as a more or less predictable, linear progression, as well as the dominant model of difference imagined in terms of race. In *Global Transformations*, Trouillot put it this way:

> Modern historicity hinges upon both a fundamental rupture between past, present, and future—as distinct temporal planes—and their relinking along a singular line that allows for continuity. I have argued that this regime of historicity in turn implies a heterology, a necessary reading of alterity. Striking then is the fact that Caribbean history as we know it starts with an abrupt rupture between past and present—for Europeans, for Native Americans, and for enslaved Africans. In no way could the enforced modernization imposed by colonization be perceived by any of these actors as a mere continuation of an immediate past. This was a New World for all involved, even for those who had lived within it before it became new to others. (2003, 44)

This relationship between historicity and alterity does not define only Caribbean societies, of course, but that is not Trouillot's point. Nor is his point a claim to the chronological primacy of modernity in the Caribbean.

To insist that features of modernization or globalization emerge first in the Caribbean is to remain trapped within the terms of a discourse about the West. From that perspective, the Caribbean is little more than a footnote to a story about the West, a story in which the West remains the subject in whose terms and against whose likeness the Caribbean—and other societies—are to be known and judged. Rather, for Trouillot, the view from the Caribbean provides important lessons not about who was modern first, but rather about the conditions of possibility of such a statement. For what the Caribbean perspective reveals is the dialectical relationship between domination and creolization and between the West and its imagined others (see chapters 1, 2, 5, 6, and 7, this volume). The Savage slot conceals this double dialectic by both silencing the history of Western power and naturalizing Western ideas of difference. How, then, might we undo that concealment?

THE FIELDS IN WHICH WE WORK: CONCEPTS, CATEGORIES, AND METHOD

> There is no stateness to states, no essence to culture, not even a fixed content to specific cultures, let alone a fixed content to the West. We gain greater knowledge of the nation, the state, the tribe, modernity, or globalization itself when we approach them as sets of relations and processes rather than ahistorical essences.
>
> MICHEL-ROLPH TROUILLOT, introduction, *Global Transformations*

The relationships between historicity and alterity and between the geography of imagination and the geography of management are themselves historical. For Trouillot, then, the question of culture—that is, of the culture concept and also of the cultural processes of making worlds—was necessarily historical, and always in a double sense. This is so because, as Trouillot argued in *Silencing the Past*, history is both a social and material process of making the world and a narrative account that people give, retrospectively, to explain what happened.

Trouillot insisted that the production of history was conditioned not only by what was "thinkable" in the past but also by what is meaningful in the present. "The Presence in the Past" (chapter 14) begins by narrating his visit to Chichén Itzá, a Mayan city in the Yucatán (now classified as a UNESCO World Heritage site). Trouillot wrote that during his visit there, he felt no connection to the past because he did not meet anyone to whom that past mattered. As he explained: "History did not need to be mine in order to engage me. It just needed to relate to someone, anyone. It could not just be The Past. It had to be someone's past" (this volume, chapter 14, 375). Trouillot argued that what endowed something with retrospective significance had less to do with the magnitude of the event at the time than with the context of its recollection: "The crux of the matter is the here and now, the relations between the events described and their public representation in a specific historical context" (this volume, chapter 14, 379).

Thus, in "Good Day, Columbus" (chapter 4), he examined how "The Discovery" of the Americas becomes a historical "fact" and "Columbus Day" a historical artifact through the efforts of actors ranging from politicians to travel agents, who endow the event with meaning for various ends. By contrast, in "The Presence in the Past," Trouillot examined how plans for a Disney theme park devoted to the history of slavery was destined for failure, not because Disney engineers would have lacked the resources to produce historical accuracy, but because the project would have been inherently inauthentic in its attempt to create a detached distance between the slave past and the present of contemporary park-goers. As he argued, "historical authenticity resides not in the fidelity to an alleged past but in an honesty vis-á-vis the present as it re-presents that past" (this volume, chapter 14, 379). He suggested that historical representations succeed or fail based not solely on their fidelity to the historical record, but on their fidelity to the present, that is, on their ability to show the connective tissue between then and now.

These lessons about history and its telling were ones Trouillot came to through direct experience. He repeatedly observed the way Haitian elites and politicians laid claim to public history to legitimize their rule (see Trouillot 1995, 1999). Trouillot demonstrated how the production of history exceeds the purview of professional historians, dwelling as much in government propaganda as in folk art, religious rites, and naming practices (Trouillot 1999). History is not the sole property of historians, but neither is it the sole property of the state. This is why Trouillot's anthropological work was always historical: it was always infused with an attention to the ways contemporary actors narrate and make use of their past. But, in turn, his historical work was always anthropological, in that he historicized not just events or narratives but also the cultural categories through which they were thought and understood.

This process was the subject of his most famous book, *Silencing the Past*, but the method by which his critique proceeded is perhaps easier to see in his earlier work, especially *Peasants and Capital*, a dense and complex monograph whose argument unfolds over several sections and across multiple "scales" or units of analysis. Rather than pulling a chapter from *Peasants and Capital* for this volume, then, we have included "Caribbean Peasantries and World Capitalism" (chapter 10), a standalone article that condenses and encapsulates the overall project of the book.

Peasants and Capital remains an underappreciated part of Trouillot's oeuvre. It is easy to read as an early and therefore still underdeveloped work, a revised dissertation, or the product of its time and of the debates within anthropology during the 1980s. It may even seem too indebted to Trouillot's graduate adviser, Sidney Mintz. The book is certainly situated within two broad fields that Mintz helped found, namely peasant studies and Marxian anthropology, and it shares with Mintz's work a commitment to a distinctively Caribbean approach to anthropology and history that foregrounds how Caribbean societies unsettle dominant theories about capitalism, culture, globalization, and modernity. In his analysis, Trouillot used historical and ethnographic research in Dominica to map out a story of global reach, showing how Caribbean cultivators are tied to markets that span several continents, and how the work of growing bananas on a small Caribbean island is implicated in the story of global capital accumulation and the rise of transnational corporations. He began by noting that the term *peasant* began to be applied to rural cultivators in the Caribbean in the nineteenth century and was used to name a type of agricultural labor over which local farmers held some measure of control (see also Trouillot 1989; chapters 12 and 13, this volume). He then showed how the historicity of the term *peasant* as used in a place like Dominica disrupts European assumptions that the term designates a distinct type of work understood to be, historically and theoretically, *precapitalist*. As Trouillot put it, the problem with the category of "peasant" is that "within the dominant historical perception of the West, the word peasant evokes a being of another age—indeed, one most typical of the Middle Ages . . . who inexplicably survived the coming of civilization" (1988, 1). In the Caribbean, however, so-called tradition came *after* modernity, and what could be called a "peasant way of life" emerged in the wake of industrial sugar production (1988, 21).[15] Rather than accepting the word *peasant* as a general category thoroughly informed by a singular history—meaning European farmers before European industrialization—Trouillot wryly concluded that such a concept of the peasant is really nothing more than "a descriptive category within a Euro-American folk view," though one with a tremendous amount of power (1988, 2). In later work, he would go on to theorize these powerful particular-qua-universal categories through which non-Western or otherwise modern societies are interpellated as "North Atlantic universals" or "North Atlantic fictions" (see chapter 5; see also 2002a and 2003).

This seemingly insignificant story of Dominican peasants and capital reverberates beyond the island's history and beyond the study of the Caribbean. In broad terms, Trouillot was insisting that our categories and concepts cannot come a priori and cannot be generalized from the historically particular experience of Europe (or elsewhere). This was a move not only to provincialize the North Atlantic (Chakrabarty 2000) but also to place marginalized parts of the world like the Caribbean back at the center of our understanding of world history. Trouillot was arguing that our categories and concepts shape our thinking and experience, and our experience in turn shapes the categories and concepts with which we think. Any adequate social analysis must therefore begin by exploring the historicity of the concepts and categories it uses; it must equally attend to the concepts and categories that operate on the ground. Such a back-and-forth mattered for more than just theoretical reasons, however. Trouillot urged us to reimagine Caribbean peasants as agents of their own history, even if they lived under harsh conditions that they certainly did not choose. By reframing the very terms of analysis, he demonstrated that peasantization was an active decision made by cultivators, a decision that came with risks and rewards, with new forms of freedom and with new constraints. He urged us to see peasantization not as "a naive response to market incentives" but instead more akin to a "strategic barrier against other forms of forced integration in a world dominated by trade and profit" (1988, 22). In essence, Dominican peasants were agents of history. Above all, the kind of analysis that he called for in *Peasants and Capital* was one in which Dominican peasants would still "be able to surprise us within the boundaries of [their] own history" (1988, 20).

On the face of it, *Peasants and Capital*, immersed as it is in the details of political economy, seems a far cry from Trouillot's later and better-known works like *Silencing the Past* and *Global Transformations*. Yet, the story it tells—of marginalized subjects who are written out of dominant Western narratives and the West's particular-qua-universal categories and concepts, but who are, nonetheless, decision-making agents of history whose stories must be told in order to understand that history—and the conceptual reversals it practices through attention to those details, and to those subjects' actions, became the bedrock to Trouillot's analytical method, to the relationship he imagined and operationalized between empirical facts and their theoretical elaboration. Indeed, it was in *Peasants and Capital*—where he was ostensibly doing a "village study"—that Trouillot initially formulated the conceptual and methodological problems with what he called the "ethnographic trilogy" that assumes "one observer, one time, one place" as "a methodological necessity, with careers hanging upon the proper performance of this ritual" (1988, 183). That critique of fieldwork, and Trouillot's broader consideration of the relationship between the empirical and the theoretical, was developed in his later work, and particularly in essays like "Making Sense: The Fields in Which We Work," the final chapter of *Global Transformations* (chapter 9, this volume).

Trouillot's early critique of the Savage slot was partly aimed at the culture concept, but it was equally concerned with the issue of the spatial and temporal relations assumed by the West's understanding of itself (as a space and place of modernity, living in historical time) and of its others (as places of tradition, living in mythic time). In *Global Transformations*, his final work, he returned to this critical anthropological project—of anthropology as the locus of an immanent critique—with a new focus not only on culture but also on the idea of "the field."

When anthropology originally emerged as a new social scientific discipline, it did so by taking up the concept of culture. As Trouillot pithily put it in "Anthropology and the Savage Slot," "anthropology inherited a disciplinary monopoly over an object that it never bothered to theorize" (2003, 19). "Making Sense," written later in his career, returns to this question of anthropology's object, arguing that the discipline also conflated its object of observation and its object of study. In the essay, Trouillot cited Margaret Mead, perhaps the best-known American anthropologist, as most clearly articulating this collapse: "'The ethnologist has defined his scientific position in terms of a field of study, rather than a type of problem, or a delimitation of theoretical inquiry. The cultures of primitive peoples are that field'" (this volume, chapter 9, 249).

Even though contemporary anthropologists no longer use the language of "primitive peoples," Trouillot held that Mead's conflation of the field as object of study, object of observation, and place in which observation occurs nonetheless persists as a result of anthropology's structural claim over the Savage slot and the concomitant restriction of its disciplinary competence to non-Western and nonwhite peoples and cultures. Moreover, fieldwork and the monograph form maintain "the treatment of places as localities, isolated containers of distinct cultures, beliefs, and practices" that can be captured between the table of contents and the index of a book (this volume, chapter 9, 247). By *localities*, Trouillot meant "site[s] defined by human content, most likely a discrete population." He argued that anthropology tends to conceive of places as localities, or, only slightly better, as *locales*, venues "defined primarily by what happens there: a temple as the locale for a ritual, a stadium as the venue for a game" (this volume, chapter 9, 246). Within this schema, anthropology's anchoring concept—culture—comes to function as a closed unit, outside power, outside history, outside a global web of political and economic connections. In lieu of *locality* and *locale*, Trouillot proposed the notion of *location*, which, he argued, is always situated, always intersectional, always in process: "One needs a map to get there, and that map necessarily points to other places without which localization is impossible" (this volume, chapter 9, 246).

Anthropology's overinvestment in the empirical can often blind us to the amorphous processes of localization—the historical and global flows, the conceptual and political conditions of possibility—that produce our objects of observation in the first place. This results in a seamless collapse of object of observation and object of study, and a lack of attention to broader configurations of power. The critique of this conflation of the object of observation and the object of study was, for example, at the center of his analysis of the way that anthropologists—not to mention political scientists or even political actors—have theorized the state (chapter 11).

What might a project that distinguished object of observation from object of study look like, then? *Silencing the Past* offers what is perhaps the clearest example of Trouillot's analytical method, the kind of theoretical reversal via the empirical that he advocated and practiced.[16] There, he pursued parallel tracks: on the one hand, he uncovered the revolutionary praxis of African slaves in colonial Haiti, like that of the Colonel Jean-Baptiste Sans Souci, who first fought French troops and then refused to submit to King Henry Christophe's new Haitian government. On the other hand, he asked why figures like Sans Souci are missing from the historical record, why the political and military actions of African slaves are usually portrayed as influenced by whites or creoles (whether at the time of the Revolution, soon afterward, or by historians now), and why the Haitian Revolution itself remains unacknowledged in various academic compendia of world revolutions. Significantly, these two parallel tracks are intertwined: by inquiring into the revolutionary praxis of African slaves, attending to their voices, and taking them seriously as revolutionaries in their own right, Trouillot was able to turn around and interrogate the historical silences about them.

Whereas the empirical facts of the Haitian Revolution are his object of observation, his object of study turns out to be the conditions of possibility of the revolution's silencing in Western historiography. "For the silencing of that revolution," Trouillot wrote, "has less to do with Haiti or slavery than it has to do with the West" (1995, 106; see also chapter 12, this volume).

Trouillot made similar moves in much of his work, shifting the focus from the problem of the Other in anthropology (can the Other be represented? how and by whom?) to the problem of the asker of such questions: the West. The question of otherness, of alterity, as posed by the West, takes for granted the very alterity it seeks to interrogate, positing otherness as a foil against which the West can speak endlessly about itself. This narcissistic "dialogue"—more aptly a monologue—goes back to anthropology's relationship to the Savage slot: "It is a stricture of the Savage slot that the native never faces the observer. In the rhetoric of the Savage slot, the Savage is never an interlocutor, but evidence in an argument between two Western interlocutors about the possible futures of humankind" (this volume, chapter 9, 260). At the same time, anthropology (and certain modes of historiography) offers the possibility of interrupting this conversation by attending to the empirical, to the Savage not as metaphor but as historical actor. As we noted earlier, there is always a gap between what has been happening over the centuries of Western conquest and colonization and what is said to have happened by those with the power to write that history. Much of Trouillot's work emerges from that gap, and from the possibilities of analytical-methodological reversal it can produce, whether that concerns Dominican peasants who are integral to global capitalism ("Caribbean Peasantries and World Capitalism," chapter 10), the modern state ("The Anthropology of the State in the Age of Globalization: Close Encounters of the Deceptive Kind," chapter 11), or the Haitian Revolution as a world-historical event enacted by African slaves, an unthinkable possibility at the time ("From Planters' Journals to Academia," chapter 12).

In many ways, then, although they are distinct disciplines in the Euro-American academy, history and anthropology were deeply intertwined for Trouillot. He worked each dialectically to interrogate the other in order to produce an account of the West as a powerful geography of imagination and management. Trouillot's historical work was always anthropological, attending empirically to those written out of the archive and out of history, so as to provincialize the narratives, concepts, and categories through which the West-as-universal has been constituted. At the same time, his anthropological work was always historical in that it took diachrony seriously, inquiring into the historical conditions of possibility for the sociocultural and political economic present. But, more than that, Trouillot also continually undertook an anthropology *of* anthropology and a history *of* historiography, though in a way that refused to understand these two projects as separate. Thus, Trouillot's version of anthropology was always both an anthropology from a Caribbean point of view—attendant to the inescapability of historicity—and an anthropology of anthropology; and, as such, it was always a critical project about the West, about its norms and forms. Looking back over the arc of his career, we can see Trouillot's oeuvre as a series of interventions not simply concerned with the discipline of anthropology, but also fundamentally directed toward an anthropology of the West, an inquiry into the conditions of possibility for the discipline's emergence and "the discursive order within which anthropology operates and makes sense" (this volume, chapter 1, 73–74). If anthropology and historiography were his objects of observation, Trouillot's ultimate object of study was the West as a political, ontological, and epistemological formation.

A NEW DUTY ARISES: UNSETTLING ANTHROPOLOGY

> While many academics agree that cross-disciplinary explorations are the path to the future, few would deny that each discipline has accumulated a huge methodological arsenal, and that it would be imprudent to reject in bloc these resources. Yet there is no widespread agreement on the specific resources to preserve or on the directions to explore.
> MICHEL-ROLPH TROUILLOT, "Discipline and Perish"

In a short reflection that takes up his own positionality as a Haitian intellectual in the halls of academe, Trouillot pointed out that "part of the problem with diversity is that most academics . . . do not really believe in its *intellectual* value" and that the academy remains "less diversified than the insurance industry or the top brass of the US Marine Corps" (this volume, interlude 4, 344). As we noted above, Trouillot's arguments about anthropology and/as the Savage slot were part of broader critiques of academe that began in the 1960s and continued through much of the 1990s. Jafari Allen and Ryan Jobson (2016) argue that his work can be understood as part of a (to some extent silenced) "decolonizing generation" of Afrodiasporic intellectuals who challenged the internal logics and the conceptual and methodological tools of various disciplines in ways that foreshadowed the more recent "decolonial turn" in academia at large.[17] Yet, Trouillot never articulated his project as an attempt to "decolonize."

Trouillot also held complex views on interdisciplinarity, which he laid out most systematically in "The Perspective of the World: Globalization Then and Now" (chapter 8). Even as he refused to restrict himself to disciplinary conventions, he remained attached to the methodological "arsenal" that particular disciplines offered (this volume, chapter 1, 76) and believed that rejecting them wholesale would be "imprudent" (this volume, interlude 3, 238). The problem, he argued, was determining what to keep and what to let go. It is telling that in "Adieu, Culture: A New Duty Arises" (chapter 13), he called for abandoning the word *culture*, unmoored as it has become from considerations of race and power, but not the conceptual kernel that lies behind it, namely, that human behavior is pattered and that those patterns are socially (not biologically) transmitted (this volume, chapter 13, 350). Thus, although he urged us to critically examine, and perhaps also give up, key aspects of anthropology, he refused to give up on disciplinarity as a whole. Why might that be? Why did he think anthropology remained a useful place from which to carry out his critique? And why did he not invoke the language of decolonization in that critical project, even as he aligned himself with figures like Faye Harrison, whose foundational edited volume *Decolonizing Anthropology* was published the same year as "Anthropology and the Savage Slot"?[18]

Trouillot was fairly explicit about his commitments to disciplinarity, as evidenced throughout this volume, and we take up below his reasoning in seeing the potential for anthropology as a critical endeavor. We can only speculate, however, about his reasons for never articulating his critique through the language of decolonization since he also never explained why. We suspect his aversion may have been due partly to the fact that early calls for decolonizing the discipline were largely focused on a critique of Eurocentrism and appeals for greater integration and valorization of so-called native anthropologists (Harrison 1997). As Harrison writes in the introduction to *Decolonizing Anthropology*, native anthropologists had long been seen as little more than "overqualified fieldwork assistants" who might provide interesting ethnographic details, but never theoretical authority (1997, 7–8). Although Trouillot certainly agreed with Harrison's diagnosis, he was less confident that incorporating native intellectuals would necessarily take the disciplines in politically progressive directions. In "The Caribbean Region," for instance, he wrote of how certain contributions by Caribbean scholars, such as "the plural society" model, were suspiciously reflective of local middle-class and elite ideologies that also underpinned the public policies these elites enacted (chapter 6). As he reminded us ominously, François Duvalier was a self-trained ethnologist and often rallied ethnographic research to political ends. Moreover, as he went on to explain, what constitutes "native" scholarship is particularly muddy in the Caribbean, where there exists little non-Western "nativeness" to speak of, and where resident intellectuals have long participated in Eurocentric debates about the region (chapter 6, this volume).

Trouillot was also deeply critical of the idea that disciplines like anthropology could deal with the enduring epistemological legacies of colonialism by simply incorporating "native" scholars. As he wrote in a footnote to "Anthropology and the Savage Slot," "I am profoundly opposed to the formulas of the type 'add native, stir, and proceed as usual' that are so successful in electoral politics inside and outside academe. Anthropology needs something more fundamental than reconstitutive surgery, and halfies, women, people of color, etc., deserve something better than a new slot" (this volume, chapter 1, 80).[19] In other words, he remained wary of how tokenism—"one skirt here, one dark skin there" (this volume, interlude 4, 344)—might serve as a mask for unaltered structures of power, and of how strategic inclusion might lead scholars of color to think of themselves as somehow outside those structures or impervious to their constraints. Trouillot would thus likely view the current "decolonial turn" as a self-congratulatory "abortive ritual" (chapter 15) that belies the particular structure of the West and the inescapable position of scholars—including nonwhite scholars in the Euro-American academy—within it.[20]

Perhaps the most logical reason, then, why Trouillot did not embrace the language of decolonizing anthropology is that he simply did not believe the discipline *could* be decolonized, given the co-constitutive relationship between the West's geography of imagination and its geography of management. Simply put, for Trouillot, there was no real way to distance anthropology from its European and colonial roots because the discipline's foundational categories, concepts, and methods are inextricably tied to the very formation of the West. (Just as important, there is no way to disembed anthropology as a system of representation from the West as a system of management and control.) As he argued in "Anthropology and the Savage Slot," the real crisis of representation is not in an academic discipline like anthropology but in the world that anthropology presumes and within which it exists (this volume, chapter 1, 73). No amount of decolonizing *within* the discipline will ever be able to do away with the broader field of power relations in which it operates. As he concomitantly argued in "Making Sense," a truly critical project must first accept that anthropology is, fundamentally, "a discourse to the West, for the West, and ultimately, about the West as project" (this volume, chapter 9, 264).

We want to suggest that what Trouillot proposed was therefore not a project of decolonization but of an epistemological *unsettling* of the disciplines, including anthropology. We use the term *unsettle* purposefully, to signal not so much an undoing as a destabilization, a shaking of foundations. To unsettle is to expose the seams, the tensions and contradictions of what appears to be an unassailable formation (Fernando 2014b). And, while not necessarily removed or toppled, what is unsettled is still fundamentally brought into question in ways that loosen its hold so that perhaps, one day, it will, in fact, fall (Bonilla 2017). Trouillot saw this mode of intellectual work as "adamantly anti-voluntarist" and insisted that individual intentions were irrelevant to structural effects. He also saw this work as a kind of war of attrition. "We do not change the world by pretending that it is different," he wrote in "Adieu, Culture." "In correctly assessing the balance of forces, I fall back on Gandhi's notion of a protracted struggle and on Gramsci's war of position" (Trouillot 2003, 153n44).

One tactic in this war of attrition involves the question of diversity—but in ways that fundamentally destabilize the epistemological conventions of anthropological knowledge. For Trouillot, the problem was less about diversifying access to an authoritative anthropological voice than about questioning "the epistemological status of the native voice" in anthropological discourse and practice, a position he most clearly articulated in "Making Sense" (chapter 9, this volume). There, he argued that the underlying schema of the Savage slot "ensures that the voice of the native is completely dominated by the voice of the anthropologist. . . . Anthropologists indeed stand behind the natives [as Clifford Geertz contended]. But we are not so much reading over their shoulders as we are writing on their backs" (this volume, chapter 9, 259). He therefore suggested that the discipline could only challenge this structural asymmetry by living up to its principle of "taking seriously" its "native" interlocutors. This means reassessing the epistemological status of the native voice and treating it not as evidence but as *theory*. It means fully recognizing native competency and making "the native a potential—if not a full—interlocutor" (this volume, chapter 9, 263). Concomitantly, it means allowing interlocutors in the non-West to "return the Western gaze," thereby unsettling the conventional relationship between author, native, and reader (this volume, chapter 9, 260).

It also means overturning the discipline's long-standing refusal to read and cite local writers, thinkers, and leaders as intellectuals in their own right, akin to scholars writing in the Western academy. As Trouillot noted, no one would dream of studying social reproduction in France without seriously engaging with (and citing) the work of Pierre Bourdieu. Yet, few North American or European anthropologists feel the need to read the Haitian intellectual tradition when they work in that country. In fact, it is all too common to hear American researchers in particular stress that they do not need to read French to do fieldwork in Haiti, and that they need only to know the language of Kreyòl (this volume, chapter 9, 259).

Trouillot saw the work of Richard Price (one of his early influences in graduate school) as exemplary of the kind of epistemological reassessments Trouillot was calling for. Price has continually stressed the importance of understanding the history of the Saramaka, in Suriname, on their own terms, going so far as to split the published pages of his book *First-Time*, with Saramaka oral history at the top and Price's commentary and archival history at the bottom (Price 2002).[21] Note the emphasis here on interlocution, on speaking, hearing, listening, and conversing, even on reading. All this stands in stark contrast to one of the main targets of Trouillot's critique and one of his main metaphors for the operation of power—namely, silencing. If the Savage slot makes it so that the native is never an interlocutor but merely metaphorical evidence in an argument between Western interlocutors about the possible futures of humankind, then the reevaluation of the epistemological status of the native voice becomes a key site for undoing the silencing produced by that slot.

Trouillot's critique of the conventions of anthropological fieldwork can be seen as analogous to the concern with citation practices that now animates much of the discussion about decolonizing the disciplines. Can we really do the critical work of decolonization without also engaging with other intellectual traditions, such as Black intellectual traditions, Indigenous intellectual traditions, Islamic intellectual traditions, or South Asian intellectual traditions? This move is essential to a renewed anthropology, even in locales where the paradigm of the Savage slot would have us believe there are no pre-existing intellectual traditions. At the same time, Trouillot underscored the importance of "return[ing] the Western gaze" by submitting Western epistemologies and authoritative reading and writing practices to the same treatment anthropologists apply to ethnographic data. Turning to Price again, this time more critically, Trouillot noted that even as Price gives his reader tips on how to "hear" his three main sources—Moravian missionaries, Dutch plants, and native Saramakas—he gives them none about how to read his own prose or that of other scholars. It may be worth asking, Trouillot wrote, which philosophy of knowledge we should use to evaluate native historical or sociological discourse, or, for that matter, the discourse of any participant to the conversation at hand (this volume, chapter 6, 166).

The question of voice and epistemology—of certain voices having an untapped epistemological potential to return the Western gaze—underpinned another tactic in Trouillot's project of unsettling anthropology, namely, his refusal to become a native anthropologist, at least not in the conventional sense. Recall that Trouillot's dissertation project was on Dominica, not Haiti, a move that upended anthropological conventions about who is supposed to study what. If, as a young graduate student, that move was unwitting—he had "unknowingly elud[ed] a gentle trap" (interlude 4, this volume)—it became more purposeful over the years; and by the time he was a professor, Trouillot consistently pushed his nonwhite graduate students to work in spaces that were not "native" to them, at least not for their first projects.[22] As Bonilla notes in the prelude to this volume, Trouillot saw great value in what he described as "learning a new dance," that is, in the epistemological and analytical importance of encountering the unfamiliar. In this vein, he encouraged his students to learn and work in foreign languages, arguing that working in one's own language gave one the impression of being on familiar territory, decreasing the chances of being "caught off guard" (this volume, chapter 6, 180) and thereby breeding incuriosity. He also argued that monolingual research promoted intellectual insularity by closing one off from scholarly debates in other languages (this volume, chapter 6, 180–81). And he emphasized that working across linguistic and political boundaries was particularly important for Caribbeanists, given the region's coming into being through multiple colonial empires. Working *across* those empires was crucial, Trouillot argued, for understanding the Caribbean as a whole.

Indeed, Trouillot argued that nonwhite scholars working in an ostensibly unfamiliar place inherently gained a comparative perspective not so much between one marginalized context and another (their own), but rather about broader structures of power in which these different marginalized spaces were imbricated. He believed that nonwhite scholars usually possessed some sense of the asymmetrical structures of power that produced their own social world, and that the precise nature of these structures of power would be thrown into relief by working elsewhere, even next door, as he did as a Haitian in Dominica. He also underscored that this inherently comparative method would produce more than the sum of its parts, that putting two social worlds side by side, if only implicitly, would reveal broader patterns about how power worked across these different worlds—how, for instance, Puerto Rico and Guadeloupe were quite different, yet both embedded within a similar political configuration of North Atlantic sovereignty and Caribbean nonsovereignty (Bonilla 2015), or how French and American secularism were quite different, yet part of a global project of secularity that takes Western Christianity as the model for any definition of "proper" religion (Fernando 2014b).

We might understand this implicitly comparative method as a way of "savaging" the West, as Harvey Neptune (2014) puts it—that is, of turning the tools of anthropology on the West as an object of knowledge. If the West constructs itself in a dyadic relation with its Other, and if it understands "particular" forms of alterity as always in relation to itself as universal, then Trouillot proposed that putting two non-Western spaces in relation with each other would reveal something about the West, about its concepts and assumptions, its claims and genealogies. To bring in a third term, so to speak, in this otherwise dyadic relation would reveal something about the pattern of relations through which the West constitutes itself. And if, as Trouillot insisted over the course of his life, "the historicization of the West . . . is a central theoretical challenge of our times" (this volume, interlude 4, 344), he also saw anthropology's potential to turn its long-standing focus on alterity against itself, and against the West, as integral to that challenge.

This position underscores Trouillot's commitment to turning anthropology into a critical anthropology of the West; it also demonstrates his lifelong focus on the twin forms of power that have most shaped not only the Caribbean but the world at large, namely: colonialism and capitalism. Those two forms of power have cast millions of people aside, tossed out of history and even out of the political formations that would ensure them a semblance of rights or recognition. Take, for instance, contemporary Haiti. The West continues to insist that Haiti does not matter to the world, that Haiti can only ever be the "poorest country in the Western hemisphere." Drawing on the insights that Trouillot offered over the arc of his work, we can see how that insistence conceals a project of domination in which a free and independent, let alone a wealthy or developed, Haiti remains just as unthinkable to the West today as the act of slaves declaring their own freedom was to the West in 1804 (Trouillot 2003; see also chapters 7,

12, and 16; see also Beckett 2013). And faced with that fact, we might also begin to see the resurgence of white supremacy around the world in a new light, not as a strange and unheralded rupture, not as an aberration, but as a long-standing system of thought and practice—of imagination and management—that has always been constitutive of the West, of North Atlantic power. Knowing what we know about Haiti, we might see that we cannot escape historicity, and we cannot embrace comfortable liberal formulations that cast the current global rise of fascism and white supremacy as a surprising turn of events, and as explicable only in presentist terms.

This is why we read Trouillot today. So that we can think with him, build upon his ideas, and draw on both his unflinching critique and his belief that such critique might have real effects. We read Trouillot today to help us expose the conditions of possibility of our own understanding. We read Trouillot to help us see our own unthinkable limits. We read his work not just for what it accomplishes, but also for what we can do with it, how we can put it to work for a more livable future.

NOTES

A few sections of this opening essay first appeared, in modified forms, in Greg Beckett, "Thinking with Others: Savage Thoughts about Anthropology and the West," *Small Axe: A Caribbean Journal of Criticism* 17, no. 3 (2013): 166–81; and Mayanthi L. Fernando, "Ethnography and the Politics of Silence," *Cultural Dynamics* 26, no. 2 (2014): 235–44.

1. For more on Trouillot's "voice," see Scott 2012.

2. *Ti dife* was originally published in 1977 as *Ti difé boulé sou istoua Ayiti* (see Trouillot 1977), before Haitian Kreyòl orthography was standardized. It was republished posthumously in 2012 with a title that reflects standard modern Kreyòl orthography. We use that standard orthography throughout the volume and cite the 2012 republication, even in Trouillot's essays (all published before that new edition). Trouillot was deeply committed to the politics of language in Haiti and to the importance of acknowledging the Haitian majority language and recognizing it as a scholarly language with its own formal properties (prior orthographical norms treated it phonetically, or as an oral language only, or as a derivative of "bad French"). Indeed, his decision to publish his first book in Kreyòl, rather than French, underscores that commitment. We honor that politics not only by using the standardized form of the title of his first book but also by referring to the language as Kreyòl (rather than Creole or Haitian Creole). Similarly, assuming that Trouillot would remain attuned to the politics of language in other domains as well, we follow contemporary

stylistic conventions and capitalize the first letter of certain terms—*Black* and *Native*, for instance—where the original text used a lowercase *b* or *n*.

3. Trouillot was obviously using the term *Savage* sardonically, referring to the concept and its circulation rather than to a "real" demographic, much as he used *The Discovery* (always with a capital *T* and a capital *D*, sometimes in quotation marks) to refer to Columbus's landing in the Americas and the way it has been named and circulates in public discourse. He likewise always capitalized the *S* in *Savage*.

4. As the Africanist anthropologist Jacques Macquet explains with seeming nostalgia: "In the former colonial countries which have recently become independent states, it is very likely that more and more studies will be devoted to present-day social phenomena, particularly to those giving rise to urgent problems. The parts of the cultures which remain influenced chiefly by traditional patterns will no longer be studied as if they existed in isolation, in a sort of timeless present, but rather as parts of the modern, literate, and industrial global society to which they now belong. Several recent publications have taken this approach. The discipline concerned with these contemporary phenomena will probably be called 'sociology' instead of 'anthropology' or 'ethnology.' As for societies of the past, traditional and colonial, they will be studied by history, using its specific methods and techniques" (Macquet 1964, 54).

5. See also Buck-Morss 2009; Eze 1997; Sala-Molins 2006; and Scott 2010.

6. Take, for instance, Michel de Montaigne's *Essays*, first published in 1588 in Paris and often considered an early example of what would become a staple of modern thought, namely, the attempt at critical self-examination. Throughout the many detailed descriptions of social life culled from his travels and his readings, Montaigne argues that both unity and difference are central to the human condition. We are all different, Montaigne writes, and yet there exists a common element by which we all "arrive at the same end" (Montaigne 1957, 3–5). Taking up the practice of cannibalism, which had emerged by this period as a central trope in debates about the so-called "barbarism" of the Indigenous populations of the New World, Montaigne suggests that barbarism and savagery are relative terms ("each man calls barbarism whatever is not his own practice"), only to then judge cannibalism in terms of the universal standard of Reason ("so we may well call these people barbarians with respect to the rules of reason, but not in respect to ourselves") (1957, 152, 156). In other words, what is seemingly an oblique critique of certain aspects of his own society culminates, ultimately, in a defense of a still-nascent universalism. That universalism would take the West as the unmarked category—Reason, in Montaigne's terms—against which all forms of difference would be known, assessed, and judged (see chapter 1, this volume).

7. Joel Robbins, for example, has suggested that Trouillot is "making a fairly simple observation: anthropology has from its start been stuck studying the savage, the primitive, and the radically other, and it needs to break out of this confining slot quickly if it is to survive into the future" (Robbins 2013, 449). Robbins argues that the discipline has since moved from the "savage slot" to the "suffering slot," a slot predicated on a shared notion of universal suffering. However, what Robbins fails to recognize is that the suffering slot is not an abandonment of the Savage slot but a continuation of the Savage *as metaphor* within broader debates about universal humanity, this time through the language of trauma.

8. In "Adieu, Culture" Trouillot wrote: "We may want to ask how the current wave of collective apologies for historical sins is propelled by the production of new sensibilities and subjectivities and the virtual presence of a Greek chorus now naively called 'the international community'" (this volume, chapter 13, 368). In "Abortive Rituals" (chapter 15) he further examined the rise and implication of these new collective apologies.

9. For more on the silencing of the United States as postcolonial society see Neptune 2015.

10. Trouillot seemed to be inspired here by Eric Wolf's (1982, 3–23) critique of the formation of the disciplines around distinct—and reified—objects of study.

11. The idea that the West was born in the Caribbean, or in the Atlantic world more broadly, is a cornerstone of Trouillot's thinking and an increasingly common idea in Caribbean studies. See Glissant 1989; Mintz 1985; Scott 2004; Williams 1961; and Wolf 1982.

12. As Kathryn Yusoff notes, "exchange" is a deliberate misnomer for "the directed colonial violence of forced eviction from land, enslavement on plantations, in rubber factories and mines, and the indirect violence of pathogens through forced contact and rape" (2018, 30).

13. Despite pioneers like Melville J. Herskovits, the region was often ignored, or, as Herskovits's own work attests, it was clumsily fit into a framework that connected it to Africa (see Herskovits 1938). A much clearer approach to Caribbean studies came later, with such works as Mintz and Price 1992. See Trouillot 1992 and chapter 6, this volume, for an extended discussion of how anthropology has framed the Caribbean region.

14. For related accounts of this "inescapable historicity" in the Caribbean, see Glissant 1989; Mintz 2010; Trouillot 2003; and Wolf 1982.

15. Sidney Mintz (1974) describes Caribbean peasantries as "reconstituted" and notes how they emerged alongside and after the intensified, protoindustrial production of the sugar plantation system. See Scott 2004 for an extended

discussion of this approach to Caribbean modernity; see also chapters 6, 7, and 10 of this volume.

16. Another particularly famous example of distinguishing between object of observation and object of study is Karl Marx's "On the Jewish Question" (Marx 1978). The Jewish Question, conventionally posed in the nineteenth century by European politicians and philosophers alike, asked whether Jews could be sufficiently emancipated from Jewishness and Judaism to become full political citizens. Whereas most answered the question by looking to Jews, Marx turned the gaze back to the asker, namely, the state. By attending to the political conditions of possibility that produced the question—and the Jew as its ostensible object—Marx interrogated the concept of political emancipation itself and revealed its immanent contradictions. See Fernando 2014a.

17. On the more recent decolonial turn see Brodkin et al. 2011; Escobar 2007; Maldonado-Torres 2007; Mignolo 2011; Mignolo and Escobar 2010; Quijano 2000, 2007; Sandoval 2000; and Todd 2018.

18. Trouillot did not cite Harrison's *Decolonizing Anthropology* in either the original 1991 publication of "Anthropology and the Savage Slot" or in its reprinted version in *Global Transformations*, nor does the word *decolonize* appear in the index to *Global Transformations*. However, in "The Caribbean Region: An Open Frontier," he described Harrison and himself as among "the few [who] dare to bring explicitly to the discipline the political or metatheoretical lessons learned on the frontier" (this volume, chapter 6, 180).

19. The term *halfies* is a reference to Lila Abu-Lughod's essay "Writing against Culture," which also appeared in *Recapturing Anthropology*. See Abu-Lughod 1991.

20. For a similar view, see Tuck and Yang 2012.

21. One could argue that Price's placement of official archival history—mostly from colonial Dutch sources—alongside Saramaka oral traditions can sometimes read like a verification of that oral history, rather than a parallel tradition in its own right. For a critique of Price, see Scott 1991. Trouillot also cited Jennie Smith's *When the Hands Are Many* (2001) and Anna Tsing's *In the Realm of the Diamond Queen* (1993) as two examples of how anthropologists might give the native voice an epistemological status beyond that of mere evidence. For our own responses to Trouillot's call to reassess the epistemological status of the native voice, see Beckett 2019; Bonilla 2015; and Fernando 2014b.

22. Yarimar Bonilla, from Puerto Rico, discusses the methodological importance of choosing to work in Guadeloupe in the preface to her first book (Bonilla 2015); Mayanthi L. Fernando, from Sri Lanka, similarly discusses her decision to write her first book about France (Fernando 2014b) in an interview on the New Books Network from January 5, 2016 (https://newbooksnetwork

.com/mayanthi-fernando-the-republic-unsettled-muslim-french-and-the
-contradictions-of-secularism-duke-up-2014/). And Viranjini Munasinghe,
also Sri Lankan and a student of Trouillot at Johns Hopkins, talks about her
experience studying Indo-Caribbean population in Trinidad in the preface to
her own book (Munasinghe 2001).

REFERENCES

Abu-Lughod, Lila. 1991. "Writing against Culture." In *Recapturing Anthropology: Working in the Present*, edited by Richard G. Fox, 137–54. Santa Fe, NM: School of American Research Press.

Allen, Jafari Sinclaire, and Ryan Cecil Jobson. 2016. "The Decolonizing Generation: (Race and) Theory in Anthropology since the Eighties." *Current Anthropology* 57, no. 2: 129–48.

Asad, Talal, ed. 1973. *Anthropology and the Colonial Encounter*. London: Ithaca Press.

Ashcroft, B., G. Griffiths, and H. Tiffin. 2003. *The Empire Writes Back: Theory and Practice in Post-colonial Literatures*. New York: Routledge.

Beckett, Greg. 2013. "The Ontology of Freedom: The Unthinkable Miracle of Haiti." *Journal of Haitian Studies* 19, no. 2: 54–74.

Beckett, Greg. 2019. *There Is No More Haiti: Between Life and Death in Port-au-Prince*. Berkeley: University of California Press.

Bonilla, Yarimar. 2013. "Burning Questions: The Life and Work of Michel-Rolph Trouillot, 1949–2012." *NACLA Report on the Americas* 46, no. 1: 82–84.

Bonilla, Yarimar. 2015. *Non-sovereign Futures: French Caribbean Politics in the Wake of Disenchantment*. Chicago: University of Chicago Press.

Bonilla, Yarimar. 2017. "Unsettling the Classics: On Symptomatic Readings and Disciplinary Agnosticism." *Hau: Journal of Ethnographic Theory* 7, no. 3: 23–28.

Brodkin, Karen, Sandra Morgen, and Janis Hutchinson. 2011. "Anthropology as White Public Space?" *American Anthropologist* 113, no. 4: 545–56.

Buck-Morss, Susan. 2009. *Hegel, Haiti, and Universal History*. Pittsburgh, PA: University of Pittsburgh Press.

Césaire, Aimé. 1972. *Discourse on Colonialism*. Translated by Joan Pinkham. New York: Monthly Review Press.

Chakrabarty, Dipesh. 2000. *Provincializing Europe: Postcolonial Thought and Historical Difference*. Princeton, NJ: Princeton University Press.

Clifford, James. 1986. "Introduction: Partial Truths." In *Writing Culture: The Poetics and Politics of Ethnography*, edited by James Clifford and George E. Marcus, 1–27. Berkeley: University of California Press.

Clifford, James, and George E. Marcus, eds. 1986. *Writing Culture: The Poetics and Politics of Ethnography*. Berkeley: University of California Press.

Crosby, Alfred W., Jr. 1972. *The Columbian Exchange: Biological and Cultural Consequences of 1492*. Westport, CT: Greenwood.

Deloria, Vine. 1969. *Custer Died for Your Sins: An Indian Manifesto*. Norman: University of Oklahoma Press, 1969.

Escobar, Arturo. 2007. "Worlds and Knowledges Otherwise: The Latin American Modernity/Coloniality Research Program." *Cultural Studies* 21, nos. 2–3: 179–210.

Eze, Emmanuel Chukwudi, ed. 1997. *Race and the Enlightenment: A Reader*. Cambridge: Blackwell.

Fernando, Mayanthi L. 2014a. "Ethnography and the Politics of Silence," *Cultural Dynamics* 26, no. 2: 235–44.

Fernando, Mayanthi L. 2014b. *The Republic Unsettled: Muslim French and the Contradictions of Secularism*. Durham, NC: Duke University Press.

Fox, Richard G., ed. 1991. *Recapturing Anthropology: Working in the Present*. Santa Fe, NM: School of American Research Press.

Glissant, Édouard. 1989. *Caribbean Discourse: Selected Essays*. Translated by J. Michael Dash. Charlottesville: University of Virginia Press.

Gough, Kathleen. 1968. "Anthropology and Imperialism." *Monthly Review* 19, no. 11: 12–27.

Harrison, Faye V., ed. 1997. *Decolonizing Anthropology: Moving Further toward an Anthropology for Liberation*. Washington, DC: American Anthropological Association.

Herskovits, Melville J. 1938. *Acculturation: The Study of Culture Contact*. New York: J. J. Augustin.

Hymes, Dell Hathaway. 1974. *Reinventing Anthropology*. New York: Vintage Books.

Macquet, Jacques J. 1964. "Objectivity in Anthropology." *Current Anthropology* 5, no. 1: 47–55.

Maldonado-Torres, Nelson. 2007. "On the Coloniality of Being: Contributions to the Development of a Concept." *Cultural Studies* 21, nos. 2–3: 240–70.

Marx, Karl. 1978. "On the Jewish Question." In *The Marx-Engels Reader*, edited by Robert C. Tucker, 22–46. New York: W. W. Norton.

Mignolo, Walter D. 2011. "Geopolitics of Sensing and Knowing: On (De)coloniality, Border Thinking, and Epistemic Disobedience." *Postcolonial Studies* 14, no. 3: 273–83.

Mignolo, Walter D., and Arturo Escobar, eds. 2010. *Globalization and the Decolonial Option*. New York: Routledge.

Mintz, Sidney W. 1974. *Caribbean Transformations*. New York: Columbia University Press.

Mintz, Sidney W. 1985. *Sweetness and Power: The Place of Sugar in Modern History*. New York: Viking.

Mintz, Sidney W. 2010. *Three Ancient Colonies: Caribbean Themes and Variations*. Cambridge, MA: Harvard University Press.

Mintz, Sidney W., and Richard Price. 1992. *The Birth of African-American Culture: An Anthropological Perspective*. Boston: Beacon.

Montaigne, Michel de. 1957. *The Complete Essays of Montaigne*. Translated by Donald M. Frame. Stanford, CA: Stanford University Press.

Munasinghe, Viranjini P. 2001. *Callaloo or Tossed Salad? East Indians and the Cultural Politics of Identity in Trinidad*. Ithaca, NY: Cornell University Press.

Neptune, Harvey. 2014. "Savaging Western Civilization: Michel-Rolph Trouillot and the Anthropology of the West." *Cultural Dynamics* 26, no. 2: 219–34.

Neptune, H. Reuben. 2015. "The Irony of Un-American Historiography: Daniel J. Boorstin and the Rediscovery of a U.S. Archive of Decolonization." *American Historical Review* 120, no. 3: 935–50.

Price, Richard. 2002. *First-Time: The Historical Vision of an African American People*. 2nd ed. Chicago: University of Chicago Press.

Quijano, Aníbal. 2000. "Coloniality of Power, Eurocentrism, and Latin America." Translated by Michael Ennis. *Nepantla* 1, no. 3: 533–80.

Quijano, Aníbal. 2007. "Coloniality and Modernity/Rationality." *Cultural Studies* 21, no. 2–3: 168–78.

Robbins, Joel. 2013. "Beyond the Suffering Subject: Toward an Anthropology of the Good." *Journal of the Royal Anthropological Institute*, n.s., 19: 447–62.

Said, Edward. 1979. *Orientalism*. London: Vintage.

Sala-Molins, Louis. 2006. *Dark Side of the Light: Slavery and the French Enlightenment*. Translated by John Conteh-Morgan. Minneapolis: University of Minnesota Press.

Sandoval, Chela. 2000. *Methodology of the Oppressed*. Minneapolis: University of Minnesota Press.

Scott, David. 1991. "That Event, This Memory: Notes on the Anthropology of African Diasporas in the New World." *Diaspora: A Journal of Transnational Studies* 1, no. 3: 261–84.

Scott, David. 2004. "Modernity That Predated the Modern: Sidney Mintz's Caribbean." *History Workshop Journal* 58, no. 1: 191–210.

Scott, David. 2010. "Antinomies of Slavery, Enlightenment, and Universal History." *Small Axe: A Caribbean Journal of Criticism* 14, no. 3 (33): 152–62.

Scott, David. 2012. "The Futures of Michel-Rolph Trouillot: In Memoriam." *Small Axe: A Caribbean Journal of Criticism* 16, no. 3: vii–x.

Smith, Jennie M. 2001. *When the Hands Are Many: Community Organization and Social Change in Rural Haiti*. Ithaca, NY: Cornell University Press.

Todd, Zoe. 2018. "The Decolonial Turn 2.0: The Reckoning." *Anthro(dendum)*, June 15. https://anthrodendum.org/2018/06/15/the-decolonial-turn-2-0-the -reckoning/.

Trouillot, Michel-Rolph. 1977. *Ti difé boulé sou istoua Ayiti*. Brooklyn, NY: Kóleksion Lakensièl.

Trouillot, Michel-Rolph. 1982. "Motion in the System: Coffee, Color, and Slavery in Eighteenth-Century Saint-Domingue." *Review (Fernand Braudel Center)* 5, no. 3: 331–88.

Trouillot, Michel-Rolph. 1988. *Peasants and Capital: Dominica in the World Economy*. Baltimore, MD: Johns Hopkins University Press.

Trouillot, Michel-Rolph. 1989. "Discourses of Rule and the Acknowledgment of the Peasantry in Dominica, W.I., 1838–1928." *American Ethnologist* 16, no. 4: 704–18.

Trouillot, Michel-Rolph. 1991. "Anthropology as Metaphor: The Savage's Legacy and the Postmodern World." *Review (Fernand Braudel Center)* 14, no. 1: 29–54.

Trouillot, Michel-Rolph. 1992. "The Caribbean Region: An Open Frontier in Anthropological Theory." *Annual Review of Anthropology* 21: 19–42.

Trouillot, Michel-Rolph. 1995. *Silencing the Past: Power and the Production of History*. Boston: Beacon.

Trouillot, Michel-Rolph. 1999. "Historiography of Haiti." In *General History of the Caribbean*. Vol. 6, *Methodology and Historiography of the Caribbean*, edited by Barry W. Higman, 451–77. London: UNESCO.

Trouillot, Michel-Rolph. 2002a. "North Atlantic Universals: Analytical Fictions, 1492–1945." *South Atlantic Quarterly* 101, no. 4: 839–58.

Trouillot, Michel-Rolph. 2002b. "The Otherwise Modern: Caribbean Lessons from the Savage Slot." In *Critically Modern: Alternatives, Alterities, Anthropologies*, edited by Bruce Knauft, 220–37. Bloomington: Indiana University Press.

Trouillot, Michel-Rolph. 2003. *Global Transformations: Anthropology and the Modern World*. New York: Palgrave Macmillan.

Trouillot, Michel-Rolph. (1977) 2012. *Ti dife boule sou istwa Ayiti*. Edited by Lyonel Trouillot. Port-au-Prince: Edisyon KIK, Invèsite Karayib.

Tsing, Anna. 1993. *In the Realm of the Diamond Queen: Marginality in an Out-of-the-Way Place*. Princeton, NJ: Princeton University Press.

Tuck, Eve, and K. Wayne Yang. 2012. "Decolonization Is Not a Metaphor." *Decolonization: Indigeneity, Education and Society* 1, no. 1: 1–40.

Williams, Eric. 1961. *Capitalism and Slavery*. New York: Russell and Russell.

Wolf, Eric R. 1982. *Europe and the People without History*. Berkeley: University of California Press.

Yusoff, Kathryn. 2018. *A Billion Black Anthropocenes or None*. Minneapolis: University of Minnesota Press.

PART I

GEOGRAPHY
OF
IMAGINATION

Between the Cracks

Academics tuned to the foundation world cannot fail to note that the hype about globalization parallels a decline in interest for area studies. Indeed, what some observers described as the scholarly assault on area studies helped to justify—if not to formulate—the shift in foundation support.

Arguments against area studies generally follow two lines. The first faults area studies for the politics that made it possible. Area studies, it is said, evolved as part of a project of Western—especially, North American—domination and never escaped the sins of the ideology that gave it birth. As a project linked to management rather than to intellectual pursuit, the geographical division of the world has little justification beyond the political and economic designs of power holders within the North Atlantic. The second type of argument insists on the lack of connection between area studies and the current world. Recent changes associated with globalization are alleged to have exhausted the relevance of area studies.

Both arguments seem sound: area studies did start as a managerial project, and the world has much changed since the 1950s. There are problems, however, when these truths are used to justify the mechanical replacement of area studies by global studies.

Clichés about *globalization* are no more immune to current ideological fads than area studies were to those of the 1950s. David Harvey suggests that the increased use of the term *globalization* and all its associated baggage exacts a severe political and analytical price. If globalization dates at least from the fifteenth-century creation of the Atlantic world (as we like to emphasize at the institute [for Global Studies in Culture, Power, and History]), why is the word so suddenly fashionable? Harvey argues that the emphasis on globalization often masks the uneven socio-spatial development of capitalism and prevents the study of that unevenness. Anthropologists and historians might add, slightly shifting the emphasis, that the "global village" often obliterates the particulars of many villages and millions of their inhabitants.

Left untheorized, globalization is no panacea. It does not fit some reality out there any more than a division of knowledge based on geopolitical entities did in the 1950s. More important, the move to global studies may not be worth much if it means giving up the substantive and theoretical gains made through area studies. These gains are worth spelling out since they are not as obvious as the flaws.

....

Area studies programs, as we know them, developed in the United States during and especially after World War II. They reorganized knowledge against the background of the Cold War with a bent toward economic and political management. Because these programs were turned to practice, they blurred many disciplinary boundaries. But in so doing, they questioned implicitly the naturalness of these disciplinary boundaries. Not all disciplines were admitted or equally involved. Historians and anthropologists who pioneered research on non-Western areas—and indeed created the few area programs before World War II—were often forgotten. Political scientists and economists took the lead in area studies programs in the era of modernization theory. Literature was a latecomer.

But insofar as area studies, as a form of knowledge organization, was tied to management projects, it also implied the use of whatever discipline would work or was available. Limited availability also ensured that the domination of some disciplines never entailed the complete silencing of the others. There were never enough economists or political scientists with expertise, say, on the Caribbean and Latin America to fully silence the humanists who had studied the history or the literature of these regions. The tension between world and disciplinary boundaries was never solved, in part because of academic politics and its reliance on disciplinary partitions. Still, in practice, *area studies provided one of the few institutionalized spaces for cross-disciplinary conversations within academia.*

Second, because of the dearth of academic experts on individual states outside the North Atlantic, area studies gathered individual scholars who worked on different, if neighboring, countries. This gathering displaced the nation-state as the self-evident framework within which the processes studied by the human disciplines occurred. Area studies programs never theorized this displacement, limited as they were both by the politics of the day and methodological assumptions dating back from the nineteenth century. Still, in practice, *area studies circumvented one of the biggest stumbling blocks of the traditional disciplines: the naturalness of the state as the central analytical building block of social action and sociocultural theory*.

Third, however much a hodgepodge of country specialists whom area programs put together, they brought into analytical existence parts of the world of which the material existence *would not have been noticed without—indeed, was not noticed before—these gatherings. There are countries within regions, regions within continents, subareas and micropopulations that made it on the intellectual map of many North American campuses only because of area studies programs*. They would have fallen between the cracks without that institutional support.

Fourth, in making the shifts just signaled, area studies accepted, implicitly and by default, that the whole disciplinary apparatus developed in the study of the so-called West was relevant to the study of areas outside the North Atlantic. In the context of the 1950s that was a methodological break, even if unplanned and untheorized.

....

Proponents of global studies should keep these gains in mind and build upon them. The institutionalization of global studies makes little sense if it does not provide a place for cross-disciplinary conversations. Without the politics of the Cold War or the pretense of development as necessary background to the study of the non-West, the dominance of economics and political science will decline in these conversations. Yet we need these disciplines, and we should be careful not to replace their dominance with the rising hegemony of "theory" as defined by literature and cultural studies.

The relative worth of disciplines is at least in part a reflection of the needs of the world outside campus walls. Do our new hegemonies reproduce the post-Reagan world in ways that the disciplines of development reproduced the world we think we left behind? Are "hybridity" and "globalization" to the world of McDonald's in Beijing and Disney in Haiti as "development" and "containment" were to the world of détente? Only an open cross-disciplinary conversation can help global studies assess the context and purpose of research in ways that area studies did not.

We need also to watch out for global studies not to reproduce the nation-state as a methodological boundary under the guise of "culture" or, worse, "multiculturalism." Academic nostalgia for state boundaries creates islands of hybridity that are often new forms of essentialism hiding behind "global" labels. Regardless of their emotional ties to Mexico, regardless of the many ways in which they crisscross—at a cost to be fully measured—political and cultural boundaries, Mexican Americans in California should not become objects of study at the expense of Latin America. Neither the study of Latin America nor that of the United States gain in the process.

Global studies' congenital disease is the tendency to focus on processes of globalization only as they currently affect the West. Thus, global studies programs are not immune to one of the main problems behind the hasty dismissal of area studies: the unquestioned centrality of the West. Yet, in timidly suggesting that the entire apparatus of the human disciplines was relevant to the non-West, area studies opened the door to the suggestion that the experience of the non-West was also relevant to sociocultural theory. When political science could not explain certain events in Africa, at least some political scientists thought that political theory had to be modified accordingly. To be sure, the resulting mixture was not always a happy one. But we should nurture the intellectual drive behind such efforts and the theoretical reach they promised.

Global studies' most immediate challenges thus recall those of area studies, with an added twist of irony. Now that the Cold War is over, will the populations that gained marginal relevance with area studies programs fall between the cracks? Will they become objects of study—and relevant to theory—only as they relate to North American capital? Will globalization be one more fancy word masking the ideology of its origins?

NOTE

Editors' Note: This chapter first appeared as "Between the Cracks," *Cross Currents: Newsletter of the Institute for Global Studies in Culture, Power, and History* 4, no. 2 (1997).

CHAPTER 1

Anthropology and the Savage Slot

The Poetics and Politics of Otherness

Anthropology faces an unprecedented wave of challenges that require an archaeology of the discipline and a careful examination of its implicit premises. The postmodernist critique of anthropology, which is now the most vocal and direct response to these challenges in the United States, falls short of building that archaeology because it tends to treat the discipline as a closed discourse. In contradistinction, I contend that the internal tropes of anthropology matter much less than the larger discursive field within which anthropology operates and upon whose existence it is premised. A cultural critique of anthropology requires a historicization of that entire field. New directions will come only from the new vantage points discovered through such a critique.

CHALLENGES AND OPPORTUNITIES

Academic disciplines do not create their fields of significance, they only legitimize particular organizations of meaning. They filter and rank—and in that sense, they truly *discipline*—contested arguments and themes that often precede them. In doing so, they continuously expand, restrict, or modify in diverse ways their distinctive arsenals of tropes, the types of statements they deem acceptable. But the poetics and politics of the "slots" within which disciplines operate do not dictate the enunciative relevance of these slots. There is no direct correlation between the "electoral politics" of a discipline and its political relevance. By "electoral politics," I mean the set of institutionalized practices and relations of power that influence the production of knowledge from within academe: academic filiations, the mechanisms of institutionalization, the organization of power within and across departments, the market value of publish-or-perish prestige, and other worldly issues that include, but expand way beyond, the maneuvering we usually refer to as "academic politics." Changes in the types of statements produced as "acceptable" within a discipline, regulated as they are—if only in part—by these "electoral politics," do not necessarily modify the larger field of operation nor the enunciative context of that discipline. Changes in the explicit criteria of acceptability do not automatically relieve the historical weight of the field of significance that the discipline inherited at birth. More likely, the burden of the past is alleviated when the sociohistorical conditions that obtained at the time of emergence have changed so much that practitioners face a choice between complete oblivion and fundamental redirection. At one point in time, alchemists become chemists or cease to be—but the transformation is one that few alchemists can predict and even fewer would wish.

Anthropology is no exception to this scenario. Like all academic disciplines, it inherited a field of significance that preceded its formalization. Like many of the human sciences, it now faces dramatically new historical conditions of performance. Like any discourse, it can find new directions only if it modifies the boundaries within which it operates. These boundaries not only predated the emergence of anthropology as a discipline, but they also prescribed anthropology's role (and ethnography's ultimate relevance) to an extent not yet unveiled. Anthropology fills a preestablished compartment within a wider symbolic field, the "Savage" slot of a thematic trilogy that helped to constitute the West as we know it. A critical and reflexive anthropology requires, beyond the self-indulgent condemnation of traditional techniques and tropes, a reappraisal of this symbolic organization upon which anthropological discourse is premised.

Anthropology's future depends much on its ability to contest the Savage slot and the *thématique* that constructs this slot. The times are ripe for such questioning. More important, solutions that fall short of this challenge can only push the discipline toward irrelevance, however much they may reflect serious concerns. In that light, current calls for reflexivity in the United States are not products of chance, the casual convergence of individual projects. Neither are they a passing fad, the accidental effect of debates that stormed philosophy and literary theory.[1] Rather, they are timid, spontaneous—and

in that sense genuinely American—responses to major changes in the relations between anthropology and the wider world, provincial expressions of
wider concerns, allusions to opportunities yet to be seized. What are those
changes? What are these concerns? What are the opportunities?

On sheer empirical grounds, the differences between Western and non-
Western societies are blurrier than ever before. Anthropology's answer
to this ongoing transformation has been typically ad hoc and haphazard.
The criteria according to which certain populations are deemed legitimate objects of research continue to vary with departments, with granting
agencies, with practitioners, and even with the mood shifts of individual
researchers. Amid the confusion, more anthropologists reenter the West
cautiously, through the back door, after paying their dues elsewhere. By
and large this reentry is no better theorized than were previous departures
for faraway lands.[2]

While some anthropologists are rediscovering the West without ever
naming it, what "the West" stands for is itself an object of debate, within
and outside the gates of academe. The reactionary search for a fundamental Western corpus of "great texts" by many intellectuals and bureaucrats
in the English-speaking world is both the reflection of a wider conflict and
a particular response to the uncertainties stirred by this conflict. Interestingly, few anthropologists have intervened in that debate. Fewer even
among those thought to be at the forefront of the discipline have deigned
to address directly the issue of Western monumentalism, with one or two
exceptions (e.g., Rosaldo 1989). Even more interestingly, anthropological *theory* remains irrelevant to—and unused by—either side of the "great
texts" debate, rhetorical references notwithstanding. Today, the statement
that any canon necessarily eliminates an unspecified set of experiences
need not come only from anthropology—thanks, of course, to the past diffusion of anthropology itself, but thanks especially to changes in the world
and to the experiences that express and motivate these changes. Minorities of all kinds can and do voice their cultural claims, not on the basis of
explicit theories of culture but in the name of historical authenticity. They
enter the debate not as academics—or not only as academics—but as situated individuals with rights to historicity. They speak in the first person,
signing their arguments with an "I" or a "we," rather than invoking the ahistorical voice of reason, justice, or civilization.

Anthropology is caught off guard by this reformulation. Traditionally,
it approached the issue of cultural differences with a monopoly over native
discourse, hypocritically aware that this discourse would remain a quote.

It is too liberal to accept either the radical authenticity of the first person or the conservative reversion to canonical truths—hence, its theoretical silence.

Here again, silence seems to me a hasty abdication. At the very least, anthropology should be able to illuminate the myth of an unquestioned Western canon upon which the debate is premised.[3] In doing so, it would certainly undermine some of its own premises; but that risk is an inherent aspect of the current wave of challenges: its numerous opportunities are inseparable from its multiple threats. Nowhere is this combination of threats and opportunities as blatant as in the postmodern admission that the metanarratives of the West are crumbling.

THE FALL OF THE HOUSE OF REASON

Whatever else postmodernism means, it remains inseparable from the acknowledgment of an ongoing collapse of metanarratives in a world where reason and reality have become fundamentally destabilized (Lyotard 1979, 1986).[4] To be sure, the related claim that "the world that made science, and that science made, has disappeared" is somewhat premature (Tyler 1986, 123). The growing awareness among literati that rationality has not fulfilled its promises to uncover the absolute becoming of the spirit does not alter the increasing institutionalization of rationality itself (Godzich 1986, xvii–xix). Indeed, one could argue that the spectacular failure of science and reason, judged on the universal grounds that scholars love to emphasize, serves to mask success on more practical and localized terrains into which academics rarely venture.

But if the world that science made is very much alive, the world that made science is now shaky. The crisis of the nation-state, the crisis of the individual, the crisis of the parties of order (liberal, authoritarian, or communist), terrorism, the crisis of "late capitalism"—all contribute to a Western malaise and, in turn, feed upon it (Aronowitz 1988; Jameson 1984). Philosophers reportedly asked: can one *think* after Auschwitz? But it took some time for Auschwitz to sink in, for communism to reveal its own nightmares, for structuralism to demonstrate its magisterial impasse, for North and South to admit the impossibility of dialogue, for fundamentalists of all denominations to desacralize religion, and for re-enlightened intellectuals to question all foundational thought. As the walls crumbled— North and South and East and West—intellectuals developed languages of postdestruction. It is this mixture of negative intellectual surprise, this postmortem of the metanarratives, that situates the postmodernist mood as primarily Western and primarily petit bourgeois.

These words are not inherently pejorative, but they are meant to historicize the phenomenon—an important exercise if we intend to have cross-cultural relevance. First, it is not self-evident that all past and present cultures required metanarratives up to their current entry into postmodernity. Second, if only the collapse of metanarratives characterized the postmodern condition, then some of the non-Western cultures that have been busily deconstructing theirs for centuries, or that have gone through megacollapses of their own, have long been "postmodern," and there is nothing new under the sun. Things fell apart quite early on the southern shores of the Atlantic, and later in the hinterlands of Africa, Asia, and the Americas. Third, even if we concede, for the sake of argument, that metanarratives once were a prerequisite of humankind and are now collapsing everywhere at equal rates (two major assumptions, indeed), we cannot infer identical reactive strategies to this collapse.

Thus, we must distinguish between postmodernism, as a mood, and the recognition of a situation of postmodernity. The acknowledgment that there is indeed a crisis of representation, that there is indeed an ongoing set of qualitative changes in the international organization of symbols (Appadurai 1991), in the rhythms of symbolic construction (Harvey 1989), and in the ways that symbols relate to localized, subjective experience, does not in itself require a postmortem. In that light, the key to the dominant versions of postmodernism is an ongoing destruction lived as shock and revelation. Postmodernism builds on this revelation of the sudden disappearance of established rules, foundational judgments, and known categories (Lyotard 1986, 33). But the very fact of revelation implies a previous attitude toward such rules, judgments, and categories—for instance, that they have been taken for granted or seen as immutable. The postmortem inherent in the postmodernist mood implies a previous "world of universals" (Ross 1988a, xii–xiii). It implies a specific view of culture and of culture change. It implies, at least in part, the Enlightenment and nineteenth-century Europe.

In cross-cultural perspective, the dominant mood of postmodernism thus appears as a historically specific phenomenon, a reaction provoked by the revelation that the Enlightenment and its conflicting tributaries may have run their course. This mood is not inherent in the current world situation, but neither is it a passing ambience, as many of the postmodernists' detractors would have—even though it ushers in fads of its own. It is a mood in the strong sense in which Geertz (1973b, 90) defines religious moods: powerful, persuasive, and promising endurance. But contrary to religions, it rejects both the pretense of factuality and the aspiration to realistic motivations. It seeks a "psychoanalytic therapeutic" from the "modern neurosis," the "Western schizophrenia, paranoia, etc., all the sources of misery we have known for two centuries" (Lyotard 1986, 125–26).

"We," here, *is* the West, as in Michael Jackson and Lionel Ritchie's international hit, "We Are the World." This is not "the West" in a genealogical or territorial sense. The postmodern world has little space left for genealogies, and notions of territoriality are being redefined right before our eyes (Appadurai 1991). It is a world where Black American Michael Jackson starts an international tour from Japan and imprints cassettes that mark the rhythm of Haitian peasant families in the Cuban Sierra Maestra; a world where Florida speaks Spanish (once more); where a Socialist prime minister in Greece comes by way of New England, and an imam of fundamentalist Iran by way of Paris. It is a world where a political leader in reggae-prone Jamaica traces his roots to Arabia, where US credit cards are processed in Barbados, and Italian designer shoes are made in Hong Kong. It is a world where the Pope is Polish, and where the most orthodox Marxists live on the western side of a fallen iron curtain. It is a world where the most enlightened are only part-time citizens of part-time communities of imagination.

But these very phenomena—and their inherent connection with the expansion of what we conveniently call the West—are part of the text that reveals the dominant mood as eventuating from a Western *problématique*. The perception of a collapse as revelation cannot be envisioned outside of the trajectory of thought that has marked the West and spread unevenly outside of its expanding boundaries. Its conditions of existence coalesce within the West. The stance it spawns is unthinkable outside of the West and has significance only within the boundaries set by the West.

If the postmodern mood is fundamentally Western in the global sense delineated above, what does this mean for an anthropology of the present? First, it means that the present that anthropologists must confront is the product of a particular past that encompasses the history and the prehistory of anthropology itself. Second, and consequently, it means that the postmodernist critique within North American anthropology remains, so far, within the very thematic field that it claims to challenge. Third, it means that a truly critical and reflexive anthropology needs to contextualize the Western metanarratives and read critically the place of the discipline in the field so discovered. In short, anthropology needs to turn the apparatus elaborated in the observation of non-Western societies on itself and, more specifically, on the history from which it sprang. That history does not start with the formalization of the discipline, but with the emergence of the symbolic field that made this formalization possible.

THE SAVAGE AND THE INNOCENT

In 1492, Christopher Columbus stumbled upon the Caribbean. The admiral's mistake would later be heralded as "The Discovery of America," the quincentennial of which two worlds will soon celebrate. To be sure, it took Balboa's sighting of the Pacific in 1513 to verify the existence of a continental mass, and Vespucci's insistence on a *mundus novus* for Christendom to acknowledge this "discovery." Then it took another fifty years to realize its symbolic significance. Yet 1492 was, to some extent, a discovery even then, the first material step in a continuously renewed process of invention (Ainsa 1988). Abandoning one lake for another, Europe confirmed the sociopolitical fissure that was slowly pushing the Mediterranean toward northern and southern shores. In so doing, it created itself, but it also discovered America, its still unpolished alter ego, its Elsewhere, its Other. The Conquest of America stands as Europe's model for the constitution of the Other (Todorov 1982; Ainsa 1988).

Yet from the beginning, the model was Janus-faced. The year 1516 saw the publication of two anthropological precursors: the Alcalá edition of the *Decades* of Pietro Martire d'Anghiera (a paraethnographic account of the Antilles, and in many ways one of Europe's earliest introductions to a "state of nature" elsewhere) and one more popular edition of Amerigo Vespucci's epistolary travel accounts. In that same year too, Thomas More published his fictional account of an "ideal state" on the island of *Utopia*, the prototypical nowhere of European imagination.

The chronological coincidence of these publications, fortuitous as it may be, symbolizes a thematic correspondence now blurred by intellectual specialization and the abuse of categories. We now claim to distinguish clearly between travelers' accounts, colonial surveys, ethnographic reports, and fictional utopias. Such cataloging is useful, but only to some extent. In the early sixteenth century, European descriptions of an alleged state of nature in the realist mode filled the writings of colonial officers concerned with the immediate management of the Other. The realist mode also pervaded travelers' accounts of the sixteenth and seventeenth centuries, before settling in the privileged space of learned discourse with eighteenth-century philosophers and the nineteenth-century rise of armchair anthropology. Even then, the line between these genres was not always clear-cut (Thornton 1983; Weil 1984). On the one hand, the realist mode pervaded fiction—so much so that some twentieth-century critics distinguish between utopias and "extraordinary voyages," or trips to the lands of nowhere with the most "realistic" geographical settings. On the other hand, even as fantasies about an ideal state increased in fiction, they also found their way into theater, songs, and philosophical treatises.

In short, classifications notwithstanding, the connection between a state of nature and an ideal state is, to a large extent, in the symbolic construction of the materials themselves. The symbolic transformation through which Christendom became the West structures a set of relations that necessitates both utopia and the Savage. What happens within the slots so created—and within the genres that condition their historical existence—is not inconsequential. But the analysis of these genres cannot explain the slots nor even the internal tropes of such slots. To wit, "utopia" has been the most studied form of this ensemble, yet there is no final agreement on which works to include in the category (Atkinson 1920, 1922; Andrews 1937; Trousson 1975; Manuel and Manuel 1979; Eliav-Feldon 1982; Kamenka 1987). Further, when reached, agreement is often ephemeral. Even if one could posit a continuum from realist ethnography to fictional utopias, works move in and out of these categories, and categories often overlap on textual and nontextual grounds. Finally, textuality is rarely the final criterion of inclusion or exclusion. From the two-hundred-year-long controversy about the *Voyage et aventures de François Leguat* (a 1708 best-seller believed by some to be a true account and by others, a work of fiction) to the Castañeda embarrassment to professional anthropology and the more recent debates on *Shabono* or the existence of the Tasaday, myriad cases indicate the ultimate relevance of issues outside of "the text" proper (Atkinson 1922; Weil 1984; Pratt 1986).

That the actual corpus fitting any of these genres at any given period has never been unproblematic underscores a thematic correspondence that has survived the increasingly refined categorizations. In the 1500s, readers could not fail to notice the similarities between works such as Jacques Cartier's *Bref récit*, which features paraethnographic descriptions of Indians, and some of Rabelais's scenes in *Gargantua*. Montaigne, an observant traveler himself within the confines of Europe, used descriptions of America to set for his readers issues in philosophical anthropology—and in the famous essay "Des cannibales," he is quick to point out the major difference between his enterprise and that of his Greek predecessors, including Plato: the Greeks had no realistic database (Montaigne 1952). Early in the seventeenth century, Tommaso Campanella produced his *Citta del sole* (1602), informed by descriptions that Portuguese missionaries and Dutch mercenaries were bringing back from Ceylon and by Jesuit reports of socialism within the Inca kingdom.

Utopias were both rare and inferior—by earlier and later standards—during the seventeenth century. Few are now remembered other than those of Campanella, Bacon, and Fénelon. But the search for an exotic ideal had not died, as some authors (Trousson 1975) seem to suggest. Fénelon's *Aventures de Télémaque* went into twenty printings. The *History of the Sevarites* of Denis Vairasse d'Alais (1677–79) was published originally in English, then in a French version that spurred German, Dutch, and Italian translations (Atkinson 1920). Utopias did not quench the thirst for fantasy lands, but only because relative demand had increased unexpectedly.

Travel accounts, of which the numbers kept multiplying, helped fill this increased demand for the Elsewhere. Some did so with reports of unicorns and floating isles, then accepted as reality by their public, including some of the most respected scholars of the time. But most did so with what were "realist" pictures of the Savage, pictures that would pass twentieth-century tests of accuracy and are still being used by historians and anthropologists. Du Tertre (1667), Labat (1722), and Gage (1648)—to take only a few recognizable authors writing on one hemisphere—familiarized readers with the wonders of the Antilles and the American mainland.

Outside of a restricted group of overzealous scholars and administrators, it mattered little to the larger European audience whether such works were fictitious or not. That they presented an elsewhere was enough. That the Elsewhere was actually somewhere was a matter for a few specialists. The dream remained alive well into the next century. Montesquieu was so much aware of this implicit correspondence that he gambled on reversing all the traditions at the same time, with considerable aesthetic and didactic effect, in his *Lettres persanes* (1721). The Elsewhere became Paris; the Other became French; the utopia became a well-known state of affairs. It worked because everyone recognized the models and understood the parody.

The thematic correspondence between utopias and travel accounts or paraethnographic descriptions was not well camouflaged until the end of the eighteenth century. The forms continued to diverge, while the number of publications within each category kept increasing. Utopias filled the century that gave us the Enlightenment, from Swift's parodic *Gulliver's Travels* (1702) to Bernadin de Saint-Pierre's unfinished *L'amazone* (1795). But so did realistic descriptions of faraway peoples, and so did, moreover, cross-national debates in Europe on what exactly those descriptions meant for the rational knowledge of humankind. In the single decade of the 1760s, England alone sent expeditions like those of Commodore Byron; Captains Cartwright, Bruce, Furneaux, and Wallis; and Lieutenant Cook to savage lands all over the world. Bruce, Wallis, and Cook brought home reports from Abyssinia, Tahiti, and Hawai'i. Byron and his companions carried back accounts "of a race of splendid giants" from Patagonia. Cartwright returned with five living Eskimos who caused a commotion in the streets of London (Tinker 1922, 5–25).

Scholars devoured such "realistic" data on the Savage with a still unsurpassed interest, while writing didactic utopias and exploring in their philosophical treatises the rational revelation behind the discoveries of the travelers. Voltaire, who read voraciously the travel descriptions of his time, gave us *Candide* and "Zadig." But he also used paraethnographic descriptions to participate in anthropological debates of his time, siding for instance with the Göttingen school on polygenesis (Duchet 1971). Diderot, who may have read more travel accounts than anyone then alive, and who turned many of them into paraethnographic descriptions for the *Encyclopédie*, wrote two utopias true to form.[5] Rousseau, whom Lévi-Strauss called "the father of ethnology," sought the most orderly link between "the state of nature" first described by Martire d'Anghiera and the "ideal commonwealth" envisioned by More and his followers. He thus formalized the myth of the "noble savage," renewing a theme that went back not only to Pope and Defoe, but also to obscure travelers of the sixteenth and seventeenth centuries. Long before Rousseau's *Social Contract*, Pietro Martire already thought that the Arawak of the Antilles were sweet and simple. Magellan's companion, Pigafetta, claimed in 1522 that the Indians of Brazil were "creduli e boni" by instinct. And Pierre Boucher, writing of the Iroquois in 1664, had confirmed that "tous les Sauvages ont l'esprit bon" (Gonnard 1946, 36; Atkinson 1920, 65–70).

The myth of the noble savage is not a creation of the Enlightenment. Ever since the West became the West, Robinson has been looking for Friday. The eighteenth century was not even the first to see arguments on or around that myth (Gonnard 1946). The verbal duel between Las Casas and Sepúlveda on the "nature" of the Indians and the justice of their enslavement, fought at Valladolid in the early 1550s in front of Spain's intellectual nobility, was as spectacular as anything the Enlightenment could imagine (André-Vincent 1980; Pagden 1982). Rather, the specificity of eighteenth-century anthropological philosophers was to dismiss some of the past limitations of this grandiose controversy and to claim to resolve it not on the basis of the Scriptures, but on the open grounds of rationality and experience. But the debate was always implicit in the thematic concordance that had tied the observation of the Savage and the hopes of utopia since at least 1516. Swiss writer Isaac Iselin, a leading voice of the Göttingen school of anthropology, criticized Rousseau's ideals and the state of savagery as "disorderly fantasy" (Rupp-Eisenreich 1984, 99). The fact that the Göttingen school did not much bother to verify its own "ethnographic" bases, or that it used travelers' accounts for other purposes than Rousseau's (Rupp-Eisenreich 1985), matters less than the fact that Rousseau, Iselin, Meiners, and De Gerando shared the same premises on the relevance of savagery. For Rousseau, as for More and Defoe, the Savage is an argument for a particular kind of utopia. For Iselin and Meiners, as for Swift and Hobbes in other times and contexts, it is an argument against it. Given the tradition of the genre being used, the formal terrain of battle, and the personal taste of the author, the argument was either tacit or explicit and the Savage's face either sketched or magnified. But argument there was.

The nineteenth century blurred the most visible signs of this thematic correspondence by artificially separating utopia and the Savage. To schematize a protracted and contested process: it is as if that century of specialization subdivided the Other that the Renaissance had set forth in creating the West. From then on, utopia and the Savage evolved as two distinguishable slots. Kant had set the philosophical grounds for this separation by laying his own teleology without humor or fiction while moving away from the *Naturinstinkt*. Nineteenth-century French positivists, in turn, derided utopias as chimeric utopianisms (Manuel and Manuel 1979).

The growing fictional literature in the United States also modified the forms of utopia (Pfaelzer 1984). To start with, America had been the imagined site of traditional utopias, Tocqueville's *feuille blanche*, the land of all (im)possibilities. Defining an elsewhere from this site was a dilemma. Ideally, its Eden was within itself (Walkover 1974). Not surprisingly, William Dean Howells brings *A Traveler from Altruria* to the United States before sending his readers back to utopia. Edward Bellamy chose to look "backward." More important, America's Savages and its colonized were also within itself: American Indians and Black Americans, only one of whom white anthropologists dared to study before the latter part of this century (Mintz 1971, 1990). With two groups of Savages to pick from, specialization set in, and Indians (especially "good" Indians) became the preserve of anthropologists.

At the same time, a Black utopia was unthinkable, given the character of North American racism and the fabric of Black/white imagery in American literature (Levin 1967). Thus the Black pastoral (the unmatched apex of which is *Uncle Tom's Cabin* [1851]—but note that the flavor is also in Faulkner) played the role that *Paul et Virginie* had played earlier in European imagination.[6] But true-to-form utopia writers in North America moved away from the specter of savagery.

Other factors were at play. The nineteenth century was America's century of concreteness, when its utopias became reachable. Of the reported 52 million migrants who left Europe between 1824 and 1924, more than ninety percent went to the Americas, mostly to the United States. In the United States, and in Europe as well, decreasing exchange among writers, who were involved in different forms of discourse and seeking legitimacy on different grounds, contributed even more to giving each group of practitioners the sentiment that they were carrying on a different enterprise. As they believed their practice and practiced their beliefs, the enterprises indeed became separated, but only to a certain extent. By the end of the nineteenth century, utopian novelists accentuated formal interests while utopianisms were acknowledged primarily as doctrines couched in nonfictional terms: Saint-Simonism, Fabian Socialism, Marxism (Gonnard 1946). Travel accounts came to pass as a totally separate genre, however Robinson-like some remained. The "scientific" study of the Savage qua Savage became the privileged field of academic anthropology, soon to be anchored in distinguished chairs, but already severed from its imaginary counterpart.

The rest of the story is well known, perhaps too well known, inasmuch as the insistence on the methods and tropes of anthropology as a discipline may obscure the larger discursive order that made sense of its institutionalization. Histories that fail to problematize this institutionalization—and critiques premised on that naive history—necessarily fall short of illuminating the enunciative context of anthropological discourse. To be sure, anthropologists to this day keep telling both undergraduates and lay readers that their practice is useful to better understand "ourselves," but without ever spelling out exactly the specifics of this understanding, the utopias behind this curiosity turned profession.

It has often been said that the Savage or the primitive was the alter ego the West constructed for itself. What has not been emphasized enough is that this Other was a Janus, of whom the Savage was only the second face.[7] The first face was the West itself, but the West fancifully constructed as a utopian projection and meant to be, in that imaginary correspondence, the condition of existence of the Savage.

This thematic correspondence preceded the institutionalization of anthropology as a specialized field of inquiry. Better said, *the constitutive moment of ethnography as metaphor antedates the constitution of anthropology as discipline* and even precedes its solidification as specialized discourse. The dominant metamorphosis, the transformation of savagery into sameness by way of utopia as positive or negative reference, is not the outcome of a textual exercise within the anthropological practice, but part of anthropology's original conditions of existence. Anthropology came to fill the Savage slot of a larger thematic field, performing a role played, in different ways, by literature and travel accounts—and soon to be played, perhaps, by unexpected media, if one takes the success of *Roots*, *Miami Vice*, or *China Beach* on North American television, or the international sales of Saddam Hussein punching balls during the Gulf War, as indications of a future. That the discipline was positivist in a positivist age, structuralist in a context dominated by structuralism, is not very intriguing; and as Tyler (1986, 128) notes acutely, the more recent "textualization of pseudo-discourse" can accomplish "a terrorist alienation more complete than that of the positivists." Thus, attempts at disciplinary reflexivity cannot stop at the moment of institutionalization or emphasize the internal tropes of late modern ethnographies, even though some rightly allude to the correspondence between savagery and utopia or to the use of the pastoral mode in anthropology (e.g., Tyler 1986; Clifford 1986b; Rosaldo 1986). Such attempts are not *wrong*. But the primary focus on the textual construction of the Other *in* anthropology may turn our attention away from the construction of Otherness upon which anthropology is premised and further mask a correspondence already well concealed by increasing specialization since the nineteenth century.

Indeed, the Savage-utopia correspondence tends to generate false candor. It rarely reveals its deepest foundations or its inherent inequality, even though it triggers claims of reciprocity. From Pietro Martire and Rousseau to the postmodernist contingent(s) of North American anthropology, the Savage has been an occasion to profess innocence. We may guess at some of the reasons behind this recurrent tendency to exhibit the nude as nakedness. Let me just say this much: in spite of such old claims, the utopian West dominated the thematic correspondence. It did so from behind the scenes, at least most of the time. It showed itself in least-equivocal terms on just a few occasions, most notably in the philosophical jousts over American colonization in sixteenth-century Spain (Pagden 1982) and in the anthropological debates of the eighteenth century (Duchet 1971).

But visible or not, naive or cynical, the West was always first, as utopia or as challenge to it—that is, as a universalist project, the boundaries of which were no-where, u-topous, non-spatial. And that, one needs to repeat, is not a product of the Enlightenment, but part and parcel of the horizons set by the Renaissance and its simultaneous creation of Europe and Otherness, without which the West is inconceivable. Thomas More did not have to wait for ethnographic reports on the Americas to compose his *Utopia*. Similarly, eighteenth-century readers of travel accounts did not wait for verification. Even today, there is a necessary gap between the initial acceptance of the most fanciful "ethnographies" and the "restudies" or "reassessments" that follow. The chronological precedence reflects a deeper inequality in the two faces of Janus: the utopian West is first in the construction of this complementarity. It is the first observed face of the figure, the initial projection against which the Savage becomes a reality. The Savage makes sense only in terms of utopia.

THE MEDIATION OF ORDER

Utopia itself made sense only in terms of the absolute order against which it was projected, negatively or not.[8] Utopias do not necessarily advance foundational propositions, but they feed upon foundational thought. Fictional "ideal states," presented as novels or treatises, suggest a project or a counterproject. It is this very projection, rather than their alleged or proven fanciful characteristics, that makes them utopias. Here again, we need to go back to the Renaissance, that fictional rebirth through which Christendom became the West, where two more snapshots may clarify the issue.

From the point of view of contemporaries, the most important event of the year 1492 was not Columbus's landing in the Antilles, but the conquest of the Muslim kingdom of Granada and its incorporation into Castile (Trouillot 1990). The gap between the three religions of Abraham had paralleled the sociopolitical fissure that split the Mediterranean, but because of that fissure, religious intolerance increasingly expressed itself in ways that intertwined religion, ethnicity, territory, and matters of state control. To put it simply, as Christendom became Europe, Europe itself became Christian. It is no accident that the fall of Muslim Granada was immediately followed by the expulsion of the Jews from the now Christian territory. It is no accident either that the very same individual who signed the public order against the Jews also signed Ferdinand and Isabella's secret instructions to Columbus. Indeed, nascent Europe could turn its eyes to the Atlantic only because the consolidation of political borders and the concentration of political power in the name of the Christian God presaged the advent of internal order.

Order—political and ideological—was high on the agenda, both in theory and in practice; and the increased use of the printing press stimulated the interchange between theory and practice. Thus, in 1513, three years before Thomas More's *Utopia*, Niccolò Machiavelli wrote *The Prince*. In retrospect, that work signified a threshold: some leaders of the emerging Western world were ready to phrase the issue of control in terms of realpolitik long before the word was coined. The Machiavelli era encompassed Erasmus's *Education of a Christian Prince*, Budé's *Education of a Prince*, and other treatises that shared an "emphasis on the workable rather than the ideal," a belief that "men's destinies were to some extent within their own control and that this control depended upon self-knowledge" (Hale 1977, 305).

The seminal writings that inscribed savagery, utopia, and order were conceived in the same era. This simultaneity is but one indication that these slots were created against the backdrop of one another. In the context of Europe, the works that set up these slots were part of an emerging debate that tied order to the quest for universal truths, a quest that gave savagery and utopia their relevance. Looming above the issue of the ideal state of affairs, and tying it to that of the state of nature, was the issue of order as both a goal and a means, and of its relation with reason and justice. Campanella's *City of the Sun*, the runner-up to *Utopia* in the critics' view, clearly engaged some of Machiavelli's proposals and those of contemporary Spanish philosophers (Manuel and Manuel 1979, 261–88). Campanella, like More, also wrote in nonfictional modes. He commented on European political regimes, in terms of their ultimate justification. He proposed to various European monarchs a nonfictional plan of rule based on his religious and philosophical views. Indeed, the opinions expressed in his treatises got him thrown into a Spanish jail, where he wrote his fictionalized utopia (Manuel and Manuel 1979; Trousson 1975, 39, 72–78). Sir Thomas More, in turn, was executed.

The relation between fictionalized utopias and matters of political power goes way back to the ancestral forms of the genre in ancient Greece (Trousson 1975, 39). So do debates on the nature of otherness. But we need not take the naive history of the West at face value: Greece did not beget Europe. Rather, Europe claimed Greece. The revisionist historiography through which the Renaissance turned Christendom into Europe and gave it its Greek heritage is itself a phenomenon that needs to be placed in history. The distinctiveness of the Renaissance was, in part, the invention of a past for the West.[9] It was also, in part, an emerging claim to universality and to an absolute order inconceivable without that claim. As Las Casas, Montesquieu, and Montaigne were quick to point out in different terms and times, a major difference between Europe and ancient Greece was the reality of the Savage as experienced by Europe after 1492. Unlike that of Greece and Rome, or that of the Islamic world, the West's vision of order implied from its inception two complementary spaces, the Here and the Elsewhere, which were premised on one another and were conceived of as inseparable.

In imaginary terms that Elsewhere could be utopia; but in the concrete terms of conquest, it was a space of colonization peopled by others who would eventually become "us"—or at the very least who *should*—in a project of assimilation antithetic to the most liberal branches of Greek philosophy. In that sense, order had become universal, absolute—both in the shape of the rising absolutist state (quite opposed, indeed, to Greek democracy), and in the shape of a universal empire stretching the limits of Christendom out into nowhere. Colonization became a mission, and the Savage became absence and negation.[10] The symbolic process through which the West created itself thus involved the universal legitimacy of power—and order became, in that process, the answer to the question of legitimacy. To put it otherwise, the West is inconceivable without a metanarrative, for since their common emergence in the sixteenth century, both the modern state and colonization posed—and continue to pose—to the West the issue of the philosophical base of order. As Édouard Glissant (1989, 2) phrases it: "The West is not in the West. It is a project, not a place," a multilayered enterprise in transparent universality.

Chronological convergences again illustrate the point. At about the time Machiavelli wrote *The Prince*, the Spanish Crown made known its supplementary laws on American colonization, and the Medici clan in 1513 secured the papacy with the nomination of Leo X—the same Leo, bishop of Rome, to whom Pietro Martire dedicated parts of his ethnography. Two years later, the accession of Francis I as king of France signaled the self-conscious invention of the traditions constitutive of the French nation-state—a self-consciousness manifested in the imposed use of the French dialect and the creation of the Collège de France.[11] One year after Francis's advent, Charles I (later Charles V) became king of Castile and of its New World possessions, and Martin Luther published the theses of Wittenberg. The second decade of the new century ended quite fortuitously with a semblance of victory on the side of order, that is, with Charles's "election" to the imperial crown in 1519. But the condemnation of Luther (1520), rural agitation within Castile itself, and the so-called Oriental menace (culminating with the 1529 siege of Vienna by the Turks) kept reminding a nascent Europe that its self-delivery was not to happen without pains. The notion of a universal empire that would destroy, through its ineluctable expansion, the borders of Christendom became both more attractive in thought and more unattainable in practice.

The fictionalized utopias that immediately followed More's and overlapped with the practical reshaping of power in a newly defined Europe were by and large reformist rather than revolutionary, hardly breaking new imaginary ground (Trousson 1975, 62–72). This is not surprising, for, just as the Savage is in an unequal relationship with utopia, so is utopia in an uneven relation with order. Just as the Savage is a metaphorical argument for or against utopia, so is utopia (and the Savage it encompasses) a metaphorical argument for or against order, conceived of as an expression of legitimate universality. It is the mediation of universal order, as the ultimate signified of the Savage-utopia relation, that gives the triad its full sense. In defense of a particular vision of order, the Savage became evidence for a particular type of utopia. That the same ethnographic source could be used to make the opposite point did not matter, beyond a minimal requirement for verisimilitude. To be sure, Las Casas had been there, Sepúlveda had not; and this helped the cause of the *procurador*. To be sure, the Rousseauists were right and Göttingen was wrong about cranial sizes. To be sure, the empirical verdict is not yet in on the Tasaday. But now as before, the Savage is only evidence within a debate, the importance of which surpasses not only his understanding but his very existence.

Just as utopia itself can be offered as a promise or as a dangerous illusion, the Savage can be noble, wise, barbarian, victim, or aggressor, depending on the debate and the aims of the interlocutors. The space within the slot is not static, and its changing contents are not predetermined by its structural position. Regional and temporal variants of the Savage figure abound, in spite of recurring tendencies that suggest geographical specialization.[12] Too often, anthropological discourse modifies the projection of nonacademic observers only to the extent that it "disciplines" them.[13] At other times, anthropologists help create and buttress images that can

```
┌─────────────────────────────────────────────────────────────┐
│         The West        The Rest                            │
│  The Observer                                   The Other   │
│  Culture                                        Nature      │
│  History                                        Stories     │
│             ORDER          SAVAGE                           │
│                              Noble                          │
│                              Barbarian                      │
│                              Wise                           │
│                              Evil                           │
│                                                             │
│             State: Justice  UTOPIA                          │
│                              Paradisiac                     │
│                              Communist                      │
│                              Innocent                       │
│                              Illusory                       │
│             Thought: Reason                                 │
│  Here                                           Elsewhere   │
└─────────────────────────────────────────────────────────────┘
```

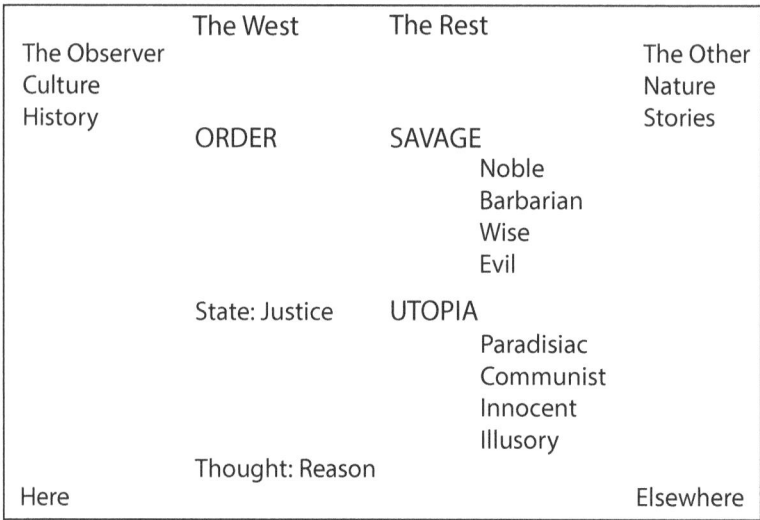

1.1 The symbolic organization of the Savage slot, ca. 1515–1990.

question previous permutations.[14] Thus, what happens within the slot is neither doomed nor inconsequential (Fox 1991; Vincent 1991). The point is, rather, that a critique of anthropology cannot skirt around this slot. The direction of the discipline now depends upon an explicit attack on that slot itself and the symbolic order upon which it is premised (figure 1.1). For as long as the slot remains, the Savage is at best a figure of speech, a metaphor in an argument about nature and the universe, about being and existence— in short, an argument about foundational thought.

PORTRAIT OF THE ARTIST AS A BUBBLE

This brings us right back to the present. I have argued so far that to historicize the West is to historicize anthropology and vice versa. I have further suggested that the postmodern condition makes that two-pronged historicization both urgent and necessary. If these two arguments are correct, together they expose the unspoken assumptions of postmodernist anthropology in North America and reveal its inherent limitations. For the portrait of the postmodernist anthropologist that emerges from this dual exercise is not a happy one indeed. Camera and notebooks in hand, he is looking for the Savage, but the Savage has vanished.

The problem starts with the fated inheritance of the moderns themselves. The world that the anthropologist inherits has wiped out the empirical trace of the Savage-object: Coke bottles and cartridges now obscure the familiar tracks. To be sure, one could reinvent the Savage, or create new Savages within the West itself—solutions of this kind are increasingly appealing. The very notion of a pristine savagery, however, is now awkward, irrespective of the Savage-object. Lingering conditions of modernity make the notion a hard one to evoke in imagination now that hordes of Savages have joined the slums of the Third World or touched the shores of the West. We are far from the days when five Eskimos caused an uproar in London. The primitive has become terrorist, refugee, freedom fighter, opium and coca grower, or parasite. He can even play anthropologist at times. Televised documentaries show his "real" conditions of existence; underground newspapers expose his dreams of modernity. Thanks to modernity, the Savage has changed, the West has changed, and the West knows that both have changed empirically.

But modernity is only part of the anthropologist's difficulty. Modern obstacles have modern (technical) answers, or so we used to think. The more serious issue is that technical solutions do not suffice anymore. At best, they can solve the problem of the empirical object by removing the Cokes and cartridges. At worst, they can fabricate an entire new face for savagery. But they cannot remedy the loss of the larger thematic field, especially since the Savage never dominated this field. He was only one of the requisite parts of a tripartite relation, the mask of a mask. The problem is not simply that the masks are torn, that true cannibals are now rare. The problem is that now—as in Norman Mailer's *Cannibals and Christians* (1966)—both are equally good, or equally evil (Walkover 1974), if evil itself can be defined (Lyotard 1986).

This is altogether a *post*modern quandary. It is part of the world of constructs and relations revealed by our juxtaposed snapshots, and it is an intrinsic dilemma of postmodern anthropology. For if indeed foundational thoughts are seen as collapsing, if indeed utopias are arguments about order and foundational thoughts, and if indeed the Savage exists primarily within an implicit correspondence with utopia, the specialist in savagery is in dire straits. He does not know what to aim at. His favorite model has disappeared or, when found, refuses to pose as expected. The fieldworker examines his tools and finds his camera inadequate. Most importantly, his very field of vision now seems blurred. Yet he needs to come back home with a picture. It's pouring rain out there, and the mosquitoes are starting to bite. In desperation, the baffled anthropologist burns his notes to create a moment of light, moves his face against the flame, closes his eyes, and, hands grasping the camera, takes a picture of himself.

TACTICS AND STRATEGY

Lest this portrait be taken to characterize the postmodernist anthropologist as the epitome of self-indulgence (as many critics, indeed, imply), let me say that narcissist labels characterize postmodernist anthropologists, as individuals, no better than they typify their predecessors or adversaries. Intellectuals as a group claimed and gained socially sanctioned self-indulgence long before postmodernism. Individual intent is secondary here. At any rate, anthropology's postmodern situation warrants more sober reflection than petty accusations of egomania across theoretical camps.

I may end up being both more lenient and more severe—thus risking the condemnation of foes and proponents alike—by saying that the perceived self-indulgence of the postmodernist anthropologists inheres in the situation itself. That is what makes it so obvious and such an easy target for opponents. If we take seriously the perception of an ongoing collapse of the Western metanarratives, the vacuum created by the fall of the house of reason in the once fertile fields of utopian imagination, and the empirical destruction of the Savage-object, then the anthropologist who is aware of the postmodern situation has no target outside of himself (as witness) and his text (as pretext), within the thematic universe he inherits.

Once phrased in these terms, the dilemma becomes manageable. One obvious solution is to confront and change the thematic field itself and claim new grounds for anthropology—which is just what some anthropologists have been doing, though without explicit programs. But the dilemma, as lived by the postmodernists, is no less real, and the epiphany of textuality cannot be reduced to a mere aggregate of individual tactics of self-aggrandizement or preservation.[15] If electoral politics may explain either overstatements or the craving for new fads in North American anthropology and elsewhere, they say little of the mechanisms leading to specific choices among myriad possibilities. Why the text? Why the sudden (for anthropologists, to some extent) rediscovery of literature, and of some literature at that? However much the (re)discovery of textuality and authorial legitimation may be associated with midterm maneuvers, it also must be seen in another context. In that context—the thematic field delineated by order, utopia, and the Savage—this emphasis on textuality represents a strategic retreat triggered by the perception of ongoing destruction. In other words, electoral politics alone cannot explain postmodernist anthropology. To propose viable alternatives, one needs to take the ideological and theoretical context of postmodernism seriously, more seriously than the postmodernists do themselves. One needs also to take more seriously both literary criticism and philosophy.

METAPHORS IN ETHNOGRAPHY AND ETHNOGRAPHY AS METAPHOR

The recent discovery of textuality by North American anthropologists is based on a quite limited notion of the text. The emphasis on "the independent importance of ethnographic writing as a genre" (Marcus 1980, 507), the dismissal of pre-text, con-text, and content, all contribute to reading the anthropological product as isolated from the larger field in which its conditions of existence are generated. Passing references aside, the course of inquiry on the relations among anthropology, colonialism, and political "neutrality," which opened in the late 1960s and early 1970s (e.g., Asad 1973), is now considered closed, because it allegedly revealed all its partial truths. Passing mentions of gender aside, feminism—as a discourse that claims the specificity of (some) historical subjects—is bypassed because it is said to deal only with "content."[16] Passing references to the Third World notwithstanding, the issues raised by Wolf's historicization of the Other (1982), an inquiry that inherently makes anthropology part of this changing world, are considered moot. Mentions of relations of textual production notwithstanding, the mechanisms and processes emphasized are those that singularize the voice of anthropology, as if anthropological discourse was either self-enclosed or self-sufficient.

Not surprisingly, the archaeological exploration that underpins the North American exercise in reflexivity tends to stop at the institutionalization of anthropology as a discipline in the Anglophone world, or at best at the delineation of a specialized anthropological discourse in the Europe of the Enlightenment. In spite of the professed renunciation of labels, boundaries are set in modern terms to produce a history of the discipline, albeit one with different emphases. The construction exposed is a discursive order *within* anthropology, not the discursive order within which anthropology operates and makes sense—even though, here again, this larger field seems to warrant passing mention. The representational aspect of ethnographic discourse is attacked with a vigor quite disproportionate to the referential value of ethnographies in the wider field within which anthropology finds its significance. In short, to use a language that still has its validity, the object of inquiry is the "simple" rather than the "enlarged" reproduction of anthropological discourse. Terminology and citations notwithstanding, the larger thematic field on which anthropology is premised is barely scratched.

But if we take seriously the proposition to look at anthropology as metaphor—as I think we can, given the thematic field outlined—we cannot just look at metaphors in anthropology. The study of "ethnographic allegory" (Clifford 1986b; Tyler 1986) cannot be taken to refer primarily to allegorical forms *in* ethnography without losing site of the larger picture. Our starting point cannot be "a crisis in anthropology" (Clifford 1986a, 3), but in the histories of the world.[17] We need to go out of anthropology to see the construction of "ethnographic authority" not as a late requirement of anthropological discourse (Clifford 1983b) but as an early component of this wider field that is itself constitutive of anthropology. Would that the power of anthropology hinged upon the academic success of genial immigrants such as Franz Boas and Bronislaw Malinowski! It would allow us to find new scapegoats without ever looking back at the Renaissance. But the exercise in reflexivity must go all the way and examine fully the enlarged reproduction of anthropological discourse.[18]

Observers may wonder why the postmodernist experiment in US anthropology has not encouraged a surge of substantive models. The question of time aside, the difficulty of passing from criticism to substance is not simply due to a theoretical aversion to content or an instinctive suspicion of exemplars. After all, the postmodernist wave has revitalized substantive production in other academic fields. It has stimulated architects and political theorists alike. At the very least, it has provoked debates on and of substance. Further, some political radicals advocate the possibility of militant practices rooted in postmodernism—although not without controversies (Laclau and Mouffe 1985; Arac 1986; Ross 1988b). More important, the implicit awareness of an expanding situation of postmodernity continues to motivate grass-roots movements all over the world, with their partial truths and partial results. In fact, an anthropologist could well read postmodernism, or at the very least the postmodern situation, as a case for the specificity of otherness, for the destruction of the Savage slot.

To claim the specificity of otherness is to suggest a residual of historical experience that always escapes universalisms exactly because history itself always involves irreducible subjects. It is to reserve a space for the subject—not the existential subject favored by the early Sartre and who keeps creeping back into the mea culpa anthropology, but the men and women who are the subjects of history.[19] It is to acknowledge that this space of the historical subject is out of reach of all metanarratives, not because all metanarratives are created equal and are equally wrong (which is the claim of nihilism and always ends up favoring *some* subjects and *some* narratives), but because metanarrative claims to universality necessarily imply the muting of first persons, singular or plural, deemed marginal. To say that otherness is always specific and historical is to reject this marginality. The Other cannot be encompassed by a residual category: there is no Savage slot. The "us and all of them" binary, implicit in the symbolic order that creates the West, is an ideological construct, and the many forms of Third Worldism that reverse its terms are its mirror images. There is no Other, but multitudes of others who are all others for different reasons, in spite of totalizing narratives, including that of capital.

Many propositions follow from this statement, not the least of which is that a discipline whose object is the Other may in fact have no object—which may lead us to take a much-needed look at the methodological specificity of anthropology. It also follows that the authenticity of the historical subject may not be fully captured from the outside even by way of direct quotes; there may be something irreducible in the first person singular. This, in turn, raises two related issues: that of the epistemological status of native discourse;[20] and that of the theoretical status of ethnography. I will turn to these issues, not so much in a purely abstract mode (though this may be also necessary), but as entwined with specific research projects.

First, anthropology needs to evaluate its gains and losses in light of these issues, with a fair tally of the knowledge anthropologists have produced in the past, sometimes in spite of themselves and almost always in spite of the Savage slot. We owe it to ourselves to ask what remains of anthropology and of specific monographs when we remove this slot—not to revitalize disciplinary tradition through cosmetic surgery, but to build both an epistemology and a semiology of what anthropologists have done and can do. We cannot simply assume that modernism has exhausted all its potential projects. Nor can we assume that "realist ethnography" has produced nothing but empty figures of speech and shallow claims to authority.

Second, armed with this renewed arsenal, we can recapture domains of significance by creating strategic points of "reentry" into the discourse on otherness: areas within the discourse where the introduction of new voices or new combinations of meaning perturbate the entire field and open the way to its (partial) recapture.[21] This chapter is not the place to expand in the directions of these many queries, so I can only tease the reader. But a few tasks seem to me urgent in this new context: an epistemological reassessment of the historical subject (the first-person singular that has been overwhelmed by the voice of objectivity or by that of the narrator and that is so important to many feminists, especially Afro-American feminists); a similar reassessment of nativeness and native discourse, now barely conceptualized; and a theory of ethnography, now repudiated as the new "false consciousness." And for the time being, at least, we need more ethnographies that raise these issues through concrete cases. Not so much ethnographies that question the author/native dichotomy by exposing the nude as nakedness, but ethnographies (ethnohistorio-semiologies?) that offer new points of reentry by questioning the symbolic world upon which "nativeness" is premised. At the very least, anthropologists can show that the Other, here and elsewhere, is indeed a product—symbolic and material—of the same process that created the West.[22] In short, the time is ripe for substantive propositions that aim explicitly at the destruction of the Savage slot.

That it has not been so among the postmodernists of North American anthropology is thus a matter of choice. In spite of a terminology that intimates a decoding of "anthropology as metaphor," we are barely reading anthropology itself. Rather, we are reading anthropological pages, and attention remains focused primarily on the metaphors in anthropology. This recurring refusal to pursue further the archaeological exercise obscures the asymmetrical position of the Savage-Other in the thematic field upon which anthropology was premised. It negates the specificity of otherness, subsuming the Other in the sameness of the text perceived as liberating cooperation. "We are the world"?

Anthropology did not create the Savage. Rather, the Savage was the raison d'être of anthropology. Anthropology came to fill the Savage slot in the trilogy of order-utopia-savagery, a trilogy which preceded anthropology's institutionalization and gave it continuing coherence in spite of intradisciplinary shifts. This trilogy is now in jeopardy. Thus the time is ripe—and in that sense, it is postmodern—to attack frontally the visions that shaped this trilogy, to uncover its ethical roots and its consequences, and to find better anchor for an anthropology of the present, an anthropology of the changing world and its irreducible histories. But postmodernist anthropologists pass near this opportunity looking for the Savage in the text. They want us to read the internal tropes of the Savage slot, no doubt a useful exercise in spite of its potential for self-indulgence. But they refuse to address directly the thematic field (and thus the larger world) that made (makes) this slot possible, morosely preserving the empty slot itself.

Times have changed since the sixteenth century: one now is innocent until proven guilty. Thus, claims of innocence can take the shape of silence. Somehow, to my surprise, I miss the faithful indignation of a Las Casas.

NOTES

My thanks to all those who commented on earlier versions of this paper, the participants at the Santa Fe Seminar, graduate students and faculty at Johns Hopkins University and at the New School for Social Research, and the readers for the School of American Research. Personal thanks to Kamran Ali, Talal Asad, Lanfranco Blanchetti, Ashraf Ghani, Ananta Giri, Richard G. Fox, Richard Kagan, and Eric Wolf, none of whom should be held responsible for the final product. An early version of this paper, "Anthropology as Metaphor: The Savage's Legacy and the Postmodern World," appeared in *Review (Fernand Braudel Center)* 14, no. 1: 29–54.

Editors' Note: This essay first appeared as "Anthropology and the Savage Slot: The Poetics and Politics of Otherness," in *Recapturing Anthropology: Working in the Present*, ed. Richard G. Fox (Santa Fe, NM: School of American Research Press, 1991), 17–44.

1. For reasons of space, I cannot retrace here all the connections between recent debates in philosophy and literary theory and recent critiques of anthropology. Our readings are too parochial, anyway—to the point that any major thinker needs to be translated into the discipline by an insider. Anthropology has much more to learn from other disciplines, notably history, literary criticism, and philosophy, than the reflexivist interpreters assume. There are blanks to be filled by the reader with proper use of the bibliographical references.

2. Other reasons aside, long-term fieldwork in the so-called Third World, after the initial dissertation, is becoming more difficult and less rewarding for a majority of anthropologists. Unfortunately, issues such as the increased competition for funds to do fieldwork abroad or the growing proportion of two-career families in and out of academe only make good conversation. Practitioners tend to dismiss them in written (and therefore "serious") assessments of trends in the discipline. The sociology of our practice is perceived as taboo, but see Wolf 1969, whose early appeal for such a sociology fell on deaf ears, and Rabinow 1991.

3. In that sense, I take exception to Renato Rosaldo's formulation that the conservative domination "has distorted a once healthy debate" (Rosaldo 1989, 223). What a certain kind of anthropology can demonstrate is exactly that the debate was never as healthy as we were led to believe.

4. See Graff 1977, Jameson 1984, Arac 1986, Lyotard 1986, Ross 1988b, and Harvey 1989 on conflicting definitions of postmodernism. I am not qualified to settle this debate. But if postmodernism only means a style, a bundle of expository devices, characterized (or not) by "double coding" (Jencks 1986), then it does not much matter to anthropologists—as long as they note that double coding has been part of the cultural arsenal of many non-Western cultures for centuries. On the connection between postmodernism and metanarratives, see Lyotard 1979, 1986; Eagleton 1987; and Harvey 1989.

5. The first consists of two chapters in *Les bijoux indiscrets*. The second is the fantastic *Supplément au voyage du Bougainville*, a primitivist utopia where Tahiti is the Other in more than one way, being both Savage and female (Trousson 1975, 140; Brewer 1985).

6. I owe my ideas on the Black or plantation pastoral to conversations with Professor Maximilien Laroche and access to his unpublished paper on the subject. In Bernadin Saint-Pierre's successful *Paul et Virginie* (1787), whose setting is a plantation island, a group of maroon slaves surprises the two lovers. But to the heroes' amazement, the chief of the runaway slaves says, "Good little whites, don't be afraid; we saw you pass this morning with a negro woman from Rivière-Noire; you went to ask her grace to her bad master; in gratitude, we will carry you back home on our shoulders."

7. Some writers have made this point. Others have assembled the necessary information to make it, without always drawing the same conclusion from their juxtapositions. I have read over the shoulders of so many of them, and imposed my reading on so many' others, that credits for this section and the next were sometimes difficult to attribute in the main text; but see Atkinson 1920, 1922, 1924; Baudet 1959; Chinard 1934; Duchet 1971; Certeau 1975; Gonnard 1946; Todorov 1982; Trousson 1975; Rupp-Eisenreich 1984; and Droixhe and Gossiaux 1985.

8. My phrasing of this issue in terms of order owes to conversations with Ashraf Ghani. I remain responsible for its use here and its possible shortcomings. Empirical elements of an analysis of the role of order within the symbolic horizons of the Renaissance are plentiful in Hale's *Renaissance Europe: Individual and Society, 1480–1520* (1977).

9. Genealogies that trace the beginnings of anthropology to Herodotus (why not Ibn Battuta?) partake of that naive history. They serve the guild interests of the "discipline," its construction of tradition, authorship, and authority and the reproduction of the Savage slot upon which it builds its legitimacy. Note, however, that it was only in the eighteenth and nineteenth centuries that

Romantics and racists abandoned the ancient Greeks' own version of their cultural origins, denying the contributions of Africans and Semites to "civilization." Classical studies then invented a new past for Greece with an Aryan model (Bernal 1987).

10. From then on, descriptions of savagery would inscribe grammatically the absence in a way now all too familiar (and unquestioned) by anthropologists. The Savage is what the West is not: "no manner of traffic, no knowledge of letters, no science of numbers . . . no contracts, no successions, no dividends, no properties" (Montaigne 1952, 94). This language is quite different from that of Polo (1958) or even from that of Pliny. But its immediate antecedents are in the very first descriptions of the Americas: Columbus, for instance, thought the "Indians" had "no religion"—by which he probably meant "none of the three religions of Abraham."

11. One cannot suggest that Francis I consciously foresaw a French nation-state in the modern sense, but the absolutist order he envisioned revealed itself historically untenable without the invented tradition necessary for the symbolic construction of the nation. It is only by one of those ironies of which history is full that this tradition became fully alive at the time of the Revolution and was solidified by a Corsican mercenary with no claim to Frankish nobility, namely, Napoleone Buonaparte.

12. One suspects that the Savage as wise is more often than not Asiatic, the Savage as noble is often a Native American, and the Savage as barbarian is often African or African American. But neither roles nor positions are always neat, and the structural dichotomies do not always obtain historically. Jews and Gypsies, for instance, are Savages "within" the West—an awkward position not accounted by the Here/Elsewhere dichotomy but resolved in practice by persecution.

13. Anthropological insistence on, say, rebellion and resistance in Latin America, economic qua material survival in Africa, or ritual expression in Southeast Asia partakes of a symbolic distribution that predates chronologically and precedes epistemologically the division of labor within the discipline. A major limitation of the work of Edward Said is the failure to read "Orientalism" as one set of permutations within the Savage slot.

14. My greater familiarity with Caribbean anthropology may explain why I find most of my positive examples in this corner of the world, but it is obvious to Caribbeanists that anthropology helped challenge the vision of the Antilles as islands in the sun peopled by indolent natives—a view popularized since the nineteenth century by racist yet celebrated writers such as Anthony Trollope (1859). How successful was the challenge is another issue, but forty years before "voodoo economics" became a pejorative slogan in North American political parlance, some North American and European anthropologists took Haitian popular religion quite seriously (e.g., Herskovits 1937b).

15. To be sure, in its current form, the alleged discovery of the text provokes transient hyperboles. We all knew that ethnography was also text if only because of the ABDs relegated to driving cabs when their lines could not see the light of day, or because of the careers destroyed when dissertations failed to sprout "publishable" books (the text/test par excellence?). That Marcus and Cushman (1982, 27) "for simplicity . . . do not consider the very interesting relationship between the production of a published ethnographic text and its intermediate written versions" is not novel. Tenure committees have been doing the same for years, also "for simplicity," while we all continued to ignore politely the electoral politics that condition academic success.

16. See Clifford's (1986a, 21) indulgent neglect of feminism on purely textual grounds: "It has not produced either unconventional forms of writing or a developed reflection on ethnographic textuality as such." Never mind that feminism now sustains one of the most potent discourses on the specificity of the historical subject and, by extension, on the problem of "voice." To be sure, some white middle-class women, especially in the United States, want to make that newfound "voice" universal, and their feminist enterprise threatens to become a new metanarrative, akin to Fanon's Third Worldism, or Black Power à la 1960. But it is at the very least awkward for Clifford to dismiss feminist and "non-Western writings" for having made their impact on issues of content alone.

17. In fact, I doubt that there is a crisis *in* anthropology as such; rather, there is a crisis in the world that anthropology assumes.

18. The limited exercises of the postmodernists would take on new dimensions if used to look at the enlarged reproduction of anthropology. For example, were we to rekindle the notion of genre to read ethnography (Marcus 1980), we would need to speculate either a metatext (the retrospective classification of a critic), or the sanction of a receiving audience of nonspecialists, or a thematic and ideological framework in the form of an archi-textual field (Genette, Jauss, and Schaffer, 1986). To speak of any of these in relation to ethnography as genre would illustrate enlarged reproduction and reexamine anthropology's own grounds.

19. I thank Eric Wolf for forcing me to make this important distinction.

20. The matter of the status of "halfies" (see Abu-Lughod 1991) can be further analyzed in these terms. We need not fall into nativism in order to raise epistemological questions about the effect of historically accumulated experience, the "historical surplus value" that specific groups of subjects-as-practitioners bring to a discipline premised on the existence of the Savage slot and the commensurability of otherness. At the same time, for philosophical and political reasons, I am profoundly opposed to the formulas of the type "add native, stir, and proceed as usual," so successful in electoral politics in and out of academe. Anthropology needs something more fundamental than reconstitutive surgery, and halfies, women, people of color, etc., deserve something better than a new slot.

21. The symbolic reappropriation that Christianity imposed on Judaism, or that liberation theology is imposing on Christianity in some areas of the world; the reorientation that the ecology movement has injected into notions of "survival"; the redirection that feminism has imposed on issues of gender; and Marx's perturbation of classical political economy from within are all unequal examples of "reentry" and recapture.

22. The anthropology of agricultural commodities as material and symbolic boundaries between human groups (along the lines opened by Mintz 1985b); the anthropology of the categories and institutions that reflect and organize power—such as "peasants," "nation," "science" (Trouillot 1988, 1989, 1990; Martin 1987), or the "West" itself (to renew with both Benveniste [1969] and Foucault); the anthropology of the transnational media and other forms of communication shaping the international organization of symbols—all can be fruitfully conceptualized within such a scheme.

REFERENCES

Abu-Lughod, Lila. 1991. "Writing against Culture." In *Recapturing Anthropology: Working in the Present*, edited by Richard G. Fox, 137–62. Santa Fe, NM: School of American Research Press.

Ainsa, Fernando. 1988. "L'invention de l'Amérique: Signes imaginaires de la découverte et construction de l'utopie." *Diogènes* 145: 405–35.

André-Vincent, Philippe. 1980. *Bartholomé de Las Casas, prophète du nouveau-monde*. Paris: Librarie Jules Tallandier.

Andrews, Charles M, ed. 1937. *Famous Utopias: Being the Complete Text of Rousseau's "Social Contract," More's "Utopia," Bacon's "New Atlantis," Campanella's "City of the Sun."* New York: Tudor.

Appadurai, Arjun. 1991. "Global Ethnoscapes: Notes and Queries for a Transnational Anthropology." In *Recapturing Anthropology: Working in the Present*, edited by Richard G. Fox, 191–210. Santa Fe, NM: School of American Research Press.

Arac, Jonathan. 1986. "Introduction." In *Postmodernism and Politics*, edited by Jonathan Arac, ix–xiii. Minneapolis: University of Minnesota Press.

Aronowitz, Stanley. 1988. "Postmodernism and Politics." In *Universal Abandon? The Politics of Postmodernism*, edited by Andrew Ross, 46–62. Minneapolis: University of Minnesota Press.

Asad, Talal. 1973. *Anthropology and the Colonial Encounter*. London: Ithaca Press.

Atkinson, Geoffroy. 1920. *The Extraordinary Voyage in French Literature before 1700*. New York: Columbia University Press.

Atkinson, Geoffroy. 1922. *The Extraordinary Voyage in French Literature from 1700 to 1720*. Paris: Librarie Ancienne Édouard Champion.

Atkinson, Geoffroy. 1924. *Les relations de voyage du XVIIe siècle et l'évolution des idées*. Paris: Librarie Ancienne Édouard Champion.

Baudet, Henri. 1959. *Some Thoughts on European Images of Non-European Man*. New Haven, CT: Yale University Press.

Benveniste, Emile. 1969. *Le vocabulaire des institutions indo-européenes*. Paris: Éditions de Minuit.

Bernal, Martin. 1987. *Black Athena: The Afroasiatic Roots of Classical Civilization*. Vol. 1 of *The Fabrication of Ancient Greece, 1785–1985*. New Brunswick, NJ: Rutgers University Press.

Brewer, David. 1985. "Diderot et l'autre feminine." In *L'Homme des Lumières et la decouverte de l'autre*, edited by D. Droixhe and P. Gossiaux, 81–91. Bruxelles: Éditions de l'Université de Bruxelles.

Certeau, Michel de. 1975. *L'ecriture de l'histoire*. Paris: Gallimard.

Chinard, Gilbert. 1934. *L'amérique et le rêve exotique dans la littérature française aux XVIIe et XVIIIe siècles*. Paris: Librairie de Medicis.

Clifford, James. 1983. "On Ethnographic Authority." *Representations* 1, no. 2: 118–46.

Clifford, James. 1986a. "Introduction." In *Writing Culture: The Poetics and Politics of Ethnography*, edited by James Clifford and George Marcus, 1–26. Berkeley: University of California Press.

Clifford, James. 1986b. "On Ethnographic Allegory." In *Writing Culture: The Poetics and Politics of Ethnography*, edited by James Clifford and George Marcus, 98–121. Berkeley: University of California Press.

Droixhe, Daniel, and Pol-P. Gossiaux, eds. 1985. *L'homme des Lumières et la découverte de l'autre*. Bruxelles: Éditions de l'Université de Bruxelles.

Duchet, Michèle. 1971. *Anthropologie et histoire au siècle des Lumières*. Paris: Maspero.

Du Tertre, Jean-Baptiste. (1667) 1973. *Histoire générale des Antilles habitées par les François*. Fort de France: Éditions des Horizons Caraïbes.

Eagleton, Terry. 1987. "Awakening from Modernity." *Times Literary Supplement*, February 20.

Fox, Richard G. 1991. "For a Nearly New Culture History." In *Recapturing Anthropology: Working in the Present*, edited by Richard G. Fox, 93–114. Santa Fe, NM: School of American Research Press.

Gage, Thomas. (1648) 1958. *Travels in the New World*. Edited by J. E. S. Thompson. Norman: University of Oklahoma Press.

Geertz, Clifford. 1973. *The Interpretation of Cultures*. New York: Basic Books.

Genette, Gérard, Hans Robert Jauss, and Jean-Marie Schaeffer. 1986. *Théorie des genres*. Paris: Éditions du Seuil.

Glissant, Édouard. 1989. *Caribbean Discourse: Selected Essays*. Translated by J. M. Dash. Charlottesville: University of Virginia Press.

Godzich, Vlad. 1986. "Foreword." In *Heterologies: Discourse on the Other*, edited by Michel de Certeau, vii–xxi. Minneapolis: University of Minnesota Press.

Gonnard, René. 1946. *La légende du bon sauvage: Contribution a l'étude des origins de socialisme*. Paris: Librarie de Medicis.

Graff, Gerald. 1977. "The Myth of the Postmodernist Breakthrough." In *The Novel Today: Contemporary Writers on Modern Fiction*, edited by Malcolm Bradbury, 217–49. Manchester: Manchester University Press.

Hale, J. R. 1977. *Renaissance Europe: Individual and Society, 1480–1520*. Berkeley: University of California Press.

Harvey, David. 1989. *The Condition of Postmodernity*. Oxford: Basil Blackwell.

Herskovits, Melville J. (1937) 1975. *Life in a Haitian Valley*. New York: Octagon Books.

Jameson, Fredric. 1984. "Postmodernism, or the Cultural Logic of Late Capitalism." *New Left Review* I/146: 53–92.

Jencks, Charles. 1986. *What Is Post-modernism?* London: Academy Press.

Kamenka, Eugene, ed. 1987. *Utopias*. Oxford: Oxford University Press.

Labat, Jean Baptiste. (1722) 1972. *Nouveau voyage aux isles de l'Amérique*. Fort de France: Éditions des Horizons Caraïbes.

Laclau, Ernesto, and Chantal Mouffe. 1985. *Hegemony and Socialist Strategy: Towards a Radical Democratic Politics*. London: Verso.

Levin, Harry. 1967. *The Power of Blackness*. New York: Alfred A. Knopf.

Lyotard, Jean François. 1979. *La Condition postmoderne*. Paris: Éditions de Minuit.

Lyotard, Jean François. 1986. *Le Postmoderne expliqué aux enfants*. Paris: Éditions Galilee.

Manue, Frank E., and Fritzie P. Manuel. 1979. *Utopian Thought and the Western World*. Cambridge, MA: Belknap Press of Harvard University Press.

Marcus, George E. 1980. "Rhetoric and the Ethnographic Genre in Anthropological Research." *Current Anthropology* 21: 507–10.

Marcus, George E., and Dick Cushman. 1982. "Ethnographies as Texts." *Annual Reviews of Anthropology* 11: 25–69.

Martin, Emily. 1987. *The Woman in the Body: A Cultural Analysis of Reproduction*. Boston: Beacon Press.

Mintz, Sidney. 1971. "Le rouge et le noir." *Les Temps Modernes* 299–300: 2354–61.

Mintz, Sidney. 1985. *Sweetness and Power: The Place of Sugar in Modern History*. New York: Viking.

Mintz, Sidney. 1990. "Introduction." In *The Myth of the Negro Past*, edited by M. J. Herskovits, ix–xxi. Boston: Beacon Press.

Montaigne, Michel Eyquem de. 1952. *Essays*. Vol. 25 of *Encyclopedia Britannica, Great Books of the Western World*. Chicago: Encyclopedia Britannica.

Pagden, Anthony. 1982. *The Fall of Natural Man: The American Indian and the Origins of Comparative Ethnology*. Cambridge: Cambridge University Press.

Pfaelzer, Jean. 1984. *The Utopian Novel in America, 1886–1896: The Politics of Form*. Pittsburgh: University of Pittsburgh Press.

Pratt, Mary Louise. 1986. "Fieldwork in Common Places." In *Writing Culture: The Poetics and Politics of Ethnography*, edited by James Clifford and George Marcus, 27–50. Berkeley: University of California Press.

Rabinow, Paul. 1991. "For Hire: Resolutely Late Modern." In *Recapturing Anthropology: Working in the Present*, edited by Richard G. Fox, 59–72. Santa Fe, NM: School of American Research Press.

Rosaldo, Renato. 1986. "From the Door of His Tent: The Fieldworker and the Inquisitor." In *Writing Culture: The Poetics and Politics of Ethnography*, edited by James Clifford and George Marcus, 77–97. Berkeley: University of California Press.

Rosaldo, Renato. 1989. *Culture and Truth: The Remaking of Social Analysis*. Boston: Beacon Press.

Ross, Andrew. 1988a. "Introduction." In *Universal Abandon? The Politics of Postmodernism*, edited by Andrew Ross, vii–xviii. Minneapolis: University of Minnesota Press.

Ross, Andrew, ed. 1988b. *Universal Abandon? The Politics of Postmodernism*. Minneapolis: University of Minnesota Press.

Rupp-Eisenreich, Britta, ed. 1984. *Histoire de l'anthropologie (XVI–XIX siècles)*. Paris: Klincksiech.

Rupp-Eisenreich, Britta. 1985. "Christophe Meiners et Joseph-Marie de Gerando: Un chapitre du comparatisme anthropologique." In *L'homme des Lumières et la découverte de l'autre*, edited by D. Droixhe and P. Gossiaux, 21–47. Bruxelles: Éditions de l'Universite de Bruxelles.

Thornton, Robert. 1983. "Narrative Ethnography in Africa, 1850–1920." *Man* 18: 502–20.

Tinker, Chauncey Brewster. 1922. *Nature's Simple Plan: A Phase of Radical Thought in the Mid-Eighteenth Century*. Princeton, NJ: Princeton University Press.

Todorov, Tzvetan. 1982. *La conquête de l'Amérique: La question de l'autre*. Paris: Éditions du Seuil.

Trollope, Anthony. (1859) 1985. *The West Indies and the Spanish Main*. New York: Hippocrene Books.

Trouillot, Michel-Rolph. 1988. *Peasants and Capital: Dominica in the World Economy*. Baltimore: Johns Hopkins University Press.

Trouillot, Michel-Rolph. 1989. "Discourses of Rule: The Acknowledgment of the Peasantry in Dominica, W.I., 1838–1928." *American Ethnologist* 16, no. 4: 704–18.

Trouillot, Michel-Rolph. 1990. "Good Day, Columbus: Silences, Power, and Public History (1492–1892)." *Public Culture* 3, no. 1: 1–24.

Trousson, Raymond. 1975. *Voyages aux pays de nulle part: Histoire littéraire de la pensé utopique*. Bruxelles: Éditions de l'Université de Bruxelles.

Tyler, Stephen. 1986. "Post-modern Ethnography: From Document of the Occult to Occult Document." In *Writing Culture: The Poetics and Politics of Ethnography*, edited by James Clifford and George Marcus, 122–40. Berkeley: University of California Press.

Vincent, Joan. 1991. "Engaging Historicism." In *Recapturing Anthropology: Working in the Present*, edited by Richard G. Fox, 45–58. Santa Fe, NM: School of American Research Press.

Walkover, Andrew. 1974. *The Dialectics of Eden*. Stanford, CA: Stanford University Press.

Weil, François. 1984. "La relation de voyage: Document anthropologique ou texte littéraire?" In *Histoire de l'anthropologie (XVI–XIX siècles)*, edited by B. Rupp-Eisenreich, 55–65. Paris: Klincksiech.

Wolf, Eric R. 1969. "American Anthropologists and American Society." In *Concepts and Assumptions in Contemporary Anthropology*, edited by S. Tyler, 3–11. Athens: University of Georgia Press.

Wolf, Eric R. 1982. *Europe and the People without History*. Berkeley: University of California Press.

CHAPTER 2

The Odd and the Ordinary

Haiti, the Caribbean, and the World

"How does one explain Haiti? What is Haiti? Haiti is the eldest daughter of France and Africa. It is a place of beauty, romance, mystery, kindness, humor, selfishness, betrayal, cruelty, bloodshed, hunger and poverty. It is a closed and withdrawn society whose apartness, unlike any other in the New World, rejects its European roots."

Nice passage, isn't it? Well, those of you who know my work may have guessed that I am trying to trick you. These words are not mine. They constitute the very first paragraph of *Written in Blood*, a sensationalist account of Haitian history written by Marine Colonel Robert Heinl and his wife, Nancy.[1] I quote this paragraph in lieu of an introduction because it typifies a viewpoint widely shared in Haitian studies, one that I wish to challenge, namely the fiction of Haiti's exceptionalism. Heinl and Heinl start with a question: "How does one explain Haiti?" The question is then set aside for a laundry list of particulars. Then, at the end of that list, the emphasis shifts to Haiti's apartness: Haiti is unique. It is unlike any other country in the New World. And indeed, if we keep reading the next seven hundred pages, we soon discover that it is unlike any other country—period.

The notion of Haitian exceptionalism permeates both the academic and popular literature on Haiti under different guises and with different degrees of candidness. At first glance, this insistence on Haiti's special status seems to be a simple acknowledgment of the country's admittedly spectacular trajectory. I suggest, however, that there are hidden agendas—intellectual and political—behind this insistence, and that these agendas, rather than genuine interest in the particulars of Haitian history, underpin Haitian exceptionalism.

Haiti is unique. Haiti is different. Haiti is special. At a superficial level, these sayings could simply mean that a particular set of environmental, historical, and social features contribute in varied ways to make Haiti quite different from other places: that Haiti is not Argentina, or Canada, or Germany, or Senegal. I have absolutely no quarrel with such a statement. I can assure you that no one born in Aquin, Gonaives, or Cité Soleil thinks of them as Buenos Aires, Frankfurt, or Dakar.

But those who insist most often on Haiti's uniqueness do not simply mean that Haiti is easily unique. For each and every society is unique, distinguishable from each and every other society. Indeed, regions within the same country can be distinguishable from other regions. Societies, countries, or regions are historical products, and all historical products are unique—by definition and by necessity. And the more we know a place or a person, the more this place or this person appears unique. But we do not keep on repeating it: life is too short for that. To my knowledge, foreign or native writers who write about, say, the Dominican Republic, Paraguay, Bolivia, Thailand, Madagascar, or Gabon—to cite only a few remarkable places—do not go on repeating ad nauseam how unique these societies are. They assume this uniqueness and proceed from there. So the celebrated uniqueness of Haitian society and culture must mean more than the distinctiveness that characterizes any historical product from any other historical product.

If all historical products are unique, not all of them are distinguishable in the same way. It is quite probable that a particular configuration of circumstances will lead to a historical product of which the uniqueness is dazzling: an individual, a group of individuals, an institution, or a phenomenon that strikes us more than otherwise similar entities. In short, some historical products are more remarkable than others, at least to certain groups of observers. However unique we may all be, it makes sense to insist that Julius Caesar, Napoleon, Shaka the Zulu, Toussaint Louverture, François Duvalier, or Mikhail Gorbachev are unique in ways that need to be noticed. It makes sense to insist upon the fact that the Holy See is a unique religious institution. That the French Academy is a unique combination of culture and politics. That German fascism was a unique political movement. That the state of Israel is a unique geopolitical entity. That the United States, Cuba, Brazil, Liberia, Tibet, or the Philippines are quite distinguishable countries, the uniqueness of which both strikes out and needs to be emphasized in the context of their own immediate environment or even perhaps in the context of world history.

In that sense, of course, Haiti seems more unique than many other countries. The list of features that makes it special is long, starting with the history of Saint-Domingue and the Haitian Revolution: first and only successful slave revolution in modern history. First independent country of the Americas and, for a long time, the only one where freedom meant freedom for everyone. First and, for a long time, sole Black republic in world history, indeed, the first nonwhite modern state. The most peasant country of the Americas. Largest creole speaking population of the world. And so on. And so on. And so on.

In that sense, of course, Haiti is indeed unique. And if we want to play semantic games, it is not just unique: it is exceptional, the result of a striking convergence of historical particulars. This is the distinctiveness that accounts for Haiti's cultural resilience. This is the distinctiveness that attracts many foreigners—tourists and academics, for good or for bad. This is the distinctiveness that succors Haitians national pride—for good *and* for bad. This is the distinctiveness that Haitian tourism officials have banked on for more than twenty years with the slogan "Vive la différénce!"

I have no quarrel with such a view of Haiti's particularisms, even though I may question the use some make of them. For all the reasons I have mentioned and probably many more, Haiti is in many ways exceptional. I would insist, though, that this exceptionalism is only one way to look at Haitian reality. There are much less petulant continuities embedded in this spectacular trajectory. The majority of Haitians live quite ordinary lives. They eat what is for them—and for many others—quite ordinary food. They die quite ordinary deaths from quite ordinary accidents, quite ordinary tortures, quite ordinary diseases. Accidents so ordinary that they could be prevented. Tortures so ordinary that the international press does not even mention them. Diseases so ordinary that they are easily treated almost anywhere else. Exceptional, is it?

Certainly more exceptional than India, Java, Burma, or Ethiopia— which are of course exceptional in their own ways. Listen to Blair Niles, the author of *Black Haiti*: "I am familiar with the measured posturing dances of Japan, of India, Java and Burma. I have watched the head-hunting dance of the Dyaks of Borneo. That was savage enough; primitive enough. . . . But savage as it was, that too had been in a way sophisticated." For Blair Niles discovered Haiti and its dances. That, says Niles, "went further back than the hunt [of Borneo]; back to the beginning" (Niles 1926, 27).

Note that Blair Niles is writing in admiration, in this passage at least. Elsewhere in the book, he heavily criticizes foreigners who denigrate the

Haitian people. Further, there is ample evidence throughout the text that Niles made a more genuine effort than many other visitors, both before and after him, to understand Haiti. At any rate, no one can accuse him of disliking Haitians. Quite the opposite: he is attracted to them. But he is attracted to them the way one can be attracted to a sexual fetish or a taboo. That is, he is attracted to Haiti as deviance. What he likes in Haiti is what he finds aberrant, the reverse image of a world of normalcy. That is not unique. That is not even exceptional. That is weird.

Listen to Professor Heinz Lehman of McGill University talking to student Wade Davis of *Serpent and Rainbow* fame: "Let me relieve you of any further suspense, Mr. Davis. We understand . . . that you are attracted to unusual places. We propose to send you to the frontier of death" (Davis 1985, 15). Davis is attracted to "unusual" places. Unusual here does not mean unique, and the reference to the frontier of death as well (as the Hollywood of the book) is there to testify to the nuance. No, unusual here means odd, strange, peculiar, freakish, queer, bizarre. Weird, indeed, don't you think?

To be sure, Davis is careful not to use these words; but that may be a reflection of the times. Even travel guides and *National Geographic* have learned not to present so-called exotic places in explicitly condescending or derogatory terminology. Further, since the nineteenth century, a Haitian tradition of sharp rebuttal has kept many foreign writers, French and North American in particular, on their guard. Thus, for instance, Davis—of all people—tries to distance himself from "sensational films and pulp fiction" (1988, 3). The Heinls (one of whom epitomized the worst of US interference in Haitian politics) dedicate their book to Haitian nationalist heroes. It has become stylish for foreign writers to denounce Haiti's bad press while contributing to it in fact.

In that context, Haitian exceptionalism tends to function at the level of the subtext in most books published outside the country in the second half of this century. While it permeates the entire work, there are very few sentences that actually articulate it, except perhaps on the back cover or in the ad copy (e.g., Davis 1985; Abbott 1989).[2] At times, however, writers— including respected academics—can be less careful, or nonchalant enough for Haitian exceptionalism to appear clearly in the text. One more quote among many: "Haiti, like eighteenth-century Sicily has always been a place apart," a place with "a penchant for the bizarre and the grotesque" (Rotberg 1971, 7, 8). As the French used to put it, with debonair condescension, "Singulier petit pays."

I am, of course, bothered by this condescension. But there is more to it. The most important problem with the overemphasis on Haiti's singularity—even if not phrased in derogatory terms—is both methodological and political. My own intolerance is less toward the narrow-mindedness often implicit in such statements (which, after all, say more about their authors than about Haiti) than toward the practical consequences of this narrow-mindedness. When we are being told over and over again that Haiti is unique, bizarre, unnatural, odd, queer, freakish, or grotesque, we are also being told, in varying degrees, that it is unnatural, erratic, and therefore unexplainable. We are being told that Haiti is so special that modes of investigation applicable to other societies are not relevant here.

In her remarkable book, *Haiti and the Great Powers*, Brenda Gayle Plummer criticizes the myth of Haitian exceptionalism and exposes some of its consequences. In Plummer's view, "The idea that Haiti could fit no paradigm prohibited the development of any but the most conservative policies" on the part of international powers, including the United States (Plummer 1988, 6). One could add that the very same view continues today to influence some policy-makers in the United States, in France, or in the Vatican—to cite only three states involved in Haitian affairs. Plummer is much more indulgent than I am, however, toward Haitian politicians and intellectuals, even though she admits that they share some of the blame. In my view, in both cases Haitian exceptionalism acts as a shield.

Though not the privy of nonnative writers, the fiction that Haiti escapes analysis and comparison emerged out of the minds of European and North American observers, mostly white males, who wrote about Haiti in the early nineteenth century, at the time when the very existence of a "Black" state that had issued from an anticolonial revolution appeared to them as an aberration. For a plethora of writers from James Franklin to Gustave d'Alaux, to Spencer St. John, to Robert and Nancy Heinl, Haitian exceptionalism has been a shield that masks the negative contribution of the Western powers to the Haitian situation. Haitian exceptionalism functions as a shield to Haiti's integration into a world dominated by Christianity, capitalism, and whiteness. The more Haiti appears weird, the easier it is to forget that it represents the longest neocolonial experiment in the history of the West.

Even James Leyburn was guilty of the same sin of omission. In the third chapter of his important book, *The Haitian People*, Leyburn (1941, 32) wrote: "If ever a country had an opportunity to start absolutely fresh in choosing its own social institutions, Haiti had that opportunity in 1804. . . . The Haitians might (theoretically, at least) have invented an entire new little world of economic, political, religious, and social life. All paths were open to them." Leyburn concluded that unfortunately Dessalines's mental limitations set the Haitians on the road to disaster.

Well, that won't do. Neither theoretically nor in practice. With one stroke of the pen, Leyburn erases three centuries of direct colonial domination and a century and a half of neocolonialism. And this from an author who remains, in my view, one of the best observers, foreign or Haitian, of Haitian society and culture.

The Haitian side is no more glorious, even though at times it looks better on paper. Indeed, many Haitian intellectuals and politicians continue to repeat the same nonsense, more loudly even than their foreign counterparts. The reality is that this fiction is as convenient to the Haitian elite as it is to many foreigners, even though for different reasons.

Before the twentieth century, Haitian writers rarely if ever promoted Haitian singularity in their studies of Haitian reality. In fact, quite the opposite, especially for the early part of the nineteenth century. Indeed, Haitian intellectuals rightly saw the theories of Haitian exceptionalism that were spreading in Europe and North America as implicitly—and often explicitly—racist. In the immediate aftermath of independence, a writer such as Baron de Vastey relied on the universalist principles of the Enlightenment to herald the Haitian Revolution and reject theories associating physical appearance and national character.[3] In the late nineteenth and early twentieth centuries, writers such as Demesvar Delorme, Louis-Joseph Janvier, Anténor Firmin, Edmond Paul, down to Jean Price-Mars and Dantès Bellegarde tried in varying degrees to make sense of Haiti in an international context and to apply some of the prevalent theories of their times to the Haitian situation. This is particularly true in the social sciences and economics. However much one may now question the economic liberalism of an Edmond Paul, the sociology of Louis-Joseph Janvier, or the ethnology of Jean Price-Mars, these authors did not think that Haiti escaped the paradigms of their times.

But even as these writers quoted famous European thinkers, political practice in Haiti fed on exceptionalism. The Haitian elites acted as if, theories aside, Haiti was exceptional and should therefore be led in an exceptional manner. Thus the politics of a Delorme or a Firmin were not that much different from the illiterate generals who supported or opposed them and may also have believed in Haitian exceptionalism. Still, the public and unchallenged assumption, in all intellectual circles, that Haiti was indeed a country like any other limited the damages inflicted by the pragmatic acceptance of practices otherwise deemed unconventional.

With the 1915–34 US occupation, however, Haitian studies took a sharp turn for the worse with increasing acceptance of theories based on Haiti's apartness. The occupation had led to a reevaluation of Haitian identity among the elites, including from writers such as Jean Price-Mars. But the ideological malaise of the times also opened the door to a possible questioning of the universals inherited from the Enlightenment. Drawing from Price-Mars but rejecting his Enlightenment heritage, the Griot school in particular—one member of which was François Duvalier—insisted on the particularities of the Haitian *mentalité*.[4]

From the 1930s on, research, political practice, and legislation emphasized Haiti's singularity, and indeed helped to increase this singularity with such aberrations as the infamous anti-Communist law of 1969. Among the many reasons cited for forbidding even the belief in Communism, the law notes "the incompatibility of *imported doctrines*, notably Marxism-Leninism, with the social, political, and economic order of Haiti" (cited in Pascal-Trouillot and Trouillot 1978, 445, emphasis added). According to Duvalier, Haiti could draw its ingredients for progress only from its own culture, a culture that is, of course, unique in the almost mystical sense emphasized by the Griot doctrine.[5]

I would be the last to say that Haitian culture is not unique, or that Haiti should not use its cultural resources. The point is that before and during the Duvalier years, the particularities of Haiti were used to shield the Haitian elites. Haiti is unique; therefore it evades foreign theories, including class analysis. Indeed, it evades all analysis in the strict sense of the term. It also evades comparison. Therefore, we can rule this country in ways that seem to defy the imagination of most foreigners and quite a few Haitians. Haiti is special; thus it deserves custom-made institutions and a custom-made government. The political maneuver is obvious. So is the intellectual fallacy upon which it rests.

It seems to me that we learn much less about Haiti if we read it as an aberration that defies any explanation than if we learn to place it in a comparative framework. One of the most serious limitations of Haitian studies, in Haiti and elsewhere, comes from the propensity of Haitianists, and especially of Haitian-born scholars, to study Haiti and nothing but Haiti. The assumption is that nothing we learn from looking at another society can teach us anything about Haiti, since Haiti is so unique. To be sure, insularism is a feature of Caribbean studies. Jamaicans study Jamaica, Cubans study Cuba, and few foreigners spread their wings over linguistic boundaries within the archipelago. Yet the irony in this case is that Haiti's exceptional history provides so many features that can benefit from the observation of other societies, especially in Latin America and more particularly in the other Antilles.

In the little space remaining, I will only mention a few of the areas where Haitian studies can surely benefit from the light of neighboring cases. I rest on the shoulders of so many colleagues that I cannot mention them all. Nor can I cover all the potential areas for comparative research.

The peasantry is one such area, and an important one. I spent fifteen months doing fieldwork among the peasantry of Dominica, and I believe that I learned much more about the Haitian peasantry during those months than I did during eighteen years in Port-au-Prince. Haiti, like the Windward Islands, like Jamaica, like Puerto Rico or, to a lesser extent, like Trinidad and Tobago, has a substantial postplantation peasantry. How do theories of the impact of the plantation economy or of the passage from plantation to peasantry in a context dominated by capitalism (Trouillot 1988) fit the Haitian case? To my knowledge Alex Dupuy may be the first Haitian scholar to have tackled this question head on. Haitian studies in general would benefit from a more systematic reading of Walter Rodney, George Beckford, Raymond Smith, and J. R. Mandle. Sidney Mintz's comparative essays on Caribbean peasantries (1979, 1990) would serve as an excellent starting point for such research.

There are so many questions left unanswered in Caribbean studies that have a direct impact on the way Haitianists could look at Haiti that I can only start such a list. Why are mating patterns similar to Haitian *plaçage*, or rural institutions similar to the Haitian *lakou* or the *konbit* present elsewhere in the Caribbean? How far do these similarities go? Are they surviving or disappearing at the same rate? For the same reasons? How do these tie in with gender? Market women in Haiti are strikingly similar to market women in Jamaica—or in Ghana, for that matter. Why? How far into social roles can we carry the postplantation paradigm, Mintz's reconstituted peasantry?

Just as there is a postplantation peasantry, there may also be a postplantation state. My own comparison of the postslavery elites of Dominica and Haiti reveals striking similarities. It is no accident that one of the most important slogans of nineteenth-century Haiti—"Le plus grand bien au plus grand nombre" ("the greatest good to the greatest number")—was the slogan of the mulatto elite in British-dominated Dominica, but it was the leitmotif of the darker Parti National in mulatto-dominated Haiti (Trouillot 1992). Does the postplantation situation lead to specific forms of state power, including specific forms of state rhetoric (Trouillot 1990)?

One could tie to that issue matters well debated in Latin American studies, such as authoritarianism and the role of the military. Is there such a thing as a social authoritarianism that can effect forms of political power? The Haitian army, just like the army in Panama, just like the army in the Dominican Republic, just like—until recently—the army in Nicaragua, is the product of a US invasion. What are the similarities and the differences between these institutions as they function in societies admittedly different but also in many ways similar?

Religion is another domain. To my knowledge, no one has yet systematically picked up the trail opened by Roger Bastide in his sketchy comparisons of Brazil and Haiti. There is also a trail to pick up in the work of Melville Herskovits on Africanisms—with the necessary corrections, of course, but also with a much-needed rereading of Price-Mars. Now that we know more about, say, both Suriname and Brazil, how "African" does Haiti appear in a hemispheric perspective? And, of course, we could push the comparison all the way to Africa.

And similarly, we should look at Kreyòl in the light of what we now know about creole languages as far away as Réunion. At the very least, Kreyòl studies would benefit much from greater familiarity with such works as that of Louis-Félix Prudent on Guadeloupe-Martinique, and especially the writings of Mervyn Alleyne on St. Lucian creole and other Afro-American languages. And I have still not said anything about music. . . .

I have scratched the tip of the iceberg to make a more general point. Haitian studies has experienced a small but noticeable revival since the late 1970s. But there is more to do. Much more. There are threads to pick up, new connections to be made. One would hope that, when the overemphasis on Duvalierism—if not on state politics—quiets down, practicing Haitianists will seriously start reading not only Bellegarde and Price-Mars (whom I consider to be the last of an intellectual lineage) but their precursors, the classics of nineteenth-century Haitian social thought.[6] In fact, all aspects of nineteenth-century life in Haiti will benefit from serious attention, since nineteenth-century studies have been unjustly outflanked by the dual emphasis on the slave revolution of 1791 and on twentieth-century politics. I emphasize social thought simply because the writers of that era, with their faith in universals and their desire to defend Haiti in a context of open ostracism, may have given us the most potent antidote to the myth of Haitian exceptionalism: specific questions, tuned to Haitian particulars but informed by the international debates of the times.

For Haitian studies cannot proceed without making a theoretical leap. Quite simply, we need to drop the fiction, inherited from the nineteenth-century racist literature, that Haiti is unique—if by unique one means that it escapes analysis and comparison. Haiti is not that weird. It is the fiction of Haitian exceptionalism that is weird.

NOTES

This text was first prepared as the keynote address at a conference titled "Haiti in Comparative Perspective," sponsored by Columbia/The New York University Consortium on Latin American and Caribbean Studies, New York University, New York, February 9, 1990. It is reproduced here with minor modifications. I thank Susan Lowes for valuable editorial suggestions.

Editors' Note: This essay first appeared as "The Odd and the Ordinary: Haiti, the Caribbean, and the World," *Cimarrón: New Perspectives on the Caribbean* 2, no. 3: 3–12.

1. The Heinls lived in Haiti in the 1960s, when the colonel acted as an adviser to François Duvalier's regime. For the introductory passage, see Heinl and Heinl (1978, 1).

2. Publishers and reviewers are less cautious and more candid than writers themselves. So Warner Books presents Davis's *The Serpent and the Rainbow* as a "journey of discovery across the border between life and death, between good and evil." The back cover of the paperback edition of the same book quotes reviews from the *Wall Street Journal* and the *Washington Post*: "Exotic and far-reaching . . . just the way Indiana Jones would tell it. . . . Replete with bizarre details to titillate the curious" (Davis 1985).

3. At the same time, yet in a more subtle way, Haitian poets and, later, novelists, replied to the negative mythification of Haitians by the West with myth-making writings of their own, a process that continues today (e.g., Dash 1988).

4. Because members of the Griot school claimed to be followers of Jean Price-Mars, Price-Mars has passed for a proponent of Haitian exceptionalism, a charge for which I find no justification in his voluminous writings. Price-Mars (1929) certainly did not at the outset reject what he took for science, not even Justin Dévot's unsuccessful tentative effort to introduce positivism in Haiti. Rather, in a move that anticipated both Bastide and Herskovits, Price-Mars

simply insisted that Haiti could not be studied as if it were an avatar of Europe with no African influence, and that Haiti's African heritage was itself amenable to scientific study. Both points are now unquestioned among anthropologists, although they may derive from them quite different conclusions. That the first point was also repeated by Duvalier as part of a new *problématique* (Denis and Duvalier 1936) does not make Price-Mars an exceptionalist. At any rate, in Price-Mars's own words, his seminal *Ainsi parla l'oncle* (1928) is "an endeavor to integrate the popular Haitian thought into the discipline of traditional ethnography" (Price-Mars 1983, 7).

5. Two preceding laws on Communist activities under Presidents Estimé (February 1948) and Magloire (September 1951) make no reference to Haitian culture as such (Pascal-Trouillot and Trouillot 1978, 443–44).

6. A good deal of this corpus is available. Further, publisher Henri Deschamps has recently issued the entire work—including hitherto unpublished volumes—of Thomas Madiou, Haiti's first comprehensive historian.

REFERENCES

Abbott, Elizabeth. 1988. *Haiti*. New York: McGraw Hill.

Dash, J. Michael. 1988. *Haiti and the United States: Stereotypes and the Literary Imagination*. London: Macmillan.

Davis, Wade. 1985. *The Serpent and the Rainbow*. New York: Warner Books.

Heinl, Robert Debs, and Nancy Heinl. 1978. *Written in Blood: The Story of the Haitian People, 1492–1971*. Boston: Houghton Mifflin.

Leyburn, James. 1941. *The Haitian People*. New Haven, CT: Yale University Press.

Mintz, Sidney W. (1974) 1989. *Caribbean Transformations*. New York: Columbia University Press.

Moral, Paul. 1961. *Le paysan haïtien: Étude sur la vie rurale en Haïti*. Paris: Maisonneuve Larose.

Niles, Blair. 1926. *Black Haiti: A Biography of Africa's Eldest Daughter*. New York: Grosset and Dunlap.

Pascal-Trouillot, Ertha, and Ernst Trouillot. 1978. *Codes de lois usuelles*. Port-au-Prince: Éditions Henri Deschamps.

Plummer, Brenda Gayle. 1988. *Haiti and the Great Powers*. Baton Rouge: University of Louisiana Press.

Price-Mars, Jean. 1929. *Une étape de l'évolution haïtienne*. Port-au-Prince: Imprimerie de la Presse.

Price-Mars, Jean. (1928) 1983. *So Spoke the Uncle*. Washington, DC: Three Continents Press.

Rotberg, Robert I., with Christopher K. Clague. 1971. *Haiti: The Politics of Squalor*. Boston: Houghton Mifflin.

Trouillot, Michel-Rolph. 1988. *Peasants and Capital: Dominica in the World Economy*. Baltimore: Johns Hopkins University Press.

Trouillot, Michel-Rolph. 1990. *Haiti: State against Nation; The Origins and Legacy of Duvalierism*. New York: Monthly Review Press.

Trouillot, Michel-Rolph. 1992. "The Inconvenience of Freedom: Free People of Color and the Aftermath of Slavery in Dominica and Saint-Domingue/Haiti." In *The Meaning of Freedom: Economics, Politics, and Culture after Slavery*, edited by Frank McGlynn and Seymour Drescher, 147–82. Pittsburgh: University of Pittsburgh Press.

CHAPTER 3

The Vulgarity of Power

Soon after he usurped the crown, King Ubu assembled the crowd in the palace yard, threw money at his happily crawling and jumping subjects, and invited them to an orgy. "Here I am, he mused, king of this land, and I have already granted myself an indigestion" (Jarry [1888] 1963, 77).

Achille Mbembe's recent reflections on the vulgarity of power in the postcolony nicely draw on the contemporary political experience of sub-Saharan Africa to decode the symbolism of scenes that constantly evoke ubuesque relations between *commandement* and peoples.[1] Mbembe goes further than isolated readings of singular scenes to contend more generally that "the grotesque and the obscene are two essential characteristics that identify postcolonial regimes of domination" (1992, 4). Postcolonial "*commandement* derives its 'aesthetics' from its immoderate appetite and the immense pleasure that it encounters in plunging in ordure" (1992, 10).

Mbembe's demonstration, much too rich to be summarized here, is thought provoking. I find myself wondering, however, about the assumptions and implications of two related lines of arguments.

The first is the issue of viewpoint. The notion of vulgarity is inherently subject-dependent. It requires an ego, active or remote, who evaluates the scene and judges it repulsive. The grotesque or the obscene is realized in this very repulsion, which accompanies or follows an initially attentive look. If the magnetism of the grotesque indeed generates conflict between attraction and disgust (and Mbembe admits that much implicitly) it is exactly because attraction and disgust are driven here by the same force: ego's recognition that a scene, otherwise familiar, has been pushed to the extremes of abnormality. Previous knowledge is also necessary to ego's judgment that the scene potentially degrades witnesses and/or participants.

Ego's acknowledgment that the scene is an outrageous breach of the norm is what authenticates the sense of aesthetic or moral degradation brought about by vulgarity. In other words, it is impossible to speak of vulgarity, obscenity, or offensiveness without some reference to a norm, both in the sense of tradition and in the sense of ethical standard.

Mbembe assumes this norm. He never says explicitly whether his judgmental ego is European, African, or a universal subject without anchor in space and time. His caveat that obscenity and vulgarity should be seen as "more than a *moral* category" (1992, 29; emphasis mine) is well taken, but it does not follow from it that the category can operate without any reference to a norm. Indeed, Mbembe does insist on "excess" and "abuse," and his analysis is often couched in terms that assume abnormality, from "promiscuous relationships" to "obsession(s) with orifices and genital organs" (1992, 8). Yet one could argue that there is nothing inherently obscene in orifices or protuberances of the body; that they have attracted attention cross-culturally; that references to such parts of the body and their functions do not imply vulgarity in many cultures, including some African ones; that metaphorical connections between body parts, bodily functions, and power are as old as power itself. To take an archetype of Western European grandeur, was not the Sun King, Louis XIV, the "body" of France (Apostolidès 1981)? References of the sort that Mbembe pulls out of the African setting have been used to speak of power in dissimilar times and places, both positively and negatively—that is, as praise or as criticism.

These counterpoints are not necessarily consistent, nor need they be. They all underline, however, a quandary that has both theoretical and empirical components, and that requires serious attention before we go further on the path of postcolonial (or African) exceptionalism. Making a case for the particular relevance of references to body functions, seized as vulgar, in postcolonial Africa (either as natural "obsessions" or as polyvalent signifiers mobilized for typically postcolonial/vulgar displays) requires the argument to flesh itself out—no pun intended—against two backgrounds: (a) a cross-cultural horizon, against which the specificity of sub-Saharan Africa could emerge, and (b) a pre- (or non-)colonial horizon against which the specificity of the postcolony would emerge.

Mbembe attempts a preemptive strike against counterpoints of this kind and suggestions of exceptionalism by stating clearly that he finds nothing specifically African about defecation, copulation, pomp, and sumptuousness, which are all in his view "classical ingredients in the production of power." The normative connotation of the article, however, and the fact that it does not suggest why or how similar things work differently in other contexts, does leave its author weak against this line of argument. Indeed, one line after rejecting African exceptionalism, Mbembe returns to what he calls "an obsession with orifices" (1992, 11). Whose obsession if not an African one? And what is that obsession measured against? What implicit backgrounds, assumptions, or comparisons reveal it to us as an obsession, as a craze or a craving? Would a survey of the literature elsewhere, carried out under similar conditions, lead to significantly different results? Is there, indeed, a sub-Saharan or a postcolonial difference?

Mbembe is perhaps most stimulating when he suggests that the postcolonial difference is in the recapture of vulgarity by the people, their taming of power through ridicule. "In the postcolony, the very display of grandeur and prestige always entails an aspect of vulgarity and the baroque that the official order always tries to hide but which ordinary people bring to its attention—sometimes intentionally, often unwittingly" (1992, 12). I almost agree with the sentence. Unfortunately, the clause "in the postcolony" seems to be a defining one in the context of Mbembe's argument. In his scheme, the people throw back at Ubu that which is inherently vulgar about power in the postcolonial context. Never mind that something may be rotten in the kingdom of Denmark, we do not know from Mbembe how vulgarity defines power outside of Africa. By inference, postcolonial vulgarity is more postcolonial than vulgar. This ambiguity on the defining character of postcolonial vulgarity (one evidently linked to Mbembe's ambiguity about viewpoint) is the source of my second reservation.

We should clear these equivocations. Power is always grotesque: Ubu is always vulgar. To parody Montaigne, however high the throne, it's never higher than the king's ass. And indeed, from Rabelais to Montaigne, to the noblemen who competed to hold Louis XIV's chamberpot, to the contemporary British fascination with the sexual frolics of Buckingham, or the US media's obsessive search for candidates in flagrante delicto, the titillation with the orifices and protuberances of the mighty may be as old as state power itself. The persistence of these metaphorical connections through history may not be accidental, though the body and its functions may evoke intimacy, familiarity, love of life, or homeliness as often perhaps as they may provoke vulgarity per se. In Africa, loosely defined, references to penis and testicles span from Dogon myths of creation to traditional (as opposed to modern or postcolonial) political institutions (Iroko 1990).

Thus, I find Mbembe closer to the truth when broaching the issue of the classical ingredients in the production of power than when defining the postcolonial difference.

To say that vulgarity is always an aspect of power reintroduces at a different level the related issue of viewpoint. To answer quickly my earlier query: power is always potentially vulgar inasmuch as it is always potentially excessive: (a) from the viewpoint of the ruled, and (b) from the viewpoint of a nonacculturated onlooker.

Vulgarity is inherent in power—unless power denies itself. To say this is not to pass moral judgment on the actors but to understand the semiotics at work. From pharaohs to popes, from armadas to stealth bombers, power feeds on exorbitance: a higher horse, a majestic panache, a tiara, a lavish banquet, golden faucets in the bathroom. The imagery of power is excess. Excess, in turn, breeds vulgarity. To be sure, power sometimes attaches a mask onto the vulgarity it generates. If the mask is half successful, power glows, the populace applauds, and vulgarity lies dormant. Yet vulgarity is always there, for power cannot live without its imagery and that imagery begs for exuberance. The king needs a throne, and it is the tension between that need and the meaning of the throne, their actual proximity and fetishized distance, that generate the potential for grotesque that Montaigne picked up.

Thus, the line is always fine between grandeur and ridicule, between sumptuosity and vulgarity. All that is required to see Ubu in every prince is the rejection, even momentary, of that prince's dominance. A slight suspension of belief either on the part of the populace or on the part of an outsider not yet tuned to the potency or rituals of this particular rule creates a perceptual distance between ego and power. Once the distance is created, any display of grandeur and prestige—indeed, even scenes not intended as displays—can turn to vulgarity. To a non-French republican questioning the divine right of the Bourbons, the *petit lever* of Louis XIV looks indeed like a buffoonery concocted by some deeply troubled child obsessed with bodily functions. To the vast majority of North Americans who did not vote for him, Michael Dukakis did look funny maneuvering that tank. For many viewers outside of the United States, George Bush's vomit on the lap of the Japanese premier did read like a metaphor for his (and America's?) future role in a changing world order. In short, step out of any ritual of power or, better, just suspend belief in the necessary ritualization of power as it affects a particular rule, and the Emperor indeed has no clothes—costumes at best.

In that light, the specificity of the postcolony is not a pathology, as Mbembe seems to suggest, but a difference morally and politically unmarked, fully open to historical-anthropological investigation. Pathologically inclined questions ("what makes the grotesque so visible in the postcolony?") can be shed aside for a more neutral agenda: Under what conditions is the vulgarity—inherent in power plays and displays—enhanced or weakened through public discourses and manifestations? Under what circumstances can the populace seize this vulgarity and throw it back at the powerful as ridicule? Under what conditions is vulgarity deflected by power? We are distant enough to see, in retrospect, that the Sun King himself was in fact carefully produced to be consumed by France and the world (Apostolidès 1981; Marin 1981). How did it work, if indeed Montaigne is right that the throne is never higher than the king's derrière?

To find out more, we need to reject explicitly, both in words and in methodologies, assumptions of pathology. We need to bring into the discussion scenes and examples from elsewhere that will reveal, through contrast and convergence, any postcolonial (or sub-Saharan) difference. Students of formerly communist European countries will be able to tell us that the mixture of distance and proximity that allows people to throw back ridicule at the *commandement* is not in itself a postcolonial distinction. In a not-too-distant past, ridicule was one of the best barometers of the domains of confrontation and accommodation between Eastern Europeans and their communist rulers.

How does the use of ridicule differ from communist regimes to liberal democracies, to so-called postcolonial polities? How much is the differential value between a Dan Quayle joke, a Gorbachev joke, and a Bokassa joke due to the fact that nothing happens to the joker in the first case, whereas suspicion arises in the second and in the third, and torture or death is around the corner? Under which circumstances are individual rulers fundamentally threatened for losing control of the vulgarity/grandeur power play? Conversely, in which kinds of situations can the mishaps of individual rulers be repaired by the state? How does the homogenization of the populace, which paved the trajectory of liberal democracies, affect Ubu and his peoples? And as far as Africa itself is concerned, it may be worth examining the historical process through which references to body parts, once associated with life, courage, grandeur, or intimacy, are increasingly viewed as vulgar by analysts and, perhaps, by larger segments of the population.

Thus, at some point in the debate, regardless of the vocabulary one chooses, the issue of the relation between state and civil society—and thus, of the nature of the postcolonial state (Trouillot 1990)—seems to me unavoidable if we care to deal with the vulgarity of power through historical particulars rather than as a general principle. If in specific cases the state does emerge as an actor, distinguishable from the rulers themselves, then so be it. Mbembe's understandable suspicion toward the traditional categories of political analysis need not lead him to dismiss the relevance of the state. Ubu rejoiced at the thought of Poland's existence: "If there was no Poland, he said, there would have been no Poles" (Jarry [1888] 1963, 180).

NOTES

Thanks to Jane Guyer for comments on this article and an ongoing conversation on its subject. This article was written while I was a guest at the Woodrow Wilson International Center for Scholars, Washington, DC.

Editors' Note: This essay first appeared as "The Vulgarity of Power," *Public Culture* 5, no. 1 (1992): 75–81.

1. I prefer not to use the word *banality*, which appears in Mbembe's title, "The Banality of Power and the Aesthetics of Vulgarity in the Postcolony," *Public Culture* 4, no. 2 (1992): 1–30. First, references to routine and banalization as such are rare in his text and not crucial to the argument. Second, in view of Arendt's powerful statement on the banality of evil (e.g., Arendt [1964] 1977), I find it judicious to avoid confusion.

REFERENCES

Apostolidès, Jean-Marie. 1981. *Le roi-machine: Spectacle et politique au temps de Louis XIV*. Paris: Éditions de Minuit.
Arendt, Hannah. (1964) 1977. *Eichmann in Jerusalem: A Report on the Banality of Evil*. New York: Penguin.
Iroko, A. Felix. 1990. "Testicules d'hommes et civilisations africaines traditionelles." *Africa* 45, no. 1: 116–39.
Jarry, Alfred. (1888) 1963. *Ubu roi*. Paris: Flasquelle.
Marin, Louis. 1981. *Le portrait du roi*. Paris: Éditions de Minuit.
Mbembe, Achille. 1992. "The Banality of Power and the Aesthetics of Vulgarity in the Postcolony." Translated by Janet Roitman. *Public Culture* 4, no. 2: 1–30.
Trouillot, Michel-Rolph. 1990. *Haiti: State against Nation; The Origins and Legacy of Duvalierism*. New York: Monthly Review Press.

CHAPTER 4

Good Day, Columbus

Silences, Power, and Public History (1492–1892)

> . . . and so to each one I gave a new name.
> **CHRISTOPHER COLUMBUS**, *The Four Voyages of Columbus*

History is messy for the people who must live it. For those within the shaky boundaries of Christendom, the most important event of the year 1492 nearly happened in 1491. Late at night on November 25, 1491, Abu al-Qasim al-Muhli signed the treaties by which the Muslim kingdom of Granada surrendered to the Catholic kingdom of Castile, ending a war the issue of which had become clear a few months earlier. The transfer of power was scheduled for May, but some of the Muslim leaders decided not to wait for the Christian takeover and left town unexpectedly. Granada's Nasrid ruler, Muhammad XII Boabdil, rushed the capitulation. Thus, it was almost by accident that the flag of Castile and the cross of Christendom were raised over the tower of the Alhambra on January 2, 1492, rather than during the previous fall, as first expected, or the following spring, as scheduled (Arié 1973; Bishko [1975] 1980; Irving [1829] 1988).

For actors and witnesses alike, the end of the *Reconquista* was a disorderly series of occurrences, neither a single event, nor a single date. The end of the war and the signing of the treaties—both of which occurred in year 1491 of the Christian calendar—were as significant as the flight of the Muslim leaders, the raising of the Christian flag, or the glorious entry of the Catholic monarchs within the conquered city, on January 6, 1492. The capitulation of Granada was, however, as close to a milestone as history in the making can get. Milestones are always set in regard to the past, and the past of Christendom projected the moving Spanish frontier as the south-ernmost rampart of the cross.

Since the Council of Clermont (1095), in part as an unexpected effect of Islamic influence, Christian militants from both sides of the Pyrenees had heralded the reconquest of the Iberian Peninsula as a sort of Christian jihad, the *via Hispania* to the Holy Land, a necessary stage on the road to the Holy Sepulcher. Popes, bishops, and kings had enlisted the limited—but highly symbolic—participation of Catholics from France to Scotland in various campaigns with such incentives as the partial remission of penance. This does not deny cultural interpenetration between Christians, Muslims, and Jews in the peninsula and even north of the Pyrenees.[1] Rather, the total ab-sence of formal boundaries between church and state in the Iberian do-minions since at least the Visigoths (Wallace-Hadrill [1965] 1988) as well as the rhetoric of the popes made the "defense of Christendom" a dominant idiom for the military campaigns (Bishko [1975] 1980; Cutler and Cutler 1986; Irving [1829] 1988). That both religious and military ardor declined in the second half of the fourteenth century did little to modify an ideological context in which religion remained the closest thing to a "public arena," and religious figures the most able crowd leaders. Thus when religious and military enthusiasm, still intertwined, climbed once more with Isabella's reign, the ultimate significance of the war for Christendom resurfaced un-questioned (Bishko [1975] 1980). Even then, however, if many of those who lived the fall of Granada saw in it an occurrence of exceptional relevance, it was a milestone only for the peculiar individuals who paid attention to such things in the first place.

It mattered little then, in comparison, that a few months after enter-ing Granada, the Catholic monarchs gave their blessing to a Genoese adventurer anxious to reach India via a shortcut through the western seas.[2] It would matter little that the Genoese was wrong, having grossly underestimated the distance to be traveled. It probably mattered less, at the time, that the Genoese and his Castilian companions reached not the Indies, but a tiny islet in the Bahamas on October 12, 1492. The landing in the Bahamas was certainly not the event of the year 1492, if only because the few who cared, on the other side of the Atlantic, did not learn about it until 1493.

How interesting, then, that 1492 has become Columbus's year, and Oc-tober 12 the day of "The Discovery." Columbus himself has become a quin-tessential "Spaniard" or a representative of "Italy"—two rather vague enti-ties during his lifetime. The landing has become a clear-cut event, much more fixed in time than the prolonged fall of Muslim Granada, the seemingly interminable expulsion of European Jews, or the tortuous consolidation of royal power in the early Renaissance. Whereas these latter issues still appear as convoluted processes—thus the favored turf of academic specialists who break them down into an infinite list of themes for doctoral dissertations—"The Discovery" has lost its processual character. It has become a single and simple moment, cut from its antecedents (the "preparations," the "voyage") and its context (the *Reconquista*, the rise of absolutism, the making of Europe). It is not a process anymore, but a "fact": on this day, in 1492, Christopher Columbus discovered the Bahamas. As a set event, void of context, it befits travel agents, airlines, politicians, the media, or the states who sell it in the prepackaged forms under which "the public" has come to expect history to present itself for immediate consumption. It is a product of power whose label has been cleansed of traces of power. The naming of the "fact" is itself a narrative of power disguised as innocence.[3] There is an arrogance (obvious, once we do not assume a Eurocentric perspective) in calling "discovery" the first European invasions of inhabited lands. Contact with the West is seen as the foundation of historicity of different cultures (Preiswerk and Perrot 1978, 105). However, more than arrogance is at stake here. Terminologies demarcate a field politically and epistemologically.[4] "Discovery" and analogous terms ensure that by just mentioning the event one enters a predetermined lexical field of clichés and predictable categories that foreclose a redefinition of the political and intellectual stakes. It is not easy to subvert from there the very language describing the "facts" of the matter.[5] "Facts" become limpid, sanitized.

Commemorations sanitize further the messy history lived by the actors. They contribute to the continuous myth-making process that gives history its more definite shapes: they help to create, modify, or sanction the public meanings attached to historical events deemed worthy of mass celebration. As rituals that package history for public consumption, commemorations play the numbers game to make the past appear both more real and more elementary.

Numbers matter at the end point, the consumption side of the game: the greater the number of participants to a celebration, the stronger the allusion to the multitude of witnesses for whom the mythicized event is supposed to have meant something from day one. The more varied the participants, the easier the claim to world historical significance. Numbers matter also as items in the calendar. Years, months, dates present history as part of the natural cycles of the world. By packaging events within temporal sequences, commemorations adorn the past with certainty: the proof of the happening is in the cyclical inevitability of its celebration.

Cycles may vary, of course, but annual cycles provide a basic element of modern commemorations: an exact date.[6] Dates anchor the event in the present. The recurrence of a predictable date severs Columbus's landfall from the context of emerging Europe on and around 1492, the day of the month (the primary part of the cycle) obliterating an entire year now subsumed within a twenty-four-hour segment. October 12 imposes a silence upon the historical past, creating a potentially endless void that comprises everything that could be said and is not being said about 1492, and about the years immediately preceding or following.

The void, however, is not left unfilled. The fixed date alone places the event within a new frame with linkages of its own. As a fixed date, October 12 is the fetishized repository for a potentially endless list of disparate events, such as the birth of US activist Dick Gregory or that of Italian tenor Luciano Pavarotti, the independence of Equatorial Guinea, the Broadway opening of the musical *Jesus Christ Superstar*, or the refusal of a Catholic monk, one Martin Luther, to repudiate assertions posted months before on the door of a church in Germany. All these events happened on October 12 of the Christian calendar, in various years from 1518 to 1971. All are likely to be acknowledged publicly by varying numbers of milestone worshipers. Each of them, in turn, can be replaced by another event judged to be equally—or more—noteworthy: Paraguay's break from Argentina in 1811, the 1976 arrest of the Chinese Gang of Four, the beginning of the German occupation of France in 1914, or the final settlement between the English Crown and its opponents on the meaning and extent of the Magna Carta and related charters in 1297.

The roster is theoretically expandable in any direction. If the Magna Carta is the most ancient icon mentioned here, that is because these examples have come from the institutionalized memory of what is now the West. For at least a few scribes elsewhere, concerned with other continuities, October 12, 1991, will mark the 2,530th anniversary of the Persian empire—next to which the 1492 landing in the Bahamas looks quite recent. October 12 thus potentially links a number of dissimilar events, all equally decontextualized and equally susceptible to mythicization. The longer the list becomes, the more it looks like an answer in a trivia game. But this is precisely because celebrations trivialize the historical process at the very same time that they mythicize history.

The myth-making process does not operate evenly, however; and the preceding list suggests as much. For if—in theory—all events can be de-contextualized to the same point of emptiness, in practice not all are re-shaped by the same power plays and not all mean the same to new actors entering the stage and busily appropriating the past. As we will see, the images and debates that surround the appropriation of Columbus vary from Spain to the United States and from both those countries to Latin America. Further, constructions vary within these areas themselves according to time, but also according to factors such as class and ethnic identification.[7] In short, celebrations are not created equal. Celebrations fill the silence that they impose upon the historical past with narratives of power, projections about the present and the future. It is telling that Columbus himself was not treated as a favorite hero by nascent Spain, and that October 12 was not marked as a special day during his lifetime. To be sure, the landing in the Bahamas, the verified existence of an American landmass, the integration of the Caribbean in the European orbit, and the imperial reorganizations that paralleled these events all imposed a symbolic reordering of the world which, in turn, contributed to the wealth of myths that now define the West—utopia, the noble savage, the white man's burden, among others (Trouillot 1991a). Still, it took quite a few years of intense struggles for political and economic power in Europe and the Americas for the narrative to unfold in ways that acknowledged the discovery as event and the discoverer as hero. Indeed, it took a living hero, Charles V, and his pretensions to a Catholic empire stretching from Tunis to Lima and from Vienna to Vera Cruz, for Columbus, then dead, to become a hero. In 1552, Francisco López de Gómara suggested to Charles that the most important event in history—after the divine Creation of the world and the Coming of Christ—was the discovery of the Americas (Hanke 1959, 2–3, 124).[8]

Even then, one can barely speak of "public" celebration. Columbus's first group of admirers was restricted, at best, to Spanish intellectuals. Further, even as Spanish arts and themes gained international attention during the reign of Philip II, the sinking of the armada in 1588 had already suggested other times and priorities. The northern Europeans who benefited the most from the rise of Caribbean plantations and transatlantic trade during the two centuries following Philip's reign tended to commission paintings of *themselves* and their families rather than writings about *conquistadores*. Meanwhile, among the intellectual elites of Europe, the mythicized faces of America overshadowed that of Columbus.[9]

Thus it was in the "New" World itself that Columbus could first emerge most strongly as myth, in the former colonies of Spain and in the United States. The United States was one of the few places where the growth of a modern public in the midst of the Enlightenment was not encumbered by a feudal past. There, as elsewhere, the constitution of a public domain reflected the organization of power and the development of the national state. But power was constituted differently from the way it took shape in most European countries. Citizens with a weakness for marching bands promoted celebrations and holidays more openly and often more successfully than in Europe.[10]

The Tammany Society, or Columbian Order, an otherwise clannish group of gentlemen incorporated in New York in 1789, had such a taste for public attention, parades, and lavish banquets. Their list of celebrations included Washington's birthday, the Fourth of July, but also Bastille Day, and other international milestones they deemed worthy of recognition. Columbus's landfall figured on their first calendar, published in 1790. More important, by what seems to be a historical accident (the joint effect of fixed dates, fundraising opportunities, and political fortunes), their most lavish ceremony occurred on October 12, 1792. On that day, members organized a memorable banquet and erected a fourteen-foot-high monument to Columbus that they promised to illuminate annually on the anniversary of the landfall. They did not keep that promise. Their banquet, however, was remembered almost a hundred years later, when new groups of worshipers searched for a North American precedent for Columbus Day.[11]

Latin America, meanwhile, kept alive Columbus's memory but treated it with ambivalence until the late 1880s. Some territories fought Europe repeatedly over Columbus's remains, both literally and figuratively. Two Caribbean colonies competed with Spain for Columbus's long-dead body.[12] The independent state that emerged from Bolívar's armed struggle on the mainland claimed Columbus's name both before and after the secession of Venezuela and Ecuador from Gran Colombia. Still, even though Latin American rejection of Spanish political tutelage did not entail a rejection of *hispanismo*, early ideologies of independence and, later, Spain's Ten Years War against Cuba (1868–1878) hampered the complete integration of Columbus into the pantheon of South American heroes.

Ethnicity—or rather, ideologies of ethnicity—added to Latin America's ambivalence toward Columbus. Latin American ideologies attribute to the New World situation an active role in the making of socioracial categories. It is not simply that categories require new names (*criollos, zambos, mestizos*) or new ingredients under old names (*mamelucos, morenos, ladinos*); the rules by which they are devised are different from those of Europe and are acknowledged as such.[13] Discourses intertwined with these rules and reproducing the creole categories give a central role, explicit or implicit, to metaphors of "blending" (Mörner 1967, 1970) in spite of the age-old denigration of certain cultural traditions (Schwartz 1987; Pagden 1987), and in spite of systems of stratification that manipulate the perception of phenotypes (Harris [1964] 1974; De Friedemann 1976). Skewed as it was, a blending did occur.[14] Brutal as it was, Spanish colonization did not nearly wipe out pre-Conquest Americans in the southern landmass as the Anglos did in the north or as Spaniards themselves did in the Caribbean islands, if only because the aboriginal populations of both Mexico and the Andes were enormous. Early cultural practices often intertwined European and Native elements. Early manifestations of a distinct local identity often included some sense of "Indianness."[15] Political doctrines of the nineteenth century incorporated both the metaphors of a blend and the acknowledgment of the Indian, even while the organization of power kept Indians and Afro-Latinos outside of the decision-making process.[16] In short, for many reasons too complex to detail here, Latin Americans did not alienate Native cultures from their myths of origin, even before the twentieth-century rise of various forms of *indigenismo*. They view themselves as *criollos* and *mestizos* of different kinds, peoples of the New World; perhaps Columbus was too much a man of the Old.[17]

In the United States, in contrast, in spite of inflated references to a melting pot, ideologies of ethnicity emphasize continuities with the Old World. The real Natives are mainly dead or on reservations. New natives (recognizable by their hyphenated group names) are numbered by generation, and their descendants fight each other for pieces of a mythical Europe. The peculiar politics of US ethnicity has proved to be a boon for Columbus's memory.

Ethnicity gave Columbus a lobby, a prerequisite to public success in US culture. The 1850 census reported only 3,679 individuals of Italian birth. Yet by 1866, Italian Americans, organized by the Sharpshooters' Association of New York, celebrated the landfall, and within three years annual festivities were being held in Philadelphia, St. Louis, Boston, Cincinnati, New Orleans, and San Francisco on or around October 12 (Tomasi 1985; Speroni [1948] 1987).[18] Italians and Spaniards were just not enough, however, to turn this celebration into a national practice. Fortunately, ethnicity gave Columbus a second—and more numerous—group of lobbyists, Irish Americans. By 1850, there were already 962,000 Americans claiming Irish descent. Many of them regrouped in organizations such as the Knights of Columbus, a fraternal society for Catholic males founded in 1881. In less than ten years, community support and the institutional patronage of the church swelled the Knights' membership. As the association spread in the northeast with the backing of prominent Irish Americans, it increasingly emphasized the shaping of "citizen culture" (Kauffman 1982).

Columbus played a leading role in making citizens out of these immigrants. He provided them with a public example of Catholic devotion and civic virtue, and thus a powerful rejoinder to the cliché that allegiance to Rome preempted the Catholics' attachment to the United States. In New Haven, the 1892 celebration of the landing attracted some 40,000 people—including 6,000 Knights and a 1,000-piece band conducted by the musical director of West Point—in a joint celebration of holiness and patriotism (Kauffman 1982, 79–81). The success of these festivities was not due solely to Catholic Americans' desire for acceptance, nor was the cult of Columbus limited to Catholics.[19] By the 1890s, Italian and Irish efforts to promote Columbus Day in the United States coincided with—and ultimately were subsumed within—the production of two mass-media events, the international celebrations of the quadricentennial of the Bahamas landfall sponsored by Spain and by the United States.

The second half of the nineteenth century saw an unprecedented attention to the systematic management of public discourse in countries that combined substantial working classes and wide electoral franchises. With the realization that "the public"—this rather vague presumption of the first bourgeois revolutions—indeed existed, government officials, entrepreneurs, and intellectuals joined in the planned production of traditions that cut across class identities and reinforced the state. Nationalist parades multiplied in Europe, while government imposed a daily homage to the flag in public schools in the United States. International fairs that attracted millions of visitors to London or Paris (and even Philadelphia), academic conferences (such as the first congress of Orientalists in 1873), historical commemorations (such as the 1880 invention of Bastille Day in France) taught the new masses who they were, in part by telling them who they were not. Socialists, anarchists, and working-class political activists replied in kind by publicizing their own heroes and promoting celebrations such as May Day. Public history was in the air (Hobsbawm 1983, 1987; Bernabeu Albert 1987; Mitchell 1988; Badger 1979).

This fast-moving fin-de-siècle era caught Spain in a state of decline. Torn by factional feuds, outflanked in Europe by nearly all the Atlantic states, and threatened in the Americas by the economic incursions of Britain, the influence of the United States, and the constant fear of losing Cuba, Spain was in dire need of a moral and political uplift (Carr 1966; Fernández Almagro 1972; Hobsbawm 1987). Conservative leader Antonio Cánovas del Castillo, architect of the Bourbon Restoration and a historian in his own right, made of Columbus and "The Discovery" the consummate metaphors for this anticipated revitalization.

Interest in Columbus had grown in the 1800s. The number of biographical sketches published in Europe and the Americas increased significantly after the 1830s; so did various suggestions about a quadricentennial in the 1880s. Cánovas turned this growing interest into an extravaganza: a political and diplomatic crusade, an economic venture, a spectacle to be consumed by Spain and the world for the sheer sake of its pageantry. In the words of its most thorough chronicler, the Spanish quadricentennial was "the apex of the Restoration" (Bernabeu Albert 1987, 19).

Spain spent more than two and a half million pesetas and four years of preparation on the celebration. Various cities were refurbished, monuments were erected, and pavilions were built on the model of recent international exhibitions.[20] A year-long series of events led to grandiose ceremonies in October and November of 1892 that involved the Spanish royal family and many foreign dignitaries.[21] Replicas of Columbus's boats sailed across the Atlantic. For at least a few weeks, Spaniards were at the center of the world. Parades in Madrid and Seville were echoed in Havana and Manila, and officials from the most powerful Western countries paid homage to Spain.

The huge international participation was due, in large part, to Cánovas's careful packaging of both the celebration and its object, "The Discovery" itself. He sold the quadricentennial not only as pageantry but as a challenge to the most enlightened minds, a year-long symposium on past and present policy, on the role of Spain in the world, on Western civilization, on the relevance of history. In a series of moves that anticipated current preparations for the coming quincentennial, the quadricentennial junta set up a series of intellectual activities that legitimized the celebration.[22] First, they made "The Discovery" and Columbus objects of learned discourse—and therefore worthy of public attention. Second, they gave anyone who spared that attention—individuals, parties, or states—an apparently neutral ground to celebrate in spite of conflicting connotations and purposes.

Connotations and purposes varied widely. Spanish urban crowds took the quadricentennial as the homage to Spain it was, in part, meant to be: the symbol of an impending revitalization.[23] Cánovas took it as such, too, but also as a unique occasion to reinforce Spain's presence west of the Atlantic.[24] Most Spanish leaders felt the need to reinforce commercial and cultural ties with Latin America in the face of US gains. At the same time, those who wanted Spanish olives or wine to enter the United States saw in the celebrations an occasion to establish contact with North American firms and agencies.

US brokers, in turn, wanted contact, but only on their own terms. Theirs was the only country whose name contained a continent—South Africa came much later—and whose imperial destiny was unfolding along manifest tracks. Thus, if for Spain the quadricentennial was an occasion to recall past splendors and imagine future glories, for many in the United States it was an opportunity to verify and celebrate their present course. Accordingly, US officials paid lip service to Cánovas's festivities, but invested their energy in *their* quadricentennial, the World's Columbian Exposition of Chicago, to which they graciously invited a Spanish Infanta as guest of honor.[25]

The Exposition actually opened in 1893, but by then, historical accuracy and even Columbus himself had become quite secondary. The intellectual aspect of the event barely mattered, in spite of contributions from Harvard's Peabody Museum and the Smithsonian Institution and the presence of then-rising star Franz Boas.[26] The point was money: to be spent and to be made. Paris 1889 and, closer to home, the 1876 centennial of United States independence in Philadelphia had proven to North American entrepreneurs that international fairs generated profits. By the late 1870s, consensus was reached among the likes of W. Rockefeller, C. Vanderbilt, J. P. Morgan, and W. Waldorf Astor that the US needed one more of these money-making events. That it occurred in Chicago one year too late was the combined result of accidents and false starts among bureaucrats and investors. That it bore Columbus's name was merely an additional attraction.

Circumstantial as he was to his own occasion, Columbus gained a lot from Chicago. Commemorations feed on numbers, and the 1893 quadricentennial was a display of the US appetite for size: more participating countries, more acreage, more exhibits, more money than any fair the world had known. Chicago won the numbers game—second only to Paris for attendance—and provided Columbus his greatest celebration to date: $28.3 million in expenses; $28.8 million in receipts; 21.5 million people in attendance. Columbus was the wrapping for an extravagant Yankee bazaar, but in the end, the bazaar was so big that the wrapping was noticed.

Latin America certainly noticed. To be sure, Columbus's metamorphosis into a Yankee hero, the lone ranger of the western seas, looked somewhat banal outside Chicago. Still, viewed from the far south, the fair belonged to a political and economic series from which it drew its symbolism. In 1889, Secretary of State James Gillespie Blaine, one of the promoters of the celebration, had convened the first meeting of American states in Washington.[27] In 1890, Minor C. Keith acquired 800,000 acres of public land in Costa Rica, the US Congress passed the McKinley Tariff, and US entrepreneurs controlled 80 percent of Cuban sugar exports. In 1891, US Admiral Bancroft Gherardi threatened to seize part of Haiti, and the US Navy prepared for war against Chile. In 1892, the Postmaster of the United States, acting as a private citizen-broker, bought the entire foreign debt of the Dominican Republic. Four centuries after Spain, the United States was taking over. The path was the same: first the Caribbean, then the continental landmass (Volwiller 1940; Manigat 1973; Langley 1989; Socolofsky and Spetter 1987; Healy 1988). Columbus as Yankee looked somewhat more real, if not necessarily less foolish, in light of that ongoing expansion.

Europe also noticed. The Pan-American strategy was designed in part to block the British (whose investments in South America exceeded those of the United States), the French (perceived as a major threat until the 1889 collapse of their canal project), and, to a lesser extent, the Germans and Italians. More specifically, from 1890 to the end of the fair, Europeans were repeatedly told how to read Columbus. The official guide to the fair dismissed as meaningless the first 280 years of the Euro-American encounter: the history of this hemisphere prior to 1776 was a mere "preparatory period" to the rise of the United States. The meaning of the discovery could be measured by the number of bushels of wheat that the United States now produced and the length of its railways. Shunning Europe and Latin America in the same stroke, the guide added: "Most fitting it is, therefore, that the people of the greatest nation on the continent discovered by Christopher Columbus, should lead in the celebration of the Four Hundredth Anniversary of that event" (Flinn 1893, 7–8).

Even US citizens were told in unmistakable terms what Columbus was *not* about, lest working-class Irish and, especially, Italian families use him as a shield to hide their own highly suspect invasion. Railroad magnate Chauncey M. Depew, having conceded in a speech that Columbus Day belonged "not to America, but to the world," went on to warn against "unhealthy immigration," urging US citizens to "quarantine against disease, pauperism and crime" (Badger 1979, 85).[28]

Vanity notwithstanding, however, those who wrote the script for Chicago could not control all the possible readings of that script. Their triumph was due, in part, to their taking Columbus further out of context than did their predecessors. Once done, however, Columbus was not theirs alone. Successful celebrations decontextualize the past successfully, but in so doing they open the door to competitive meanings. The richer the ritual, the easier it is for subsequent performers to change parts of the script or impose new interpretations. Further, as rituals of a special kind, commemorations build upon each other, and each celebration raises the stakes for the next one. Cánovas's *fiesta* and the earlier parades of Italian Americans and Irish Americans had unwittingly promoted the Chicago fair. The Chicago fair, in turn, was read as an acknowledgment of immigrants in the melting pot—clearly an unexpected effect from the point of view of the magnates. From then on, Catholic Americans felt partly vindicated by their hero's national recognition.[29] Three years after the fair, Italians in New York founded the Sons of Columbus Legion, which celebrated Columbus Day the following year (Tomasi 1972, 78). The Knights also worked particularly hard for their chosen ancestor, petitioning successive state legislatures to make October 12 a legal holiday. By 1912, they were victorious;[30] and Columbus himself, further out of the context of 1492 Europe, became more Irish than ever—until Italian Americans made new gains in the continuing contest with the mass migrations that followed each of two world wars.

Latin Americans also appropriated Columbus in unexpected ways, skewing plans made both in Madrid and in Washington. The Spanish government had promoted emigration to South America in the late nineteenth century, as part of a larger movement to promote *hispanismo* in the region. From Madrid's viewpoint, attachment to Spanish culture and veneration of the Spanish past would counteract the growing political and economic influence of the United States. Madrid's promotion of Columbus Day as the day of Hispanism in the colonies and former colonies fitted well into this scheme. The scheme, however, was in obvious conflict with the dominant image of Columbus promoted in the United States. Latin Americans, who participated in both quadricentennials, resolved these conflicts in their own favor.

The image of Columbus with a cowboy hat escorting Wells Fargo wagons was simply not convincing south of Texas, but it did challenge the

Columbus as Renaissance monk favored by Cánovas's Spain. In trying to make of Columbus a North American, the Chicago fair made of him a man of the Americas. That was due to a confusion of tongues, deliberate only in part. From the US viewpoint, turning the discoverer into an "American" was equivalent to putting on him a "made in USA" label, for the United States *is* America.[31] Latin Americans, for their part, could not appropriate Columbus from Spain. Their cultural heritage, their views on blending, their semiperipheral position in the world economy simply did not lead to this takeover: they had neither the means nor the will. Thus, they had watched from the sidelines the Americanization of Columbus. For them, however, the hemisphere is not the exclusive property of *norteamericanos*. *American* means neither *gringo* nor *yankee*—at least not necessarily. An "American" Columbus belonged to the hemisphere. Adding their own line to two different scripts, South Americans forced both the Spanish and the US figures into their "blending" discourse. Throughout Latin America, October 12 became the day either to honor Spanish influence or to honor its opposite or, more often, to celebrate a blending of the two: Discovery Day, the Day of the Americas, or simply El Día de la Raza, the Day of the Race, the day of the people—a day for ourselves, however defined, for ethnicity however constructed.[32] La Raza has in Merida or Cartagena accents unknown in San Juan or Santiago de Chile, and Columbus wears a different hat in any of these places.[33]

Will the real Columbus please stand up?

The problem is, of course, in the injunction itself. Academics and power brokers, diplomats and travel agents will soon again claim to have found the true Columbus. They will assert ownership of his remains and tell various audiences how to read the Bahamas landfall. With the internationalization of "the public" that characterizes this moment in the life of capitalism, with the sophisticated techniques now available to image makers, the quincentennial celebrations promise new twists in the contest for Columbus's persona.[34] Power brokers will talk to us about themselves while feigning to speak of Columbus. Others will denounce the maneuver as "cheating."[35]

It will be cheating—but only to a certain extent. The production of history for mass consumption in the form of commercial and political rituals has become increasingly manipulative. With worldwide changes in the nature of the "public," public history is often now a tale of sheer power clothed in electronic innocence and lexical clarity.[36] Such manipulations, however, are possible because of the contradictions inherent in history itself. As process and as reflection on the very process of which it is part, history is always—to some extent—about oneself. This does not suggest that history is never honest but rather that it is always confusing because of its constitutive mixes.

History involves peoples in three distinct capacities: (1) as occupants of structural positions, or *agents*; (2) as *actors* in constant interface with a context; (3) as *subjects*, that is, as voices aware of their vocality. The subjective capacity, the very one that makes human beings "historical," ensures confusion. Peoples are the subjects of history the way workers are subjects of a strike: they define the very terms under which the situation can be described. Since subjects are never created equal, history is always a partial invention in the sense that genealogies, traditions, or nations are always "invented" (Hobsbawm and Ranger 1983; Trouillot 1990a). The production of history thus necessarily involves the production of silences, erasures, preferences, exaggerations.

If history is as messy as I think it is for its subjects, the "real" Columbus would have no final reading of the events he generated—certainly not at the time of their occurrence. Genoese by birth, Mediterranean by training, Castilian by necessity, Cristóbal Colón had no final word on things much more trivial than his landfall. He contradicted himself many times—much like other historical actors, sometimes more than other historical actors. He left some blanks on purpose; he left others because he did not know better; and yet others because he could not do otherwise. In Columbus's travel journal, there is a description of the first sighting of land on Thursday, October 11, 1492. In his log entry for the day Columbus (1989, 63) hints about the tense evening, the long night that followed, the first views of land at two in the morning. "At two hours after midnight, land appeared, from which they were about two leagues distant. They hauled down the sails . . . passing time until daylight Friday," when they reached an islet and descended. There is no clear-cut milestone in the log (Columbus 1981, [1492–] 1989). It was a messy night; not Thursday anymore, but not yet Friday. At any rate, there is no separate entry in Columbus's journal for Friday, October 12, 1492.

NOTES

I am grateful to Carol A. Breckenridge, Nancy Farriss, Richard Kagan and Sidney W. Mintz for their valuable comments on this essay. Special thanks to Arjun Appadurai for suggesting its theme and providing comments, and to Anne-Carine Trouillot for her research assistance. My continuous involvement with the International Roundtables in Anthropology and History since 1986 and our ongoing exchanges on "The Production of History" influenced my grasp of some of the issues treated here. I remain responsible for the final result. *Editors' Note:* This chapter's epigraph is from Columbus ([1493–] 1988, 2). This chapter first appeared as "Good Day, Columbus: Silences, Power, and Public History (1492–1892)," *Public Culture* 3, no. 1 (1990): 1–24.

1. The influence of nearly eight centuries of Islamic control over one or another of the dominions of Europe is undeniable (Imàmuddin 1981; Burns 1984; Cutler and Cutler 1986; Sánchez-Albornoz [1946–73] 1985). Also, whereas the Christian victors expelled the Jews, the capitulation treaties protected Islamic cultural practices, including religion (Arié 1973; Irving [1829] 1988; Bishko [1975] 1980). Bums (1984) summarizes nicely the different approaches to the study of Muslim-Christian contact.

2. Isabella had summoned Columbus to Santa Fe, the town she had built near Granada during the siege to serve as military headquarters and as a symbol of Christian determination. Rumeu de Armas (1985, 50) contends that serious negotiations between royal secretary Juan de Colomba and Father Juan Perez, Columbus's sponsor, started on January 2, 1492, the very day the Christian flag was raised over the Alhambra. The final mandate was drawn up in April 1492.

3. For heuristic purposes, I have suggested to distinguish within the process of historical production the moment of fact creation (the making of sources) from the moment of fact assembling (the making of narratives). Yet the distinction is useful only if we keep in mind that both feed on each other: facts are always created in relation, that is, as part of narratives in the making. This means that the invention of tradition is also the invention of "events." It always imposes new facts upon the past, new ways of cutting, naming, defining "what actually happened." At the same time, the making of sources, as a historical process itself marked by power, imposes certain limits on future interpretations (Trouillot 1986, 1989b).

4. On naming and power, see Trouillot 1988, 27; 1989a.

5. For this reason, I confess to prefer "discovered the Bahamas," or "stumbled on the Antilles," to "discovered America," or "landed in the New World." The first two phrases may raise some eyebrows if only because they decenter the official narrative—which is more than the last two will ever do. (See note 7.)

6. Centennials themselves are elaborate variations on the annual theme. They are most often fashioned around an event that has been celebrated yearly at a fixed date—even if by a few. They may, in turn, revitalize an annual cycle, as we will see later.

7. These three ensembles are dealt with unequally here, and I do not claim to exhaust all modes of appropriation of Columbus and his landfall within each

of them. Latin America in particular, where constructions about Columbus are complex and numerous (O'Gorman 1961; Phelan 1970), is shortchanged in the discussion. But my point is not to show what images of Columbus look like in each of these three ensembles or even to construct an equilateral triangle with sketches from the three. Rather, this is a narrative about narratives of power that aims at no center itself—except, of course, the nondescript place that Columbus stumbled upon in the middle of this nowhere they now call the Caribbean.

8. Sidney Mintz called my attention to the significance of López de Gómara's statement.

9. Up to the 1830s, for instance, there may have been three times more literary or musical works about an American figure like Montezuma (including that of Vivaldi) than about Columbus.

10. Reflecting on the invention of traditions in the United States, Eric Hobsbawm (1983, 279) rightly insists that "Americans had to be made" in ways Europeans did not need to be. This production of traditions, however, started in the United States much earlier than Hobsbawm seems to think, and perhaps earlier than in Europe since North America was perceived as having no past.

11. On the Tammany Society, see Kilroe 1913 and Mushkat 1971. Columbus's landfall was also celebrated in Baltimore and Boston in 1792 (Adams 1892; Badger 1979). The first permanent monument to Columbus in the United States may have been that erected by the Chevalier d'Anmour, the French consul to Baltimore (Adams 1892: 30–31). Still, New York tends to be the most popular reference to early Columbian celebrations, proving that even traditions about traditions are created unequal. On early monuments to Columbus in the United States, see Bump 1892.

12. Columbus died in Spain in 1505. More than thirty years later, his remains were transferred to Santo Domingo, then supposedly to Havana and/or Seville. Where they are nowadays remains a matter of controversy in spite of Santo Domingo's edge among the favorite locations.

13. The acknowledgment that the rules for classification had changed was quite candid on the part of the early colonists. It declined somewhat in the eighteenth and nineteenth centuries, only to reappear with political and cultural nationalisms of various kinds in the twentieth century (Pagden 1987; Schwartz 1987; Mörner 1967, 1970).

14. This does not suggest that Latin America stands outside of the international hierarchy of races, religions, and cultures, or that Native Americans in that region do not encounter prejudice. Rather both discourses and institutionalized practices of discrimination allow much more flexibility to the actors than, say, the rigid US system—to the point where phenotype alone does not deter-

mine the socioracial denomination of specific individuals. In fact, at times, the reverse can be true: individuals of known "Indian" ancestry can become "white" (Wolf 1959, 236). The treatment of Black populations and the ways that boundaries defining Blackness and whiteness are erected is also relevant to this argument.

Marvin Harris, who rightly criticizes naive claims of Latin American racial harmony, admits that "it is definitely verifiable that all hybrids were not and are not forced back into a sharply separated Negro group by application of a rule of descent. This was true during slavery and it was true after slavery" (Harris [1964] 1974, 79). This was even truer of the Native Americans.

15. Schwartz (1987, 30) draws on Fernando de Azedevo to observe that in certain regions of Brazil "Tupí, the predominant Indian language, was more widely spoken than Portuguese . . . even by the colonists." See also Pagden 1987.

16. Hence, Bolívar declared in 1815: "We are . . . neither Indian nor European, but a species midway between the legitimate proprietors of this country and the Spanish usurpers" (cited by Mörner 1967, 86). A few decades later, nineteenth-century scientific racism did influence Latin American opinions and practices (e.g., Mörner 1967; Nash 1970, 181–83) without always negating, however, the stress on mixes rather than pure sets, on differences of degrees rather than differences of kind (Mörner 1970).

17. These ideological traits of the discourse on culture and ethnicity in Latin America are so strong that they spill over in the academic literature. Many scholars speak of Latin American groups as if they were peculiar biological blends—*café au lait* mixtures—of otherwise "pure" pre-Conquest entities: Indian, African, Spanish, Portuguese (e.g., Mörner 1967, 1970). Similarly, "the Indian Legacy" of Spanish America is often assumed, rather than demonstrated, by "Native" cultural historians in particular (e.g., Picón-Salas 1967).

18. There are vague mentions of Columbus Day celebrations by Italian Americans as early as the 1840s, especially after the creation of the Colombo Guard by Genoese immigrants in New York (Tomasi 1972, 79).

19. The introduction of history into the school curriculum as a required subject in the early nineteenth century, and its slow growth before the Civil War (Pierce 1926) also contributed to familiarize a larger audience with Columbus. So did the few biographical sketches published in the first half of the century. Nevertheless, the Catholic connection was crucial in that Catholics provided the bodies that made possible the mass celebrations of Columbus Day before the 1890s.

20. My account of the quadricentennial activities is drawn primarily from Bernabeu Albert 1987. On Spain at the time, see Carr 1966; on Cánovas, see Fernández Almagro 1972.

21. On October 9, Cánovas, his wife, and members of the royal family took part in a mock-trip off the Andalusian coast with escort ships from twelve foreign countries. At least twenty-four countries (France, the United Kingdom, Italy, Belgium, Russia, Austria, Holland, Denmark, Germany, Portugal, Mexico, Argentina, the Dominican Republic, El Salvador, Guatemala, Costa Rica, Colombia, Uruguay, Bolivia, Peru, Chile, Brazil, Haiti, and the United States) participated officially in the Spanish quadricentennial.

22. The quadricentennial junta created at least one serious academic journal, influenced others, dealt with learned societies, and commissioned research that still inspires European and American studies. From February 1891 to May 1892, more than fifty public lectures were delivered in the Ateneo de Madrid alone. Topics in Madrid and elsewhere varied from "Marriage and Divorce in Private International Law" to the possibility of a military alliance tying Spain and Portugal to Latin America, to the relevance of philosophical positivism for the writing of history. Many titles show the role of the quadricentennial in shaping the categories under which the conquest of the Americas is still discussed: the differential impact of various colonial systems on conquered populations, the accuracy of the Black Legend, the cultural legacies of pre-Conquest Americans, Spain's treatment of Columbus, Columbus's role as compared to that of other European explorers, his exact landing place, his exact burial place, and so forth (Bernabeu Albert 1987; Vorsey and Parker 1982).

23. Spanish journalist Angel Stor then spoke in the name of many when he wrote: "There is in the discovery of America a character much greater than Isabella and Ferdinand the Catholic . . . much greater than Columbus himself, for never was an individual able to do what a people can. This character is Spain, the true protagonist of this wonderful epic" (cited by Bernabeu Albert 1987, 123).

24. Cánovas also used the quadricentennial to consolidate his personal power. In a political context marked by Spain's first experiment with "universal" (male) suffrage and nearly obsessional fears of losing face in Europe and elsewhere, he came out of the celebrations as a bona fide representative of the nation and a guarantor of her honor. Finally, token gifts were made to the colonies—such as schools and dispensaries opened in the Philippines.

25. US appropriations for the 1892 celebration in Madrid were a mere $25,000, thus one tenth of US appropriations for the 1889 fair in Paris and a mere trifle compared to the $5.8 million for the Chicago Exposition (Badger 1979, 132). On the Chicago Exposition, see Flinn 1893; Rand, McNally 1893; Badger 1979; and Rydell 1984.

26. Henry Adams later wrote in his *Education*: "The Exposition denied philosophy. . . . [S]ince Noah's Ark, no such Babel of loose and ill-jointed, such vague and ill-defined and unrelated thoughts and half-thoughts and

experimental outcries . . . had ruffled the surface of the Lakes" (cited by Badger 1979, 120).

27. Years before, the United States had boycotted a similar project by Bolívar. Blaine himself did not witness the opening of the fair. He died in January 1893, months after submitting his resignation to President Harrison.

28. The number of immigrants from Europe had doubled between 1860 and 1893. At the same time, the countries of origin were increasingly non-English-speaking areas of what passed for "Southern Europe": Italy, Russia, Poland, Bohemia, and so forth. (By 1890, the number of Italian immigrants was over 300,000.) Ideas suggesting the biological inferiority of the "Southern" immigrants and the threat they constituted to the "future race" of the United States became widespread. Progressive journals taking the "new" immigrants' side published articles with titles such as "Are the Italians a Dangerous Class?" (Howarth 1894). Thus Depew's remarks were part of a debate (Tomasi 1972).

29. In the 1890s the appropriation of Columbus in the United States truly became a national phenomenon, a process in which professional historians played their part. By 1892, for instance, historians were listing Columbus, Ohio, as proof of Columbus's recognition in the United States (Bump 1892, 70). How interesting, then, that a comprehensive history of Columbus, Ohio, published less than twenty years before does not underscore the connection between the Genoese navigator and the Ohio town (Studer 1873).

30. Columbus Day did not become a federal holiday in the United States until 1968.

31. This "American" Columbus was modified somewhat in Old World territories taken by the United States. Further decontextualized, October 12 became Discovery Day in Hawai'i and Guam—places where Columbus never set foot alive, but where chunks of the myth followed US power.

32. October 12 is a fixed holiday in at least twelve former colonies of Spain, under different labels, including "Day of the Americas" in addition to those cited above. There are numerous variations on the theme. Panama, whose Latin legitimacy has sometimes been questioned because of its US-sponsored birth, celebrates Latin American Nations Day on October 12. In Cuba, discovery-oriented celebrations were toned down by the revolutionary government which, in turn, promoted the celebration of the launching of the war of independence on October 10. Peru does not set Columbus Day as a fixed holiday but celebrates National Dignity Day on October 9. The situation is quite different in countries where the influence of Spain is less obvious. Except for the United States and Canada, none of the American countries that bears more strongly the imprint of one of Spain's former colonial competitors celebrates October 12. For instance, Trinidad celebrates the first European landfall on its shores on August 4. Haiti celebrates its own "discovery" on December 5.

33. There are many twists to the manipulation of past history and the current calendar in the construction of ethnicity. In Caño Mochuelo, Colombia, October 12 is "The Day of the Indian," the occasion for one of the many regional fiestas which, according to De Friedemann (1976, 293), perpetuate Indian stereotypes and act as a "cultural mechanism of subordination."

34. Already, the realm of the contest has been expanded: in a bold move, Spain's economic and political magnates have, for the first time, made public apologies for the 1492 persecution of the Jews and call on Sephardics to join in the extravaganza. Some Jewish American lobbies seem ready to jump on Columbus's quincentennial bandwagon.

35. Jean-François Revel contends that "cheating in history consists of speaking of oneself while feigning to speak about others" (cited by Preiswerk and Perrot 1978).

36. The speed at which commodities, information, and individuals travel and, conversely, the decreasing significance of face-to-face interaction (two worldwide trends with numerous local variations) influence both the kinds of communities people wish to be part of and the kinds of communities to which they think they belong. Image makers use this tension—and its historical components—as a springboard: a flag, a memorial, an anniversary.

REFERENCES

Adams, Herbert B. 1892. "Columbus and His Discovery of America." In *Columbus and His Discovery of America*, edited by H. B. Adams and H. Wood, 7–39. Baltimore, MD: Johns Hopkins University Press.

Arié, Rachel. 1973. *L'Espagne musulmane au temps des Nasrides (1232–1492)*. Paris: Éditions E. de Brocard.

Badger, Reid. 1979. *The Great American Fair: The World's Columbia Exposition and American Culture*. Chicago: N. Hall.

Bernabeu Albert, Salvador. 1987. *1892, el IV centenario del descubrimiento de America en España: Coyuntura y conmemoraciónes*. Madrid: Consejo Superior de Investigacicónes Científicas.

Bishko, Charles Julian. (1975) 1980. "The Spanish and Portuguese Reconquest, 1095–1492." In *Studies in Medieval Spanish Frontier History*. London: Variorum Reprints. (repr. from Setton and Hazard [eds.], *A History of the Crusades*, 396–456. Madison: University of Wisconsin Press.)

Bump, Charles Weathers. 1892. "Public Memorials to Columbus." In *Columbus and His Discovery of America*, edited by H. B. Adams and H. Wood, 69–88. Baltimore, MD: Johns Hopkins University Press.

Bums, Robert I. 1984. *Muslims, Christians, and Jews in the Crusader Kingdom of Valencia*. Cambridge: Cambridge University Press.

Carr, Raymond. 1966. *Spain, 1808–1939*. Oxford History of Modern Europe. Oxford: Clarendon Press.

Columbus, Christopher [Colomb, Christophe]. 1981. *La découverte de l'Amérique: Journal de bord, 1492–1493*. Paris: Maspero.

Columbus, Christopher [Colomb, Christophe]. (1493–) 1988. *The Four Voyages of Columbus*. Edited by Cecil Jane. New York: Dover Publications.

Columbus, Christopher [Colomb, Christophe]. (1492–) 1989. *The Diario of Christopher Columbus: First Voyage to America*. Transcribed and translated by Oliver Dunn and James E. Kelley Jr. Norman: University of Oklahoma Press.

Cutler, Allan Harris, and Helen Elmquist Cutler. 1986. *The Jew as Ally of the Muslim: Medieval Roots of Anti-Semitism*. Notre Dame, IN: University of Notre Dame Press.

De Friedemann, Nina S. 1976. "The Fiesta of the Indian in Quibdó, Colombia." In *Ethnicity in the Americas*, edited by F. Henry, 291–300. The Hague: Mouton Publishers.

Fernández Almagro, Melchor. 1972. *Cánovas: Su vida y su política*. Collección políticos y financieros. Madrid: Ediciónes Tebas.

Flinn, John Joseph, ed. 1893. *Official Guide to the World's Columbian Exposition*. Chicago: The Columbian Guide Co.

Hale, J. R. (1971) 1977. *Renaissance Europe: Individual and Society*. Berkeley: University of California Press.

Hanke, Lewis. 1959. *Aristotle and the American Indians*. London: Hollis and Carter.

Harris, Marvin. (1964) 1974. *Patterns of Race in the Americas*. New York: Norton Library.

Healy, David, 1988. *Drive to Hegemony: The United States in the Caribbean, 1898–1917*. Madison: University of Wisconsin Press.

Hobsbawm, Eric. 1983. "Mass-Producing Traditions: Europe, 1870–1914." In *The Invention of Tradition*, edited by Eric Hobsbawm and Terence Ranger, 263–307. Cambridge: Cambridge University Press.

Hobsbawm, Eric. 1987. *The Age of Empire, 1875–1914*. New York: Pantheon.

Hobsbawm, Eric, and Terence Ranger, eds. 1983. *The Invention of Tradition*. Cambridge: Cambridge University Press.

Howarth, I. W. 1894. "Are the Italians a Dangerous Class?" *Charities* 4: 17-40.

Imàmuddin, S. M. 1981. *Muslim Spain, 711–1492 A.D.* Medieval Iberian Peninsula Texts and Studies. Leiden: E. J. Brill.

Irving, Washington. (1829) 1988. *The Complete Works of Washington Irving*. Vol. 13, *A Chronicle of the Reconquest of Granada* [by Fray Antonio Agapida]. Boston: Twayne Publishers.

Johnson, John. 1990. *A Hemisphere Apart: The Foundations of United States Policy toward Latin America*. Baltimore, MD: Johns Hopkins University Press.

Kauffman, Christopher. 1982. *Faith and Fraternalism: The History of the Knights of Columbus, 1882–1982*. New York: Harper and Row.

Kilroe, Edwin Patrick. 1913. *Saint Tammany and the Origin of the Society of Tammany or Columbian Order in the City of New York*. New York: Columbia University Press.

Langley, Lester D. 1976. *The Struggle for the American Mediterranean*. Athens: University of Georgia Press.

Langley, Lester D. 1989. *America and the Americas: The United States in the Western Hemisphere*. Athens: University of Georgia Press.

Manigat, Leslie F. 1973. *L'Amérique latine au XXe siècle, 1889–1929*. Paris: Éditions Richelieu.

Mitchell, Timothy. 1988. *Colonizing Egypt*. Cambridge: Cambridge University Press.

Mörner, Magnus. 1967. *Race Mixture in the History of Latin America*. Boston: Little, Brown.

Mörner, Magnus, ed. 1970. *Race and Class in Latin America*. New York: Columbia University Press.

Mushkat, Jerome. 1971. *Tammany: The Evolution of a Political Machine, 1789–1865*. Syracuse, NY: Syracuse University Press.

Nash, Manning. 1970. "The Impact of Mid-Nineteenth Century Economic Change upon the Indians of Middle America." In *Race and Class in Latin America*, edited by M. Mörner, 170–83. New York: Columbia University Press.

O'Gorman, Edmundo. 1961. *The Invention of America: An Inquiry into the Historical Nature of the New World and the Meaning of Its History*. Bloomington: Indiana University Press.

Pagden, Anthony. 1982. *The Fall of Natural Man: The American Indian and the Origins of Comparative Ethnology*. Cambridge: Cambridge University Press.

Pagden, Anthony. 1987. "Identity Formation in Spanish America." In *Colonial Identity in the Atlantic World*, edited by N. Canny and A. Pagden, 51–93. Princeton, NJ: Princeton University Press.

Phelan, John Leddy. 1970. *The Millennial Kingdom of the Franciscans in the New World*. Berkeley: University of California Press.

Picón-Salas, Mariano. 1967. *A Cultural History of Spanish America from Conquest to Independence*. Berkeley: University of California Press.

Pierce, Bessie Louise. 1926. *Public Opinion and the Teaching of History in the United States*. New York: Alfred A. Knopf.

Preiswerk, Roy, and Dominique Perrot. 1978. *Ethnocentrism and History: Africa, Asia, and Indian America in Western Textbooks*. New York: Nok Publishers.

Rand, McNally & Co. 1893. *Handbook of the World's Columbian Exposition*. Chicago: Rand, McNally & Co.

Rumeu de Armas, Antonio. 1985. *Nueva luz sobre las capitulaciónes de Santa Fe de 1492 concertadas entre los reyes católicos y Cristóbal Colón: Estudio institucional y diplomático*. Madrid: Consejo Superior de Investigaciónes Científicas.

Rydell, Robert W. 1984. *All the World's a Fair: Visions of Empire at American International Expositions, 1876–1916*. Chicago: University of Chicago Press.

Sánchez-Albornoz, Claudio. (1946–73) 1985. *L'Espagne musulmane*. Translated by Claude Farragi. Paris: OPU/Publisud.

Schwartz, Stuart. 1987. "The Formation of a Colonial Identity in Brazil." In *Colonial Identity in the Atlantic World, 1500–1800*, edited by N. Canny and A. Pagden, 15–50. Princeton, NJ: Princeton University Press.

Socolofsky, Homer E., and Allan B. Spetter. 1987. *The Presidency of Benjamin Harrison*. Lawrence: University of Kansas Press.

Speroni, Charles. (1948) 1987. "The Development of the Columbus Day Pageant of San Francisco." In *The Folklore of American Holidays*, edited by H. Cohen and T. P. Coffin, 301–2. Detroit: Gale Research.

Studer, Jacob Henry. 1873. *Columbus, Ohio: Its History, Resources and Progress*. Columbus: J. H. Studer.

Tomasi, Lydio F., ed. 1972. *The Italian in America: The Progressive View, 1891–1914*. New York: Center for Migration Studies.

Tomasi, Lydio F. 1985. *Italian Americans: New Perspectives in Italian Immigration and Ethnicity*. New York: Center for Migration Studies of New York.

Trouillot, Michel-Rolph. 1986. "So Spoke the Muffled: Notes on the Conditions of Possibility of the Historical Narrative." Paper prepared for the Fifth International Roundtable in Anthropology and History, The Production of History, Maison des Sciences de l'Homme, Paris, France, July 3–5.

Trouillot, Michel-Rolph. 1988. *Peasants and Capital: Dominica in the World Economy*. Baltimore, MD: Johns Hopkins University Press.

Trouillot, Michel-Rolph. 1989a. "Discourses of Rule and the Acknowledgment of the Peasantry in Dominica, W.I., 1838–1928." *American Ethnologist* 16, no. 4: 704–18.

Trouillot, Michel-Rolph. 1989b. "Glory and Silences in the Haitian Revolution: The Three Faces of Sans-Souci." Paper presented at the Sixth International Roundtable in Anthropology and History, The Production of History: Silences and Commemorations, Rockefeller Conference Center, Bellagio, Italy, August 29–September 2.

Trouillot, Michel-Rolph. 1990. *Haiti: State against Nation; The Origins and Legacy of Duvalierism*. New York: Monthly Review Press.

Trouillot, Michel-Rolph. 1991. "Anthropology as Metaphor: The Savage's Legacy and the Post-modern World." *Review (Fernand Braudel Center)* 14, no. 1: 29–54.

Volwiller, Albert T., ed. 1940. *The Correspondence between Benjamin Harrison and James G. Blaine, 1882–1893*. Memoirs of the Society, vol. 14. Philadelphia: American Philosophical Society.

Vorsey, Louis de, Jr., and J. Parker, eds. 1982. *The Columbus Landfall Problem: Islands and Controversy*. Detroit, MI: Wayne State University Press.

Wallace-Hadrill, J. M. (1965) 1988. *The Barbarian West, 400–1000*. Oxford: Basil Blackwell.

Wolf, Eric R. 1959. *Sons of the Shaking Earth*. Chicago: University of Chicago Press.

PART II

THE
OTHERWISE
MODERN

TRANSLATED AND ANNOTATED BY LAURA WAGNER

Ti dife boule: Radio
Haiti Interview, 1977

In 1977, a twenty-seven-year-old undergraduate student named Michel-Rolph Trouillot was living at his aunt's apartment in Brooklyn, working as a taxi driver while earning his bachelor's degree from Brooklyn College. That year, he published his Kreyòl-language history of the Haitian Revolution, Ti dife boule sou istwa Ayiti.[1] In the book, Grenn Pwomennen, a wandering storyteller from traditional Haitian folklore, sets out to understand the mysteries of life, death, and suffering and, after a long time away, returns to his village to recount what he has learned, focusing on the story of the Haitian Revolution. In July of that year, Trouillot sat down with Radio Haiti's Richard Brisson in Port-au-Prince to discuss the book. The following year, Trouillot would receive his bachelor's degree and move to Johns Hopkins University to begin a PhD in anthropology.

Throughout history, including today, most of Haiti's literary, academic, and journalistic writing has been produced in French, despite the fact that the vast majority of Haitian people are monolingual Kreyòl speakers. Two months after the 1977 interview, Radio Haiti's director, Jean L. Dominique, reviewed Ti dife boule sou istwa Ayiti on the air. "Our history had long remained the privilege of the educated elites: Francophone scholars," Dominique observed. This "deprived Ti Jozèf and Lamèsi of all the richness of studying their own past."[2] Trouillot's book was, according to Dominique, a most important intervention, one that would allow the long-excluded Kreyòl-speaking Haitian majority to at last understand the glories and the complexities of their country's history. As the first radio station to broadcast serious reporting and intellectual debate in Kreyòl, Radio Haiti shared this mission. "My duty, now, is to make every child understand this book," Dominique declared. "My duty is to make every Lamèsi and every Sedènye and every Ti Jozèf hear Grenn Pwomennen telling them the history of Haiti. This is the pledge I am making, before everyone. Wowo,[3] you have done your duty as a historian. You have written a proper book. And now I am going to do my own duty as a radio journalist for this station to broadcast the story of Sedènye and Lamèsi just as it broadcast the story of Manuel and Anaïse last year.[4] Thank you, Wowo."

Trouillot had gone into exile in the United States in 1968, one of many student activists to flee the dictatorship of François Duvalier. Brisson, Radio Haiti's poet-journalist, would likewise be exiled, along with the rest of Radio Haiti's team, after the government of Jean-Claude Duvalier unleashed a wave of violent repression on the independent press beginning on November 28, 1980. Brisson was killed during a doomed and quixotic effort to invade Haiti and overthrow Duvalier in 1982.

RICHARD BRISSON: Michel-Rolph Trouillot, a young man trying to survive in New York City, has just released his latest text, his latest book. This book is called *Ti dife boule sou istwa Ayiti*. Two-hundred twenty-four pages, from front to back, about a period of time gone by. Michel-Rolph Trouillot makes us relive a beautiful moment—if not one of the most beautiful moments—of our country's history. Grenn Pwomennen hoists up his sack and sets out to understand why the spirits have gone back to Ginen.[5] Many of them returned, after a long time. If we didn't have to stand on formality, I'd let him simply say his piece and be done with it but, thankfully, this issue deserves to be broken down over a cup of coffee. So, in the meantime, let's see what Michel-Rolph Trouillot himself has to say about this book. Wowo, I would like you to tell us the story of this book you've put into my hands here.

MICHEL-ROLPH TROUILLOT: This book took root amid all the work I was trying to do at *Lakansièl* magazine.[6] My first attempt at theoretical work in Kreyòl appeared in the second volume of *Lakansièl* magazine in July 1975. In it, I attempted to make a few clarifying points in an ongoing debate at the time about the issue of sexuality. That article was called "Pou drese kozman" (To set the record straight). As a result of that article and the effect it had, I became interested in continuing to write theory in Kreyòl. In October

'75, in the third volume of *Lakansièl*, I published an article on the death of Dessalines.[7] This was for the anniversary of the death of Dessalines, October 17. From that moment on, the book itself started to come to life, as I continued to receive ideas and critiques on those two articles, both that first theoretical article in Kreyòl and the article on the death of Dessalines.

> **BRISSON:** *Monchè*,[8] I'd like you to tell us how long it took you to write this book.

TROUILLOT: The book started to come alive, if you will—well, the better part of the material that makes up the book had been taking shape in my mind for some time, but I really sat down to write it, well, around the time I wrote that article about the death of the Emperor [Dessalines], so around September or October '75. That's when I really started writing the book, the book itself. So it took me about a year and six months, more or less.

> **BRISSON:** But before you even sat down to write it, when you had just started to work on the book, what problems did you have with documents?

TROUILLOT: I didn't have any trouble *finding* documents, if that's what you mean. Because, you see, there are plenty of documents abroad about the history of our country. There's enough for someone to retrace these events, whether in general or in detail. So that's not really the problem. Moreover, lots of guys have delved into the history of Haiti, guys who have the perseverance to dig into those musty old papers, and they find the majority of events. The problem is sorting through those documents, reading those documents, seeing what those documents contain—I would say consuming the documents, down to the last drop, and seeing what they can impart to us today.

> **BRISSON:** So you didn't have any problems at all, then!

TROUILLOT: Well, I didn't have any problem finding documents, but there were other problems, especially the problem of finding time to do it, because I had other activities, you understand, school and so on.

> **BRISSON:** In any case, when I opened *Ti dife boule*, I saw that you began with the history of the Code Noir.[9] What about the Indians? What about Columbus?

TROUILLOT: Do you mean Christopher Columbus?

> **BRISSON:** Mmm-hmm.

TROUILLOT: Well, if you look closely, I don't begin—I begin with the Code Noir but at the same time I don't begin with the Code Noir. The essence of the book is to trace the history of the revolution in Saint-Domingue. And the chapter on the Code Noir helps me, if you will, delve into the conflicts of that society, how that society took shape, how the conflicts themselves took shape, so that the reader could understand how that society came to be, before the society itself crumbled. The course of the book is to deconstruct the revolution in Saint-Domingue. Seeking to understand, if you will, what social classes the revolution put in power, which other social classes the revolution unseated, which social groups took advantage of the revolution, and so on. I could say, well, the first part [of the book] follows the development of the revolution, examining the pauses it took, especially from 1789 to 1801, because I believe that the revolution slowed in 1801, and it slowed again in 1804, and it stopped for the last time from around 1820 to around 1825, from when the last of the maroons, Goman, Malfêt, and Malfou disappeared from the Grand'Anse,[10] until France finally recognized Haiti's independence in 1825. So I would say, in essence, that the fundamental work of my text is that, tracing the path of the Revolution.

BRISSON: Has there never been any other work like this?

TROUILLOT: Well, I wouldn't rush to say that my work is the first work of its kind. True, this work breaks with a lot of books that have already been written about the history of Haiti, but it also builds upon certain other books that have tried, well, to trace the class conflicts in Saint-Domingue, from 1789 to 1804, or to go even further than that. There are several works that come to mind just now as I'm speaking: there are people like [C. L. R.] James, a Trinidadian who wrote a book called *The Black Jacobins*. He wrote a book, he tries to trace the movement of social classes, you understand, and he tries to trace the social forces that moved the revolution in Saint-Domingue forward! There are other books that come to mind too, like Roger Dorsinville's *Toussaint Louverture ou la vocation de la liberté*; there's the work Ambroise and Rameau did in their book,[11] there are a few other guys who try to show, I believe, the foundation of the revolution, which is to show the path the revolution took, and who try especially, I would say, to insist that this was a matter of class war in Saint-Domingue.

BRISSON: Mmm-hmm. But, even so, wouldn't you say your book is a bit different from these books you've just spoken of?

TROUILLOT: Well, of course there are differences between every book and every other book, because each book is its own book! But, well, I think I could say, if you will, in my opinion: despite all the good work they've done digging deep into the subject, they don't dig deep enough into certain problems that I would say I focus on more. For example, they don't look deeply enough, I think, at the work that Toussaint was doing. They focus a bit too much on Toussaint himself, Toussaint Louverture, I would say, the individual, you know, François Dominique Toussaint Bréda, who he was, and so on, rather than digging deep beneath the surface to see the real work Toussaint was doing. Furthermore, all of them, both James and Dorsinville—I'm thinking especially of those two—go a long way in explaining how Toussaint's team took control of the population, they try to explain the conflicts between the population and Louverture's government in 1801. But because they don't, I would say, center those conflicts from 1791 onward, they don't manage to reveal the problems that were at the heart of that strategy, the problems that were at the heart of Louverture's government, and especially the problems of Louverture's ideology. So I believe there's a difference there.

> **BRISSON**: Well, you told us that you're going to school; I know you're studying anthropology. Isn't that what made you decide to write a history of Haiti, rather than devoting yourself to something else, another subject?

TROUILLOT: Well, I don't know, I wouldn't rush to say it's one or the other. But certainly, everything a man or a woman does is connected, nothing we do in life is an isolated act, and no one is an island, there's always a ripple effect.[12] So everything I've picked up along the way, everything I've learned up to this point has helped me bring this book to fruition. Well, as for the matter of anthropology in particular, anthropology helped me, for example, to make a special effort to lay out various concepts, various ways of speaking, various ways of thinking, various ways of reflecting, that are in tune with the culture of the Haitian people and the mores of the Haitian people. Anthropology helped me, if you will, embrace language that doesn't look 100 percent like Western theoretical language! You can see, for example, the book is filled with songs, proverbs, and *langaj*,[13] which according to the formal conventions of Western readers, isn't supposed to be part of scientific prose! But anthropology shows us that according to African mores or Antillean mores—hence the mores of the Haitian people—those ways of speaking are not inconsistent with one another. Those ways of speaking are not separate. So I believe that, yes, it [anthropology] helps us in certain ways.

> BRISSON: *Monchè*, there's something else I'd like to know. If you were living in Haiti, do you think you would have been able to write the book as well as you did?

TROUILLOT: Well, I'm not living in Haiti right now, so I can't say how I would have written the book if I had written it in Haiti. But here, again, one can see that every single thing someone does can help them do the things they will eventually do. So living in New York helped the book come out the way it did. Haitians living in France or in Canada—Montreal, Paris, and so on—for example, would have less of a problem speaking French. But for a man or a woman trying to make it in the United States, the Dominican Republic, or the Bahamas—you can see as clear as day that if you want to speak so that anyone, old or young, within Haiti or abroad, can understand you, you have to speak Kreyòl! For example, if you want a kid who is finishing up high school in the United States to understand you, or if you want a Haitian laborer in the Dominican Republic or the Bahamas to understand you, and, at the same time, you want someone taking his final high school exams in Haiti to understand you, and for another guy trying to get by in Africa[14] to understand you—if you want the majority of all those Haitians to understand you, there's no question about it, you've got to do it in Kreyòl.

> BRISSON: But given the book's price, and the size of this book, for whom did you write it?

TROUILLOT: Well, that's a real problem. Myself, I'd rather the book was shorter, I'd be happier that way, if you will, and I'd much rather the book be a little bit cheaper, even though the book isn't really all that expensive. But I can say, too, that the book went where it wanted to go! As I was writing the book, I discovered a series of foundations that hadn't yet been dug! So as I went along, I had to dig those foundations as I was writing the book. Bit by bit, piece by piece. I couldn't move forward, if you will, so long as I didn't establish those foundations. You can't build a house if you haven't built a good foundation. As a matter of fact, I can tell you: the book might seem long, but, well, it couldn't have come out any shorter. It could have been *longer*, certainly, but it couldn't have been shorter. And so it couldn't have been any cheaper, either, because it's the length of the text that makes it cost more at the printer. Furthermore, I believe that the way the book is written, well, the book has a bunch of chapters, and these chapters are distinct, and at the same time, well, the information unfolds the same way that Grenn Pwomennen is laying it out. But at the same time, too, someone can read this book bit by bit. You understand? The people I think could read this book, well, I would hope that they can manage to read this book bit by bit.

BRISSON: Who are these people you're speaking of?

TROUILLOT: Well, I would like for everyone who can read the book to read the book! There's no question about that. But there are certain people I have in mind, if you will, who would interest me more than others! I don't know if they will be the ones who read this book. I envision, for example, a young man or a young woman getting a diploma from some institution of dubious quality,[15] who's struggling through high school and who isn't too clear on things, but who is making an effort to better understand their own reality. I envision, as well, students who are going through the baccalaureate exam in their final year of high school, who are just memorizing lessons by heart, you know, who think these things don't concern them, who don't have any real interest in what they are doing—I think that the book can make them a little bit interested in what they are forced to study in school, and they will try to understand it better, and they will come to love what they're learning, too.[16]

BRISSON: You wrote the book in Kreyòl, true. But—what Kreyòl is it?

TROUILLOT: Well, the Kreyòl of *Ti dife*, if you will, is a blend of a bunch of different Kreyòls—if I can say there are several Kreyòls, because I don't actually believe there are several Kreyòls. But *within* Kreyòl, there are several branches, there are several—if you will, there are many different ways of speaking. So the Kreyòl of *Ti dife boule*—if there *is* a Kreyòl of *Ti dife boule*— is a blend of many of the ways the people speak—proverbs, songs, tales, *langaj*, and so on, which, if you will, is the essence of the Kreyòl language of the countryside, mixed with Kreyòl I took, if you will, from studying the work of other guys who had already written in Kreyòl, like Frankétienne in *Dézafi*,[17] or work by guys like Rassoul Labuchin,[18] Morisseau-Leroy,[19] Franck Fouché,[20] or work that appeared in *Sèl* magazine[21] or in other journals like *Bon Nouvèl*[22]—guys who work, if you will, from dusk 'til dawn on the issue of Kreyòl. I borrowed from those guys, too. So I can't say that there's a specific Kreyòl but there is a distinctive blend that's mixed with storytelling, and I tried to take what I could from those guys, especially that which helps me push [social] theory further.

BRISSON: Let's change the subject for a moment.[23] You spoke of *Lakansièl*. We all know that *Lakansièl* is a cultural magazine published by a group of young men and women every three months in New York. But I see that the book appeared in the Lakansièl Collection. What is that?

TROUILLOT: The Lakansièl Collection is an effort we've undertaken to push the work that was begun in the magazine a bit further. Because, well, the magazine has its limits, which it cannot exceed—there are texts of a certain length you can't put in the magazine, you know. You can manage to put a complex text in a magazine, but it can't be too complex. So there are some special pieces that will be taken further in their respective areas, in their respective fields. And those pieces, well, you can do them a bit more easily in books, they can take up all the space they need better than in a magazine.

BRISSON: So the first publication of the Lakansièl Collection is *Ti dife boule sou istwa Ayiti*.

TROUILLOT: Yes, the first part of *Ti dife boule* is the first book in the collection. And there are more books to follow, there are other parts of *Ti dife boule*.

BRISSON: What are these other parts of *Ti dife boule* you've referred to?

TROUILLOT: Well, when we examine the revolution in Saint-Domingue closely, we see that the foundation of the revolution began to be laid, if you will, from the society's inception, from around the time of the Code Noir of 1785, but especially from 1789 onward. So what the first part of *Ti dife boule* does is that it encompasses the situation on the island around 1789, and ends in 1791, when the slaves began to set fire to the plantations, sparking the revolution. In 1801, if you will, there was a lull in the revolution in Saint-Domingue. And in the first section of *Ti dife boule*, well, since both myself and Grenn Pwomennen were a bit exhausted, we took a break along with the revolution. Now, well, the revolution had other phases. I believe the revolution started up again for a second time from 1801, if you will, the end of 1801 and the beginning of 1802, you see, particularly with the arrival of Leclerc at the beginning of 1802, the Moïse affair at the end of 1801, and then there was another lull in the revolution in 1804. And now, after independence, the revolution got set for its third phase, you see, and that's when it began its greatest contest. And it stopped for the last time in 1825, when the last card had been played, according to the will of the class that had taken advantage of the revolution.

BRISSON: So, if you stop with that third pause, that means that *Ti dife boule* will have only three parts.

TROUILLOT: Well, I can't say that, because, well, the book will stop where it wants to stop. I wouldn't want to say ahead of time, myself, where it's going, you know, because history itself is always moving forward.

BRISSON: So . . . it might never stop, then?

TROUILLOT: Well, history itself never stops.

BRISSON: But, Wowo, I would like to think that the majority of books you will write, and the majority of books that will appear in the Lakansièl Collection, are going to be books in Kreyòl.

TROUILLOT: Well, I would hope so. I don't know exactly, you know, in which languages all the other books will be written. But as for myself, I know, well, I can, I can certainly write books in other languages, in French for example. But the rest of *Ti dife boule* will be written in Kreyòl. And I would hope that most of the other Lakansièl books, in the Lakansièl Collection, will be in Kreyòl!

BRISSON: Why?

TROUILLOT: Well, writing books in Kreyòl is a matter of great importance. A bevy of scholars who specialize in linguistics and sociolinguistics have demonstrated the importance of language in the lives of a people, in the culture of a people. Take, for example, what sociolinguists and linguists call the Sapir-Whorf hypothesis. Whorf in particular says that a people's spoken language allows them to make sense of their reality. It determines how that people perceives reality, how they act within that reality. If we accept that hypothesis, it is obvious that we cannot help the [Haitian] people see their reality more clearly, get to the heart of that reality, if we don't have those tools, the tools of everyday life in that reality—namely the Kreyòl language—to help us see the issue at hand. And more recently, after Sapir, after Whorf, there are people like Noam Chomsky, another linguist, who goes even further. Chomsky says that the main work a language does is not that it allows one individual in a society speak to another. The main work a language does is that it allows a society to think, it allows a society to make sense of itself, to make sense of its reality. And the work of speaking about that reality is something that language does less often than the work of deconstructing reality. So, that is the main work a language does, according to Noam Chomsky, who says that when we speak our own language, we speak to ourselves more often than we speak to other people. And every time we speak to ourselves, we are deconstructing reality, and every time we talk to ourselves, we do so in our native language. So if the main work language does is deconstructing that reality, when we reject Kreyòl—and most, I would say, of the Haitian petty bourgeoisie, middle class, and bourgeoisie reject Kreyòl—if we reject Kreyòl, as it were, we are casting aside our main tool for deconstructing reality, and we choose instead to use someone else's tools. And as we all know, borrowed tools are never as good as our own.[24]

> BRISSON: Aha! But, whatever the case may be, Rolph Trouillot, if you hadn't been the one to write this book, if someone else had written *Ti dife boule*, what would you think of it?

TROUILLOT: That's a difficult question you're asking me. I can't say it's impossible, but it's hard because I am the one who wrote the book, so you're asking me to pretend that I didn't write it, to sort of step back and look at the book from a distance. Myself, I can say that if I were to look at the book from the point of view of someone who is reading the book and doesn't know where it came from, I could say that I see three different kinds of work that the book is doing: the work of telling the story, the story of the events of the revolution in Saint-Domingue, especially from 1789 to 1802. The work, I would say, that all historical studies must do, both broadly and in detail. The second kind of work I see it doing is the work of concrete analysis. That is to say, well, beyond the storytelling, there is an analysis of those events mixed in with the storytelling, with the telling of the events. How those events came to be, what those events mean, and so on, you see. The relationships between all these events, the relationship between one event and another. And the third kind of work I see is the work of theoretical analysis, which is to say, well, an abstract kind of work, a kind of work that draws out, well, a series of elements, based upon, I would say, the concrete analysis.

> BRISSON: I think I understand what you mean. But, in that case, is this the first work, is this the first book of its kind to be published in Kreyòl?

TROUILLOT: Yes, I believe it is the first book of its kind to be published in Kreyòl, a book that tries to, that uses Kreyòl to do both concrete analysis and theoretical analysis together. I believe there are books published in Kreyòl that are neither novels nor poems—I'm thinking of *Bon Nouvèl*'s entire collection of books—but, in a certain sense, they are not books of concrete analysis. Most of them, I would say, are technical books. That does not mean that they are not important—I think they are hugely important—but they are technical books, they are different from a book that does concrete analysis. And this book, well it's not only doing concrete analysis, it also tries to do theoretical analysis to underpin the concrete analysis.

> **BRISSON:** Well, Michel-Rolph Trouillot, I think we'll end there. Thank you very much for agreeing to this interview on Radio Haïti-Inter, and we hope that someday all Haitians will be able to read *Ti dife boule sou istwa Ayiti.*

NOTES

Translator's Note: I would like to thank Tanya Emma Thomas and Gaspard Louis for their assistance with this translation. Any errors that remain are mine and mine alone.

Editors' Note: This interview was transcribed and translated from the following source: "Michel-Rolph Trouillot sou *Ti difé boulé sou istoua Ayiti*. Entèvyou Richard Brisson," Radio Haiti Collection, David M. Rubenstein Rare Book and Manuscript Library, Duke University, https://repository.duke.edu /dc/radiohaiti/RL10059-RR-0094_02 and https://repository.duke.edu/dc /radiohaiti/RL10059-RR-0094_01.

1. Michel-Rolph Trouillot, *Ti dife boule sou istwa Ayiti*, ed. Lyonel Trouillot (Port-au-Prince: Edisyon KIK, Inivèsite Karayib 2012). Originally published in 1977 as *Ti difé boulé sou istoua Ayiti* (Brooklyn, NY: Koleksion Lakansièl). For clarity's sake, I have used standard modern Kreyòl orthography throughout this translation. Trouillot wrote the book before the orthography was standardized in 1979.

2. Sedènye, Lamèsi, and Ti Jozèf are three of the villagers who listen to Grenn Pwomennen's tale; they represent the Haitian everyman and everywoman.

3. Nickname for Michel-Rolph Trouillot.

4. In 1976, Radio Haiti broadcast a Kreyòl adaptation of Jacques Roumain's novel *Gouverneurs de la rosée* (*Masters of the Dew*). It tells the story of a young man from rural Haiti who returns to his native village after living in Cuba, and who saves his community from drought through collective labor and solidarity before meeting with a tragic end. The radio play—adapted from the French by Jean Dominique and his sister Madeleine Paillère—made the text available to a far wider public.

5. In vodou cosmology, Ginen is both the African homeland across the sea from which Haitian people's ancestors were stolen and the spiritual realm to which people's souls return after death. Elsewhere in the Radio Haiti Archive, a vodou patriarch tells Jean Dominique that the spirits fled back to Ginen when François Duvalier came to power in 1957, and that when the spirits return to Haiti, that means "the time has come" for the Haitian people to rise up against their oppressors.

6. *Lakansièl* ("Lakansyèl" in modern Kreyòl orthography, meaning "rainbow") was a bilingual cultural journal published by a group of Haitian intellectuals in New York, including Michel-Rolph Trouillot and his brother and sister, the novelists Lyonel and Évelyne Trouillot.

7. Jean-Jacques Dessalines (1758–1806), one of the leaders of the Haitian Revolution. He was emperor of Haiti from 1804 until his murder in 1806.

8. Familiar term of address for a man, similar to "buddy" or "my man."

9. The decree that regulated the conditions of slavery in the French empire.

10. Maroons were Africans and their descendants who escaped slavery and fled to remote mountainous regions, where they created small autonomous communities. Goman, Malfèt, and Malfou were three rebel leaders in the area of Jérémie in the Grand'Anse department of Haiti. When Haitian President Jean-Pierre Boyer invaded Jérémie in 1820, he crushed the remaining maroons.

11. Mario Rameau and Jean-Jacques Dessalines Ambroise, *La révolution de Saint-Domingue, 1789–1804* (1963; repr., Port-au-Prince: Société Häitienne d'Histoire et de Géographie, 1990). Rameau, Ambroise, and Ambroise's pregnant wife, Lucette Lafontant, were all killed by the government of François Duvalier in August 1965.

12. Trouillot uses a Kreyòl expression: "Pa genyen zak nan lavi a, kankou grenn senk, kòm ki dire gwo pous pa mele" (literally, "No act in life is on its own, as when we say, the thumb isn't involved [with the other fingers on the hand]").

13. The words traditionally used in vodou ceremonies, much of which comes from African languages; the language of the spirits.

14. During the Duvalier regime, many Haitians fled to Francophone Africa.

15. Trouillot says, "Yon sètifika maltaye."

16. In his introduction to the 2012 edition of *Ti dife boule*, Michel-Rolph Trouillot's brother, the novelist Lyonel Trouillot, describes how the book circulated *an kachèt* (clandestinely) after its initial publication, passed around by students, schoolteachers, and university professors during the regime of Jean-Claude Duvalier.

17. Frankétienne (born Franck Étienne in 1936) is a Haitian writer, poet, playwright, and painter. His 1975 work *Dézafi* was the first novel published in Kreyòl.

18. Rassoul Labuchin (born in 1938) is a Haitian actor, writer, theater director, and filmmaker.

19. Félix Morisseau-Leroy (1912–98) was a Haitian playwright and poet who was one of the first prominent artists to write in Kreyòl.

20. Franck Fouché (1915–78) was a Haitian journalist, writer, literary scholar, poet, and playwright.

21. *Sèl: Jounal Ayisyen Aletranje* was a Kreyòl-language journal by and for Haitians living abroad in the 1970s and 1980s.

22. *Bon Nouvèl* is a Kreyòl-language periodical, originally created by Catholic missionaries, that has been published monthly since 1967.

23. Brisson uses the Kreyòl expression: "Ann kite lapriyè yon ti moman, ann voye kò nou sou kantik la" (literally, "Let's leave the prayer alone for a moment; let's throw ourselves into the hymn").

24. Trouillot uses the Kreyòl expression: "Chodyè prete pa kwit pwa" ("A borrowed pot can't cook peas").

REFERENCES

Trouillot, Michel-Rolph. 1977. *Ti difé boulé sou istoua Ayiti*. Brooklyn, NY: Koleksion Lakensièl.
Trouillot, Michel-Rolph. (1977) 2012. *Ti dife boule sou istwa Ayiti*. Edited by Lyonel Trouillot. Port-au-Prince: Edisyon KIK, Inivèsite Karayib.

CHAPTER 5

The Otherwise Modern

Caribbean Lessons from the Savage Slot

Modernity is a murky term that belongs to a family of words we may label "North Atlantic universals." By that, I mean words inherited from what we now call the West—which I prefer to call the North Atlantic, not only for the sake of geographical precision—that project the North Atlantic experience on a universal scale that they have helped to create. North Atlantic universals are particulars that have gained a degree of universality, chunks of human history that have become historical standards. Words such as *development*, *progress*, *democracy*, and indeed the *West* itself are exemplary members of that family that contracts or expands according to contexts and interlocutors.[1]

North Atlantic universals so defined are not merely descriptive or referential. They do not describe the world; they offer visions of the world. While they appear to refer to things as they exist, rooted in a particular history, they are evocative of multiple layers of sensibilities, persuasions, cultural assumptions, and ideological choices tied to that localized history. They come to us loaded with aesthetic and stylistic sensibilities, religious and philosophical persuasions; cultural assumptions that range from what it means to be a human being to the proper relationship between humans and the natural world; and ideological choices that range from the nature of the political to its possibilities of transformation. To be sure, there is no unanimity within the North Atlantic itself on any of these issues, but there is a shared history of how these issues have been and should be debated, and these words carry that history. Yet since they are projected as universals, they deny their localization, the sensibilities, and the history from which they spring.

Thus, North Atlantic universals are always prescriptive inasmuch as they always suggest, even if implicitly, a correct state of affairs—what is good, what is just, what is desirable—not only what is, but what should be. Indeed, that prescription is inherent in the very projection of a historically limited experience—that of the North Atlantic—on the world stage. Thus also, North Atlantic universals are always seductive, at times even irresistible, exactly because they manage, in that projection, to hide their specific—localized, North Atlantic and, thus, parochial—historical location.

The ability to project universal relevance while hiding the particularities of their marks and origins makes North Atlantic universals as hard to conceptualize as they are seductive to use. Indeed, the more seductive these words become, the harder it is to specify what they actually stand for, since part of the seduction resides in that capacity to project clarity while remaining ambiguous. Even if we believe that concepts are merely words—a questionable assumption (Trouillot 2002), a quick perusal of the popular press in any European language demonstrates that North Atlantic universals are murky references: they evoke rather than define. More seriously, attempts to conceptualize them in the scholarly literature reveal little unanimity about their scope, let alone denotation (Knauft 2002; Gaonkar 1999; Dussel 1993).

This chapter therefore is quite ambivalent about the extent to which modernity can be fully conceptualized. Yet at the same time, it would be disingenuous not to acknowledge that the word *modernity* evokes sensibilities, perceptions, choices, and indeed states of affairs that are not captured as easily by other words. Thus, my aim here is less to provide a conceptualization of modernity—or an illustration based on a shared conceptualization—than to bring to the table some issues we should discuss on our way to such conceptual attempts, and to evaluate both their terms and feasibility. If the seduction of North Atlantic universals has to do with their power to silence their own history, then our most immediate task is the unearthing of such silences. Only after bringing such silences to the fore will we know if and when claims to universal relevance and descriptive objectivity vanish into thin air.

This chapter thus argues that in its most common deployments as a North Atlantic universal, modernity disguises and misconstrues the many Others that it creates. A critical assessment of modernity must start with the revelation of its hidden faces. I set the ground by contrasting modernity and modernization as distinct, yet necessarily entangled. The global expansion of the North Atlantic juxtaposes a geography of imagination and a geography of management that are both distinctive and intertwined. Modernity and modernization overlap and contradict one another as epitomes of these two geographies. Then, I suggest that as a moment of a geography of imagination, modernity is necessarily plural. It is structurally plural: it requires an alterity, a referent outside of itself—a pre- or nonmodern in relation to which the modern takes its full meaning. It is historically plural: it produces that alterity through both the management and the imaginary projection of various populations within—and especially outside—the North Atlantic. Yet the case of the Caribbean at the time of slavery shows that many of the features associated with North Atlantic modernity could actually be found in areas thought to be pre- or nonmodern. The point is not to insist that the Antilles or other regions of the world were as modern as Europe in the eighteenth and nineteenth centuries—though a legitimate argument can be made along those lines (Mintz 1971a, 1998). Rather, if my sketchy narrative about the Caribbean holds true, it suggests much less the need to rewrite Caribbean history than the necessity to question the story that the North Atlantic tells about itself.

MANAGEMENT OF IMAGINATION

From their joint beginnings in the late Renaissance to the recent dislocations attributed to globalization, the development of world capitalism and the cultural, ideological, and political expansion of the North Atlantic can be read through two different sets of lenses, two related mappings, two intertwined yet distinct geographies: a geography of imagination and a geography of management. Modernity and modernization each call to mind one of these two geographies and their necessary coexistence.

Commenting on the cultural domination of the North Atlantic, Martinican writer Édouard Glissant writes: "The West is not in the West. It is a project, not a place" ([1989] 1992, 2). Indeed, the geography of imagination inherent in that project did not need the concreteness of *place*. Rather, it emphasized *space*. More precisely, it required from the beginning two complementary spaces, the Here and the Elsewhere, which premised one another and were conceived as inseparable (Trouillot 1991). Yet inasmuch as Renaissance imagination entailed a universal hierarchy, control and order were also premised in the enterprise. So was colonization. That is to say, the geography of imagination went hand in hand with a geography of management, the elaboration and implementation of procedures and institutions of control both at home and abroad. That the two maps so produced do not fully overlap should not surprise us. Indeed, it is in the very disjuncture between these two geographies that we are likely to identify processes most relevant to the joint production of sameness and difference that characterizes the dual expansion of the North Atlantic and of world capitalism.

As moments and aspects within the development of world capitalism, yet as figures within two distinctive geographies, modernity and modernization are thus both discrete and intertwined. Thus, a rigid distinction between societal modernization and cultural modernity can be misleading (Gaonkar 1999, 1), especially when it couches them as separate historical developments that can be judged on their own terms. The distinction remains useful only if we keep in mind that the bundle of facts and processes we can package under one label was at any moment of world history, *as a package*, a condition of possibility of the processes and phenomena that we cover with the second label. Better, the distinction becomes necessary inasmuch as it illuminates specific historical moments and processes.

To speak of modernization is to put the accent on the material and organizational features of world capitalism in specific locales. It is to speak of that geography of management, of these aspects of the development of world capitalism that reorganize space for explicitly political or economic purposes. We may note among the continuities and markers along that line the French Revolution as a moment in the modernization of the state—that is, a reorganization of space for political management. We may read the English Industrial Revolution as a moment in the reorganization of labor relations—here again a reorganization of space, primarily for economic purposes. Similarly, the wave of decolonization after World War II can be read as a moment in the modernization of the interstate system— one more moment of reorganization of space on a world scale, one that provides a new geography of management. Finally, and closer to our times, what we now call globalization—and which we too often reduce to a concoction of fads and slogans—inheres in a fundamental change in the spatiality of capital (Trouillot 2001a). In short, modernization has everything to do with political economy, with a geography of management that creates *places*: a place called France, a place called the third world, a place called the market, a placed called the factory or, indeed, a workplace.

If modernization has to do with the creation of place as a relation within a definite space, modernity has to do with the projection of that place—the local—against a spatial background that is theoretically unlimited. To put it differently, modernity has to do not only with the relationship between place and space but also with the relation between place and time. For in order to prefigure the theoretically unlimited space—as opposed to the space within which management occurs—one needs to relate place to time, or, better said, to address a unique temporality, that is, the position of the subject located in that place. Thus, modernity has to do with these aspects and moments in the development of world capitalism that require the projection of the individual or collective subject against both space and time. It has to do with historicity.

I will further expand on that argument by discussing the work of Reinhart Koselleck (1985) and by discussing features of Caribbean history. For now, we may note as markers of modernity historical moments that both localized the individual or collective subject while opening its spatial and temporal horizons and multiplying its outside references. The invention of private life in the Renaissance and the accompanying features noted by Chartier (1993) and others, such as the spread of silent reading, of personal journals, of private libraries, the translation of the Bible in vernacular languages, the invention of the nation and national histories, and the proclamation of the United States Bill of Rights, can all be read as key moments in the spread of modernity. Closer to our times, the global production of desire, spurred by the unification of the world market for consumer goods (Trouillot 2001a), expands further the geography of imagination of which modernity is part.

This last example is telling. That this global production of desire, as a moment of modernity, parallels globalization as a moment in the spatial history—and thus the management—of capital suggests that although modernity and modernization should not be confused, they are inherently intertwined. Indeed, one could take the two lists of markers that I have just suggested, extend them appropriately, and draw lines across them that spell out this inextricability. From the printing press to silent reading, from the political rise of the bourgeoisie to the expansion of individual rights, from the elusiveness of finance capital to the elusiveness of global desires, the geography of management and the geography of imagination are intertwined. Just as the imaginary projection of the West constantly refuels managerial projects of modernization, so is modernization itself a condition of possibility of modernity.

As part of the geography of imagination that constantly recreates the West, modernity always required an Other and an Elsewhere. It was always plural, just like the West was always plural. This plurality is inherent in modernity itself, both structurally and historically. Modernity as a structure requires an Other, an alter, a native—indeed, an alter-native. Modernity as a historical process also created this alter ego, as modern as the West, yet otherwise modern.

If we follow the line of argument drawn from Reinhart Koselleck (1985) that modernity implies first and foremost a fundamental shift in regimes of historicity, most notably the perception of a past radically different from the present and the perception of a future that becomes both attainable (because secular) and yet indefinitely postponed (because removed from eschatology), we come to the conclusion that modernity requires a localization of space. Koselleck does not reach that conclusion himself, yet those of us who claim that modernity requires a geography of imagination (Mudimbe 1988; Trouillot 1991) are not necessarily at odds with his analysis. For as soon as one draws a single line that ties past, present, and future and yet insists on their distinctiveness, one must inevitably place actors along that line. In other words, not everyone can be at the same point along that line. Some become more advanced than others. From the viewpoint of anyone anywhere in that line, others are somewhere else, ahead or behind. Being behind suggests in and of itself an elsewhere that is both in and out of the space defined by modernity—*out* to the extent that these others have not yet reached that place where judgment occurs, and *in* to the extent that the place they now occupy can be perceived from that other place within the line. To put it this way is first to note the relation between modernity and the ideology of progress (Dussel 1993), between modernity and modernism, but there is more to the argument.

In his treatment of modernity, Koselleck insists upon historicity—that is, in part, a relation to time of which the chronologization, the periodization, the distanciation, the increasing speed and range of affective relations from hope to anxiety help to create a new regime. But if he is correct, as I believe he is, this new regime of historicity requires also a localization of its subject. Time here creates space. Or more precisely, Koselleck's historicity necessitates a locale, a *lieu* from which springs this relation to time. Yet, by definition, the inscription of a lieu requires an Elsewhere—a space of and for the Other. That this space can be—indeed, often is—imaginary merely suggests that there may be more continuities than we think between the geography of imagination of the Renaissance and that of the Enlightenment.

Within that geography, elaborations of a state of nature in Hobbes, Locke, or Rousseau, as varied as they indeed are between and across these authors, emerge as alternative modernities—places, locales against which we can read what it means to be modern. Rousseau is the clearest on this for two reasons. First, he is not a modernist. He does not believe in either the inevitability or the desirability of linear progress. Indeed, critics wrongly accuse him of naïveté vis-à-vis the noble savage and earlier stages of human history. Second, that critique notwithstanding, Rousseau explicitly posits his state of nature as a structural and theoretical necessity of which the historical reality is largely irrelevant. He needs that fictional time to mark his own space as a modern one. Later observers will be less perceptive. Indeed, as the line that ties past, present, and future gets more acute and more relevant, as both the momentum behind it and the goal to which it aspires become clearer—otherwise said, as teleology replaces eschatology—from Condorcet to Kant and from Hegel to Marx, the place assigned to the Other may fall not only within the line but also *off* the line. Hegel's dismissal of Africa and Marx's residual "Asiatic" mode of production—maybe his most unthought category—are exemplars of a hierarchy of spaces created through a relation to time. Not only does progress and its advance leave some people "behind" (an elsewhere from within), but increasing chunks of humanity fall off its course (an elsewhere on the outside that can be perceived only from within). In short, the temporal-historical regime that Koselleck associates with modernity creates multiple spaces for the Other.

If that is so, modernity necessitates various readings of alterity, what Michel de Certeau calls a heterology. The claim that someone—someone else—is modern is structurally and necessarily a discourse on the Other, since the intelligibility of that position—what it means to be modern—requires a relation to otherness. The modern is that subject which measures any distance from itself and redeploys it against an unlimited space of imagination. That distance inhabits the perspectival look to and from the painted subject in Raphaël or Titian's portraits. It fueled the quarrel of the Ancients and Moderns in Louis XIV's France. It is crucial to Baudelaire's (re)definition of modern art and poetry as both recognition and rejection of time.

Idiosyncratic as it may be, the case of Baudelaire suggests in miniature the range of silences that we need to uncover for a critical assessment of modernity that would throw light on its hidden faces. As is well known, Baudelaire had just turned twenty when his stepfather forced him to embark for Calcutta. He went only as far as Mauritius and Bourbon (now Réunion), then part of France's plantation empire. That trip inspired—and may have seen the first drafts of—many of the poems that would later be published in *Les fleurs du mal*. Back in Paris, Baudelaire entered into a relationship with a "mulatto" actress, better known as Jeanne Duval, widely said to have been of Haitian descent. Although Baudelaire's liking of dark-skinned females seems to have preceded that liaison, his tumultuous affair with the woman he called his "Black Venus" lasted over twenty years, during which she was for him a major source of poetic inspiration.

Only recently has the relationship between Duval and Baudelaire become a central object of scholarly research.[2] Emmanuel Richon (1998) points out that Baudelairian scholarship has not even bothered to verify the most basic facts about Duval, including her actual origins. The many sketches of Duval by Baudelaire and other portraits, such as Édouard Manet's *La Maitresse de Baudelaire Couchée*, only confirm her constant presence in his life. Many visitors recount entering the poet's place and finding him reading his unpublished poetry to Jeanne. Literary scholarship has attributed some of Baudelaire's work to a "Jeanne Duval cycle" while insisting on her role as "femme fatale" and relishing the assertion that Duval infected Baudelaire with syphilis. Richon, who demolishes that assertion, convincingly argues that the opposite was more likely.

However, the main lesson of Richon's work goes beyond biographical rectification. His claim that the Indian Ocean trip, and especially the relationship with Duval, fundamentally shaped Baudelairian aesthetics suggests that Baudelairian scholarship may have produced what I call a "silence of significance" through a procedure of banalization. Well-known facts are recounted in passing, yet kept in the background of the main narrative or accorded little significance because they "obviously" do not matter (Trouillot 1995). Yet can it not matter that Baudelaire was living a racial taboo in the midst of a Paris sizzling with arguments for and against the abolition of slavery and the equality of human races? Slavery was abolished in Bourbon and other French possessions less than seven years after he had been there and while he was enthralled in his relationship with Duval. Can it not matter that the eulogist of modernity was also Jeanne Duval's eulogist?

The issue is even more intriguing in light of Baudelaire's own disdain for the modernization—here, the concrete management of places and populations by the French state, republican and imperial as it was—that was a condition of possibility of his own modernity. As in Rousseau, Baudelaire's relation to time, a hallmark of his modernity, does not imply a blind faith in either the desirability or the inevitability of progress. Indeed, Baudelaire is resolutely antimodernist (Froidevaux 1989). His modernity is founded upon the search for a furtive yet eternal present. The past has no legacy; the future holds no promises. Only the present is alive. With Baudelaire, we are thus quite far from either side of the quarrel between the Ancients and the Moderns and from Koselleck's regime of historicity. Baudelaire's historicity is indeed a new brand.

How interesting, then, that this new brand of modernity also leads to "the spatialization of time" (Froidevaux 1989, 125). Baudelaire's escape from chronological temporality is space—more specifically, the space of the Elsewhere. Here again, time creates space, and here again, space generates a heterology. Literary scholars have long noted the importance of themes and metaphors of space and of travel, as well as the role of exoticism, in Baudelaire's poetry. While we should leave to specialists the task of mapping out further the many locations in a geography of imagination that links space and time, the Here and the Elsewhere, routine and exoticism, we may want to provoke them in finding out the extent to which the modernity of Baudelaire, the critic, establishes itself against the background of an ethereal Elsewhere that Baudelaire, the poet, inscribes somewhere between Jeanne's body and the islands of the Indian Ocean.

DIFFERENTLY MODERN: THE CARIBBEAN AS ALTER-NATIVE

I have argued so far that modernity is structurally plural inasmuch as it requires a heterology, an Other outside of itself. I would like to argue now that the modern is also historically plural because it always requires an Other from within, the otherwise modern, created between the jaws of modernity and modernization. Here again, that plurality is best perceived if we keep modernity and modernization as distinct yet related groups of phenomena, with the understanding that the power unleashed through modernization is a condition of possibility of modernity itself. I will draw on the sociohistorical experience of the Caribbean region to make that point.

Eric Wolf once wrote in passing but with his usual depth that the Caribbean is "eminently a world area in which modernity first deployed its powers and simultaneously revealed the contradictions that give it birth."[3] Wolf's words echo the work of Sidney W. Mintz (1971a, 1974a, 1974b, 1996, 1998), who has long insisted that the Caribbean has been modern since its early incorporation in various North Atlantic empires. Teasing out Wolf's comments and drawing from Mintz's work, I want to sketch some of the contradictions from the Caribbean record to flesh out a composite picture of what I mean by the "otherwise modern."

Behold the sugar islands from the peak of Barbados's career to Cuba's lead in the relay race—after Jamaica and Saint-Domingue—thus roughly from the 1690s to the 1860s. At first glance, Caribbean labor relations under slavery offer an image of homogenizing power. Slaves were interchangeable, especially in the sugar fields, which consumed most of the labor force, victims of the most "depersonalizing" side of modernization (Mintz 1971a). Yet as we look closer, a few figures start to emerge that suggest the limits of that homogeneity. Chief among them is the slave striker, the one who helped decide when the boiling of the cane juices had reached the exact point when they could be transferred from one vessel to the next.[4] Some planters tried to identify that moment by using complex thermometers. Yet since the right moment depended on temperature, on the intensity of the fire, on the viscosity of the juice, and on the quality of the original cane itself and its state at the time of cutting, other planters thought that a good striker was much more valuable than the most complex technology. Indeed, the slave who acquired such skills would be labeled or sold as "a striker." Away from the sugar cane, especially on the smaller estates that produced coffee, work was often distributed by task, thus allowing individual slaves at times to exceed their quota and to gain additional remuneration.

The point is not that plantation slavery allowed individual slaves much room to maneuver in the labor process; it did not. Nor is the point to conjure images of sublime resistance. Rather, Caribbean history gives us various glimpses at the production of a modern self—a self producing itself through a particular relation to material production—even under the harshest possible conditions. For better *and* for worse, a sugar striker was a modern identity, just as being a slave violinist, a slave baker, or a slave midwife (Higman 1984; Debien 1974; Abrahams 1992, 126–30).

That modern self takes firmer contours when we consider the provision grounds of slavery. Sidney Mintz (1974b) has long insisted on the sociocultural relevance of these provision grounds, small plots in which slaves were allowed to grow their own crops and raise animals on the margins of the plantations on land unfit for the main export crops. Given the high price of imported food, the availability of unused lands, and the fact that slaves worked on these plots in their own free time, these provision grounds were in fact an indirect subsidy to the masters, lessening their participation to the reproduction of the labor force.

Yet Mintz and others—including myself—have noted that what started as an economic bonus for planters turned out to be a field of opportunities for individual slaves. I will not repeat all these arguments here (Trouillot 1988, 1996, 1998). Through these provision grounds, slaves learned the management of capital, the planning of family production for individual purposes. How much to plant of a particular food crop and where, how much of the surplus to sell in the local market, what to do with the profit involved decisions that required an assessment of each individual's placement within the household. Thus the provision grounds can be read not only as material fields used to enhance slaves' physical and legal conditions—including at times the purchase of one's freedom—but also as symbolic fields for the production of individual selves by way of the production of material goods.

Such individual purposes often found their realization in the colonial slave markets, where slaves—especially female slaves—traded their goods for the cash that would turn them into consumers. Here again, one can only guess at the number of decisions that went into these practices, how they fed into a slave's habitus, how they impacted on gender roles then and now in the Caribbean. Individual purposes also realized themselves through patterns of consumption from the elaborate dresses of mulatto women to the unique foulard that would distinguish a slave woman from another one. The number of ordinances regulating the clothing of nonwhites, free and enslaved, throughout the Caribbean in the days of slavery is simply amazing. Their degree of detail—for example, "with no silk, gilding, ornamentation or lace unless these latter be of very low value" (Fouchard [1972] 1981, 43)—is equally stunning. Yet stunning also is the tenacity of slaves who circumvented the regulations and used clothing as an individual signature.

Moreau de St.-Méry, the most acute observer of Saint-Domingue's daily life, writes: "It is hard to believe the height to which a slave woman's expenses might rise. . . . In a number of work gangs the same slave who wielded tools or swung the hoe during the whole week dresses up to attend church on Sunday or to go to market; only with difficulty would they be recognized under their fancy garb. The metamorphosis is even more dramatic in the slave woman who has donned a muslin skirt and Paliacate or Madras kerchief" (quoted in Fouchard [1972] 1981, 47). Moreau's remarks echo numerous observations by visitors and residents of the Americas throughout slavery's long career.

If modernity is also the production of individual selves through patterns of production and consumption, Caribbean slaves were modern, having internalized ideals of individual betterment through work, ownership, and personal identification to particular commodities. It was a strained and harsh modernity, to be sure. Otherwise modern they were—yet still undoubtedly modern by that definition.

One could argue—although the argument is not as easy as it seems—that the selves on which I just insisted may have existed elsewhere without the forced modernization imposed by colonialism. I would readily concede that point if it leads to the realization that the modern individual self claimed by North Atlantic consciousness is not unique to the North Atlantic. At the extreme opposite, one could also argue that the detached individual self is only a fiction of the North Atlantic geography of imagination, an ideological by-product of the internal narrative of modernity. Surprisingly, perhaps, I am even more willing to concede that point. Indeed, in either case, the central issue is not that of an allegedly modern individual subjectivity—whatever that may be—but the insertion of that subjectivity into a particular regime of historicity. Clothing as individual signature may be as old as human society. So may be the production of identity through labor. At any rate, I doubt that these two features—or any of the markers usually claimed to signify the rise of the modern self—first obtained as such in Renaissance or post-Renaissance Christendom. Intellectual and art history, literature, and philosophy may have misled us in overrating these individual attributes of the modern self to the detriment of the historical context within which these selves were fashioned. François Hartog (1980) sets the projection of alterity as the context for self-identification as far back as Herodotus. Horkheimer and Adorno (1972) see in Odysseus the precursor of the modern subject. Closer to ground, Ariès and Duby (1988) and their collaborators in the *History of Private Life* project effectively extend notions of privacy or even intimacy back into the Middle Ages. I suspect that with similar data, one could make just as potent discoveries outside of

Christendom, thus relativizing the narrative that makes the modern individual self such a Eurocentric product.[5]

Yet again, necessary as this revisionist narrative is, it is not the central issue. Too often, critics of Eurocentrism flesh out their arguments in terms of chronological primacy. They spend much energy demonstrating that such-and-such a feature claimed by North Atlantic narratives to have been a European first could actually be found elsewhere before European presence. The mistake here is to forget that chronological primacy is itself a central tenet of North Atlantic imagination. That is, the value of being the first comes from a particular premium on time, a specific take on historicity. The existence of certain social features outside of Europe matters less than the inscription of these features in social and political regimes *then* and much less even than the inscriptions of these same features—as found in Europe then—in North Atlantic narratives *now*. From that perspective, the modern self may be less a matter of the content of an individual subjectivity than that of the insertion of that subjectivity into a particular regime of historicity and sociopolitical management. On that latter issue, the most crucial one in my view, the Caribbean story is most revealing.

Modern historicity hinges on both a fundamental rupture between past, present, and future—as distinct temporal planes—and their relinking along a singular line that allows for continuity. I have argued that this regime of historicity in turn implies a heterology—that is, a necessary reading of alterity. Striking, then, is the fact that Caribbean history as we know it starts with an abrupt rupture between past and present—for Europeans, for Native Americans, and for enslaved Africans. In no way could the enforced modernization imposed by colonization be perceived by any of the actors as a mere continuation of an immediate past. This was a New World for all involved, even for those who had lived within it before it became new to others.

For indeed, the consciousness that times had changed, that things were falling apart and coming together in new ways, was both inescapable and yet inseparable from the awareness that others were fundamentally different—different in where they came from, in the positions they occupied along any of the intersecting hierarchies, in the languages they spoke, in the costumes they wore, in the customs they inhabited, in the possible futures they could envision. The sensibility to time and the recognition of heterogeneity associated with modernity are inescapable here. Indeed, they have been central themes of Caribbean scholarship (Trouillot 1992, 2001b).

Here again the slave quarters are telling. There was imposed the sudden discovery of a common African past but also the awareness that this commonality barely covered fundamental differences. One could not address that Other next door, who looked so strikingly similar, without using a language derived at least in part from that of the masters. Was not that as modern as the vulgate version of the Bible? More modern than the quarrel between seventeenth-century French intellectuals as to whether the king's engravings were best written in French or in Latin? If the awareness of one's position in history not just as an individual but as part of a group and against the background of a social system brought to consciousness is a fundamental part of what it means to be modern, the Caribbean was modern from day one—that is, from the very day colonialism imposed its modernization. If the awareness of sociocultural differences and the need to negotiate across such differences are part of what we call modernity, then the Caribbean was modern since at least the sixteenth century—that is, from day one of North Atlantic modernity. But if that is so, the chronological primacy of the North Atlantic falters.

Yet chronology here is only an index. My goal is not to replace North Atlantic chronological primacy over the rest of the world with a Caribbean chronological primacy over other colonies and postcolonies. To be sure, historical particulars made the Caribbean, for better and for worse, the area longest under European control outside of Europe itself and the only one where Europeans moved as if it was indeed empty land, *terra nullius*, to be fashioned along modern lines. To be sure, now-dominant North Atlantic narratives—reflecting the international reach of the English language, the expansion of Protestantism as a variant of Christianity, and the spread of Anglo-Saxon and Teutonic sensibilities—reduce the crucial role of Portugal and Spain in the creation of the West. To be sure, a related emphasis on the Enlightenment and on the nineteenth century and the downplaying of the Renaissance as a founding moment also lead to a neglect of the role of the Caribbean and Latin America in the production of the earliest tropes associated with modernity, a chronological amnesia that crucially impedes our understanding of the North Atlantic itself (Trouillot 1991, 1995; Dussel 1993).

Yet I want to insist that the lessons learned from the Caribbean are applicable elsewhere. As a historical process inherently tied to modernization, modernity necessarily creates its alter-native in Asia, in Africa, in Latin America—in all these areas of the world where the archetypal Caribbean story repeats itself with variations on the theme of destruction and creolization. Modernity creates its Others—multiple, multifaced, multilayered. It has done so from day one: *we* have always been modern, differently modern, contradictorily modern, otherwise modern—yet undoubtedly modern.

I don't want to conclude with this pun on Bruno Latour's famous title, however tempting a *bon mot*. In *We Have Never Been Modern*, Latour (1993) suggests that the North Atlantic's "modern constitution" rests on a divide between scientific power, meant to represent things as they are, and political power, meant to represent subjects as they wish to be. Latour sees the formulation of this divide (science/politics, object/subject, nature/culture) as the impossible dream of modernity, since the world so neatly divided is actually made of hybrids. Nevertheless, Latour does admit, almost in passing, that blind faith in this divide also makes the moderns invincible. I am interested in this invincibility. Latour's witty title could be misread as to imply that we could have been modern according to definition. But if modernity is as much blind faith in this narrative as its global consequences, we have long been modern, except that the we here is not only the North Atlantic but also the hidden faces of modernity necessary to North Atlantic hegemony—if not invincibility.

Ultimately, however, that modernity has long obtained outside of the North Atlantic is only a secondary lesson from the Caribbean Savage slot, a conclusion that still makes us ask what is there to be explained. Yet is the alter-native really what needs to be explained? Is the puzzle the female slave who used her kerchief as individual signature, or the laws that repeatedly tried to curb her individual expression? Is the puzzle the resilience of the creolization process under slavery, or the expectation that enslaved Africans and their descendants would be either a tabula rasa or mere carriers of tradition (Trouillot 1998)? In short, is not the puzzle within the West itself?

The Caribbean story as I read it is less an invitation to search for modernity in various times and places—a useful yet secondary enterprise—than an exhortation to change the terms of the debate. What is there to be analyzed further, better, and differently is the relation between the geography of management and the geography of imagination that together spurred and underpinned the development of world capitalism. And in the context of that reformulation, the Caribbean's most important lesson is a formidable one indeed. For that lesson, as I see it, is that modernity never was—never could be—what it claimed to be.

Editors' Note: This chapter first appeared as "The Otherwise Modern: Caribbean Lessons from the Savage Slot," in *Critically Modern: Alternatives, Alterities, Anthropologies*, ed. Bruce Knauft (Bloomington: Indiana University Press, 2002), 220–37.

1. Belonging to that class does not depend on a fixed meaning. It is a matter of struggle and contest about and around these universals and the world they claim to describe. For instance, only time will tell if newly popular expressions such as "globalization" or "the international community" will become North Atlantic universals.

2. That relationship provides the thread of Haitian novelist Fabienne Pasquet's *L'ombre de Baudelaire* (1996), whose title I borrow here.

3. *Editors' Note:* Trouillot did not give a reference for this citation.

4. According to Higman (1984, 170–72), the head sugar boiler added lime, controlled evaporation, and decided when to strike the sugar at the point of crystallization. He "was depended on by the planters to make correct decisions in what required 'practical chemical knowledge' but remained more an art than a science" (1984, 172). Mintz (1985, 49–50), who discusses striking at length, notes: "boiling and 'striking' . . . required great skill, and sugar boilers were artisans who worked under difficult conditions" (1985, 49).

5. Sometimes the data are there and only the perspective is missing. Reversing the dominant perspective, Sidney Mintz asks, "Who is more modern, more western, more developed: a barefoot and illiterate Yoruba market woman who daily risks her security and her capital in vigorous individual competition with others like herself; or a Smith College graduate who spends her days ferrying her husband to the Westport railroad station and her children to ballet classes? If the answer is that at least the Smith girl is literate and wears shoes, one may wonder whether one brand of anthropology has not been hoisted by its own petard" (1971b, 267–68).

REFERENCES

Abrahams, Roger D. 1992. *Singing the Master: The Emergence of African American Culture in the Plantation South*. New York: Pantheon Books.

Ariès, Philippe, and G. Duby, eds. 1988. *A History of Private Life II: Revelations of the Medieval World*. Cambridge, MA: Belknap Press of Harvard University Press.

Chartier, Roger, ed. 1993. *A History of Private Life III: Passions of the Renaissance*. Cambridge, MA: Belknap Press of Harvard University Press.

Debien, Gabriel. 1974. *Les esclaves aux Antilles françaises (XVIIe–XVIIIe siècles)*. Fort de France: Sociétés d'histoire de la Guadeloupe et de la Martinique.

Dussel, Enrique. 1993. "Eurocentrism and Modernity: Introduction to the Frankfurt Lectures." *boundary 2*, no. 20: 65–76.

Fouchard, Jean. (1972) 1981. *The Haitian Maroons: Liberty or Death*. New York: Blyden Press.

Froidevaux, Gérald. 1989. *Baudelaire: Représentation et modernité*. Paris: José Corti.

Gaonkar, Dilip Parameshwar. 1999. "On Alternative Modernities." *Public Culture* 11, no. 1: 1–18.

Glissant, Édouard. (1989) 1992. *Caribbean Discourse: Selected Essays*. Translated by J. Michael Dash. Charlottesville: University of Virginia Press.

Hartog, François. 1980. *Le miroir d'Herodote: Essai sur la représentation de l'autre*. Paris: Gallimard.

Higman, B. W. 1984. *Slave Populations of the British Caribbean 1807–1834*. Baltimore, MD: Johns Hopkins University Press.

Horkheimer, Max, and Theodor W. Adorno. 1972. *Dialectic of Enlightenment*. New York: Seabury Press.

Knauft, Bruce M. 2002. "Critically Modern: An Introduction." In *Critically Modern: Alternatives, Alterities, Anthropologies*, edited by Bruce M. Knauft, 1–54. Bloomington: Indiana University Press.

Koselleck, Reinhart. 1985. *Futures Past: On the Semantics of Historical Time*. Cambridge, MA: MIT Press.

Latour, Bruno. 1993. *We Have Never Been Modern*. Cambridge, MA: Harvard University Press. First published 1991.

Mintz, Sidney W. 1971a. "The Caribbean as a Socio-Cultural Area." In *Peoples and Cultures of the Caribbean: An Anthropological Reader*, edited by Michael M. Horowitz, 17–46. Garden City, NY: American Museum of Natural History Press.

Mintz, Sidney W. 1971b. "Men, Women, and Trade." *Comparative Studies in Society and History* 13, no. 3: 247–69.

Mintz, Sidney W. 1974a. "The Caribbean Region." In *Slavery, Colonialism, and Racism: Essays*, edited by Sidney W. Mintz, 45–71. New York: Norton.

Mintz, Sidney W. 1974b. *Caribbean Transformations*. Chicago: Aldine Publishing.

Mintz, Sidney W. 1985. *Sweetness and Power: The Place of Sugar in Modern History*. New York: Penguin Books.

Mintz, Sidney W. 1996. "Enduring Substances, Trying Theories: The Caribbean Region as Oikoumene." *Journal of the Royal Anthropological Institute* 2, no. 2: 289–311.

Mintz, Sidney W. 1998. "The Localization of Anthropological Practice: From Area Studies to Transnationalism." *Critique of Anthropology* 18, no. 2: 117–33.

Mudimbe, V. Y. 1988. *The Invention of Africa: Gnosis, Philosophy, and the Order of Knowledge*. Bloomington: Indiana University Press.

Pasquet, Fabienne. 1996. *L'ombre de Baudelaire*. Paris: Actes Sud.

Richon, Emmanuel. 1998. *Jeanne Duval et Charles Baudelaire: Belle d'abandon*. Paris: L'Harmattan.

Rousseau, Jean-Jacques. (1775) 1984. *A Discourse on Inequality*. Harmondsworth: Penguin.

Trouillot, Michel-Rolph. 1988. *Peasants and Capital: Dominica in the World Economy*. Baltimore, MD: Johns Hopkins University Press.

Trouillot, Michel-Rolph. 1991. "Anthropology and the Savage Slot: The Poetics and Politics of Otherness." In *Recapturing Anthropology: Working in the Present*, edited by Richard G. Fox, 17–44. Santa Fe, NM: School of American Research Press.

Trouillot, Michel-Rolph. 1992. "The Caribbean Region: An Open Frontier in Anthropological Theory." *Annual Review of Anthropology* 21: 19–42.

Trouillot, Michel-Rolph. 1995. *Silencing the Past: Power and the Production of History*. Boston: Beacon Press.

Trouillot, Michel-Rolph. 1996. "Beyond and below the Merivale Paradigm: Dominica's First 100 Days of Freedom." In *The Lesser Antilles in the Age of European Expansion*, edited by Robert L. Paquette and Stanley L. Engerman, 302–23. Gainesville: University Press of Florida.

Trouillot, Michel-Rolph. 1998. "Culture on the Edges: Creolization in the Plantation Context." *Plantation Society in the Americas* 5, no. 1: 8–28.

Trouillot, Michel-Rolph. 2001a. "The Anthropology of the State in the Age of Globalization: Close Encounters of the Deceptive Kind." *Current Anthropology* 42, no. 1: 125–38.

Trouillot, Michel-Rolph. 2001b. "Caribbean: Sociocultural Aspects." In *International Encyclopedia of the Social and Behavioral Sciences*, edited by Neil J. Smelser and Paul B. Baltes, 1484–88. New York: Elsevier Science.

Trouillot, Michel-Rolph. 2002. "Adieu, Culture: A New Duty Arises." In *Anthropology beyond Culture*, edited by Richard G. Fox and Barbara J. King, 37–60. Wenner-Gren International Symposium Series. Oxford: Berg.

CHAPTER 6

The Caribbean Region

An Open Frontier in Anthropological Theory

The encounter between anthropological theory and any region of the globe says as much about anthropology as it does about that region. Caribbean anthropology is a case in point. This region where boundaries are notoriously fuzzy has long been the open frontier of cultural anthropology: neither center nor periphery, but a sort of no man's land where pioneers get lost, where some stop overnight on their way to greater opportunities, and where yet others manage to create their own "new" world amidst First-World indifference. Accordingly, the object of this essay is dual: I write here about the Caribbean as viewed by anthropologists, but also about anthropology as viewed from the Caribbean. My review dwells on the coincidence between some zones of weakness in anthropological theory and areas of concern for Caribbeanists. I claim neither exhaustiveness nor statistical representativeness in dealing with the literature, and my boundaries are both arbitrary and fuzzy. I emphasize a present that encompasses most of the last twenty years, but my framework—not to mention the absence of any Caribbean focus in previous issues of this series—justifies forays into more distant pasts. I concentrate on works available in English, which happens to be the predominant language of Caribbean ethnology; but this emphasis here is no less arbitrary. More importantly, since I am addressing outsiders and insiders alike, I flatten some rough edges and overlook inevitably some segments of the corpus, notably the anthropology of healing and that of religion, and urban studies as such (but see Fisher 1985; Laguerre 1982; Simpson 1980; Thoden van Velzen and van Wetering 1988). Issues in creole linguistics, the ethnography and politics of language in the Caribbean, have generated many solid studies and deserve separate treatment. So does the literature on migration. The reader can consult other review essays on specific topics or earlier periods, bibliographies, as well as bibliographies of bibliographies (Banck 1988; Berleant-Schiller 1981; Comitas 1977; Mintz 1975; R. Price 1971; Smith 1970).

The essay is organized around three major themes: "heterogeneity," "historicity," and what I refer to as "articulation" (matters relating to levels, boundaries—the nature and limits of the unit of observation or analysis) and their ramifications. I do not see these themes as natural groupings of a self-contained Caribbean corpus but as markers highlighting the encounter between Caribbean studies and anthropology, scattered posts on the open frontier.

AN UNDISCIPLINED REGION

Christopher Columbus's landing in the Caribbean in 1492 provided a nascent Europe with the material and symbolic space necessary to establish its image of the Savage Other (Trouillot 1990a, 1991). Not surprisingly, it is in the Caribbean islands and in the surrounding mainland that a certain kind of comparative ethnography was born in the sixteenth century with the writings of Spanish scholars (Pagden 1982). But the Caribbean was also where Europe first achieved the systematic destruction of the Other, with the genocide of the Caribs and Arawaks of the Antilles. By the time the Enlightenment returned to the myth of the noble savage, recycling with a vengeance the debates in philosophical anthropology that had marked the Renaissance, most of the Antilles were inhabited by African peoples who had crossed the Atlantic in chains, and their Afro-Creole descendants, also enslaved. Many of these slaves worked on plantations run by profit-conscious Europeans on quite "modern" lines (Mintz 1985a).

Slavery ended in the Caribbean at about the same time that the social sciences diverged from law and history in Europe and the United States; but by then the Caribbean had become an oddity in Western scholarship. The swift genocide of the aboriginal populations, the early integration of the region into the international circuit of capital, the forced migrations of enslaved African and indentured Asian laborers, and the abolition of slavery by emancipation or revolution all meant that the Caribbean would not conform within the emerging divisions of Western academia. With a predominantly nonwhite population, it was not "Western" enough to fit the concerns of sociologists. Yet it was not "native" enough to fit fully into the Savage slot where anthropologists found their preferred subjects. When E. B. Tylor published the first general anthropology textbook in the English language in 1881, Barbados had been "British" for two and a half centuries, Cuba had been "Spanish" for almost four, and Haiti had been an independent state for three generations—after a long French century during which it accounted for more than half of its metropolis's foreign trade. These were hardly places to look for primitives. Their very existence questioned the West/non-West dichotomy and the category of the native, upon both of which anthropology was premised.

The entire corpus of Caribbean cultural anthropology from the early decades of this century up to the present can be read against the background of this basic incongruity between the traditional object of the discipline and the inescapable history of the region. In that light, many riddles of the encounter fall into place, including North American anthropology's relative avoidance of the Caribbean (Mintz 1975). Up to the fourth decade of this century, native scholars from Haiti, Cuba, or Puerto Rico were more willing than foreigners to apply the tools of anthropological analysis to the study of their own folk. Later on, as Caribbean anthropology developed its specific interests, some of the weakest zones of anthropological theory came to overlap with concerns that Caribbeanists could not fully escape. Even the increased interest in Afro-American anthropology in the early 1970s (Horowitz 1971; Whitten and Szwed 1970) failed to accord full legitimacy to the Caribbean within the guild. Today, as anthropology continues to nurture a legacy of tropes and concepts honed through the observation of societies once deemed "simple" (if not "primitive"), outsiders continue to confront the fact that Caribbean societies have long been awkwardly, yet definitely, "complex" (if not "modern").

No Gates on the Frontier

Three related features of this complexity sustain the lines of tension between anthropological discourse and Caribbean ethnology. First, Caribbean societies are inescapably heterogeneous. If savages elsewhere once looked the same to most anthropologists, the Caribbean has long been an area where some people live next to others who are remarkably distinct. The region—and indeed particular territories within it—has long been multiracial, multilingual, stratified, and some would say, multicultural (Deosaran 1987a, 1987b; Mintz and R. Price 1992; Safa 1987; Smith 1965, 1984b; Lier 1950). Second, this heterogeneity is known to be, at least in part, the result of history. Caribbean societies are inescapably historical, in the sense that some of their distant past is not only known, but known to be different from their present, and yet relevant to both the observers' and the natives' understanding of that present (Alexander 1984; Bernabé, Chamoiseau, and Confiant 1989; McWatt 1982; R. Price 1990b). There is no general agreement on the extent of this relevance, but some of the earliest attacks on "the fallacy of the ethnographic present" (Smith 1962, 76–77) were launched from the Caribbean.

To be sure, the Caribbean is not the only area where heterogeneity and historicity have haunted the practitioners of a discipline that once made sociohistorical depth the exclusive attribute of Western societies. Elsewhere, however, anthropologists often blocked the full investigation of that complexity by posting "gatekeeping concepts": hierarchy in India, honor and shame in the Mediterranean, etc. (Appadurai 1986), a maneuver that, in my view, reflected, as well, the West's ranking of certain Others. Anthropological gatekeeping notwithstanding, "Sinology" was—and is— more likely to be taken as a separate field, and any reunion of "Orientalists" is more likely to be taken as an academic meeting than similar bodies or institutions of knowledge—and power—dealing with many other parts of the world. Would anyone open Pandora's box by suggesting that such implicit rankings are based on "objective" grounds?

Still, gatekeeping as a specific anthropological strategy was relatively successful in many complex societies outside of the Caribbean because anthropologists dealing with these regions could pay lip service to history while using that same history as a buffer against historical investigation (cf. Abu-Lughod 1989). With history kept at a comfortable distance, anthropologists could resurrect the "native" while forsaking the primitive. Gatekeeping concepts are so-called native traits mythified by theory in ways that bound the object of study. They act as theoretical simplifiers to restore the ethnographic present and protect the timelessness of culture.

Gatekeeping has never been successful in the Caribbean. Here, heterogeneity and historicity opened up new vistas, deflecting energies from theoretical simplification. Each in its own way pointed to a third feature of the sociocultural landscape: the fact that Caribbean societies are inherently colonial. It is not only that all Caribbean territories have been conquered by one or another Western power. It is not only that they are the oldest colonies of the West and that their very colonization was part of the material and symbolic process that gave rise to the West as we know it. Rather, their social and cultural characteristics—and, some would say, individual idiosyncrasies of their inhabitants (Fisher 1985)—cannot be accounted for, or even described, without reference to colonialism.

This inescapable feature precludes the resurrection of the native, even when colonialism is not evoked explicitly. Here, there is no way to satisfy anthropology's obsession for "pure" cultures (Mintz 1974a; Rubenstein 1983; Smith 1978). Even populations such as the Island Caribs of Dominica and St. Vincent or the mainland Garifuna are known to be products of complex mixtures (Gonzalez 1984, 1988; Gullick 1985; Taylor 1946). Whereas anthropology prefers "pre-contact" situations—or creates "no-contact" situations—the Caribbean is nothing but contact.

Understandably, disciplinary fences are quite flexible. Anthropologists engage historians, economists, and policy makers (Bolles 1983; Handler 1982, 1984; Marshall 1990; Moya Pons 1986; Trouillot 1984), and many publish as much in historical or regional journals as in publications regimented by the guild. Gatekeeping themes never muster a partisan following large enough within the discipline to allow for fermentation. Anthropological master tropes have rather short tenures on the frontier, as competing topics sneak through the open lands and establish new lines of exchange. Theory alone cannot enclose the object of study, not because Caribbean reality is messier than any other but because anthropological theory has yet to deal with the mess created by colonialism with handles as convenient as honor and shame, the caste system, or filial piety. Yet, in part also because of colonialism, empirical boundaries are no clearer in this region of prefabricated enclaves and open frontiers where the very "unit of empirical existence" (Smith 1988, 2), let alone that of analysis, is a matter of open controversy.

HETEROGENEITY

If complexity is what first strikes the anthropologist when looking at Caribbean societies, and if heterogeneity is at least one marker of this complexity, what, then, holds these societies together? Michael G. Smith's answer to this question has remained consistent over the years. "The monopoly of power by one cultural section is the essential precondition for the maintenance of the total society in its current form," writes Smith (1984a, 183), quoting himself twenty-four years later. For Smith, Caribbean societies are "plural": they exhibit antagonistic strata with different cultures. They stand as essentially political shells, filled with juxtaposed—and incompatible—value-systems, different sets of institutions being held together solely by the vertical power of the state (Smith 1965, 1984b).

The debate over Smith's use of the "plural society" concept has been long—much too long, some would say (Austin 1984b; Baber 1987; Deosaran 1987a, 1987b; Robotham 1980, 1985; Smith 1983, 1984a, 1987). Caribbeanists of various persuasions fail to see the insurmountable wall that Smith erects between his corporate groups. Moreover, the distinction between plural and nonplural societies never seemed convincing to the rest of the guild, and few scholars (Despres 1975; Nettleford 1979) embraced Smith's framework. Yet, his inflexibility notwithstanding, Smith does raise eloquently the issue of the relation between heterogeneity and power, an issue that remains to be taken more seriously by anthropologists in the Caribbean and elsewhere. For Smith is right in suggesting that in the Caribbean case, at least, one cannot presume "culture," if by this we mean a principle of homogeneity, determined by fiat, that would somehow find its parallel in an equally bounded entity referred to as "society."

Cite, Praise, or Paraphrase?

M. G. Smith makes much of the respective birthplaces, nationalities, and races of his various opponents. Smith himself is Jamaican-born and faces continuous insinuations that his application of the plural society is local middle-class ideology passing for social theory (Robotham 1980, 1985; Smith 1983, 1984b, 1987). Unfortunately, the serious issue of the status of native discourse remains only in the subtext of this debate. For although many Caribbean-born scholars have rightly questioned some of the assumptions behind the plural society framework, we need to ask why approaches that emphasize ethnic or cultural segmentation constitute a cross-generational stream in Caribbean studies and letters (Nettleford 1979; Pedreira 1968; Price-Mars 1983). These approaches are singularly effective when translated into the realm of state politics by a self-trained ethnologist such as Haiti's François Duvalier, by self-anointed "natives" such as Forbes Burnham in Guyana or Balaguer in the Dominican Republic, or by dissidents and potential coup leaders in Suriname and Trinidad. In an obvious reference to the local persuasiveness of his views, Smith himself notes that those "who participate in those processes and who are most directly affected by them" implicitly know which side is right (Smith 1984b, 35). This "proof of the pudding" argument is not convincing to those of us who believe that social science is possible and that Goebbels does not necessarily provide the best analysis of Nazism. Yet the fact that Smith's viewpoint indeed reflects Jamaican elite ideology does not change by an iota the fact—equally "obvious"—that the presumption of order and homogeneity that has been a hallmark of Western social science is itself a reflection of dominant Euroamerican consciousness, a by-product of the ideological invention of the nation-state.

The issue is not trivial. Even a superficial inquiry reveals that the pronouncements of Caribbean peoples of various origins have long made their way into anthropological accounts with unequal value added. Recently, Richard Price has systematically undertaken to record the Saramaka Maroons' voices and narratives from and about the past and present them to an academic audience (R. Price 1983, 1990a). Price excels at inventing intellectual quotation marks, new ways of marking on the published page both the boundaries and the dialogues between voices; but he keeps prudently away from epistemological issues. Advancing along the path Price broke with *First-Time*, *Alabi's World* masterfully mixes four voices on the page. Price gives us tips on how to "hear" three of these voices (Moravian missionaries, Dutch planters, and native Saramakas) but none on how to read his own prose and "passages from other scholars." Yet it may be worth asking which philosophy of knowledge we should use to evaluate native historical or sociological discourse or, for that matter, that of any participant (Price and Price 1988). How do we handle the overlaps and incompatibilities of participants' judgments with Euroamerican scholarship (Dominguez 1986; Vega 1981)? How does anthropology handle the similarities between, say, Puerto Rican discourses on virility and nationalism and Peter Wilson's construct on reputation and respectability (about which more below), or the affinities between the social criticism of Haitian scholars in the 1930s and Herskovits's notion of "socialized ambivalence"? To identify scholars independently of nativeness reopens the epistemological issues we might have wanted to postpone. Yet even if we set aside the issue of knowledge qua truth, who is the outsider who assigns differential semiotic relevance to alternative native voices (R. Price 1990b)? And who is to bestow nativeness, anyway (Dominguez 1986; Nettleford 1972; Vega 1981)? In the Caribbean, there is no "native" viewpoint in the sense that Geertz assumes nativeness (1976), no privileged shoulder upon which to lean. This is a region where Pentecostalism is as "indigenous" as Rastafarianism, where some "Bush Negroes" were Christians long before Texans became "American," where some "East Indians" find peace in "African" rituals of Shango (Austin-Broos 1987; Henry 1983; R. Price 1990a).

Anthropology has yet to reach a consensus on both the epistemological status and semiotic relevance of native discourse anywhere. Is native discourse a citation, an indirect quote, or a paraphrase? Whose voice is it once it enters the discursive field dominated by the logic of academe? Is its value referential, indexical, phatic, or poetic? The problem is compounded in the Caribbean by colonial domination whose duration and intellectual reach defy most understandings of nativeness. At least some resident intellectuals have long been interlocutors in European debates about the region (Glissant 1989; Lewis 1983; Price-Mars 1983; Robotham 1985). No discursive field is fully "ours," or "theirs." Diane Austin's suggestion that Caribbean anthropology is marked by an analytical antinomy between, on the one hand, conflict-resistance and, on the other, integration-domination is telling (Austin 1983), for similar dualities obtain in Caribbean intellectual discourse (Lewis 1983). But such dualities stand correct only if we do not try to push every single author toward one or the other pole.

At any rate, the real debate is not over whether heterogeneity exists but about where to locate it and—quite literally—what to do with it. The answer to that question turns on one's idea of what Caribbean societies are about and, equally important, on one's theory of culture and society. This is also what I mean by saying that the inescapable fact of Caribbean heterogeneity poses fundamental questions for anthropological theory that most anthropologists have chosen to ignore. Raymond T. Smith, one of M. G. Smith's earliest intellectual opponents, said as much long ago, though in more muted terms and in a different context.

Gender, Social Organization, and the Wider World

In a 1963 review of family and kinship studies in the Caribbean, then the dominant field of Caribbean ethnology, R. T. Smith states: "The major problem is what it has always been; to relate patterns of familial and mating behavior to other factors in the contemporary social systems and to the cultural traditions of the people concerned. Here progress is less impressive because we are still unclear about the nature of these societies" (1971, 472).

Smith's concern should not be read only as the reflection of a functionalist's search for structuring principles. The assumption that fieldwork will somehow reveal the nature of the entity under study, however persuasive it may look in cases of apparent homogeneity, breaks down completely on the frontier. Smith's statement shows how the inescapable manifestations of complexity turn the anthropologist's eye toward a larger horizon. It suggests why the glut of kinship studies did not lead in turn to enduring gatekeeping concepts in Caribbean anthropology: the heterogeneity of the ensemble precluded the domestic unit, the matrifocal family, or the allocation of gender roles to generate theoretical simplifiers, in spite of a flow of publications recycling a restricted number of themes.

I cannot do justice to this abundant corpus (more than two hundred titles between 1970 and 1990), which has sparked, in turn, a number of anthologies, bibliographies, and reassessments (e.g., Loroña 1987; R. Price 1971; Rawlins 1987; Rubenstein 1983; Cohen 1985). The streams are multiple, though they tend to crisscross around the role—or the plight—of women as mothers, as child-bearers and rearers, and as mates. In their own way, Caribbean kinship studies have always been gender studies, and they have always insisted that gender is a two-way street. This had to do, ironically, with an early concern for policy on the part of officials who saw Afro-Caribbean families as "deviant" simply because they did not fit the nuclear folk-model of Western consciousness (Rubenstein 1983, 1987; Smith 1982a, 1987). Just as in the United States, these bureaucrats' views were echoed by social scientists who wanted to explain—or explain away—such "abnormalities" as "missing fathers."

Two early studies continue to influence the tone of the research: Edith Clarke's *My Mother Who Fathered Me* (1957) and R. T. Smith's *The Negro Family in British Guiana* (1956). Smith's legacy may well be, to his despair, the often misused notion of matrifocality. Smith insists that he coined the word not to mean female-headed or even consanguineal families, as others would believe, but to underline the role of women as mothers (Smith 1973, 1978). Clarke's legacy goes more in the direction of a social pathology. More recently, Peter Wilson's construct of "reputation and respectability," which neatly ties gender roles to the wider society, came close to becoming the master trope of Caribbean anthropology, precisely because it did not treat the domestic as a closed domain. Criticizing the fact that "social organization" was a code word for limited studies of the purely "domestic," Wilson postulates a pan-Caribbean opposition between an internal value system ("reputation"), emphasizing equality, virility, and lower-class norms, and an external one emphasizing ranking, womanhood, and elitist respectability (Wilson 1969, 1973). The scheme is more ingenious than most of the dualities that plague Caribbean studies; hence its continuous impact on the literature (e.g., Abrahams 1983; Rubenstein 1987). But it is too neat for comfort; hence the reluctance of most Caribbeanists to use it as an overall simplifier. Wilson's polarity requires strong qualifications when the observer tackles the historical and social particulars of specific territories and especially the relations among gender, the dual value system, and colonialism (Olwig 1990).

New paradigms have yet to emerge in spite of an abundance of refreshing positions on gender and the family. I can note only a few: the call to incorporate an emic approach to kinship into ethnographies of "social organization" (Lowenthal 1987; R. Price 1971; S. Price 1984); the call for yet more careful distinctions between household and family (Rubenstein 1983), or for a reconceptualization of the consanguineal household (Gonzalez 1984); the call for a more systematic study of the wide realm of female responsibility (Durant-Gonzales 1982), or for the delineation of gender-specific estates, spheres, or domains against the background of economic roles (Berleant-Schiller 1977). The last two strategies do not always point to a simplistic division that would consign women to the home and leave the world to men. Neither among the relatively isolated Maroons of Suriname nor in Barbados, arguably one of the most Westernized islands, do the cultural ideals and the practice of gender roles duplicate fully dominant Western patterns (Dann 1987; S. Price 1984; Sutton and Makiesky-Barrow 1981). Further, the case for female-centered domains, material or symbolic, is usually made on more sophisticated grounds than a base/superstructure model where gender would duplicate the division of labor (Austin-Broos 1987; Stubbs 1988; Wilson 1973). Furthermore, the division of labor itself does not always operate as most Westerners would expect. Specialization in independent economic activities, notably marketing, often helps open for rural *women* certain gender-specific vistas upon the wider world (Mintz 1971c, 1990; Murray and Alvarez 1975). Men may occupy street corners and engage in lewd behavior in nonfamilial settings (Brana-Shute 1989; Lieber 1981; Manning 1973), but the woman's world is by no means *private*, as North Americans would understand this word (Barrow 1986a, 1986b; Lazarus-Black 1991). The evidence does not prove that gender equality is a widespread Caribbean phenomenon, but it does indicate indigenous forms and designs of female autonomy. In that context, female independence does not necessarily mean the breaking of traditional ties; it may signify the reinforcement of certain "networking" practices (Barrow 1986a). Nor does modernization always mean the demise of a putative "feudal" patriarchy. On the contrary, recent Western inroads often create or renew forms of gender inequality. Off-shore industries, Christian churches, professionalization, monetization, or remittances from migrants may reduce traditional female autonomy or increase gender-specific risks (Bolles 1983; Griffith 1985; Harrison 1987; Leo-Rhynie and Hamilton 1983; Mintz 1971c; Safa 1986; Sutton and Makiesky-Barrow 1981; Trouillot 1988). The complexity of gender roles recorded by Caribbean ethnographers implicitly begs feminist theory to de-Westernize its premises further.

Caribbean analyses of kinship and gender keep encroaching upon the wider world. Sally Price's rich ethnography of Saramaka shows how the production and flow of art reflect and reinforce cultural understandings about gender (S. Price 1984). In an equally acclaimed study of mating patterns in nineteenth-century Cuba, Martinez-Alier centers on the relationship between sexual values and social inequality. She argues convincingly that the battles between sexes, races, and classes intertwine and that, in the final analysis, it is "the hierarchical nature of the social order" (Martinez-Alier 1974, 128) that generates sexual codes as well as gender roles and relations. One cannot adequately abridge Martinez-Alier's superb exposition of these arguments. I note here that, in the end, they echo R. T. Smith's earlier intimation to look at "the nature" of these societies. How revealing, then, it is of the relationship between the Caribbean frontier and the discipline that a leading feminist theorist found it necessary to state five years ago that "analyses of marriage must be based on analyses of entire social systems" (Collier 1987, 197).

If Martinez-Alier's work remains the concrete standard for studies tying marriage and the family to the entire social system, Raymond Smith remains the most consistent advocate for studies that meet this standard. For him, the strongest critique levied against any analysis of Caribbean kinship, including his earlier work on Guyana, is that which undermines the linkages that the researcher establishes between family and society (Smith 1978). Smith repeatedly emphasizes that kinship relations are not mere derivatives of a larger social structure, and especially not epiphenomena or consequences of the economic order (Smith 1973, 1978, 1982a, 1987, 1988). Rather he sees domestic organization tied to the wider world by way of multiple subsystems (households, sex roles, etc.), each of which can be explored more systematically as potential linkages to the totality.

Smith's views of that totality and of the ways to deal with it reflect changes in emphasis and a capacity to incorporate multiple influences. One detects a distinct shift from structure and stratification (Smith 1956, 1970) to culture, and at times, a less clear-cut move from culture to culture-history.

The second mode pervades Smith's recent essay on race, class, and gender in the Americas, one of his most powerful to date (Smith 1992). In the first and more familiar mode, Smith distinguishes culture as an analytically distinct system of symbols and meanings, but he replaces David Schneider's "conglomerate" cultural level with a plane of "ideas in action," the "norms which mediate" (rather than govern) behavior. Smith then tends to locate on an intermediary level the two messy fields that I call here heterogeneity and historicity.

Heterogeneity and Hegemony

The intermediate level has served as the emergency exit of social science since at least Talcott Parsons. If Smith, to his credit, tries not to treat it as residual, it took younger scholars to make the very heterogeneity that this level embodies the stuff of anthropological inquiry. Lee Drummond draws on fieldwork in Guyana to question the homogeneity of culture and on creole linguistics to propose a "creole metaphor" that posits a set of intersystems with no uniform rules, no invariant properties, and no invariant relationships between categories (Drummond 1980). The proposal is refreshing in light of the dominance of Western folk-models of cultural homogeneity in anthropological theory but, as Brackette Williams notes, Drummond's continuum is unidimensional and overlooks hierarchy. For Williams, who also did fieldwork in Guyana, the construction of mixed hierarchies is a chief concern, and multidimensional complexity a theoretical litmus test. Multidimensionality is what makes the hitherto intermediate level—where putative purities evaporate, where neither thought nor action constitutes an unruffled web, let alone a harmonious system—both pivotal and amenable to study. Williams's research strategy on ethnicity (partly colored through Gramscian lenses) emphasizes the process of homogenization of national cultures (Williams 1989, 1991).

Williams seems unaware of Andrès Serbin's work on ethnicity and politics in Guyana, published in Venezuela in 1981. This unawareness would confirm that various anthropologists now tackling the relationship between heterogeneity and power in the Caribbean consider Gramsci a stimulating interlocutor, since Serbin's treatment of Guyana is explicitly Gramscian. Yet if both Serbin and Williams agree on the limits of hegemony (in the Gramscian sense) in Guyana, Serbin insists on the state-wide mechanisms that foster both dominant and counter "ethnic ideologies," while Williams documents the cultural struggle in a back-and-forth movement from the "community" to the national scene.

Race, class, and power—and Gramsci—are also present in the work of Austin-Broos. Austin's theoretical reformulations include a distinction between culture (values and their embodiments) and ideology (the interpretation of that culture in a contested field); a rejection of the old oppositions between ideology and knowledge, between the symbolic and the structural-practical (Austin 1979, 1981, 1983; Austin-Broos 1987). Austin's ethnographic comparison of two Jamaican neighborhoods exposes a situation where conflict is constrained by a dominant (and, in her view, hegemonic) ideology of education (Austin 1984b).

The conflation of color, class, and power and the fiction of the nation-state return in my book on the Haiti of the Duvaliers, which rests on a reevaluation of Benedict Anderson's notion of the nation as "imagined community" and on yet one more reading of Gramsci that emphasizes the role of the state (Trouillot 1990b). The nation is not a political fiction but a fiction in politics, culture-history projected against the background of state power. In both Haiti and Dominica, the state is part of the stakes and yet, at times, it is an actor competing for the very stakes that it helps to define (Trouillot 1992). The requisite gap between state and nation creates a field where both homogeneity and heterogeneity are simultaneously created and destroyed.

The contention that sameness and heterogeneity intermesh necessarily in so-called "complex" societies was not always a given of anthropological practice. Nor is it an explicit premise of most anthropological strategies today. It is thus further illustration of the ambiguous relationship between the Caribbean frontier and the discipline that an early quest to untangle the roots of heterogeneity remained for long on the outer orbit of anthropological discourse. Individual assessments of *The People of Puerto Rico* vary (*Revista/Review Interamericana* 1978; Wolf 1990); but when Steward and his associates launched that seminal project, it was an extraordinary attempt to look beyond the singular community study and treat an entire society as a complex structural whole. Further, in spite of its intellectual contradictions, the collective book did set out a proposition central to the themes that structure this review: communities need to be studied in reference to a "larger context" that includes networks of local institutions but also the development of colonies and empires (Steward et al. 1956, 32, 505–6). In short, heterogeneity cannot be grasped without serious reference to history.

The Puerto Rico project did not introduce historicity in debates about Caribbean cultures, even though two of its participants, Sidney W. Mintz and Eric Wolf, have become well-known proponents of a historically oriented anthropology (Mintz 1975, 1985b; Wolf 1982). Dutch scholar Rudy Van Lier, a pioneer of twentieth-century Caribbean studies, also leaned toward history in his dealings with Caribbean heterogeneity, as would his compatriot H. Hoetink, later in the century (Hoetink 1971, 1982; Lier 1971). In the 1920s and 1930s, many Caribbean-born writers, such as Price-Mars in Haiti and Pedreira in Puerto Rico, saw the study of culture as inevitably tied to history (Pedreira 1968; Price-Mars 1983). In 1940, anteceding some of Mintz's work, Cuban writer Fernando Ortiz (1970) saw in the history of export crops the framework within which to look at sociocultural patterns in Cuba.

In the United States, by the mid-1930s, Melville Jean Herskovits had also concluded that Caribbean heterogeneity made the use of historical data "almost mandatory" (Herskovits 1971, 329). Herskovits saw the Afro-Americas and especially Caribbean territories as ideal laboratories for anthropologists suspicious of the theoretical assumptions underpinning analyses of "simple" societies. Within the framework of acculturation studies, anthropologists could map out the differential evolution of European and African traits in the Americas and, ultimately, discover the nature of culture, understood as a continuous process of retention and renewal.

This research program paralleled a political agenda marked by the US experience. Herskovits was anxious to demonstrate that cultural legacies were innate entitlements of all humans; they were neither the exclusive property of whites, as believed by the general public, nor an awkward accoutrement of some American Indians, as demonstrated by anthropologists (Herskovits 1971, 297–330). Herskovits saw culture-history as one of the most powerful antidotes to North American racism. It is fair to say, however, that in spite of this political goal and in spite of an explicit attention to the workings of culture under strain, the model itself cannot deal with the differential access to power that conditioned the encounter between Europeans and Africans in the Americas—only with its consequences. Thus, the investigation of slave culture can take on a life of its own; the description of past or present cultural traits (or their ascription to African, European, or Creole roots) can become an end in itself.

The extent to which Caribbeanists still engage in such exercises and manage to avoid the Herskovitsian pitfalls depends very much on their view of the region, but also on their perspective on both racism and the nature and role of culture theory (e.g., Moreno Franginals 1984). Holland and Crane (1987) rely more on industrialization than on the past in studying current developments in Trinidadian Shango. For Roger Abrahams and John Szwed, the vision of Americans of African descent as misadapted individuals, stripped of their cultural heritage, is very much alive and should be challenged on Herskovitsian grounds (Abrahams and Szwed 1983, 1–48). Abrahams and Szwed's compilation of travel accounts and residents' journals from the British Caribbean shows enslaved Africans and their descendants busily building a distinctive Afro-American culture patterned after African models. The extracts cover various aspects of slave life, with an emphasis on religion, patterns of performance, and expressive continuities (Abrahams and Szwed 1983). One or another of these emphases returns in a number of works published in the 1980s (Dance 1985; Dirks 1987; Simpson 1980; Thoden van Velzen and van Wetering 1988)—but see Glazier (1983) for an exception to Herskovits's influence, and Dirks (1987) for a more narrowly materialistic treatment of a slave ritual.

The rigidity of Herskovits's model became an open secret after developments in the historiography of slavery in the 1960s and early 1970s, but few anthropologists before Sidney Mintz and Richard Price (1992) dared to revise the scheme. Rejecting the backward search for the retention of alleged African forms, Mintz and Price argue that the African influence on Afro-American cultures is best defined in terms of underlying values and "grammatical" orientations, and that the culture-history of the Afro-Americas should rest upon historical knowledge of the concrete conditions under which the slaves operated and interacted with Europeans. Although they do not address frontally the role of power in the making of Afro-American cultures, Caribbeanists from various disciplines addressing the issue of African and European continuities in the New World must now take into account their influential reevaluation of the Herskovits model (Carnegie 1987). Mintz and Price's methodological framework for the study of culture contact also has important implications for the guild, now that anthropologists admit, more readily than in Herskovits's time (Herskovits 1937), that we are living in a global village. Richard Price's subsequent work, often in collaboration with Sally Price, greatly advances our knowledge of the Afro-Caribbean past (R. Price 1983, 1990a, 1990b; Price and Price 1988).

The explicit reevaluation of Herskovits and the reevaluation of Steward implicit in the addenda to—and contradictions of—the Puerto Rico book are the intersecting lines with which Sidney Mintz scissors his space on the

Caribbean frontier. For Mintz, heterogeneity cannot be grasped without history (as knowledge) because heterogeneity is the product of history (as process). Historical knowledge is not just a succession of facts—though its empirical grounds must be sound; nor can it pass as explanation—though it illuminates patterns and trends (Mintz 1971d, 1975). Rather, history provides the only context within which to make sense of human beings as subjects (Mintz 1990). Thus, the historical study of the material and symbolic rise of sugar in the modern world provides the context within which to observe the connection between culture and power (Mintz 1985b). What is true for a world commodity is also true for a localized religion: "*Vaudou* cannot be interpreted apart from its significance for the Haitian people, and for Haitian history" (Mintz 1971b, 11).

Mintz's view of historicity thus encompasses the natives' conscious sense of the past emphasized by Price, the "conditioning fact of historicity" emphasized by Alexander Lesser (Mintz 1985a, 59), and the sweeping movements so well captured by Eric Wolf (1982). Mintz's historicism reminds us of C. L. R. James and E. P. Thompson (but note that the former influenced the latter), insofar as it takes the great tides of history (Mintz 1971d, 1977b, 1979, 1985b) as seriously as it does the petty details of individual lives (Mintz 1974c). But individuals manifest themselves only in cultural guise and within the constraints of historically defined social roles. Indeed, social positioning can steer the employment of the same cultural materials in opposite directions (Mintz 1982, 1984). Mintz repeatedly uses Afro-American slavery, as the most repressive and influential institution of recent Western history, to underscore the necessary dialectics between institutions and individuals, system and contingency, adaptation and resistance, and structure and creativity (Mintz 1978, 1990): "The house slave who poisoned her master's family by putting ground glass in the family food had first to become the family cook" (Mintz 1971d, 321).

From that viewpoint, history is never just about the past; that is, the historical process never stops. History is, altogether, part of anthropology, part of what anthropology studies, and part of why anthropology matters; it is material, tool, and context of anthropological discourse. "Culture must be viewed historically if it is to be understood at all" (Mintz 1982, 508). Culture itself is cleansed of ahistorical assumptions of homogeneity. Mintz agrees with Wolf that "culture" and "society" are neither "perfectly coherent in themselves nor necessarily congruent with each other" (Mintz 1982, 509). A favorite axis along which to follow the play between the social and the cultural is the plantation-peasantry complex. Mintz sees Caribbean peasantries and the cultural patterns they recreated, developed, or renewed, over time as one of the most vibrant signs of resistance on the part of Caribbean peoples (especially Afro-Caribbeans) against a system imposed from the outside and dominated by the capitalist plantation (Mintz 1973, 1978, 1979, 1990).

Unfortunately, many of the metatheoretical insights that Mintz draws from the Caribbean and that serve him so well in the study of the plantation-peasantry complex are hidden in over one hundred publications, most of which stand outside disciplinary lines. He rarely packages theory for immediate consumption (but see Mintz 1973, 1974b, 1985b, 1990). Understandably, some students of the Caribbean freely adopt any combination of the themes that he refines or generates: the proto-peasantry, slave marketing and its impact on social organization, etc. Others follow similar directions but on parallel lines. Still, the peasant-plantation complex is a major theme in the anthropology of the region, in part because of Mintz's work. Historians, sociologists, geographers, and anthropologists continue to raise cognate questions about the transition from slavery to free labor in the Caribbean, about the relation between the cultural and the social before and after slavery, and about the relation between agrarian systems and cultural traditions (Besson 1979, 1984a, 1984b; Besson and Momsen 1987; Brierly and Rubenstein 1988; Cross and Marks 1979; Marshall 1990; McGlynn and Drescher 1992; Thomas-Hope 1982; Trouillot 1984). Accommodation and resistance are the organizing themes of Karen Fog Olwig's monographic study of St. John, a work that spans three centuries and combines effectively oral history, archival research, and ethnographic fieldwork (Olwig 1985). Marilyn Silverman (1980) retraces the factional politics in a rice-producing village of East Indians in Guyana over a seventy-year period. My own book on Dominica spans more than two centuries, combining historical and ethnographic research to situate a Caribbean peasantry in a changing world. I explicitly use the case as a contribution to peasant studies and social theory (Trouillot 1988). In richly different ways, Jean Besson, Hymie Rubenstein, and Drexel Woodson look at customary forms of land tenure and the perception of land in Jamaica, St. Vincent, and Haiti. Woodson's work is well grounded in history and explores the dialectic of similarity and dissimilarity as it relates to person, place, and forms of tenure (Woodson 1990). Besson emphasizes "family land" as an institution of resistance in Martha Brae, Jamaica; but Carnegie, in turn, sees customary tenures as probable African retentions (Besson 1979, 1984a, 1984b; Besson and Momsen 1987; Carnegie 1987). Rubenstein's contributions to the field are numerous. His monograph on a St. Vincent village uses primarily ethnographic data to address both the Caribbean and general literature on issues of livelihood, kinship, and household structure and social life outside the family. But, as Robert Manners long insisted, even community studies in the Caribbean must take cognizance of the past and use archival materials (Manners 1957).

BOUNDARIES AND ARTICULATIONS

Historicity, once introduced, is the nightmare of the ethnographer, the constant reminder that the groupings one tends to take for natural are human creations, changing results of past and ongoing processes. Caribbean ethnography long faced the issue of the boundaries of observation and analysis (Clarke 1957; Steward et al. 1956), but this concern increased lately with the greater awareness of history. I disagree with Rubenstein's statement that Caribbean ethnography has been marked by too much theory running after too little descriptive data (Rubenstein 1987, 3–4). Caribbean ethnographers are no worse than others. Rather, the complexity of the frontier makes the application of many models inherited from the guild simplistic—a realization often deterred in other regions of the world by gatekeeping and the adoption of unproblematized units. To Radcliffe-Brown's search for a "convenient locality of suitable size," Baber replies (1987, 95) that "social boundaries can never be a matter of convenience" and that their setting is crucial in analyses of multicultural situations. Elsewhere, Baber warns us that Turner's notion of social drama may be misleading without proper attention to the context within which this drama is played out (Baber 1985).

But in the Caribbean, context is not uniform and the individual actor, this basic unit of methodological individualism, not an obvious entity of which the boundaries are known—even though individualism may be quite evident (Despres 1975; Mintz 1990; Wilson 1969; Woodson 1990). Ever since Comitas's influential article (Comitas 1964), Caribbean anthropology has tried to deal with "occupational multiplicity," the simultaneous or sequential engagement in a number of economic activities. Of course, there are obvious reasons why the urban and rural poor, women heads of households, migrants, and other people eking out a living under social and economic strain would want to be skeptical and bank on multiple adaptive strategies (Barrow 1986a; Carnegie 1982; Chibnik 1980). Yet I suspect that what strikes most ethnographers is something more than risk management. First, the systematicity with which people maintain multiplicity is prevalent enough for observers to phrase it not in terms of movement between roles or types but in terms of types or roles that include movement (Comitas 1964; Frucht 1967). Second, Caribbean peoples seem to have fewer problems than most in recognizing the fuzziness and overlap of categories, and multiplicity is not confined to the economic realm or to the poor. What appears to some as divided political, economic, or social loyalties has a long history on the frontier (Bibly 1989; Pedreira 1968; R. Price 1990b; Price-Mars 1983). Middle-class individuals engage in behavior similar to the economic strategies of the poor—but further research is required because few anthropologists have enhanced our knowledge of the Caribbean middle classes (Alexander 1984; Lowes 1987). Still, what seems to be at stake here is a way to live what the post-Enlightenment West calls—and anthropology uncritically accepts as—individual oneness. Herskovits's comments on Haitian "socialized ambivalence" seem to rest on an assumption of universal univalence, and a good deal of symbolic anthropology is premised on individual oneness.

The presumption of a microcosm, to paraphrase Manners (1957), is no easier to maintain when studying a "community" on the frontier. The village tradition of the anthropological monograph becomes problematic in the Caribbean, where the line between rural and urban folk is not clear-cut (Mintz 1953). Anthropologists have noted the scarcity of book-length community studies in the region (Carnegie 1987; Rubenstein 1987). This deficiency is not just a reflection of the politics of the guild; it is also a healthy sign that Caribbean ethnographers often realize that the story they were after does not end with their village. How does one package ethnography with such an awareness? Williams ties her descriptions of Cockalorum to the national space in Guyana. Rubenstein admits that his village is open to the world (Rubenstein 1987, 83–84) but stops short of drawing from this confession any fundamental shift in the scope of description. Still, Rubenstein goes much further than the expected chapter on history and the nation. He takes seventy-eight pages to get to his village and, once there, he returns to history for a proper introduction of his core unit of observation. Woodson also rejects the perfunctory historical introduction: in his dissertation, historical chapters spanning the Haitian space come after the ethnographic introduction of his community and before his institutional analysis (Woodson 1990). My own study of Dominica also takes on the joint issues of historicity and boundaries. I use three units of description and analysis, The Nation, The World, and The Village—three different vantage points from which to look at Dominican peasants. History generates the first unit; political economy helps make sense of the second. The reader enters the village-level ethnography only two-thirds of the way through the book (Trouillot 1988).

The simultaneous use of multiple units of analysis by a single author or a team is one of the many strategies that reveals the search by many Caribbeanists for a way to tie their immediate units of observation to the wider world (Clarke 1957; Mintz 1985b; Steward et al. 1956; Trouillot 1982, 1988, 1989). The overwhelming evidence for the intrusion of outside forces makes Caribbean anthropologists attentive to—if not always uncritical of—world-systems theory, dependency theory, or cognate approaches that allow them to read their data beyond the traditional boundaries of the colonial or national state (Baber 1985; Bolles 1983, 1986; Farmer 1988a; Griffith 1985; Harrison 1987, 1988; McGlynn and Drescher 1992; Murphy 1991; Silverman 1979; Smith 1978, 1982a, 1988; Trouillot 1982). But once the world is acknowledged, one must deal with "local response," of which the Caribbean is a powerful illustration precisely because it is so colonial (Mintz 1977b). Potential methodologies include analyses moving down, through concentric circles, from the level of the world system to as small a unit as the plantation by way of increasingly smaller units, such as the region or the territory (Trouillot 1982).

Fortunately, at the level of the region, the conceptualization of units and boundaries is well advanced. Mintz's overview of the Caribbean stands as one of the most sophisticated conceptualizations of a sociocultural area in the anthropological literature. Neither a laundry list of necessary particulars nor a covert reference to an immanent essence, it is doubly open. First, it ties the Caribbean to the rest of the world, notably to the continental Americas, and to Europe and Africa, by way of the Atlantic. Second, it does not superimpose homogeneity upon its internal units but views Caribbean territories along a multidimensional continuum informed by history. Colonial domination, African substrata, ecological limits, forms of labor extraction, cultural and ideological ambiance, and now US domination intermix in this scheme, which I read as an exemplar of "family resemblance" à la Wittgenstein (Mintz 1971a, 1971d, 1974a; Mintz and R. Price 1992).

The concern for a regional multilevel methodology is explicit in the Women in the Caribbean Project, a multidisciplinary study covering a number of Caribbean territories that is the focus of two special issues of *Social and Economic Studies* (1986a, 1986b) and that has already spurred one book (Senior 1991). Unfortunately, in line with most of the works published or sponsored by the University of the West Indies (but see Allman 1985), the project concentrates on territories where English is the official language, a weak commonality if we take seriously the idea of family resemblance. What makes Guadeloupe look like St. Lucia is not what makes Dominica look like Antigua; what makes Barbados look like Cuba is not what makes Cuba look like the Dominican Republic; and even Haitian exceptionalism is, to a large extent, a myth (Trouillot 1990c). There are good grounds for arguing that a comparison of women in Jamaica and Haiti would be at least as interesting as one between women in Jamaica and Trinidad; good grounds to suggest that we may understand better the degree to which Barbados is British if we also look at Martinique; good reasons to suppose that studies of local consciousness in Curaçao may throw a better light on Puerto Rican nationalism. More important, everything we know about each of these territories confirms one thing: it is as a complex package that the Caribbean presents such stimulating challenge to Western social science and to anthropology in particular.

CONCLUSION

The domination of English on Caribbean studies reflects and reinforces boundaries and rankings inherited from the colonial past, as well as current US domination. It is also a scholarly handicap that amplifies intellectual parochialism within disciplinary, linguistic, or colonial spheres. It restricts the range of comparison and the number of territories studied (Jamaica, Barbados, Guyana, Trinidad), and promotes superficial similarities. Few students of Caribbean culture (especially Caribbean-born or African American scholars) dare to cross linguistic or colonial borders, with only a few exceptions in recent years (e.g., Baber 1985, 1987; Woodson 1990). Few dare to bring explicitly to the discipline the political or metatheoretical lessons learned on the frontier (Harrison 1991; Trouillot 1990c, 1991). Fewer dare to be comparative across linguistic boundaries (McGlynn and Drescher 1992; Mintz 1990; Mintz and S. Price 1992; R. Price 1990b). Yet as language gives fieldworkers the impression of being on familiar territory, chances increase for them to be off guard and also to ignore works done in other languages.

Yet Dutch scholars continue to produce a small but steady stream of works on the Caribbean, only a few of which are available in English (e.g., Hoetink 1971, 1982; Hoogbergen [1984] 1990). In the 1970s, PhD theses on the Caribbean outnumbered those dealing with every other non-Western area in departments of anthropology and sociology in the Netherlands (Banck 1988). Works in Dutch and in other languages are covered in the yearly update on Caribbean Studies of the *Boletín de estudios latinoamericanos y del Caribe*. A few titles by historians in Spanish (e.g., Moreno Fraginals, Rivero Calle, and Dacal 1987) and a number of works in French, on the French Antilles, Guyane, and Haiti, should be also of interest to English-speaking anthropologists (Affergan 1983; André 1987; Bastien [1951] 1985; Bébel-Gisler 1985, 1989; Benoist 1972; Bernabé, Chamoiseau, and Confiant 1989; d'Ans 1987; Giraud, 1979; Helly 1979; Jolivet 1986; Labelle 1978; Louillot and Crusol-Baillard 1987). To be sure, while the Dutch tend to match North Americans in empiricism, works in Spanish and French are rarely based on the kind of ethnographic fieldwork required by most US universities. On the other hand, the latter works often partake of an ancient and fundamental debate about the nature of Caribbean societies and their relation to the West. A number of writers (mostly linguists and literary critics writing in French, many of whom are Caribbean-born) are asking questions about *creolité*, or what it means for Caribbean people to be part of societies and cultures born out of contact (e.g., Bernabé, Chamoiseau, and Confiant 1989; Glissant 1989; Jolivet 1986). The multidisciplinary periodical *Etudes créoles* extends beyond the technical issues of creole linguistics and ties the Caribbean to societies and cultures of Africa and the Indian Ocean. In short, the concerns that I have highlighted here as scattered posts on the frontier are not the exclusive domain of Caribbean anthropologists nor are they exclusively expressed in English. A number of academics and intellectuals, writing in at least four languages, have dealt in different ways with what I here call heterogeneity, historicity, and articulation. That some think this endeavor possible without anthropology reveals their intellectual preference and prejudices. Yet it also suggests some of the limits to anthropological theory, at least as seen from the frontier.

NOTE

I thank Flor Ruz, Sara M. Springer, and especially Paul Kim for their research assistance. I am grateful to Suzan Lowes, Sidney W. Mintz, and Drexel G. Woodson for their comments on an early version of the manuscript. I alone remain fully responsible for the substance of the argument and the final text. *Editors' Note:* This chapter first appeared as "The Caribbean Region: An Open Frontier in Anthropological Theory," *Annual Review of Anthropology* 21 (1992): 19–42.

REFERENCES

Abrahams, Roger D. 1983. *The Man-of-Words in the West Indies: Performance and the Emergence of Creole Culture*. Baltimore, MD: Johns Hopkins University Press.

Abrahams, Roger D., and John F. Szwed, eds. 1983. *After Africa: Extracts from British Travel Accounts and Journals of the Seventeenth, Eighteenth, and Nineteenth Centuries concerning the Slaves, Their Manners, and Customs in the British West Indies*. New Haven, CT: Yale University Press.

Abu-Lughod, Lila. 1989. "Zones of Theory in the Anthropology of the Arab World." *Annual Review of Anthropology* 18: 267–306.

Affergan, Francis. 1983. *Anthropologie à la Martinique*. Paris: Anthropos.

Alexander, Jack. 1977. "The Culture of Race in Middle-Class Kingston, Jamaica." *American Ethnologist* 4, no. 3: 413–36.

Alexander, Jack. 1984. "Love, Race, Slavery, and Sexuality in Jamaican Images of the Family." In *Kinship, Ideology, and Practice in Latin America*, edited by Raymond T. Smith, 147–80. Chapel Hill: University of North Carolina Press.

Allman, James. 1985. "Conjugal Unions in Rural and Urban Haiti." *Social and Economic Studies* 34, no. 1: 27–57.

André, Jacques. 1987. *L'inceste focal dans la famille noire antillaise*. Paris: Presses Universitaires de France.

Appadurai, Arjun. 1986. "Theory in Anthropology: Center and Periphery." *Comparative Studies in Society and History* 28: 356–61.

Austin, Diane J. 1979. "History and Symbols in Ideology: A Jamaican Example." *Man* 14: 447–514.

Austin, Diane J. 1981. "Born Again . . . and Again and Again: Communities and Social Change among Jamaican Pentecostalists." *Journal of Anthropological Research* 37, no. 3: 226–46.

Austin, Diane J. 1983. "Culture and Ideology in the English-Speaking Caribbean: A View from Jamaica." *American Ethnologist* 10, no. 2: 223–40.

Austin, Diane J. 1984a. "Reply to M. G. Smith." *American Ethnologist* 11, no. 1: 185.

Austin, Diane J. 1984b. *Urban Life in Kingston, Jamaica: The Culture and Class Ideology of Two Neighborhoods*. New York: Gordon and Breach.

Austin-Broos, Diane J. 1987. "Pentecostals and Rastafarians: Cultural, Political, and Gender Relations of Two Religious Movements." *Social and Economic Studies* 36, no. 4: 1–39.

Baber, Willie L. 1985. "Political Economy and Social Change: The Bissette Affair and Local-Level Politics in Morne-Vert." *American Ethnologist* 12, no. 3: 489–504.

Baber, Willie L. 1987. "The Pluralism Controversy: Wider Theoretical Implications." *Caribbean Quarterly* 33, no. 1–2: 81–94.

Banck, Geert A. 1988. "Anthropological Research on the Caribbean and Latin America." *Boletín de estudios latinoamericanos y del Caribe* 44: 29–38.

Barrow, Christine. 1986a. "Finding the Support: A Study of Strategies for Survival." *Social and Economic Studies* 35, no. 2: 131–76.

Barrow, Christine. 1986b. "Male Images of Women in Barbados." *Social and Economic Studies* 35, no. 3: 51–64.

Bastien, Rémy. (1951) 1985. *Le paysan haïtien et sa famille*. Paris: ACCT-Karthala.

Bébel-Gisler, Dany. 1985. *Leonora: L'histoire enfouie de la Guadeloupe*. Paris: Éditions Seghers.

Bébel-Gisler, Dany. 1989. *Le défi culturel guadeloupéen: Devenir ce que nous sommes*. Paris: Éditions Caribbéennes.

Benoist, Jean. 1972. *L'archipel inacheve: Culture et societe aux antilles francaises*. Montreal: Les Presses de l'Université de Montreal.

Berleant-Schiller, Riva. 1977. "Production and Division of Labor in a West Indian Peasant Commune." *American Ethnologist* 4, no. 2: 253–72.

Berleant-Schiller, Riva. 1981. "Plantation Society and the Caribbean Present." *Plantation Society in the Americas* 1, no. 3: 387–409.

Bernabé, Jean, Patrick Chamoiseau, and Raphaël Confiant. 1989. *Éloge de la créolite*. Paris: Gallimard.

Besson, Jean. 1979. "Symbolic Aspects of Land in the Caribbean: The Tenure and Transmission of Land Rights among Caribbean Peasantries." In *Peasants, Plantations and Rural Communities in the Caribbean*, edited by Malcolm Cross and Arnaud F. Marks, 86–116. Leiden: Royal Institute of Linguistic Anthropology and University of Surrey.

Besson, Jean. 1984a. "Family Land and Caribbean Society: Toward an Ethnography of Caribbean Peasantries." In *Perspectives on Caribbean Regional Identity*, edited by Elizabeth M. Thomas-Hope, 57–83. Liverpool, UK: Center for Latin American Studies, University of Liverpool.

Besson, Jean. 1984b. "Land Tenure in the Free Villages of Trelawny, Jamaica: A Case Study in the Caribbean Peasant Response to Emancipation." *Slavery Abolition* 5, no. 1: 3–23.

Besson, Jean, and Janet Momsen. 1987. *Land and Development in the Caribbean*. London: Macmillan.

Bilby, Kenneth M. 1989. "Divided Loyalties: Local Politics and the Play of States among the Aluku." *Nieuwe West-Indische Gids/New West Indian Guide* 63, nos. 3–4: 143–74.

Bolland, O. Nigel. 1986. "Labour Control and Resistance in Belize in the Century after 1838." *Slavery and Abolition* 7, no. 2: 175–87.

Bolles, A. Lynn. 1983. "Kitchens Hit by Priorities: Employed Working-Class Jamaican Women Confront the IMF." In *Women, Men, and the International Division of Labor*, edited by June Nash, Maria P. Fernandez-Kelly, 138–60. Albany: SUNY Press.

Bolles, A. Lynn. 1986. "Economic Crisis and Female-Headed Households in Jamaica." In *Women and Change in Latin America*, edited by June Nash and Helen Safa, 65–83. South Hadley, MA: Bergin and Garvey.

Brana-Shute, Gary. 1989. *On the Corner: Male Social Life in a Paramaribo Creole Neighborhood*. Prospect Heights, IL: Waveland.

Brierley, John S., and Hymie Rubenstein, eds. 1988. *Small Farming and Peasant Resources in the Caribbean*. Winnipeg: Department of Geography, University of Manitoba.

Carnegie, Charles V. 1982. "Strategic Flexibility in the West Indies: A Social Psychology of Caribbean Migration." *Caribbean Review* 11, no. 1: 10–13, 54.

Carnegie, Charles V., ed. 1987. *Afro-Caribbean Villages in Historical Perspective*. ACIJ Research Review No. 2. Kingston: African Caribbean Institute of Jamaica.

Chibnik, Michael. 1980. "Working Out or Working In: The Choice between Wage Labor and Cash Cropping in Rural Belize." *American Ethnologist* 7, no. 1: 86–105.

Clarke, Edith. 1957. *My Mother Who Fathered Me: A Study of Three Selected Communities in Jamaica*. London: George Allen and Unwin.

Cohen Stuart, Bertie A. 1985. *Women in the Caribbean: A Bibliography*. Leiden: Royal Institute of Linguistics and Anthropology, Department of Caribbean Studies.

Collier, Jane Fishburne. 1987. "Rank and Marriage: Or Why High-Ranking Brides Cost More." In *Gender and Kinship: Essays toward a Unified Analysis*, edited by Jane Fishburne Collier and Sylvia Junko Yanagisako, 197–220. Stanford, CA: Stanford University of Press.

Comitas, Lambros. 1964. "Occupational Multiplicity in Rural Jamaica." In *Proceedings of the American Ethnological Society*, edited by Viola E. Garfield and Ernestine Friedl, 41–50. Seattle: University of Washington Press.

Comitas, Lambros. 1977. *The Complete Caribbeana*. Millwood, NY: KTO Press.

Cross, Malcolm, and Arnaud F. Marks, eds. 1979. *Peasants, Plantations and Rural Communities in the Caribbean*. Leiden: Royal Institute of Linguistics and Anthropology and University of Surrey.

Dance, Daryl Cumber. 1985. *Folklore from Contemporary Jamaica*. Knoxville: University of Tennessee Press.

Dann, Graham. 1987. *The Barbadian Male: Sexual Attitudes and Practice*. Kingston: Macmillan Caribbean.

d'Ans, André-Marcel. 1987. *Haïti: Paysage et société*. Paris: Karthala.

Deosaran, Ramesh. 1987a. "The Social Psychology of Cultural Pluralism: Updating the Old." *Caribbean Quarterly* 33, nos. 1–2: 1–19.

Deosaran, Ramesh. 1987b. "Some Issues in Multiculturalism: The Case of Trinidad and Tobago in the Post-colonial Era." *Caribbean Quarterly* 33, nos. 1–2: 61–80.

Despres, Leo A., ed. 1975. *Ethnicity and Resource Competition in Plural Societies*. The Hague: Mouton.

Dirks, Robert. 1987. *The Black Saturnalia: Conflict and Its Ritual Expression on British West Indian Slave Plantations*. Gainesville: University Press of Florida.

Dobbin, Jay D. 1986. *The Jombee Dance of Montserrat: A Study of Ritual Trance in the West Indies*. Columbus: Ohio State University Press.

Dominguez, Virginia. 1986. "Intended and Unintended Messages: The Scholarly Defense of One's 'People.'" *Nieuwe West-Indische Gids/New West Indian Guide* 60, nos. 3–4: 208–22.

Drummond, Lee. 1980. "The Cultural Continuum: A Theory of Intersystems." *Man* 15: 352–74.

Durant-Gonzales, Victoria. 1982. "The Realm of Female Familial Responsibility." In *Women and the Family*, edited by Joycelin Massiah, 1–27. Cave Hill, Barbados: Institute of Social and Economic Research, University of the West Indies.

Farmer, Paul. 1988a. "Bad Blood, Spoiled Milk: Bodily Fluids as Moral Barometers in Rural Haiti." *American Ethnologist* 15, no. 1: 62–83.

Farmer, Paul. 1988b. "Blood, Sweat, and Baseballs: Haiti in the West Atlantic System." *Dialectical Anthropology* 13, no. 1: 83–99.

Fisher, Lawrence E. 1985. *Colonial Madness: Mental Health in the Barbadian Social Order*. New Brunswick, NJ: Rutgers University Press.

Frucht, Richard. 1967. "A Caribbean Social Type: Neither Peasant nor Proletarian." *Social and Economic Studies* 16, no. 3: 295–300.

Geertz, Clifford. 1976. "From the Native's Point of View": On the Nature of Anthropological Understanding." In *Meaning in Anthropology*, edited by Keith H. Basso and Henry A. Selby, 221–37. Albuquerque: University of New Mexico Press.

Giraud, Michel. 1979. *Race et classes à la Martinique*. Paris: Anthropos.

Glazier, Stephen D. 1983. *Marchin' the Pilgrims Home: Leadership and Decision-Making in an Afro-Caribbean Faith*. Westport, CT: Greenwood.

Glissant, Édouard. 1989. *Caribbean Discourse: Selected Essays*. Translated by J. Michael Dash. Charlottesville: University of Virginia Press.

Gonzalez, Nancie L. 1983. "New Evidence on the Origin of the Black Carib with Thoughts on the Meaning of Tradition." *Nieuwe West-Indische Gids/New West Indian Guide* 57, no. 3–4: 143–72.

Gonzalez, Nancie L. 1984. "Rethinking the Consanguineal Household and Matrifocality." *Ethnology* 23: 1–12.

Gonzalez, Nancie L. 1988. *Sojourners of the Caribbean: Ethnogenesis and Ethnohistory of the Garifuna*. Urbana: University of Illinois Press.

Griffith, David C. 1985. "Women, Remittances, and Reproduction." *American Ethnologist* 12, no. 4: 676–90.

Gullick, C. J. M. R. 1985. *Myths of a Minority: The Changing Traditions of the Vincentian Caribs*. Assen, Netherlands: Van Gorcum.

Handler, Jerome S. 1982. "Slave Revolts and Conspiracies in Seventeenth-Century Barbados." *Nieuwe West-Indische Gids/New West Indian Guide* 56, nos. 1–2: 5–42.

Handler, Jerome S. 1984. "Freedmen and Slaves in the Barbados Militia." *Journal of Caribbean History* 19, no. 1: 1–25.

Harrison, Faye V. 1987. "Gangs, Grassroots Politics, and the Crisis of Development Capitalism in Jamaica." In *Perspectives in US Marxist Anthropology*, edited by David J. Hakken, Hanna Lessinger, June Nash, and Florence Babb, 186–210. Boulder, CO: Westview Press.

Harrison, Faye V. 1988. "Women in Jamaica's Urban Informal Economy: Insights from a Kingston Slum." *Nieuwe West-Indische Gids/New West Indian Guide* 62, no. 3–4: 103–28.

Harrison, Faye V. 1991. "Ethnography as Politics." In *Decolonizing Anthropology: Moving Further toward an Anthropology of Liberation*, edited by Faye V. Harrison, 88–109. Washington, DC: American Anthropological Association.

Helly, Denise. 1979. *Idéologie et ethnicité: Les Chinois Macao à Cuba, 1847–1886*. Montréal: Les presses de l'Université de Montréal.

Henry, Frances. 1983. "Religion and Ideology in Trinidad: The Resurgence of the Shango Religion." *Caribbean Quarterly* 29, nos. 3–4: 63–69.

Herskovits, Melville J. 1937. "The Significance of the Study of Acculturation for Anthropology." *American Anthropologist* 39, no. 2: 259–64.

Herskovits, Melville J. 1971. *Life in a Haitian Valley*. Garden City, NY: Anchor Books.

Hoetink, Harry. 1971. *Caribbean Race Relations: A Study of Two Variants*. Translated by Eva M. Hooykaas. London: Oxford University Press.

Hoetink, Harry. 1982. *The Dominican People, 1850–1900: Notes for a Historical Sociology*. Translated by Stephen K. Ault. Baltimore, MD: Johns Hopkins University Press.

Holland, Dorothy C., and Julia G. Crane. 1987. "Adapting to an Industrializing Nation: The Shango Cult in Trinidad." *Social and Economic Studies* 36, no. 4: 41–66.

Hoogbergen, Wim S. M. (1984) 1990. *The Boni Maroon Wars in Suriname*. Leiden: Brill.

Horowitz, Michael, ed. 1971. *Peoples and Cultures of the Caribbean: An Anthropological Reader*. Garden City, NY: Natural History Press.

Horowitz, Michael. 1983. *Morne Paysan, Peasant Village in Martinique*. New York: Irvington.

Jolivet, Marie-José. 1986. *La question créole: Essai de sociologie sur la Guyane*. Paris: Orstrom.

Labelle, Micheline. 1978. *Idéologie de couleur et classes sociales en Haïti*. Montréal: Les presses de l'Université de Montréal.

Laguerre, Michel S. 1982. *Urban Life in the Caribbean*. Cambridge, MA: Schenkman.

Lazarus-Black, Mindie. 1991. "Why Women Take Men to Magistrate's Court: Caribbean Kinship Ideology and Law." *Ethnology* 30, no. 2: 119–33.

Leo-Rhynie, Elsa, and Marlene Hamilton. 1983. "Professional Jamaican Women: Equal or Not?" *Caribbean Quarterly* 29, nos. 3–4: 70–85.

Lewis, Gordon K. 1983. *Main Currents in Caribbean Thought: The Historical Evolution of Caribbean Society in Its Ideological Aspects, 1492–1900*. Baltimore, MD: Johns Hopkins University Press.

Lieber, Michael. 1981. *Street Scenes: Afro-American Culture in Urban Trinidad*. Cambridge, MA: Schenkman.

Lier, Rudolf Asveer Jacob van. 1950. *Development and Nature of Society in the West Indies*. Koninklijke Institut voor de Tropen, Mededeling and Afdeling Culturele en Physische Anthropologie No. 37. Amsterdam: Uitgave van Het Indisch Institut.

Lier, Rudolf Asveer Jacob van. 1971. *Frontier Society: A Social Analysis of the History of Surinam*. The Hague: Martinus Nijhoff.

Loroña, Lionel V, ed. 1983–1987. *Bibliography of Latin American and Caribbean Biblio-graphies*. Madison: Seminar on the Acquisition of Latin American Library Materials (SALALM), University of Wisconsin-Madison.

Louillot, Germaine, and Danielle Crusol-Baillard. 1987. *Femmes martiniquaises: Mythes et realités*. Fort-de-France, Martinique: Éditions Caribéennes.

Lowenthal, David. 1972. *West Indian Societies*. London: Oxford University Press.

Lowenthal, Ira P. 1987. "Marriage Is 20, Children Are 21: The Cultural Construc-tion of Conjugality and the Family in Rural Haiti." PhD diss., Johns Hopkins University.

Lowes, Suzan. 1987. "Time and Motion in the Formation of the Middle Class in Antigua, 1834–1940." Paper presented at the Annual Meeting of the American Anthropological Association, Chicago, IL, November.

Manners, Robert A. 1957. "Methods of Community Analysis in the Caribbean." In *Caribbean Studies: A Symposium*, edited by Vera Rubin, 80–92. Seattle: Univer-sity of Washington Press.

Manning, Frank E. 1973. *Black Clubs in Bermuda: Ethnography of a Play World*. Ithaca, NY: Cornell University Press.

Marshall, Woodville K. 1990. *The Post-slavery Labour Problem Revisited: The 1990 Elsa Goveia Memorial Lecture*. Kingston, Jamaica: University of the West Indies.

Martinez-Alier, Verena. 1974. *Marriage, Class and Colour in Nineteenth-Century Cuba: A Study of Racial Attitudes and Sexual Values in a Slave Society*. Cambridge: Cam-bridge University Press.

McGlynn, Frank, and Seymour Drescher, eds. 1992. *The Meaning of Freedom: Economics, Politics, and Culture after Slavery*. Pittsburgh, PA: University of Pittsburgh Press.

McWatt, Mark. 1982. "The Preoccupation with the Past in West Indian Literature." *Caribbean Quarterly* 28, nos. 1–2: 12–19.

Mintz, Sidney W. 1953. "The Folk-Urban Continuum and the Rural Proletarian Community." *American Journal of Sociology* 59, no. 2: 136–43.

Mintz, Sidney W. 1971a. "The Caribbean as a Socio-Cultural Area." In *Peoples and Cultures of the Caribbean: An Anthropological Reader*, edited by Michael Horo-witz, 17–46. Garden City, NY: Natural History Press.

Mintz, Sidney W. 1971b. "Introduction." In *Voodoo in Haiti*, by Alfred Métraux, 1–15. New York: Schocken Books.

Mintz, Sidney W. 1971c. "Men, Women, and Trade." *Comparative Studies in Society and History* 13, no. 3: 247–69.

Mintz, Sidney W. 1971d. "Toward an Afro-American History." *Cahiers d'Histoire Mondiale* 13: 317–32.

Mintz, Sidney W. 1973. "A Note on the Definition of Peasantries." *Journal of Peasant Studies* 1: 91–106.

Mintz, Sidney W. 1974a. "The Caribbean Region." In *Slavery, Colonialism, and Rac-ism*, edited by Sidney W. Mintz, 45–71. New York: Norton.

Mintz, Sidney W. 1974b. "The Rural Proletariat and the Problem of Rural Proletar-ian Consciousness." *Journal of Peasant Studies* 1: 291–325.

Mintz, Sidney W. 1974c. *Worker in the Cane: A Puerto Rican Life History*. New York: Norton.

Mintz, Sidney W. 1975. "History and Anthropology: A Brief Reprise." In *Race and Slavery in the Western Hemisphere: Quantitative Studies*, edited by Stanley L. Engerman and Eugene D. Genovese, 477–94. Princeton, NJ: Princeton University Press.

Mintz, Sidney W. 1977a. "North American Anthropological Contributions to Caribbean Studies." *Boletín de estudios latinoamericanos y del Caribe* 22: 68–82.

Mintz, Sidney W. 1977b. "The So-Called World System: Local Initiative and Local Response." *Dialectical Anthropology* 2, no. 4: 253–70.

Mintz, Sidney W. 1978. "Was the Plantation Slave a Proletarian?" *Review* 2, no. 1: 81–98.

Mintz, Sidney W. 1979. "Slavery and the Rise of Peasantries." *Historical Reflections* 6, no. 1: 135–242.

Mintz, Sidney W. 1982. "Culture: An Anthropological View." *Yale Review* 71: 499–512.

Mintz, Sidney W. 1984. "American Anthropology and the Marxist Tradition." In *On Marxian Perspectives in Anthropology: Essays in Honor of Harry Hoijer, 1981*, edited by Sidney W. Mintz, Maurice Godelier, and Bruce Graham Trigger, 11–34. Malibu, CA: Undena Publications.

Mintz, Sidney W., ed. 1985a. *History, Evolution, and the Concept of Culture: Selected Papers by Alexander Lesser*. Cambridge: Cambridge University Press.

Mintz, Sidney W. 1985b. *Sweetness and Power: The Place of Sugar in Modern History*. New York: Viking.

Mintz, Sidney W. 1990. *Caribbean Transformations*. New York: Columbia University Press.

Mintz, Sidney W., and Richard Price. 1992. *The Birth of African-American Culture: An Anthropological Perspective*. Boston: Beacon Press.

Mintz, Sidney W., and Sally Price, eds. 1992. *Caribbean Contours*. Baltimore, MD: Johns Hopkins University Press.

Moreno Fraginals, Manuel R., ed. 1984. *Africa in Latin America: Essays on History, Culture, and Socialization*. Translated by Leonor Blum. New York: Holmes and Meier.

Moreno Fraginals, Manuel R., Manuel Rivero Calle, and Ramón Dacal. 1987. "Apuntes para una historía económico-social de la cultura cubana: Cultural indocubana." *Temas* 12: 53–66.

Moya Pons, Frank. 1986. *El batey: Estudio socioeconómico de los bateyes del consejo estatal del azúcar*. Santo Domingo, Dominican Republic: Fondo para el Avance de las Ciencias Sociales.

Murphy, Martin Francis. 1991. *Dominican Sugar Plantations: Production and Foreign Labor Integration*. New York: Praeger.

Murray, Gerald, and Maria D. Alvarez. 1975. "Haitian Beans Circuits: Cropping and Trading Maneuvers among a Cash-Oriented Peasantry." In *Working Papers in Haitian Society and Culture*, edited by Sidney W. Mintz, 85–126. New Haven, CT: Antilles Research Program, Yale University.

Nettleford, Rex. 1972. *Mirror, Mirror: Identity, Race and Protest in Jamaica*. Kingston, Jamaica: W. Collins and Sangster/William Morrow.

Nettleford, Rex. 1979. *Caribbean Cultural Identity: The Case of Jamaica*. Los Angeles: Center for Afro-American Studies and UCLA Latin American Center.

Olwig, Karen Fog. 1985. *Cultural Adaptation and Resistance on St. John: Three Centuries of Afro-Caribbean Life*. Gainesville: University Press of Florida.

Olwig, Karen Fog. 1990. "The Struggle for Respectability: Methodism and Afro-Caribbean Culture on 19th Century Nevis." *Nieuwe West-Indische Gids/New West Indian Guide* 64, nos. 3–4: 93–114.

Ortiz, Fernando. 1970. *Cuban Counterpoint: Tobacco and Sugar*. New York: Vintage.

Pagden, Anthony. 1982. *The Fall of Natural Man: The American Indian and the Origins of Comparative Ethnography*. Cambridge: Cambridge University Press.

Pedreira, Antonio S. 1968. *Insularismo: Ensayos de interpretacíon puertorriqueña*. San Juan: Edil.

Price, Richard. 1971. "Studies of Caribbean Family Organization: Problems and Prospects." *Dédaldo revista de arte e arqueologia* 4, no. 14: 23–58.

Price, Richard. 1983. *First-Time: The Historical Vision of an Afro-American People*. Baltimore, MD: Johns Hopkins University Press.

Price, Richard. 1990a. *Alabi's World*. Baltimore, MD: Johns Hopkins University Press.

Price, Richard. 1990b. *Ethnographic History, Caribbean Pasts*. Working Papers No. 9. College Park, MD: University of Maryland.

Price, Richard, and Sally Price, eds. 1988. *Narrative of a Five Years' Expedition against the Revolted Negroes of Suriname in Guiana on the Wild Coast of South America from the year 1772 to the year 1777 . . .* , by John Gabriel Stedman. Baltimore, MD: Johns Hopkins University Press.

Price, Sally. 1984. *Co-wives and Calabashes*. Ann Arbor: University of Michigan Press.

Price-Mars, Jean. 1983. *So Spoke the Uncle*. Translated by Magdaline W. Shannon. Washington, DC: Three Continents Press.

Rawlins, Joan M. 1987. *The Family in the Caribbean, 1973–1986: An Annotated Bibliography*. Cave Hill, Barbados: Institute of Social and Economic Research.

Revista/Review Interamericana. 1978. 8, no. 1.

Robotham, Don. 1980. "Pluralism as an Ideology." *Social and Economic Studies* 29, no. 1: 69–89.

Robotham, Don. 1985. "The Why of the Cockatoo?" *Social and Economic Studies* 34, no. 2: 111–51.

Rubenstein, Hymie. 1983. "Caribbean Family and Household Organization: Some Conceptual Clarifications." *Journal of Comparative Family Studies* 14, no. 3: 283–98.

Rubenstein, Hymie. 1987. *Coping with Poverty: Adaptive Strategies in a Caribbean Village*. Boulder, CO: Westview.

Safa, Helen I. 1986. "Economic Autonomy and Sexual Equality in Caribbean Society." *Social and Economic Studies* 35, no. 3: 1–21.

Safa, Helen I. 1987. "Popular Culture, National Identity, and Race in the Caribbean." *Nieuwe West-Indische Gids/New West Indian Guide* 61, nos. 3–4: 115–26.

Senior, Olive. 1991. *Working Miracles: Women's Lives in the English-Speaking Caribbean.* Bloomington: Indiana University Press; and Cave Hill, Barbados: Institute of Social and Economic Research, University of the West Indies.

Serbin, Andrés. 1981. *Nacionalismo, etnicidad y politica en la república cooperativa de Guyana.* Caracas, Venezuela: Bruguera.

Serbin, Andrés. 1985. "Procesos etnoculturales y percepciones mutuas en el desarrollo de las relaciones entre el Caribe de habla inglesa y América Latina." *Boletín de estudios latinoamericanos y del Caribe* 38: 83–98.

Silverman, Marilyn. 1979. "Dependency, Mediation, and Class Formation in Rural Guyana." *American Ethnologist* 6, no. 3: 466–90.

Silverman, Marilyn. 1980. *Rich People and Rice: Factional Politics in Rural Guyana.* Leiden: Brill.

Simpson, George. E. 1980. *Religious Cults of the Caribbean: Trinidad, Jamaica, and Haiti.* Caribbean Monograph Series No. 15. Rio Piedras: Institute of Caribbean Studies, University of Puerto Rico.

Smith, Michael G. 1962. "History and Social Anthropology." *Journal of the Royal Anthropological Institute of Great Britain and Ireland* 92: 73–85.

Smith, Michael G. 1965. *The Plural Society in the British West Indies.* Berkeley: University of California Press.

Smith, Michael G. 1983. "Robotham's Ideology and Pluralism." *Social and Economic Studies* 32: 103–39.

Smith, Michael G. 1984a. "Comment on Austin's 'Culture and Ideology in the English-Speaking Caribbean.'" *American Ethnologist* 11, no. 1: 183–85.

Smith, Michael G. 1984b. *Culture, Race and Class in the Commonwealth Caribbean.* Mona, Jamaica: School of Continuing Studies, University of the West Indies.

Smith, Michael G. 1987. "Pluralism: Comments on an Ideological Analysis." *Social and Economic Studies* 36, no. 4: 157–91.

Smith, Raymond T. 1956. *The Negro Family in British Guiana.* London: Routledge and Kegan Paul.

Smith, Raymond T. 1970. "Social Stratification in the Caribbean." In *Essays in Comparative Stratification*, edited by Leonard Plotnicov and Arthur Tuden, 43–76. Pittsburgh, PA: University of Pittsburgh Press.

Smith, Raymond T. 1971. "Culture and Social Structure in the Caribbean." In *Peoples and Cultures of the Caribbean: An Anthropological Reader*, edited by Michael Horowitz, 448–75. Garden City, NY: The Natural History Press.

Smith, Raymond T. 1973. "The Matrifocal Family." In *The Character of Kinship*, edited by Jack Goody, 121–44. Cambridge: Cambridge University Press.

Smith, Raymond T. 1978. "The Family in the Modern World System: Some Observations from the Caribbean." *Journal of Family History* 3: 337–60.

Smith, Raymond T. 1982a. "Family, Social Change and Social Policy in the West Indies." *Nieuwe West-Indische Gids/New West Indian Guide* 56, nos. 3–4: 111–42.

Smith, Raymond T. 1982b. "Race and Class in the Post-emancipation Caribbean." In *Racism and Colonialism*, edited by Robert Ross, 93–119. The Hague: Martinus Nijhoff.

Smith, Raymond T. 1987. "Hierarchy and the Dual Marriage System in West Indian Society." In *Gender and Kinship: Essays toward a Unified Analysis*, edited by Jane F. Collier and Sylvia J. Yanagisako, 163–96. Stanford, CA: Stanford University Press.

Smith, Raymond T. 1988. *Kinship and Class in the West Indies*. New York: Cambridge University Press.

Smith, Raymond T. 1992. "Race, Class, and Gender in the Transition to Freedom." In *The Meaning of Freedom: Economics, Politics, and Culture after Slavery*, edited by Frank McGlynn and Seymour Drescher, 257–90. Pittsburgh, PA: University of Pittsburgh Press.

Social and Economic Studies. 1986a. 35, no. 2. Special Issue: Women in the Caribbean, Pt. 1.

Social and Economic Studies. 1986b. 35, no. 3. Special Issue: Women in the Caribbean, Pt. 2.

Stephen, Henri J. M. 1985. *Winti: Afro-Surinaamse religiee en magische rituelen in Suriname en Nederland*. Amsterdam: Karnak.

Steward, Julian, et al. 1956. *The People of Puerto Rico: A Study in Social Anthropology*. Urbana: University of Illinois Press.

Stubbs, Jeans. 1988. "Gender Constructs of Labour in Prerevolutionary Cuban Tobacco." *Social and Economic Studies* 37, nos. 1–2: 241–69.

Sutton, Constance, and Susan Makiesky-Barrow. 1981. "Social Inequality and Sexual Status in Barbados." In *The Black Woman Cross-Culturally*, edited by Filomina C. Steady, 469–98. Cambridge, MA: Schenkman.

Taylor, Douglas. 1946. "Kinship and Social Structure of the Island Caribbean." *Southwestern Journal of Anthropology* 2, no. 2: 180–212.

Thoden van Velzen, Hendrik Ulbo E., and Wilhelmina van Wetering. 1988. *The Great Father and the Danger: Religious Cults, Material Forces, and Collective Fantasies in the World of the Surinamese Maroons*. Dordrecht, Netherlands: Foris Publications.

Thomas-Hope, Elizabeth M., ed. 1982. *Perspectives on Caribbean Regional Identity*. Liverpool: Center for Latin American Studies, University of Liverpool.

Trouillot, Michel-Rolph. 1982. "Motion in the System: Coffee, Color, and Slavery in Eighteenth-Century Saint-Domingue." *Review (Fernand Braudel Center)* 5, no. 3: 331–88.

Trouillot, Michel-Rolph. 1983. "The Production of Spatial Configurations: A Caribbean Case." *Nieuwe West-Indische Gids/New West Indian Guide* 57, nos. 3–4: 215–29.

Trouillot, Michel-Rolph. 1984. "Labour and Emancipation in Dominica: Contribution to a Debate." *Caribbean Quarterly* 30, nos. 3–4: 73–84.

Trouillot, Michel-Rolph. 1988. *Peasants and Capital: Dominica in the World Economy*. Baltimore, MD: Johns Hopkins University Press.

Trouillot, Michel-Rolph. 1989. "Discourses of Rule and the Acknowledgment of the Peasantry in Dominica, W.I., 1838–1928." *American Ethnologist* 16, no. 4: 704–18.

Trouillot, Michel-Rolph. 1990a. "Good Day, Columbus: Silences, Power and Public History (1492–1992)." *Public Culture* 3, no. 1: 1–24.

Trouillot, Michel-Rolph. 1990b. *Haiti: State against Nation; The Origins and Legacy of Duvalierism*. New York: Monthly Review Press.

Trouillot, Michel-Rolph. 1990c. "The Odd and Ordinary: Haiti, the Caribbean, and the World." *Cimarrón: New Perspectives on the Caribbean* 2, no. 3: 3–12.

Trouillot, Michel-Rolph. 1991. "Anthropology and the Savage Slot: The Poetics and Politics of Otherness." In *Recapturing Anthropology: Working in the Present*, edited by Richard G. Fox, 17–44. Santa Fe, NM: School of American Research Press.

Trouillot, Michel-Rolph. 1992. "The Inconvenience of Freedom: Free People of Color and the Aftermath of Slavery in Dominica and Saint-Domingue/Haiti." In *The Meaning of Freedom: Economics, Politics, and Culture after Slavery*, edited by Frank McGlynn and Seymour Drescher, 147–82. Pittsburgh, PA: University of Pittsburgh Press.

Vega, Bernardo, ed. 1981. *Ensayos sobre cultura dominicana*. Santo Domingo: Fundacíon cultural dominicana and Meseo del hombre dominicano.

Warner, Keith. Q. 1982. *Kaiso! The Trinidad Calypso: A Study of the Calypso as Oral Literature*. Washington, DC: Three Continents Press.

Watts, David. 1987. *The West Indies: Patterns of Development, Culture and Environmental Change since 1492*. Cambridge: Cambridge University Press.

Whitten, Norman E., and John F. Szwed, ed. 1970. *Afro-American Anthropology: Contemporary Perspectives*. New York: Free Press.

Williams, Brackette F. 1989. "A Class Act: Anthropology and the Race to Nation across Ethnic Terrain." *Annual Review of Anthropology* 18: 401–44.

Williams, Brackette F. 1991. *Stains on My Name, War in My Veins: Guyana and the Politics of Cultural Struggle*. Durham, NC: Duke University Press.

Wilson, Peter J. 1969. "Reputation and Respectability: A Suggestion for Caribbean Ethnology." *Man* 4: 70–84.

Wilson, Peter J. 1973. *Crab Antics: The Social Anthropology of English-Speaking Negro Societies of the Caribbean*. New Haven, CT: Yale University Press.

Wolf, Eric. 1982. *Europe and the People without History*. Berkeley: University of California Press.

Wolf, Eric. 1990. "Facing Power: Old Insights, New Questions." *American Anthropologist* 92, no. 3: 586–96.

Woodson, Drexel G. 1990. "Tout Mounn se Mounn, Men tout Mounn pa Menm: Sociocultural Aspects of Land Tenure and Marketing in a Northern Haitian Locality." PhD diss., University of Chicago.

Yamaguchi, Masao, and Masao Naito, eds. 1987. *Social and Festive Space in the Caribbean*. Tokyo: Institute for the Study of Languages and Cultures of Asia and Africa, Tokyo University of Foreign Studies.

CHAPTER 7

Culture on the Edges

Creolization in the Plantation Context

Le lieu est incontournable.

ÉDOUARD GLISSANT

Creolization is a miracle begging for analysis. Because it first occurred against all odds, between the jaws of brute and absolute power, no explanation seems to do justice to the very wonder that it happened at all. Understandably, the study of creole cultures and languages has always left room for the analyst's astonishment. Theories of creolization or of creole societies, assessments of what it means to be "creole" in turn, are still very much affected by the ideological and political sensibilities of the observers (Bolland 1992; Le Brun 1996).

It may not be possible or even meritorious to get rid of these sensibilities, but the knowledge of creolization can benefit from a more ethnographic approach that takes into account the concrete contexts within which cultures developed in the Americas. The plantation-society, the plural-society and the creole-society models—and even Bolland's (1992) "dialectical" approach—all seize creolization as a totality, thus one level too removed from the concrete circumstances faced by the individuals engaged in the process. All these models invoke history; some even use it at times. Yet the historical conditions of cultural production rarely become a fundamental and necessary part of the descriptions or analyses that these models generate. Calls for a more refined look at historical particulars (e.g., Mintz 1971; Mintz and Price 1992) remain unheeded. Worse, current apologists for *créolité* (e.g., Bernabé, Chamoiseau, and Confiant 1989) pay even less attention to the historical record than their predecessors in cultural nationalism, perhaps because the historiography of slavery is much weaker in French than in Dutch, or especially, English.

This article, which draws primarily from the experience of Afro-Caribbean peoples, tries to give due credit to the creativity that Africans and their descendants demonstrated right from the beginning of plantation slavery. However, praise for the creativity of Afro-Caribbeans may mask the struggles that are also inherent in creolization unless we take the analysis one step closer to changing historical contexts. From a wide range of changing historical circumstances I abstract three contexts as key heuristic devices: a plantation context; an enclave context; and a modernist context. I then return to the plantation context to illustrate the many ways in which such a framework may improve our knowledge of creolization.

THE AFRO-AMERICAN MIRACLE

From the family plots of the Jamaican hinterland, the Afro-religions of Brazil and Cuba, or the jazz music of Louisiana to the vitality of Haitian painting and music or the historical awareness of Suriname's maroons, manifestations of Afro-American cultures appear to us as the product of a repeated miracle. For those of us who keep in mind their conditions of emergence and growth, the very existence of cultural practices associated with African slaves and their descendants in the Americas is a continuing puzzle. Afro-American cultures were born against all odds. Even if we define culture in the restricted sense of artistic and intellectual production ultimately sanctioned by power (what some anthropologists call "high culture"), the Antilles alone suffice as exemplars of the repeated wonder: in relation to their size, the Caribbean islands have given birth to an impressive array of individuals who left their intellectual marks on the international scene. But the real achievement is, of course, that of the anonymous men and women who have woven, along the centuries, in spite of slavery and other forms of domination, the cultural patterns upon which rest the highly individualized performances of the intellectuals.

Afro-Caribbean cultures came to life unexpectedly, unforeseen developments of an agenda set in Europe, by Europe, and for Europe. Caribbean territories have experienced Western European influence longer than any other area outside of Europe itself. They are territories that Europe claimed to shape to fit its particular goals, territories through which Europeans moved as if they were empty lands. And indeed, they were emptied, in so far as the Native population had been wiped out without even the dubious privilege of slow death on a reservation. Almost everything that we now associate with the Caribbean—from sugarcane, coffee, mangoes, donkeys, and coconuts, to the people themselves, whether African or Asian in origin—was brought there as part of the European conquest.

Cultural concerns did not figure among European priorities during most of the conquest. For more than a century, the search for gold and the rivalries it provoked obliterated most other issues. Then, from the seventeenth century on, European attention slowly turned to the production of agricultural commodities in the tropical areas of the mainland and in the Antilles. Cultural considerations entered into the design of plantation America, but only as prerequisites of political and economic domination, as corollaries of the plantation system. Thus, although the Afro-Caribbean world came to life on the plantation and, in part, because of the plantation, Afro-Caribbean cultural practices emerged against the expectations and wishes of plantation owners and their European patrons. They were not meant to exist.

Because Afro-Caribbean cultures were not meant to exist, many observers came to believe that they did not exist, in spite of all evidence to the contrary. Up to the second part of this century, most observers and many speakers viewed the creole languages of the Caribbean as burlesque versions of European tongues, "français petit nègre," "patois," "broken English," unworthy of serious attention from linguists and writers.

Interestingly, however, Caribbean cultural practices never became exactly what Europeans planners and owners might have expected. From the very beginnings of slavery, it was clear that the Africans and their descendants were shaping modes of behavior, patterns of thought and their expression. Caribbean languages provide good examples of this creativity. Africans brought to the Caribbean during the slave trade spoke a wide variety of African languages. Yet, in many circumstances, which we have yet to specify, they were also forced to draw from the vernacular of their respective masters. That itself is not surprising. More interesting is the fact that, once taken over by the slaves and their descendants, European languages did not remain the same. They acquired sounds, morphological and syntactic patterns unknown in Europe. More important, they were shaped to express the joys, pains and reflections of hundreds of thousands of humans. In one word, they were creolized.[1]

For a number of reasons, these creole languages became the first products of the creolization process to attract the attention of scholars.[2] First, creole languages were obvious. The features that demarcated them from European vernaculars could not be denied (Magens 1770). On the contrary, these features had to be acknowledged if only for the purpose of communication. Even when the linguistic status of creoles was denigrated, such denigration also reinforced the acknowledgment that they were different. Second, a vibrant tradition in the observation of non-Western languages existed in Europe since at least the seventeenth century. Lastly, language was politically safe—or thought to be so. It was thought to be amenable to study without long encounters with a mass of natives. It was one of the few products of creolization least likely to engage the scholar in immediate political controversies about the people who had been creolized.

Controversies there were, however, especially on the matter of origins. Here also, wonderment played its role. Since the early nineteenth century, analysts felt the need to explain the puzzle of the emergence of creole languages, to ponder the significance of their existence (Gilbert 1986). This obsession with origins, still central to creole linguistics (Alleyne 1980; Muysken and Smith 1986), gave rise to two methodological tendencies.

First, since actual slave speech was—for all practical purposes—inaccessible, creolists had to infer the past from the present. Current Caribbean speech or changing patterns in more recent non-Caribbean creoles supposedly documented what must have happened in some undetermined pan-Caribbean past. Second, since the ultimate purpose of the exercise was, more often than not, to explain or dissipate the wonder of creole emergence, creolists tended to use one exclusive all-encompassing theory after another. Either all creoles had evolved from a singular source, most probably a Portuguese pidgin (monogenesis theory); or all followed the same "West African" grammatical principles (substratum theory); or again the same genetically programmed elementary structures (bioprogram theory).

From an epistemological and methodological viewpoint, the striking similarity between these theories is their exclusiveness. Their adherents, past and present, right or wrong, tend to be virulently monocausal. In the words of Claire Lefebvre (1986, 282), creolists "[try] to explain everything the same way at the same time." Fidelity to a unique explanation in turn tended to preclude detailed examination of changing historical contexts in spite of Sidney Mintz's (1971) crucial demonstration at the first international conference on creole languages—in Mona in 1968—that the study of linguistic change had to take into account "the sociohistorical background" of creolization. Available documents were not used to their full potential. Known historical facts, periodization, empirical questions of space and time, demography and social norms, took secondary positions within pre-developed schemes. Even when creole linguistics focused on the past, even though it emphasized the process of linguistic change, it generally ignored the sociohistorical process. History was always evoked, often used, yet rarely treated in its complexities.

Since the mid-1980s, in part in response to Derek Bickerton's bioprogram hypothesis, in part because of the influence of non-Caribbean creolists (e.g., Romaine 1988; Sankoff 1980; and Siegel 1987), linguists are increasingly aware of the historical complexities involved in Afro-Caribbean creolization. The distance between two hallmark conferences (Hymes 1971; and Muysken and Smith 1986) reveals a tremendous growth in historical sophistication between the late 1960s and the mid-1980s. However, such sophistication (e.g., Cérol 1992; Gilbert 1986; Lefebvre 1986; and Rickford 1986, 1987) has yet to inform fully the study of specific linguistic changes.

The linguistic stalemate is reinforced by the lack of exchange between linguists and nonlinguists and by the weaknesses of cultural theories of creolization. First, students of sociocultural history have yet to provide as detailed answers as the more sophisticated linguists have questions. Moreover, in recent years, grand pronouncements by some cultural and literary critics have increased the gap between many linguists' empirically-oriented inquiries and sociocultural theories of creolization. For instance, the repeated announcement that the world is now in—or moving toward—a state of hybridity or creolization (e.g., Bernabé, Chamoiseau, and Confiant 1989; Hannerz 1987, 1992) is too sweeping to reinforce a dialogue between the cultural theorists who make such statements and historical linguists interested into knowing who actually taught what to whom and when in particular Caribbean territories (e.g., Rickford 1986, 1987; and Cérol 1992). On the contrary, such sweeping statements reinforce, perhaps inadvertently, the proclivity to treat creolization as a totality, thereby reinforcing the worst tendencies of the sociocultural theorists.

Indeed, both the tendency to infer the past from the present and the predilection for all-encompassing explanations, which together characterize creole linguistics, reappear in sociocultural studies of creolization with some noteworthy differences. First, the technical apparatus of creole linguistics could not be transferred to studies of creolization outside of language. Whereas linguists generally agree on micro-methodologies and definitions (e.g., what noun phrases are and how to break them down), social scientists and cultural theorists do not have this fundamental agreement on a technical apparatus. Thus, second, nonlinguist students of creolization find themselves in the awkward situation of having fewer tools (at least apparently) to do yet a larger job. Sociocultural life is an object of study admittedly more fluid and harder to delimit than language, which it encompasses. Without a common technical apparatus, the theoretical claims made by students of sociocultural creolization are even less controllable than those of the linguists. Or, to put it differently, the distance between these claims and the organization of the facts into a coherent object of study is greater than in linguistics. Faced with the wonder of creolization and the need to explain a cultural emergence that seems to defy their implicit assumptions about culture, social scientists used strokes as broad as those of the linguists but on a greater range of topics. The range of topics has actually increased with time. With methodological issues further relegated to the back burner, current studies of creolization return, in a cycle, to the wonder of origins with the added value of the ideologies of the day.

The increased relevance of ideology is understandable. First, social scientists are increasingly aware that creolization still goes on. Even though analysts are not much closer to an agreement in defining creolization as an object of study than they were, say, in the 1950s, they have both the increased feeling of being witness to the ongoing wonder and the conviction that it matters how they explain it. Second, indeed, the ongoing denigration of many Afro-American populations continues to incite praise for the "creoleness" that they are said to typify (Bernabé, Chamoiseau, and Confiant 1989). Third, now that globalization and hybridity have become suspiciously fashionable (Harvey 1995; Williams 1995)—some would say too fashionable—the creolization process in the Afro-Americas appears, in retrospect, as an early state of grace only now accessible to the rest of humanity (Gilroy 1993; Hannerz 1992). The cultural idealism that now so happily masks increased inequalities worldwide further fuels the ahistorical tendencies of creolization studies (di Leonardo 1997). Indeed, if there is a difference between the créolité movement of the 1990s and predecessors such as Haitian *indigénisme* of the 1930s (Trouillot 1993) and the Jamaican creole-society school of the 1950s and 1960s (Bolland 1992), it is the increased persistence to further divorce the wonder of creolization from the very history that made it possible. As social theory becomes more discourse-oriented, the distance between data and claims in debates about creolization and créolité increases. Historical circumstances fall further into a hazy back-ground of ideological preferences.

THE CONTEXTS OF CREOLIZATION

Historical circumstances are what I would like to emphasize here: creoliza-tion cannot be understood outside of the various contexts within which it occurred.

Many features shaped such contexts. First among these was the regimen-tation of the populations involved, including their regimentation as labor force. The nature and degree of such regimentation necessarily skewed the daily expressions of cultural creativity. In the second half of the eighteenth century, the kind of materials needed, available, and used to "produce cul-ture" were quite different for the member of a cane-field gang in Barbados than for an enslaved coffee grower in Dominica or in Saint-Domingue. Reg-imentation, including labor regimentation, crystallized such differences. Differences in labor regimes in turn, proceeded from the crops involved, but also from the number of years a particular crop had been cultivated in a territory (Berlin and Morgan 1993; Higman 1984). Regimentation, so con-strued, thus centers around labor but includes all the factors that limited daily activities of the laboring populations both before and after slavery.

Second, the frequency and nature of outside contact—in and out mi-grations, communications, the ease or difficulty of individual movement—also helped to define the context of creolization. Clearly, creolization must have proceeded differently in contexts marked by constant influx of enslaved Africans than in situations where such influx was negligible. Third, creoliza-tion cannot be understood without some attention to its participants as sub-jects of history. Édouard Glissant suggests that creolization implies some awareness of heterogeneity, the impossibility of denying mixed origins (Glissant 1996). But surely, that awareness includes both an implicit sense of cultural ideals—what Mintz (1971) calls target cultures—and an implicit attentiveness to facts of power on the ground, which Glissant himself tends to neglect. Cultural ideals and power relations, including actors' under-standings and interpretations of the stakes and forces available to reach their self-defined goals, fundamentally shape the context of creolization.

A short example may make the point. We can assume that to practice what is now known as Haitian vodou is to engage knowingly or not in creolization. Yet even if we assume an unchanging content to vodou—a dubious assumption indeed—we must concede that what it meant to serve the gods changed in space and in time. Imagine first, the negotiations, trials, and tactics necessary for African-born slaves just to set a ritual in colonial Saint-Domingue: how to do it away from the masters' ears; whom to include and on what grounds; which gods to evoke or invoke. Imagine, then, the relative freedom of association and the related freedom of choice in the isolated mountains of independent Haiti, away from memories of both Europe and Africa before the growth of the Catholic clergy at the end of the nineteenth century. Imagine, in turn, the fears unleashed by the US occupation of 1915–34 and renewed by the repressive campaigns of the 1930s and 1940s. Today, the change is monumental: the holders of state power in Haiti officially recognize vodou as a religion. Even before that recognition, vodou had become truly transnational; some of its canonical rituals are routinely held in Cuba's Oriente or in Brooklyn, New York. Not all its practitioners are Haitian. Some are white North Americans. Yet the poverty of the Haitian countryside has also undermined vodou at its base, limiting its ritual possibilities among the peasantry (Murray 1977). Through-out all this, nevertheless, vodou has figured and continues to figure as a key manifestation of Haitian culture, an emblem of its successful creolization. There is no way to follow that thread of continuities and breaks without evaluating these changing contexts.

In short, we need a framework to approach the changing contexts of creolization. Using time, space, and power relations as my main markers, I suggest three such contexts for the study of creolization: (a) a plantation context; (b) an enclave context; (c) a modernist context.

Each of these contexts emphasizes, in turn, one of the factors high-lighted earlier. The regimentation of populations is the defining moment of the plantation context. The frequency and nature of outside contact help to distinguish the enclave context. The awareness of heterogeneity and power are inherent in the context of modernity. Since all three factors are always relevant, it follows that these contexts are heuristic devices. Further, in the case of the Spanish Caribbean, it may be useful to devise a preplantation context that would help to account for the markedly different base and outcome of the creolization process there.

At any rate, the contexts described here are not meant to duplicate real life situations, but they may help us understand such situations by focus-ing attention on "the specific sorts of community settings within which groups became further differentiated or intermixed" (Mintz 1971, 481). They do not delineate fixed periods: often they overlapped in historical time within the same territory. What I hope they do best is to sketch with broad strokes the notably different historical dynamics of creolization as a cultural process so as to bring forward the particulars of the populations involved.

By *plantation context*, I have in mind situations defined primarily by plantation slavery both during and immediately after the centuries of legal enslavement. Most enslaved Africans and their immediate descendants throughout the Americas engaged in creolization within a plantation context until—and at times way into—the second half of the nineteenth century.

By *enclave context*, I mean situations marked by the relative autonomy and isolation of the populations under study. Early maroon societies from St. Vincent to Suriname, the Haitian peasantry from 1804 to the 1880s, highland villagers in the Windward Islands up to the first decades of this century creolized mainly within such enclaves.

The *modernist context* became dominant only with the decline of the plantation. I do not mean by this that modernity itself came late to the Caribbean or is a postplantation phenomenon. On the contrary, the Caribbean was in many ways as modern as Europe by the first quarter of the seventeenth century, especially because of the plantation. Indeed, creolization itself is a modern phenomenon if only because it implies the awareness and even the expectation of cultural differences (Thompson 1975; see also Glissant 1996). Further, frequency and ease of contact with the outside world marked the daily routine of many urban slaves, especially in the port cities where news of other territories circulated to an extent we have yet to appreciate (Scott 1986).

My modernist context combines elements of both modernity and modernization. It implies a different kind of technical and institutional support to creolization. It implies also a sense of global history and the awareness of progress—or backwardness—which are part of modernity, and which spread quite unevenly among Caribbean populations from early conquest until the second third of the twentieth century. The degree to which the awareness of both target cultures and facts of power become explicit and voiced and the degree to which organic intellectuals harness institutional and technical support for cultural practices help define a modernist context.[3]

These three contexts bring us closer to actual situations, yet we need to specify them further by way of a number of changing parameters. The relative proportion of populations of diverse origins, including individuals of mixed descent (see Mintz 1971); the impact of prior moments of creolization, including the spread of institutions that solidified that creolization; and the extent of social differentiation are among such parameters. Their relevance will vary with the case under study, but the point is precisely to use these three contexts as starting points and to refine them with the relevant particulars so as to get closer to actual situations.

Thus the scheme outlined here puts on hold most theories of creolization and creole societies for trying to do too much, too fast. In that sense, I am not proposing an alternative model. Rather, I am suggesting that we have not thought enough about what went on in specific places and times to produce a framework sensitive enough to time, place, and power. I now turn to the plantation context to illustrate the complexities that we need to address.

THE PLANTATION AS CULTURAL MATRIX

During the long centuries of the slave trade, Africa was no more static or culturally unified than Europe was at the time. We simply do not know enough of African variations and change. Ignorance and ethnocentrism may explain the general tendency to acknowledge differences among Europeans and ignore them when referring to Africans. Second, whereas European residents of particular territories usually came from similar—when not the same—milieux, enslaved Africans did not necessarily end up among tribal fellows. Further, the Middle Passage had cut the African-born slaves from their roots, without the possibility, open to many Europeans, of maintaining regular contact with their original milieu. Thus, although they kept their memories, they could not reproduce the societies whence they came.

Only since the 1980s have we begun to acknowledge the restrictions imposed by the trade and plantation slavery on African cultural transfers, but the achievement seems even more spectacular against this limiting background. As Sidney Mintz and Richard Price (1992, 10) argue in the pathbreaking essay that launched this new awareness: given the conditions of their passage, the enslaved "were not able to transfer the human complement of their traditional institutions to the New World. Members of tribal groups of differing status, yes; but different status systems, no. Priests and priestesses, yes; but priesthoods and temples, no. Princes and princesses, yes; but courts and monarchies, no."

Limitations applied as much to the collective as to individuals. Surely, no African slave came to the Caribbean carrying a drum from the motherland. But the memory of African music lingered long enough to catch up with the memory of drum making; and Afro-Caribbeans used their new environment to create drums and music that were close to those of Africa yet distinctively Caribbean. Likewise their dances may have been influenced by the minuets and waltzes they learned to play sometimes for their European masters, but their own Sunday performances were not likely to be minuets and waltzes—though some musicologists may rightfully argue that these were also influenced by minuets and waltzes. In short, Africans and their descendants had to create, so to speak, a new cultural world, with elements gathered from the many African cultures they came from and the European cultures of those who dominated them.

How was such a process of selective creation and cultural struggle—in one word, creolization—possible among the enslaved? How could Africans and Afro-Americans forge entirely new cultures out of the remnants of Old World values and patterns, both African and European? How did they come to dominate the process of cultural formation in societies such as those of the Caribbean where they were kept by daily terrorism at the bottom of the sociopolitical ladder?

Sidney Mintz and Richard Price (1992, 9–10) suggest that the West African cultural heritage is to be found mainly in unconscious, underlying "grammatical" principles: cognitive orientations, attitudes, expectations common to the diverse communities whence most of the enslaved came. They argue that these underlying principles ordered the process of creolization by making certain choices more appealing or more significant than other possible ones.

This argument needs to be refined in light of more sustained research on the institutional impact of African ethnicity on slave practices in specific territories. In other words, the underlying principles that Mintz and Price highlight had to work through tensions among Africans in order to produce meaningful practices, and we need to know how and when they did so. More important, however a modus vivendi on cultural grammar was obtained among slaves, shared principles—old and new—had to survive the European exercise of power. How did they do so? When and how were they given space and time to breathe and to breed? How did they survive and reproduce themselves enough to generate new institutions?

Answers to these questions, tentative as they may be, require that we turn to the plantation. Afro-American slavery was plantation slavery. The plantation was the institution around which the system was built; it provided the model after which were shaped the actual units on which slaves labored. But to phrase it this way is already to suggest that the word *plantation* covers in fact different types or realities that we may want to keep separate even if for heuristic purposes: the institution itself, in the restricted sense of a type of agricultural enterprise; the socioeconomic and political system built upon it (in this particular case, plantation slavery); and the actual units of production modeled after this ideal type.

As a form of labor organization, the plantation is an agricultural enterprise, distinguished by its massive use of coerced or semicoerced labor, producing agricultural commodities for markets situated outside of the economy within which the plantation itself operates. One of the better treatments of the type comes from sociologist Edgar T. Thompson (1935). Thompson suggests that, as a unit of production, the plantation is an economic institution, an agricultural unit operating with an industrial dynamic. It is also, in his view, a settlement institution, in the sense that it arranges peoples in a "new" territory; and a political institution, inasmuch as it operates as a small state, with an authoritarian structure. Plantation owners claim a monopoly of violence, control over the life of the people who inhabit the plantation. The plantation is, finally, a cultural institution. It tends to generate a distinguishable way of life for owners and workers alike, but it also divides them along racial and ethnic lines. It is a race-making institution (Thompson 1935, 31–38, 115–17).

Needless to say that few if any actual plantations ever exactly matched the prototype. Whether inferred or planned, social models are peculiar kinds of abstraction, the dual products of the typological exercise that projects them and the historical units through which they are actualized. In other words, the plantation, as such, never existed historically, not even in the Americas of slavery. Rather, thousands of plantations did, that tried to conform to the ideal type, but always within the limitations imposed by specific circumstances. This is an obvious enough assertion; but it implies that in almost every instance there were varying limits to economic efficiency, to the organization of settlement, to planters' political power, or to the cultural apartheid premised in the organization of labor. The very actualization of the institution, whether or not premised on the planter's pursuit of the ideal type, allowed the slaves much more room to maneuver than implied by the type itself.

Latitude came also from elsewhere and perhaps in more important ways. Units of production never operate alone. As units of production serving distant markets within the strict order of slavery, the plantations of the Americas felt even more the pressures of the system. Indeed, we can conceptualize an inherent tension between plantation slavery as a system and the actual units of production. This is not to suggest that the units and the system belong to the same order of things; but the fact that the system is a construct does not make it any less real than actual estates. It had its requirements, its logic; but the very fact that this logic and these requirements were not of the same kind as the daily exigencies that masters and overseers had to face within individual units of production created an inherent tension.

Reactions to *marronage* provide us with a good entry point in this world of tensions and broken lines. In principle, throughout the Americas, slaves were forbidden to leave the plantations without authorization, and infractions to this code were punished. On the ground, however, planters' attitudes varied, according to the particulars of the case at hand: the time of the infraction, its mode of discovery, the climate of the colony, the individual slave involved, or indeed the personality of the owner or overseer. More important, beyond these variations, planters often acknowledged a difference between desertions intended to be final and temporary absences. The French even distinguished them by name, coining the former *grand marronage* as opposed to the more benign forms of *petit marronage*. Throughout the Americas, whereas system and practice tended to overlap in cases of the first kind, planters sometimes closed their eyes on instances of petit marronage, when slaves ran away to visit relatives, to take part in certain rituals, or sometimes even to make a symbolic gesture of protest.

This indulgence did not necessarily come from kindness. Its deepest roots were systemic: planters knew that the code was not always enforceable, that not all instances of unauthorized absence could be punished without encroaching on the working routine of their particular plantation. One suspects that slaves came to the same realization and took repeated risks at manipulating this systemic fissure, often to their detriment, but as often perhaps with the expected results. Communication across plantations, for instance, must have depended on such "illegal" absences as much as on the "free" time officially allotted by the planters. And as slaves repeated such manipulations, on the one hand acknowledging the system, on the other circumventing its actualization in carefully chosen instances, they solidified the *détour*, the social time and space that they controlled on the edges of the plantations.

Thus, even though grand marronage stands as a privileged example of Afro-American resistance under slavery, maroon societies are better seized within what I call the enclave context (Price 1979). Petit marronage, in turn, stands as a more accurate model for the kind of behavior through which most slaves established the institutional continuity of creole patterns within the plantation context. For a majority of enslaved Africans and Afro-Americans, prior to the mid-nineteenth century, creolization did not happen away from the plantation system, but within it.[4]

I suggest that this creation was possible because slaves found a most fertile ground in the interstices of the system, in the latitude provided by the inherent contradictions between that system and specific plantations, historically situated. Afro-Caribbean cultural practices developed within the plantation system, but on the margins of the units through which the ideal type was actualized. They were born within the plantation but on the edges of particular plantations. The tensions between the logic of the system and the daily life of actual estates provided a context full of minute opportunities for initiatives among the enslaved. We need to look closely at the mechanisms by which slaves seized upon these contradictions and repeatedly turned latent opportunities to their advantage, further stretching the time and space that they controlled. But even before further empirical research on the so-called slave sector illuminates these mechanisms, we can assess the opportunities. I will give one more example of an opportunity seized upon by the slaves, one quite different from planters' attitudes to petit marronage, but which ultimately makes the same point.

In many Caribbean societies, slaves were allowed by their masters to grow their own food and, at times, to sell portions of what they harvested. This was a fundamental contradiction within the plantation system. The practice of allowing slaves to cultivate their own gardens whenever they were not working on plantation crops emerged because particular planters wanted to save money, given the high cost of imported food (see Mintz 1978; Trouillot 1988). Planters were not in the business of feeding slaves. The name of the game was profit; and it was to enhance their profits that many planters passed on to the slaves the responsibility of feeding themselves. Indeed, the extent and viability of slave provision grounds depended on a series of factors operating within the unit of production and on the impact of these factors on the planter's cost accounting. Steep and broken terrain, less fertile lands not used for the production of plantation staples, the flexibility of work regimen, all worked to reinforce the use of provision grounds within a unit. Within a given territory so did the unavailability of cash, and the availability and acclimation of imported plants and animals.

Eventually however, these practices, which first emerged because they provided concrete advantages to particular owners, went against the logic of the plantation system itself. Provision grounds provided both time and space that were both within the order dictated by the plantation and yet detached from it. They provided a space quite distinct from the plantation fields congested with sugarcane, coffee, and cotton. Space where one learned to cherish root crops, plantains, and bananas; space to raise and roast a pig, to run after a goat, or to barbecue a chicken; space to bury the loved ones who passed away, to worship the ancestors, and to invent new gods when the old ones were forgotten.

Time used on the provision grounds was also slave-controlled time to a large extent. It was time to develop new practices of labor cooperation, reminiscent of—yet different from—African models of work. Time to talk across the fences to a passing neighbor. Time to cross the fences themselves and fish in the adjacent rivers. It was time to create culture knowingly or unknowingly. Time to mark the work tempo with old songs. Time to learn rhythm while working and to enjoy both the rhythm and the work. Time to create new songs when the old ones faded way. Time to take care of the needs of the family. Time to meet a mate. Time to teach children how to climb a tree. Time indeed to develop modes of thought and codes of behavior that were to survive plantation slavery itself.[5]

Such survival, in turn, depended on the consolidation of institutions. For instance, we know that in some colonies—Saint-Domingue, for instance—slaves sold part of their produce at urban markets. We can assume that the practice of producing, and especially producing for sale, involved a number of individual and economic decisions. Slaves not only had to engage in a cost-benefit analysis—as any petty producer would—but in a cost-benefit analysis that took into account their ideals (what and when to cultivate; how to profit; what to buy with the profit, for whom, and why). Such a culturally informed cost-benefit analysis, in turn, necessarily implied the distribution and consolidation of roles within the household, the distribution and consolidation or statuses across households. In short, practices of that kind—and there were many more we need to think about—influenced also the institutions that would survive slavery.

How they did so remains, of course, open to serious concrete investigation. Such investigation can only benefit from analyses that try to integrate the three contexts suggested here. As enclaves and plantations slowly gave way to populations that experienced creolization mainly in a modernist context, how did cultural content and, especially, patterns of accommodation, resistance, and struggle change? For instance, how did the transformation of target cultures accommodate the perception of past practices? We can already assume that here again historical particulars played their role. Contact between different populations within and across political boundaries, influx of newcomers, impact of prior creolization, political control, and social differentiation enter into the process. But my main point is that we need to rehistoricize creolization.

Creolization is a process rather than a totality. To enable us to seize it in its movement, I have suggested the use of three contexts as heuristic devices, bearing in mind that these contexts often overlapped in particular places and times. My longer exploration of the plantation context is meant as an illustration or the complexities we need to acknowledge at the very beginning. Ideally, the analysis would need to integrate the overlap of the three contexts in historically specific cases.[6] The point remains that we need to look at creolization as a process, constantly influenced not only by prior history but by the numerous factors that characterized the times, the territories, and the peoples to which it bears witness.

CONCLUSION: PLANTATION CODA

The provision grounds of slavery, the reluctant tolerance toward petit marronage, and the unequal ranking and treatment of slaves constitute only conspicuous examples of tension among many to be found in the plantation context. The general lesson remains the same. Cultural practices markedly Afro-American emerged, at least in part, because of the slaves' ability to use the contradictions inherent in the fundamentals of the system and the daily workings of specific plantations. Time and space matter enormously here—that is, social time and social space seized within the system and turned against it.

This ability to stretch margins and circumvent borderlines remains the most amazing aspect of Afro-American cultural practices. It encapsulates their inherent resistance. Afro-American cultures are cultures of combat in the strongest possible sense: they were born resisting. Otherwise they would not have existed at all. For they were not meant to exist. But the resistance they encapsulate is not best seized by the epics that typify cultural nationalist treatments of creolization. The heroism of the creolization process is first and foremost the heroism of anonymous men, women, and—too often forgotten—children going about the business of daily life. And for more than three centuries, such daily life was conditioned primarily by the plantation.

Afro-American cultural practices emerged on the edges of the plantations, gnawing at the logic of an imposed order and its daily manifestations of dominance. Filtering in the interstices of the system, they conquered each and every inch of cultural territory they now occupy. In that sense, the plantation was the primary cultural matrix of Afro-American populations. But it was so against the expectations of the masters. It was an imposed context, and quite a rigid one at that, an institution forced upon the slaves but one within which they managed their most formidable accomplishment, that of creating what has indeed become a New World.

NOTES

This article started as a contribution to the colloquium The Plantation System in the Americas, Louisiana State University, Baton Rouge, April 27–29, 1989. It was revised in 1996–97, mainly at the Center for Advanced Study in the Behavioral Sciences (CASBS), Stanford, California, and at Johns Hopkins University. I thank Édouard Glissant, who invited me to the Baton Rouge colloquium, and all the participants who commented on the original version. Thanks also to the National Science Foundation, which supported my fellowship at the CASBS, to Marie Espelencia Baptiste, and Niloofar Haeri for sharing their views on creolization. Haeri and A. James Arnold also commented on later versions.
Editors' Note: This chapter first appeared as "Culture on the Edges: Creolization in the Plantation Context," *Plantation Society in the Americas* 5, no. 1 (1998): 8–28.

1. The extent of linguistic creolization varied. In some cases, creolization led to the rise of entirely new languages spoken by the entire population, like Haitian Kreyòl, now the language of Haiti, or Lesser Antillean (also a French-based creole, common to Martinique, Guadeloupe, and to a lesser extent Dominica and St. Lucia). Sranan (Tongo) emerged in Suriname, Papiamento in Curaçao. In many of the former British territories, we witness a different phenomenon. The linguistic spectrum presents itself more like a continuum with the more creolized forms at one end and the forms closer to the European standard at the other.

2. Of course, sociohistorical studies of the Caribbean have dealt with creolization since colonial times (Lewis 1983), but the delineation of creolization and of its products as a specific object of scholarly research, and the subsequent

labeling of creolists as specialists of the field so defined, first happened in linguistics.

3. Late twentieth-century developments in linguistic ideology and speech practice in Haiti and the geographical and social expansion of both reggae music and Rastafarianism within and beyond Jamaica are two cases that may illustrate the point even briefly. The increased technical and institutional support to Haitian as a language—from its use in print and audiovisual media in Haiti and abroad to its official recognition as one of the two national languages—is part of a process of modernization. (This modernization is now obvious, but keep in mind that Napoleon's army issued proclamations in Kreyòl to the revolutionary slaves.) But these recent technical and institutional changes intertwine with modernity, with the recognition of indifference and the recognition of an identity that claims to be specifically Haitian. Similarly, reggae music and, by extension, Rastafarianism have benefited from the profound changes in both electronics and communication that have affected the music industry worldwide. But the opportunity that these changes offered had to be seized by artists, cultural nationalists, and local entrepreneurs quite aware of Jamaican modernity. In Jamaica and Haiti, organic intellectuals have integrated the knowledge that the world is now their context if not always their interlocutor.

4. Even the Haitian Revolution, which stands as the most significant act of resistance against slavery, does not actually fit the grand marronage model. To start with, there is no evidence of a continuous maroon community in the northern part of Saint-Domingue, where the revolution started. Rather, in part because the local topography prevented the establishment of permanent camps where fugitives could regroup, the slaves from that region could not escape the contradictions of the system through organized forms of grand marronage (Trouillot [1977] 2012). Indeed, our knowledge so far suggests that the original rebellion involved primarily slaves located on the plantations that were burned, even though some historians infer maroon participation. Further, there are indications that slave drivers and privileged slaves established the interplantation network of communication without which the widespread revolt that destroyed the northern plains and launched the revolution would have been impossible.

5. It is not at all surprising that when slavery ended, Caribbean slaves did the most to maintain access to their provision grounds. And almost everywhere after the end of slavery, planters unanimously condemned the former slaves' attachment to these provision grounds.

6. For instance, although a society such as eighteenth-century Saint-Domingue (between 1763 and 1789) was primarily a plantation society, one would need to examine both the impact of port cities, where creolization had a strong

modernist component, and the impact of Le Maniel's enclave and of coffee frontier areas, which operated as cultural enclaves on the creolization process. Given the location of these port cities and enclaves and the history of settlement (Debbasch 1979; Trouillot 1982), this immediately suggests that the research should eventually look at specific regions within the territory. In the 1770s, creolization around Jacmel—close to Le Maniel and close to new coffee areas—could not have worked the same way on the ground as in the northern plains.

REFERENCES

Alleyne, Mervyn C. 1980. *Comparative Afro-American: An Historical-Comparative Study of English-Based Afro-American Dialects of the New World*. Ann Arbor, MI: Karoma.

Berlin, Ira, and Philip D. Morgan, eds. 1993. *Cultivation and Culture: Labor and the Shaping of Slave Life in the Americas*. Charlottesville: University Press of Virginia.

Bernabé, Jean, Patrick Chamoiseau, and Raphaël Confiant. 1989. *Éloge de la créolité*. Paris: Gallimard and Presses Universitaires Créoles.

Bolland, O. Nigel. 1992. "Creolization and Creole Societies: A Cultural Nationalist View of Caribbean Social History." In *Intellectuals in the Twentieth-Century Caribbean*, edited by Alistair Hennessy, 50–79. London: Macmillan Caribbean.

Cérol, Marie-Josée. 1992. "What History Tells Us about the Development of Creole in Guadeloupe." *Nieuwe West-Indische Gids/New West Indian Guide* 66, nos. 1–2: 61–76.

Debbasch, Yvan. 1979. "Le Maniel: Further Notes." In *Maroon Societies: Rebel Slave Communities in the Americas*, edited by Richard Price, 143–48. Baltimore, MD: Johns Hopkins University Press.

di Leonardo, Micaela. 1997. "It's the Discourse, Stupid." Review of *The Magic of the State*, by Michael Taussig. *Nation*, March 17.

Gilbert, Glenn. 1986. "The Language Bioprogram Hypothesis: Déjà Vu?" In *Substrata versus Universal in Creole Genesis: Papers from the Amsterdam Creole Workshop, April 1985*, edited by Pieter Muysken and Norval Smith, 15–24. Amsterdam: John Benjamins.

Gilroy, Paul. 1993. *The Black Atlantic: Modernity and Double Consciousness*. Cambridge, MA: Harvard University Press.

Glissant, Édouard. 1996. *Introduction à une poétique du divers*. Paris: Gallimard.

Hannerz, Ulf. 1987. "The World in Creolization." *Africa: Journal of the International African Institute* 57, no. 4: 546–59.

Hannerz, Ulf. 1992. "The Global Ecumene as a Network of Networks." In *Conceptualizing Society*, edited by Adam Kuper, 34–56. London: Routledge.

Harvey, David. 1995. "Globalization in Question." *Rethinking Marxism* 8, no. 4: 1–17.

Higman, Barry W. 1984. *Slave Populations of the British Caribbean 1807–1834*. Baltimore, MD: Johns Hopkins University Press.

Hymes, Dell. 1971. *Pidginization and Creolization of Languages*. London: Cambridge University Press.

Le Brun, Annie. 1996. *Statue cou coupé*. Paris: Jean-Michel Place.

Lefebvre, Claire. 1986. "Relexification in Creole Genesis Revisited: The Case of Haitian Creole." In *Substrata versus Universals in Creole Genesis: Papers from the Amsterdam Creole Workshop: April 1985*, edited by Pieter Muysken and Norval Smith, 282. Amsterdam: John Benjamins.

Lewis, Gordon K. 1983. *Main Currents in Caribbean Thought: The Historical Evolution of Caribbean Society in Its Ideological Aspects, 1492–1900*. Baltimore, MD: Johns Hopkins University Press.

Magens, Joachim Melchior. 1770. *Grammatica over det creolske sprog: Som bruges paa de trende danske eilande, St. Croix, St. Thomas og St. Jans i America; Sammenskrevet og opsat af en paa St. Thomas jndföd mand*. Copenhagen: Trykt udi det Kongelige wäyenshusets bogtrkkerie, af Gerhard Giese Salikath.

Mintz, Sidney W. 1971. "The Socio-Historical Background to Pidginization and Creolization." In *Pidginization and Creolization of Languages*, edited by Dell Hymes, 481–96. London: Cambridge University Press.

Mintz, Sidney W. 1978. "Was the Plantation Slave a Proletarian?" *Review* 2, no. 1: 81–98.

Mintz, Sidney W., and Richard Price. 1992. *The Birth of an African-American Culture: An Anthropological Perspective*. Boston: Beacon Press.

Murray, Gerald F. 1997. "The Evolution of Haitian Peasant Land Tenure: A Case Study in Agrarian Adaptation to Population Growth." PhD diss., Columbia University.

Muysken, Pieter, and Norval Smith, eds. 1986. *Substrata versus Universals in Creole Genesis: Papers from the Amsterdam Creole Workshop, April 1985*. Amsterdam: John Benjamins.

Price, Richard, ed. 1979. *Maroon Societies: Rebel Slave Communities in the Americas*. Baltimore, MD: Johns Hopkins University Press.

Rickford, John R. 1986. "Short Note." *Journal of Pidgin and Creole Languages* 1, no. 1: 159–63.

Rickford, John R. 1987. *Dimensions of a Creole Continuum: History, Texts, and Linguistic Analysis of Guyanese Creole*. Palo Alto, CA: Stanford University Press.

Romaine, Suzanne. 1988. *Pidgin and Creole Languages*. London: Longman.

Sankoff, Gillian. 1980. *The Social Life of Language*. Philadelphia: University of Pennsylvania Press.

Scott, Julius Sherrard, III. 1986. "A Common Wind: Currents of Afro-American Communications in the Era of the Haitian Revolution." PhD diss., Duke University.

Siegel, Jeff. 1987. *Language Contact in a Plantation Environment: A Sociolinguistic History of Fiji*. Cambridge: Cambridge University Press.

Thompson, Edgar T. 1935. *The Plantation*. Chicago: University of Chicago Libraries.

Thompson, Edgar T. 1975. *Plantation Societies, Race Relations, and the South: The Regimentation of Populations*. Durham, NC: Duke University Press.

Trouillot, Michel-Rolph. 1982. "Motion in the System: Coffee, Color, and Slavery in the Eighteenth-Century Saint-Domingue." *Review (Fernand Braudel Center)* 5 no. 3: 331–88.

Trouillot, Michel-Rolph. 1988. *Peasants and Capital: Dominica in the World Economy*. Baltimore, MD: Johns Hopkins University Press.

Trouillot, Michel-Rolph. 1993. "Jeux de mots, jeux de classe: Les mouvances de l'indigénisme." *Conjonction: Revue Franco-Haïtienne* 197 (January–March): 29–44.

Trouillot, Michel-Rolph. (1977) 2012. *Ti dife boule sou istwa Ayiti*. Edited by Lyonel Trouillot. Port-au-Prince: Edisyon KIK, Invèstie Karayib.

Williams, Brackette F. 1995. "Review of *The Black Atlantic*." *Social Identities* 1, no. 1: 175–92.

CHAPTER 8

The Perspective of the World

Globalization Then and Now

Globalization is a fuzzy word. What hidden histories are silenced by this fuzziness? What would the many phenomena heavily packaged and heavily publicized under the word *globalization* look like from a world perspective? In particular, what would a world perspective tell us about cultural flows and processes?

INTRODUCTION: COFFEE . . . CON LECHE?

Whereas the word *globalization* has been defined at least by some economists (see M.-R. Trouillot 2001), its increasing use by students of culture and society has generated little attention for—and even less agreement on—what it actually means. The further we move away from economics, the more anecdotal and impressionistic our vision of globalization seems to be. Thus anthropology and literary and cultural studies in particular have yet to spell out what, if anything, globalization means to culture. Indeed, throughout the human disciplines, the relation between culture and globalization is as evanescent as it is pervasive (but see Ohnuki-Tierney 2001; Tsing 2000; Appadurai 1996).

It is not easy to fight a spook. Yet cultural globalization is a spook insofar as it is impossible to locate *in thesis* [*sic*] in academic discourse and almost as difficult to find in the world outside of academia. There are reasons for this which suggest why cultural globalization is a dream for advertisers ("United Colors of Benetton"?), and I will allude to some of them. But first I will give flesh to the thesis. The enterprise is opinioned but intellectually honest. In making explicit a number of tacit but pervasive propositions about cultural globalization, I hope to render a dominant narrative more real and more conscious of its premises but, indeed, more vulnerable.

In synthetic form, the cultural globalization thesis goes as follows: economic and technological transformations since the 1970s have led to an unprecedented flow of capital, goods, ideas, and people across state and continental borders. These flows, in turn, have contributed to the demise of institutions of power, notably the state. Our times are thus marked by the incapacity of state-built or state-sponsored boundaries (borders, citizenship, ethnicity) to regiment populations and affect cultural practices and identities. In short, the world is fast turning into a single cultural unit.

At this point, the cultural globalization thesis splits into two parts, best captured in two subliminal images. The first image is that of a blending, a coffee increasingly *con leche*, at the end of which awaits cultural homogeneity across states and continents. The second is that of a shopping mall of cultures within which individuals and groups will be able to pick their preferred components and return home, as it were, to self-construct the culture(s) of their choice—with, indeed, the capacity to return the next day if the shoe does not fit.

There is a tension between these two images, but it is exactly because the images are subliminal that this tension rarely surfaces explicitly, even in scholarly studies of globalization, let alone in the public arena. When it does, notably in the hands of advertisers, spin doctors, or media handlers, it is hyped and projected in such terms that its harmonious resolution denies the very contradictions that produced the tension in the first place. Thus golf prodigy Tiger Woods, the blend of blends, the mixture of mixtures, can successfully shop for the cultural attributes of his choice—notably the American Dream—and sell some of his wares back to us in the form of shoes that fit all. The tension between story one (the unending blending) and story two (I am what I decide to be) is happily resolved because of the boldness of the move. That is, both images revel in the alleged newness of the phenomenon, and that mutual newness is exactly what makes one support the other. Thus we buy the image—and the shoes. Again, Benetton comes to mind as a precursor, daring to juxtapose the obviously incompatible and claiming to resolve the incompatibility in a future marked by congenital innocence.

Yet claims of innocence are suspicious when it comes to globalization. Indeed, a narrative of political and economic change is fundamental to these images. These images work in part because we are convinced that the world is changing—fast, too fast—and that the motor of change is the inexorable hand of technology and trade (Gibson-Graham 1996). A critical reading of cultural globalization should therefore never lose sight of the political economy against which the narrative is deployed.

IS GLOBALIZATION UNPRECEDENTED?

Back to economics, therefore, to check on that feeling of newness. Is globalization unprecedented? We may approach the answer with this quote:

> International finance has become so interdependent and so interwoven with trade and industry . . . that political and military power can in reality do nothing. . . . These little recognized facts, mainly the outcome of purely modern conditions (rapidity of communication creating a greater complexity and delicacy of the credit system) have rendered the problems of modern international politics profoundly and essentially different from the ancient. (Angell 1910)

The elements of a thesis are there: new technology—especially the speed of communication—creates an interdependence that in turn leads to a fundamentally different world. Does this suggest a radical break? Yes, except that the quote is from Norman Angell's *The Great Illusion*, published in 1910. Thus in the first decade of this century, some knowledgeable observers had already proposed that the main features we associate today with globalization fully obtained in the world of finance and politics. Were they wrong?

The figures that best measure economic globalization reveal that, in relative terms, the flow of goods and capital across state boundaries was at least as high during the period immediately preceding World War I as it is today. Ratios of export trade to GDP may have been higher in 1913 than in 1973. In the period from 1913 to 1914, Foreign Direct Investment (FDI) was around 11 percent, about the same level as in 1994. Capital flows relative to output were higher during the Gold Standard period than in the 1980s. To sum up a number of authors and arguments:

(1) There is absolutely no evidence to suggest that the economic facts we most often associate with globalization are unprecedented;

(2) There is evidence to indicate that the changes of the last twenty years are not as massive as we think they are;

(3) There also is evidence that they are much more limited in geographical scope than the ideology of today suggests (Banuri and Schorr 1992; M.-R. Trouillot 2001; Weiss 1997).

We should not draw from the figures highlighting the period preceding World War I that globalization first happened then—if only because two world wars should help temper such presumption. Rather, the most important lesson of the comparison between the first and last decades of this century is about the sense of newness that the awareness of global flows provoked then and now. Angell's pompousness is indeed refreshing when we know the date of his statement. Yet we need also to remember that at about the same date, Rosa Luxemburg (1968, 1972) was insisting that capitalism had always been a global process, needing from its inception new spaces to devour. Read as a process, economic globalization is inherent in capitalism and therefore as old as that system (Harvey 1995; Luxemburg 1972).

The lesson is thus one of humility, a mere suggestion that we may need eyeglasses to see things that are too near. If the economic flows we now associate with globalization are not as different or as massive as we may believe, should we not question the apparent newness of the cultural, social, and demographic flows that supposedly derive from this globalized economy?

In economics as in politics, in cultural studies as in social studies, the main narrative of globalization hides the very facts of power that make it both desirable and possible. All narratives impose silences (M.-R. Trouillot 1995). The particularity of the narrative of globalization when it touches culture-history is a massive silencing of the past on a world scale, the systematic erasure of continuous and deeply felt encounters that have marked the last five hundred years of human history. For sushi in Chicago to amaze us, we need to silence that the Franciscans were in Japan as early as the fifteenth century. For Muslim veils in France to seem out of place, we need to forget that Charles Martel stopped Abd-al-Raman only three hundred miles south of Paris, two reigns before Charlemagne. To talk of a global culture *today*, we need to forget that Chinese chili paste comes from Mexico, French fries from Peru, and Jamaican Mountain Blue from Yemen.

TIME, SPACE, AND HISTORY

Studies of globalization have been eminently parochial in their premises, eminently limited in their handling of either time or space and the time-space conflation itself. It is thus both ironic and necessary to insist that studies of globalization need to develop a global perspective. How do we do it? To start with, we need a better handle on two sets of issues that I will call, for short, temporality and historicity.

Narratives of globalization say something about the history of the world, but they often assume naively as their premises the state of affairs of the *Wall Street Journal*. If globalization is about world history, scholars of globalization need to ask: Which world? Whose history? We cannot answer the first question, "Which world?" without a firm handle on temporality and the time-space relation.

You may have noticed that my title alludes to Fernand Braudel's *The Perspective of the World* ([1979] 1992). Yet Braudel was less interested in the perspective *of* the world than in a perspective *on* the world. The original French title of the third volume of *Civilisation matérielle* . . . is *Le temps du monde*, "World time" or, more accurately, "the pace of the world." Mistranslation aside, Braudel focused on that duration whose tempo was set by the global development of capitalism.

Still, Braudel's perspective on the world is a crucial step in a search for a perspective of the world. For can we talk about globalization without taking seriously the various paces and temporalities involved? Braudel himself was careful to insist that there were temporalities other than the tempo of world capitalist development. World time does not affect the entire world in the same way. World time is not universal time. The pace of the world is uneven on the ground. Indeed, Braudel insisted, following Marx-Luxemburg and anticipating Harvey, that world time itself necessarily created spatial hierarchies.

There are lessons here for those of us interested in the movement of global flows. Which temporalities do we privilege? Which spaces do we ignore? How do we set the criteria behind these choices? A world perspective on globalization requires attention to differential temporalities and the uneven spaces that they create.[1]

Having distinguished, as we should, the temporalities involved, we need to return to the ground where those temporalities overlap. We need to observe how these temporalities coalesce, mix, disjoint, and contradict themselves among historically situated populations. Just as world space is not everyone's space, the history of the world is not everyone's history. We need to ask whose history is being told by the most fashionable narratives of globalization, and whose history is being silenced?

If temporalities overlap in inherently uneven spaces, this overlap enables and limits sensibilities and subject positions that can arise from within these spaces. In other words, we need to move from temporality to historicity, that two-pronged field in which human beings become both actors and narrators of their own story.

The rules of the game being what they are, it is no accident that the temporalities most successfully isolated by economic history are most successfully mixed in literature. I will not dare discuss Third World literature, whatever that may be, but I will dare suggest that Caribbean literature in all languages, of which I know something, is a world where time collapses into historicity.

> Five hundred years that je cooperate, je pacify, je collaborate, that je dream American, socialize old-Europe style, that euros penetrate my ass with dollars a la leche. Here I am plexiglass prostitute from Curaçao to Amsterdam, soccer player on the French team, sweeper of all sixtine chapels in the chassé-croisé of exotic transfers. Ah, if for once I was the world, how they would laugh in Nigger's Corner! (L. Trouillot 1997, 31)

THE FIRST MOMENT OF GLOBALITY

The world became global five centuries ago. The rise of the West, the conquest of the Americas, New World slavery, and the Industrial Revolution can be summarized as "a first moment of globality," an *Atlantic moment*, culminating in US hegemony after World War II. Europe became Europe in part through severing itself from what lay south of the Mediterranean, but also in part through a westward move that made the Atlantic the center of the first truly global empires.

I cannot deal here with the empirical details of that moment, which encompass five centuries of world history and the shrinking of huge continental masses, including Asia. Indeed, my Atlantic moment is not restricted geographically to societies bordering the Atlantic Ocean. The designation does not refer to a static space but to the locus of a momentum. Spain's conquest of the Philippines, the British conquest of India, and the United States' control of Korea all fall within that moment. I will insist, however, that it is no accident that such non-Atlantic ventures often took place when the respective power claimed partial or total control of the Atlantic Ocean.

This Atlantic moment of globality entailed at the onset massive flows of money, capital, goods, ideas, motifs, and people not only across states but across continents.

Global flows of population include, of course, the Castilian invasion of the Americas, the nearly twelve million enslaved Africans taken to the

New World, and the hundreds of thousands of Asians brought to succeed the slaves on Caribbean plantations. As the North Atlantic states forcibly moved populations all over the world, their own citizens also moved from one continent to another, most often from temperate to temperate climate. Australia, Canada, New Zealand, Southern Africa, and the United States bear the marks of these demographic flows.

As peoples moved, so did goods. Massive flows of gold and silver, crops and spices, and plants and diseases, from tobacco to coconuts, from syphilis to smallpox, and from the mines of Peru to the Kews sprinkled over the British Empire and enmeshed world populations into encounters and confrontations unrestricted by physical distance. Economically these flows of goods and money sustained the life of the North Atlantic both before and after its Industrial Revolution. By the late eighteenth century, almost two-thirds of France's external trade rested on the shoulders of the Caribbean colony of Saint-Domingue/Haiti and the slaves who died there. Similarly, in the nineteenth century, the opium trade proved vital to the British economy. Crops such as sugar, coffee, tea, or cocoa concretely tied together populations separated by oceans (M.-R. Trouillot 1980; Mintz 1985; Brockway 1977).

This first moment of globality also produced its self-proclaimed hybrids, from the many *convertos* who joined the Castilian venture, to the early Americans who discovered they had become Indians, to the mulattos of Cuba, Brazil, or Saint-Domingue. *Cafe con leche* is not new, certainly not in Latin America. Already in 1815 Simón Bolívar had officialized a narrative of hybridity: "We are . . . neither Indian nor European, but a species midway between the legitimate proprietors of this country and the Spanish usurpers." Assessing the cultural evolution of the Caribbean, Édouard Glissant insists that creolization requires the consciousness of mixed origins, but he also contends that the notion of hybridity is too narrow to capture the richness of the situation.

THE HUMAN DISCIPLINES AND THE LEGACIES
OF THE NORTH ATLANTIC

The initial reaction of the men of robes and letters of the North Atlantic to this first moment of globality was one of intellectual curiosity. The new geography of imagination that arose during the Renaissance (and made possible the conversion of Latin Christendom into Europe) implied a global projection of power. That projection, which still serves as the foundation of what we call "the West," inherently divides and segregates populations, cultures, areas, religions, and races. Yet it would be a mistake to think that it did so then the way it does now. From the sixteenth to the early nineteenth century, a number of writers expressed wonder at the globality just discovered but took it seriously enough to explore its social, moral, and cultural implications across a wide spectrum of philosophical and political positions.

From Amerigo Vespucci's letters and the debates between Las Casas and Sepulveda through the sixteenth-century proponents of a total history, the reflections of Montaigne and Montesquieu, down to Diderot-Raynal or even Adam Smith on colonization, there is indeed an "us" and a "them." But the "us" keeps changing, and the "them" is open-ended, for there is also a sense that what we say about "them" says something about "us." To that extent, the Atlantic moment of globality was handled, at least by some of the most prominent European thinkers, as a truly global—that is, open if not open-ended—phenomenon.[2]

A precision is necessary. I am not arguing that Renaissance and Early Modern European thinkers were *not* ethnocentric. On the contrary, I have suggested elsewhere that the roots of scientific racism, as it first appears in the early 1700s before gaining full speed during the nineteenth century, go back to the ontology and geographical imagination of the Renaissance (M.-R. Trouillot 1995, 74–78). This does not contravene the proposition that in the scholarly world, the impact of that geography was not homogenous. It implied closure and segregation, but it also implied degrees and forms of openness. Las Casas's position at Valladolid was intellectually and *politically* defensible. It would look insane today.

When did this break occur?

In the nineteenth century, right at the moment when the North Atlantic nurtured jointly and with equal ardor nationalist rhetorics and myths of "scientific" racial supremacy, the scholarly world took what increasingly appears in retrospect as a "wrong turn" in the institutionalization of the human disciplines.

In a context marked by the increasing evocation and deployment of state power outside of academia and the reorganization of power within institutions of knowledge, the nineteenth century saw a qualitative break in both the notion and practice of "social science" as objective knowledge of the human world. Three fundamental changes sealed that break: the search for objectivity itself; the use of that "objective" knowledge as a guide for the management of social change, now perceived as inevitable; and the sense that such change would occur in a context where (political) sovereignty resided in the people (Wallerstein 1991). Objectivity and the manageability of data *and* populations fed on each other, separating the task into "disciplines" increasingly removed from the humanities and from each other (Wallerstein et al., 1996).

So stated, the project created major zones of exclusion inherent in its aims and claims. To start with, in practice and for purposes of management, the bulk of the data to be analyzed came from the five countries where that institutionalization took place: Britain, France, the Germanies, the Italies, and the United States. More important, the project left out *by definition* the populations thought to be impervious to change by nature or by practice, including most of the non-West, which became the purview of a particular discipline, anthropology (M.-R. Trouillot 1991). It left out by definition, also, populations—often the same—that were not thought to be worthy of self-sovereignty. Indeed, sovereignty and the capacity for progress went hand in hand in North Atlantic social thought, if not from the days of Las Casas, certainly at least from the days of Condorcet. The project also left out the populations—again, often the same—that were thought to be (or, later on, chose to be) outside of the capitalist order as defined from the North Atlantic.

Tailing along, fighting for their own institutional space and micro-sites of power, the humanities tended to mimic the parcellation of the social sciences. The result is still horrific. The human disciplines rewrote their past and polished their theoretical apparatus, drawing primarily from the North Atlantic experience, as though what we now call the West encapsulated the entire richness of humankind. They did not simply neglect the experience of the non-West—and, some would add, that of quite a few fellow Westerners. Rather, they actively silenced that experience within their self-designed domains. They made it inconsequential to theory.

Within the self-designed domains, theoretical segregation paralleled the closure of human populations within the political boundaries designed by the North Atlantic or—in the lack of such—within the boundaries that most resembled home in the minds of North Atlantic observers. Tribes, nations, regions, and ethnicities became not only natural units of analysis, which is bad enough, but they became the real thing. Not only was what was here to be studied, but it was what was "out there," entities imbued with an internal life and enclosed in fixed boundaries. Anthropologist Eric R. Wolf evaluates the intellectual disaster thus:

The habit of treating named entities such as Iroquois, Greece, Persia, or the United States as fixed entities opposed to one another by stable internal architecture and external boundaries interferes with our ability to understand their mutual encounter and confrontation. . . . We seem to have taken a wrong turn in understanding at some critical point in the past, a false choice that bedevils our thinking in the present.

That critical turning point is identifiable. It occurred in the middle of the past century, when inquiry into the nature and varieties of humankind split into separate (and unequal) specialties and disciplines. This split was fateful. (Wolf 1982, 7)

CULTURE IN A BOTTLE

One consequence of that discursive narrowness is an essentialist approach to cultures, the borders of which supposedly overlap with the imagined community of the nation-state or similar political boundaries within it. Anthropology, notably American cultural anthropology, played its part in this theoretical segregation, making culture not only both an object and a unit of analysis—an enterprise intellectually doubtful at best—but something "out there" that people obviously similar shared somewhat in their head when not through their practice.

To be sure, in the mind of many Boasians, the enterprise was partially intended to sever race from culture. Yet a century later it is not at all certain that cultural determinism's possible victory over biology has done much to destroy racism. At any rate, willingly or not, anthropology, and American cultural anthropology in particular, sold the general public an ahistorical, classless, essentialist notion of culture that breeds determinism. Culture became something evanescent and yet palpable, shared by a community whose borders just happened to replicate political boundaries. One nation, one state, one culture. One subnation, one subculture. Where racial boundaries were also fundamental political boundaries, as in the United States, culture and race became conflated. If a number of North Americans now think that there is more cultural affinity between a Black boy from inner-city Detroit and a Kalahari bushman than between that boy and his white Bostonian counterpart, American anthropologists have to take part of the blame.

The notion of single, isolated, and identifiable cultures thus channeled the geographical imaginary of the Renaissance through some of the worst intellectual catheters designed by the nineteenth century. Never mind that this notion of an isolated culture was never adequate to describe any population in or out of the North Atlantic. It fit nationalist ideologies of what the world should look like.

But suddenly, alas, the world does not look as it should. The problem is not that cultures are suddenly changing: they have always been changing. Nor is it new that cultures are porous. Human groups have always been open, in various degrees, to new experiences, outside influences, borrowings, and impositions. The difference now is that the fiction of isolated cultures built by the nineteenth century on the assumptions of the Renaissance no longer fits the lived experiences of the populations of the North Atlantic. I now turn to this second moment of globality.

THE SECOND MOMENT OF GLOBALITY: MASS AND VELOCITY

Since the end of World War II, a number of changes have deeply affected the globalization process. The first major change is not in the nature of global flows. As I suggested earlier, capital, goods, populations, ideas, motifs, and sensibilities have traveled across state and continental borders for a long time. They continue to do so. But they now do it at speeds and in quantities unthinkable just fifty years ago. It is not the relative importance of global flows that is unique to our times. Rather, it is the sheer volume of these flows and the speed at which these masses move. Mass and velocity are unique to our times. Unique also is the widespread awareness of global flows. That awareness grows everywhere, largely because of the increase in both size and velocity.

We can now start reading the unspoken tensions that characterize a number of cultural icons of our times, from Tiger Woods to postcolonial theorists. Capital, populations, and information move in much greater mass and at increasing speed, producing a centripetal effect of perception: we are the world; we are at its center, since everything around us moves. But that imaginary center is also the eye of a hurricane, for not only does everything move around us, but everything moves too fast and too soon.

To phrase the proposition in slightly different terms, while global flows increase in speed and velocity, most human beings continue to think and act locally. There is thus a disjuncture between the awareness of globalization and the capacity to come to terms with its consequences. While the first moment of globality produced tremendous cultural upheavals felt deeply in the colonies, in the second moment of globality globalization hits consciousness as a never-ending shock, the echoes of which seem to circle around the world.

Two contradictory reactions thus dominate the popular responses to global flows: wonderment and fragmentation.

WONDERS AND FRAGMENTATION

The most visible products of the two moments of globality do not fit the essentialist categories we inherited from the nineteenth century. They disturb the sense we had of what the world was or should have been. Thus wonder emerges as one of the reactions among the public.

We knew—we thought we knew—that a Chinese looks Chinese, speaks Chinese, and acts Chinese—until we walk into a Cuban restaurant, say, on New York's Upper West Side or in Miami's Little Havana—and discover a Chinese face with Latin flavors and Spanish accent. We think: the world has changed. But the world has not changed. We have simply moved closer to it. Chinese laborers stood next to African slaves on Cuban sugarcane plantations without much surprise on their or their masters' parts.

The example brings home a difference of our times set in three propositions: (1) wonder is premised in the incompatibility between essentialist categories and the products of global processes; (2) the nineteenth century has left us with the habit of conceptualizing humankind fundamentally in essential terms; (3) the speed of the late twentieth century makes it impossible for us not to notice the nonessentialist products of global flows. Wonder and puzzlement increase accordingly.

Academics reproduce this wonder in part by providing new labels that attempt to reconcile the world we face and the one we think we left behind. Used uncritically, these labels couch the treatment of globalization—or some of its avatars: hybrids, transnationals (corporations or peoples), diasporas—in an essentialist mode that tries to recover the assurance of nineteenth-century pronouncements. Their fluidity once stated, we treat our new hybrids as entities—as givens rather than as moments to be unpacked.

The political danger is obvious. One of the least banal effects of the Tiger Woods, Hybrid qua Star phenomenon is a thicker mask on the formation of racial identity and the workings of racism in the United States. There is a mess out there, and the temptation to order the mess by inventing new labels, by naming the result rather than deciphering the process, is great. From nominalization to essentialism, the bridge is rather short.

Wonder does not exhaust our dominant responses to the second moment of globality. A second reaction is a feeling of fragmentation.

Since the end of World War II, a number of political and intellectual leaders have promised us, intermittently and with varying degrees of certitude, an end to racial and ethnic conflicts, both within and across political borders. Yet during that same period, such conflicts have erupted repeatedly in various parts of the globe, pushing millions of individuals to unexpected levels of verbal and physical violence. That violence does not exempt Western democracies such as the United States, Germany, or France. Further, even when mass violence is absent, race and ethnicity creep into personal relations, often with surprising twists of perversity. From the vote of the United Nations Charter in 1945 to today's headlines from Bosnia or Los Angeles, these last fifty years can be read as an ongoing tension between the promise of a future where religion, language, and phenotype would become increasingly immaterial and the reality of a present where differences, presumed irrelevant, would become suddenly pristine. The twenty-first century is likely to be marked by the speed and brutality of similar conflicts.[3]

Academics also have reproduced this tension both within and across disciplinary lines. Whereas some disciplines can be said to have emphasized the processes of integration rather than the facts of fragmentation, all have had to take both into account, albeit to different degrees. Overlapping the disciplines are, again, the labels that tie this new world together: globalization, global culture, and diasporas.

One danger in these labels is the extent to which they replace the old universalisms of nineteenth-century thought—or of development studies—with a new universalism that is equally blind to its parochial roots. The experience of globality is always that of historically situated individuals with specific resources and limits.

I am not convinced that we gain more understanding of globalization by suggesting that the world is now moving to a "global culture," or that cultures are now engaged in flows of exchange that propel them as equal partners in a global market of patterns and ideas. McDonald's in Beijing is not the same as sushi in Evanston. Or at least we should not assume so until we do the research that would confirm this assumption. The challenge is to face the reality that cultural landscapes are open, that their openness has always been an occasion for exchanges and flows, and that these exchanges have always been modulated by power. In better words, how do we study the cultural practices of human populations and take power into account?

THE HISTORICIZATION OF THE WEST

We cannot start with a clean deck. The history of the last five hundred years has marked us all in ways that we cannot deny. Indeed, if there is proof of what I call the Atlantic moment of globality, the proof is that few of us can think about the last five hundred years as though they were not inevitable, as if North Atlantic hegemony was not in the very premises of human activity. Thus the first task is to ask how and why that hegemony became not only so pervasive but also so convincing, and the ideal tool for that task is the parochialization of the North Atlantic. The historicization of the West—its practices, concepts, assumptions, claims, and genealogies—is a central theoretical challenge of our times.

That has been said by many, including notable subaltern and postcolonial theorists. My own insistence is that this historicization, properly conceived, requires a global perspective. It cannot be reduced to an empirical focus on the successive geographical areas or populations (Greece, Rome, Latin Christendom, or the North Atlantic) that the West now claims in its genealogies. To limit the investigation to the physical West would be to accept naively the West's own genealogies and forget that the current challenge comes to the human sciences, in part, from changes in the globalization process.

Theoretical ethnocentrism is not intellectually equipped to face that situation, nor are the marginal responses, such as Afrocentrism, that this ethnocentrism provokes. Nor can ethnic studies, legitimate in their own terms, fill that void, unless we are willing to argue that North American minorities can serve as historical proxies for the vast chunks of humankind abandoned by the Latin and Teutonic canons. Chicano studies, as legitimate as they are, cannot replace Latin American studies. Black studies, as legitimate as they are, cannot replace African or Caribbean studies. In short, we need to cross political and linguistic boundaries to place whichever population we study, and the very places we come from, in a global perspective.

The difficult in achieving such a global perspective may be the Achilles heel of postcoloniality, the main reason it has not delivered on the promises of a new theory and politics. To put it differently, postcolonial theory has broken a silence less than it has generated a new position within an ongoing conversation. The postcolonial intellectual *her*self entered the conversation only inasmuch as her positioning via-à-vis that center demanded a generous attention that denies the facts of power that made this positioning necessary in the first place. As such, she may have changed the themes but not the terms of a conversation that preceded her entry and will likely continue after her departure.

The capacity to read one's own position and generate from that reading multiple, shifting, and questioning new locations seems to me the singular lesson from the most progressive academic trends of the last few years. The deployment of that capacity—in what I insist should be a global perspective—may be the key difference in evaluating the effectiveness of recent strategies of discourse and practice in and out of academia. If so, the difficulties that self-described postcolonials have in developing a critical reading of their own conditions of possibility may be a testimony to the limits of the enterprise.[4] As others have suggested (Ahmad 1992, 1995; Harvey 1989, 350–52), the need remains for a more critical reading of the context of intellectual production in and around academia.

CROSSING BOUNDARIES

Within academia itself we need to cross disciplinary boundaries much more often than we do now. Today, no single discipline has the capacity to conceptualize the experience of the people dismissed by the nineteenth century. Anthropologist Eric R. Wolf (1983, 5) again says it best: "It is only when we integrate our different kinds of knowledge that the people without history emerge as actors in their own right. When we parcel them out among several disciplines, we render them invisible."

While parochialism, including that of the disciplines, leads to obvious dead ends and centrisms of all kinds—including the renewed search for universalist paradigms, such as rational choice theory—these now convince mostly the believers. The human sciences are going through what historian Jacques Revel (1995) calls a time of "epistemological anarchy," in part because of the greater empirical basis available for theory. Yet if we make use of that empirical base, this very anarchy is an opportunity for new conversations that take into account the entire historical experience of the world, with the various sensibilities and viewpoints that this experience implies.

NOTES

This chapter was written in 1998, when versions of it were presented at Stanford University, the University of Chicago, West Virginia University, Duke University, and at the workshop Theory and Politics after Postcoloniality (Institute for Global Studies, Johns Hopkins University). Since then I have substantially refined my thoughts on these issues in later articles noted in the bibliography below. I have also added later references to the text for the benefit of the reader. My thanks to Michael Dorsey, Jeffrey Mantz, Nabiha Megateli, and Clare Sammells, whose research tips inform this text, and to Vivek Dhareshwar, for the ongoing conversation that provoked some of these lines.

    Editors' Note: This chapter first appeared as "The Perspective of the World: Globalization Then and Now," in *Beyond Dichotomies: Histories, Identities, Cultures, and the Challenge of Globalization*, edited by Elisabeth Mudimbe-Boyi (Albany: State University of New York Press, 2002), 3–20.

1. Yet when we turn to most of the literature on globalization, from the *Wall Street Journal* to the liberal-minded literature of anthropology and literary and cultural studies, we discover a peculiar handling of the space-time relation: a silencing of the past, an obsession with what Annales historians called derisively "la conjoncture," a patchwork of current headlines projected as the duration of the future over a world unfettered by mountains and other sinuosities. The world started this morning when sushi first reached Peoria, and guess what—it is a flat world.

2. Trails of this wonderment can still be found in studies of the Americas, notably creolization studies focusing on Brazil or the Caribbean.

3. In February 1998, Zapatista Indians seized control of the Web page of Mexico's Ministry of Finance. What could be more global than a Web page? Yet what is more grounded in locality and historicity than the claim of the Zapatistas?

4. Yet some of these are rather obvious: England's difficulties in sustaining the Commonwealth as an economic and intellectual umbrella; the uncontested dominance of English as the Latin of the late twentieth century; the ideological and personnel relay points between the United Kingdom and the United States—from Thatcher-Reagan to Clinton-Blair—however weak the structural

parallels; and the conditions of academic production in the United States, including the politics of racism, all seem parts of a landscape begging for critical description.

REFERENCES

Ahmad, Aijaz. 1992. *In Theory: Classes, Nations, Literatures*. London: Verso.

Ahmad, Aijaz. 1995. "Postcolonialism: What's in a Name?" In *Late Imperial Culture*, edited by Roman de la Campa, E. Ann Kaplan, and Michael Sprinker, 11–32. London: Verso.

Angell, Norman. 1910. *The Great Illusion*. New York: G. Putnam's Sons.

Banuri, Tariq, and Juliet R. Schorr, eds. 1992. *Financial Openness and National Autonomy: Opportunities and Constraints*. Oxford: Oxford University Press.

Braudel, Fernand. (1979) 1992. *The Perspective of the World*. Translated by Siân Reynolds. Berkeley: University of California Press.

Gibson-Graham, J. K. 1996. *The End of Capitalism (As We Know It): A Feminist Critique of Political Economy*. Oxford: Blackwell.

Harvey, David. 1989. *The Condition of Postmodernity: An Enquiry into the Origins of Cultural Change*. Oxford: Blackwell.

Harvey, David. 1995. "Globalization in Question." *Rethinking Marxism* 8, no. 4: 1–17.

Luxemburg, Rosa. 1968. *What Is Economics?* Translated by T. Edwards. London: Merlin.

Luxemburg, Rosa. 1972. *The Accumulation of Capital: An Anti-Critique*. New York: Monthly Review Press.

Mintz, Sidney W. 1985. *Sweetness and Power: The Place of Sugar in Modern History*. New York: Viking.

Ohnuki-Tierney, Emiko. 2001. "Historicization of the Culture Concept." *History and Anthropology* 12, no. 3: 231–54.

Revel, Jacques, and Lynn Hunt, eds. 1995. *Histories: French Constructions of the Past*. Translated by Arthur Goldhammer. New York: New Press.

Trouillot, Lyonel. 1997. *Les dits du fou de l'île: Nouvelles*. Port-au-Prince: Éditions de l'Ile.

Trouillot, Michel-Rolph. 1991. "Anthropology and the Savage Slot: The Poetics and Politics of Otherness." In *Recapturing Anthropology: Working in the Present*, edited by Richard G. Fox, 17–44. Santa Fe, NM: School of American Research Press.

Trouillot, Michel-Rolph. 1995. *Silencing the Past: Power and the Production of History*. Boston: Beacon Press.

Trouillot, Michel-Rolph. 1998. "Culture on the Edges: Creolization in the Plantation Context." *Plantation Society in the Americas* 5, no. 1: 8–28.

Trouillot, Michel-Rolph. 2001. "The Anthropology of the State in the Age of Globalization: Close Encounters of a Deceptive Kind." *Current Anthropology* 42, no. 1: 125–38.

Tsing, Anna Lowenhaupt. 2000. "The Global Situation." *Cultural Anthropology* 15, no. 3: 327–60.

Wallerstein, Immanuel. 1991. *Unthinking Social Science: The Limits of Nineteenth-Century Paradigms*. Cambridge: Polity Press.

Wallerstein, Immanuel, et al. 1996. *Open the Social Sciences: A Report of the Gulbenkian Commission on the Restructuring of the Social Sciences*. Stanford, CA: Stanford University Press.

Weiss, Linda. 1997. "Globalization and the Myth of the Powerless State." *New Left Review* I/225: 3–27.

Wolf, Eric R. 1982. *Europe and the People without History*. Berkeley: University of California Press.

Wolf, Eric R. 1983. "The People without History." Lecture to the University Faculty Senate, 125th Plenary Session, City University of New York, December 13.

PART III

THE FIELDS
IN WHICH WE
WORK

Discipline and Perish

Michel Foucault says that the work of an intellectual is "to question over and over again what is postulated as self-evident, to disturb people's mental habits . . . to dissipate what is familiar and accepted." If so, can an academic be an intellectual?

Academic institutions are indispensable to intellectual life as we know it. They provide a privileged context for critical enquiry about the world and our place within it. They are sites of research, of exchange, and of accumulation of knowledge. Yet academic institutions, especially universities, *discipline* both the knowledge they inherit and that which they help to produce. They regulate the privilege of enquiry through departmental structures that mimic and sustain disciplinary boundaries. The disciplines so enforced secure mental habits no less familiar or self-evident within their walls than those of the populace outside.

This inherent tension between the academic and the intellectual reaches new heights now that few intellectuals can afford not to be academics. The intellectual as member of the Court died with the advent of the republic. The intellectual as public figure has become a syndicated TV show. Disciplines are, by default, reluctant guarantors of intellectual life at the very time when their power to guarantee anything, even a job, is itself questioned.

The questions are multiple. First, the exchange value of the major—the first stamp of disciplinary worth, reportedly introduced in the United States by Johns Hopkins University—is decreasing. Leading employers now question openly the assumed correspondence between a given academic discipline and the regimentation of a particular workplace.

Second, the increasing skepticism of the market parallels that of scholars who are experiencing in new ways the intellectual limits to academic hospitality. Disciplines do not fit the world any worse than before but, for once, professors *and students* are aware of the huge gap between worldly chaos and the order of knowledge—thanks, in part, to the very knowledge accumulated within disciplinary boundaries. That awareness has engendered contradictory reactions in most fields, from despair to collage, from dilettantism to increased specialization.

Third, if some natural scientists can assume that the world has not changed and that we need only to get a better fix on it, the humanities and the social sciences cannot escape the fact that their role within the world has changed. The crisis of representation is also a crisis of legitimacy, the context of emergence of new voices—feminists, "minorities," gays, "postcolonies." In short, the humanities and social sciences now age much faster than the natural sciences because they also age from within.

The humanities and the social sciences bear gauchely the weight of a nineteenth century soon to be twice removed. Their development during that century paralleled the political and economic expansion of the North Atlantic. These disciplines rewrote their past and polished their theoretical apparatus, drawing primarily from that experience, as if what we now call the West encapsulated the entire richness of humankind. They did not simply neglect the experience of the non-West—and that of quite a few fellow Westerners. Rather, they actively silenced that experience. They made it inconsequential to theory.

The price of that erasure is a hefty one. Today, no single discipline has the capacity to conceptualize the experience of the people dismissed by the nineteenth century. Anthropologist Eric R. Wolf says it best: "It is only when we integrate our different kinds of knowledge that the people without history emerge as actors in their own right. When we parcel them out among several disciplines, we render them invisible."

One understands, then, why mechanical formulas of intellectual emancipation—"add women, color, stir and proceed as usual"—are doomed from the start. One understands also the panic that makes them appealing. But the politics of discovery should not mislead us on the strategies for remedy. There is no reason why the guilt of white liberals and the anger of nonwhite students, deep and relevant as they may be, should substitute for an intellectual agenda on this issue—*and on this issue alone*. Such assumption is suspicious in a society where *culture* is now the polite word for *race*, and *an alibi for racism*. In her Spring Distinguished Lecture, Brackette F.

Williams suggests that the impasses of multiculturalism are often due to its convenient blending of effects and causes. Multiculturalism, even of the best kind, can only be a limited program because it is not likely to emancipate Dick and Jane. Yet Dick and Jane are the ones truly in need of enlightenment.

Many seek this enlightenment through a comparative perspective. This is Marcel Detienne's position, which encapsulates a distinctively "French" universalism. But as Detienne points out, France itself is not as universalist as it sometimes seems from this side of the Atlantic. There, as here, disciplines can stifle fertilization in spite of institutions such as the Collège de France or the Centre national de la recherche scientifique (CNRS) that palliate the rigors of the university system.

Few such havens exist in the United States, where graduate programs and national associations jealously protect disciplinary boundaries now indispensable to their reproduction. As Ali Khan suggests, the academic who trespasses such boundaries may find no home away from home. Luckily, the competitiveness of the system, and the very size of the United States, allows much room for individual maneuvering.

Such maneuvering may lead to "multidisciplinary" ventures that are nothing more than the juxtaposition of traditional lines, especially at the undergraduate level. The humanities and the social sciences do not feel as much the pressures for cross-disciplinary *research* that scientists encounter from government and industry. Thus, multidisciplinary packaging is often relegated to the undergraduate level, where it reflects much more the short-term demands of students, as translated by administrators, than an intellectual agenda prompted by research.

Outside pressures complicate the picture. Today, African American studies and women's studies lead the way to institutional recognition across the human disciplines, however reluctantly granted. Ethnic, cultural, and global studies follow in disparate order, depending upon their immediate constituency. This institutionalization suggests impending orthodoxies, loci of power to be challenged by new generations. Whether these reconfigurations are worth the effort depends on their impact on the production of knowledge by individual researchers anxious to cross traditional boundaries.

For, while orthodoxies come and go, serious intellectual travel remains a solitary venture inasmuch as it is always in part a move away from self (Foucault). Cross-disciplinary travel is no exception. Disciplines provide safety; moving away may also mean fading away. While many academics agree that cross-disciplinary explorations are the path to the future, few would deny that each discipline has accumulated a huge methodological arsenal, and that it would be imprudent to reject in bloc these resources. Yet there is no widespread agreement on the specific resources to preserve or on the directions to explore.

Thus, intellectuals who cross disciplinary lines do so at their own risk. Fortunately, somewhere beyond the boundaries, fellow travelers appear, ready to share the perilous pleasures of exploration. For the time, however short, that their paths intersect with ours, the conversation is worth the risks.

What we hope to provide here is a forum for such conversations.

NOTE

This chapter first appeared as "Discipline and Perish," *Cross Currents: Newsletter of the Institute for Global Studies in Culture, Power, and History* 1, no. 2 (1994).

CHAPTER 9

Making Sense

The Fields in Which We Work

Anthropology could not have simply landed where it did had the deployment of the culture concept not influenced its disciplinary path. To ask where anthropology is—or should be—going today is to ask where anthropology is coming from and to assess critically the heritage that it must claim. But it is also to ask about changes in the world around us, inside and outside of academe, and how those changes should affect our use of that heritage, and what is best left behind as obsolete, redundant, or simply misleading in this new context of global transformations.

When Charles Darwin wrote *The Descent of Man* (1871), the humanity he purported to connect with its animal cousins counted about a billion individuals. *Homo sapiens* had grown at first haphazardly over more than 200,000 years to reach close to two hundred million during the lifetime of Jesus of Nazareth.[1] As humanity strengthened its mastery over a growing number of species, it took only 1,500 years for that number to double. With the global transformations of modernity, the pace of demographic growth accelerated further. World population jumped to 750 million by 1750; a century later it was over one billion; a century later it had more than doubled. In 2003 world population reached the 6.3 billion mark. By the end of the twentieth century humanity added more members in any single year than it had in any of the *centuries* before Columbus reached the Americas. By 2025 we will have surpassed the ten billion mark, barring no major catastrophe.

Many observers see in these numbers the harbinger of further massive changes, especially when juxtaposed with the rate of technological growth, including increases in communications technology. Others have insisted on the effects of speed rather than mass. As the speed of change increases, so does the speed of immediate response, as we have seen earlier; but so too does the gap between the devastation caused by new problems and the application of long-term strategies. Humanity faces an increasing inability to envision and implement durable solutions to the transformations it generates (Bodley 1976).

Does sociocultural anthropology—a painstaking enterprise that requires slow years of preparation and relishes in the long-term observation of small groups—have a role in that speeding and massive world? The answer to that question depends largely on what kind of anthropology one has in mind and who takes part in the conversation that shapes it. As of yet, the situation is equivocal. Most anthropologists aspire to fundamental change in the discipline: indeed, they see it as inevitable. Yet there is little open debate about the heritage to claim or the directions to pursue.

Anthropologists may agree more easily than other academics that the world has changed and that our discipline must face those changes, first because—for better and often for worse, and for reasons yet unclear—the discipline has valued newness over accumulation as far as theory is concerned (Barrett 1984). Second, the traditional populations of anthropological study are among those most visibly affected by recent global flows. With refugees at the gates, diasporas in the midst, and peasant kids dreaming of Nike shoes, most anthropologists cannot deny that the world has changed and that therefore the discipline that claims to cover the whole of humankind must also change.

Anthropological practice itself, however, tends to vacillate between an overly loud rejection of previous thinkers and a quiet reproduction of the very same research techniques and methodological assumptions. In announcing their new products to a market increasingly attuned to change, quite a few anthropologists feel the need to distance themselves from their predecessors. Claims that the wheel has just been invented are now common within academe: newness sells everywhere, from literary criticism to the epistemology of science. Promotion and search committees in all disciplines now insist on such claims as a condition of advancement.

In anthropology, at least, it is striking that these claims are not always supported once the package is opened.[2] The loud repeal of the elders and the reproduction of their practice also weaken the guild as an intellectual force. But together they enhance individual recognition, which partly explains their resilience: The claim to newness with the guarantee of normal science combine to produce great careers. Yet as far as the future of anthropology is concerned, a third strategy may be more productive—one that explicitly embraces a disciplinary legacy as a necessary condition for present practice, but systematically identifies specific changes that would help redefine that practice.

This admittedly formulaic proposition immediately raises two sets of questions. First, since the past is always a construction, a choice that silences some antecedents to privilege others, which legacy should anthropology claim? And why? How does one establish a critical distance vis-à-vis that legacy? Second, since not all innovations can be equally beneficial, how do we measure their relative intellectual worth? How do we distinguish between the fads that appeal to our academic sensibilities and the ideologies of our times, and the methods, approaches, and themes that are likely to be relevant in a distant future at which we can only guess? What are the zones of last retreat and the risks worth taking? Finally, how do we help achieve, if not a better future, at least a better reading of possible futures? Obviously, these are public questions and my answers to them can only be contributions to a public debate.

My initial response about the legacies for anthropology to claim is that we need to arc back to those disciplinary traditions that best help us understand the world today. If our age is indeed marked by changes in the size, velocity, and directions of global flows—and the fragmentation and confusion those changes create—anthropology should claim anew the traditions that paid special attention to such flows. If our age is also marked by the death of utopia, and if the geography of imagination of the West links utopia, order, and savagery, then anthropology should also claim the legacies most likely to challenge the Savage slot from within and from without. The deep-rooted connection between history and anthropology takes new relevance in that light.

HISTORY AND POWER: THE SHAPING OF THE MODERN WORLD

Throughout most of its career as a distinct intellectual practice, anthropology has overlapped with history. F. W. Maitland's famous line that anthropology will be history or it will be nothing—altogether plagiarized and misunderstood (Cohn 1987, 53)—still resonates in the discipline because it reflected not only a wish but also a perception of a state of affairs. When anthropology began to emerge as a separate profession in the 1870s and 1880s, the few anthropologists practicing in the United States were historians of a kind, collecting either material history—mostly non-European arti-facts for museums or oral histories of Native Americans for government agencies. The academic figures who towered intellectually over the newly emerging field in Europe as in the United States saw history, cultural or legal, as their prime material. Henry Maine (1861), Lewis Henry Morgan (1877), Edward B. Tylor (1881)—to cite only three names now recognized as founding figures—wrote treatises about "ancient societies," or "the early history of mankind."

Early on, anthropology's history differed from that of most guild his-torians, who were then increasingly obsessed with the nationalized past of their states of origins. Instead, the first historical anthropologists stressed world history. That "world," however, was a residual category, a variation of the Savage slot that encompassed potentially anything that was deemed safely outside the newly nationalized memories of North Atlantic populations. The relevance of anthropology's universal history was its very vagueness, its capacity to speak *to* "mankind" without speaking to anyone in particular. Yet it did speak *of* mankind in the context of the times, and universal history continued to influence anthropological works well into the twentieth century (White 1949; Wolf 1982).

At the end of the nineteenth century, anthropology took a second and much more precise historical turn. New trends—such as diffusionism in Germany and the historically oriented anthropology that emerged with Boas in the United States—prompted a growing number of practitioners to investigate, in varied ways and often for quite different purposes, how par-ticular groups of people came to possess the cultural attributes that were said to characterize them.[3] It is fair to say that by the beginning of the last century most anthropologists knew that local "traditions are invented" long before that phrase became fashionable in the late 1980s.

Yet it is fair also to concede that this acknowledgment, however wide-spread in theory, became less relevant to anthropological practice with the institutionalization of the discipline in degree-granting departments. In North America, where Boasian practitioners focused almost exclusively on American Indians, anthropology's history became the story of a pre-conquest past, the remoteness of which guaranteed that the people under study would be severed "from the modern industrial society in which they lived, from which they could hardly escape, and to which they were clearly subject" (Mintz 1984, 15).

In the United States as in Europe, institutionalization also meant a very limited geographical specialization. One became an expert on a subcontinent, on a culture area, or even on a single tribe. The further narrowing of geographical specialization reinforced historical blindness. As we have noted elsewhere, the more doctoral students produced monographs devoted to supposedly discrete groups and cultures, the more the ethnographic trilogy emphasized culture or structure at the expense of history [see chapter 13, this volume].

It took the political tremors of the late 1960s for history to return vigorously to the center of anthropological practice. The political and ideological clashes of the times raised vital questions to which many anthropologists felt their disciplinary tradition had no answers (Gough 1968a, 1968b; Hymes 1972). How did the world turn out the way it is, so varied yet so unified? What should be the terms of the relations between the North Atlantic and the rest of the world? Should anthropology's contribution to shaping these relations be ethical and practical, or safely academic? Did anthropologists have a duty to be on the side of the people they study? These questions, which resonated throughout the North Atlantic, were exacerbated in the United States when news of the clandestine use of anthropologists for intelligence purposes in Latin America and Southeast Asia shook the American Anthropological Association.

Looking for answers while striving to "reinvent anthropology," a growing minority of practitioners returned to history, including the history of anthropology itself. But that third historical turn in the evolution of the discipline differed from its predecessors in two related ways. First, it was a history meant to put the past in direct relation with the present, rather than a bifurcation meant to discount or even to hide the immediacy of that relation. In sharp contrast to the earlier Boasians, history served to bridge distances between cultures rather than to isolate them.[4]

Second, power—until then a theoretical oxymoron outside of the reserved area of political anthropology—became the key mediator of the new relation between past and present. Since power launched on a global scale was what tied world populations, power became the theoretical axis connecting anthropology and history, the central concept—sometimes implicit, often explicit—in accounting for the many ways in which the past helped to shape the present.

The repeated appearances of words hitherto absent from anthropology's standard vocabulary—such as colonialism, racism, imperialism, domination, or resistance—is only a superficial sign of that turn to a history of power that started in the late 1960s. More fundamental was the now widespread acknowledgment that the world in which we live is a product of a capitalist expansion, of which the domination of non-European peoples is an inherent chapter. For a growing number of anthropologists, non-European peoples stopped being "primitive" and became oppressed, marginalized, colonized, or racial minorities somewhere in the 1970s (Hymes 1972; Whitten and Szwed 1970). At about the same time the relation between anthropology and forms of domination—notably colonialism—was repeatedly exposed (Asad 1973; Leclerc 1972), generating no small amount of soul searching—and guilt—among some North Atlantic practitioners.

But neither guilt nor political stance alone could generate a fecund research program. As the excitement of the 1960s withered, the sober exploration of the links between colonialism, capitalism, and European expansion soon became the most tangible development within the new historically oriented anthropology. Since the mid-1970s that exploration has generated a substantial share of anthropological production within the North Atlantic.

In that context, Marx, who had been largely absent from anthropology—and kept at bay in the United States by the era of McCarthyism—became both a key interlocutor and a claimed predecessor (Godelier 1973; Meillassoux 1975; Mintz, Godelier, and Trigger 1984; O'Laughlin 1975).[5] Anthropologists engaged various blends of Marxism with world historical pretensions, such as dependency theory (Frank 1969) and world-system theory (Wallerstein 1976). The least controversial yet most fundamental propositions of these schemes, notably the historical unity of the modern world, have now been integrated into the discipline. Currently anthropology assumes constitutive links between the past and the present, the Here and the Elsewhere, the colonizers and the colonized, the North Atlantic and the postcolony (Alexander and Alexander 1991; Blanchetti-Revelli 1997; Carter 1997; Chatterjee 1989; Comaroff and Comaroff 1991; Feierman 1990; Heath 1992; Nash 1992; Ong 1988; Smith 1984; Stoler 1985; Trouillot 1988).

Yet even when they are openly sympathetic to world historical schemes, anthropologists seldom adopt them without serious modifications. Practicing anthropologists are rarely satisfied with affirming or even demonstrating that the world today is a product of power, or that colonialism within a loosely defined capitalist world system was a crucial manifestation of that power on a global scale. Rather they tend to pay attention—at least more attention than others—to the less obvious ways in which power is deployed and subtly impacts global interactions. They favor the less obvious mechanisms of North Atlantic domination—dress codes, religious campaigns, cuisine, literacy programs, linguistic change, and botanical gardens—over more blunt military and political deployments of power (Brockway 1979; Heath 1992).

Most anthropologists working in the historical mode also tend to focus their research on local dynamics within the colony and the postcolony, paying great attention to the particulars of what Sidney Mintz (1977) calls "local initiative and local response."[6] Local dynamics and global power are indeed what best distinguish this historical turn from preceding ones in anthropology. Early anthropologists such as Maine or Tylor were interested in universal history. The first Boasians focused on particular histories severed from the world. Historical anthropologists today deal with global history in local contexts. They are anxious to demonstrate how the global deployment of power never fully achieves, on the ground, the results expected by those who unleashed that power. Juxtaposing structures and events, necessity and contingency, they aim to document how local responses vary from relative retrenchment to relative incorporation within the world system, from relative accommodation to subtle or overt resistance (Comaroff and Comaroff 1991; Price 1983; Trouillot 1982). At times, local response can be the integration of the colonizer's presence into symbolic structures that preceded contact and conquest—a reinforcement, albeit awkward and perhaps temporary, of the very tradition challenged by the deployment of North Atlantic power (Sahlins 1985). At other times, resistance can take the form of a newly invented tradition adopted by colonized groups, a reworking of the past in response to that deployment of power.

Such an anthropology is by definition multidisciplinary, reaching out to historians and other human scientists (Cohn 1987).[7] It has developed strong ties with other attempts to write a history from below, such as subaltern studies (Chatterjee 1989; Said 1993; Trouillot 1995), and ends up questioning the North Atlantic historicity that made it possible in the first place. Ultimately, the analysis of power problematizes the very power to write the story.

. . . AND THEN CAME FIELDWORK

Anthropology's long-standing interest in time and history overlaps with a more ambiguous relation with space and place. A naive conception made spaces into places—or more exactly, into locales and localities: things that existed out there, the reality of which, although central to anthropological practice, was not to be questioned or analyzed. Spurred by an empiricist epistemology that often equated the object of observation with the object of study, anthropology's overemphasis on localities preceded the rise of fieldwork as a marker of the discipline. Fieldwork reinforced both the influence of that epistemology and the centrality of localities in anthropological practice. Critiques and eulogies of fieldwork today reach their full potential only to the extent that they address both the assumptions of empiricism and the naive construction of locales and localities.

When anthropology solidified as a discipline in the nineteenth century, the naive treatment of space paralleled a general tendency in the human sciences to empirically set the boundaries of the object of study and to take for granted the unit of analysis. Both that object and that unit were thought to be contained within the place observed. Various disciplines defined or redefined themselves by imposing their mark on the preferred object of observation: the body, the nation-state, the surface of the earth, language, social organizations, or political institutions.

None of these could be anthropology's reserved domain to the extent that it claimed most of them. More importantly, the Savage slot restricted anthropology's claims of specialized competence to non-Western peoples. Increasingly anthropology's object of observation turned out to be defined primarily as a locality—especially after the relative decline of the universal history championed by the likes of Maine and Tylor.

The nuances between location, locale, and locality, subtle as they may be, are crucial here. We can see *location* as a place that has been situated, localized if not always located. One needs a map to get there, and that map necessarily points to other places without which localization is impossible. We can see the *locale* as a venue, a place defined primarily by what happens there: a temple as the locale for a ritual, a stadium as the venue for a game. *Locality* is better perceived as a site defined by its human content, most likely a discrete population. A fishing locality is one thought to be populated by fishermen and their families, a farming locality is said to be populated by farmers, and a culture area is a locality populated by people who are said to share similar cultures. Both locale and locality, therefore, are places where something or someone can be located even if their own situatedness as locations remains vague. Anthropology's weak treatment of the field as a site for our work has to do with the fact that it always tended to conceive places at best as locales, and at worst as localities, rather than as locations.

When anthropologists write that the Tolai of New Britain and the Rukuba of Plateau State contribute to bridewealth while the Kekchi of Pueblo Viejo prefer bride service, it matters little that Pueblo Viejo is in Belize, Plateau State in Nigeria, and New Britain in Papua New Guinea. The geographical names index localities rather than locations; they are specific places, but relevant mainly because of the kinds of marriage arrangements that occur there and their classificatory effects on the populations. For the statement on bridewealth to make sense and be operative in anthropological discourse, it need not address the fact that the three places just cited are contested locations. It does not matter that their names, limits, and forms of incorporation within the larger world have been and are still open to often quite bloody debates. That in 1943 the Fifth and Thirteenth US Air Force bombers shelled New Britain so much that they set a new record for bomb loads in the history of warfare is absolutely and objectively irrelevant within that discourse.[8]

Similarly, the listings of early armchair anthropologists who drew information from occasional observers can be read as various catalogues of localities and locales. In their treatment of these places, some anthropologists—notably the universalist historians and the diffusionists—did lay the groundwork for a problematization of space that could eventually question the naturalness of both locales and localities. However, as British and French anthropologists specialized along colonial lines and as culture-areas in the Americas became collections of localities and peoples, the reduction of the object of study to a place defined by its discrete human content became even more consequential. Cultures and localities were like hand and glove, perfect content for the most fitting container. By the time fieldwork became a constitutive moment of anthropological practice, it only made obvious the treatment of places as localities, isolated containers of distinct cultures, beliefs, and practices.

Fieldwork is not the theoretical villain here, only an accessory to a theoretical erasure. First, as noted above, the naive treatment of space as locales or localities preceded the fetishization of ethnographic fieldwork. Second, the notion of the field as a source of data was shared across the human and natural sciences in the nineteenth century (Kisklick 1997; Stocking 1987). Third, the reduction of anthropological practice to fieldwork itself and the related reduction of fieldwork to ethnographic data gathering are more recent than most anthropologists recognize. Fourth, this double reduction did not proceed from a theoretical reassessment. On the contrary, fieldwork merely confirmed the crossing out of locations.

When Bronislaw Malinowski's *Argonauts of the Western Pacific*, now held or criticized as the ethnography par excellence, first came out in 1922, only a minority saw it as a methodological watershed in anthropological practice. Those who did see it as such did not insist so much on the unusual length and carefulness of the ethnographic fieldwork behind it. Rather, their immediate methodological praise was focused on Malinowski's exhortation to anthropologists to lay bare the means through which they gathered their facts and the relations they produced between facts and statements.[9] The consecration of Malinowski or Boas as archetypal fieldworkers, the reduction of ethnography to fieldwork, and the fetishization of fieldwork itself as the defining moment of sociocultural anthropology belong more to the second than to the first part of the twentieth century.[10] Only after World War II does ethnography become synonymous with fieldwork, especially in the English-speaking world, and the anthropologist become primarily a fieldworker.[11] Only then do we find the proliferation of statements as strong as that of S. F. Nadel (1951, 9): "Like the practical sociologist, the anthropologist is primarily a field worker."[12] A decade later Joseph Casagrande was even more emphatic: "For the anthropologist the field is thus the fountainhead of knowledge, serving him as both laboratory and library" (1960, x).[13]

More than a theoretical reflection on the epistemological status of ethnography, changes in the world at large were behind this new euphoria. Coming on the heels of a world depression and ending with a victory against evil, World War II fundamentally transformed both the mood and the composition of North Atlantic campuses. A different world opened up to the young men who joined graduate school in those times and who shaped various fields of knowledge for the next fifty years. In anthropology, the war increased both the desire for and the feasibility of fieldwork, at least in the English-speaking world (Cohn 1987, 26–31; Penniman 1974). The 1960s built upon that base. The demographic boom in North American social science—propelled by tighter relations between the federal state and academe and the expansion of the world economy—offered anthropologists, among others, what Bernard Cohn (1987, 30) calls with biting humor "irresistible opportunities" for growth. With increased specialization justifying expansion, ethnographic fieldwork became the first credential of the specialist, the proof of *his* expertise on *his* locality.[14]

However, localities—just like locales—preceded fieldwork, which cannot be blamed for artificially isolating them from global flows and transformations. That isolation was first premised in the Savage slot. Recall that the geography of imagination inherent in the West requires a complementary space, but recall also that this space need not be localized. As place, it can be anywhere. Recall also that anthropology's relative disregard for the geography of management, which is also inherent in the West, severed the study of populations deemed non-Western from the deployment of North Atlantic power.

The inability to construct places as locations derives from these two fundamental choices. It also derives from an empiricist epistemology that reduced the object of study to the thing observed. It also rests on a refusal to address the epistemological status of the native voice. The specificity of anthropology is not "the field" but a certain way of doing fieldwork that is premised on the locality as a place both severed from the world and constitutive of the object of study. The emphasis on fieldwork, prompted as it was by institutional reproduction and expansion, only fused the locality as the place observed with the place within which observation occurred.

Margaret Mead understood quite well the connections criticized here—except that she approved of them. She concludes a 1933 article on field methods with these words: "The ethnologist has defined his scientific position in terms of a field of study rather than a type of problem, or a delimitation of theoretical inquiry. The cultures of primitive peoples are that field" (Mead 1933, 15). The entire article is premised upon the triangular relation and equivocation between the field as object of study, the field as object of observation (the place observed), and the field as the place within which observation occurs.

CONSTRUCTING "THE FIELD"

Seen from that viewpoint, the critiques of fieldwork that sprang up in the 1980s and 1990s (e.g., Gupta and Ferguson 1997; Marcus 1997; Marcus and Fischer 1986; Ruby 1982) launched a much-needed reevaluation of anthropology's most acclaimed practice. Their relentless assault on the naive notion of space on which fieldwork rests leads to a reevaluation of the assumptions that made *a certain kind of fieldwork* so central to anthropology's claims and practice. The problem is not fieldwork per se, but the taking for granted of localities upon which the fetishization of a certain kind of fieldwork was built and the relationship between such supposedly isolated localities and supposedly distinct cultures.

The two illusions are intertwined, and a full reevaluation of ethnography requires a critique of the culture concept (Abu-Lughod 1991; Trouillot 2003 [and chapter 13 of this volume]). But whereas the illusion of self-enclosed cultures still attracts many anthropologists, the obviousness of massive global flows makes it impossible for anthropologists to maintain the illusion of detached localities. Not surprisingly, a number of new topics, emerging themes or—more rarely—explicit proposals coalesce into a new tendency to bypass the traditional localities once seen as necessary sites of anthropological research. I welcome these new trends: complex objects of observations may indeed lead to complex studies. Yet if localities are only the byproducts of a naive treatment of the object of study, these new turns in anthropological practice can fully succeed only to the extent that they lead to new modes of constructing *both* the object of observation and the object of study.

One example will make the point: that of multisited ethnography, a practice that somewhat preceded the critique of the 1980s (Steward et al. 1956) and reemerged as a more systematic proposal in the 1990s (e.g., Marcus 1997). Just like team-ethnography, a multisited ethnography can be a partial answer to the limitations of the ethnographic trilogy (one observer, one time, one place). That partial answer is insufficient, however, if it does not address head-on the role of localities as objects of observation. After all, nineteenth-century anthropologists collected data from more than one site. There is no theoretical ground for claiming that an ethnography of Haitian vodou sited simultaneously in New York City, southern Cuba, and rural Haiti would inherently address the issue of locality any better than an ethnography that follows Haitian peasants from house to farm to town. To assume this is to assume that multisited means to cross the boundaries of national states, an assumption that sends us right back to nineteenth-century postulates. A multisited ethnography is quite reconcilable with an empiricist epistemology if it constructs the object of study as a mere multiplication of the places observed. The multiplication of localities does not solve the problem of their construction as given entities "out there."

Another move away from the traditional locality is the ongoing development of an anthropology that tries to capture global encounters in their very movement, an anthropology of streams and flows in the making, which takes the linkages, junctures, and borders created or transformed by global movements, when not the actual movement itself, as the object of observation (Clifford 1994; Hannerz 1992; Heyman 1995; Pi-Sunyer 1973; Rouse 1991). That anthropology takes the commodities, institutions, activities, or populations that constitute central—though not always obvious—linkages or streams in the movement of global flows as its favorite sites. Thus a commodity like seaweed, unfamiliar to most individuals yet a key additive for the food industry, links the Philippines and the United States by way of McDonald's hamburgers (Blanchetti-Revelli 1997). A McDonald's restaurant in Beijing, in turn, becomes a privileged site to access not "Chinese culture" per se but the cultural transformations brought about by what many Chinese perceive as a new and top-notch form of eating and socializing (Yan 1997).

This latter example is the sort of occurrence that common sense identifies as a major sign of globalization, and that the food, clothing, and entertainment industries clamor as proof of a new global culture. Yet a close ethnography of that linkage raises a number of issues that go beyond the obvious, including the extent to which that new presence is a cultural intrusion. How much is the sociocultural direction of McDonald's in Beijing redirected by Chinese groups and individuals of various ages and classes? In this case as in others—such as ethnographies based on the observations of NGO-run clinics, immigration offices, advertising agencies, and banks—the move from traditional ethnographic localities to sites where global flows are empirically inescapable does not by itself solve the need for localization. On the contrary, the visibility of global flows in these new sites begs the question of their situatedness: What else is there for me to know about the individuals seen in that place?

Empirical global markers make these places fascinating sites for fieldwork in our times. They provide clearer opportunities for localizing the places they so mark, but they can also blind the ethnographer to the situatedness of these sites and their local conditions of possibility. Anthropologists cannot fall for the obvious sameness of airport lounges. A Nike shop in Mumbai is not the same site as a Nike shop in Johannesburg, and it should not be treated the same. On the contrary, the ethnographic challenge is to discover the particulars hidden by this sameness. Empirical global markers alone cannot transform these newly found *localities* of new consumers of global products into historically situated *locations*, each exhibiting global markers, yet unique nonetheless.

The move to bypass traditional localities is also inherent and most obvious in the growing number of studies that focus on human global flows such as tourists, migrants, diasporas, and refugees: people caught between the Here and the Elsewhere and carriers of multiple directions. Here again, the opportunities are numerous, but the pitfalls are plenty, if only because of the sensibilities involved.[15]

Flows of population have marked the history of humankind since its beginnings, and the conquest of the Americas produced some of the most important diasporas of all time. Thus, in some ways mass migrations are not new (see Trouillot 2003, 29–46). Furthermore, current flows are not as massive as they sometimes seem. The vast majority of human beings continue to be raised and buried within the same immediate area of their birth. This is true even in the North Atlantic states and even more so in Latin America and the Caribbean, Africa or Asia.

In another way, however, demographic growth and the transformations emphasized in this book together point to qualitative differences. World population grew from a contested three hundred million to over six billion in the five hundred years between the start of the Castilian conquest of the Americas and our times. The very definition of what constitutes a mass migration changes in light of that growth. Flows of population take on different meanings in that changing context. Those meanings are shaped not only by the numbers involved but also by the specific history of those who move and those who see them leave or arrive. To put it this way immediately suggests that the object of observation cannot be only the individuals who compose the diasporic population in the present they live or in the space they occupy. It suggests a necessary turn to multiple places and times, all of which are relevant to our understanding of the management of a specific diaspora by local and transnational institutions, of its responses to these institutional pressures, and of the changing meanings that precede, follow, or accompany this reception and these responses. Just as the ethnography of the state cannot take the state as a given object of observation "out there" [see chapter 11], an ethnography of diasporas cannot assume the conflation of the object of study and the object of observation.

The lesson is worth spelling out because diasporas, as a topic, bypass the naive notion of the isolated locality premised in traditional ethnographic fieldwork better than any of the other new themes, topics, or sites spurred by the empirical visibility of global flows today. One could write the ethnography of a tourist village as a mere locality through which populations flow. One could pretend to study a refugee camp as a self-enclosed temporary site for transplanted populations. In both of these cases, as in that of banks, agencies, or restaurants, the most obvious empirical facts do not necessarily force us outside of the site—seen as a locality. They push us in this direction, but we could resist and refuse to see the signs of a larger world, just like previous anthropologists sometimes refused to see the links between their villages and the world around them. Compare the possibility of two ethnographies: one of a fishing village (locality defined by content) that happens to be on the Caribbean island of Dominica, and a Pakistani neighborhood (locality also defined by content) that happens to be in Leeds.

Leeds here is much more operational than Dominica. It is much more difficult to pretend that a Pakistani neighborhood in Leeds is not located in Leeds and that Leeds itself is not located in England. Everything about that neighborhood keeps reminding us of its localization. Although the theoretical and methodological issues are the same in these two situations, our perception of the situations makes some shortcuts harder in the case of the Pakistani neighborhood. Because the situatedness of diasporas is obvious and indeed part of their definition, the ethnography of diasporas inherently bypasses the locality.[16] Yet at the same time this situatedness forces us to admit that the disappearance of the locality does not erase the need for localization, and that the object of study—here as elsewhere—cannot be reduced to the object of observation.

If everything about Leeds's Pakistani neighborhood evokes localization, everything there and around also reminds us that this localization is not an empirical given. In my ethnography of that neighborhood I need not, in fact cannot, say everything I know, let alone everything that is there to be known, about Leeds, England, or Pakistan. Yet everything I would want to say about that neighborhood has to do with the fact that it is located.[17] Thus it is not only that I need to be selective empirically. The impossibility of clinging to a fictitiously closed locality imposes upon me the fact that *localization is not an empirical process*. Localization is part of the process through which I construct my "field"; it is part of the construction of the object of observation as it relates to the object of study.

While empirical data never speak for themselves, anthropologists cannot speak without data. Even when couched in the most interpretive terms, anthropology requires observation—indeed, often field observation—and relies on empirical data in ways and to degrees that distinguish it as an academic practice from both literary and cultural studies. That such data is always constituted and such observation is always selective does not mean that the information they convey should not pass any test for empirical accuracy. The much welcome awareness that our empirical base is a construction in no way erases the need for such a base. On the contrary, this awareness calls upon us to reinforce the validity of that base by taking more seriously the construction of our object of observation. Ideally this construction also informs that of the object of study in a back and forth movement that starts before fieldwork and continues long after it. But the preliminary conceptualization of the object of study remains the guiding light of empirical observation: "What is it that I need to know in order to know what I want to know?"[18]

What I want to know in this case is never merely an empirical fact, let alone what I could learn from someone else—from a book, for instance. It is the knowledge that I want to produce. It is what I want to say about this topic, this site, these people—the "burning questions" I want to share even with myself as interlocutor. In that sense, the construction of the object of study is always dialogical.[19] But if that is so, then issues of methodology and epistemology are inherently tied to issues of purpose. What is the purpose of this dialogue? Who are the interlocutors? To whom does it—and should it—make sense?

BURNING QUESTIONS

To the extent that anthropologists have shared their burning questions, our dialogues have been between interlocutors within the North Atlantic. The limitation is in part practical: the vast majority of our readers reside in Europe and North America. It has also a political dimension: the distribution of writers and readers reflects the uneven distribution of economic and political power on a world scale. I would like to insist, however, on an epistemological dimension of this limitation that is directly related to the discussion of ethnography as a knowledge-producing practice—the issue of the status of the native voice in anthropological discourse. That issue opens the door to a critical appraisal of both the privileges and limitations of anthropology's position between the social sciences and the humanities.

The Scholar and the Text

Academic discourse never gives full epistemological status to speech produced outside of academe. Since universities—and like institutions—became the primary centers of scholarly production in the North Atlantic in the mid-nineteenth century, part of the distinction of academe is its claim to a level of competency—a relationship to truth, established through a specialized construction of the object of study—that cannot be reached outside of that institutionalized frame.[20]

We should not be surprised that anthropologists never give the people they study the right to be as knowledgeable or, more precisely, to have the same kind of knowledge about their own societies as ethnographers. North Atlantic sociologists, economists, or political scientists do not extend such a right to the people of Norway, Germany, Italy, or Canada.

They only concede that the populations under observation have empirical information and phenomenological experiences. French scholars may unanimously agree that the residents of Normandy know how to produce the best raw cheese in the world. They may also agree that these villagers have strong feelings about the United States's ban on raw cheese from France. Few French chemists, however, will claim that the villagers of Normandy understand the chemical process behind cheese production the way a chemist does, and no French economist will admit that the villagers' understanding of the economic stakes behind the US ban is equal to that of a graduate of the École nationale d' administration. On the humanities end of the continuum, part of the claim of literary criticism is a competency over the meaning of an author's voice that extends beyond any autobiography or self-analysis produced by the author in question.

Social scientists and literary critics differ in their construction of authorship and authority. The claim of the most quantitative sociologists, economists, and political scientists with a positivist bent is that they have summarized the voice of the participants in such ways that the lived experience embedded in that voice has become inconsequential. Affect has been transformed into a reference. Beliefs can be reduced to actions. At the other end of the spectrum, most literary critics are eager to convince us that if we read them we will be better able to understand or appreciate the voices of a Joyce or a Baudelaire. But few literary scholars are likely to tell us that we do not need to read Baudelaire or Joyce if we read their critiques. None would venture to suggest that the effect of reading their work is the same as reading Baudelaire or Joyce. While statisticians—the extreme summarizers—may tell us that lived experience does not matter once it has been summarized in a referential language, literary critics as interpreters are telling us that lived experience—in this case our aesthetic encounter with an author's voice—can only be consumed raw, that is, by reading the text.

For different reasons, these two constructions of authority allow some autonomy to the voice of the observed—or the voice observed, as in the case of literary criticism. Even the most epistemologically naive economists, sociologists, and political scientists assume—often implicitly—that in summarizing the voice contained in lived experience, they somehow must create an object of study that is slightly different from that voice. Raw experience cannot encapsulate fully the object of study: it becomes data.[21] At the other end of the continuum, literary scientists concede that their own object of study is different from what the voice of the author says in and of itself or about itself. In both cases, the claim to a unique competency goes through a dual acknowledgment. The observer acknowledges a minimal difference between the object of study and the object of observation and a relative autonomy of voice to the first actor. Even when that double acknowledgment comes as a reluctant compromise, as it does for most positivists, and even when it is implicit, as it is for many literary scholars, it is necessary to the scholar's claim of competency.

The Native in the Text

Projected against that background, anthropology's control over the native voice seems unique. Caught between the hard social sciences and the humanities, anthropology makes claims of competency that span the entire spectrum of the human disciplines. Ethnography's distinction is that it claims to summarize the voice of the native in a manner akin to that of a pollster, yet it also claims to encapsulate the lived experience embodied in this voice in ways that would make the reading of Baudelaire or Joyce redundant. This is the deep claim behind Clifford Geertz's famous comment that the cockfight is "a Balinese reading of Balinese experience, a story they tell themselves about themselves" (1973, 448) and that the ethnographer reads over the natives' shoulders.

Geertz's prose is so enticing that we may miss the fact that the same word *read* refers to two different operations or experiences. The three "texts" treated here do not have the same status. As a reading of the Balinese experience to be itself read by the ethnographer, the cockfight is not a primary text. It is a commentary on that experience. A first construal of that passage would have the ethnographer looking at a Balinese textual commentary (the cockfight) over the primary text of Balinese cultural production (Balinese daily experience). The Balinese collectivity here is both Baudelaire and Joyce writing their primary texts and commenting on their writing—as both authors and critics. But if that is so, then what is Geertz doing there? Is he merely reporting to us as readers what the Balinese commentators have written about their own texts? If so, then contrary to both pollsters and literary critics, the ethnographer is not producing new knowledge. He is reading in the most literal sense.

Naive as it may seem today, this vision of ethnography as mere reportage would have satisfied quite a few anthropologists for nearly a century—from about the 1880s to the early 1980s.[22] Today, however, the vision of ethnography as mere realist reportage is unsatisfying to most ethnographers.[23] Most anthropologists would opt for the solution that makes the second reading or the third text—that of the ethnographer—also an interpretation. The emphasis on ethnography as realist description and the ethnographer as observer has been replaced by an emphasis on ethnography as genre and the ethnographer as author. Clearly that is the direction Geertz (1988) himself prefers. In that second construal, the ethnographer qua critic reads both Baudelaire and Joyce *and* what Baudelaire and Joyce have written about their own work.

But if that is the case, the status of the first two texts in relation to their author(s) is quite different than the status of the texts produced by Baudelaire and Joyce as viewed by literary critics. Both Baudelaire and Joyce were not only aware of their primary production, but they were also aware of any commentary they made about it as being commentaries. The literary critic needs to assume that double awareness in order to proceed with a third level of analysis that constructs differently the object of study.

The ethnographer is in the opposite position. Geertz writes: "The culture of a people is an ensemble of texts, themselves ensembles, which the anthropologist strains to read over the shoulders of those to whom they properly belong" (1973, 452). There is some fuzziness here. Is the ethnographer actually reading the Balinese daily experience—the primary text as culture—or the cultural commentary on that primary text, or both? One could concede that the line between the primary text and a metatext (as commentary) is blurry—that Baudelaire did comment on writing within his writing. Yet that concession still requires that we afford Baudelaire's voice a degree of autonomy and self-definition. Quite the opposite occurs in the claims of ethnography, whether mere reportage or interpretation. The Balinese need not be aware that they are producing a culture that is an ensemble of texts, nor that they are commenting upon that text, in order for the ethnographer to proceed. The Balinese may not know—and need not know—that the cockfight is a story they are telling themselves about themselves.[24] Worse still, the less the Balinese know about the cockfight as commentary, the more relevant the ethnography.

This extraordinary claim is not due to anthropologists' arrogance. Nor does it start with Geertz whose fame and brilliance at formulations make his the most obvious illustration. Geertz's interpretive stance only highlights a relation of domination that was always part of anthropology but that was masked by the illusions of positivist social science. That domination over the native voice comes first from anthropology's position within the human disciplines.[25] It stems also from anthropology's constitutive relation with the Savage slot. While anthropologists draw consequences—some quite debatable—from their academic hybridity, we rarely consider the academic consequences of our insertion into the Savage slot.

Anthropologists are quite aware of the ambiguity inherent in the fact that we straddle the humanities and the social sciences. Geertz himself (1988) has written: "Anthropology is going to have to find out if it is to continue as an intellectual force in contemporary culture . . . if its mule condition (trumpeted scientific mother's brother, disowned literary father) is not to lead to mule sterility." But are anthropologists willing to go as far as their disowned literary fathers? Once Baudelaire's correspondence was published, literary critics had to integrate his personal statements about his work into their discourse. This incorporation required that the critics attribute to Baudelaire what some of them call a "competency effect"; a limited recognition of Baudelaire's authority on Baudelaire as writer. The passages in Baudelaire's letters to his mother, his mistresses, and his friends that speak of literature do not become "scientific." They do not have the epistemological status of the critics' own prose, but they cannot be ignored. Thus, Baudelaire has become an interlocutor, although at a lower level of exchange. When Baudelaire takes upon himself the right to write about aesthetics and modernity, albeit not as an academic, he becomes a full-fledged interlocutor insofar as the critic cannot escape the issue of the relation between Baudelaire's scholarly discourse and his writings.

Geertz is thus quite wrong: anthropology's dual inheritance from the social sciences and the humanities is not an impediment. It is a blessing that need not lead to sterility. However, the luxury of that mixture has too often been used to protect the anthropologist against the native, regardless of theoretical positions within anthropology. While anthropologists with a positivist bent tended to assume the epistemological passivity of their object of observation, anthropologists with an interpretive bent construct that passivity by silencing the competency effect of the native voice in their commentary. Although Geertz insists that the treatment of the cockfight as text makes obvious the "use of emotions for cognitive ends" (1973, 449), the reader does not actually know what the Balinese know, think they know, or aim to know about Balinese society. Ultimately the Balinese cockfight is a Geertzian play, more Geertzian than Balinese. It matters more in the world of the ethnographer than in the world that it supposedly describes. It is staged in that first world.

The location of this stage has little to do with Geertz as an individual scholar, or even with his extreme interpretive stance. It has to do with anthropology's relation to the Savage slot. The rhetoric of the Savage slot is what ensures that the voice of the native is completely dominated by the voice of the anthropologist. Geertz has the right positions: anthropologists indeed stand behind the natives. But we are not so much reading over their shoulders as we are writing on their backs.

This positioning is confirmed by anthropology's flagrant contempt for the most obvious and recognized forms of metasocial commentary emanating from local voices: the discourse of local politicians, local media, and especially local scholars. The usual alibi that local scholarly voices are, by definition, elitist does not hold up to scrutiny. There is no reason to decide a priori that elitist origins make such voices theoretically irrelevant. Few of us would dare to study social reproduction in France without taking Pierre Bourdieu or Alain Touraine as serious interlocutors, especially if we disagree with their analysis of France. The argument is disingenuous inasmuch as the distance between intellectuals and the lay population is measured differently in countries where intellectuals cannot make a living protected by the ivory towers of academe and must also work as journalists, lawyers, medical doctors, or politicians, as they do, for instance, in Haiti. There are other pitfalls in this positioning. Yet when a North American anthropologist tells me that she can study Haiti with a bare knowledge of French because French is the language of the elites, she is affirming her right to dismiss local knowledge that most Haitians think necessary to study their own country.[26] Worse, she is affirming her right to decide which Haitians belong to the Savage slot.

A sparkling minority of anthropological writings demonstrates vividly that while the native cannot face the anthropologist, some anthropologists have tried to face the native. The ways and means of a disciplinary encounter that takes the native voice more seriously—as knowledge, as affect, or as project—are varied. They reflect the moral, political, and aesthetic choices of individual anthropologists. Still the choices are there to explore and debate. I will mention only three cases that reflect the range of this exploration and the possibilities for such a debate.

Richard Price's work on Saramaka historical consciousness (1983, 1990) gives Saramaka historical discourse a competency effect rarely seen in anthropology. Price does remain the dominant voice in this encounter (Trouillot 1992, 24), just like a critic who takes Baudelaire as a serious interlocutor retains the epistemological high ground and the power to reorganize Baudelaire's voice. But this reorganization goes beyond the mere collection of what Baudelaire wrote about his work or what the Saramaka say about history, and immediately gives a new status to the quoted voice. Because Price attempts to face his natives, his readers can read over *his* shoulders and glimpse the Saramaka as historians directly and long enough to pretend to become a third interlocutor. In a different vein and with different purposes, Jennie Smith's ethnography of rural Haiti (2001) systematically searches for a vision of Haitian development, social justice, and social change that would give equal competence to Haitian peasants. On yet a different register, Anna Lowenhaupt Tsing (1993) uses creative shifts in positioning author, native, and reader to allow the Meratus Dayaks of Indonesia to return the Western gaze. The reader can develop the impression that the gaze is returned because we can read over Tsing's shoulders.

Each of these examples demonstrates that ethnographers can do much more than most have done so far to give to the native voice a competency effect that makes it an inescapable and thus specific—even if partial—interlocutor. In restoring the specificity of Otherness—if taken seriously Haitian voices cannot be the same as those of the Dayaks or of the Saramaka—these strategies undermine the stability of the Savage slot. Each of these strategies also has its limits, since above and beyond the ethnographer's choice, the Western gaze remains the stumbling block that makes it impossible for the native to become a full interlocutor.[27]

THE RHETORIC OF THE SAVAGE SLOT

It is a stricture of the Savage slot that the native never faces the observer. In the rhetoric of the Savage slot, the Savage is never an interlocutor but evidence in an argument between two Western interlocutors about the possible futures of humankind. More than five hundred years after the debate at Valladolid about the humanity of the American Indians, Las Casas's brief against the arguments of Sepulveda remains a most powerful—and brilliant—example of that rhetoric.

We can summarize its three steps as follows:

(1) You have suggested that there are different levels of humanity because the Savage is a cannibal, a pagan;

(2) I will show you that the Savage is human because his behavior demonstrates that he is perfectible and thus open to Christ's word;

(3) So that you (my Christian interlocutor) and I can envision a future in which humanity becomes one under God.

The first proposition recaps the interlocutor's argument—an argument often backed by evidence from the life of the Savage or evidence deemed universal. The second proposition challenges that argument on the basis of empirical evidence supposedly collected through meticulous observation—or evidence that leads to a more accurate analysis—of the Savage. The third proposition returns to the possible future envisioned with the interlocutor, a future in which the Savage is neither an active participant nor deciding subject, since he has fulfilled his role as evidence and has no further epistemological or decisional relevance.

With slight changes and the necessary dose of humor, we can reproduce the scheme ad infinitum in North Atlantic discourses about non-Western peoples inside and outside of anthropology:

(1) You have argued that human beings can only be controlled by fear by pointing to past or contemporary states of savagery;

(2) I will show you cases in which savages organize themselves through choice;

(3) So that you and I can envision a future based on our own free will.

(1) You have suggested that human behavior proceeds from individual greed;

(2) I will show you savages whose behavior cannot be explained in either individualistic or material terms;

(3) So that you and I can envision a future where individual human behavior is driven by values other than money.

(1) You have suggested that biological descent determines behavior;

(2) I will show you that beliefs, attitudes, and actions vary within and across racial lines even among savages;

(3) So that you and I can envision a future where one race does not dominate another.

(1) You have argued that Haiti cannot attain democracy because Haitians are culturally challenged or are too ignorant to conceive of such a state of affairs;

(2) I will show you that Haitian peasants have a sophisticated sense of social justice and that Haitian predicaments are in fact due to foreign hegemony;

(3) So that you and I can envision a world where the United States government does not have to impose its will on the Americas.

(1) You have suggested that capitalism is invincible by pointing to its conversion (or domination) of non-Western people;

(2) I will show you how savages resist capitalist indents into their world;

(3) So that you and I can envision a future that is not driven by sheer accumulation.

Two points are worth making about this rhetoric. First, it is most powerful when it does not hide its grounds, that is, when the stakes become immediately public, either because the interlocutor is identified or because the rhetorical use of the Savage is explicit. The power of the Valladolid debate is that the fight was public, the positions explicit, and the opponents well known. That publicity advertises the fact that the ultimate stake was not the range of reasons behind the Indians' alleged cannibalism, nor even their humanity, but Latin Christendom's own conception of humankind and whether that conception allowed for a Catholic (i.e., universal) Church compatible with colonial control. On a different model, the power of Rousseau's Savage in *A Discourse on Inequality* is that the philosopher is very aware and, indeed, makes dear—although some readers miss the point—that the transition from savagery to civilization is a necessary construction. What Rousseau builds on the back of the Savage is a platform from which to envision a social contract based on free will that does not proceed either from Locke's individualist drives or from Hobbes's Leviathan.

Rousseau's uneasy position illustrates the second point about this rhetoric: it often stems from—and appeals to—a moral optimism about humankind. That optimism is sharpened, in this case, by Rousseau's social and political skepticism. Rousseau does not share in the certainty of progress or the necessary improvement of humanity along teleological lines. Contrary to many thinkers of his time, he does not see the inevitability of the great march forward. Yet Rousseau leaps anyway, but backward—as it were—into savagery: if I cannot bet on the Savage, how can I bet on us? He must assume, for no reason, that humanity is essentially good, its history notwithstanding.

This moral optimism permeates anthropology to different degrees. It lurks behind the mock list of arguments above. It sustained anthropology's defense of cultural relativism from Boas to Mead to Geertz's magisterial lecture on "Anti Anti-Relativism" (1984)—one of his best pieces precisely because he does not hide the stakes for anthropologists and for nonanthropologists. Yet anthropologists rarely make that optimism explicit. First, a false construction of objectivity—one that denies the observer the right to sensibilities, as if these sensibilities could disappear by fiat—pushes anthropologists into deep denial about that moral leap, in spite of the fact that this leap—and the generosity it implies toward humanity as a whole—may be the discipline's greatest appeal for entering graduate students. Second, as these graduate students mature, they learn—incorrectly—to associate that moral optimism with social optimism, with teleology, or worse, with political naïveté. Moral optimism need not produce political naïveté. The two become close only when that optimism is shameful, when it refuses to present itself as a primal act of faith in humankind, however qualified by history and politics.

FACING THE NATIVE, FACING THE WEST

This moral optimism is anthropology's best bet in these times of fragmented globality that are marked by the death of utopia and where futures are so uncertain (Trouillot 2003 [and chapter 5 of this volume]). But this optimism comes with duties, responsibilities, and some personal discomfort. We cannot bury it under weak social analysis flavored by political optimism, the way we sometimes do in studies of resistance that any semi-illiterate dictator in the Caribbean or in Africa can easily dismiss as exemplars of liberal political naïveté. When we do that, we add insult to injury for we merely aestheticize the natives' pain to alleviate our own personal uneasiness. Instead, optimism requires that we abandon some of the comforts of the Savage slot and take some risks. I see four worth taking:

(1) an explicit effort to reassess the epistemological status of the native voice in ethnography, to recognize its competency so as to make the native a potential—if not a full—interlocutor;

(2) an explicit effort to publicly identify anthropology's hidden interlocutors in the West who are the ultimate targets of our discourse;

(3) an explicit effort to publicize the stakes of this exchange about humankind within the West;

(4) an explicit claim to the moral optimism that may be this discipline's greatest appeal and yet its most guarded secret.

I have already mentioned examples of strategies that pay more attention to the status of the native voice and aim at restoring the specificity of Otherness in ethnography. In addition to the always limited promotion of such native interlocutors, anthropology also needs to abandon its contempt for local scholarly discourse. All societies produce a formalized discourse about themselves within which there is a scholarly component. Touraine sees this metacommentary as indispensable to a society's historicity. If he is correct in that regard, it means that anthropology has produced not only peoples without history, but also people without historicity. If we acknowledge local scholarly discourse as part of that commentary—as we do for North Atlantic societies—we necessarily construct that commentary as changing, contested, and multiple. We thus recognize the society's historicity and thus pluralize the native. Once we pluralize the native, the category itself becomes untenable and the Savage slot becomes open to deconstruction.

Anthropology also needs to clearly identify its inescapable interlocutors within the West itself. If in the rhetoric of the Savage slot the Savage is evidence in a debate between two Western interlocutors, if indeed that rhetoric is most powerful when couched as a response to a clearly identified addressee, then anthropology should abandon the fiction that it is not primarily a discourse to the West, for the West, and ultimately, about the West as project. On the contrary, we should follow the steps of Las Casas in addressing the Sepulvedas of our times directly, in identifying clearly the ultimate listeners. Some prominent anthropologists have done this in different ways. Margaret Mead and Claude Lévi-Strauss are two strikingly different examples. I have argued that Franz Boas saw his work on race and culture as contrapuntal and saw the need to make this contrapuntal stance more explicit toward the end of his life. Yet the more anthropology solidified as a degree-granting discipline, the more the mechanics of institutionalization made anthropologists act as if their primary interlocutor was not the West and as if the primary goal of the discipline was not a contrapuntal argument—even if inherently diverse and always renewed, enriched, and recapped—to some primary Western narrative. We need to return as confidently as Boas had wished—too late—to the identification of these primary interlocutors without whom the detour into the Savage slot remains a self-congratulatory exercise.

The better we identify such interlocutors—inside and outside of anthropology, and indeed outside of academe, from rational choice theorists, historians, and cultural critics to World Bank officials and well-intentioned NGOs—the more chance there is for savages to jump into the discussion, establish themselves as interlocutors, and further challenge the slot by directly claiming their own specificity.[28] The identification of the interlocutors and their premises facilitates the identification of the stakes. Las Casas and especially Rousseau are spectacular precursors who showed great political and intellectual courage in spelling out what they saw as the stakes behind their contrapuntal arguments. Institutionalized anthropology has tended to choose comfort over risk, masking the relevance of its debates and positions and avoiding a public role.[29]

The time is gone when anthropologists could find solace in the claim that our main civic duty—and the justification for our public support—was the constant reaffirmation that the Bongobongo are "humans just like us." Every single term of that phrase is now publicly contested terrain, caught between the politics of identity and the turbulence of global flows. Too many of the Bongobongo are now living next door, and a few of them may even be anthropologists presenting their own vision of their home societies, or studying their North Atlantic neighbors. The North Atlantic natives who reject them do so with a passion. Those who do accept them do not need anthropologists in the welcoming committee. The political field within which the discipline operates is fundamentally different from that of colonial eras and the world of the 1950s. Not enough dust has yet settled to point to a safe haven of unequivocal neutrality. Anthropology's substantive contributions in this modified context should be a matter of debate among anthropologists inside and outside of academe, but relevance will likely depend on the extent to which the discipline rids itself of some of its shyness and spells out its stakes for a wider audience.

That will not be easy. The last two decades of the twentieth century saw an opening of anthropological discourse to other disciplines, with anthropologists such as Geertz influencing practitioners in all the human sciences. Yet the same period also saw a closing of academic discourse to the problems felt by the majority of the world population. Media claims notwithstanding, the influence of academic research that can be labeled politically "progressive" has decreased—if only because these works are increasingly inaccessible to lay readers. Beyond the absolute need for a technical vocabulary to which research contributes and without which it cannot be sustained, beyond the specific need for syntactic structures that express the complexity of thought and the gracefulness of language, academics—especially in the humanities—have basked in what I call "the aestheticization of theory." By that I mean a process through which theory not only acquires a birthright of its own—a legitimate claim, indeed—but spends its life spinning in a proselytical circle, the main purpose of which is to verify its own beauty.

This retrenchment, more critically felt in the United States and Britain, may be a delayed consequence of the Reagan-Thatcher era as academe slowly adapts to larger economic and institutional changes. More widely, it may also be linked to the perception that capitalist laissez-faire has eliminated all possible alternatives to its own rules of survival. The market economy now reigns supreme in the worldwide distribution of consumer goods. The temptation to read into that domination the omen of a global *market society* is understandable, wrong-headed though it is (see Trouillot 2003, 47–78). Torn between suspicion and seduction, and dazed by the speed and multiple directions of global flows, the retreat of alarmed academics into an aesthetics of theory is also understandable.

That solution, however, is not the only one at reach. It is not even the safest one, inasmuch as the life expectancy of irrelevance tends to be short. More courageous and healthier is the acknowledgment of the many dead ends within the human disciplines brought about or brought to light by current global transformations, including the death of utopia. We might as well admit that all the human sciences may need more than a mere facelift; most will be deeply modified and others, in their current institutional shape, might disappear. As the world changes, so do disciplines.

Anthropologists are well placed to face these changes, first by documenting them in ways that are consistent with our disciplinary history. The populations we traditionally study are often those most visibly affected by the ongoing polarization brought about by the new spatiality of the world economy. They descend directly from those who paid most heavily for the transformations of earlier times. We are well placed to detail the ongoing effects of the power unleashed over five centuries by the West's twin geographies. We are particularly well placed to document these effects on the lived experience of real people everywhere, but especially among those who happen to be the ones most disposable from the viewpoint of capital. The need to renew our topical interests is real, but it should not lead into the temptation to aestheticize the native or to study only natives that suddenly look like us. We cannot abandon the four-fifths of humanity that the Gorbachev Club sees as increasingly useless to the world economy, not only because we built a discipline on the backs of their ancestors but also because the tradition of that discipline has long claimed that the fate of no human group can be irrelevant to humankind.

The claim is somewhat philosophical, but values are among the highest stakes in and behind all arguments about our fragmented globality. Anthropologists are well placed to make those stakes public because they coalesce into topics over which we have some claim of competency: conceptions of humankind, religious differences, cultural relativism, and the ideals, ideologies, and social models specific to particular groups, to name a few among such stakes. While prominent social scientists are urging cultural homogenization as the sole path to global happiness (Harrison and Huntington 2000), anthropologists are well placed to show what conceptions of humankind are behind this call, what vision of the future it promotes, and what imaginary it evokes. When powerful financiers, politicians, and economists tell billions of humans that they should adopt the market as sole social regulator, anthropologists are well placed to show that what is presented as a logical necessity is actually a choice. We can demonstrate that this choice serves the material interests of certain groups and may not be beneficial, even in material terms, to the majority of humankind. We can expose the historical and cultural specificity of this new faith: Why and how is this secular religion emerging here and now, and who are its priests? What is its language of conversion, what are its ritual practices? We can remind our readers inside and outside of academe that one cultural specificity of this new faith is the ability to predict social futures, one that North Atlantic leaders have claimed since the sixteenth century—and especially since the nineteenth—with a resounding rate of failure. We can compare these new omens to older ones and see how they overlap or differ. We can study their charisma without falling for the attraction (Ohnuki-Tierney 2001; Tsing 2000).

A thick description of this new religion also requires that we expose its foundation in a vision of humanity that constructs economic growth as the ultimate human value. We owe it to ourselves and to our interlocutors to say loudly that we have seen alternative visions of humankind—indeed more than any academic discipline—and that we know that this one may not be the most respectful of the planet we share, nor indeed the most accurate, nor the most practical. We also owe it to ourselves to say that it is not the most beautiful nor the most optimistic.

At the end of the day, in this age where futures are murky and utopias mere reminders of a lost innocence, we need to fall back on the moral optimism that has been anthropology's greatest—yet underemphasized—appeal. But we need to separate that optimism from the naïveté that has been liberalism's most convenient shield. We need to assume it as a choice—whether we call it moral, philosophical, or aesthetic in the best sense. We need to hang on to it not because we are historically, socially, or politically naive—indeed, as social scientists we cannot afford such naïveté—but because this is the side of humanity that we choose to prefer, and because this choice is what moved us to anthropology in the first place. We need to assume that optimism because the alternatives are lousy, and because anthropology as a discipline is the best venue through which the West can show an undying faith in the richness and variability of humankind.

NOTES

Editors' Note: This chapter first appeared as "Making Sense: The Fields in Which We Work," chapter 6 of *Global Transformations: Anthropology and the Modern World* (New York: Palgrave Macmillan, 2003), 117–39.

1. World population figures are always contested, but especially before the seventeenth century because of debates about the population of the Americas before the conquest.

2. I used to ask graduate students in theory classes not to read the prefaces and introductions of books based on dissertations, but to try to guess a posteriori from the readings of the ethnographic sections how innovative the authors were. This was by no means a scientific study, but it did confirm my own prejudice that empiricist strategies were being deployed with the same naïveté that was their hallmark since at least the eighteenth century, in spite of self-congratulatory nods to deconstruction and many references to the likes of Foucault or Derrida.

3. Boas ([1920] 1940, 284) writes, "The whole problem of cultural history appears to us [American anthropologists] as a historical problem. In order to understand history it is necessary to understand not only how things are, but how they have come to be."

4. Contrary also to the history of Maine or Tylor, the chronological interest turned to post-Renaissance, rather than to ancient history.

5. Citations of Marx are extremely rare in anthropology in the first half of the twentieth century. In the United States, where the human disciplines were stifled by the anticommunist witch hunt, passing and timid mentions of Marx start a few years after the official end of the hunt and Senator McCarthy's censure (e.g., Wolf 1959, 252).

6. The loudest controversies have been about the nature of that response and the ways in which it matters (Obyesekere 1992; Price and Price 1999; Sahlins 1995).

7. See in particular the first two chapters of Cohn 1987 for a penetrating and lively discussion of the relationship between history and anthropology and the state of historical anthropology up until the mid-1980s.

8. The devastation of Cape Gloucester (New Britain) was so total that *Gloucesterizing* came to mean the complete destruction of a target in Fifth Air Force parlance.

9. Malinowski (1922, 3) wrote: "In Ethnography, the distance is often enormous between the brute material of information . . . and the final authoritative presentation of the results." "Wholesale generalisations are laid down before us, and we are not informed at all by what actual experiences the writers have reached their conclusion. . . ."

Inasmuch as anthropologists—like all professional researchers, from art historians to physicists—draw principled conclusions from privileged information, Malinowski's admonition remains relevant in spite of three related issues to which it cannot be reduced: (1) whether Malinowski himself heeded his own call; (2) whether art historians, anthropologists, and physicists construct information in the same way; (3) whether they build—or should build—the same kind of connections between information and conclusion.

10. T. K. Penniman (1974, 9–17) of Oxford, writing originally in 1935, defines ethnography as "the study of a particular race, people or area *by any of the methods of anthropology*. . . . It furnishes the data required by anthropology, and employs the methods based on such data" (emphasis added).

11. In a 1955 addendum to the same book (1974, 366), Penniman singles out Malinowski's long fieldwork as having given him a unique opportunity to analyze social structures in light of Durkheimian principles.

12. Nadel's own life work strongly qualifies that statement.

13. Both Nadel and Casagrande see anthropology through the nineteenth-century model of a natural science, and Casagrande skirts over the fact that both the library and the laboratory are scholarly constructions.

14. "The field" is gendered, with the dominance of male figures within the discipline and the preeminence of Margaret Mead in the public sphere, at least in the United States. The tension between public sphere and guild practices permeates other aspects of fieldwork. Public claims notwithstanding, fieldwork alone, while often a necessary condition of access to the guild, is rarely a sufficient condition of preeminence. Few anthropologists have gained notoriety *within* the discipline with a monograph based on traditional fieldwork in exotic lands—especially after the 1950s, that is, during the very era when fieldwork is heralded as the distinctive practice of the discipline.

15. Refugees, diasporas, and indeed tourism have become suddenly visible to academics in part because of their growing role in shaping the social and geographical consciousness of North Atlantic populations. Diasporas in particular are poised to stand as archetypes of the current state of cultural transformations on a world scale in part because of their impact on receiving countries,

including their academic institutions. An anthropology of diasporas thus requires not only an awareness of change and continuity but also the awareness of its own conditions of possibility, including the sensibilities that drive the research. Yet how much of the scholarly research on diasporas—as research on other obvious global flows—merely reflects North Atlantic common sense?

16. One could consciously restore the locality, for instance by looking at a specific diasporic neighborhood on the anachronistic model of the closed corporate community. Few anthropologists are tempted to do this today, if only because of the ridicule they would attract.

17. The sensibilities that drive and shape our work may be at play in ways yet to be determined. Why it is possible to write about a fishing village in the Caribbean or to describe a ritual in Indonesia as if they were not localized, while it is obvious that we cannot describe a Pakistani neighborhood in Leeds as if it was not in England, may have less to do with the facts on the ground—the empirical markers—than with our reaction to certain kinds of markers.

18. I owe this phrasing to Niloofar Haeri.

19. Both the content and the phrasing of this paragraph reflect years of sharing "burning questions" with Brackette F. Williams.

20. In the natural sciences, private laboratories, the eminence of which goes back only to the twentieth century, play by the same rules. The only two differences with government sponsored research centers is the financing and the explicit possibility of profit. By the second decade of the twentieth century, even intellectuals whose individual fame did not generate directly from an institutional location became full interlocutors of academics through their institutional recognition. Furthermore, such recognition—always posthumous—is actually quite rare. In the human disciplines, Antonio Gramsci is a spectacular exception for the twentieth century, as he had no institutional location within academe.

21. We see this most clearly on postelection nights when pollsters and journalists pose at being social scientists. They must say something more than the results themselves, lest the results "speak" for themselves. Yet these analysts must also concede—at least in democratic contexts—that, whatever their second reading, the people have indeed spoken.

22. First, reportage in and of itself was satisfying because for a long time anthropologists, along with Orientalists, were the only North Atlantic scholars to pay serious empirical attention to non-Europeans. Second, the possibility of mere reportage was premised on a naive realism: the facts were there to be observed and collected by the ethnographer. To be sure, such "facts" included ideas, motifs, cosmologies, marriage practices, myths, or stories, all the items that collectively constitute "the cultures of primitive peoples" (Mead 1933) and interpretation or analysis could follow. But they were not always necessary.

23. This dissatisfaction did not originate from a theoretical debate about the status of the native. Rather, the second moment of globality, including the spread in communications, made realist ethnography as a reportage on the culture of primitive peoples a redundant exercise. The critique of representation followed (see Trouillot 2003, 7–28 [and chapter 1 of this volume]).

24. Geertz concludes the list of rules for the Balinese cockfight with this unusually awkward statement: "Finally, the Balinese peasants themselves are quite aware of all this and can and, at least to an ethnographer, do state most of it in approximately the same terms as I have" (1973, 440).

25. Not accidentally, the discipline in which we are most likely to encounter similar claims is history, especially in its treatment of events.

26. In contradistinction, just imagine academe's contempt for a researcher who does not speak or read the dominant language in any diglossic situation within the North Atlantic.

27. None of these authors address satisfactorily the issue of local scholarly discourse or explain its irrelevance, although in his later work Price deals with Martinican intellectuals as serious interlocutors, even though he disagrees with them.

28. Only they can gain this status for themselves. No anthropologist—not even anthropologists born and raised outside of the North Atlantic, who risk becoming anthropology's new comfort zone as indeed they have quickly become in literary criticism and cultural studies—can confer this right upon them. We can only facilitate their entry.

29. The number of anthropologists practicing in and out of academe has increased tremendously in the last decades of the twentieth century. Anthropologists have brought their specialized knowledge to governments, international agencies, grassroots organizations, and high-class advertisers. Yet those individualized engagements do not coalesce into trends in part because academic anthropology, the institutional core of the discipline, has not meditated much on its public role. Just as anthropology protected its "primitives" and their pristine "cultures," it also protected itself from the public eye, or at least avoided as much as possible entering the public sphere by the front door (di Leonardo 1998).

REFERENCES

Abu-Lughod, Janet. 1991. "Writing against Culture." In *Recapturing Anthropology: Working in the Present*, edited by Richard G. Fox, 137–62. Santa Fe: School of American Research Press.

Alexander, Jennifer, and Paul Alexander. 1991. "Protecting Peasants from Capital-ism: The Subordination of Javanese Traders by the Colonial State." *Comparative Studies in Society and History* 33: 370–94.

Asad, Talal, ed. 1973. *Anthropology and the Colonial Encounter*. London: Ithaca Press.

Barret, Stanley R. 1984. *The Rebirth of Anthropological Theory*. Toronto: University of Toronto Press.

Baudelaire, Charles. (1857) 1999. *Les fleurs du mal*. Paris: Hazan.

Blanchetti-Revelli, Lanfranco. 1997. "Keeping Meat and Dairy Consumers Slim: Philippine Seaweed, American Carrageenan and the USFDA." *Anthropology Today* 13, no. 5: 6–13.

Boas, Franz. (1920) 1940. *Race, Language, and Culture*. New York: Macmillan.

Boas, Franz. 1932. *Anthropology and Modern Life*. New York: W. W. Norton & Company.

Bodley, John. 1976. *Anthropology and Contemporary Human Problems*. California: Cummings Publishing Company.

Brockway, Lucille H. 1979. "Science and Colonial Expansion: The Role of British Royal Botanic Gardens." *American Ethnologist* 6, no. 3: 449–65.

Carter, Donald Martin. 1997. "Media Politics and the Migrant." In *States of Grace: Senegalese in Italy and the New European Immigration*, edited by Donald Carter, 133–44. Minneapolis: University of Minnesota Press.

Casagrande, Joseph B, ed. 1960. *In the Company of Man: Twenty Portraits of Anthropological Informants*. New York: Harper.

Chatterjee, Partha. 1989. "Colonialism, Nationalism, and Colonized Women: The Context in India." *American Ethnologist* 16, no. 4: 622–33.

Clifford, James. 1994. "Diasporas." *Cultural Anthropology* 9, no. 3: 302–38.

Cohn, Bernard S. 1987. *An Anthropologist among the Historians and Other Essays*. New York: Oxford University Press.

Comaroff, Jean, and John Comaroff. 1991. *Christianity, Colonialism, and Consciousness in South Africa*. Vol. 1 of *Of Revelation and Revolution*. Chicago: University of Chicago Press.

Darwin, Charles. 1871. *The Descent of Man*. New York: Humboldt Publishing Company.

Di Leonardo, Micaela. 1998. *Exotics at Home: Anthropologies, Others, American Modernity*. Chicago: University of Chicago Press.

Feierman, Steven. 1990. *Peasant Intellectuals: Anthropology and History in Tanzania*. Madison: University of Wisconsin Press.

Frank, Andre Gunder. 1969. *Latin America: Underdevelopment or Revolution; Essays on the Development of Underdevelopment and the Immediate Enemy*. New York: Monthly Review Press.

Geertz, Clifford. 1973. *The Interpretation of Cultures*. New York: Basic Books.

Geertz, Clifford. 1984. "Distinguished Lecture: Anti Anti-Relativism." *American Anthropologist* 86, no. 2: 263–78.

Geertz, Clifford. 1988. *Works and Lives: The Anthropologist as Author*. Stanford, CA: Stanford University Press.

Godelier, Maurice. 1973. "Horizon, trajets marxistes en anthropologie." In *Heterologies: Discourse on the Other*, edited by Michel de Certeau, vii–xxi. Minneapolis: University of Minnesota Press.

Gough, Kathleen. 1968a. "Anthropology: Child of Imperialism." *Monthly Review* 19, no. 11: 12–27.

Gough, Kathleen. 1968b. "New Proposals for Anthropologists." *Current Anthropology* 9, no. 5: 403–7.

Gupta, Akhil, and James Ferguson, eds. 1997. *Anthropological Locations: Boundaries and Grounds of a Field Science*. Berkeley: University of California Press.

Hannerz, Ulf. 1992. "The Global Ecumene as Network of Networks." In *Conceptualizing Society*, edited by Adam Kuper, 34–56. New York: Routledge.

Harrison, Lawrence E., and Samuel P. Huntington, eds. 2000. *Culture Matters: How Values Shape Human Progress*. New York: Basic Books.

Heath, Deborah. 1992. "Fashion, Anti-fashion, and Heteroglossia in Urban Senegal." *American Ethnologist* 19, no. 1: 19–33.

Heyman, Josiah. 1995. "Putting Power in the Anthropology of Bureaucracy: The Immigration and Naturalization Service at the Mexico–United States Border." *Current Anthropology* 36, no. 2: 261–77.

Hymes, Dell H., ed. 1972. *Reinventing Anthropology*. New York: Pantheon Books.

Kisklick, Henrika. 1997. "After Ishmael: The Fieldwork Tradition and Its Future." In *Anthropological Locations: Boundaries and Grounds of a Field Science*, edited by Akhil Gupta and James Ferguson, 47–65. Berkeley: University of California Press.

Las Casas, Bartolomé de. (1552) 1992. *In Defense of the Indians: The Defense of the Most Reverend Lord, Don Fray Bartolomé de Las Casas, of the Order of Preachers, Late Bishop of Chiapa, against the Persecutors and Slanderers of the Peoples of the New World Discovered across the Seas*. Translated and edited by Stafford Poole. Dekalb: Northern Illinois University Press.

Leclerc, Gérard. 1972. *Anthropologie et colonialisme: Essai sur l'histoire de l'africanisme*. Paris: Fayard.

Maine, Henry Summer. 1861. *Ancient Law: Its Connection with the Early History of Society, and Its Relation to Modern Ideas*. London: Jay Murray.

Malinowski, Bronislaw. 1922. *Argonauts of the Western Pacific: An Account of Native Enterprise and Adventure in the Archipelagoes of Melanesian New Guinea*. London: Routledge.

Marcus, George E. 1997. *Cultural Producers in Perilous States: Editing Events, Documenting Change*. Chicago: University of Chicago Press.

Marcus, George E., and Michael M. J. Fischer, eds. 1986. *Anthropology as Cultural Critique: An Experimental Moment in the Human Sciences*. Chicago: University of Chicago Press.

Mead, Margaret. 1933. "More Comprehensive Field Methods." *American Anthropologist* 35, no. 1: 1–15.

Meillassoux, Claude. 1975. *Femmes, greniers et capitaux*. Paris: Maspero.

Mintz, Sidney W. 1977. "The So-Called World System: Local Initiative and Local Response." *Dialectical Anthropology* 2, no. 4: 253–70.

Mintz, Sidney W. 1984. "American Anthropology in the Marxist Tradition." In *On Marxian Perspectives in Anthropology: Essays in Honor of Harry Hoijer*, edited by Sidney W. Mintz, Maurice Godelier, and Bruce Trigger, 11–34. Malibu, CA: Undena Publications.

Mintz, Sidney W., Maurice Godelier, and Bruce Trigger, eds. 1984. *On Marxian Perspectives in Anthropology: Essays in Honor of Harry Hoijer*. Malibu, CA: Undena Publications.

Nadel, S. F. 1951. *The Foundations of Social Anthropology*. Glencoe, IL: Free Press.

Nash, June. 1992. "Interpreting Social Movements: Bolivian Resistance to Economic Conditions Imposed by the International Monetary Fund." *American Ethnologist* 19, no. 2: 275–93.

Obeyesekere, Gananath. 1992. *The Apotheosis of Captain Cook: European Mythmaking in the Pacific*. Princeton, NJ: Princeton University Press.

Ohnuki-Tierney, Emiko. 2001. "Historicization of the Culture Concept." *History and Anthropology* 12, no. 3: 231–54.

O'Laughlin, Bridget M. 1975. "Marxist Approaches in Anthropology." *Annual Review of Anthropology* 4: 341–70.

Ong, Aihwa. 1988. "The Production of Possession: Spirits and the Multinational Corporation in Malaysia." *American Ethnologist* 15, no. 1: 28–42.

Penniman, T. K. 1974. *A Hundred Years of Anthropology*. New York: William Morrow.

Pi-Sunyer, Oriol. 1973. "Tourism and Its Discontents: The Impact of a New Industry on a Catalan Community." *Studies in European Society* 1: 1–20.

Price, Richard. 1983. *First-Time: The Historical Vision of an Afro-American People*. Baltimore, MD: Johns Hopkins University Press.

Price, Richard. 1990. *Alabi's World*. Baltimore, MD: Johns Hopkins University Press.

Price, Sally, and Richard Price. 1999. *Maroon Arts: Cultural Vitality in the African Diaspora*. Boston: Beacon Press.

Rouse, Roger. 1991. "Mexican Migration and the Social Space of Postmodernism." *Diaspora* 1, no. 1: 8–23.

Rousseau, Jean-Jacques. (1755) 1984. *A Discourse on Inequality*. Translated by Maurice Cranston. New York: Penguin Books.

Ruby, Jay, ed. 1982. *A Crack in the Mirror: Reflexive Perspectives in Anthropology*. Philadelphia: University of Pennsylvania Press.

Sahlins, Marshall. 1985. *Islands of History*. Chicago: University of Chicago Press.

Sahlins, Marshall. 1995. *How "Natives" Think: About Captain Cook, for Example*. Chicago: University of Chicago Press.

Said, Edward W. 1993. *Orientalism*. New York: Pantheon.

Smith, Carol A. 1984. "Local History in Global Context: Social and Economic Transitions in Western Guatemala." *Comparative Studies in Society and History* 26, no. 2: 193–228.

Smith, Jennie Marcelle. 2001. *When the Hands Are Many: Community Organization and Social Change in Rural Haiti*. Ithaca, NY: Cornell University Press.

Steward, Julian Haynes, Robert A. Manners, Eric R. Wolf, Elena Padilla Seda, Sidney W. Mintz, and Raymond L. Scheele. 1956. *The People of Puerto Rico: A Study in Social Anthropology*. Urbana: University of Illinois Press.

Stocking, George W., Jr., ed. 1987. *A Franz Boas Reader: The Shaping of American Anthropology, 1883–1911*. Chicago: University of Chicago Press.

Stoler, Ann L. 1985. "Perceptions of Protest: Defining the Dangerous in Colonial Sumatra." *American Ethnologist* 12, no. 4: 642–58.

Trouillot, Michel-Rolph. 1982. "Motion in the System: Coffee, Color, and Slavery in Eighteenth-Century Saint-Domingue." *Review (Fernand Braudel Center)* 5, no. 3: 331–38.

Trouillot, Michel-Rolph. 1988. *Peasants and Capital: Dominica in the World Economy*. Baltimore, MD: Johns Hopkins University Press.

Trouillot, Michel-Rolph. 1992. "The Caribbean Region: An Open Frontier in Anthropological Theory." *Annual Review of Anthropology* 21: 19–42.

Trouillot, Michel-Rolph. 1995. *Silencing the Past: Power and the Production of History*. Boston: Beacon Press.

Trouillot, Michel-Rolph. 2003. *Global Transformations: Anthropology and the Modern World*. New York: Palgrave Macmillan.

Tsing, Anna Lowenhaupt. 1993. *In the Realm of the Diamond Queen: Marginality in an Out-of-the-Way Place*. Princeton, NJ: Princeton University Press.

Tsing, Anna Lowenhaupt. 2000. "The Global Situation." *Cultural Anthropology* 15, no. 3: 327–60.

Tylor, Edward B. 1881. *Anthropology: An Introduction to the Study of Man and Civilization*. New York: D. Appleton and Company.

Wallerstein, Immanuel. 1976. *The Modern World-System*. New York: Academic Press.

White, Leslie. 1949. *The Science of Culture*. New York: Grove Press.

Whitten, Norman E., and J. F. Szwed, eds. 1970. *Afro-American Anthropology: Contemporary Perspectives*. New York: Free Press.

Wolf, Eric R. 1959. *Sons of the Shaking Earth*. Chicago: University of Chicago Press.

Wolf, Eric R. 1982. *Europe and the People without History*. Berkeley: University of California Press.

Yan, Yunxiand. 1997. "McDonald's in Beijing: The Localization of Americana." In *Golden Arches East: McDonald's in East Asia*, edited by James L. Watson, 39–67. Stanford, CA: Stanford University Press.

CHAPTER 10

Caribbean Peasantries and World Capitalism

An Approach to Micro-level Studies

The existence, in the Caribbean, of populations generally conceived as "peasantries" raises many questions for practitioners of different disciplines engaged in so-called peasant studies. Some of these questions have not yet been confronted. Within the dominant historical perception of the West, the word *peasant* usually evokes a being of another age—indeed, one most typical of the "Middle" ages—some specimens of whom have inexplicably survived "civilization" in the most "backward" areas of Europe. The presence of similar beings in Asia, Africa, and Latin America is integrated in that linear vision with the implication that the technologically advanced West first encountered such groups while the societies in which they lived were still going through their own equivalents of such "Dark" ages.[1]

The empirical record suggests that the Caribbean does not easily fit such a mold. The preconquest Carib and Arawak populations do not come close to any general or specific notion of "peasantries" the way some precolonial mainland groups might. But in addition, European violence reached such proportions in the Antilles that the preconquest populations were virtually wiped out before the massive introduction of African slaves. Caribbean peasantries, then, are peasantries whose emergence and growth came with the penetration of the Antilles by the West. Caribbean peasantries are peasantries that depend principally upon plants and animals brought into the region in the course of that penetration. With such notable exceptions as maize, cotton, manioc, and sweet potatoes, the flora that sustain these peasantries have come not only from other regions, but from other continents altogether, after the so-called discovery of the New World. Sugar cane and coffee, of course (Deerr 1949; Trouillot 1982)—but also coconuts, rice, mangoes, breadfruit, and bananas exemplify the point (Mintz 1983). Caribbean peasantries are made up of populations whose very physical presence in the territories they now occupy came as a consequence of world capitalist development: the ancestors of today's peasants crossed the Atlantic under the supervision of merchant capitalists. What we have in the Caribbean may thus be a unique historical record of peasantries emerging socially and *physically* after the penetration of a peripheral area by the West—a sort of zero-degree of peasant evolution within the sphere of Euro-American capitalism, where no reference can be made to a past within the past.

That history challenges in various degrees and from different angles more sophisticated definitional approaches to "peasants" that nevertheless confirm, in part, the dominant linear perception. S. Silverman (1979) rightly suggests that the notion of a "peasant tradition" is based on the idea of a perpetuation of cognitive and behavioral patterns such that the final object of inquiry turns out to be the disruption of such patterns by outside forces. But in the Caribbean, "tradition," in any given sense of the word, succeeded modernity: the "peasant way of life" fully blossomed only upon the ruins of the plantations, amid the remains of the developed technology and the highly stratified social structure that King Sugar had fostered. Here, the "disruption" is our starting point.

The variety of situations under which peasant-like behavior occurred in the Caribbean and the time span covered by such occurrences (Mintz 1974a, 1978, 1979) also seriously undermine any conceptualization based on an empirical assemblage of economic or cultural qualifiers. If our approach to real "peasants" presents them as tokens of an ideal type, then the slaves who cultivated their provision grounds and sold part of their product in local markets were tokens of two types, not one. Even aside from the epistemological problems raised by such an approach, the category "peasants" becomes nonoperational, not because actual analysis would then require a potentially endless list of subdivision (peasant-slaves, peasant-proletarians, etc.), but because, in that context, the first half of any such binomial would still not provide a basis for comparison, having no independent roots outside of the binomial itself.[2]

The particular history of the Caribbean also calls into question the growing tendency to couch conceptualizations of "peasantries" in terms of a "precapitalist" mode (or modes) of production. To be sure, the debate continues over whether any such mode of production to which "peasants" belonged can or does, survive capitalism.[3] But in the Caribbean, faced with the material impossibility of establishing an empirical connection with a preconquest past, we would be forced to suggest that capitalism had generated "precapitalist" modes of production. Such a theoretical leap seems dubious.[4] Yet, if it could be made, one would face the dilemma of explaining the new "articulation" in terms consistent with the historical record. The question of operational validity again raises its ugly head: How could such a theoretical distortion enhance our understanding of particular events, past and present, on the ground?

Thus, the Caribbean record helps us emphasize three major areas of inquiry in the field of peasant studies:

(1) Given that the record seems antithetic to the notion of a precapitalist mode of production, at what level of the socioeconomic structure can we start a conceptualization of peasantries?

(2) If Caribbean peasantries could emerge and grow at times when the region was fully integrated in the capitalist world economy, what is the logic of that coexistence?

(3) Since that logic—in view of what we know of both the Caribbean and capitalism—seems to suggest the overarching relevance of world-historical processes, how does one move down from such macro-processes to micro-level studies?

The following pages will try to clarify these three issues; particular stress will be placed on the third, the sphere of human agency, where any conceptualization should reach its full operational relevance. But the starting suggestion here is that most people usually covered by the empirical generalization "peasant" do indeed share a common practice, and that there is an operational concept in the critical literature on political economy that could serve to isolate this practice—the concept of labor process.

The notion of labor process encompasses all human activity destined to produce useful objects (use-values). At such a general level, the elementary factors of the labor process are human activity (i.e., *work* itself), the *object* on which that work is performed, and the *instruments* used for that performance (Marx [1867] 1967, 178). But the universal necessity of organizing production only enhances the diversity of forms that such an organization can take. All human beings must produce, but they do not do so in the same manner, and the empirical conditions under which they act encapsulate as many labor processes as we can distinguish specific types of work organizations. We can speak of different labor processes because we can conceive of and identify particular organizations of labor that recur with structural consistency. Indeed, the material and social conditions under which labor is applied are often such that the technical processes they delineate constitute, through time, a micro-ensemble regularly grouping the same categories of workers and similar means of work (Bettelheim 1976, 93–94).

Defined as such, *a* labor process implies specific instruments of labor regularly deployed on a particular object, in a particular unit of production, with a particular organization of the workers, toward the production of particular items. We can apply the concept to different organizations of labor and identify, say, a manufactural labor process, a plantation labor process, or a peasant labor process. A peasant labor process then appears as an institutionalized process of work through which:

(1) a discrete domestic group;
(2) performs agricultural labor;
(3) in a unit of production of which it has *possession;*[5]
(4) with instruments of work that it also controls, but which generally constitute a lesser input than the living labor itself.

Obviously, the concept of a peasant labor process, as couched here, is one with modest applications. As such, it does not exhaust the conceptualization built around it and necessarily calls attention to the larger socioeconomic networks in which the units of production that it isolates are embedded. Yet, before giving full attention to that embedding, we can already sketch some of the social tendencies that the work arrangement itself is likely to nurture.

The fundamental trait that emerges from the peasant work process is the overlap of the unit of production with a unit of consumption, an overlap that emphasizes the paramount importance of the domestic group for all peoples engaged in that type of work. The priority of living labor over labor embodied in the tools also reinforces the already crucial role of the domestic group. Thus we can suggest a tendency for all units engaged in that process to achieve, maintain, or restore a proper balance between the needs of the domestic group as a productive team and its consumptive needs. Types of "peasant" families will likely vary, at least in part, according to the contextual modalities of achieving that balance (Wolf 1966). Household composition will often reflect that need for additional security by taking the form of variably organized extended families (Shenton and Lehinnan 1981).

The paramount importance of the domestic group as a productive and consumptive team and the preeminence of living labor over labor congealed or crystalized in technology suggest a complementary tendency to maintain and reinforce solidarity among the members. Of course, conflicts do arise and, at times, threaten the fragile balance between production and consumption. So do sudden environmental changes, especially in light of the relatively low input of technology. Such broad and inherent vulnerability of the production/consumption unit thus calls for external insurance that can be normative as well as economic.[6] Finally, a relatively firm set of rules and obligations, and their continuous reinforcement, are likely to reduce, if not the chances of conflict, at least the ways in which particular conflicts can be solved.

A second general set of tendencies can be derived from the multifold importance of land in "peasant" activities. All human actions require portions of the surface of the Earth as their spatial base; but there are several factors that distinguish the peasant labor process. The first, its agricultural character, seems obvious; but it is less obvious that, as a consequence, land is *both* object and instrument of labor in addition to being the place of work. Second, the preeminence of living labor enhances the importance of land among the instruments of production.[7] Third, the overlap between the productive and consumptive domains implies that the domestic group shares discrete portions of the Earth's surface in both types of activities, even when the field is spatially distinguishable from the dwelling place. In the peasant unit of production, the family that works together stays together. Land thus stands as a social identifier of those who participate in the work process and share the same dwelling area.

To be sure, many of the traits sketched above—and others that could be derived from the factors inherent in the work process—have been previously drawn in various forms in the literature on peasantries.[8] The point here is not to claim major empirical discoveries but to suggest, on the one hand, that many of the sociocultural commonalities derive their impetus from the common work process and, on the other, that one cannot derive from those tendencies their specific modes of actualization, since the degrees and forms of engagement of any "peasant" family in that process vary.[9] As noted before, the concept of a peasant labor process is one of limited range, but its very limitations allow us a greater flexibility in historical analyses and, eventually, comparative studies.[10]

In a stimulating article on definitional treatments of peasantries, Mintz (1973) suggested a reorientation of "peasant studies" toward the production of historically derived "middle-level" categories that would flesh out the historical diversity of peasant groups within a national society or a specific peripheral area such as the Caribbean. While Mintz had long demonstrated his powerful insight in deriving such subgroups from the Caribbean record (1961b, 1974a), little has been done systematically, since then, to enable others to further such a categorization, or even to repeat the feat in the Caribbean or elsewhere. An approach rooted in the concept of a peasant labor process may allow us to move to that middle level and produce such categories, since the concept of a labor process inherently points to that of *relations of production* which, in turn, restore historicity.

A few pages after sketching the notion of labor process, Marx ([1867] 1967, 184; emphasis added) pointed out its inherent limitations:

> As the taste of the porridge does not tell you who grew the oats, no more does this simple process tell you *of itself* what are *the social conditions under which it is taking place.*

The concept of a peasant labor process thus necessarily calls attention to the social embedding of the peasant unit of production and to the structural ties that bind the domestic group to larger social ensembles. Wolf (1966) had already emphasized the importance of such ties, but a most effective first step to their systematic discovery may be a study of the manner in which the peasant labor process is subsumed within diverse relations of production.

Limitations of time and space do not allow here for a comprehensive treatment of the distinction between formal and real subsumption of a labor process within capitalist relations of production (Marx [1867] 1967, [1863–66?] 1971, [1863–66?] 1976; Banaji 1978; Dallemagne 1978, 84–96; Faure 1978). Still, for our purposes, couching the coexistence of "peasantries" and capitalism in terms of the subsumption of a peasant labor process within capitalist relations of production has several related advantages. First, as noted before, we remain consistent with the particular historical data on the Caribbean. Second, though we acknowledge a common material base for "peasant" activities, human beings and their historically derived social relations remain at the center of the analysis. Thus, we give precedence to the circulation of values and the accumulation of capital as social processes (Dallemagne 1978; Salama 1975). Our starting point, the productive forces, remains secondary (Pouillon 1976), and we thus avoid any "technologism" or the "agronomic determinism" (Somers and Goldfrank 1979) for which Paige (1976) has been rightly criticized. Third, we can nevertheless integrate the rich fruits of particular studies couched in terms of mode(s) of production (Scott 1976; Cliffe 1977; Hedley 1981; Soifer and Howe 1982; Bennholdt-Thomsen 1982) that have followed anthropologist Pierre-Philippe Rey's seminal treatment of articulation (1973). Finally, and most importantly for our purposes, we can more easily produce the particular historical categories necessary to bridge the gap between our understanding of trends within the world system and that of particular "peasants" of different times and places.

Such categorizations should enable us to determine the particular historical trajectory of each group defined, the logic of its coexistence with capitalism, and the levers of its economic, political, or cultural resistance. Yet the specific criteria that differentiate any two groups are not necessarily operative in shaping the distinctions between those two groups and any third group. Thus, the production of such historical categories implies a procedure that not only organizes an extensive range of factors leading to the discovery of the characteristics noted above but also allows for the differential relevance of such factors in particular situations. Such a procedure, then, requires at least:

(1) the identification of the particular historical conditions under which the group defined first engaged in the peasant labor process and maintained that engagement;

(2) a study of the degrees and forms of that engagement, as determined by the relations of production, that is, property and labor relations, as well as surplus relations or relations of distribution (Cliffe 1977);

(3) a determination of the means and degree of integration by which that three-prong set of relations inserts the group within a process of valorization (Dallemagne 1978, 85)—that is, a process of value circulation and, ultimately, of surplus-value production and capital accumulation (Marx [1867] 1976, 985–92).

That integration in the process of valorization might, in turn, occur in varying degrees:

(a) through the direct sale of labor power by those otherwise engaged in the peasant work process (Mintz 1974b);

(b) through the indirect sale of labor power by way of usurers' or merchants' capital (Roseberry 1976; Shennton and Lehinnan 1981);

(c) through the production of commodities outside of the peasant labor process, for example, handicrafts (Wolf 1955);

(d) through the production, within the peasant unit, of commodities taken over directly by foreign capital (Trouillot n.d.);

(e) through taxation (Paul 1876; Tanzi 1976).

Obviously, such mechanisms are not mutually exclusive (Trouillot 1980) and serve as criteria of differentiation only in terms of their unequal importance. The chronological precedence of a mechanism of integration likely affects the subsequent emergence of others. Furthermore, the last three criteria imply an evaluation of the degree to which "outside capital" (Wolf 1955) is necessary to production. Also, while cases (b) and (d) nearly fit the model of formal subsumption of a labor process by capital, cases (a) and (c) suggest a slightly different form of symbiosis. Only empirical studies can reveal the predominant conditions under which wage labor or handcraft production coexist with the peasant labor process.[11] But the point is exactly that the procedure for differentiating within the "peasantry" must be applicable to particular historical contexts.

Indeed, the first major advantage of this procedure may be its utility for producing or verifying long-range historical categories. Agrosocial groupings such as Mintz's "early yeomen," "protopeasants," or "reconstituted peasantries" of the Caribbean can all be differentiated, first of all, according to the conditions under which they engaged in the peasant labor process and the subsequent degree of their engagement. The procedure thus expands our chronological, spatial, and social boundaries, since we can isolate, at that first level of differentiation, groups that spanned several centuries, on a multinational base—some of whom do not even fit the traditional image of the "peasant."[12] But more interestingly, one could also produce subgroups within those long-range historical categories themselves, especially by differentiating in more detail, according to varied mechanisms of integration.

Indeed, since our first criterion rests on the historical evolution of the peasant labor process, we can always reduce that historical base, so to speak, to produce categories of a smaller range by applying the procedure to ever smaller segments of population. (Extensive use of those criteria within that narrower scope is likely to produce categories that may fall within the range of the two types usually treated as "middle" and "poor" peasants; but that is precisely where further differentiation seems most needed [e.g., Wolf 1955; Patnaik 1978; Bernstein 1979]). That increasingly detailed differentiation of the peasantry (in terms of the embedding of the labor process) brings us closer to bridging the gap between local particulars and world-historical forces. On the one hand, we can produce categories manageable at the micro-level but, on the other, the smaller groups so produced have been identified primarily in terms of their integration within macrolevel processes.

Still, this identification does not consummate a micro-level analysis, if only because it does not inherently enable us to engage in, or profit from, the meticulous observation of the groups engaged in the peasant labor process in ways that would bring out the relevance of individual actions. Yet such actions accelerate, duplicate, or, at times, counteract the mechanisms of economic integration. Even if individual deeds eventuate directly from the particular embedding of the peasant labor process—and they rarely spring up as mechanically as this formulation would imply—they always influence the actualization of that process, if only by establishing new areas of emergent loyalties or conflicts for the groups involved. Most important among such actions are those that bring into contact members of the different groups defined by the mechanisms of integration in an empirical encounter among themselves or between themselves and the larger order. In the second part of this paper, I will suggest complementary means to integrate in the analysis the effects of human agency on the actualization of the peasant labor process and the form of its embedding.

AN EMPIRICAL FIELD

The principle suggested here in the organization of the ethnographic data is that of *mediation*, understood as a broad empirical field. Yet before laying out the modalities of use of that principle, and before building somehow on a particular "critical moment of mediation" in the Caribbean island of Dominica, it is perhaps best to denote, by way of a very cursory example, the potential results of the procedure of differentiation suggested above. One will perhaps first see more clearly the kinds of groups likely to emerge from an analysis of the mechanisms that integrate the peasant labor process, and then turn to the field of mediation where various linkages between such groups are not only observable by the fieldworker, but also subjected to change.

In the Caribbean island of Dominica, most peasants first appear to be integrated in capitalist relations primarily through the sale of the bananas produced in their gardens to a British-based transnational company. Further, most are primarily dependent on the peasant labor process for the food that they consume: their diets include a high proportion of home-grown root crops, including plantains and, for that matter, bananas. Yet despite this appearance of structural homogeneity in a nationwide rural population of about 72,000, closer attention to the relative importance of diverse mechanisms of integration reveals further differentiation. The other mechanisms of integration rarely take precedence over the sale of bananas (and bananas still constitute the bulk of Dominican exports), but the existence of those secondary mechanisms, and their relative importance for particular subgroups, do enable us to isolate subgroups within that small population.

In the Mahaut area, for instance, which is relatively close to the capital town of Roseau and to industrial plants, integration through the direct sale of labor power (our mechanism *a*, above) predominates among subsections within some villages, as many "peasants" intermittently or regularly engage in plantation or industrial work or provide domestic or other services to noncultivating classes. The subsequent population surplus that those activities fostered, eventuated in the creation of what I dub a *lumpen-peasantry*, torn between the security of the peasant unit on the one hand and individual ventures in a totally commoditized world on the other. Transistors and sweat suits abound in the area, but most villagers seem to hold to "a piece of land," through kinship or alliance ties, while desiring to benefit as individuals from the greater cash flow of wages. In the southeast of the island, the production and sale of bay leaf and bay oil lead to patterns of indebtedness toward richer peasants or landlords (often indebted in turn to urbanites). Peasants there depend on a few individuals even to bring their bananas to the buying points. A markedly different ecotype, historical isolation, and the juxtaposition of mechanisms of economic integration has led there to the formation of a much more *clientized* subgroup—not just "poorer," but more bound as well. Farther south, on the west coast, peasants in the villages of Souffrière and Scotts Head are integrated in the valorization process not only through the sale of bananas and occasional labor on citrus estates, but also through the sale of fish on the national market. One could argue that the *fishermen-peasants* are often as "poor" as the bay leaf gardeners, and often in debt (especially when boat-engines are not fully amortized)—but also that the particular mechanisms of integration, notably the sale of fish (our type *c*, above) allows them more room to maneuver. They are not as threatened by the immediate presence of other rural groups, nor by the national contractions of the banana industry. Finally, all these subgroups could be fruitfully contrasted with the *yeomanry* of Saint Andrew parish (the most northern parish), whose integration occurs primarily through the sale of commodities independently produced on peasant farms (our type *d*, above). Yet while in the district of Saint Andrew South (also known as La Soye),[13] in the area around Marigot, Wesley, and Woodford Hill, such commodities are usually restricted to bananas and coconuts, both of which are subject to monopsonistic control, peasants in the more northern Vieille Case area have long maintained a tradition of independent exchange, notably with Guadeloupe and Marie Galante, which often bypasses government control. This secondary outlet gives the same mechanism of integration through the market a different impetus in the case of the partly *independent traders* of Vieille Case from that of the equally "middle" peasants of Wesley or Marigot.

This sketch overlaps spatial differentiation within Dominica, but only because the island's particular history of difficult internal communications has tended to produce or reinforce remarkable subregional differences. The procedure can be carried forward, with greater precision, at the level of the village itself, providing that one clears the historical grounds for such a choice. Subgroups within Wesley and Marigot, for instance, do present some of the characteristics of the lumpen-peasantry, particularly because of the proximity of the Melville Hall airport. Some fishermen in Marigot are integrated in the valorization process in a manner very similar to what happens to those of Souffrière. The point remains that the exercise of differentiation according to the criteria proposed above does permit the production of categories of diverse spatial and historical ranges that can then be contrasted with each other, with other rural groups not at all engaged in the peasant labor process (e.g., a landless rural proletariat) and, ultimately, with nonrural groups as well.

The illumination provided by the juxtaposition of those categories in a particular historical context, in turn, sets the stage for empirical studies that could further bridge the gap between micro and macro levels. A broadening of the concept of mediation may provide the organizing principle necessary to classify the ethnographic data. The procedure suggested here involves a systematic search, during fieldwork, for *the empirical elements of mediation*, the observable links that tie the rural groups engaged in the peasant labor process among themselves to other rural groups, to urban classes, and to other areas of the world economy.

M. Silverman rightly argues that mediation not only links societal levels but also competing subgroups within the countryside and, in so doing, affects the "dynamic of economic differentiation" (1979, 482). She draws on the history of Rajgahr, Guyana, to demonstrate the multifold roles of mediators in faction and class formation. But agents of mediation are not always at the front of the stage, and primordial loyalties (Alavi 1973) do not always coalesce on the political scene. Thus, if (following Silverman) we suggest that mediation turns out to be a sum of unequal and contradictory processes, we will further insist that its various elements—and their differential relevance—are neither obvious nor predictable. *Mediation*, as such, does not have a logic: individual mediating processes may lead to dead ends; and mediation as an empirical field, is full of holes and broken lines, for it is the social "coefficient" of *integration*.

Two factors explain this empirical "disorder." First, though studies of mediation have emphasized formal economic or political ties (e.g., patronage, clientage), the actual liaisons from which individual mediating processes eventuate may belong to any "sphere" of human activity or overlap different arenas of social life. For instance, a particular marriage or christening may reinforce economic and/or political arrangements, but it remains, in its own right, a marriage or a christening. Second, not all the events that may constitute individual mediating processes are the results or products of conscious and rational decisions. Many come as unintended results of routine actions in which people might engage without any transactional aim.

The field of mediation, understood in such broad terms, is by definition, then, empirical, and we penetrate it by way of the discovery of *the empirical elements of mediation*. Such elements, characterized by their function at particular points in time (rather than by their functional nature), can be spatially fixed or mobile. Mobile elements of mediation can, in turn, be material (*instruments of mediation*) or human (*agents of mediation*).

Spatially fixed elements of mediation can be first located within the village or the community itself. First among those are the economic "relay points" (Girault 1981) of distribution and circulation: for instance, the banana boxing plants of the Windward Islands, where peasants weekly deliver their products to be loaded on trucks that will carry them to the docks; or the shops of various kinds and sizes where peasants buy imported goods. But churches, post offices, health and police stations, schools, or, indeed, the frequently visited house of a broker are also, in different ways, spatial elements of mediation.

Other spatial elements may be located in rural towns, like the coffee-buying point of the Haitian *spéculateurs* (Girault 1981). An empirical survey might also list locations in the cities (banks, financial, administrative, religious or political headquarters, or the house of a major absentee land-owner) inasmuch as such places physically bring together diverse sub-groups of the peasantry in a common encounter with the larger order. Spatial elements do not always facilitate encounters in the most obvious and expected manner: many police stations in the rural Caribbean are traditional loci for domino contests that bring together players from di-verse subgroups of the peasantry and nonpeasants alike. Such activities cannot be inferred from the nature of the station and require empirical observation.

Likewise, any mobile object can function, at times, as an *instrument of mediation*. Commodities, obviously, most often fit that category; but so do newspapers, trucks, letters, and, at times, musical instruments or remit-tances. In many Caribbean countries, specific radio programs bring to the peasants messages from relatives or friends in town or abroad. It is not at all unusual to hear the announcer appeal to listeners in Trou to transmit to Janet X the message that her sister, now in Guadeloupe, wants her to pick up a package from the boat *Cecilia*, due to land in town the next day. Again, the range of interlocked individual actions implied in such an event, and the consequences of the long-term repetition of events of that kind, remain subject to empirical verification.

Yet anyone contributing to those empirical linkages can be seen, for that particular moment, as an *agent of mediation*. The older child of a peasant family working as a cook on a nearby plantation or as a gardener in town, pre-teenagers who daily walk to another village to attend the nearest elementary school, or the urban housewife who participates in a *pratik* relationship with a rural market woman (Mintz 1961a)—all contribute to the general process of mediation. The term *agent of mediation* should not evoke, then, the image of a petty investor in social relations; nor is it restricted to the "mediators" traditionally favored by the anthropological literature.

To be sure, many agents of mediation may consciously partake of trans-actional aims (Barth 1963); and political leaders, brokers, middlemen, and hucksters do function more visibly and more systematically in the global mediating process. Their preponderant role in articulating group rela-tions should be emphasized, especially since the tools for analyzing such preponderance have been increasingly refined (Wolf 1956; M. Silverman, 1979; Soiffer and Howe 1982). But a whole range of other people who may not systematically function as brokers or middlemen may, because of their occupations, participate in the invasion of the village by outside forces:

teachers, police and health officers, truck drivers, missionaries, hikers and campers, or, indeed, anthropologists. In cases where the preponderance of traditional "mediators" is low, their presence may strongly affect the cultural or political balance. At other times, they may unintentionally contribute to the erosion of the traditional mediators' power. Other people provide empirical linkages among the peasants themselves with various degrees of systematicity: owners of rum shops, organizers of cockfights, local choir leaders, village calypsonians, or policemen supervising domino contests, and so on.

The differential weight of diverse elements of mediation can sometimes be perceived at *critical moments of mediation*, that is, during those periods of time when diverse individual mediating processes coalesce and agents of mediation are more likely to appear at the front stage. Political rallies are such obvious moments. But so also are the "banana days" in Dominica—and, likewise, in the other Windward Islands—when the purchase of bananas in "boxing plants," usually located in the confines of the village, sets in motion crossing mediating processes.

In Wesley, Dominica, for instance, the actual manner in which a particular family's fruits reach the plant reveals ties between and across rural subgroups. The vehicle used might belong to a distant "cousin," and the fees for that use vary in light of reciprocal obligations; it might be hired from a richer peasant, a civil servant, or a shopkeeper, and its owner-driver might be paid by the bunch. But vehicles are in such demand on "fig day" that, at equal volumes, the order in which the owner decides to meet individual requests also reveals his own social priorities. Further, vehicle owners are not necessarily "richer" than their clients of the day: many are heavily indebted; others are civil servants with better credit but not necessarily greater income. The efficiency with which bananas are brought to the plant, then, is not always a function of one's financial situation but often an indication of social standing.

At the boxing plant itself, ties are constantly reinforced, broken, or established. Bananas are evaluated, accepted, or rejected by fellow villagers temporarily working for the government trade board that functions as an agent of the transnational. Occasional employment as a "selector" may well improve a poor peasant's standing and bring him the friendship or the wrath of fellow villagers. But the proportion of "rejects" that a particular grower is forced to accept is also a measure of his/her social influence. The repetition of the constant power play between "selector" and grower, in turn, creates grounds for further differentiation: in any given year, the returns of a more outspoken peasant are likely to surpass those of a quieter individual with similar technical and economic resources. Older men also tend to obtain fewer "rejects" than older women or younger men. Moreover, such displays of influence occur in front of a relatively large audience. Out of a village population of some 3,500 people, 800 individuals may gather at the boxing plant in the course of one day, some selling bananas, others selling food or drinks, others accompanying a friend or relative, and others—most often adolescent males—just "checking the scene." The continuous formation and breakup of groups at the plant provide to those participant-observers a mirror in which to perceive their own alignments across the boundaries of economic differentiation; but that consciousness itself may be put to use in reinforcing or changing those very alignments.

The accumulation of ethnographic material of that sort will not necessarily lead to the discovery of the structural linkages between the actors engaged in the peasant labor process and world capitalism, especially if differences of scale are treated in terms of a quantitative continuum rather than as the occasional manifestations of different levels of organization (Barth 1978). Often, the very perception of size will deter the observer from an analysis of the complex networks involved (Trouillot 1983), and the nation or the village will be held, a priori, as the "obvious" unit of analysis.

Yet the hope is that the systematic search for the empirical elements of mediation will at least bring to the surface events, people, and objects often missed at the time of fieldwork. Second, one also presumes that these data will necessarily include material not easily washed away at the micro-level and will force the analyst to recognize the limitations of his/her boundaries or pursue the empirical track up to the discovery of larger processes. Ideally, the search for those empirical elements should be done in light of the differentiation proposed above. The study of those elements could then allow the empirical re-evaluation of the historical categories that first lead to their discovery. A return to those middle-level categories with the more documented knowledge of their interaction on the ground may perhaps help us flesh out more satisfactorily the peculiar coexistence of "peasantries" and capitalism. At any rate, the above suggestions remain tentative and should be read as a partial contribution to the continuous and multidisciplinary search for a methodology that is sensitive to world-historical forces yet able to acknowledge particulars as sources of change in their own right (Trouillot 1982, 334).

Editors' Note: This chapter first appeared as "Caribbean Peasantries and World Capitalism: An Approach to Micro-Level Studies," *Nieuwe West-Indische Gids/ New West Indian Guide* 58, nos. 1–2 (1984): 37–59.

1. The fieldwork in the Commonwealth of Dominica from which some of the following material is drawn was carried out in 1979, 1980, and 1981, and was supported by the Program in Atlantic History and Culture of John Hopkins University, the Inter-American Foundation, and the Social Science Research Council. I wish to thank Sidney Mintz, Sally Price, and Brackette Williams for comments and criticisms on this paper, even though I was unable to incorporate some of their suggestions. Finally, I did not have access, at the time of writing, to Chevalier's article (1983) on petty commodity production, which enlightens some of the issues raised here.

2. A list of such binomials cannot help us determine, for instance, whether similarities and differences between eighteenth-century slaves and contemporary peasant-proletarians have roots in their common participation in plantation work or in their common engagement in "subsistence" production.

3. Many reject such survival as a mere "guise" or "form" (Ennew et al. 1977); but that solution begs the question of the nature and function of such "form." Moreover, to posit a necessary linkage between contemporary "peasantries" and "precapitalist" modes or forms still evades the questions raised by the Caribbean data.

4. Hedley (1981) comes close to such a leap in discussing petty commodity production in the Canadian Prairies, but one might also want to further the distinction between relations of work and relations of production.

5. *Possession* here does not imply jural ownership, but rather a power to dispose of, a form of control that excludes similar control by group(s) of the same kind (Bettelheim 1976, 93–101).

6. Kinship, alliance, and patronage ties, may, for instance, provide additional use-values or money when the consumption level falls too low, or additional labor when production falls. But they often act also to reinforce from the outside the cohesion of the domestic group by providing forums where internal conflicts can be aired and diffused.

7. That importance strongly differentiates, for instance, the peasant techniques from those of the capitalist farmer who generally relies much more on the dead labor embodied in tools.

8. Chayanov (1966), Redfield (1956), and Wolf (1966) have emphasized in various ways the production/consumption balance, the importance of land, the role of the domestic group, and the inherent vulnerability of the unit.

9. Thus, the disagreement with the marginalists or neo-populist approaches rests on our contention that no labor process can fully account for the social ensembles in which the units of production are embedded, that no "society" is an addition of enterprises. Likewise, this conceptualization differentiates itself from the moral economists' approach by emphasizing the practical "basis" of peasant behavior, yet also by acknowledging that those tendencies are not to be found in any pristine form in the real world and can even be reversed under certain conditions. Thus, rather than claiming that the peasant "aims" at subsistence (Wolf 1955, 454), we suggest that the relative importance of living labor gives rise to a tendency to secure the reproduction of the domestic group before any expansion or renewal of the instruments of work. The argument is not simply about terminology: in certain cases, a "peasant" family may very well use the wages of one of its members to face those reproductive needs. At equal income, a capitalist-farming family may very well cut down on "subsistence" as the only means of acquiring new tools. Still, we cannot derive from the "laws of motion" of the labor process itself any peasant "culture" or "tradition" (Redfield 1956) that would recur, mutatis mutandis, in all peasant "communities."

10. That flexibility does solve, for instance, the theoretical dilemma raised by the "peasant breach" (Lepkowski 1968–69) in plantation slavery. While it is difficult to imagine how and why "capitalism" would have created a separate mode of production (Cardoso 1979), one can easily understand the pragmatism of local planters who allowed or even encouraged an organization of work that shifted the responsibility of reproducing labor power from the master to the slave. Moreover, whether we call such laborers "peasant-slaves" or "proto-peasants" (Karasch 1979; Mintz 1961b, 1974a), we can effectively compare them with other historically derived groups engaged in the same type of activities.

11. It is clear that in many cases, low wages or low prices of handicrafts can be explained only in light of the secondary engagement of the producers in a peasant-type activity that contributes to their reproduction. In such cases, the subsidiary nature of the peasant household—as a unit of production sustaining laborers otherwise integrated in the valorization process—allows us to speak of the formal subjugation of the peasantry. In other cases, we might want to keep the notion of an articulation of modes of production (Taylor 1979).

12. "Protopeasants," for instance, did not engage in this labor process to the same extent as the early yeomen, or the postslavery peasantry. Property relations particularly ensured that the slaves' gardens were only appendages of larger units of production, the plantations. Yet one could also argue that the planters' emphasis on the plantation work process may have allowed the slaves a greater control of distribution than some of their free successors. Likewise, property and surplus relations generally imposed more stringent conditions on the post-slavery groups than on the early yeomen.

13. *Editors' Note:* The parish as a whole is called Saint Andrew. The parish has several districts, including Saint Andrew South, also known as La Soye (which is how Trouillot refers to it in other writing).

REFERENCES

Alavi, Hamza. 1973. "Peasant Classes and Primordial Loyalties." *Journal of Peasant Studies* 1, no. 1: 23–62.

Banaji, Jairus. 1978. "Capitalist Domination and the Small Peasantry: Deccan Districts in the Late Nineteenth Century." In *Studies in the Development of Capitalism in India*, edited by Ashok Rudra et al., 351–428. Lahore: Vanguard Books Limited.

Barth, Fredrik. 1963. *The Role of the Entrepreneur in Social Change in Northern Norway*. Oslo: Universiteitsforlaget.

Barth, Fredrik, ed. 1978. *Scale and Social Organization*. Oslo: Universiteitsforlaget.

Bennholdt-Thomsen, Veronica. 1982. "Subsistence Production and Extended Reproduction: A Contribution to the Discussion about Modes of Production." *Journal of Peasant Studies* 6, no. 4: 241–54.

Bernstein, Henry. 1979. "African Peasantries: A Theoretical Framework." *Journal of Peasant Studies* 6, no. 4: 421–43.

Bettelheim, Charles. 1976. *Calcul économique el forms de propriété*. Paris: Maspero.

Cardoso, Ciro F. 1979. *Agricultura, esclavidão e capitalismo*. Petrópolis, Brazil: Vozes.

Chayanov, Alexander V. 1966. *The Theory of Peasant Economy*. Edited by Daniel Thorner, Basile Kerblay, and R. E. F. Smith. Homewood, IL: R. D. Irwin.

Chevalier, Jacques M. 1983. "There Is Nothing Simple about Simple Commodity Production." *Journal of Peasant Studies* 10, no. 4: 153–86.

Cliffe, Lionel. 1977. "Rural Class Formation in East Africa." *Journal of Peasant Studies* 4, no. 2: 195–224.

Dallemagne, Jean-Luc. 1978. *L'économie du Capital*. Paris: Maspero.

Deerr, Noel. 1949. *The History of Sugar*, Vol. 1. London: Chapman and Hall.

Ennew, Judith, et al. 1977. "'Peasantry' as an Economic Category." *Journal of Peasant Studies* 4, no. 4: 295–322.

Faure, Claude. 1978. *Agriculture et mode de production capitaliste*. Paris: Anthropos.

Girault, Christian A. 1981. *Le commerce du café en Haiti: Habitants, spéculateurs, exportateurs*. Paris: Centre national de la recherche scientifique.

Hedley, Max, 1981. "Relations of Production of the 'Family Farm': Canadian Prairies." *Journal of Peasant Studies* 9, no. 1: 71–85.

Jahangir, B. K. 1979. *Differentiation, Polarisation and Confrontation in Rural Bangladesh*. Dacca: Centre for Social Studies.

Karash, Mary. 1979. "Commentary on 'Slavery and the Rise of Peasantries' by Sidney W. Mintz." *Historical Reflections* 6, no. 1: 248–51.

Lepkowski, Tadeusz. 1968–69. *Haiti*, 2 vols. Havana: Casa de las Americas.

Marx, Karl. (1867) 1967. *Capital: A Critique of Political Economy, Volume 1*. New York: International Publishers.

Marx, Karl. (1863–66?) 1971. *Un chapitre inédit du Capital*. Paris: Pion.

Marx, Karl. (1863–66?) 1976. *Results of the Immediate Process of Production: Appendix to Capital, Volume 1*. New York: Vintage.

Mintz, Sidney W. 1961a. "Pratik: Haitian Personal Economic Relationships." In *Proceedings of the 1961 Spring Meeting of the American Ethnological Association*, edited by Viola E. Garfield, 54–63. Seattle: University of Washington Press.

Mintz, Sidney W. 1961b. "The Question of Caribbean Peasantries: A Comment." *Caribbean Studies* 3: 31–34.

Mintz, Sidney W. 1973. "A Note on the Definition of Peasantries." *Journal of Peasant Studies* 1, no. 1: 91–106.

Mintz, Sidney W. 1974a. *Caribbean Transformations*. Chicago: Aldine.

Mintz, Sidney W. 1974b. "The Rural Proletariat and the Problem of Rural Proletarian Consciousness." *Journal of Peasant Studies* 1, no. 3: 201–325.

Mintz, Sidney W. 1978. "Was the Plantation Slave a Proletarian?" *Review (Fernand Braudel Center)* 2, no. 1: 81–98.

Mintz, Sidney W. 1979. "Slavery and the Rise of Peasantries." *Historical Reflections* 6, no. 1: 213–42.

Mintz, Sidney W. 1983. "Reflections on Caribbean Peasantries." *Nieuwe West-Indische Gids/New West Indian Guide* 57: 1–17.

Paige, Jeffrey. 1976. *Agrarian Revolution*. New York: Free Press.

Patnaik, Utsa. 1978. "Class Differentiation within the Peasantry: An Approach to Analysis of Indian Agriculture." In *Studies in the Development of Capitalism in India*, edited by Ashok Rudra et al., 259–322. Lahore: Vanguard Books Limited.

Paul, Edmond. 1876. *De l'impot sur le café*. Kingston: Cordova.

Pouillon, François. 1976. "La détermination d'un mode de production: Les forces productives et leur appropriation." In *L'anthropologie économique: Courants et problems*, edited by Lucien Démonio and François Pouillon, 57–85. Paris: Maspero.

Redfield, Robert. 1956. *The Little Community: Peasant Society and Culture*. Chicago: University of Chicago Press.

Rey, Pierre-Philippe. 1973. *Les alliances de classe*. Paris: Maspero.

Roseberry, William. 1976. "Rent, Differentiation, and the Development of Capitalism among Peasants." *American Anthropologist* 78, no. 1: 45–58.

Salama, Pierre. 1975. *Sur la valeur*. Paris: Maspero.

Scott, C. D. 1976. "Peasants, Proletarianization and the Articulation of Modes of Production: The Case of Sugar Cane Cutters in Northern Peru, 1940–69." *Journal of Peasant Studies* 3, no. 3: 321–41.

Shenton, R. W., and Louise. Lehinnan, 1981. "Capital and Class: Peasant Differentiation in Northern Nigeria." *Journal of Peasant Studies* 9, no. 1: 47–70.

Silverman, Marilyn. 1979. "Dependency, Mediation, and Class Formation in Rural Guyana." *American Ethnologist* 6, no. 3: 466–90.

Silverman, Sydel. 1979. "The Peasant Concept in Anthropology." *Journal of Peasant Studies* 7, no. 1: 49–69.

Soiffer, S. M., and G. N. Howe. 1982. "Patrons, Clients and the Articulation of Modes of Production: An Examination of the Penetration of Capitalism into Peripheral Agriculture in Northeastern Brazil." *Journal of Peasant Studies* 9, no. 2: 176–206.

Somers, M. R., and W. L. Goldfrank. 1979. "The Limits of Agronomic Determinism." *Comparative Studies in Society and History* 21: 443–58.

Tanzi, Vito. 1976. "Export Taxation in Developing Countries: Taxation of Coffee in Haiti." *Social and Economic Studies* 25: 66–76.

Taylor, John G. 1979. *From Modernization to Modes of Production: A Critique of the Sociologies of Development and Underdevelopment*. London: Macmillan.

Trouillot, Michel-Rolph. 1980. "Review of *Peasants and Poverty*, by Mats Lundahl." *Journal of Peasant Studies* 8, no. 1: 112–16.

Trouillot, Michel-Rolph. 1982. "Motion in the System: Coffee, Color, and Slavery in Eighteenth-Century Saint-Domingue." *Review (Fernand Braudel Center)* 5, no. 3: 331–88.

Trouillot, Michel-Rolph. 1983. "The Production of Spatial Configurations: A Caribbean Case." *Nieuwe West-Indische Gids/New West Indian Guide* 57, no. 3–4: 215–29.

Trouillot, Michel-Rolph. n.d. "Peasants and Capitalism: The Peculiar Coexistence." Paper presented at the Faculty Seminar on Marxism, Duke University, Durham, NC, February 1984.

Wolf, Eric R. 1955. "Types of Latin American Peasantry: A Preliminary Discussion." *American Anthropologist* 57, no. 3: 452–71.

Wolf, Eric R. 1956. "Aspects of Group Relations in a Complex Society: Mexico." *American Anthropologist* 58, no. 6: 1065–78.

Wolf, Eric R. 1966. *Peasants*. Englewood Cliffs, NJ: Prentice Hall.

CHAPTER 11

The Anthropology of the State in the Age of Globalization

Close Encounters of the Deceptive Kind

Sociocultural anthropology often arises from the banality of daily life. I will start this essay with three banal stories.

In January 1999, Amartya Sen, Nobel Laureate in economics, on his way to a conference in Davos, was stopped at the Zürich airport for entering Switzerland without a visa. Never mind that he was carrying credit cards and his US resident green card. Never mind that he claimed that the organizers had promised him a visa delivered to the airport. North Americans and Western Europeans can, of course, enter Switzerland without a visa, whether or not on their way to a conference, but Sen uses his Indian passport. The Swiss police were worried that he would become a dependent of the state, as Indians are likely to be. The irony of the story is that Sen was on his way to the World Economic Forum, the theme of which that year was "Responsible Globality: Managing the Impact of Globalization."

Less amusing but just as banal is the story of the fourteen-year-old "Turk" who was sent *back* to Turkey by the German government when in fact he had never set foot there, having been born and raised in Germany. The French and US governments routinely expel "aliens" whose school-age children are citizens by birth.

Less amusing still is the encounter between one Turenne Deville and the US government in the 1970s. At the news that the Immigration and Naturalization Service was to send him back to Haiti, Deville hanged himself in his prison cell. Deville's suicide is no more dramatic than the wager of hundreds of Haitian refugees who continue to dive—both literally and figuratively—into the Florida seas, betting that they will beat the sharks, the waves, and the US Coast Guard.

Are these encounters with the state? In all three cases, we see a government—or a government agency—telling people where they should or should not be. If, as James Scott (1998), among others, argues, the placement of people, including their enforced sedentarization, is a major feature of statecraft, the encounters I have just described do seem to be cases in which state power was wielded to enforce physical placement.

My three stories speak of borders—of the space between centralized governments with national territorial claims, where encounters between individuals and state power are most visible. Yet millions of encounters of the same kind also occur within national or regional boundaries: a car owner facing state emission laws in California; a family facing school language in Catalonia, India, or Belize; a couple dealing with a new pregnancy in China; a homeless person deciding where to sleep in San Francisco, Rio de Janeiro, or New York; a Palestinian in the Occupied Territories having to decide which line to cross and when; or a citizen of Singapore or Malaysia having to conform to prescribed behavior in a public building.

Behind the banality of these millions of encounters between individuals or groups and governments we discover the depth of governmental presence in our lives, regardless of the regimes and the particulars of the social formation. The opening sentence of Ralph Miliband's (1969, 1) opus on the state still rings true: "More than ever before men now live in the shadow of the state." One can even argue that the penal state has actually increased in size and reach in a number of countries since Miliband wrote—notably in the United States, with the increase of prison space and the routinization of the death penalty.

This, however, is only one side of the story. Indeed, while signs of the routinization of governmental presence in the lives of citizens abound everywhere, this turn of century also offers us images of governmental power challenged, diverted, or simply giving way to infra- or supranational institutions. From Chiapas and Kosovo to Kigali and Trincomale, separatist movements have become increasingly vocal on all continents. Further, and on a different scale, analysts increasingly suggest that globalization renders the state irrelevant not only as an economic actor but also as a social and cultural container. They point to the significance of practices that reject or bypass national state power—such as the "new" social movements—or to the power of trans-state organizations from NGOs and global corporations to the World Bank and the International Monetary Fund (IMF) as concrete signs of that relative decline.

Thus this century opens on two sets of contradictory images: the power of the national state sometimes seems more visible and encroaching and sometimes less effective and less relevant. This essay explores how as anthropologists we can make sense of this tension and fully incorporate it into our analysis of the state. To do so, we need to recognize three related propositions: (1) state power has no institutional fixity on either theoretical or historical grounds; (2) thus, state effects never obtain solely through national institutions or in governmental sites; and (3) these two features, inherent in the capitalist state, have been exacerbated by globalization. Globalization thus authenticates a particular approach to the anthropology of the state, one that allows for a dual emphasis on theory and ethnography.

If the state has no institutional or geographical fixity, its presence becomes more deceptive than otherwise thought, and we need to theorize the state beyond the empirically obvious. Yet this removal of empirical boundaries also means that the state becomes more open to ethnographic strategies that take its fluidity into account. I suggest such a strategy here, one that goes beyond governmental or national institutions to focus on the multiple sites in which state processes and practices are recognizable through their effects. These effects include: (1) *an isolation effect*, that is, the production of atomized individualized subjects molded and modeled for governance as part of an undifferentiated but specific "public"; (2) *an identification effect*, that is, a realignment of the atomized subjectivities along collective lines within which individuals recognize themselves as the same; (3) *a legibility effect*, that is, the production of both a language and a knowledge for governance, and theoretical and empirical tools that classify and regulate collectivities; and (4) *a spatialization effect*, that is, the production of boundaries and jurisdiction. This essay is an exploratory formulation of this strategy.

THINKING THE STATE

Exploratory though it may be, this exercise requires a conceptual baseline. First, we need to determine at what level(s) best to conceptualize the state. Is the state a "concrete-concrete," something "out there"? Or is it a concept necessary to understand something out there? Or, again, is it an ideology that helps to mask something *else* out there, a symbolic shield for power, as it were?

Unfortunately, sociocultural anthropologists have not given these questions the attention they deserve. In a major review of the anthropology of the state, Carole Nagengast (1994, 116) wrote: "Insofar as anthropology has dealt with the state, it has taken it as an unanalyzed given." Interestingly, Nagengast's own treatment of the state in the context of her assessment does not attempt to turn this unanalyzed given into an object of study.[1] Indeed, is there an object to study?

The anthropologist A. R. Radcliffe-Brown answers this question with a resounding "no" that should give us food for thought even if we disagree with its extremism. Introducing Meyer Fortes's *African Political Systems* in 1940, Radcliffe-Brown ([1940] 1995, xxiii) wrote:

> In writings on political institutions there is a good deal of discussion about the nature and origin of the State, which is usually represented as being an entity over and above the human individuals who make up a society, having as one of its attributes something called "sovereignty," and sometimes spoken of as having a will (law being defined as the will of the State) or as issuing commands. The State in this sense does not exist in the phenomenal world; it is a fiction of the philosophers. What does exist is an organization, i.e., a collection of individual human beings connected by a complex system of relations. . . . There is no such thing as the power of the State. . . .

One could call this death by conceptualization inasmuch as Radcliffe-Brown conceptualizes the state into oblivion.

To be sure, this answer carries the added weight of both empiricism and methodological individualism. Yet Radcliffe-Brown is not simply saying that "army" is merely the plural for "soldiers." Nor is he saying that the state does not exist because we cannot touch it. Governmental organizations have different levels of complexity, even if for the sake of functionality, when not for the sake of functionalism. Thus, a generous reading of Radcliffe-Brown, which would prune out the added philosophical baggage of his school and times, still leaves us with a powerful answer. The state is neither something out there nor a necessary concept. Each and every time we use the word, words such as *government* would do the conceptual job, and they would do it better.

I do not agree with this answer, but it seems to me that anthropologists cannot continue to ignore it. Radcliffe-Brown's answer to the state question contains a warning that anthropologists should keep in mind. Since the state can never be an empirical given, even at the second degree (the way, say, particular governments can be thought to be), where and how does anthropology encounter the state, if at all? What can be the terms of our analytical encounter with the state? What can we possibly mean, for instance, by an ethnography of the state?

In an important article, Philip Abrams revives Radcliffe-Brown's warnings. Abrams provides a sophisticated demonstration of the reasons for rejecting the existence of the state as an entity and raises some serious doubts about the analytical purchase of the state concept. He writes (1988, 76):

> The state . . . is not an object akin to the human ear. Nor is it even an object akin to human marriage. It is a third-order object, an ideological project. It is first and foremost an exercise in legitimation. . . . The state, in sum, is a bid to elicit support for or tolerance of the insupportable and intolerable by presenting them as something other than themselves, namely, legitimate, disinterested domination.

Contrary to Radcliffe-Brown, Abrams admits an object for state studies, the very process of power legitimation that projects the image of an allegedly disinterested entity—"the state-idea."[2] As stated, Abrams's state-idea is not immediately conducive to ethnography, but it does provide a warning that balances Radcliffe-Brown. Something happens out there that is more than government. The question is what.

Theorists have provided different answers to this question, which I will not survey here. For the purposes of this essay, let me only say that my own evolving view of the state starts with the "enlarged" notion of the state first put forward by Antonio Gramsci. I also find extremely fruitful Nicos Poulantzas's reworking of Marx and Gramsci. I continue to gain also from various writers such as Ralph Miliband (1969), Louis Althusser ([1969] 1971), Paul Thomas (1994), James Scott (1998), and Étienne Balibar (1997).[3] All this is to say that I do not claim to provide an original conceptualization. Rather, I hope to make a contribution to an ongoing dialogue with an eye to the kind of research best performed by sociocultural anthropologists (see also Trouillot 1997).

Most of the writers I have mentioned have insisted that the state is not reducible to government. In Miliband's (1969, 48) words, "what 'the state' stands for is a number of particular institutions which, together, constitute its reality, and which interact as part of what may be called the state system." Miliband's overly sociological treatment of that system needs to be backed by Poulantzas's and Gramsci's more elaborate conceptualizations of the state as a privileged site of both power and struggle. Gramsci's insistence on thinking state and civil society together by way of concepts such as hegemony and historical bloc is fundamental to this approach. I read Gramsci as saying that, within the context of capitalism, theories of the state must cover the entire social formation and articulate the relation between state and civil society. One cannot theorize the state and then theorize society or vice versa. Rather, state and society are bound by the historical bloc that takes the form of the specific social contract of—and, thus, the hegemony deployed in—a particular social formation. "A social contract is the confirmation of nationhood, the confirmation of civil society by the state, the confirmation of sameness and interdependence across class boundaries" (Trouillot 1997, 51). Yet even that phrasing needs to be qualified lest it seem to reinforce the nineteenth-century homology of state and nation.

As institutionalized in degree-granting departments in a context in which faith in progress was unquestioned, nineteenth-century social science built its categories on the assumption that the world in which it was born was not only the present of a linear past but the augur of an ordained future. For most of its practitioners, the world may not have been eternal, but the referents of the categories—if not the categories themselves—used to describe that world were eternal. Thus the conflation of state and nation was naturalized because it seemed so obvious within that present— evidence to the contrary notwithstanding. But what if the correspondence between statehood and nationhood, exemplified by the claimed history of the North Atlantic and naturalized by its social science, was itself historical?[4] Indeed, there are no theoretical grounds on which to assert the necessity of that correspondence, and there are some historical grounds for questioning it.

If we suspend the state-nation homology as I suggest we should, we reach a more powerful vision of the state, yet one more open to ethnography, since we discover that, theoretically, there is no necessary site for the state, institutional or geographical. Within that vision, the state thus appears as an open field with multiple boundaries and no institutional fixity—which is to say that it needs to be conceptualized at more than one level. Though linked to a number of apparatuses not all of which may be governmental, the state is not an apparatus but a set of processes. It is not necessarily bound by any institution, nor can any institution fully encapsulate it.

At that level, its materiality resides much less in institutions than in the reworking of processes and relations of power so as to create new spaces for the deployment of power. As I have put it elsewhere (Trouillot 1990, 19), "At one level the division between state and civil society has to do with content. . . . At another level it has to do with methodology in the broad sense."

I will return later to the particular consequences of this position in the age of globalization. First, however, I need to make explicit what I mean by *globalization*.

A FRAGMENTED GLOBALITY

If by *globalization* we mean the massive flow of goods, peoples, information, and capital across huge areas of the earth's surface in ways that make the parts dependent on the whole, the world has been global since the sixteenth century. To acknowledge these earlier global flows is not to claim that there is nothing new under the sun. Rather, the reference to a massive empirical record of global flows helps us, first, to expose what I call *globalitarism* as a dominant ideology of our times and, second, to insist on the political and scholarly need to establish a critical distance from that ideology.

If we approach globalization naively as the recent emergence of "a world without boundaries," we find ourselves repeating advertising slogans without knowing how we ended up doing so. We overlook the fact that words like *global* and *globalization* in their most current use were first broadcast most aggressively by marketing agents and marketing schools. Masaki and Helsen (1998) locate what they candidly call "the globalization imperative" in the search for new marketing strategies.[5] Scholarly analysis needs to go beyond the slogans, clichés, and narratives that sustain these strategies. These tropes not only silence the histories of the world but also veil our understanding of the present—including their own conditions of possibility—by hiding the changing story of capital. Changes in the composition and spatialization of capital are crucial in shaping the uniqueness of our present. In this essay, I reserve the word *globalization* for the conflation of these changes.[6]

Capitalism has always been transnational. Crossing political borders is inherent in its historical trajectory. Indeed, some analysts have long suggested that capitalism is necessarily prone to cross borders inasmuch as it must find new places to integrate into the sphere of capital (Luxemburg

[1914] 1951). Today as in the past, most firms that operate in more than one country have a distinguishable home base. What is new is not the internationalization of capital as such but the changes in the spatialization of the world economy and changes in the volume and, especially, the kinds of movements that occur across political boundaries.

Indeed, present world history is characterized by a series of fundamental changes in spatialization, many of which are both captured and obscured by the word *globalization*. Changes in the spatialization of markets—the market for capital (both financial and industrial), the market for labor, and the market for consumer goods—create overlapping spatialities that are not synchronized but together help to give the world economy its current shape. The world economy now looks like what Ohmae (1985) called "the Triad"—a triangle with three major regional centers as its poles, one in North America (the United States and Canada), one in Asia (with Japan at the epicenter), and one in Western Europe (with Germany as the epicenter).[7]

A major change is in the dynamism of international investments. The magnitude of foreign direct investment—for instance, capital deployed from one country into branches and subsidiaries located in another country—was reportedly US $317 billion in 1995, dwarfing records from all past eras. Further, in spite of some yearly fluctuations, notably in 1992 and in 1998 after the Asian crisis, the long-term rise seems continuous. Indeed, foreign direct investment is becoming the primary form of exchange across state borders, a place traditionally occupied by commerce, and is thus influencing more than ever the rhythm and direction of international exchanges.

Within this foreign direct investment, the major transfers have moved away from manufacturing to target "nonproductive" assets such as real estate, tourism, department stores, banking, and insurance (Weiss 1997, 8). Among the leading countries, only Japan's foreign investments remain relatively high in manufacturing. The major profits, national and transnational, are now in rent form, notably in the financial markets. As many transnational holdings involved in manufacturing become, in fact, "financial groups with an industrial concentration" (Chesnais 1994, 61–66), the logic of finance capital—which, both Marx and Keynes warned us, is very close to the logic of usury—becomes the dominant logic of the system. The fragility of unregulated financial markets combines rumors of immediate doom with hopes of extravagant profits. Indeed, quick profit anywhere, by any means, a goal inherent in the logic of capital itself, becomes the explicit ethos of managers. At the same time and for the very same reasons, capital does not move freely across borders. Rather, the spatial distribution of capital is increasingly selective. Most world economic movement and especially foreign direct investment occurs between or within the poles of the Triad.[8] Outside of the Triad, exchange tends to take the minor form of subcontracting.

That global exchange remains concentrated among a few countries, mainly in the North Atlantic, China, and Japan, is one of many aspects of a third major feature of our times—the increasing concentration of economic power. Exchange occurs primarily between the same countries, between firms of the same sectors, between branches of the same firm. Far from moving toward more open markets, the world economy has witnessed in the 1980s and '90s the emergence of "private markets" that dominate its most important exchanges.

Likewise, we have not witnessed the global integration of the price of labor that some optimists promised in the 1960s. On the contrary, the world labor market has become more differentiated. It is differentiated by region, with the highest prices in the North Atlantic and the lowest in most of Asia, Latin America, and, especially, Africa. It is also differentiated within countries. Only at a lower level, that of consumer products, is the global economy moving, at great speed, toward a single integrated market. And even there, a few industries account for most of that integration.

In short, globalization does not mean that the world economy is now integrated into a single space. Rather, it means that that economy is developing three contradictory but overlapping modes of spatialization: (1) increased, though selective, flexibility of capital, mainly financial capital, within or between the poles of the Triad; (2) differentiated labor markets within and across national borders; and (3) increased but uneven integration of consumer markets worldwide.

A major socioeconomic consequence of these overlaps is global polarization. This polarization takes many forms. Between sellers and buyers we are witnessing the rise of world oligopolies: a few firms now control the world market for most major commodities. Polarization has also increased between countries. Gone are the developmentalist dreams that assumed all countries to be on the same path. A majority of countries and some continental chunks (notably sub-Saharan Africa) are becoming poorer every day. Even more important, what happens there is becoming irrelevant to the world economy. Given the declining significance of geopolitics in the post–Cold War era, this means, quite concretely, that chunks of humankind are seen by world political and economic leaders as superfluous. The global map increasingly has large black holes.

Polarization occurs also within borders, even in the North Atlantic. According to former US secretary of labor Robert Reich (1992), one-fifth of the population of the United States is doing increasingly well while the remaining four-fifths are on a downward path. Socialist-oriented programs are slowing down similar trends in Europe, but they are under serious political attack from big business and their allies. There, as here, the debate continues about the number of citizens who will fall on the bad side of the gap. Still, the public acknowledgment that populations within the same industrialized countries are headed in different directions is a new feature.

To make matters worse, academic, political, and corporate leaders in most of the world have joined in what Linda Weiss (1997, 1998) calls "the political construction of hopelessness," telling citizens that they cannot do anything about the social consequences of globalization. Once-unequivocal assumptions that citizens of Western democracies had some control over the fate of their neighborhoods, their towns, or their children are now being questioned.[9]

We are far from the idyllic vision of a global village in which everyone is connected to everyone else. Rather, our times are marked by an increasing awareness of global flows and processes among fragmented populations. World histories and local histories are becoming both increasingly intertwined and increasingly contradictory. Homogenization is at best superficial.

To be sure, a few corporations from the United States, Japan, Italy, and France now seem to share global cultural control through the distribution of entertainment and clothing. The planetary integration of the market for consumer goods does link the world's populations in a web of consumption in which national ideals are becoming more similar even as the means to achieve them elude a growing majority. The integration of that market, the speed of communications, and the oligopolies in media and entertainment help to project the same image of the good life all over the world. In that sense, we are truly witnessing for the first time, especially among the youth, the global production of desire.

At the same time, this global production of desire does not satisfy the cultural needs of specific populations. In fact, it exacerbates tensions because of the social polarization noted above, the limited means available to satisfy those new desires, and the always-specific discrepancies between global models and local ones. Further, there is no global culture model to attenuate those discrepancies, in part because there is no agreement on long-term meanings. Indeed, with the demise of the Soviet bloc, North Atlantic societies in general and the United States in particular find it increasingly difficult to generate a unified meaning and purpose to social life for their own citizens, let alone agree on an ideal that they can sell to others (Reich 1992; Laïdi 1993). In short, within and across state boundaries, polarization and entanglement now create new ways of perceiving distance—temporal, spatial, social, and cultural—thus shaping a new horizon of historicity that I call "a fragmented globality."

CHANGING CONTAINERS

It is against the background of this fragmented globality that we may best evaluate changes in the effectiveness of the national state as a primary site for economic exchange, political struggle, or cultural negotiation. Further, we need to assess these changes with a sober awareness that the national state was never as closed and as unavoidable a container—economically, politically, or culturally—as politicians and academics have claimed since the nineteenth century. Once we see the necessity of the national state as a lived fiction of late modernity—indeed, as possibly a brief parenthesis in human history—we may be less surprised by the changes we now face and be able to respond to them with the intellectual imagination they deserve.[10]

These changes cannot be measured quantitatively on a single scale. Even if we were to reduce states to governments, a quick comparison of Iran, Mexico, India, France, Iraq, and the United States within and across their recognized borders suggests that one cannot measure governmental power on a continuum. Thus claims of the declining relevance of the state along globalitarist lines are at best premature if only because they presume such a continuum.[11] Rather than unilinear, the changes are multiple and, as I have suggested, sometimes contradictory (see also Comaroff and Comaroff 2000). I will note only a few of the most significant ones.

First, and directly related to globalization as defined here, the domains of intervention of national governments are rapidly changing. Second, and quite important for sociocultural anthropologists, national states are now performing less well as ideological and cultural containers, especially—but not only—in the North Atlantic. Third, new processes and practices that seem to reject or bypass the state form—such as the new social movements—are creeping into the interstices thus opened. Yet, fourth, statelike processes and practices also obtain increasingly in nongovernmental sites such as NGOs or in trans-state institutions such as the World Bank. These practices, in turn, produce state effects as powerful as those of national governments.

To complicate matters, none of this means that national governments have stopped intervening in the economic or in other walks of life. Indeed, the number of sovereign states has more than quadrupled between 1945 and the end of the last century. Yet, the kinds of intervention national governments perform have changed—at times considerably. For instance, as Terry Turner (n.d.) astutely notes, we can see in retrospect that since the end of World War II military intervention within the North Atlantic has become obsolete as the means to capture the leadership of the capitalist world economy.[12] More recently, changes in the composition and spatialization of capital have rendered government interventions in international commerce both less necessary and less effective.[13]

Most crucial for sociocultural anthropologists, the national state no longer functions as the primary social, political, and ideological container of the populations living within its borders. To be sure, it was never as solid a container as we were led to believe. However, in the North Atlantic at least and, to a lesser extent, in the American states that saw the first wave of decolonization, it often secured the outer limits of political struggle, economic exchange, and cultural negotiation. More important, their performance notwithstanding, national governments were often expected—and often pretended—to act as cultural containers. Now, neither citizens nor governmental leaders expect the state to play that role effectively.[14]

This is in part because of governments' inability (especially in the South) or unwillingness (especially in the North Atlantic) to deal with the increased inequality ushered in by globalization and, more important, the citizenry's perception of that inability or unwillingness. It is also, relatedly, because of the increased inability of national governments from Iran and China to France and the United States to play a leadership role in the shaping of cultural practices, models, and ideals. Further, almost everywhere both the correspondence between the state system and what Althusser ([1969] 1971) calls the "ideological state apparatuses" has declined as these apparatuses increasingly reflect rather than deflect locally lived social tensions, notably those of race and class.[15] The fiction of isolated national entities constructed by nineteenth-century politicians and scholars no longer fits the lived experiences of most populations.

Cracks in the fiction appeared soon after World War II. In the North Atlantic, the declining relevance of war as the path to global economic leadership meant a decline in the use and effectiveness of nationalist rhetoric—partly masked and delayed, especially in the United States, by the existence of the Soviet bloc. Elsewhere, the deep tremors experienced in Africa and Asia during the second wave of decolonization augured ill for the presumed national homogeneity.[16] Where and how to establish the borders of the new African and Asian polities often proved an unforeseen predicament. Partition by decree in cases as varied as India-Pakistan, Israel-Palestine, and French and German Togo exposed the artificiality and the use of power inherent in border-making practices. Cases such as Algeria's *pieds noirs* suggested that even the distinction between home and elsewhere was not as easy as once thought.

From the 1950s to the 1990s, the Cold War, in spite of its rhetoric, also brought home the relevance of events happening in other regions of the globe. In North America, Vietnam—as later the taking of hostages in Tehran—played a key role in producing that understanding. In the 1970s and '80s, citizens throughout the North Atlantic discovered their partial dependency on foreign imports after most OPEC countries assumed ownership of their oil fields.

One can safely suggest, however, that geopolitical and economic changes on the world scene as such were less crucial in breaking down the fiction of impermeable entities than the manner in which those changes were brought home to ordinary citizens in the North Atlantic and affected their daily lives. To give but one example, the objective degree of US involvement in Indochina in the 1960s was arguably less than that of Spain in seventeenth-century Mexico, that of France in eighteenth-century Saint-Domingue/Haiti, or that of Britain in nineteenth-century India. It might not have been enough to change the imagination of North Americans if not for the fact that television made the Vietnam War a daily occurrence in their homes, just as it would later make the Iran-US confrontation a matter of nightly routine. Even more than television, refugees knocking at the door, new patterns of immigration, and the reconfiguration of the ethnic and cultural landscape in major North Atlantic cities brought the "elsewhere" to the home front. The speed and mass of global flows—including the flow of populations deemed to be different and often claiming that difference while insisting on acceptance—profoundly undermined the notion of bounded entities, and not just on an abstract level. The barbarians were at the door, which was bad enough, but they were also claiming that "our" home could be theirs.

North Atlantic natives, in turn, both rejected and accommodated that daily presence. Thus, segregationist practices notwithstanding, the commodification of exotic customs and products from Zen and yoga to Mao shirts and dashikis facilitated a guarded cultural acceptance. Food played a major role in that process. Korean vegetable shops in the United States and Arab groceries in France provided needed services. More important may have been the wave of "ethnic" restaurants that swamped Paris, London, Amsterdam, and New York beginning in the 1970s and now brings couscous, curry, or sushi to inland cities once thought impermeable to Third World cultural imports. The daily presence of the Other, mediatized, commodified, tightly controlled, yet seemingly unavoidable—as Other—on the screen or on the street, is a major trope of globalitarist ideology. Yet this trope functions at least in part because it illustrates for local populations the national state's increasing difficulty in functioning as a container, even in the North Atlantic.[17]

TOWARD AN ETHNOGRAPHY OF THE STATE

None of this means that the relevance of the state is declining, if by "state" we mean more than the apparatus of national governments. If the state is indeed a set of practices and processes and their effects as much as a way to look at them, we need to track down these practices, processes, and effects whether or not they coalesce around the central sites of national governments. In the age of globalization, state practices, functions, and effects increasingly obtain in sites other than the national but never entirely bypass the national order. The challenge for anthropologists is to study these practices, functions, and effects without prejudice about sites or forms of encounters. I will note the possibilities of this approach by further sketching the state effects mentioned at the beginning of this essay as grounds for an ethnography of the state.

Nicos Poulantzas (1972) identified what he called the "isolation effect," which I read as the production of a particular kind of subject as an atomized member of a public—a key feature of statecraft. Through the isolation of socioeconomic conflicts, notably class divisions, the state not only guarantees its own relative autonomy vis-à-vis dominant classes but also produces atomized, individualized citizens who all appear equal in a supposedly undifferentiated public sphere. In many societies today, the national public sphere is fractured differently from when Poulantzas wrote. At the same time, the relative increase in judicial power in almost all the North Atlantic countries suggests that individual atomization is accompanied by new forms of homogenization. Identity politics notably signals new configurations of the citizenry. The development of notions of universal human rights and the global spread of North Atlantic legal philosophy and practices—to cite only one example—are producing isolation effects, North and South, at times with the backing of national governments or with the still timid support of transnational statelike institutions. In short, the isolation effect—including the masking of class divisions and the joint production of a public and the atomized subjects that constitute it—still obtains, but the processes and practices—and hence the power—that produce it are being deployed in unexpected sites.

Following Poulantzas's approach and terminology, we can identify a number of state effects that he did not identify by name. To the isolation effect we can add, as suggested earlier, an identification effect, a legibility effect, and a spatialization effect. In all these cases we observe a *déplacement* of state functions, a move away from the state system described by Miliband or even from the state apparatuses described by Althusser. State power is being redeployed, state effects are appearing in new sites, and, in almost all cases, this move is one away from national sites to infra-, supra-, or transnational ones. An ethnography of the state can and should capture these effects.

For instance, we may call an identification effect the capacity to develop a shared conviction that "we are all in the same boat" and therefore to interpellate subjects as homogeneous members of various imagined communities (Poulantzas 1972; Balibar 1997; Scott 1998; Trouillot 1997). This homogenizing process, once thought the fundamental purview of the national state, is now shared by the national state and a number of competing sites and processes from region to gender, race, and ethnicity. Here again, identity politics helps redefine the national for better and—often—for worse. The so-called new social movements have also become sites for accumulating, redirecting, or deploying social and political power that often tries to bypass or challenge national states, albeit with limited success.[18] Many are both parochial and global, with multiple boundaries.[19] Few see national borders as the main line of demarcation of their activities.

The national state also produces what I call a legibility effect, following Scott's (1998) development on legibility practices. However, as Scott himself suggests, governments are not the only actors who "see like a state." Notably in the South, NGOs and trans-state institutions from the World Bank to the IMF now perform—sometimes better—on that score and produce similar if not more potent legibility effects. UNESCO or International Labour Organization (ILO) statistics are more reliable than those of quite a few national governments. NGOs' capacities to plan effectively at the local and regional level all over the South and the World Bank's or the IMF's power to envision and promote everywhere a future based on their assessment—however questionable—of the present have now moved a number of state practices away from the national. For better and for worse, these are all, analytically, statelike institutions.

Since most state effects can be captured in part through the subjects they help to produce, ethnographers are well positioned to follow this worldwide displacement of state functions and practices. To give one obvious example, we are well equipped to follow NGOs "on the ground," to evaluate their capacity to interpellate and the conscious acceptance or rejection of that interpellation. Kamran Ali's ethnography of a family-planning campaign in Egypt—which involves USAID, internationally funded NGOs, and the national government—suggests that one of the potential outcomes of the campaign is the production of newly atomized "modern" subjects (Ali 1996, 2000). I read Ali as saying that nongovernmental and governmental practices combine in the production of quite new but quite "Egyptian" citizens. Similarly, NGOs attempting to reform "street children" in Mexico City are also producing new but Mexican subjects, with a different mixture of accommodation and resistance on the part of the citizenry so shaped (Magazine 1999). Indeed, the extent to which the emerging subjects recognize the statelike nature of nongovernmental organizations and institutions varies. Still, there are indications that awareness of their role is increasing.[20]

NGOs are only the most obvious cases begging for an ethnography of state effects. We need to note, however, that they fit within a more general movement of privatization of state functions (e.g., Hibou 1999) of which the rise of privately-run prisons, the proliferation of private armies in Africa and Latin America, and the privatization of public enterprises worldwide are other evident manifestations. Only careful ethnographies will tell us the extent to which these—or less visible emergent manifestations—produce state effects.

Are national governments left only to guard their borders—and quite ineffectively at that? The three stories with which I started this essay suggest that government still performs this role.[21] More important, regardless of the relative effectiveness of governments at border patrol, the national state still produces—and quite effectively among most populations—a spatialization effect. Citizens all over the world may reject the slogan that all nationals are in the same boat, but they remain aware that "we" (however defined) do live in a place usually defined in part by a political border.

While the spatialization effect may also be produced in other sites, national governments are less likely to let go of their power in this domain. Indeed, with the spectacular exception of the European Union—a truly innovative and changing formation of which we cannot even guess the long-term political consequences within and outside of Europe—national states are likely to hold onto their power to define political boundaries. First, in a context marked by the obvious incapacity of national states to function as cultural containers, the protection of borders becomes an easy political fiction with which to enlist support from a confused citizenry. Second, the right to define boundaries remains a fundamental component of sovereignty to which national governments must cling in an age in which many state functions are being performed elsewhere. To put it bluntly, national states produce countries, and countries remain fundamentally spatial. Hence, quite understandably, most human beings continue to act locally most of the time, even while many more now claim to think globally. Anthropology's challenge for this century may very well be to pay deserved attention to the tensions inherent in that contradiction.

The respatialization of various state functions and effects is taking place in a context already marked by the differential respatialization of markets. These incongruent spatialities inevitably produce tensions in the location of state power and in citizens' perception of and reaction to its deployment. An anthropology of the state may have to make these tensions a primary focus of its research agenda. These tensions will be found not only in organized politics but in the many practices through which citizens encounter not only government but also a myriad of other statelike institutions and processes that interpellate them as individuals and as members of various communities. In short, anthropology may not find the state ready-made, waiting for our ethnographic gaze in the known sites of national government. Government institutions and practices are to be studied, of course, and we can deplore that anthropology has not contributed enough to their study. However, we may also have to look for state processes and effects in sites less obvious than those of institutionalized politics and established bureaucracies. We may have to insist on encounters that are not immediately transparent. We may indeed have to revert to the seemingly timeless banality of daily life.

NOTES

Editors' Note: This chapter first appeared as "The Anthropology of the State: Close Encounters of a Deceptive Kind," *Current Anthropology* 42, no. 1 (2001): 125–38.

1. Anthropological attempts to look at institutions of the national state ethnographically since the publication of her review include Gupta 1995; Heyman 1998, 1999; and Nugent 1994.

2. Since the state is an ideological projection, the purpose of state studies is to decipher this exercise in legitimacy—the processes behind the idea of the state and its cultural acceptance.

3. Gramsci's enlarged view of the state, inseparable from concepts such as hegemony, civil society, and historical bloc, offers the fundamental point of departure that, in the context of capitalism, theories of the state must cover the entire social formation because state and civil society are intertwined. The intellectual and political implications of that starting point cannot be overestimated. See Bucci-Glucksman 1975; Macchiocci 1974; Thomas 1994; and Trouillot 1990, 1996. Miliband launched the Marxist critique of Leninism and its implication that seizing control of government meant seizing control of state power. That critique, implicit in Gramsci, arose timidly in the '60s and grew in the '70s, especially in England and France. For Miliband, although government is invested with state power, the state is not reducible to government. Further, the leadership of the state elite includes individuals who are not in government proper but who often belong to the privileged classes. Miliband barely cites Lenin, but the critique is evident. He also suggests (1969, 49) that the study of the state must start with the preliminary problem that "'the state' is not a thing, that is, does not, as such, exist." On Poulantzas's contribution, see Thomas 1994 and Jessop 1985. On Althusser, see Resch 1992.

4. For a critical assessment of the state-nation homology, see Trouillot 1990, 23–26.

5. Both *globalization* and *global village* date at least from the 1960s, with Zbigniew Brzezinski and Marshall McLuhan emphasizing respectively the universal status of the North American model of modernity and the technological convergence of the world (Mattelart 2000).

6. Economists do not fully agree on the list of changes that make up globalization. I have tended to rely on the more critical observers. François Chesnais (1994) and Serge Cordellier (2000) provide two accessible summaries and Linda Weiss (1997) one of the most brutal critiques of globalization. See also Adda 1996a, 1996b; Reich 1992; Sassen 1998; and Wade 1996.

7. In 1970, 64 of the world's top 100 corporations were based in the United States. The United Kingdom was a distant second with 9, followed by Germany, Japan, and France. By 1997, 29 corporations on *Fortune*'s top-100 list were based in Japan, 24 in the United States, 13 in Germany, and 10 in France.

8. The capital invested tends to come from six countries: the United States, Japan, the United Kingdom, Germany, France, and the Netherlands, more or less in that order. More important, the investments reach mainly the same countries with the notable addition of China. Of the US $317 billion invested across state boundaries in 1995, US $194 billion stayed in the North Atlantic (in the United States, Canada, and the European Union). Outside of the North Atlantic, only China's share (US $37.7 billion) was significant. Latin America as a whole received about as much as Sweden alone. China was Japan's second-largest trading partner and Japan China's largest trading partner.

9. Right-wing populism feeds on this despair, silencing the fact that social polarization is not something handed down to us by an anonymous world market but the partial and predictable result of conscious political decisions made by North Atlantic states since the Reagan-Thatcher era.

10. As part of their bold move to link economy, society, and the ideological-cultural tenets of neoliberalism in our times, Comaroff and Comaroff (2000, 318–30) provide a more ambitious summary of the debate about state and globalization than I can here.

11. There are other problems. These theses also rest on the illusion that the political is an analytically distinct sphere, a proposition long questioned by Talcott Parsons (1951, 126) and explicitly rejected by most of the state theorists I have used here, notably Gramsci. A second theoretical slip is the illusion that states are equivalent to governments. Since many of the kinds of intervention traditionally thought to be within the purview of governments are less easily achieved or simply impossible today, globalitarians conclude that the state has declined. A third theoretical rejoinder to the declining-relevance thesis is that the state and the international system of states—without which each state is, in turn, unthinkable—are necessary conditions for globalization. Globalization is inconceivable theoretically or historically without a number of strong states and especially a strong international state system.

12. Ironically, the two big losers of World War II formalized this new trend better and faster than their competitors. Japan and West Germany reaped the benefits of having to renounce, both by choice and by force, the threat of war.

This argument does not invalidate the benefits of a war machine in revamping a national economy, as both Reagan and Clinton administrations demonstrate.

13. There are areas of great controversy, as the ongoing banana wars between the United States and the European Community suggest. Also, trans-state government interventions to remove trade barriers tend to pressure the South much more than the North to remove its tariffs and protections.

14. The recent history of France makes the point. From Francis I to Louis XIV to Napoleon, de Gaulle, and Mitterrand, French governments have always taken seriously the role of the state as a cultural container. Against that background, the rate of decline of expectations in this regard in recent years is telling.

15. The overall erosion of ideological state apparatuses in the former colonies is obvious. An overview of either the Catholic Church in France or the educational system in the United States from the 1950s to the present could illustrate the point for the North Atlantic.

16. The first wave of decolonization occurred, of course, in the Americas in the nineteenth century with the successive independences of the United States, Haiti, the former Spanish colonies, and Brazil.

17. There are plenty of other signs of the tension between the visibility of groups clearly marked as Others and the homogenizing claims of the state. The consolidation of "ethnic" votes in the United States is among the most blatant. I have concentrated on the North Atlantic here not because similar signs are lacking in the South but because the fiction of homogeneous entities never fully obtained in the South or in Eastern Europe. To put it otherwise, the peripheral state was never as competent in producing an identification effect as the state in France, Britain, Germany, or the United States.

18. Emily's List and the Sierra Club in the United States and the German Greens suggest that the capacity of social movements—feminist, ecological, or other—to avoid national-state-like institutionalization is not as evident as once thought.

19. Thus, almost all separatist movements have branches outside the geopolitical borders of the state they contest.

20. Beatrice Pouligny (personal communication) reports that some Haitians say in reference to NGOs: "yo fè leta" (literally, "they make the state"), which in Haitian parlance suggests that they have identified a site of power equal to and capable of challenging the state but also the makings of a potential bully. (The same word can mean "state" or "bully" in Haitian.) At least some street children in Mexico seem to be aware of the social overlap and flows between the personnel of state agencies and that of NGOs, an overlap that is not unique to Mexico; I read Magazine (1999) as saying that the governmental/nongovernmental divide is not significant for the street children.

21. They also suggest that it is not always efficient—or at least that its performance is now marred by increased ambiguity. After all, Sen did go to Davos and receive a public apology from the Swiss government. Since 1999 Germany has recognized *jus solis* (citizenship right by birth) as well as *jus sanguinis* (right by descent). Other difficulties of ethnic Turks are now being addressed by German courts—one more sign if needed of this global expansion of judicial rhetoric and reach.

REFERENCES

Abrams, Philip. 1988. "Notes on the Difficulty of Studying the State." *Journal of Historical Sociology* 1, no. 1: 58–89.

Adda, Jacques. 1996a. *La mondialisation de l'économie*. Vol. 1, *La genèse*. Paris: La Découverte.

Adda, Jacques. 1996b. *La mondialisation de l'économie*. Vol. 2, *Les problèmes*. Paris: La Découverte.

Ali, Kamran Asdar. 1996. "The Politics of Family Planning in Egypt." *Anthropology Today* 12, no. 5: 14–19.

Ali, Kamran Asdar. 2000. "Making 'Responsible' Men: Planning the Family in Egypt." In *Fertility and the Male Life-Cycle in the Era of Fertility Decline*, edited by Caroline Bledsoe, Susana Lerner, and Jane Guyer, 119–43. Oxford: Oxford University Press.

Althusser, Louis. (1960) 1971. *Lenin and Philosophy, and Other Essays*. Translated by Ben Brewster. New York: Monthly Review Press.

Balibar, Étienne. 1997. *La crainte des masses: Politique et philosophie avant et après Marx*. Paris: Galilée.

Bermann, George A., et al. 1993. *Cases and Materials on European Community Law*. St. Paul, MN: West Academic.

Bucci-Glucksman, Christine. 1975. *Gramsci et l'état: Pour une théorie matérialiste de la philosophie*. Paris: Fayard.

Chesnais, François. 1994. *La mondialisation du capital*. Paris: Syros.

Comaroff, Jean, and John L. Comaroff. 2000. "Millennial Capitalism: First Thoughts on the Second Coming." *Public Culture* 12, no. 2: 291–343.

Cordellier, Serge, ed. 2000. *La mondialisation au-delà des mythes*. Paris: La Découverte.

Gupta, Akhil. 1995. "Blurred Boundaries: The Discourse of Corruption, the Culture of Politics, and the Imagined State." *American Ethnologist* 22, no. 2: 375–402.

Heyman, Josiah McC. 1998. "State Effects on Labor Exploitation: The INS and Undocumented Immigrants at the Mexico–United States Border." *Critique of Anthropology* 18: 155–79.

Heyman, Josiah McC. 1999. "United States Surveillance over Mexican Lives at the Border: Snapshots of an Emerging Regime." *Human Organization* 58, no. 4: 429–37.

Hibou, Béatrice, ed. 1999. *La privatisation des états*. Paris: Karthala.

Jessop, Bob. 1985. *Nicos Poulantzas: Marxist Theory and Political Strategy*. New York: St. Martin's Press.

Laïdi, Zaki. 1993. *L'ordre mondial relaché: Sens et puissance aprés la guerre froide*. Paris: Presses de la Fondation nationale des sciences politiques.

Luxemburg, Rosa. (1914) 1951. *The Accumulation of Capital*. New York: Monthly Review Press.

Macchiocci, Maria-Antonietta. 1974. *Pour Gramsci*. Paris: Éditions du Seuil.

Magazine, Roger. 1999. "Stateless Contexts: Street Children and Soccer Fans in Mexico City." PhD diss., Johns Hopkins University.

Masaki, Kotabe, and Kristiaan Helsen. 1998. *Global Marketing Management*. New York: John Wiley.

Mattelart, Armand. "La nouvelle idéologie globalitaire." In *La mondialisation au-delà des mythes*, edited by Serge Cordellier, 81–92. Paris: La Découverte.

Miliband, Ralph. 1969. *The State in Capitalist Society*. New York: Harper Books.

Nagengast, Carol. 1994. "Violence, Terror, and the Crisis of the State." *Annual Review of Anthropology* 23: 109–36.

Nugent, David. 1994. "Building the State, Making the Nation: The Bases and Limits of State Centralization in 'Modern' Peru." *American Anthropologist* 96, no. 2: 333–69.

Ohmae, Ken'ichi. 1985. *Triad Power: The Coming Shape of Competition*. New York: Free Press.

Parsons, Talcott. 1951. *The Social System*. New York: Free Press.

Poulantzas, Nicos. 1972. *Pouvoir politique et classes sociales*. Paris: Maspero.

Radcliffe-Brown, A. R. (1940) 1955. "Preface." In *African Political Systems*, edited by Meyer Fortes and E. E. Evans-Pritchard, xi–xxiii. Oxford: Oxford University Press.

Reich, Robert B. 1992. *The Work of Nations: Preparing Ourselves for 21st-Century Capitalism*. New York: Knopf.

Resch, Robert Paul. 1992. *Althusser and the Renewal of Marxist Social Theory*. Berkeley: University of California Press.

Sassen, Saskia. 1998. *Globalization and Its Discontents: Essays on the New Mobility of People and Money*. New York: New Press.

Scott, James C. 1998. *Seeing Like a State: How Certain Schemes to Improve the Human Condition Have Failed*. New Haven, CT: Yale University Press.

Thomas, Paul. 1994. *Alien Politics: Marxist State Theory Retrieved*. New York: Routledge.

Trouillot, Michel-Rolph. 1990. *Haiti: State against Nation; The Origins and Legacy of Duvalierism*. New York: Monthly Review Press.

Trouillot, Michel-Rolph. 1996. "Démocratie et société civile." In *Les transitions démocratiques: Actes du colloque international de Port-au-Prince*, edited by Laënnec Hurbon, 225–31. Paris: Syros.

Trouillot, Michel-Rolph. 1997. "A Social Contract for Whom? Haitian History and Haiti's Future." In *Haiti Renewed: Political and Economic Prospects*, edited by Robert Rotberg, 47–59. Washington, DC: Brookings Institution Press.

Turner, Terence. n.d. "Globalization, the State, and Social Consciousness in the Late Twentieth Century." Unpublished manuscript.

Wade, Robert. 1996. "Japan, the World Bank, and the Art of Paradigm Maintenance: The East Asian Miracle in Political Perspective." *New Left Review* 217: 3–36.

Weiss, Linda. 1997. "Globalization and the Myth of the Powerless State." *New Left Review* I/225: 3–27.

Weiss, Linda. 1998. *The Myth of the Powerless State*. Ithaca, NY: Cornell University Press.

CHAPTER 12

From Planters' Journals to Academia

The Haitian Revolution as Unthinkable History

INTRODUCTION

In 1790, just a few months before the beginning of the insurrection that shook Saint-Domingue and eventuated in the revolutionary birth of independent Haiti, French colonist La Barre reassured his metropolitan wife of the peaceful state of life in the tropics.[1] He wrote: "There is no movement among our Negroes. . . . They don't even think of it. They are very tranquil and obedient. A revolt among them is impossible." And again: "We have nothing to fear on the part of the Negroes; they are tranquil and obedient." And again: "The Negroes are very obedient and always will be. We sleep with doors and windows wide open. Freedom for Negroes is a chimera" (Dorsinville 1965, 56).

Historian Roger Dorsinville, who cites these words, notes that a few months later the most important slave insurrection in recorded history had reduced to insignificance such abstract arguments about Negro obedience. I am not so sure. When reality does not coincide with deeply held beliefs, human beings have the rather curious tendency of phrasing interpretations that force reality within the scope of these beliefs. They devise formulas to repress the unthinkable and to bring it back within the realm of accepted discourse.

La Barre's views were by no means unique. Witness this manager who constantly reassured his patrons in almost similar words: "I live tranquilly in the midst of them without a single thought of their uprising unless that was fomented by the whites themselves" (Cauna 1987, 204). There were doubts at times. But the planters' practical precautions aimed at stemming individual actions, or at worst, a student riot. No one in Saint-Domingue or elsewhere worked out a plan of response to a general insurrection.

Indeed, the contention that enslaved Africans and their descendants could not envision freedom—let alone formulate strategies for gaining and securing such freedom—was based not so much on empirical evidence as on an ontology, an implicit organization of the world and its inhabitants. Although by no means monolithic, this world view was widely shared by whites in Europe and the Americas and by many nonwhite plantation owners as well. Although it left room for variations, none of these variations included the possibility of a revolutionary uprising in the slave plantations, let alone a successful one eventuating in the creation of an independent state.

The Haitian Revolution thus entered history with the peculiar characteristic of being unthinkable even as it happened. Publications of the times, including the long list of pamphlets on Saint-Domingue published in France from 1790 to 1804, reveal the incapacity of most contemporaries to understand the ongoing Revolution on its own terms.[2] They could read the news only with their ready-made categories, and these categories were incompatible with the idea of a slave revolution.

The discursive context within which news from Saint-Domingue was discussed as it happened has important consequences for the historiography of Saint-Domingue/Haiti. How does one write a history of the impossible? The key issue is not ideological. Ideological treatments are now more current in Haiti itself (in the epic or bluntly political interpretations of the Revolution favored by some Haitian writers) than in the more rigorous handling of the evidence by professionals in Europe or in North America. The international scholarship on the Haitian Revolution has been sound by modern standards of evidence since at least the 1940s. The issue is rather epistemological and, by inference, methodological in the broadest sense. Standards of evidence notwithstanding, to what extent has the modern historiography of the Haitian Revolution, as part of a continuous Western discourse on slavery and colonization, broken the iron bonds of the philosophical milieu in which it was born?

The West was created somewhere at the beginning of the sixteenth century in the midst of a global war of material and symbolic transformations. What we call the Renaissance, much more an invention in its own right than a re-birth, ushered in a number of philosophical questions to which politicians, theologians, artists, and soldiers provided both concrete and abstract answers. What is Beauty? What is Order? What is the State? But also and above all: What is Man?

Philosophers who discussed that last issue could not escape the fact that colonization was going on as they spoke. Men (Europeans) were conquering, killing, dominating, and enslaving other beings equally human. The contest between Las Casas and Sepúlveda was only one instance of this debate where the symbolic and the practical merged. Whence the very ambiguities of the early Las Casas who believed both in colonization and in the humanity of the Indians and found it impossible to reconcile the two. But despite Las Casas and others, the Renaissance did not—could not—settle the question of the ontological nature of conquered peoples. As we well know, Las Casas himself offered a poor and ambiguous compromise that he came to regret later: freedom for the savages (the Indians), slavery for the barbarians (the Africans). Colonization won the day.

The ambiguity lingered way into the eighteenth century. By the time of the American Revolution, Man (with a capital *M*) was of European ancestry and male. On this single point everyone who mattered agreed. Men were also, to a lesser degree, females of European origins, for example, the French "citoyennes." Further down were peoples tied to strong state structures: Chinese, Persians, Egyptians—evil men. On reflection, and only for a timid minority, Man could also be westernized man, the complacent colonized. The benefit of doubt did not extend very far: westernized (or more properly, "westernizable") humans were at the lowest level of this nomenclature.

Thus the Enlightenment did not remove the fundamental ambiguity that dominated the encounter between ontological discourse and colonial practice. If the philosophers did reformulate some of the answers inherited from the Renaissance, the question "What is Man?" kept stumbling against the practices of domination and of merchant accumulation. The gap between abstraction and practice grew or, better said, the handling of the contradictions between the two became much more sophisticated. The Age of the Enlightenment was an age in which the slave drivers of Nantes bought titles of nobility to better parade with philosophers, an age in which a freedom fighter such as Thomas Jefferson owned slaves without bursting under the weight of his intellectual and moral contradictions.[3] Jacques Thibau doubts that contemporaries found a dichotomy between the France of the slavers and that of the philosophers. "Was not the western, maritime France, an integral part of France of the Enlightenment?" Louis Sala-Molins further suggests that we distinguish between the advocacy of slavery and the racism of the time: one could oppose the first (on practical grounds) and not the other (on philosophical ones). Voltaire, notably, was racist but opposed slavery (Thibau 1989; Sala-Molins 1987, 49). Likewise, David Hume opposed slavery, not because he believed in the equality of Blacks, but because, like Adam Smith, he thought the whole business to be too expensive.

The Enlightenment, nevertheless, brought a change of perspective. The idea of progress, now confirmed, suggested that men were perfectible. More important, the slave trade itself was running its course and the economics of slavery were questioned increasingly as the eighteenth century came to its end. Perfectibility became an argument in the practical debate. A memoir of 1790 summarized the issue: "'It is perhaps not impossible to civilize the Negro, to bring him to principles and *make a man out of him*: there would be more to gain than to buy and sell him'" (quoted in Duchet 1971, 157, emphasis added). Finally, we should not underestimate the loud anticolonialist stance of a small but vocal group of philosophers and politicians (Duchet 1971; Benot 1987, 1992).

Note, however, that few at the time attacked racism, colonialism, and slavery in a single blow and with equal vehemence. In France as in England colonialism, proslavery rhetoric and racism intermingled and supported one another without ever becoming totally confused. So did their opposites. That allowed much room for multiple positions.

Such multiplicity notwithstanding, there was no doubt about Western superiority, only about its proper use and effect. *L'histoire des deux Indes*, signed by Abbé Raynal with philosopher and encyclopedist Denis Diderot acting as ghost—and some would say, premier—contributor, was perhaps the most radical critique of colonialism from the France of the Enlightenment (Duchet 1978; Benot 1970, 1987). Yet it never fully questioned the ontological principles behind the colonialist enterprise, namely that the differences between forms of humanity were not of degree but of kind, not historical but primordial. Bonnet rightly points that the *Histoire* is a book that reveres at once the immobile vision of the noble savage and the benefits of industry and human activity. Behind the radicalism of Diderot and Raynal stood, ultimately, a project of colonial management. It included for sure the abolition of slavery, but only in the long term, and as part of a process that aimed at the better control of the colonies (Bonnet 1984, 416; Sala-Molins 1987, 254–61).

Political and philosophical breakthroughs aside, Man (with a capital M) was thus undeniably Western at the end of the eighteenth century. Below and beyond the West, there was debate about degrees of humanity. The vocabulary of the times reveals that gradation. When one talked of the biological product of Black and of white intercourse, one spoke of "man of color" as if the two terms did not necessarily go together: unmarked humanity was white. The lexical Man-vs.-Native (or Man-vs.-Negro) tinted the European literature on the Americas from 1492 to the Haitian Revolution and beyond. Even the radical duo Diderot-Raynal did not escape it. Recounting an early Spanish exploration, they write: "Was not this handful of *men* surrounded by an innumerable multitude of *natives* . . . seized with alarm and terror, well or ill founded?" (Bonnet 1984, 316, emphasis added).

One will not castigate long-dead writers for using the words of their time or for not sharing ideological views that we now take for granted. Yet to the extent that categories do express world views, it is fair to suggest that the Haitian Revolution did challenge the ontological assumptions of the most radical writers of the Enlightenment. *The events that shook up Saint-Domingue from 1791 to 1804 constituted a sequence for which not even the extreme political left in France or in England had a conceptual frame of reference.* They were "unthinkable" facts in the framework of Western thought.

Pierre Bourdieu defines the unthinkable as that for which one has no adequate instruments to conceptualize. He writes: "In the unthinkable of an epoch, there is all that one cannot think for want of ethical or political inclinations that predispose to take it in account or in consideration, but also that which one cannot think for want of instruments of thought such as problematics, concepts, methods, techniques" (Bourdieu 1980). The unthinkable is that which one cannot conceive within the range of possible alternatives, that which perverts all answers because it defies the terms under which the questions were phrased. In that sense, the Haitian Revolution was unthinkable in its time: it challenged the very framework within which proponents and opponents had examined slavery and colonialism in the Americas.

Between the first slave shipments of the early 1500s and the 1791 insurrection of northern Saint-Domingue, most Western observers had treated manifestations of slave resistance and defiance with the ambivalence characteristic of their overall treatment of colonization and slavery. On the one hand, resistance and defiance did not exist, since to acknowledge them was to acknowledge the humanity of the enslaved.[4] On the other hand, since resistance occurred, it was dealt with quite severely on the ground, within or around the plantations. Thus, next to a discourse that claimed the contentment of slaves, a plethora of laws, advice, and measures, both legal and illegal, tried to curb the very resistance denied in theory.

Publications by and for planters, as well as plantation journals and correspondence, often mixed both tendencies. Close as some were to the real world, planters and managers could not fully deny resistance, but they tried to provide reassuring certitudes by trivializing all its manifestations. Resistance did not exist as a global phenomenon. Rather, each case of unmistakable defiance, each possible instance of resistance, was treated separately and drained of its political content. Slave A ran away because he was particularly mistreated by his master. Slave B was missing because he was not properly fed. Slave X killed herself in a fatal tantrum. Slave Y poisoned her mistress because she was jealous. The runaway or the rebellious slave emerges from this literature—which still has its disciples—as an animal driven by biological constraints, at best as a pathological case. This is not "a man in revolt"—signs of humanity are doubtful—but a maladjusted Negro, a mutinous adolescent who eats dirt until he dies, an infanticidal mother, a pathological escapee, a deviant.

In retrospect, this argument is not very convincing to anyone aware of the infinite spectrum of human reactions to forms of domination. It is at best an anemic caricature of methodological individualism. Were each single explanation true, the sum of all of them would say little of the causes and effects of the repetition of such cases.

In fact, this line of argument never convinced the planters themselves. They held on to it because it was the only scheme that allowed them not to deal with the issue as a mass phenomenon. Yet, as time went on, the succession of plantation revolts, and especially the consolidation—in Jamaica and in the Guianas—of large colonies of runaways with whom colonial governments had to negotiate, gradually undermined the image of submission and the complementary argument of pathological maladaptation.

However much some observers wanted to see in these massive departures a sign of the attraction that nature exerted on the animal-slave, the possibility of mass resistance penetrated Western discourse.

The penetration was nevertheless circumspect. When Louis-Sebastien Mercier announced an avenger of the New World in 1771, it was in a novel of anticipation, a utopia.[5] The goal was to warn Europeans of the fatalities that awaited them if they did not change their ways. Similarly, when the duo Raynal-Diderot spoke of a Black Spartacus, it was not a clear prediction of a Louverture-type character, as some would want with hindsight.[6] In the pages of the *Histoire des deux Indes* where the passage appears, the threat of a Black Spartacus is as a warning. The reference is not to Saint-Domingue but to Jamaica and to Guyana, where "there are two established colonies of fugitive negroes. . . . These flashes of lightning announce the thunder, and the negroes lack only a chief courageous enough to drive them to *revenge and to carnage*. Where is he, this great man whom nature owes *perhaps* to the honor of the human species? Where is this new Spartacus?" (Benot 1970, 214; Duchet 1971, 175, emphasis added).

In this version of the famous passage, which Diderot modified in successive editions of the *Histoire*, the most radical stance is in the unmistakable reference to a single human species. But just as with Las Casas, the practical conclusions from what looks like a revolutionary philosophy are ambiguous. Indeed, the political appeal—if appeal there was—is murky. To start with, Diderot's interlocutors are not the enslaved masses nor even the Spartacus who may or may not rise in an uncertain future. Diderot here is the voice of the enlightened West admonishing its colonialist counterpart.

Second and more important, "slavery" was at that time an easy metaphor, accessible to a large public who knew that the word stood for a number of evils, except perhaps the evil of itself. Slavery in the parlance of the philosophers could be whatever was wrong with European rule in Europe and elsewhere. To wit, the same Diderot applauded US revolutionaries for having "burned their chains," for having "refused slavery." Never mind that some of them owned slaves. The *Marseillaise* was also a cry against "slavery."[7] This metaphorical usage permeated the discourse of various nascent disciplines from philosophy to political economy up to Marx and beyond. References to slave resistance must thus be regarded in light of the rhetorical clichés of the time. For if today we can read the US Bill of Rights or the successive "Declarations of the Rights of Man" as naturally including every single human being, it is far from certain that this revisionist reading was the favored interpretation of the "men" of 1776 and 1789 (Jaume 1989).

Third, here as in the rarer texts that speak clearly of the right to insurrection, the possibility of a successful rebellion by slaves or colonized peoples is in a very "distant" future, still a specter of what might happen if the system remains unchanged (e.g., Diderot, in Benot 1970, 187). The implication is, of course, that improvement within the system could prevent change, surely not the philosophers' favorite outcome.

Fourth and finally, this was an age of change and inconsistency. Few thinkers had the politics of their philosophy. Radical action on the issue of slavery often came from unsuspected corners, notably in England or in the United States. After examining the contradictions of the *Histoire*, Michèle Duchet concludes that the book is politically reformist and philosophically revolutionary (Duchet 1971, 177). This dichotomy characterized public discourse on slavery and the colonial question in Europe and the Americas throughout the eighteenth and early nineteenth century. Contradictions were plenty, even within the radical left.[8] Thus, even though a number of radical writers were willing to acknowledge at times the full humanity of the enslaved, even though some of the same, also intermittently, acknowledged the possibility of conscious mass resistance, none dared to link the two assertions and to draw from this linkage its most obvious conclusion: *the right of nonwhite peoples to achieve full self-determination by way of armed resistance*. By 1791, the evocation of a slave revolution had become an occasional rhetorical device in the discourse of the West, yet the possibility of such a revolution was still part of the unthinkable.

Not only was the revolution unthinkable and, therefore, unannounced in the West, it was also—to a large extent—unspoken among the slaves themselves. By this I mean that the revolution was not preceded or even accompanied by an explicit intellectual discourse.[9] One reason is, of course, that most slaves were illiterate and that the printed word was not a realistic means of propaganda in the context of a slave colony. But another reason was that the claims of the revolution were indeed too radical to be formulated in advance of its deeds. Victorious practice could assert them only *after the fact*. In that sense, the revolution was indeed at the limits of the thinkable, even in Saint-Domingue, even among the slaves, even among its own leaders.

We need to recall that the key tenets of the political philosophy that became explicit in Saint-Domingue/Haiti between 1791 and 1804 were not accepted by world public opinion until World War II. Claims about the fundamental uniqueness of humankind, claims about the ethical irrelevance of racial categories or geographical situation to matters of governance, and, above all, claims about the right of *all* peoples to self-determination—all went against received wisdom in the Atlantic world and beyond. Each could reveal itself in Saint-Domingue only through practice. In that sense, the Haitian Revolution thought itself out politically and philosophically as it was taking place. Its project, increasingly radicalized throughout thirteen years of combat, was revealed in successive spurts. Between and within its unforeseen stages, discourse always lagged behind practice: the revolution expressed itself mainly through its deeds.

This meant that the Haitian revolutionaries were not overly restricted by previous ideological limits set by professional intellectuals in the colony or elsewhere, that they could break new ground—and, indeed, they did so repeatedly. But it meant also that philosophical and political debate in the West, when it occurred, could only be reactive. It dealt with the impossible only after that impossible had become fact; and even then, the facts were not always accepted as such.

DEALING WITH THE UNTHINKABLE

When the news of the massive uprising of August 1791 first hit France, the most common reaction among interested parties was disbelief: the facts were too unlikely, the news had to be false. Only the most vocal representatives of the planter party took it seriously, in part because they were the first to be informed via their British contacts, in part because they had the most to lose if indeed the news were verified. Others, including colored plantation owners then in France and most of the left wing of the French assembly, just could not reconcile themselves with the idea of a large-scale Black rebellion.[10] In an impassioned speech delivered to the French assembly on October 30, 1791, delegate Jean-Pierre Brissot, member of the *Amis des Noirs* and moderate anticolonialist, outlined the reasons why the news had to be false: (a) anyone who knew the Blacks had to realize that it was simply impossible for 50,000 of them to get together so fast and act in concert; (b) slaves could not conceive of rebellion on their own, and mulattoes and whites were not so insane as to incite them to full-scale violence; (c) even if the slaves had rebelled in such huge numbers, the superior French troops would have defeated them. Brissot went on:

> What are 50,000 men, badly armed, undisciplined and used to fear when faced with 1,800 Frenchmen used to fearlessness? What! In 1751, Dupleix

and a few hundred Frenchmen could break the siege of Pondichéri and beat a well-equipped army of 100,000 Indians, and M. de Blanchelande with French troops and cannons would fear a much inferior troop of Blacks barely armed? (Raimond et al. 1791).

So went majority opinion from left to center-right within the Assembly until the news was confirmed beyond doubt. Confirmation itself did not change the dominant views. When detailed news reached France, many observers were frightened not by the revolt itself but by the fact that the colonists had appealed to England (Blackburn 1988, 193). A serious long-term danger coming from the Blacks was still unthinkable. Slowly though, the size of the uprising sunk in. Yet even then, in France as in Saint-Domingue, as indeed in Jamaica, Cuba, and the United States before, planters, administrators, politicians, or ideologues found explanations that forced the rebellion back within their world view, shoving the facts in the proper order of discourse. Since Blacks could not have generated such a massive endeavor, the insurrection became an unfortunate repercussion of planters' miscalculations. It did not aim at revolutionary change, given its royalist influences. It was not supported by a majority of the slave population. It was due to outside agitators. It was the unforeseen consequence of various conspiracies concocted by nonslaves. Every party picked its favorite enemy as the most likely conspirator behind the slave uprising. Royalist, British, mulatto, or Republican conspirators were seen or heard everywhere by dubious and interested witnesses. Conservative colonialists and antislavery republicans accused each other of being the brains behind the revolt. Inferences were drawn from writings that could not have possibly reached or moved the slaves of Saint-Domingue even if they knew how to read.[11]

For thirteen years at least, Western public opinion pursued this game of hide and seek with the news coming out of Saint-Domingue. With every new threshold, the discourse accommodated some of the irrefutable data, questioned others, and provided reassuring explanations for the package so created. By the spring of 1792, for instance, even the most distant observer could not deny any more the extent of the rebellion, the extraordinary number of slaves and plantations involved, the magnitude of the colonists' material losses. But then, many even in Saint-Domingue argued that the disaster was temporary, that everything would return to order. Thus, an eyewitness commented: "If the whites and the free mulattoes knew what was good for them, and kept tightly together, it is quite possible that things would return to normal, *considering the ascendancy that the white has always had over the negroes*" (Cauna, 1987, 223, emphasis added). Note the doubt (the witness is tempted to believe his eyes); but note also that the ontological nomenclature has not moved. Worldview wins over the facts: white hegemony is natural and taken for granted; any alternative is still in the domain of the unthinkable. Yet this passage was written in December 1792. At that time, behind the political chaos and the many battles between various armed factions, Toussaint Louverture and his closest followers were building up the avant-garde that would push the revolution to the point of no return. Indeed, six months later, civil commissar Léger Félicité Sonthonax was forced to declare free all slaves willing to fight under the French republican flag. A few weeks after Sonthonax's proclamation, in August 1793, Toussaint Louverture raised the stakes with his proclamation from Camp Turel: unconditional freedom and equality for all.

Similarly, as it became increasingly clear that none of the major revolutionary leaders was willing to take orders from colonists or foreign powers, the old conspiracy theories became largely irrelevant. It did not much matter if the idea of rebellion had been suggested by nonslaves; what was going on in Saint-Domingue was, by all definitions the most important slave rebellion ever witnessed. But then, few writers bothered to ask whether or not the earlier allegations had been false and, if so, why they were accepted so readily. Rather, every party struggled to convince itself and others that the achievements of the Black leadership would ultimately benefit someone other than the former slaves. The new Black elite had to be, willingly or not, the pawn of a "major" international power. Or else, the colony would fall apart, and a legitimate international state would pick up the pieces. Theories assuming chaos under Black leadership continued even after Louverture and his closest lieutenants took over the military, political, and civil apparatus of the colony. If some foreign governments—notably the United States—were willing to maintain a guarded collaboration with the Louverture regime, it was in part because they "knew" that an independent state led by former slaves was an impossibility. Toussaint himself may have not believed in the possibility of independence even though, for all practical purposes, he was ruling Saint-Domingue as if it were independent.

Opinion in Saint-Domingue and in Europe constantly dragged after the facts. Predictions, when they were made, revealed themselves useless. Once the French expedition of reconquest was launched in 1802, pundits were easily convinced that France would win the war. In England, the *Cobbett's*

Weekly Political Register doubted that Toussaint would even oppose a resistance: he was likely to flee the country.[12] Leclerc himself, the commander of the French forces, predicted in early February that the war would be over in two weeks. He was wrong by two years, give or take two months. Yet planters in Saint-Domingue apparently shared his optimism. Leclerc reported to the minister of the Marine that French residents were already enjoying the smell of victory. Newspapers in Europe, North America, and Latin America translated and commented on these dispatches: restoration was near.

By mid-1802, the debacle of Louverture's army seemed to verify that prophecy. The rejection of the truce by a significant minority of armed rebels, and the full-scale resumption of the war in the fall of 1802, did little to change the dominant views. Despite the alliance between the forces of Dessalines, Pétion, and Christophe, and the repeated victories of the new revolutionary army, few outside of Saint-Domingue could foresee the outcome of this Negro rebellion. As late as the fall of 1803, a complete victory by the former slaves and the creation of an independent state was still unthinkable in Europe and North America. Only much after the 1804 declaration of independence would the fait accompli be ungraciously accepted.

Quite ungraciously, indeed. The international recognition of Haitian independence was even more difficult to gain than military victory over the forces of Napoleon. It took more time and more resources, more than a half century of diplomatic struggles. The United States and the Vatican, notably, recognized Haitian independence only in the second half of the nineteenth century.

Diplomatic rejection was only one symptom of an underlying denial. The very deeds of the revolution were incompatible with major tenets of the dominant Western ideologies. They remained so up to at least the first quarter of the twentieth century. Between Haitian independence and World War I, in spite of the successive abolitions of slavery, little changed within the ontological ladder that ranked humankind in the minds of the majorities in Europe and the Americas. In fact, some views deteriorated (Benot 1992). The nineteenth century was, in many respects, a century of retreat from the Enlightenment. Scientific racism reinforced the ontological nomenclature inherited from the Renaissance. The carving up of Asia and, above all, of Africa reinforced both colonial practice and ideology. Thus in most places outside of Haiti, more than a century after it happened, the revolution was still largely unthinkable history.

The curious career of the Haitian Revolution in Western thought has important implications for its treatment by the historical guild. It comes as no surprise that the majority of books on Haiti produced by foreigners in the nineteenth century reflected or encouraged racism, cultural denigration, and political ostracism. Yet it may be less obvious that the figures of discourse that contemporary observers used to read the Haitian Revolution as it was unfolding have crossed the nineteenth century to penetrate, almost without modification, the historical writings of our time.

The treatment of the Haitian Revolution in written history outside of Haiti reveals two families of tropes that are identical, in formal (rhetorical) terms, to figures of discourse of the late eighteenth century. The first kind of tropes are formulas that tend to erase the fact of the revolution. I call them, for short, formulas of silence.[13] The second kind tends to empty a number of singular events of their revolutionary content so that the entire string of facts becomes trivialized. I call them formulas of banalization. The first tropes characterize mainly the generalists and the popularizers, textbook authors, for example. The second are the favorite tropes of the specialists. The first recall the general silence on resistance of yore. The second recall the explanations of the specialists of the times, overseers and administrators in Saint-Domingue, or politicians in Paris.

The general silence that Western historiography has produced around the Haitian Revolution originally stemmed from the incapacity to express the unthinkable, but it was ironically reinforced by the significance of the revolution for its contemporaries and for the generation immediately following. From 1791 to 1804 to the middle of the century, many Europeans and North Americans came to see that revolution as a litmus test for the Black race, certainly for the capacities of Afro-Americans. Haitians did likewise. But if the revolution was significant for Haitian elites as its self-proclaimed inheritors, to most foreigners it was primarily a lucky argument in a larger issue. Thus apologists and detractors alike, abolitionists and avowed racists, liberal intellectuals, economists, or slave owners used the events of Saint-Domingue to make their case, irrelevant of Haitian history itself. Haiti mattered to all of them, but only as pretext to talk about something else.

With time, the silencing of the revolution was strengthened by the fate of Haiti itself. Ostracized for the better part of the nineteenth century, the country deteriorated both economically and politically—*in part* as a result of this ostracism (Trouillot 1990). As Haiti declined, the reality of the revolution seemed increasingly distant, an improbability that took place in an awkward past and for which no one had a rational explanation. The revolution that was unthinkable became a nonevent.

This silencing of Saint-Domingue/Haiti by the generalists is still widely displayed in the textbooks and popular writings that are the prime sources on global history for the literate masses in Europe, in America, and in large chunks of the Third World. This corpus has taught generations of readers that the period that goes from 1776 to 1848 should properly be called "The Age of Revolutions." At the very same time, this corpus has kept quiet on the most radical political revolution of that age.

In the United States, for example, up until recently very few textbooks mentioned the Haitian Revolution. When they did, they made of it a "revolt," a "rebellion." The ongoing silence of the Latin American textbooks is still more tragic. In England, the *Penguin Dictionary of Modern History*, a pocket encyclopedia with a mass circulation that covers the period from 1789 to 1945, has neither Saint-Domingue nor Haiti in its entries. Likewise, historian Eric Hobsbawm, one of the best analysts of this era, managed to write a book called *Age of Revolutions, 1789–1848*, where the Haitian Revolution scarcely appears.[14] One could extend the list.

As this silence of the generalists goes on, increased specialization within the historical guild leads to a second trend. Saint-Domingue/Haiti emerges at the intersection of various interests: colonial history; Caribbean or Afro-American history; the history of slavery; the history of New World peasantries. In any one of these subfields, it has now become impossible to silence the fact that a revolution took place. Indeed, the revolution itself, or even strings of facts within it, have become legitimate topics for serious research within any of these subfields.

How interesting then, that many of the rhetorical figures used to interpret the mass of evidence accumulated by modern historians recall tropes honed by planters, politicians, and administrators both before and during the revolutionary struggle. Examples are plenty, and I will only cite a few. Many analyses of marronage ("desertion" some still would say) sometimes come close to the biophysical explanations preferred by plantation managers. Conspiracy theories still provide many historians with a deus ex machina for the events of 1791–92, just as in the rhetoric of the assemblymen of the times.[15] In that same vein historian Robert Stein acknowledges the fact of a revolution but places most of the credit for the 1793 liberation of the slaves on Sonthonax. The commissar was a zealous Jacobin and, no doubt, a revolutionary in his own right. We have no way to estimate the probable course of the revolution without his contribution. But the point is not empirical. The point is that Stein's rhetoric echoes the very rhetoric first laid out in Sonthonax's trial. Implicit in that rhetoric is the assumption that the French connection is both *sufficient and necessary* to the Haitian Revolution. Other writers tend to stay prudently away from the word *revolution* itself, more often using words such as *insurgents*, *rebels*, *bands*, etc.[16]

Yet since at least C. L. R. James's classic, *The Black Jacobins* (but note the title), the demonstration has been well made to the guild that the Haitian Revolution is indeed a "revolution" in its own right by any definition of the word, and not an appendix of Bastille Day.[17] Until the 1970s, however, the banalization of the events of 1791–1804 was near total within modern Western historiography. The banalization of singular events within that string remains a common trope among specialists.

There is, nevertheless, a counterdiscourse. It goes back to the historiography produced in Haiti and draws on the popular second edition of James's classic (James 1962). It was revitalized in the 1980s. Then, Eugene Genovese and, later, Robin Blackburn insisted on the central role of the Haitian Revolution in the collapse of the entire system of slavery (Genovese 1981; Blackburn 1988).

The impact of this counterdiscourse remains limited, however, especially since Haitian researchers are increasingly distant from these international debates. Since the early nineteenth century, the Haitian elites have chosen to respond to attempts at denigration with an epic discourse lauding their historical past. The empirical value of that historical tradition has steadily declined after its spectacular launching by nineteenth-century giants such as Madiou (1987–89) and Ardouin (1958), and in spite of individual achievements of the early twentieth century. Unequal access to archives—products and symbols of neocolonial domination—and the secondary role of empirical exactitude in this epic discourse continue to handicap Haitian researchers.[18]

Thus, the historiography of the Saint-Domingue revolution now finds itself marred by two unfortunate tendencies. On the one hand, most of the literature produced in Haiti remains respectful—too respectful, I would say—of the ideological and political project elaborated through an extraordinary struggle by the revolutionary leaders who led the masses of former slaves to freedom and independence. The empirical monuments of the Haitian tradition date back to the nineteenth century: it has benefited little from recent archival research. That corpus excels at putting facts into perspective, but its facts are weak, sometimes wrong, especially since the Duvalier regime explicitly politicized historical discourse.

On the other hand, the history produced outside of Haiti is increasingly sophisticated and rich empirically. Yet its vocabulary and, at times, its discursive framework, recalls frighteningly the discourse of the eighteenth century. Papers and monographs take the tone of plantation records; analyses of the revolution recall the letters of a La Barre, the speeches of French politicians, the messages of a Leclerc. If we are willing to concede that the intentions are not the same, we still cannot fail to notice that this kind of history cannot do justice to the revolution.

The solution may be for the two traditions to merge or to generate a new perspective that encompasses the best of each. There are indications of a move in this direction. Carolyn Fick remains much too close to the epic rhetoric of the Haitian tradition (Fick 1990). Her treatment of resistance is overly ideological and skews her reading of the evidence in the direction of heroism. Nevertheless, her book adds more to the empirical bank on Saint-Domingue than most recent works in the epic tradition. David Geggus's ongoing research remains empirically impeccable. One wishes that it continues to move further away from the discourse of banalization and that it spells out explicitly, one day, some of its hidden assumptions. The work by the Auguste brothers on the French expedition comes closer to finding a tone that treats its material with ideological respect without falling into a celebration or extrapolating from the evidence. It is well grounded in archival research, yet it does not make concessions to the banalizing discourse (Auguste and Auguste 1985).

These recent trends and titles suggest both room and hope for improvement. It may become possible, sometime in the near future, to write the history of the revolution that was, for long, unthinkable.

NOTES

Editors' Note: This chapter first appeared as "From Planters' Journals to Academia: The Haitian Revolution as Unthinkable History," *Journal of Caribbean History* 25, nos. 1–2 (1991): 81–99.

1. The shell of this argument was first presented at the conference Révolution Haïtienne et Révolution Française, Port-au-Prince, Haiti, December 12, 1989, under the title "Penser l'impensable: La Révolution Haïtienne et les limites intellectuelles de l'occident." Empirical research was conducted in Paris in 1991–92 by a generous fellowship from the John Simon Guggenheim Foundation.

2. Most of these pamphlets are included in the Lk12 series at the Bibliothèque nationale de France, in Paris, where I read them. Others were reproduced by the French government. See also Raimond 1791 and note 11 below.

3. Jefferson followed from afar the example of John Locke, abolitionist in principle, who had no fewer shares that he [sic] in a slave trade monopoly, the Royal African Company.

4. There is no term in the vocabulary of the times either in English or in French that would account for the practices—or encapsulate a generalized notion—of resistance. I used *resistance* here in the rather loose way it appears nowadays in the literature. I have dealt elsewhere with the necessary distinction between resistance and defiance and the concept of resistance: Michel-Rolph Trouillot, "In the Shadow of the West: Power, Resistance, and Creolization in the Caribbean," keynote address to the congress "Born out of Resistance," Utrecht University, Utrecht, the Netherlands, March 25, 1992.

5. "Nature has at last created this stunning man, this immortal man, who must deliver a world from the most atrocious, the longest, the most insulting tyranny. . . . He has shattered the irons of his compatriots. So many oppressed slaves under the most odious slavery seemed to wait only for his signal to make such a hero. . . . This heroic avenger . . . has set an example that sooner or later cruelty will be punished, and that Providence holds in store these strong souls, which she releases upon earth to reestablish the equilibrium which the inequity of ferocious ambition knew how to destroy" (Mercier, "The Year 2440," cited in Bonnet 1984, 331).

6. Whether Louverture himself had read Raynal in 1791 and was convinced of his own future role in history is unproven and beside the point.

7. "Ces fers dès longtemps prepares . . . pour nous. . . . / C'est nous qu'on ose méditer / De rendre à l'antique esclavage," etc. (*La Marseillaise*).

8. Diderot hailed nearly without reservation the North American revolution, which was anticolonialist but retained slavery. Marat and—to a much less extent—Robespierre aside, few of the leading French revolutionaries recognized the French colonies' right to revolt, the application of which they admired in North America.

9. To be sure, there were oral and written texts of which the philosophical import became increasingly explicit as the Revolution advanced, from the speeches reportedly given at the gatherings that preceded the insurrection to the Haitian Constitution of 1805. But these are primarily political texts marking immediate goals or recent victories. Up to the first post-independence writings of Boisrond-Tonnere, there were no full-time intellectuals to engage in speech acts one step removed from the political battles, as in the French and the American revolutions, the later anticolonial

struggles of Latin America, Asia or Africa, or the revolutions that claimed a Marxist ancestry.

10. *Editors' Note:* By "colored plantation owners," Trouillot is referring to *gens de couleur libres*, many of whom owned plantations and, therefore, slaves.

11. See, for example, Anonymous (n.d. [1791?]), *Le mot du vrai législateur sur la révolte et les incendies arrivés à Saint Domingue au mois d'août 1791*; Anonymous (n.d. [1792?]), *Nouvelles de Saint Domingue, arrivées par deux bâtiments du commerce partis du Cap les 26 septembre et 10 octobre*; see also Baillio 1791a, 1791b; Milscent 1791; and Garran-Coulon 1797–99.

12. See *Cobbett's Weekly Political Register* 1802, 286.

13. I see silence in history not as a dead time but an active and transitive process: one "silences" a fact or an individual, as a silencer silences a gun. One makes history keep quiet; one engages in the practice of "silencing."

14. Saint-Domingue is mentioned once in the notes, twice in the text: the first time to say, in passing, that Toussaint Louverture was the first independent revolutionary leader of the Americas—as if that was not important; the second time (in parentheses) to note that the French Revolution "inspired" colonial uprisings. See Hobsbawm 1962, 93, 115. If we accept that Hobsbawm is at the extreme left of Western historiography, the parallel with Diderot-Raynal is amazing.

15. One example among others. David Geggus and Jean Fouchard agree in suggesting that a royalist conspiracy could have provoked the revolt of 1791. But Fouchard notes this possibility in a book that remains one of the epic monuments of Haitian history. Geggus, in turn, concludes that if royalist participation is proved, "the autonomy of the slave insurrection will find itself considerably diminished." Robin Blackburn, who notes this disparity between the two authors, rightly finds Geggus's conclusion "curious" (Blackburn 1988, 210).

16. See Cauna 1987 and Geggus 1982. The *revolution* in Geggus's title is the French revolution. He has since extended his use of the word to include Haitian achievements.

17. James's book was published, in France, by Gallimard, so French historians cannot claim an accidental failure of transmission in this case. But old habits die hard. Even though James's subtitle contains the word *revolution*, in 1968, his Italian editor turned it into "The first revolt against the white man."

18. The Haitian historian "proves" very few "facts" in this epic discourse, which is in many ways an instrument of class domination in Haiti. The epic of 1791–1804 is one of the rare historical alibis of the Haitian elites, an indispensable reference to their claims to power.

REFERENCES

Ardouin, Beaubrun. 1958. *Études sur l'histoire d'Haïti*. Port-au-Prince: François Dalencour.

Auguste, Claude B., and Marcel B. Auguste. 1985. *L'expédition Leclerc*. Port-au-Prince: Imprimerie Henri Deschamps.

Baillio [citoyen du Cap-François]. 1791a. *L'Anti-Brissot, par un petit blanc de Saint Domingue*. Paris: Chez Girardin, Club Littéraire et Politique, au Palais Royal.

Baillio [citoyen du Cap-François]. 1791b. *Un mot de vérité sur les malheurs de Saint-Domingue*. Paris: n.p.

Benot, Yves. 1970. *Diderot, de l'athéisme à l'anti-colonialisme*. Paris: F. Maspero.

Benot, Yves. 1987. *La revolution française et la fin des colonies*. Paris: La Découverte.

Benot, Yves. 1992. *La démence coloniale sous Napoléon*. Paris: La Découverte.

Blackburn, Robin. 1988. *The Overthrow of Colonial Slavery*. London: Verso.

Bonnet, Jean-Claude. 1984. *Diderot, textes et débats*. Paris: Le Livre de Poche.

Bourdieu, Pierre. 1980. *Le sens pratique*. Paris: Éditions de Minuit.

Cauna, Jacques. 1987. *Au temps des isles à sucre*. Paris: Karthala.

Cobbett, William. 1802-17. *Cobbett's Weekly Political Register*. London: R Bagshaw.

Dorsinville, Roger. 1965. *Toussaint Louverture ou la vocation de la liberté*. Paris: Julliard.

Duchet, Michèle. 1971. *Anthropologie et histoire au siècle des Lumières*. Paris: F. Maspero.

Duchet, Michèle. 1978. *Diderot et l'histoire des deux Indes, ou l'écriture fragmentaire*. Paris: Nizet.

Fick, Carolyn. 1990. *The Making of Haiti: The Saint Domingue Revolution from Below*. Knoxville: University of Tennessee Press.

French National Assembly. 1791–92. *Pièces imprimées par ordre de l'Assemblée Nationale: Colonies*. Paris: Imprimerie Nationale.

Garran-Coulon, Jean-Phillippe. 1797–99. *Rapport sur les troubles de Saint-Domingue*. Paris: Imprimerie Nationale.

Geggus, David. 1982. *Slavery, War and Revolution: The British Occupation of Saint Domingue, 1793–1798*. Oxford: Claredon Press.

Genovese, Eugene. 1981. *From Rebellion to Revolution*. New York: Vintage.

Hobsbawm, Eric J. 1962. *The Age of Revolution: Europe 1789–1848*. New York: New American Library.

James, C. L. R. 1962. *The Black Jacobins: Toussaint Louverture and the San Domingo Revolution*. New York: Vintage.

Jaume, Lucien. 1989. *Les déclarations des droits de l'homme*. Paris: G. F. Flammarion.

Madiou, Thomas. 1987–89. *Histoire d'Haiti*. 7 vols. Port-au-Prince: Henri Deschamps.

Milscent de Mussé, Claude L. M. 1971. *Sur les troubles de Saint-Domingue*. Paris: Imprimerie du Patriote Française.

Raimond, Julien, et al. 1791. "Première lettre écrite de la partie de l'ouest." *Paris*, October 21.

Sala-Molins, Louis. 1987. *Le Code Noire ou la calvaire de Canaan*. Paris: Presses Universitaires de France.

Thibau, Jacques. 1989. *Le temps de Saint-Domingue: L'esclavage et la Révolution française*. Paris: Éditions Jean-Claude Lattès.

Trouillot, Michel-Rolph. 1989. "Penser l'impensable: La révolution Haïtienne et les limites intellecutalles de l'occident." Paper presented at the conference Révolution Haïtienne et Révolution Française, Port-au-Prince, Haiti, December 12.

Trouillot, Michel-Rolph. 1990. *Haiti: State against Nation; The Origins and Legacies of Duvalierism*. New York: Monthly Review Press.

PART IV

A NEW DUTY ARISES

Theorizing a Global Perspective

Had I stayed in Haiti or moved on to France, I would probably hold a degree in philosophy or perhaps in history. I have a penchant—almost aesthetic—for theoretical reflection grounded in historical concreteness, regardless of discipline or persuasion. I view theory as that which emerges in the back-and-forth movement between concepts and history, as in Hegel and Marx, as in Eliade, Lévi-Strauss, or Foucault. But this updated and disparate list suggests my dilemma back in the early 1970s: my intellectual horizon was European, yet unforeseen events had thrown me into the United States.

The year 1969 was the worst of the Duvaliers' dictatorship. The Haitian exile community in New York provided a sanctuary where I combined artistic and intellectual pursuits with political activism.

That apprenticeship reinforced earlier propensities: a desire to reach an audience not defined by academic membership; a conviction that an intellectual is so much more than a mere academic and the member of multiple overlapping communities. I had absorbed these beliefs growing up within the so-called intellectual elite so closely tied to the state in Haiti. Political activism in New York turned this heredity into conscious choices.

The most lasting product of these choices is my first book, *Ti dife boule sou istwa Ayiti*, a history of the Haitian Revolution of 1791–1804. This was a natural evolution: my father and my uncle both wrote history. In a deeper sense, it was going against class origins and attitudes. *Ti dife* questions the "great men" tradition of Haitian historiography. More important, it is also the first nonfiction book written in Haitian. Except a handful of poets and even fewer novelists, Haitian intellectuals write books in French.

With a book and an undergraduate degree in hand, access to graduate school was relatively easy. Yet what to do and where to do it remained serious questions. Cultural studies and comparative literature had not yet discovered "theory" or gained the legitimacy they now enjoy.

Luckily, Sidney Mintz had just helped found the anthropology department at Johns Hopkins University. The special character of the department, its interdisciplinary take on the profession, and its ties to history and what was then the Atlantic Program tipped the balance toward anthropology.

I remember Mintz asking me: "Of course, were you to come here, you would want to work on Haiti?" "Of course not," I said, unknowingly eluding a gentle trap. Haiti was in me—the work of a lifetime. I needed something else from graduate school. I went on to live among the peasants on the island of Dominica. Some of my best insights on slavery and on world peasantries owe much to that fieldwork, its preparation, and its aftermath.

Dominica made me feel the Caribbean and its diversity and touch firsthand—a resilience that I knew only through its intellectual echoes. Dominica was also a methodological threshold. I became convinced that the study of peasant dependency that I was following could not be told or understood fully from within the present of the island. So I followed the story to England and the Netherlands. The resulting book, *Peasants and Capital*, ties global and crossdisciplinary perspectives.

The book is divided into three parts: The Nation, The World, and The Village. Each part privileges a particular disciplinary lens: historiography, political economy, and ethnography. As Columbus discovered, when you look for the Caribbean you find the world. My research now expands to such "European" topics as the cultural underpinnings of the first Atlantic empires in the Renaissance.

Some people would ask: Is this anthropology? I would reply: It's in the best tradition of Hopkins anthropology. Now that I serve as chair of the department, I am more than ever aware of its unique position in the North American intellectual landscape. This uniqueness comes from the combination of three major traits: a sensitivity to world history best expressed as a search to integrate the local and the global; a serious concern for sociocultural theory grounded in empirical research; and a particular relationship to the Atlantic world.

That latter relationship has much to do with the history of Johns Hopkins in the last twenty-five years and the research interests of colleagues, notably in history, as Jack Greene and Sidney Mintz noted in an earlier issue of *Cross Currents*. Given its small size, this university has produced an extraordinary proportion of PhDs on Africa and the Afro-Americas in the last two decades. That track record, with its international reach, has special value for search committees and many graduate students.

We could do better at the undergraduate level. Today, the Homewood campus has more faculty working on Africa and the African Diaspora than on Latin America and Asia combined, with at least six scholars with expertise on slavery. Yet while we have undergraduate programs in East Asian and Latin American studies, we have no single umbrella for students interested in Africa or the African diaspora.

The relation between faculty interests and undergraduate programs is changing at all research universities. This has to do with global trends that affect the relationship between institutions of higher learning and society in the entire North Atlantic. In the United States, the low level of accountability that recently characterized academia is becoming untenable.

That is not necessarily a bad thing. It is not unfair to ask that universities maintain a more articulate dialogue with the society that feeds them. The real issue is who is to set the terms of this dialogue and how. Should faculty have a say in the public mission of academia? In the absence of greater faculty involvement, the impulses of donors or the changing tastes of undergraduates who are increasingly treated as mere clients may affect intellectual programming much more than they should.

I think we can make a case for who we are and what we do. That case need not be made with linear connections as in "art history is good for you because it will make you a better physician or the best manager at IBM." I am not sure I can quantify what I gained from six years of Latin and five years of Greek in high school. Nor do I want to do so. Yet I believe that a case can be made for the space that intellectual research occupies in society and for what happens in that space when scholars share their professional views with graduate and undergraduate students alike.

We can make a case for integrating undergraduates in a community of inquiry rather than treating them as consumers of education. That case requires, however, a public defense of intellectual work. It requires the acknowledgment that part of that work is to disturb mental habits, including rules of discourse. It requires the realization that an intellectual has a deeper ethical base and a wider conceptual frame than the most competent academic. Indeed, if successful, we may contribute to the reemergence in American life of public intellectuals outside academia.

The relative isolation of academia has perverse effects. We are often blamed for sins we do not commit. Take race. The outside perception is that universities are at the vanguard of the fight against racism in the United States. That's true as far as speech codes and the publicity about ethnic studies are concerned. But many recent studies debunk such myths as the relative advantage of minority PhDs in the academic market. In fact, a comprehensive survey suggests that nearly 91 percent of university faculty in the United States is white. Professionally, we are less diversified than the insurance industry or the top brass of the US Marine Corps!

Thus while academia may be a bastion of liberal speech—at some cost, indeed, to itself and society—its politics, measured by their results, are less progressive than they seem. And I do want to distinguish between liberals and progressives, as much as I want to distinguish between academics and intellectuals, on grounds of purpose, reach, and effectiveness.

These distinctions are inevitably rooted in a *morale politique*, but they are not narrowly political. Further, they are intellectually significant. In my case, they allow me to understand the ambiguous relationship between the Caribbean and the West it helped to create.

Foucault suggests that one draws from the past to write the history of the present because of what one finds intolerable (morally, politically) in that present. My moral turn to history may begin with the extraordinary capacity of liberals, since at least the Enlightenment, to feel good about themselves while history goes on its merry bloody way.

If we bracket the liberal discourse and look freshly at the results, we can see old problems in new light. Again, take diversity. Part of the problem with diversity is that most academics—liberals or not—do not really believe in its *intellectual* value. They back diversity—when they do—for social and political reasons, some noble, some suspicious. They view it mainly in terms of physical attributes—one skirt here, one dark skin there, necessary diversions on their way to matters of essence: let's hear the Black or the female viewpoint and move along.

Thus, beyond paying a reluctant homage to the often-unfortunate politics of identity, the social sciences and the humanities have yet to theorize the experience of the world outside the North Atlantic. Hype about the postcolonial gaze notwithstanding, most humanists see the historical experience of the majority of humankind only as an avatar of something of which the true face can be seen only in what we now call the West. Theory is done at the center; color comes from the margins.

Global studies should help us go beyond this theoretical ethnocentrism that is intellectually more perverse than the racism of *The Bell Curve*. The historicization of the West—its practices and its concepts, its assumptions, its claims and its genealogies—is a central theoretical challenge of our times.

That historicization requires a global perspective. It cannot be reduced to an empirical focus on the successive geographical areas or populations (Greece, Rome, Latin Christendom, or the North Atlantic) that the West now claims in its genealogies. To limit the investigation to the physical West would be to accept naively the West's own genealogies and forget that the current challenge comes to the human sciences in part because of changes in the globalization process.

The global village is now a cliché. But those of us who work on the Caribbean know that the world was global since at least 1492. Europe became Europe, in part through severing itself from what lay south of the Mediterranean, but in part also through a westward move that made the Atlantic the center of the first truly global empires.

What is new today is not globalization as such—we are too late for that. Rather, what is unique to our times is the widespread awareness of global processes among increasingly fragmented populations. That awareness grows everywhere, largely because of the increase in both the size and the velocity of global flows. Capital, populations, and information move in much greater mass and at increasing speed. At the same time, most human beings continue to act locally.

Thus, we are witnessing the rise of what I call "a fragmented globality." World histories and local histories are at once becoming both increasingly intertwined and increasingly contradictory. The twenty-first century is likely to be marked by the speed and brutality of these contradictions.

Theoretical ethnocentrism is not intellectually equipped to face that situation. Nor are the marginal responses, such as Afrocentrism, that this ethnocentrism provokes. Nor can ethnic studies, legitimate in their own terms, fill that void—unless we are willing to argue that North American minorities can serve as historical proxies for the vast chunks of humankind abandoned by the Latin and Teutonic canons.

In short, while parochialism leads to obvious dead ends, centrisms of all kinds—including the renewed search for universalist paradigms, such as rational choice theory—now convince mostly the believers. The human sciences are going through what historian Jacques Revel calls a time of "epistemological anarchy" in part because of the greater empirical base available for theory.

Yet this anarchy is also an opportunity for new conversations that take into account the entire historical experience of the world, with the various sensibilities and viewpoints that this experience implies. I see global studies as a space for theoretical developments based on this new empirical richness, a space for both tough talk and hope, inasmuch as it seizes the current contradictions as a starting point to imagine a new world. Here at the Institute, such a space is being built in the ebb and flow of three overlapping theoretical movements:

(1) a back-and-forth movement between the global and the local;
(2) a back-and-forth movement between economic and political structures and expressive forms, which itself parallels;
(3) a continuous exchange between the social sciences and the humanities.

I am gratified to contribute to these conversations.

NOTE

Editors' Note: This chapter first appeared as "Theorizing a Global Perspective," *Cross Currents: Newsletter of the Institute for Global Studies in Culture, Power, and History* 4, no. 1 (1996).

CHAPTER 13

Adieu, Culture

A New Duty Arises

A new duty arises. No longer can we keep the search
for truth the privilege of the scientist.
FRANZ BOAS

The conceptual kernel behind the word *culture*, as deployed in North American anthropology, provides a useful and fundamental lesson about humankind. Yet the word culture today is irretrievably tainted by both the politics of identity and the politics of blame—including the racialization of behavior that it was meant to avoid. Contrary to many of the critics reviewed by Robert Brightman (1995), I do not see the concept as inherently flawed on theoretical grounds. I agree with Richard A. Shweder and Les Beldo (2015) that something akin to a culture concept remains necessary to anthropology as a discipline and to social science in general.[1] The distinction between concept and word, however, is central to my argument. So is a related emphasis on the sites and processes in which the word and concept are deployed and on the modes of engagement that mediate between concepts and words. For if concepts are not just words, then the vitality of a conceptual program cannot hinge upon the sole use of a noun.

Culture's popular success is its own theoretical demise. Its academic diffusion has generated new institutional clusters on North American campuses: cultural—and multicultural—studies. Culture has also entered the lexicon of advertisers, politicians, businesspeople, and economic planners, up to the high echelons of the World Bank and the editorial pages of the *New York Times*. Culture now explains everything: from political instability in Haiti to ethnic war in the Balkans, from labor difficulties on the shop floors of Mexican *maquiladoras* to racial tensions in British schools and the difficulties of New York's welfare recipients in the job market. Culture explained both the Asian miracle of the 1980s and the Japanese economic downturn two decades later (Jomo 2001).

As the explanatory power of culture increases, many anthropologists react negatively to what they see as the abuse of one of their favorite categories by the general public, journalists, and, especially, colleagues—reserving their most emotional attacks for practitioners of cultural studies.[2] I confess a triple weakness: the narrative and the solutions sketched here are valid only to the extent that we have both a conceptual problem and a *public*—and therefore political—problem; to the extent that these problems are intertwined and urgent; and to the extent that the massive exportation of essentialized and racialized views of culture(s) from the United States increases both the theoretical and the political urgency.

The massive diffusion of the word *culture* in recent times awaits its ethnographer, but even the trivia are revealing. One internet search engine found more than five million pages linked to the keyword *culture*, after exclusion of most references to cultivation and agriculture. When *culture* was coupled with *anthropology* or *ethnography*, however, the total fell to 61,000 pages. Similarly, whereas the search engine of a major internet bookseller produced more than 20,000 titles containing the word *culture*, the list dropped to 1,350 titles when *culture* was coupled with *anthropology* or *ethnography* in the subject index. *Culture* is out there, and anthropologists have no control over its deployment.

Prominent among the 20,000 titles is *Culture Matters* (Harrison and Huntington 2000), an anthology praised by the *Wall Street Journal*, *Time* magazine, and political heavyweights such as Daniel Patrick Moynihan and the president of the World Bank. The underlying argument of most of the essays, quite explicit in Harrison's introduction, is that culture explains the state of affairs in the world today, especially economic inequalities between countries and even continents. Culture matters, indeed, but in ways few anthropologists would recognize. Yet the success of the word is in part a reflection of the corporate success of anthropology in the United States, and to that extent we may wonder whether the anthropological critique of culture's deployment should not start at home.

Words are not concepts, and concepts are not words. Thus the same word can express various conceptualizations. Similarly, a conceptualization can survive the demise of the word that once encapsulated it. Further, conceptualizations, whether or not encapsulated by a single word, take full significance only in the context of their deployment.

That context is inherently multilayered. It extends beyond the walls of academe. It includes not only other concepts—academic, lay, and political deployments of key words (Williams 1989)—but also the very social milieu that is a condition of possibility for any conceptualization. Theories are built on words and with words, but what ties those words together is always a specific moment in the historical process. In short, conceptualizations are always historically situated.

So historicized, the North American trajectory of the concept of culture seems to offer a contradiction. The kernel of the conceptualization teaches fundamental lessons about humanity that were not as clearly stated before its deployment and that cannot easily be unlearned. Yet the deployment of the word *culture* today, while evoking this conceptual kernel, carries an essentialist and often racialist agenda outside and especially within the United States.

The connection between these two states of affairs is not the misappropriation of an otherwise "clean" concept by nonanthropologists. Rather, North American anthropology's theoretical disregard for the very context of inequality—and especially the racism—that allowed the emergence of the conceptualization also doomed its deployment. Thus, the contradiction is apparent only if we take concepts as disembodied truths. If we turn to context as a condition of possibility of any conceptualization, a different story emerges, that of a political move in theory that denied the culture concept its very conditions of possibility. The trajectory of culture is that of a concept distancing itself from the context of its practice. As it did so, a concept created in part as a theoretical answer to an American political problem lost both its theoretical bite and its progressive political potential—and in doing so, its universalism.

For purposes of this chapter, I distinguish two contexts: academe and society at large. Within the first, the culture concept appears as an anticoncept, what I call here a *political move in theory*, the benefits of which become increasingly restricted by the status of anthropology as a discipline, by the state-centrism of the human sciences, and by micropractices of reproduction. Within the second, the culture concept appears as a *theoretical move from politics*, that is, a theoretical practice that silences its own conditions of possibility.

Two substantive propositions are central to the conceptualization of culture as deployed in North American anthropology. First, human behavior is patterned. There exist within historically specific populations recurrences in both thought and behavior that are not contingent but structurally conditioned and that are, in turn, structuring. Second, those patterns are learned. Recurrences cannot be tied to a natural world within or outside the human body but to constant interaction within specific populations. Structuration occurs through social transmission and symbolic coding with some degree of human consciousness.

These two propositions are indispensable to the most influential definitions of culture proposed by anthropologists in the United States. They are likely to be agreed upon, as premises of their practice, by a majority of individuals who have earned anthropological degrees in the United Sates. Yet they are not unique to North American anthropology or even to anthropology as a discipline. The first is necessary to Machiavelli's politics and fundamental to Montesquieu's sociocultural geography. The second echoes European thinkers again from Machiavelli, Montaigne, or Montesquieu to Kant and Vico. Nor do these two propositions exhaust all anthropological definitions of culture.[3]

The conceptual kernel made up of these two propositions does not impose an essentialist reading on either the definition or the use of the word *culture*. Nor does it predispose the word to racialist interpretations. How culture found itself on the essentialist track with a racialist bent is less about definitional truth than about context, and much less about intellectual history than about the history of power that the concept itself was used to silence. Central to that context is race and racism.

North American anthropologists love to claim with no small pride that Boasian anthropology's answer to American racism was its theoretical drive to separate race, language, and culture. If that claim is true, as I believe it is, then the culture concept is not just an intellectual product remotely connected to society—if indeed such a thing could exist—but an intellectual maneuver against the background of a social, political, and intellectual context. I describe that maneuver as a political move in theory.

In its initial context of deployment, culture was first and foremost an anticoncept. It was inherently tied to race, its nemesis. Culture is race repellent—it is not only what race is not, but it is what prevents race from occupying in anthropological discourse the defining place that it otherwise occupies in the larger American society. Within that privileged space, the culture concept can limit the impact of notions and descriptions linked to biological inheritance.

The consequences of this positioning are far-reaching yet unavoidable. As an anticoncept, the peculiarity of culture in North American anthropological theory stems less from its possible German predecessors or its distance from Malinowski's abstractions than from the peculiarity of North American notions of race and practices of racism. What makes culture unique in the US academic context is not a definitional feature or a combination of such features but its deployment in a society with a peculiar one-drop rule (Harris 1964), a society in which either of the two Alexandre Dumases would have been a "Black writer," in which Black blood becomes a thing—that is, as Marx would say, an objectified relation—and in which that relation supersedes others. What makes Boasian and post-Boasian "culture" peculiar and necessary is the white American gaze on Blackness—the centerpiece of American racial consciousness—that justifies culture's gatekeeping function.

Unfortunately, culture's academic career only reinforced the gatekeeping qualities that made its birth possible and necessary. Launched as the negation of race, culture also became the negation of class and history. Launched as a shield against some of the manifestations of racial power, culture eventually protected anthropology from all conceptual fields and apparatuses that spoke of power and inequality. Culture became what class was not, what evaded power and could deny history. How it became so has much to do again with context. The political move in theory was further restricted by anthropology's position within the human disciplines and its practitioners' temptation to mimic the state-centered social "sciences." Its essentialist potential was also enhanced by micropractices of reproduction within the discipline. "Culture" was part of the price sociocultural anthropology paid to gain a legitimate foothold in North American academe.

THE PRICE OF POWER

I formulated earlier two propositions that constitute the substantive kernel of the culture concept. But the career of the concept was also tied to a third proposition, epistemological and methodological, that propelled if not required the use of the word and its cognates. One can summarize that proposition as follows: cultural analysis is a legitimate lens of observation that relates to a distinguishable domain of human activity. Culture, like economics, is a way to look at populations.

So stated, this methodological proposition is no more essentialist than the substantive propositions at the core of the conceptualization. Indeed, one can derive from it very strong positions against both essentialism and philosophical empiricism. At best, the domain of culture as practiced by the analyst does not exist independently in the phenomenal world. That reading is a legitimate interpretation of the work of Franz Boas and his followers up to the 1920s. Yet as early as perhaps the 1910s, most certainly by the 1920s, and especially in the four ensuing decades, culture shifted from being a domain of analysis to being something out there (Stocking 1968).

Anthropology's disciplinary emergence was part of the institutionalization of the social sciences that took place from the mid-nineteenth century to the start of World War II. That institutionalization followed closely the rise of nationalism and the consolidation of state power in the North Atlantic countries in which the social science disciplines first solidified. It paralleled the partition of the world mainly by the same countries (Wallerstein et al. 1996). Eurocentric ideas, developed or nurtured successively by the Renaissance, the first wave of colonialism, the Enlightenment, and the practice of plantation slavery in the Americas, had gathered new momentum with colonialism's second wave. By the time the social sciences became standardized in degree-granting departments, non-Western areas and peoples were thought to be fundamentally different both in essence and in practice. They could not be known through the same scientific procedures or submitted to the same rules of management as Western areas and peoples. At the same time, the desire to know and to manage them had increased.

It was in that context that cultural anthropology became, by default, a discipline aimed at exposing the lives and mores of the Other to the people of the North Atlantic. Anthropologists became specialists in the "Savage slot" (Trouillot 1991), a necessary position within the geography of imagination that paralleled the self-invention of the "West" in the late Renaissance. Wise or innocent, noble or barbarian, the Savage was a condition of possibility of the West, an indispensable alter ego to its universalist pretensions.

In the second half of the nineteenth century, the new discipline brought to the Savage slot some of the methodological assumptions shared by fields such as history, sociology, and economics that studied the North Atlantic. One such assumption was that state boundaries provided the natural frameworks within which the processes studied by social scientists occurred (Wallerstein et al. 1996, 80). That assumption, equally shared by literary scholars, ran along the following lines: France was obviously a nation-state. It had, therefore, a single economy, a single history, and a single social life, all of which could be studied by the appropriate discipline, and all of which were also fundamentally circumscribed within the distinct political territory called France.

Anthropology easily avoided that assumption when it turned to ancient times. Yet when it came to the study of contemporary "primitives," anthropology mimicked the state-centrism of the other social sciences, often assuming for these peoples a waterish version of the nation-state, the borders of which were alleged to be as obvious and as impermeable as those of the North Atlantic entities.

Since that watered-down polity was only a copy, and a bad one at that, it could provide neither the methodological stability nor the naturalness of borders that made North Atlantic countries obvious units of analysis. From the 1890s to the 1950s, anthropologists increasingly made up for that fuzziness. In France and Britain, notably, they emphasized the rigidity of such concepts as the "total social fact" and the "social structure," each of which supposedly brought to the observer's mind a closure otherwise hard to demonstrate on the ground. In the United States, "culture" provided an even thicker closure.

The solidity of that closure came less from the methodological proposition sketched above than from the way it was used. Culture as a domain became what North American anthropologists could cling to in contradistinction to, say, sociologists or economists (Cole 1999; Darnell 1997, 1998; Stocking 1968). But the emphasis on the distinction also entailed the acceptance of a model: the production of self-evident units of analysis of the kind produced by these "harder" social sciences, and the implicit acknowledgment of an essence within those boundaries. In short, culture became a *thing*, in the footsteps of thing-like entities such as the market, the economy, the state, and society.

As culture became a thing, it also started doing things. Parodying the market and the model set by economists, culture shifted from being a descriptive conceptual tool to being an explanatory concept. And the more it explained, the more rigid and reified it became, just like the market or the state. In the process, North American anthropologists grafted onto the self-evident units of the Savage slot an essentialist notion of culture that reproduced the state-centrism of the other human sciences. Just as France

or the United States obviously had one economy, one history, and one social life, the Iroquois, the Samoans, the Dobu, the Zuni, or the Japanese,
for that matter, could have only one of each of these. The extent to which
their economy or their history mattered depended very much on the interests and benevolence of the observer. The extent to which inequality among
them mattered was partly silenced by the liberal aversion toward Marxism
and by the preconditions of the Savage slot, which made the people without
history "classless societies."

Here again, culture functioned as an anticoncept, just as the Savage had
functioned as an anticoncept in earlier times. For Columbus as for Montaigne, Las Casas, or Rousseau, savages were those who had no state,
no religion, no clothes, no shame—because they had nature. For North
American anthropologists, primitives became those who had no complexity, no class, no history that really mattered—because they had culture.
Better, each group had a single culture whose boundaries were thought to
be self-evident. Thus, North American cultural anthropology reconciled the
Boasian agenda with both the state-centrism of the strong social sciences
and the taxonomic schemes (Silverstein 2000) of the even stronger natural
sciences, notably zoology and biology.

Not every anthropologist welcomed the essentialist turn. Some, notably Edward Sapir, rejected it quite loudly (Brightman 1995; Darnell 1997).
Many acknowledged outside influences (Stocking 1968). Their deep knowledge of history often led early anthropologists to recognize diffusion
and thereby to circumvent at times the borders they had erected around
culture. The overemphasis on culture was doubly tactical: it helped to
inscribe the discipline within academe, and it provided a response to
biological determinism. Yet its noblest goals notwithstanding, as North
American anthropology became both more powerful and more popular,
cultural centrism—if not determinism—obscured the finer points of the
intellectual program for the public and graduate students alike.

First, increased specialization made it impossible for single writers or
even a group of writers to maintain the back-and-forth movement between
race and culture that characterized the early work of Boas. Specialization
facilitated a mind-body dualism. Man the symbol maker was freed from
the physical realities of his being and of his world. Culture, in turn, was left
on its own even within anthropology. Its boundaries became thicker; its
negative reference to race blurrier. Anthropologists such as Ruth Benedict
(1938) and Ralph Linton (1955) emphasized the "wholeness" of distinct cultures, a theme later revived in the work of Clifford Geertz (1973).

Slanted as it became toward closure, theory alone would not have sufficed to sustain the notion of cultures as isolated wholes. Extreme isola-
tionist pronouncements such as those of Benedict and Linton did not
necessarily gain unanimity within the discipline (Brightman 1995; Darnell
1997). Further, the very practice of fieldwork belied the possibility of a cultural quarantine.

Yet whatever individual doubts emerged from field practice crashed
against the corporate wall of institutionalization. Disciplines necessarily
impose rites of passage that ensure and confirm professionalization. As
anthropology gained in demographic and institutional power, the ethnographic monograph became a major proof of professionalization in France,
England, and especially the United States, where support for fieldwork was
more available. The production of one such work became the privileged rite
of access to the profession. In North America, it became the sole credential
unanimously recognized for entry into the guild (Cohn 1987).

The institutionalization of the monographic tradition in turn reinforced
what I call the ethnographic trilogy: one observer, one time, one place.
Since what is accessible to the gaze of a single observer staying in one place
for a limited amount of time is inherently limited, the ethnographic trilogy,
inscribed in a rite of passage, invited a practical closure.

Contrary to recent critics, I do not see this closure as inherent in fieldwork. Rather, a naive epistemology, strongly influenced by empiricism,
predisposed anthropologists to fetishize fieldwork—first, by avoiding the
issue of the epistemological status of the native voice, and second, by blur-
ring the necessary distinction between the object of study and the object of
observation (Trouillot 1992a, 2001). Further, in the first half of the twentieth century, procedures of acceptance within the guild provided additional
corporate and individual incentives to fetishize fieldwork. By the middle of
the twentieth century, the units of analysis were most often taken, on both
sides of the Atlantic, as natural, obvious, and, for all practical purposes,
impermeable, and "culture" became, in the United States, the impenetrable
boundary of these units.

A THEORETICAL REFUGE

The story described so far is academic in most senses of the word. It happens within academe. Its consequences may seem commonplace both
within and outside of that context. The parallel between the deployment

of *culture* and the deployment of terms such as *economy*, *state*, and *society* is evident. Each of the last three words has been as thoroughly reified as has *culture*. Yet none of these terms today suggests the exact opposite of what it was first intended to question. The paradox of *culture*, as promoted by North American anthropology, is unique. A word deployed in academe to curb racialist denotations is often used today in and out of academe with racialist connotations. A word intended to promote pluralism often becomes a trope in conservative agendas or in late liberal versions of the civilizing project. The story of how that happened is not merely academic. It is the story of a move away from politics, the story of a conceptualization whose deployment denied its very conditions of possibility.

The political move in theory described earlier was not necessarily fatal, even with the limitations mentioned. Within academe, culture could be read as a step back from politics, but this step backward could have been healthy if the privileged space it created had become one from which to address power, even if indirectly. Unfortunately, the pendulum never swung back. The privileged space became a refuge. Culture never went out to speak to power.

I am not suggesting that sociocultural anthropologists should have become political activists. Nor am I blaming them for avoiding "correct" political positions. Indeed, the American Anthropological Association has taken quite a few positions that can be described as politically progressive. I am willing to concede a lot on mere political grounds. Rather, my contention is that within the terms of its own history of deployment, the culture concept failed to face its context. What I see as a move away from politics inheres in that deployment and the silences it produced. Those on which I insist are not political silences as such. They are silences in *theory* that shielded theory from politics.

Two of them are most telling: first, the benign theoretical treatment of race, and second, the failure to connect race and racism in the United States and elsewhere and the related avoidance of Black-white relations in the United States as an ethnographic object.

Race for Boas was a biological fact. It did not need to be conceptualized, but it had to be documented. It was between that careful documentation—in the terms of the times—and the development of a program of cultural research that the race-culture antinomy played out in Boas's work (Darnell 1998; Stocking 1968). Yet as biological determinism seemed to fade out of public discourse with the decline of scientific racism, as nineteenth-century definitions of race became questioned in academe, and as anthropologists themselves subspecialized further within the discipline, culture and race each went its own way (Baker 1998, 168–87). The result is that today there is more conceptual confusion about race among anthropologists than there was at the beginning of the last century.

After a careful survey of anthropological textbooks, Eugenia Shanklin (2000) argued that "American anthropologists deliver inchoate messages about anthropological understandings of race and racism." Echoing the pioneering work of Leonard Lieberman and his associates (Lieberman, Stevenson, and Reynolds 1989; Lieberman et al. 1992), she documented inconsistencies and lacunae that combine to make anthropology "look ignorant, backward, deluded, or uncaring" about race and racism. Should we be worried? Sociocultural anthropologists have also proposed myriad definitions of culture. That they would not agree on definitions of race should come as no surprise.

Yet this response to Shanklin's judgment makes sense only if we reduce conceptualizations to mere definitions. If we return to the kernel I sketched earlier, the two cases—culture and race—are diametrically opposed. Behind the definitional differences over culture is a core understanding of the notion. Indeed, definitional debates about culture are battles over control of that conceptual core. The very opposite is true of race. Definitional divergences reveal the lack of a conceptual core.

The absence of a conceptual core is verified by numerous entries in the *Anthropology Newsletter* on and after October 1997, when the American Anthropological Association presented its chosen theme for 1997–98: "Is It 'Race'? Anthropology and Human Diversity." Both the statement that announced this theme and the following debates confirmed what we might already have concluded from Lieberman: something on the order of the kernel sketched earlier for culture is blatantly missing.

Both Lieberman's and Shanklin's research confirms my intuition that few within anthropology want control over a concept of race, except for a few politically naive or conservative biological anthropologists. It is as if North American anthropologists—especially those who see themselves as politically liberal—are worried about stating bluntly what race is, even as a matter of intellectual debate. The consensus is that biological inheritance cannot explain the transmission of patterns of thought and behavior; culture (and/or social practice) does. It even explains the transmission of the belief that biological inheritance plays such a role.

That may seem to be good news, and indeed it is. Still, that statement brings us back to our starting point. For in a way we have gone full circle, as far as the race-culture antinomy is concerned. We have restated our belief in the conceptual kernel. Yet in spite of that kernel, within the antinomy itself, culture is what race is not, and race, in turn, is what culture is not. In other words, we have gained nothing *conceptually* on the race-culture relation. Worse yet, culture has been freed from its original milieu of conception, from the political tension that made its deployment necessary. It can function alone. It has become a theoretical refuge.

Some may object to the apparent harshness of this judgment. Have we not learned that race is a "construction"? Indeed, we may have. Yet this catchword states only that race is a proper object of study for sociocultural anthropologists, like other kinds of constructions such as language, history, marriage, ritual, gender, and class. It says little about how to conceptualize this particular construction, about the specific mechanisms of its production or its special modes of operation. To put it most simply, if race does not exist, racism does, and the mere coining of race as a construction fails to give us much of a handle on racism.

Yet mentions of racism are rarer than mentions of race in North American textbooks. The dominant trend is not divergence but neglect. While disagreeing on what race is, North American anthropologists often overlook practices of racism. That outcome was predictable. Studies of racism by anthropologists in North America are extremely rare. So are works on Blacks in the United States.[4]

That anthropologists traditionally study people in faraway places is not enough to explain this avoidance. Native Americans have long been favorite objects of anthropological enquiry. Sidney W. Mintz (1971), who juxtaposed North American anthropology's aversion toward the study of the Black victims of white domination with its predilection for the "red" ones, had a number of suggestions to explain this bizarre polarity. Most notably, Indians fitted quite well the Savage slot. Black Americans did so less well. The combined reasons are theoretical and political in the way addressed here. Whereas each "Indian culture"—enforced isolation abetting—could be projected as a distinct unit of analysis, it is impossible to describe or analyze patterns of thought and behavior among the people who pass for Black within the United States without referring to racism and its practices. Without that reference, anthropology will continue to look irrelevant to most Blacks.[5] With that reference, the pendulum would swing back. Culture would have to address power.

Why does power seem to provide the stumbling block to anthropological theory at almost each point of this story? I contend that a recurring assumption behind the difficulties and silences we have encountered here regarding both culture and race is the illusion of a liberal space of enlightenment within which words-as-concepts can be evaluated without regard for their context of deployment.

On the same front page of the October 1997 *Anthropology Newsletter* is another headline: "AAA Tells Feds to Eliminate 'Race.'" The Association recommended to the US Office of Management and Budget that race be eliminated from Directive 15, "Race and Ethnic Standards for Federal Statistics and Administrative Reporting." The rationale was that race and ethnicity are indistinguishable and commonly misunderstood and misused. Thus, the Census Bureau should stop classifying Americans on the basis of race. Restating proposals first made by Ashley Montagu (e.g., 1946), the AAA suggested first coupling race and ethnicity and then phasing out race altogether.

The coupling seems awkward: native informants are likely to feel that one is not African American the way one is Italian American, especially since a reconsolidation of whiteness occurred in the half century between Montagu's writings and our times (Jacobson 1998). Thus, in the United States, as elsewhere, ethnicity and race need to be conceptualized together (Trouillot 1995, 133; Williams 1989), not evened out empirically or theoretically. Shanklin (2000) rightly castigated textbook authors who subsumed race under ethnicity. Yolanda Moses, who drafted the AAA statement, rightly implied that the change of labels might prove meaningless so long as "white" remained an unquestioned category. But can we really erase whiteness by a mere stroke of the pen?

A major contention of the official AAA position in 1997 was that the public was misusing ethnic categories and, especially, the concept of race. Thus, anthropology needed to reclaim race and provide a better concept in order to enlighten the public. But the only way we can accept this solution is to assume a liberal space of enlightenment—a space blind to the world, isolated from the messiness of social life, within which the concept of race would go through its own intellectual cleansing and whence it would emerge with the purity of whiteness to edify a world all too social and political.

Left out of the discussion of Directive 15 were the practices within which these concepts and categories are mobilized and reach full realization. Yet the problem with these concepts is not one of scientific exactitude, their purported referential relation to entities existing out there. The crux of the matter is the uses to which these categories are put, the purposes for which they are mobilized, and the political contests that make this mobilization necessary in the first place. Here the academic, lay, and political lives of concepts (Williams 1989) intertwine. Not to address this overlay is to assume the imperviousness of the privileged space. That is a huge assumption. Yet it is a common one in anthropological practice—indeed, the very one that overlies the deployment of the culture concept itself.

In separating race and culture, Boas consistently noted the "errors" of racialist theories. Unlike many of his followers, he did mention race discrimination in both his academic and his popular writings (e.g., Boas 1945). Yet his fundamental strategy was to disconnect race and culture in anthropology, not to connect race and racism in or out of anthropology.

The evidence is overwhelming that Franz Boas, the individual, wanted to go beyond that space and its rules of engagement (Hyatt 1990), especially at the end of his life. When read chronologically, the essays collected posthumously in *Race and Democratic Society* (Boas 1945) hint at a dual progression. From about 1925 to 1941, their themes—as well as a gradual shift in vocabulary—register a move from the description of politically neutral states of affairs (e.g., race, 1925; race feelings, 1932) to *inherently political categories* (e.g., prejudice, 1937; racial injustice, 1937; racism, 1940 [Boas 1932, 1945]). Equally important, the introduction and the concluding essay interrogate the purported isolation of academic institutions—and thus their role as mere exporters of good concepts. Indeed, Boas wondered to what extent academic knowledge was influenced by "demagogues" and by both the prejudices and the institutional structure of the society at large. If this is not a full agenda, it is the closest anthropology came to the real thing in the first half of the last century.

As a rule, however, theory in sociocultural anthropology never followed that agenda. Perhaps the political will was missing in—or poorly channeled through—the discipline as an institutional site. Perhaps the need to establish anthropology as an objective "science" limited the terms of engagement.[6] At any rate, the study of "race relations," relinquished by anthropology, remained a purview of sociology—often with the unfortunate premise that race is a biological given. Sandwiched between Ruth Benedict and Gene Weltfish's "Races of Mankind" (1943) and Boas's *Race in a Democratic Society* (1945), the publication of Gunnar Myrdal's much more influential *American Dilemma* (1945) signaled both the absorption of culture by race and their twin capture from anthropologists in the public arena. Myrdal saw "American Negro culture" as a pathological distortion of the general (i.e., white) American culture.

The public resonance of Myrdal's thesis only verified an old division of labor within academe rarely acknowledged by historians of anthropology (but see Baker 1998). Anthropology's monopoly over both the word and the concept of culture obtained only when the use of either was restricted to the Savage slot. When it came to Black Savages in the cities, white immigrants, or the majority population, other social scientists, such as political scientists or sociologists—notably of the Chicago school—took the lead. Their varying notions of culture sometimes challenged the Boasian race-culture divide. Further, even when nonanthropologists accepted this divide, the politics of race and assimilation and the belief in American exceptionalism led these scholars to emphasize the "white American culture" that Myrdal assumed.

To say that sociologists coined the wrong concept or distorted the right one for a general public obsessed by race is to miss the point. The political persona and professional career of Clark Wissler illustrate how much these public developments came from anthropology's own theoretical ambiguities. Wissler's writings on culture areas and "American Indian cultures" fit broadly within the Boasian paradigm. When Wissler turned his gaze to "Euro-American culture," however, his conceptual handling reveals the extent to which the conceptual and political ambiguities overlapped. He identified three main characteristics of "our American culture," one of which was the practice of universal suffrage and the belief that the vote is one of the "inalienable and sacred rights of man" (1923, 10). This proposition becomes blatantly suspicious when we recall that, at that time, about forty states had laws against miscegenation, and grandfather, poll, and literacy laws kept most Blacks from voting throughout the US South.

Wissler's position becomes both conceptually stranger and politically clearer when he backs his reserve toward miscegenation by evoking this major tenet of "our" American culture, universal suffrage. He writes: "If it can be shown that negroes may under favorable conditions play an equal part *in the culture of whites*, it is yet proper to question the social desirability of such joint participation" (emphasis added). The first issue is amenable to "scientific treatment." The second depends only on "the preferences of a majority of the individuals concerned" (Wissler 1923, 284–87). Thus, miscegenation is not a topic for anthropological study but a political matter best left to voters. It may not be surprising, then, that the same Wissler, a member of the Gaitan Society, also sat on the executive committee of the Second International Congress of Eugenics in 1921 and on the advisory council of *Eugenics: A Journal of Race Betterment*.[7]

I am not arguing that Wissler was a standard representative of the Boasians—if there was such a being. I am arguing that his positions demonstrate not only the inability to produce from the space carved out by the Boasians a clear *theoretical reply to racist practices* but also the possibility of short-circuiting culture as an anticoncept both from within (Wissler, Benedict) and from without (e.g., Davenport et al. 1930; Myrdal 1962; Murray and Herrnstein 1994). The space Wissler used between politics and "science" was carved out by the two moves described here, which fully isolated culture (best dealt with in academe) from issues of power, including racism, which were relevant only to the world around the ivy walls. Wissler's position could be made theoretically consistent with Boasian anthropology, just as racist practices today can very well accommodate the belief that "race" is a construction.[8]

Current reactions among many anthropologists to the misuse of the culture concept rely on the same assumption of a privileged space. Worse, they nurture it. If only culture could get back where it belongs, the world would be edified. But who is to say where culture belongs?

The desire to occupy a privileged space of enlightenment is a frequent feature of both philosophical and political liberalism, though it is not unique to them. It echoes dominant ideologies of North American society, notably the will to power. Liberalism wishes into existence a world of free, willing individual subjects barely encumbered by the structural trappings of power. Hence the dubious proposition that if enlightened individuals could get together within their enlightened space, they could recast "culture" or "race" and, in turn, discharge other free, willing individuals of their collective delusions. But is racism a delusion about race? Or is race made salient by racism? That is the crux of the matter.

Albert Memmi ([1982] 2000, 143) may have been the first scholar to proclaim loudly that "racism is always both a discourse and an action," a structuring activity with political purposes. Semantic content and scientific evidence thus matter less than the denunciation of those purposes. Similarly, Étienne Balibar (1991) asked how we might get rid of some of the practices of power rooted in ambiguous identities when we disagree with the politics of those practices. Balibar argued that we cannot get rid of these practices by repression, that is, by forbidding some kinds of thoughts or some kinds of speech. He went on to say that we cannot eliminate these practices through predication, either, that is, by the mere infusion of new kinds of thoughts and new kinds of speech.

One need not put a low premium on the value of thought and speech to recognize that the primary solution anthropological theory has tended to propose to the problems many anthropologists genuinely want to solve is the infusion of new kinds of words. Worse, from the early Boasian wager to more recent recommendations about either race or culture, the reduction of concepts to words has worsened—hence the fetishization of "culture" to the detriment of its conceptual kernel. The distance between theory and its context of deployment has widened as well, and not only in anthropology.

The last two decades of the twentieth century saw a closing of academic discourse to problems felt by a majority of the world's population. Media claims notwithstanding, the influence of academic research that could be labeled politically "progressive" has decreased—if only because these works are increasingly inaccessible to lay readers. Far beyond the absolute need for a technical vocabulary to which research contributes and without which it cannot be sustained, far beyond the specific need for syntactic structures that express the complexity of thought or the gracefulness of language, academics now bask in "the aestheticization of theory." By that I mean a process through which theory not only acquires a birthright of its own—a legitimate claim, indeed—but spends its life spinning in a proselytical circle, the main purpose of which is to verify its beauty. In short, the pressures are much greater now than in Boas's time to find refuge in a privileged space of enlightenment where words are protected and, in turn, protect their writers.

That space does not exist. Once launched, the concepts we work with take on a life of their own. They follow trajectories that we cannot always predict or correct. We can place them in orbit, design them with a direction in mind, but we know they will be challenged in and out of academe. There is no guarantee that the final meaning will be ours. Yet without prior attention to the wider context of deployment, the words that encapsulate our concepts are most likely to become irretrievable for us. That, I think, is what happened to *culture*.

OUT OF ORBIT?

The deployment of the culture concept echoes a voluntarism distinctive of the liberal ideologies that permeate US society. If culture had remained tied to the race-culture antinomy even as circuitously as it was in Boas's early writings (therefore maintaining an engagement with biology and biological anthropologists), or, more importantly, if its anthropological deployment had compelled references to sociohistorical processes such as mechanisms of inequality, it would have been more difficult to displace. Launched on some conceptual path, it still could have been nabbed in orbit. But as set, a self-generating, singularized, and essentialized entity, it was literally up for grabs.

The complexity of the Boasians' private debates (Brightman 1995; Darnell 1997) was not immediately accessible to the general public. Even within the discipline, groups of specialists integrated different parts of an increasingly vast corpus and inherited only portions of an increasingly broad agenda. While some cultural anthropologists successfully questioned biological determinism so far as group behavior was concerned, some biological anthropologists may have reinforced biological determinism as it pertained to individual behavior.[9] Further and more important, the separation of race and culture heralded by Boas, the major public purpose of the culture concept, filtered down quite slowly to parts of the citizenry (Baker 1998). Not only did racism survive the Boasians, but it survived them quite well. Worse, it turned culture into an accessory.

Although the culture concept helped in questioning the theoretical relevance of race in some learned circles, it has not much affected racism in the public space. At best, the racism that evokes biological determinism simply made room for a parallel racism rooted in cultural essentialism. At times, the two forms of racism contradict each other. Most often, they reinforce each other in and out of academe. The biological determinism of a Charles Murray or a Vincent Sarich implies an essentialist notion of culture without which the biological package does not hold up. In turn, many of the chapters in *Culture Matters* imply an essentialist take on racial, religious, or geoethnic clusters projected as cultural isolates. Instead of the culture versus race effect that Boas expected, many in American society now espouse a culture qua race ideology that is fast spreading to the rest of the world.

Indeed, culture has become a preferred explanation of socioeconomic inequality within and across countries (Banfield 1990; Harrison and Huntington 2000). It has become an argument for a number of politically conservative positions and been put to uses that quite a few anthropologists would question, from the disapproval of cross-racial adoptions to the need for political representation based on skin color. It has also revived, with much less criticism from anthropologists, versions of the white man's burden.

Both the politically conservative use of culture and the late liberal versions of the white man's burden have theoretical roots in anthropology itself: first, in the unchecked explanatory power with which many anthropologists endowed culture, and second, in the use of culture to delineate ever smaller units of analysis. These delineations ("the culture of science," "the culture of academe," "political culture," etc.) make the concept of society and the entire field of social relations less relevant both analytically and politically to any topic under study. The social order need not be analyzed, let alone acted upon; we need only to change the morally dubious or politically ineffective subcultures. On a different scale but in a similar manner, the burden of the North Atlantic today can be formulated as a duty to bring to the rest of the world the enlightenment of Protestant liberalism (Harrison and Huntington 2000).

Many cultural anthropologists are appalled by these uses, which they tend to discover too late anyway. For indeed, few people outside anthropology now bother to ask anthropologists what they mean by culture. Since the early 1980s, a vibrant discussion has been going on in economics about the relationship between culture and development (e.g., Buchanan 1995; Mayhew 1987), with little participation from anthropologists. In policy circles, we are often left out of the debates about multiculturalism, which we all know are "really" about race. Or when solicited, we reject the engagement, preferring the isolation of our place of enlightenment. Even within academe we are losing ground to cultural studies in the debate over the appropriation of the word *culture*, a loss that seems to irritate anthropologists more than the political capture of the word in the world outside. We keep telling all sides, "You've got it wrong." But a lot of it they got from us—not only through our epiphany of culture but also through our clinging to a space where we feel conceptually safe. If some Afrocentrists today believe that an inner-city Chicago kid is culturally closer to a Kalahari bushman than to her white counterpart on the North Side of town—and if the inequalities between the two are ascribed to culture, however misdefined—then anthropology has to take part of the blame.

ADIEU, CULTURE

Blame is not enough, nor is it the most effective attitude. Solutions are necessary. They will not come from a single individual or group but from the discipline's collective engagement with the context within which we operate.

I do not mean by this a political engagement, which remains a matter of individual choice. Anthropology's primary response as a discipline cannot be a political statement, however tempting or necessary that solution may be in critical circumstances. Yet while the primary context of our practice as professionals remains the academic world, the ultimate context of its relevance is the world outside, starting most likely with the country within which we publish, rather than those we write about.[10] Thus, while not suggesting that anthropologists abandon theory for political discourse, I am arguing for a theory that is aware of its conditions of possibility, which include the politics of its surroundings.

The nineteenth century generated a particular model of the relations between academe and politics premised on an alleged difference of nature between scientific and social practices. Challenged as it has been at times, this model continues to dominate North Atlantic academic life. The most visible alternative emerged in the 1960s and remains alive under various guises, including some trends of identity politics. That alternative model negates the autonomy and specificity of academic life and research. It solves the problem of the relationship between academe and politics by collapsing the two: science is politics and theory is insurgency. One does one's politics in the classroom or in academic journals. There is no need to problematize a relation between academe and its context because the two entities are the same, except that the first is a disguised version of the second.

Neither model is convincing. While the first assumes a liberal space of enlightenment where concepts can be cleansed by academics, the second belittles academe's specific rules of engagement and the relative power of different institutional locations. It perniciously allows academics to claim the social capital of political relevance while comforting them in their privileged space. A major hope behind this chapter is that anthropologists might explore the possibility of a third model of engagement.

Until that collective engagement manifests itself forcefully, what do we do about culture? If the story told here is reasonably accurate, then the word is lost to anthropology for the foreseeable future. To acknowledge this is not to admit defeat. It is to face the reality that there is no privileged space within which anthropologists alone can refashion the word. Culture is now in an orbit where chasing it can be only a conservative enterprise, a rearguard romance with an invented past (when culture truly meant culture—as if culture ever meant culture only). If concepts are not words, then Brightman (1995) is correct that strategies of "relexification" are not useful either. There is a conceptual kernel to defend, but that defense need not be tied to a word that the general public now essentializes on the basis of anthropologists' own fetishization.[11] We need to abandon the word while firmly defending the conceptual kernel it once encapsulated. More important, we need to use the power of ethnographic language to spell out the components of what we used to call culture.

Even more importantly, we need to rethink the terms of sociocultural anthropology's engagement with other disciplines and with the world outside of academe. It is not accidental that our increasingly parochial discussions interest fewer social scientists and even less the public at large at a time when the ethical drive of the discipline is not only unclear but not even open to debate. Nor is it accidental that sociocultural anthropology is slowly turning away from the very same populations that globalization now makes irrelevant to the accumulation of capital (Trouillot 2001, 128–29). Thus again, the long-term and most crucial issue is that of a collective engagement.

It is only with this caveat in mind that I reluctantly propose a few examples of midterm solutions. In my current efforts to describe the global flows that characterize our times and their impact on localized populations (e.g., Trouillot 2000, 2001), I find that the word *culture* often blurs rather than elucidates the facts to be explained—especially since globalization itself has become thing-like much faster than culture. Words such as *style, taste, cosmology, ethos, sensibility, desire, ideology, aspirations,* and *predispositions* often better describe the facts to be studied on the ground, because they tend to limit better the range of traits and patterns covered. They actually allow a better deployment of the conceptual kernel to which I hold.

Do we gain or lose by describing clashes between *beur* and white youths in France as clashes between Arab (or Muslim) and French (or Western) culture? How close do we want to get to Harrison and Huntington's clash of civilizations? Is the spread of McDonald's in France or China proof of the globalization of American "culture"—whatever that may be? We may be more precise in exploring how successfully North American capitalists export middle-class American consumer tastes. We may want to investigate how US corporations—often dominated by white males—are selling speech forms, dress codes, and performance styles developed under conditions of segregation in North American cities as "Black culture." What are the mechanisms through which these forms and styles are accepted, rejected, or integrated in the US South, in the rest of the anglophone world, in Africa, Brazil, or the Caribbean, or in European neighborhoods with substantial numbers of African or Caribbean immigrants? We may want to look at how the expansion and consolidation of the world market for consumer goods, rather than creating a "global culture," fuels a "global production of desire" (Trouillot 2001). What forces and factors now reproduce the same image of the good life all over the world and push people in very different societies to aspire to the same goods? We may want to ask how the current wave of collective apologies for historical sins is propelled by the production of new sensibilities and subjectivities and the virtual presence of a Greek chorus now naively called "the international community" (Trouillot 2000). The production of these new subjects, the rise of new forces and new sites, make it increasingly perilous to hang our theoretical fate on a single word over whose trajectory we have absolutely no control.

Abandoning the word would actually free practitioners in all the subfields of anthropology. It would enhance the dialogue between sociocultural anthropologists, on the one hand, and archaeologists and—especially—biological anthropologists, on the other. Biological anthropologists would not have to find "culture" in the behavior of humans or other primates. Rather, they would have to specify the role of biology in patterning particular instances of cognition, volition, and activity among the groups—human or otherwise—that they study and the degree to which symbolic constructions inform those patterns. The debate would turn on specifics, not on generalities.

Urging fellow physical anthropologists to abandon the word *race*, Ashley Montagu (1964, 27) once wrote that "the meaning of a word is the action it produces," suggesting that the only reasons to deploy racial terms were political. Sociocultural anthropologists need to demonstrate a similar courage. The intellectual and strategic value of *culture* depends now as then on use and historical context (Knauft 1996, 43–45). Today, there is no reason to enclose any segment of the world's population within a single bounded and integrated culture, except for political quarantine. The less culture is allowed to be a shortcut for too many things, the more sociocultural anthropology can thrive within its chosen domain of excellence, documenting how human thought and behavior is patterned and how those patterns are produced, rejected, or acquired. Without culture, we will continue to need ethnography. Without culture, we may even revitalize the Boasian conceptual kernel, for we will have to come to the ground to describe and analyze the changing heads of the hydra that we once singularized.

This adieu took a long time to say. My uneasiness with the race-culture complex in North American anthropology goes back to graduate school. I first put it into words at the presidential session on race at the annual meeting of the American Anthropological Association in San Francisco in 1991. My arguments were revived for the paper "Exploring the Limits of Liberal Discourse: American Anthropology and U.S. Racism," presented at the symposium Anthropologists of Color Speak Out: Perspectives on Race and Public Anthropology at American University on October 25, 1997. This chapter itself was first proposed at Ben-Gurion University in Israel in April 2000 and was discussed at the Wenner-Gren symposium from which this book springs. I thank participants in all these venues. Xavier Andrade, Lee D. Baker, Bruce Knauft, Sam Kaplan, Richard A. Shweder, George W. Stocking Jr., and especially Richard G. Fox provided substantial comments. Clare Sammells provided comments and assistance. Special thanks to Brackette F. Williams, from whom I continue to learn both in print and in talk, and to the students who have taken my "Concepts and Categories" seminar over the last sixteen years at Duke, Johns Hopkins, and Chicago. I claim full and sole responsibility, however, for what some will see as the outrageous conclusions of the chapter.

Editors' Note: This chapter first appeared as "Adieu, Culture: A New Duty Arises," in *Anthropology beyond Culture*, ed. Richard G. Fox and Barbara J. King (Oxford: Berg, 2002), 37–60.

1. *Editors' Note:* In the original work, Trouillot cites Shweder (n.d.). In the version of this essay that appears in *Global Transformations*, Trouillot cites Shweder's work in the *International Encyclopedia of the Social and Behavioral Sciences*. Since that work has now been updated, we here cite the latest version, which includes a coauthor.

2. The exaggerated focus on cultural studies, which turns fellow academics into prime political targets, and reactions to earlier versions of this chapter, though obviously different in scope and relevance, include some dominant themes: we do not have a *public* problem, only an academic one that can be solved within academe; we have a public problem, but it can be solved with conceptual adjustment; we have only a North American problem: culture and cultural studies are quite healthy everywhere else.

3. Indeed, as conceptual foundations of North American anthropology, these propositions preceded by a decade at least—notably in Franz Boas's writings—the routine use of the word that came later to embody them.

4. Exceptions include Gregory 1998, Gregory and Sanjek 1994, Sanjek 1998, and classics such as Herskovits's *Myth of the Negro Past* (1958). Yet Herskovits's own move from the proposition that "[Negroes] have absorbed the culture of

America" to the celebration of a distinct Afro-American culture (Mintz 1990) poignantly reveals the political dilemma of cultural essentialism and augurs the recapture of culture by race.

5. The relationship between anthropology and Black Americans has deteriorated greatly since the first generation of Black students Boas attracted to the field. Today the number of PhDs in anthropology climbs much faster than in other fields, with a majority of the diplomas going to women. Yet while we attract increasing numbers of Asians, American Indians, and Latinos (except Puerto Ricans, whose numbers are shamefully small), Blacks received merely 3.5 percent of our doctoral degrees in 1999. The national average for that year was 5.9 percent, excluding professional schools. Clearly, in comparison with peer disciplines, anthropology is becoming less attractive to Blacks (Sanderon et al. 1999, 2000).

6. Many among the individuals least willing to accept anthropology as refuge—St. Clair Drake, Otto Klineberg, Allison Davis, Eugene King—never became its tenors. Yet it would be futile for us today to divide anthropological ancestors along Manichean lines. Ruth Benedict's pamphlet "Races of Mankind" (1943), coauthored with Gene Weltfish and later a victim of McCarthyism, was banned by the army as "communist propaganda" (di Leonardo 1998, 196). Yet in spite of her antiracist activism, Benedict rarely questioned the implicit evaluation of white advancement.

7. Wissler was most likely the influence behind the presence of Melville J. Herskovits in the pages of *Eugenics*, where Herskovits provided a rather polite rebuttal to those who saw interracial mixture as a recipe for undesired mutants (Davenport et al. 1930).

8. A political climate that mixed nativism and exceptionalism is also part of the story of culture's road to essentialism. Although North Americans have no monopoly on exceptionalism or essentialism, there is a quite specific mixture of the two in North American social science. Drawing from Dorothy Ross (1991), I read the American particularity as the confluence of three trends: a methodological reliance on natural science models, a political reliance on liberal individualism, and an ideological reliance on American exceptionalism. Liberalism and exceptionalism permeate Benedict's dismissal of racism as an aberration of North American democracy.

9. Lest readers think I am singling out biological anthropology as the fall guy, let me remind them that most biological anthropologists—including a majority of those who believe in the existence of biological races—were trained in four-field departments dominated by culturalists. The real issue is how anthropology connects culture and racism, not the biological boundaries of race.

10. Given the power of the United States, the relative responsibility of those of us privileged to write in the United States is obvious.

11. Powerful arguments for the defense of that kernel—rather than for the defense of culture as a unit of analysis—can be found in Wolf 1999. I disagree, however, with Wolf's implicit equation of word and concept, an equation belied by his own work, including the cases treated in that book.

REFERENCES

Baker, Lee D. 1998. *From Savage to Negro: Anthropology and the Construction of Race.* Berkeley: University of California Press.

Balibar, Étienne. 1991. "Racism and Nationalism." In *Race, Nation, Class: Ambiguous Identities*, edited by Étienne Balibar and Immanuel Wallerstein, 37–68. London: Verso.

Banfield, Edward C. 1990. *Unheavenly City Revisited.* New York: Waveland Press.

Benedict, Ruth. 1934. *Patterns of Culture.* Boston: Houghton Mifflin.

Benedict, Ruth, and Gene Weltfish. 1943. *The Races of Mankind.* New York: Public Affairs Committee, Inc.

Boas, Franz. 1932. *Anthropology and Modern Life.* New York: W. W. Norton.

Boas, Franz. 1945. *Race and Democratic Society.* New York: J. J. Augustin.

Brightman, Robert. 1995. "Forget Culture: Replacement, Transcendence, Relexification." *Cultural Anthropology* 10, no. 4: 509–46.

Buchanan, James M. 1995. "Economic Science and Cultural Diversity." *Kyklos* 48, no. 2: 193–200.

Cohn, Bernard S. 1987. *An Anthropologist among the Historians and Other Essays.* New York: Oxford University Press.

Cole, Douglas. 1999. *Franz Boas: The Early Years, 1858–1906.* Vancouver: Douglas and McIntyre; Seattle: University of Washington Press.

Darnell, Regna. 1997. "The Anthropological Concept of Culture at the End of the Boasian Century." *Social Analysis* 41, no. 3: 42–54.

Darnell, Regna. 1998. *And Along Came Boas: Continuity and Revolution in Americanist Anthropology.* Amsterdam: John Benjamins.

Davenport, Charles B., Ales Hrdlicka, Louis I. Newman, Melville J. Herskovits, Frank H. Hankins, and C. M. Goethe. 1930. "Eugenics and Racial Intermarriage: A Symposium." *Eugenics: A Journal of Race Betterment* 3, no. 2: 58–62.

di Leonardo, Micaela. 1998. *Exotics at Home: Anthropologies, Others, American Modernity.* Chicago: University of Chicago Press.

Geertz, Clifford. 1973. *The Interpretation of Cultures.* New York: Basic Books.

Gregory, Steven. 1998. *Black Corona: Race and the Politics of Place in an Urban Community.* Princeton: Princeton University Press.

Gregory, Steven, and Roger Sanjek, eds. 1994. *Race.* New Brunswick, NJ: Rutgers University Press.

Harris, Marvin. 1964. *Patterns of Race in the Americas.* New York: Walker.

Harrison, Lawrence E., and Samuel P. Huntington, eds. 2000. *Culture Matters: How Values Shape Human Progress*. New York: Basic Books.

Herskovits, Melville J. 1958. *The Myth of the Negro Past*. Boston: Beacon Press.

Hyatt, Marshall. 1990. *Franz Boas, Social Activist: The Dynamics of Ethnicity*. New York: Greenwood Press.

Jacobson, Matthew Frye. 1998. *Whiteness of a Different Color: European Immigrants and the Alchemy of Race*. Cambridge: Harvard University Press.

Jomo, K. Sundaram. 2001. "Asian Values and the East Asian Crisis." Paper presented at the conference Identidade e Diferença na era Global, Candido Mendes University, Rio de Janeiro, May 21–23.

Knauft, Bruce M. 1996. *Genealogies for the Present in Cultural Anthropology: A Critical Humanist Perspective*. New York: Routledge.

Lieberman, Leonard, Blaine W. Stevenson, and Larry T. Reynolds. 1989. "Race and Anthropology: A Core Concept without Consensus." *Anthropology and Education Quarterly* 20: 67–73.

Lieberman, Leonard, et al. 1992. "Race in Biology and Anthropology: A Study of College Texts and Professors." *Journal of Research of Science Teaching* 29: 301–21.

Linton, Ralph. 1955. *The Tree of Culture*. New York: Knopf.

Mayhew, Anne. 1987. "Culture: Core Concept under Attack." *Journal of Economic Issues* 21, no. 2: 587–603.

Memmi, Albert. (1982) 2000. *Racism*. Translated by Steve Martinot. Minneapolis: University of Minnesota Press.

Mintz, Sidney W. 1971. "Le rouge et le noir." *Les Temps Modernes* 299–300: 2354–61.

Mintz, Sidney W. 1990. "Introduction." In *Myth of the Negro Past*, by Melville Herskovits, ix–xxi. Boston: Beacon Press.

Montagu, Ashley. 1946. "What Every Child and Adult Should Know about 'Race.'" *Education*: 262–64.

Montagu, Ashley. 1964. "The Concept of Race." In *The Concept of Race*, edited by Ashley Montagu, 12–28. New York: Free Press.

Murray, Charles, and Richard J. Herrnstein. 1994. *The Bell Curve: Intelligence and Class Structure in American Life*. New York: Free Press.

Myrdal, Gunnar. 1962. *An American Dilemma: The Negro Problem and Modern Democracy*. New York: Harper and Row.

Ross, Dorothy. 1991. *The Origins of American Social Science*. New York: Cambridge University Press.

Sanderon, Allen R., Bernard Dugoni, Thomas Hoffer, and Sharon Myers. 2000. *Doctorate Recipients from United States Universities: Summary Report, 1999*. Chicago: National Opinion Research Center.

Sanderon, Allen R., Bernard Dugoni, Thomas Hoffer, and Lance Selfa. 1999. *Doctorate Recipients from United States Universities: Summary Report 1998*. Chicago: National Opinion Research Center.

Sanjek, Roger. 1998. *The Future of Us All: Race and Neighborhood Politics in New York City*. Ithaca, NY: Cornell University Press.

Shanklin, Eugenia. 2000. "Representations of Race and Racism in American Anthropology." *Current Anthropology* 41, no. 1: 99–103.

Shweder, Richard A., and Les Beldo. 2015. "Culture: Contemporary Views." In *International Encyclopedia of the Social and Behavioral Sciences*, 2nd ed., vol. 5, edited
by James D. Wright, 582–89. Oxford: Elsevier.

Silverstein, Michael. 2000. "Languages/Cultures Are Dead! Long Live the
Linguistic-Cultural!" Paper presented at the annual meeting of the American
Anthropological Association, San Francisco, November 15–19.

Stocking, George W., Jr. 1968. "Franz Boas and the Culture Concept in Historical
Perspective." In *Race, Culture, and Evolution: Essays in the History of Anthropology*,
edited by George W. Stocking Jr., 195–233. New York: Free Press.

Trouillot, Michel-Rolph. 1991. "Anthropology and the Savage Slot: The Poetics and
Politics of Otherness." In *Recapturing Anthropology: Working in the Present*,
edited by Richard G. Fox, 17–44. Santa Fe, NM: School of American Research
Press.

Trouillot, Michel-Rolph. 1992. "The Caribbean Region: An Open Frontier in Anthropological Theory." *Annual Review of Anthropology* 21: 19–42.

Trouillot, Michel-Rolph. 1995. *Silencing the Past: Power and the Production of History*.
Boston: Beacon Press.

Trouillot, Michel-Rolph. 2000. "Abortive Rituals: Historical Apologies in a Global
Era." *Interventions: International Journal of Postcolonial Studies* 2, no. 2: 171–86.

Trouillot, Michel-Rolph. 2001. "The Anthropology of the State in the Age of Globalization: Close Encounters of the Deceptive Kind." *Current Anthropology* 42,
no. 1: 125–38.

Wallerstein, Immanuel, Calestous Juma, Evelyn Fox Keller, Jurgen Kocka, V. Y. Mudimbe, Kinhide Miushakoji, Ilya Prigogine, Peter J. Taylor, and Michel-Rolph
Trouillot. 1996. *Open the Social Sciences: A Report of the Gulbenkian Commission for
the Restructuring of the Social Sciences*. Stanford, CA: Stanford University Press.

Williams, Brackette F. 1989. "A Class Act: Anthropology and the Race to Nation
across Ethnic Terrain." *Annual Review of Anthropology* 18: 401–44.

Wissler, Clark. 1923. *Man and Culture*. New York: Thomas Y. Crowel.

Wolf, Eric R. 1999. *Envisioning Power: Ideologies of Dominance and Crisis*. Berkeley:
University of California Press.

CHAPTER 14

The Presence in the Past

They came long before Columbus. For reasons we can only guess, they had stopped in this arid land where their sole sources of water were gigantic sinkholes nature had carved into the limestone. Here, in the province of Chichén, they had built their temples between two of these wells. They had surveyed the skies from these heights, master astronomers, aware of mathematical secrets that Europeans barely guessed. They were practiced warriors. Most strikingly, they were devout. They had kept one well for themselves and given to their gods the deep one with the green waters.

I knew all these stories. I had done my homework before coming to Maya land. Now, I wanted something real. Hunting, my eyes descended the limestone walls eighty feet down into the well. This was the Cenote of Sacrifice, the Sacred Well of Chichén Itzá.

The still green waters did not speak of war and murder. Not a ripple of blood disturbed their cool surface. Here and there a dead leaf, dropped from the air far above, left a patch of dark green over the underground lake. But there was no movement on the water surface. Here, the past was hidden by a verdant coat of silence.

I coughed nervously, sweeping the water with my binoculars. I was in search of evidence. I was eager to see a corpse, a skull, some bones, any gruesome trace of history. But the belly of the earth uttered only the echo of my cough.

Yet history had to be there. Below the water, hundreds of corpses melted into the earth—women, men, and children, many of them thrown alive to deities now forgotten, for reasons now murkier than the bottom of this well. Stories about these sacrifices spanned at least ten centuries. Scavengers of all sorts—colonists, diplomats, warriors, and archaeologists—had unearthed the proofs behind these narratives. Still, I felt disappointed: there was nothing here to touch, nothing to see except a dormant green liquid.

I retraced my steps along the ancient path to the central pyramid. That, at least, seemed concrete, and I had not yet made the journey to the top. Up there, as in the well, history required bodily donations. I had to pay my part of sweat for the encounter to be sincere. Stoically, I climbed the stairs, all 354 of them, and I ventured into the ruins. Inside, for a long time, I ran my fingers on the walls, probing mysteries unresolved, longing for recognition. But as much as I was touched by the magnificence of the structure, I never came to feel that I was touching history. I climbed down the pyramid, careful not to look into the void, blaming myself for this failure to communicate with a past so magnificently close.

Many exotic lands later, I understood better my trip to Chichén Itzá. History was alive and I had heard its sounds elsewhere. From Rouen to Santa Fe, from Bangkok to Lisbon, I had touched ghosts suddenly real, I had engaged people far remote in time and in space. Distance was no barrier. History did not need to be mine in order to engage me. It just needed to relate to someone, anyone. It could not just be The Past. It had to be someone's past.

During my first trip to the Yucatan, I had failed to meet the peoples whose past Chichén Itzá was. I could not resuscitate a single mathematician viewing the skies from the Caracol, a single sacrificial victim pushed toward the green waters. And I knew even less then how to relate the Mayas to the architects of the pyramids. That, no doubt, was my fault, my lack of imagination, or a shortfall of erudition. At any rate, I had missed a vital connection to the present. I had honored the past, but the past was not history.

SLAVERY IN DISNEYLAND

The controversies about EuroDisney had not yet faded when the mammoth transnational revealed its plans for Disney's America, a new amusement park to be built in Northern Virginia. Aware that environmental and historical tourism are among the fastest growing branches of that industry, Disney emphasized the historical themes of the park. Afro-American slavery was one of them.

Protests immediately erupted. Black activists accused Disney of turning slavery into a tourist attraction. Others intimated that white corporate types were not qualified to address the subject. Others wondered whether the subject should be addressed at all. Disney's chief imagineer tried to calm the public: activists need not worry, we guarantee the exhibit to be "painful, disturbing and agonizing."

William Styron, a popular novelist, author of such best-sellers as *Sophie's Choice* and *The Confessions of Nat Turner*, denounced Disney's plans in the pages of the *New York Times* (Styron 1994). Styron, whose grandmother owned slaves, asserted that Disney could only "mock a theme as momentous as slavery" because "slavery cannot be represented in exhibits." Whatever the images displayed and the technical means deployed, the artifacts of cruelty and oppression "would have to be fraudulent" because they would be inherently unable to "define such a stupendous experience." The moral dilemmas of many whites and especially the suffering of Blacks would be missing from the exhibit, not because such experience could not be displayed, but because their very display would beget a cheap romanticism. Styron concluded: "At Disney's Virginia park, the slave experience would permit visitors a shudder of horror before they turned away, smug and self-exculpatory, from a world that may be dead but has not really been laid to rest."

When I first read these lines, I wished a practicing historian had written them. Then it occurred to me that few historians could have done so. Indeed, my second thought was for another novelist writing about yet a third one.

In a story often evoked in debates about authenticity, Jorge Luis Borges imagines that a French novelist of the 1930s produces a novel that is word for word a fragmentary version of *Don Quixote de la Mancha*. Borges insists: Pierre Ménard did not copy *Don Quixote*, nor did he try to be Miguel de Cervantes. He rejected the temptation to mimic both Cervantes's life and style as too facile. He achieved his feat after many drafts, at the end of which his text was the same as that of Cervantes (Borges 1969). Is that second novel a fake and why? Is it, indeed, a "second" novel? What is the relationship between Ménard's work and that of Cervantes?

Disney dropped its plans for the Virginia park, much less because of the controversy about slavery than in reaction to other kinds of pressure.[1] Still, the plans for the park can be interpreted as a parody of Borges's parody. Indeed, read against one another, the respective projects of the transnational and of Borges's fictitious writer provide a pointed lesson about the fourth moment of historical production, the moment of retrospective significance.[2]

Neither in the case of the park nor in that of the book is empirical exactitude a primary issue. Disney could gather all the relevant facts for its planned exhibits, just as the words in Ménard's final draft were exactly the same as those in Cervantes's *Don Quixote*. Indeed, the Disney corporation flaunted its use of historians as paid consultants—proof, as it were, of its high regard for empirical exactitude. The limitless possibility for errors remained but, other things being equal, one could imagine a version of Disney's America as empirically sound as the average history book. Styron, who wrote a controversial novel about slavery, knows this. He expresses concerns about empirical issues, but his emphasis is elsewhere. Styron even admits, although reluctantly, that Disney could duplicate the mood of the times. Modern images have enough means to stage virtual reality. Yet Styron remains indignant, and it is this indignation that helps him stir his way through his previous objections toward a conclusion that follows the tourists until *after* they turn away.

Deconstruction's most famous line may be Jacques Derrida's sentence: *il n'y a pas de hors-texte*. How literally can we take the claim that there is no life beyond the text? To be sure, we may decide not to get out of the amusement park. We can argue that if Disney's imagineers had produced the virtual reality of slavery, the paying tourist would have been projected in history. It would have mattered little then, if that projection were a short or even short-sighted representation. Similarly, we may tell Borges that the issue of authenticity is irrelevant and that both novels are the same, however awkward this phrasing. Yet if such answers are unsatisfactory, then, we need to get out of the text(s) and look for life after Disney. And, I would argue, getting out the text enables us also to get out of the tyranny of the facts. The realization that historical production is itself historical is the only way out of the false dilemmas posed by positivist empiricism and extreme formalism.

In the subtext of Styron's objection is a fundamental premise: Disney's primary public was to be white middle-class Americans. They are the ones for whom the park was planned, if only because their aggregate buying power makes them the prime consumers of such historical displays. They are the ones most likely to have plunged into the fake agony of Disney's virtual reality. Styron does not spell out this premise, expressed only through innuendos. Perhaps he wants to avoid accusations of bending to "political correctness." Perhaps he wants to avoid the issue of collective white guilt. He is careful to suggest, quite rightly in my view, that the exhibit would have misrepresented the experiences of both Blacks and whites.

The value of a historical product cannot be debated without taking into account both the context of its production and the context of its consumption.[3] It may be no accident that this insight comes from a popular novelist in the pages of a mass market daily. At any rate, few academic historians would have set the problem in those terms; for academic historians are trained to neglect the very actor that Styron or the *New York Times* cannot ignore, the public. The nature of that public is at the center of Styron's objections.

To phrase the argument in these terms is immediately to reintroduce history, or, better, to refuse to get out of it for the seraphic comfort of the text or the immutable security of The Past. Styron refuses to sperate the history of slavery from that of the United States after Civil War. He devotes just a few lines to the time after Union cavalry men invaded his grandmother's plantation, to the fate of the ex-slaves, to Jim Crow laws and the Ku Klux Klan, and to illiteracy among Blacks. He adds, almost in passing, that this postslavery period is what actually haunts him.

The time that elapsed between the demise of slavery and the planning of the Virginia park shaped the meaning of Disney's representation of slavery. Time here is not mere chronological continuity. It is the range of disjointed moments, practices, and symbols that thread the historical relations between events and narrative. Borges's Ménard makes this complex point in simpler terms: "It is not in vain that three hundred years have passed, charged with the most complex happenings—among them, to mention only one, that same *Don Quixote*" (Borges 1969, 23). We could parody him further: it is not irrelevant that a century of complex occurrences has passed in the United States, while slavery hangs on as an issue. That US slavery has both officially ended, yet continues in many complex forms—most notably institutionalized racism and the cultural denigration of Blackness—makes its representation particularly burdensome in the United States. Slavery here is a ghost, both the past and a living presence; and the problem of historical representation is how to represent that ghost, something that is and yet is not.

I disagree, therefore, with Styron's comment that the Holocaust Museum in Washington is illuminating and that displays of slavery in Virginia would be obscene because of some inherent difference in magnitude or complexity between the two phenomena described. That argument rests on the assumption of a fixed past. But the cost accounting of historical suffering makes sense only as a presence projected in the past. That presence ("look at me now") and its projection ("I have suffered") function together as a new exhibit for claims and gains in a changing present. Many European Jews who condemn projects of parody at Auschwitz or elsewhere in Poland, Germany, France, or the Soviet Union deploy the same moral arguments that Styron uses against mock plantations today in Virginia.

Do displays of Jewish genocide run greater risks of being obscene in Poland than Virginia? The illuminating value of the Holocaust Museum in Washington may be tied as much to the current situation of American Jews as to the real bodies in and around Auschwitz. Indeed, many Holocaust survivors are sure that such a museum would be illuminating at Auschwitz itself. The crux of the matter is the here and now, the relations between the events described and their public representation in a specific historical context.

These relations debunk the myth of The Past as a fixed reality and the related view of knowledge as a fixed content. They also force us to look at the purpose of their knowledge. What is scary about tourist attractions representing slavery in the United States is not so much that the tourists would learn the wrong facts, but rather, that touristic representations of the facts would induce among them the wrong reaction. Obviously, the word *wrong* has different meanings here. It denotes inaccuracy in the first case. In the second, it suggests an amoral or, at least, unauthentic behavior.

Cascardi suggests that "authenticity is not a type or degree of knowledge, but a relationship to what is known" (1984, 289). To say that "what is known" must include the present will seem self-evident, but it may be less obvious that historical authenticity resides not in the fidelity to an alleged past but in an honesty vis-á-vis the present as it re-presents that past. When we imagine Disney's project and visualize a line of white tourists munching on chewing gum and fatty food, purchasing tickets for the "painful, disturbing and agonizing" experience promised by television ads, we are not in The Past. And we should not ask these tourists to be true to that past: they were not responsible for slavery. What is obscene in that image is not a relation to The Past, but the dishonesty of that relation as it would happen in our present. The trivialization of slavery—and of the suffering it caused—inheres in that present, which includes both racism and representations of slavery. Ironically, a Klan member actively promoting racial inequality would have stood a better chance of authenticity. At least, it would not have trivialized slavery.

One understands why many practicing historians kept silent. The denunciation of slavery in a presentist mode is easy. Slavery was bad, most of us would agree. But, presentism is by definition anachronistic. To condemn slavery alone is the easy way out, as trivial as Pierre Ménard's first attempt to become Cervantes. What needs to be denounced here to restore authenticity is much less slavery than the racist present within which representations of slavery are produced. The moral incongruence stems from this uneasy overlap of the two sides of historicity.

Not surprisingly, survivors of all kinds are more likely than historians to denounce these trivializations. Thus, Vidal-Naquet warns us that if Holocaust narratives, even if empirically correct, lose their relationship to the living present, Jews and perhaps non-Jews would have suffered a moral defeat, and Holocaust survivors would have been returned symbolically to the camps. Pierre Weill approves in different terms: there is no purpose to the speeches and banners that marked the fiftieth celebration of Auschwitz's liberation by Soviet troops. The celebrations were a vain effort by state officials throughout the West to commemorate an impossible anniversary.

Survivors carry history on themselves, as Vidal-Naquet well knows. Indeed, a key difference between US slavery and the European Holocaust is that no former slaves are alive today in the United States. This physical embodiment, a historical relation carried on the self, is crucial to Vidal-Naquet's distinction between history and memory. Thus, Vidal-Naquet worries about representations of the Holocaust once his generation is gone. But we should be careful not to push too far the distinction between various kinds of survivors. Weill, indeed, refuses to do so: as long as every living Jew, "regardless of age" remains an Auschwitz survivor, one cannot celebrate the liberation of Auschwitz (Vidal-Naquet 1987; Weill 1995).[4]

We are back into this present that we thought we could escape after the death of the last man (Fukuyama 1992). It is from within this present that survivors, actors, and fellow narrators are asking us: what for? The meaning of history is also in its purpose. Empirical exactitude alone is not enough. Historical representations—be they books, commercial exhibits or public commemorations—cannot be conceived only as vehicles for the transmission of knowledge. They must establish some relation to that knowledge. Further, not any relation will do. Authenticity is required, lest the representation becomes a fake, a morally repugnant spectacle.

By authenticity, I do not mean a mere simulacrum, a remake of Columbus's caravels, a mock battle on an anniversary, or an exact model of a slave plantation. Neither do I mean a plunge into The Past. For how far can we plunge without trying to become Miguel de Cervantes in the way that Ménard first tried and found cheap and too easy? To be sure, injustices made to previous generations should be redressed: they affect the descendants of the victims. But the focus on The Past often diverts us from the present injustices for which previous generations only set the foundations.

From that viewpoint, the collective guilt of some white liberals toward "the slave past" of the United States, or the "colonial past" of Europe can be both misplaced and inauthentic. As a response to current accusations, it is misplaced inasmuch as these individuals are not responsible for the actions of their chosen ancestors. As a self-inflicted wound, it is comfortable inasmuch as it protects *them* from a racist present.

Indeed, none of us today can be true to Afro-American slavery—whether for or against it—as we can be true to ongoing practices of discrimination. Similarly, individuals in the Old World or in Latin America today cannot be true or false to a colonialism they did not live. What we know about slavery or about colonialism can—should, indeed—increase our ardor in the struggles against discrimination and oppression across racial and national boundaries. But no amount of historical research about the Holocaust and no amount of guilt about Germany's past can serve as a substitute for marching in the streets against German skinheads today. Fortunately, quite a few prominent German historians understand that much.

Authenticity implies a relation with what is known that duplicates the two sides of historicity: it engages us both as actors and narrators. Thus, authenticity cannot reside in attitudes toward a discrete past kept alive through narratives. Whether it invokes, claims, or rejects The Past, authenticity obtains only in regard to current practices that engage us as witnesses, actors, and commentators—including practices of historical narration. That the foundations of such practices were set by our precursors with the added value of their respective power is an inherent effect of the historicity of the human condition: none of us starts with a clean slate. But the historicity of the human condition also requires that practices of power and domination be renewed. It is that renewal that should concern us most, even if in the name of our pasts. The so-called legacies of past horrors—slavery, colonialism, or the Holocaust—are possible only because of that renewal. And that renewal occurs only in the present. Thus, even in relation to The Past our authenticity resides in the struggles of our present. Only in that present can we be true or false to the past we choose to acknowledge.

If authenticity belongs to the present, academic historians—and quite a few philosophers—may have lured themselves into a corner. The traditions of the guild, reinforced by a positivist philosophy of history, forbid academic historians to position themselves regarding the present. A fetishism of the facts, premised on an antiquated model of the natural sciences, still dominates history and the other social sciences. It reinforces the view that any conscious positioning should be rejected as ideological. Thus, the historian's position is officially unmarked: it is that of the nonhistorical observer.

The effects of this stance can be quite ironic. Since historical controversies often revolve on relevance—and therefore, at least in part, on the positioning of the observer—academic historians tend to keep as far away as possible from the historical controversies that most move the public of the day. In the United States, a few have intervened in the historical debates that made news in the early 1990s: the alleged role of Jews as slave owners, the Holocaust, the Alamo, the Smithsonian exhibits on the American West and on Hiroshima, or the Virginia park project.[5] But many more qualified historians have kept public silence on these and similar issues. That silence even extends to debates about the national standards for history that academics seem to have abandoned to pundits and politicians.

To be sure, the distance between scholarly and public discourses in the United States is extreme when compared, for instance, with the situation in France or in Germany.[6] American scholars have largely abandoned the role of public intellectual to pundits and entertainers. But the US extreme tells us something about the continuum to which it belongs. At the heart of the noninvolvement of US historians is the guild's traditional attachment to the fixity of pastness.

Professional historians have made good use of the creation of the past as a distinct entity, a creation that paralleled the growth of their own practice (Le Goff 1992). That practice, in turn, reinforced the belief that made it possible. The more historians wrote about past worlds, the more The Past became real as a separate world. But as various crises of our times impinge upon identities thought to be long established or silent, we move closer to the era when professional historians will have to position themselves more clearly within the present, lest politicians, magnates, or ethnic leaders alone write history for them.

Such positions need not be fixed, nor should they imply the ideological manipulation of empirical evidence. Practicing historians who advocate a history aware of its purpose—from the presentists of the first half of this century to the leftists of the 1970s—never suggested such manipulation.[7] Most of these advocates, however, assumed the possibility of an unambiguous present. With varying degrees of certitude, they envisioned that narratives about the past could expose with utmost clarity positions solidly anchored in the present. We now know that narratives are made of silences, not all of which are deliberate or even perceptible as such within the time of their production. We also know that the present is itself no clearer than the past.

None of these discoveries entails an absence of purpose. They certainly do not entail an abandonment of the search and defense of values that distinguish the intellectual from a mere scholar.[8] Positions need not be eternal in order to justify a legitimate defense. To miss this point is to bypass the historicity of the human condition. Any search for eternity condemns us to the impossible choice between fiction and positivist truth, between nihilism and fundamentalism, which are two sides of the same coin. As we move though the end of the millennium, it will be increasingly tempting to seek salvation by faith alone, now that most deeds seem to have failed.

But we may want to keep in mind that deeds and words are not as distinguishable as we often presume. History does not belong only to its narrators, professional or amateur. While some of us debate what history is or was, others take it in their own hands.

NOTES

Editors' Note: This chapter first appeared as "The Presence in the Past," chapter 5 of *Silencing the Past: Power and the Production of History* (Boston: Beacon Press, 1995), 141–53.

1. Many historians and Civil War buffs had fought the project because they felt that the proposed park would blot out important war sites. Environmentalists, in turn, had raised an uproar about crowding and traffic congestion. In both cases, the loudest objections focused more on the proposed site than on the intrinsic value of the project. In the same tone, Disney's official announcement was that the company would look for a "less controversial" site. Some analysts saw in the announcement a graceful way for Disney to abandon the project altogether (Hofmeister 1994; Pérez-Peña 1994; Turner 1994).

2. I am not assuming that either Ménard or Borges himself espouses or expresses a coherent philosophy or history. I am not even assuming that Borges's main theme here is history. Obviously, I am using the parody within my own frame. I am satisfied, however, that this use is justifiable (for extended treatments of "Pierre Ménard," see Latouche 1989, 170–210; Carilla 1989, 20–92. For Ménard and the history of texts, see Schaeffer 1989, 131–54.

3. For a similar conclusion on the text as literary product drawing from a reading of Borges, see Schaeffer 1989.

4. The divergence between Vidal-Naquet's stance and mine are mostly—but not only—terminological. He calls "memory" a living relation to the past,

in part because he only believes in a scientific history based implicitly on a nineteenth-century model of science. I explicitly reject that model both for the natural sciences and for the systematic historical investigations performed by professionals. For the record, Weill's statement should not be dismissed as the individual complaint of a Jew maladjusted within France's social structure: he is the president of the powerful Sofres group.

5. David McCullough, James McPherson, and David Brian Davis are among the historians who addressed wide audiences on some of these controversies in public forums or in newspapers.

6. In France, leading members of the guild expressed themselves regularly in daily or weekly publications. François Furet or Emmanuel Leroy Ladurie are not penalized for writing in *Le Nouvel Observateur* or *Le Monde*. Some of the most famous names in German history fought the Historiker dispute on the uniqueness of the Holocaust in the pages of daily and weekly newspapers. And the public debate itself was launched by philosopher-sociologist Jürgen Habermas.

7. In the 1970s, some professional historians, notably Jean Chesneaux and Paul Thompson, made a passionate case for academic historians to explicitly position themselves vis-à-vis their present (see Chesneaux 1976; Thompson 1978).

8. See Todorov 1991 on the ethical differences between scholars and intellectuals.

REFERENCES

Borges, Jorge Luis. (1938) 1969. "Pierre Ménard, Author of Don Quixote." In *The Overwrought Urn: A Potpourri of Parodies of Critics Who Triumphantly Present the Real Meaning of Authors from Jane Austen to J. D. Salinger,* edited by C. Kaplan, 17–26. New York: Pegasus.
Carilla, Emilio. 1989. *Jorge Luis Borges autor de 'Pierre Ménard' (y otros estudios borgesianos).* Bogota: Instituto Caro y Cuervo.
Cascardi, A. J. 1984. "Remembering." *Review of Metaphysics* 38: 275–302.
Chesneaux, Jean. 1979. *Du passé faisons table rase.* Paris: Maspero, 1976.
Fukuyama, Francis. 1992. *The End of History and the Last Man.* New York: Free Press.
Hofmeister, Sally. 1994. "Disney Vows to Seek Another Park Site, but Analysts Ask Whether Company Should Go on with Project." *New York Times,* September 30.
Latouche, Raphaël. 1989. "L'oeuvre invisible: Pierre Ménard auteur du Quichotte." In *Borges ou l'hypothèse de l'auteur III,* 170–210. Paris: Balland.
Le Goff, Jacques. 1992. *History and Memory.* New York: Columbia University Press.
Pérez-Peña, Richard. 1994. "Disney Drops Plan for History Theme Park in Virginia." *New York Times,* September 29.

Schaeffer, Jean-Marie. 1989. *Qu'est-ce qu'un genre littéraire?* Paris: Éditions du Seuil.

Styron, William. 1994. "Slavery's Pain, Disney's Gain." *New York Times*, August 4.

Thompson, Paul. 1978. *The Voice of the Past: Oral History*. Oxford: Oxford University Press.

Todorov, Tzvetan. 1991. *Les morales de l'histoire*. Paris: Bernard Grasset.

Turner, Richard. 1994. "Disney to Move Planned Theme Park to 'Less Controversial' Site in Virginia." *Wall Street Journal*, September 29.

Vidal-Naquet, Pierre. 1987. *Les assassins de la mémoire: "Un Eichmann de papier" et autres essais sur le révisionnisme*. Paris: La Découverte.

Weill, Pierre. 1995. "L'anniversaire impossible." *Le Nouvel Observateur*, February 9.

CHAPTER 15

Abortive Rituals

Historical Apologies in the Global Era

PRELUDE: THE CRUSADERS OF FORGIVENESS

They are the crusaders of the twenty-first century. Caught between a present they denounce and a past they did not live, they vow to shape a future in accordance with their faith. Devoted Christians, they chose Jerusalem for their millennial rendezvous, but their march started long before and their hopes will live long after. They believe that faith requires action now more than ever. So from Cologne to Istanbul, from Vienna to Beirut, from Macedonia to Palestine, they followed the path of war, just like other Christians before them.

But contrary to the crusaders of long ago, they did not carry swords. Nor did they carry guns like other Europeans and North Americans before them. Humbly yet honorably, they carried a message. They gave it to the Imam of Cologne, to Turkish delegates to the European Parliament, to passersby in Slovakia, to the mayor of Beirut, and to Chief Rabbi Yisrael Meir Lau of Jerusalem. Again and again, to all Muslims and Jews they met along the road, they repeated that same message: "I am sorry."

The Reconciliation Walk, as its organizers call it, started on Easter Sunday 1996, in Cologne, Germany, the very town from which the First Crusade began its bloody march in the spring of 1096. In a solemn commemoration at the cathedral of Cologne, 150 Christians, mostly evangelical Protestants, vowed to retrace the path of the early crusaders all the way to Jerusalem. Reaching over two thousand miles and nine centuries of tension, they aimed at reconciliation with all non-Christians. Since 1996, more than two thousand participants have joined the initial group. Breaking down into small crews, numbers dwindling or reinforced as they cross unquiet borders, town after town, they have apologized for the crimes committed in the name of Christ since the First Crusade.

To many of us caught in the mundane demands of modern life the Reconciliation Walk may seem like repentance gone amok, historicity gone childish. Yet, we may want to pause and wonder why the marchers seem to have been taken more seriously by the political and religious leaders throughout the Middle East than by those in the countries whence they came. Further, we cannot easily dismiss the walkers' apology on empirical or technical grounds. Their starting point that a historical wrong was committed is a quite reasonable interpretation of the facts we know. Their statement of repentance is in as good a form as any now offered or demanded.[1]

The peculiarity of the Reconciliation Walk comes from the time and road traveled since Pope Urban II gave the initial order for the First Crusade in 1095 in what is now Clairmont-Ferrant. The material traces are thinner, the descent lines more blurred than in most cases of collective apologies. Thus few of us can relate to the need for an apology, let alone think of its modalities, especially from outside of the Middle East. It took a religious sentiment, faith, rather than an abstract principle (such as a transcendental notion of right) or a pragmatic sense of reparation to propel the marchers. Raw faith—if such a thing exists—is what bridges an otherwise insurmountable gap between past and present for these walkers. Yet that others may question this particular bridge only reveals that all apologies require such a temporal bridge. Further, since the difficulty here is the adequacy of that bridge in linking collectivities with spatial-temporal borders that are fuzzy in the extreme, the Reconciliation Walkers, aberrant as they may seem, bear witness to an age where collective apologies are becoming increasingly common.

RITUALS IN HISTORY, RITUALS FOR HISTORY

The Reconciliation Walk is only a small and peculiar case within an ongoing wave of collective apologies. Since the late 1980s an increasing number of collectivities throughout the world seem to face one another, demanding, offering, denying, or rejecting the explicit recognition of guilt for offenses committed from a few years to many centuries ago. Any offer, any request, brings out another one. There is little indication that the wave is likely to stop in the near future.

This essay focuses on the conditions of possibility of that wave. I am not addressing the relative merits of cases on moral or legal grounds—others have engaged in that important exercise. Rather, my interest is in the wave itself as a phenomenon unique to our times, which both reveals and impels new stakes in the construction of collective subject positions and identities—and therefore new takes on historicity. Taking all cases of collective apologies—offered, denied, accepted, or requested—as part of an ongoing trend, I want to explore some of the historical and conceptual constituents of that trend.

Some prime constituents are the subjects involved. Collective apologies in our late modern age imply a transfer to collectivities of the attributes that a dominant North Atlantic discourse had hitherto assigned to the liberal subject. Ever since the independent self emerged in liberal discourse in the seventeenth century, it has accumulated a number of properties and attributes, from identity to free will to personality. I contend that the attribution of features of that liberal self to states, ethnic groups, and nations is a major condition of possibility of collective apologies as late modern rituals.

Second, this transfer of attributes from individual to collective subjects testifies to the changes in historical perception that make it possible. Third, this transfer and those changes project the protagonists against the background of a global stage where the apology takes on its full significance. We may not have reached the universal history dreamed of by Enlightenment thinkers, but collective apologies are increasing in part because offers, demands, denials, or rejections are all projected on to a global stage that is now the ultimate horizon of a new historicity.

In that framework, no case is insignificant on legal merits alone since the task is to explore the conditions that make it possible to enunciate any request, offer, denial, or rejection with some resonance. Indeed, cases where the actual perpetrators or victims of the initial wrong are absent from the scene—of which the Reconciliation March, or plantation slavery in the Americas, however different on other grounds, are archetypes—assume great significance in that context. Clearly, no white person alive today took part in plantation slavery, just as none of the Reconciliation Walkers took part in the Crusades. Similarly, no direct victim of these past wrongs is around to ask for compensation. The moral or legal case for redress—as well as for an admission of guilt—can be made only through a genealogical construction, that is, on a particular composition of the subjects involved and on a particular interpretation of history.

The implication is not that cases with more historical depth are less clear-cut on moral grounds than cases that can firmly stand the test of law—where individual victims, witnesses, and perpetrators are alive and identifiable as individuals. Rather, exactly because of their moot legal prospects, cases that span long periods of time reveal both the needs and the difficulties inherent in the constitution of collective subjects. They expose more clearly the fact that collective apologies are rituals in history, for history, which engage their participants as doers and as narrators, thus on both sides of historicity. Yet collective apologies cannot fulfill the promises of their purported assumptions and fail to reconcile these two sides of historicity even as they claim them both. They are abortive rituals, meant to remain infelicitous.[2]

A PAST FOR THE PRESENT

We can conceptualize apologies as illocutionary events denoting to an addressee the repentance of a speaking subject. As such, they belong to a loose family of related speech acts, the members of which should be differentiated on the basis of the particular affects they claim to project, the kinds of acknowledgments and relations they presume, and the consequences for which they call.[3]

As transformative rituals, apologies always involve time—even apologies between individuals. They mark a temporal transition: wrong done in a time marked as past is recognized as such, and this acknowledgment itself creates or verifies a new temporal plane, a present oriented toward the future. Strictly speaking, I cannot apologize for a wrong being—or about to be—inflicted, although I can excuse or explain myself. I can only apologize for things already done. My apology sets a temporal marker between those things—and the past to which they belong—and a present characterized by my new relation to my interlocutor. It creates a new era: I repent, let us now be friends. Or, it registers that a new era has indeed been launched: I can now tell you how remorseful I am, I was wrong. In short, apologies are premised on the assumption that the state of affairs to which they refer does not, or should not, obtain in the present of the actors involved. In claiming a past, they create pastness.

Pastness is, of course, a relation, in the same way that distance is a relation. In the case of an apology, that relation involves four positions and two

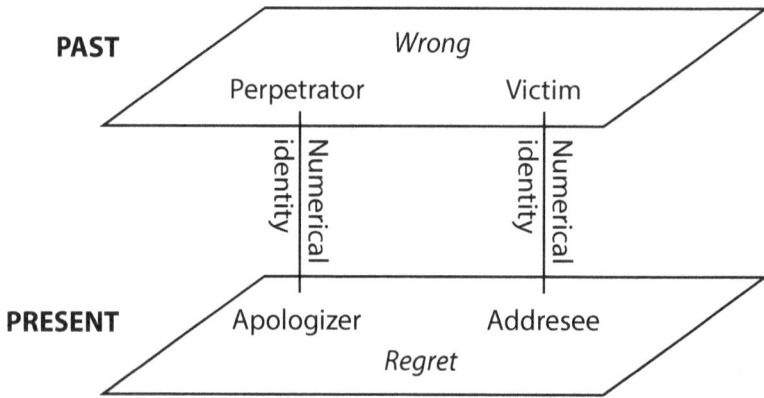

PAST

Wrong

Perpetrator   Victim

identity   Numerical   identity   Numerical

PRESENT

Apologizer   Addresee

Regret

15.1 The structure of an apology.

temporal planes: the perpetrator and the victim in a first temporal plane—the past; and the repentant and the addressee in a second temporal plane—the present. The necessary differentiation of these two temporal planes correlates to a double recognition of numerical identity across time: the perpetrator is the repentant apologizer; the victim is the addressee (figure 15.1).

To put it schematically, as transformative rituals, apologies require at least six distinguishable operations: (1) the establishment of a wrong; (2) the creation of a temporal plane by way of the creation of pastness; (3) a first operation of numerical identity involving perpetrator and apologizer; (4) a second operation involving victim and addressee; (5) an utterance conveying some form of remorse or repentance; (6) the production of a partial or complete erasure, ideally verified by both sides.[4] In this formal scheme, the first two operations set the stage. The last two produce a transformation of that stage. The double recognition of numerical identity (steps 3 and 4), which links the two temporal planes, thus emerges as a necessary condition of the transformation promised by the ritual. Indeed, it distinguishes the apology proper from related speech acts that express commiseration without implicating the speaker in the first temporal plane. At its most felicitous, an apology turns the perpetrator's expressed regret into remorse acknowledged by the addressee.

Two points need to be made about this felicitous performance. First, it is always culturally specific: what obtains as a satisfactory expression of remorse between two parties involved in an automobile accident in New York may not work between two Caribbean peasants involved in a land feud.

Second, the dual need for numerical identity across time is met between two individuals on pragmatic grounds in part because of the need to assume spatiotemporal continuity on both sides.[5] Yet while all human beings need such an assumption of continuity in order to go through their daily lives, the issue of identity through time remains a perplexing one for philosophers since Hume and Locke first reopened it (Hume [1748] 1950; Locke [1690] 1997; Wiggins 1967). What makes any particular "the same" if that particular is going through changes (Ferret 1996)? Further, if that particular is imbued with consciousness, how much does this consciousness account for its sameness (Alexander 1997)? How can I be the same, thus a perpetrator, and yet different, thus repentant?

Whatever the answers we provide to these questions, new problems arise when the particular is a collective subject. To start with, collective subjects never meet each other physically as both collectives and subjects. They cannot therefore assume identity on pragmatic grounds as do individual subjects.

Collective subjects are by definition historical products. They cannot precede their own experience. They are not naturally given. This means that we cannot assume the first temporal plane of a collective apology to be a zero degree of history in which the particulars existed as such in an eternal present. We need to establish their existence within that past. We need to establish when and how our perpetrators—Latin Christendom, the white race, the Japanese nation, or the Hutu *ethnie*—became single historical actors, responsible, as independent subjects, for the wrongs committed in that first temporal order. Second, we need to replicate the operation in the present, aware of the new difficulties of this second temporal order. What is Christendom today, regardless of what it may have been in 1492? And third, only after the first two operations can we try to demonstrate a numerical identity between perpetrator and repentant subject. Christendom has changed, yet it is still the same: it must apologize. Then, of course, we would need to repeat the steps on the other side of the wrong and establish the numerical identity of victim and addressee, to make sure that repentant Christendom is indeed apologizing to the right entity.

In short, when we move from the individual to the collective, that which involved at least six distinguishable operations now requires eight steps, four of which become highly problematic since they involve the construction and continuous identification of collective entities that are necessarily historical. Needless to say, few individuals and even fewer collectivities go through these complicated operations even at times of historical crisis. Historians, philosophers, legal scholars, or political leaders themselves rarely adhere to this tangled procedure and the many steps that it implies.

This, of course, is my point. On purely formal grounds, collective apologies imply more than a simple jump from the one to the many. To be felicitous and transformative, they require a perplexing relation of identity between subjects who are themselves already very difficult to construct as subjects. They further require that we maintain these constructions while recognizing their historical nature.

The difference between agent and subject is crucial here because the basis on which we construct both historical continuity and responsibility—and thus acknowledge the legitimacy of a spokesperson—for collective agents and subjects is different. On pragmatic grounds we do assume the identity of groups and institutions through time, as agents.[6] Indeed, we rightly allow the possibility for an agent who is not an individual person to shoulder some form of responsibility for past actions without assuming an affective register in the encounter between perpetrator and victim. Thus agents representing collectivities can be held accountable, and that accountability is central to the possibility of historical reparations. Yet to speak of subjects is to invoke affective characteristics that are hard to encompass with the public sphere of late liberal representation and accountability—in spite of Habermas (Markell 2000). To put it simply, it is one thing for a state or a bank—as agent—to provide compensation, it is something else for the state—as subject—to commiserate or show remorse. The identity requirements for the two gestures are different.

Not surprisingly, then, collective apologies have not been a hallmark of human history. Indeed, *they have been rather rare*.[7] During most of its history humankind dealt with clashes between groups and the aftermath of these clashes mainly on pragmatic terms. To be sure, morality, justice, and their absence—as lived and defined in specific times and places—played their role in prolonging or ending those clashes. Yet even when such clashes solidified into long-term feuds and enmities, the expression or resolution of these enmities rarely took the new ritualized forms that typify our times. Indeed, an inherent feature of this ritual wave of collective apologies is its very novelty. Why here? Why now?

We catch a glimpse of an answer when we go beyond the easy attraction of the "why" and its linear causality for a richer examination of the "how." If the formal requirements for collective apologies to obtain as felicitous performatives and transformative rituals are so complicated as to make them rare in history, what makes so many apologies historically possible today?

Do current apologies somehow manage to meet the complicated formal requirements outlined above? If not, how do they bypass them?

The public discourse that shapes the formulations of current proposals for or against apologies is revealing here. Why should Germany apologize for the atrocities of the Second World War? Because Germany is not "a normal country," and indeed it may never become one according to Günter Grass, who himself is seen to stand as "the painful consciousness of Germany." Even if the legal grounds for and implications of German collective guilt are complicated, some legal experts acknowledge that an apologetic attitude helps to clean "the moral stain on the German soul." Some Japanese, in turn, reject the proposition of an apology for wrongs committed during the same era because such a collective admission would taint Japanese "dignity." However, such retreat into dignity may make it harder to eradicate "the guilt that haunts Japan." Meanwhile, of course, a minority of North Americans favor an apology for plantation slavery because it may indeed reinstate the soiled dignity of perpetrator or victim.[8]

The repeated references and appeals to dignity, pride, shame, or guilt in the media and in the legal and scholarly literature, point to a symbolic overlap in current debates over collective apologies. Behind that language of an internally renewable guilt is a fundamental assumption about the nature of the collectivities discussed, an assumption reinforced by the language itself.

Collective apologies today circumvent the difficulty of establishing numerical identity across time by setting up their subjects as particular kinds of individuals. Ethnicities, races, states, and especially nations have character, personality, consciousness, will, memories, and desires—notably the desire to join in a new collectivity with similarly inclined individuals. Above and across its inner discordant voices, the discourse of collective apologies tends to treat collectivities as if they were a kind of organic particular. Further, the model for the construction of this new kind of particular is a folk composite of the individual subject of liberal discourse.

THE NORTH ATLANTIC LIBERAL AS COLLECTIVE SUBJECT

Although practices that personalize collectivities by ascribing to them attributes constructed to define or describe individuals may be as old as human society, they took on a different import after the global rise of the North Atlantic in the sixteenth century. As North Atlantic hegemony moved from the Iberian states to Northern Europe, the physical overlap between state and nation, already premised in various versions of the absolutist state, reached a new threshold of both material and symbolic concreteness in the nineteenth century.[9] By the middle of that century, political issues were increasingly couched in nationalist language, and the emerging social sciences, in turn, were becoming increasingly state-centric (Wallerstein et al. 1995). Divergent interests aside, social theorists and politicians both assumed the state-nation conflation and sold it to a general public. The habit of treating collectivities as fixed entities, already entrenched in the spheres of knowledge and power (Wolf 1982), slowly made its way into North Atlantic common sense. The stage was set for collectivities, especially nation-states and ethnic groups—now taken as fixed entities—to be treated as individuals. Yet although some historians and anthropologists ascribed to these individualized collectivities attributes of the subject (such as national character), both the public at large and international law rarely went beyond the need to treat collectivities or institutions such as the state as responsible agents.[10]

Indeed, neither the nineteenth nor the first three-quarters of the twentieth century—which saw an increase in demands for international reparations—witnessed anything close to the wave of apologies that marks our times. Again, this is not surprising when we look back at the formal requirements for a collective apology to obtain as a felicitous performative. Since visions of the person vary considerably across and within populations (Carrithers et al. 1985), any vision of the individual as even remotely constituted in history doubles the requirements for the construction of a collective self that could survive its own history. In short, most visions of the individual make it nearly impossible to move easily from agent to subject and to generate a collective apology as a felicitous transformative ritual.

But let us suppose that the individual self is an unencumbered one, existing prior to its environment and fully formed on its own terms. Collective selves with full attributes of the person become much easier to build on that model since all historical constituents of—and limits to—a fixed identity of the subject have disappeared.

Current collective apologies are premised exactly on that supposedly autoregulating and unencumbered self. Those who propose or request them increasingly ascribe to institutions and collectivities attributes unique to the subject—such as mood, memory, moral responsibility, and feelings, down to the possibility of repentance—rather than the practical liability and communal responsibility through time that has long been an attribute of agents. Further, the current wave of apologies does not simply treat collectivities as individuals but as a particular type of individual; more exactly, as a liberal person. Finally, *not any form of liberalism will do*. Rather, behind the discourse about collective apologies today stands the figure of the person in the composite vision of classical liberalism. It is a vision that ties Locke to Kant rather than Montesquieu to Rousseau or to current proponents of a more communitarian liberalism (Sandel 1982; Shklar 1984; Taylor 1992; Walzer 1983). It is a liberalism of rights rooted in the individual. The collectivities projected in these apologies are not merely subjects. Rather, they are subjects with specific attributes that evoke in turn or together the subject of the market, the subject of civil or criminal law, the ego of psychology, and indeed, the ultimate subject of liberal individualism, an individual united by the memory of past actions yet unburdened by any history that precedes its consciousness.

A caveat is in order. I am not suggesting a single vision of the self among individualist philosophers, let alone a single descent line between intellectual constructions and a coherent popular version now consciously shared by all the populations involved. I am not claiming global cultural change as intellectual history trickling down to the masses. Rather, I would insist that these theorists and these populations overlap through time and space by way of practices—including linguistic or other highly symbolic practices—which, in turn, reinforce, cancel, or modulate certain philosophical viewpoints. Practices both require and impose a vision. They help to rearrange a particular field of forces.

If we see the global domination of the North Atlantic since the sixteenth century as setting up exactly a unique field of forces—perhaps the first global one in human history (Trouillot 2003)—we can also see that practices embedded in this field of forces generate or reinforce conceptual overlaps. From the Caribbean to China, from the spread of plantation work regimes to the diffusion of modern state forms, from the rise of English as lingua franca to the daily renewals of Evangelical commitments, overlapping bundles of practices continue to push forward particular visions of the self.

Central here is the spread of North Atlantic Christianity and its penitent practices. In spite of denominational differences in liturgy and theology, these penitent practices share fundamental assumptions about the redemptive possibilities of singular individuals and the capacity of particular speech acts to actualize this redemption. Yet more obviously material practices, such as wage labor, also presume and reinforce particular framings of the individual. The more such practices spread, the more the visions they embody—and the core they share—compete, on the ground, with pre-existing or parallel visions of the self. Whatever dominant notions of the self may have been in China, Kashmir, or sub-Saharan Africa (Carrithers et al. 1985), these localized notions must now accommodate a composite figure of growing international reach.

Key to that composite figure is the unity of consciousness long ago assumed by Locke on the basis of memory of past actions. Here again a reading of the media is useful. Thus a discussion of Jane Taylor's play, *Ubu and the Truth Commission*, by Desmond Tutu and Wole Soyinka at Emory University boiled down to their conceptualization of the nation as individual, with Tutu arguing that the nation was a single individual both guilty and innocent and Soyinka advocating the position that the nation was composed of two individuals, only one of whom was guilty.[11] Closer to Tutu's position, a commentator in the *Glasgow Herald* reads the apology that British prime minister Tony Blair offered for the Great Famine of Ireland in terms of a soul-searching exercise into memory land:

> The apology that Tony Blair made in Ireland last year for Britain's role in the Great Famine had been a long time coming. It had taken a century-and-a-half for one country to look into its soul and admit its crime against another. The Irish nation, however, has been no swifter to look into its own soul to examine its reactions to that holocaust.[12]

The soul of nations—quite a different construct from Montesquieu's spirit—has become, at once, the site of that memory-consciousness and the engine behind both the recognition of past failures and the will to reach a higher moral plane. One need not espouse all the tenets of postmodernism to note with appropriate humor that in the media, debates about collective apologies and notions of soul and character have become pastiches of pastiches. Thus "nearly 136 years after President Lincoln signed the Emancipation Proclamation, slavery remains the unhealed wound on the American soul." Thus newspapers in both South Africa and the United States attribute to Bishop Desmond Tutu the belief that "acts of contrition are good for the soul of the 'rainbow nation.'" But "is Japan on the verge of baring its soul?"[13]

The "soul" here is free to choose. Character is self-designed. Inner regulation is in command of change. The collectivities projected in the current wave of apologies are framed outside of history—except, of course, the history of the encounter on which the apology is premised. Not that this framing denies all historicities. Rather, it requires a particular kind of historicity, notably the possibility of freezing chunks of an allegedly unified past, as in the storage model of memory and history (Trouillot 1995, 14–18). In other words, history is both denied and heralded.

On the one hand, history is denied as an experience constitutive of the collectivity: no structure precedes the subject. Thus, not accidentally, the current wave favors collectivities assumed to be altogether obvious, eternal, and continuous through biological reproduction, such as races and ethnic groups. On the other hand, the history that ties the initial wrong to the possibility of—or need for—an apology is brandished as the sole relevant story. Steeped in a language of blood and soul, collectivities are now defined by the wrongs they committed and for which they should apologize, or by the wrongs they suffered and for which they should receive apology. Further, the historical necessity of joining a collectivity of collectivities best known as "the international community" prompts these newly redefined subjects to play out the liberal social contract on a global scale. Collective apologies today are global apologies inasmuch as they are projected onto a global stage.

LOCAL STORIES, GLOBAL STAGE

The spectacular developments in communications that marked the last two decades of the twentieth century have made possible the creation of a virtual yet global stage on which historical actors—both individual and collective—play out scenarios that are shaped in part by the nature of the stage itself. The "global village" may be an illusion but, if so, it is an illusion through which an increasingly large part of humanity takes consciousness of the new links and hierarchies created by an unprecedented alliance between capital and technologies of communication. The "international community" may be communal only in name, shaped as it is by sheer economic and military force from the North Atlantic, but it remains a powerful trope for the recognition of a new moment in world history.

Particular to this moment is the virtual acceptance that "the whole world is looking at me," a privilege once reserved for the most powerful, who even then retained the right to reject that gaze. That gaze, now virtual yet increasingly hard to escape, global in its pretensions yet parochial in its instrumentalities, frames all discussions of collective responsibility today. It thus helps to set the stage on which collective apologies are performed.

Future historians may debate if, when, and how our newest born imagined collective, "the international community," solidified in the minds of a majority of humankind. One can safely suggest that the notion has yet to be inscribed fully in the daily routine of a majority of human beings. At the same time, the endless repetition of this vague and changing concept each and every time collectivities, states, or trans-state institutions are involved, the repeated tactical deployment of the phrase, gives this imagined super-community practical and symbolic value.[14] Media references are so frequent that examples may be superfluous here: mentions of the omnipresent "international community" now punctuate all discussions of collective apologies, even those otherwise framed in the most parochial terms.

Further, similar mentions accompany the construction of collective subjects even in cases where the reference does not seem to make much sense on practical grounds. Thus in reversing a federal court decision and allowing three war crime cases to resume, the Canadian Supreme Court felt compelled to admonish the lower judges: "What is at stake here, in however small a measure, is Canada's reputation as a responsible member of the community of nations."[15] Beyond the legal merit of the case, the highest judicial body of the Commonwealth was pointing to the symbolic value of the virtual global gaze.

Quite differently, yet as evocatively, the reprobatory gaze of this newly imagined international community is constantly evoked in reference to political leaders—notably in the south—whom we know to have the tacit approval of the leaders of that community or who clearly care little about such approval. Thus, rejoicing at the creation of the East Timor Independent National Commission on Human Rights, yet doubting its effectiveness, a local commentator warned the Indonesian authorities that they "should realize that they are now being tried by world public opinion."[16]

It is in front of this nebulous entity that collective apologies are being requested, denied, accepted, or rejected. Part witness, part audience, this international community functions like a Greek chorus in late modern virtual reality. It is the ultimate listener, presumed yet unseen by the actors, so limited as enforcer yet so powerful as a trope. Some of its limitations come from the nature of apologies as rituals. If, as mentioned above, felicitous apologies between individuals always obtain in a culturally specific context, by whose cultural criteria should a collective apology be judged felicitous? Appeals to the international community as witness presume but cannot deliver this alleged "global culture."

Still, with the development in communications, this assumed international audience helps remove one major obstacle to the performance: the difficulty for collectivities to meet face to face. The virtual chorus is there to fill the gap in communication between the groups involved, wherever they are. Only through it do the actors speak to one another. Thus, it is unfair to ask if Mr. Clinton's near apology for slavery was directed at Africans or at Blacks in the United States.[17] It was directed at neither group, although it spoke of, and implicated, both of them. Mr. Clinton spoke to the world in an internationally televised speech.

Central here is that world, a ghost community, yet the calibrator of a relevance deemed at the same time unique and universal. For on the victim's side one must claim both a unique memory of a unique experience and the universal relevance of that uniqueness.[18] On the perpetrator's side one must deny or validate that very same combination with the whole world witnessing. The internet plays its role in this disrobing of souls on a world stage: an amazing number of apologies have inspired web pages, pro and con, official and unauthorized. The Reconciliation Walkers, although harking back to the Middle Ages, keep the world informed of their activities through web technology. The South African Truth Commission has set up a web page, a virtual "confession box," so that white South Africans can publicly yet privately apologize for apartheid. The enhanced gaze, in turn, feeds new symbolic demands. The debate about slavery in the United States provoked a demand for a Jim Crow apology. Thus the hit parade of victims and penitents continues, each claim or denial topping the other.

It is tempting but wrong to think that such victims are not real because of the display. The very concrete issue of reparations does matter, at some times more than others. Yet there is an inherent irony—as well as many practical obstacles—in framing that issue in the language of collective apologies. The very discourse of liberal individualism, the tropes of which now allow for the projection of apologetic collective subjects, is fundamentally opposed to the recognition of collective rights, including therefore reparative "affirmative" actions. Further, we need to sever the matter of reparations from the linear relation between time and responsibility that assumes that the effects of past wrongs are necessarily more concrete when the actual victims are still on the ground. That approach rests on a legalistic framework and on a notion of guilt, both of which reproduce the reduction of collectivities to individuals. Yet just as historical authenticity can obtain only in the present of the actors (Trouillot 1995, 148–51), historical responsibility cannot hark back to an original sin that the collective-individual supposedly committed. Rather, it needs to take into account the structures of privilege unleashed by a history of power and domination and to evaluate the current losses induced by the reproduction of these structures.[19]

In short, the matter of collective reparations cannot be assessed on the basis of supposedly cold and ahistorical standards of justice shared by a suddenly unified world. At the very least, it requires an active notion of justice (Sandel 1982; Shklar 1990; Walzer 1983; Yack 1996). At best, it should be addressed frontally as a historical and *political* issue.

Yet the dual tendency to present passive justice and shared individual guilt as the defining moments of collective apologies, while stressing the merits of globalization, functions exactly as an obstacle to any such political debate about the reproduction of historical structures of which globalization itself is an example (Trouillot 2003). Just as the rhetoric of sharing pain within state boundaries obscures relations of power in the national imaginary (Berlant 1999), the emphasis on shared feelings of remorse obscures the reproduction of worldwide structures of inequality. The emphasis on passive justice, in turn, sets up the current wave of apologies as the expression of a global legal sea change with ritual overtones. However, that legalistic framework cannot reconcile its universalistic pretensions and the ritualistic and affective dimensions of the apologetic gesture. Apologies are inherently about affect. Yet liberalism encounters overwhelming difficulties in "making affect safe for democracy" (Markell 2000). To be sure, the legal framework within which the cases that now involve collective apologies are argued is changing fast, both within and across state boundaries. In addition, notions of sovereignty and polity keep changing. These two sets of changes, in turn, parallel efforts to redeploy affect within or across the laws of nations. Yet jurisprudence is not the drive behind the wave. Rather, that wave can be read as the ritual overflow of a political impasse in this moment of world history when the inability to face structures of inequality—or even to find a language that describes those structures and their consequences—eventuates in the repetition of gestures that cannot meet their own criteria of performance. From within that perspective, both the ritual and the forensic difficulties of collective apologies reflect the global spread and the unevenness of late liberalism. I will conclude by insisting on the consequences of that unevenness for collective apologies as rituals.

ABORTIVE RITUAL

From a symbolic viewpoint, indeed, collective apologies offer an inherent ambiguity: the request, the offer, the rejection or the acceptance of an apologetic gesture is deemed to be felicitous inasmuch as it claims to tie two collective subjects, yet it is incapable of fulfilling that claim because of the nature of the subjects involved.

The fundamental problem is not one of hypocrisy, although sheer hypocrisy does play a role in the construction of the international community as Greek chorus.[20] My point, however, is subtler. Apologies can be read as rituals in the strictly anthropological sense of a regulated, stylized, routinized, and repetitive performance that tends to have both demonstrative and transformative aspects. Their transformative aspect depends fundamentally on a dual identity relation across temporal planes, easily met on pragmatic grounds in individual apologies. Yet in collective apologies, identity is always questionable. It is hard to establish on formal grounds, hard to assume on pragmatic ones. The problem is bypassed through formulas that patch upon collective subjects attributes of a particular kind of liberal individual. Yet the repetition of these formulas has yet to convince the populations involved that the problem has been solved. Think about going to a mass not doubting the sincerity of the priest, but doubting whether or not he is truly a priest regardless of what he himself may think. Beyond the matter of Mr. Clinton's own sincerity, a common point of discussion in the debate about his near apology for plantation slavery was whether or not he had the power to apologize for it. Or even commiserate. To whom? And, especially, in whose name?

Until and unless the liberal formulas now fundamental in the changing constitution of collective subjects manage to convince the populations on both sides that identity obtains in ways that make the performance meaningful, collective apologies will have little transformative power. For now at least, they are born without the capacity to meet their inherent purpose. The very formulas they use to create their collective subjects—the attribution of the features of the liberal individual—though successful in placing these subjects on stage, make it impossible for them to act. Thus collective apologies are meant not to succeed—not because of the possible hypocrisy of some of the actors but because their very conditions of emergence deny the possibility of a transformation. They are abortive rituals.

In that context, the Reconciliation Walk, which appears as one of the oddest apologies within the current waves and with which this essay began, takes on a different significance. "We may not be guilty of the Crusaders' sins, but are nevertheless responsible to repair the damage in any way we can" says Lynn Green, an early organizer from Britain.[21] The problem with the Reconciliation Walkers is not only in the distance between the alleged wrong and the present. It also inheres in their determination to bridge that gap and to assume on both sides identities that are impossible to demonstrate on logical grounds or to make up on pragmatic grounds. The walkers are true believers. They mean their apology. Unlike most current cases of apologies offered, rejected, or denied, their whole enterprise makes sense only if it is meaningful to them. They are indeed performing what is, at least in their own minds, a felicitous ritual, a mid- if not premodern religious dance with full transformative power. Perhaps they convinced some of the individuals whom they met face to face, as opposed to their internet interlocutors; but can they convince any collectivity? The rest of the world chuckles: We never *really* meant this, did we?

NOTES

Editors' Note: This chapter first appeared as "Abortive Rituals: Historical Apologies in the Global Era," *Interventions: International Journal of Postcolonial Studies* 2, no. 2 (2000): 171–86.

1. "Nine hundred years ago, our forefathers carried the name of Jesus Christ in battle across the Middle East. . . . On the anniversary of the First Crusade, we also carry the name of Christ. We wish to retrace the footsteps of the Crusaders in apology for their deeds and in demonstration of the true meaning of the Cross. We deeply regret the atrocities committed in the name of Christ by our predecessors. We renounce greed, hatred and fear, and condemn all violence done in the name of Jesus Christ." [*Editors' Note:* Trouillot did not provide a source for this quotation.]

2. The conceptualizations of the past, of history and historical authenticity, as well as the crucial differentiation between subject and agent that inform this essay, are all developed more fully in Trouillot 1995.

3. In English vernacular, the noun *apology* (even more than the French *excuse* or the Spanish *excusa*) covers a wide range of speech acts, not all of which denote a repentant subject. Similarly, much like the French *désolé*, the adjective *sorry* can express from sadness and sympathy to commiseration and contrition, requiring Spanish translations as different as *triste* and *arrepentido*. Clearly, not all instances where these words are used meet the criteria for a formal apology as conceptualized here. However, the family resemblance between these various acts creates a space for ambiguity crucial to the following discussion.

4. Of course, this formal order does not necessarily reproduce the actual chronology of all apologies.

5. I wronged my neighbor yesterday. I apologize this morning as we bump into each other on our way to work. In so doing, I am assuming that my neighbor

is my neighbor by eliminating all other possibilities as too complicated. There is no way for me to *know*, but I need that assumption for the continuity of my routine.

6. I expect my bank to honor my checks regardless of changes in its personnel. On agents, actors, and subjects, see Trouillot 1995, 23.

7. There is no record that apologies between human collectivities immediately and automatically followed the quite ancient recognition of such collectivities. Nor did collective apologies become normalized in the nineteenth century when the consolidation of the ideal of the nation-state placed specific names, and putatively solid borders and identities, throughout the North Atlantic.

8. I have synthesized here a number of articles, mostly from print media. See "Un citoyen écrivain," *Le Monde*, October 1, 1999; "Guilt Haunts Japan," *New York Times*, November 30, 1998.

9. Louis XIV's famous "L'Etat c'est moi" assumes a process of francization that dates back to at least Francis I. The long process of Spanish "unification" suggests similar assumptions. Indeed, it is against the background of France and Spain as specters that Machiavelli set up a unified Italy as both an assumption and a wish to fulfill.

10. Academic disciplines played different supportive roles in different times and places. For instance, from the 1930s to the 1980s, the most popular versions of North American anthropology promoted in different ways notions of culture as closed, integrated, or personality-like systems, twice removed from the sociological, playing an indirect yet important role in reaffirming the treatment of collectivities as a kind of individual (e.g., Benedict 1946; Geertz 1973).

11. Special thanks to Brian Axel for providing me with a videotape of that debate.

12. "A Time to Live, a Time to Die, a Time to Talk," *Glasgow Herald*, December 10, 1998.

13. "Book reviews," *Boston Globe*, September 27, 1998; "White South Africans Apologize for Apartheid via Internet," *Arizona Republic*, January 4, 1998; "Stop the Denial, Says Hosokawa; Prime Minister Wants Japan to Face Its Past," *Los Angeles Times*, August 17, 1993. See also "The Far East," BBC *Summary of World Broadcasts*, September 24, 1984; "China Still Trails Russia in What Matters Most," Editorial Desk, *New York Times*, July 2, 1998; "Comment," *Independent* (London), February 15, 1999.

14. To be sure, the notion harks back to the Age of Revolutions when various documents from France, the United States, or Haiti took "humanity" as an audience and the "opinion(s) of mankind" as an arbiter.

15. "Nazi Cases to Resume," *Canadian Jewish News*, October 1, 1997.

16. "More Problems in East Timor," *Jakarta Post*, April 20, 1999.

17. "Clinton's Comments on Slavery and on Mistreatment of Africa Seemed Directed at African-Americans, not Africans," *Arizona Republic*, March 29, 1998.

18. For an incisive discussion of that model in relation to the Holocaust, see Chaumont 1997; see also Trigano 1989.

19. As I put it elsewhere: "The historicity of the human condition requires that practices of power and domination be renewed. It is that renewal that should concern us most, even in the name of our pasts. The so-called legacies of past Horrors—slavery, colonialism, or the Holocaust—are possible only because of that renewal. And that renewal occurs only in the present. Thus, even in relation to The Past, our authenticity resides in the struggles of our present. Only in that present can we be true or false to the past we choose to acknowledge" (Trouillot 1995, 151).

20. To be sure, couching the issues in terms of a collective blame that clearly cannot be shared, the legalistic frame, and the liberal drive behind the wave all revive the suggestion of an inherent connection between hypocrisy and liberal democracy (Shklar 1984; Thompson 1996). For instance, when P. W. Botha toured Europe in 1985, members of the party that accompanied him confided to journalists that their most pleasurable discovery was what they saw as European hypocrisy vis-à-vis South African apartheid. "Europe no longer really cared about apartheid. European leaders had gone through the motions of criticism, but were now making it clear that this was all it was: a ritual" ("Fighting Talk on Apartheid—But No Action," *Manchester Guardian Weekly*, March 31, 1985). "Ritual" in that journalistic language suggests a conscious dissimulation, hypocrisy at its fullest.

21. *Nashville Tennessean*, June 27, 1999.

REFERENCES

Alexander, Ronald G. 1997. *The Self, Supervenience and Personal Identity*. Aldershot, UK: Ashgate.
Benedict, Ruth. 1946. *The Chrysanthemum and the Sword: Patterns of Japanese Culture*. Boston: Houghton Mifflin.
Berlant, Lauren. 1999. "The Subject of True Feeling: Pain, Privacy, and Politics." In *Cultural Pluralism: Identity Politics and the Law*, edited by Austin Sarat and Thomas R. Kearns, 49–83. Ann Arbor: University of Michigan Press.
Candau, Joël. 1998. *Mémoire et identité*. Paris: Presses universitaires de France.
Carrithers, Michael, Steven Collins, and Steven Lukes, eds. 1985. *The Category of the Person: Anthropology, Philosophy, History*. Cambridge: Cambridge University Press.

Chaumont, Jean-Michel. 1997. *La concurrence des victimes: Génocide, identité, reconnaissance*. Paris: La Découverte.

Ferret, Stéphane. 1996. *Le bateau de Thésée: Le problème de l'identité à travers le temps*. Paris: Éditions de Minuit.

Geertz, Clifford. 1973. *The Interpretation of Cultures*. New York: Basic Books.

Hume, David. (1748) 1950. *An Inquiry concerning Human Understanding*. Indianapolis: Bobbs-Merrill.

Locke, John. (1690) 1997. *An Essay concerning Human Understanding*. New York: Penguin.

MacIntyre, Alasdair C. 1981. *After Virtue: A Study in Moral Theory*. Notre Dame, IN: University of Notre Dame Press.

Markell, Patchen. 2000. "Making Affect Safe for Democracy? On Constitutional Patriotism." *Political Theory* 28, no. 1: 38–63.

Rorty, Richard. 1983. "Postmodernist Bourgeois Liberalism." *Journal of Philosophy* 80: 583–89.

Sandel, Michael. 1982. *Liberalism and the Limits of Justice*. Cambridge: Cambridge University Press.

Shklar, Judith N. 1984. *Ordinary Vices*. Cambridge, MA: Harvard University Press.

Taylor, Charles. 1992. *Multiculturalism and "The Politics of Recognition": An Essay*. Princeton, NJ: Princeton University Press.

Thompson, Dennis F. 1996. "Hypocrisy and Democracy." In *Liberalism without Illusions: Essays on Liberal Theory and the Political Vision of Judith N. Shklar*, edited by Bernard Yack, 173–90. Chicago: University of Chicago Press.

Trigano, Schmuel. 1989. "Les juifs comme peuple à lépreuve de la Shoah." Special issue, *Pardès: Penser Auschwitz* 9–10.

Trouillot, Michel-Rolph. 1995. *Silencing the Past: Power and the Production of History*. Boston: Beacon Press.

Trouillot, Michel-Rolph. 2003. *Global Transformations: Anthropology and the Modern World*. New York: Palgrave Macmillan.

Wallerstein, Immanuel, et al. 1995. *Open the Social Sciences: Report of the Gulbenkian Commission on the Restructuring of the Social Sciences*. Palo Alto, CA: Stanford University Press.

Walzer, Michael. 1983. *Spheres of Justice: A Defense of Pluralism and Equality*. New York: Basic Books.

Wiggins, David. 1967. *Identity and Spatio-temporal Continuity*. Oxford: Blackwell.

Wolf, Eric R. 1982. *Europe and the People without History*. Berkeley: University of California Press.

Yack, Bernard, ed. 1996. *Liberalism without Illusions: Essays on Liberal Theory and the Political Vision of Judith N. Shklar*. Chicago: University of Chicago Press.

CHAPTER 16

The Interrupted March to Democracy

The first mass demonstrations against the regime, in 1984, were food riots during which provincial slum dwellers attacked customhouses and the warehouses of charitable organizations where food was stored or reported to be stored. It is no accident that the riots snowballed in the old port-city of Gonaïves, now a dusty provincial town wedged between a bay and two rocky chains of hills, and remarkable primarily for the size of its slums and its isolation from the hinterland that had once provided its daily food. The first slogans, prudently limited to "Aba lamizè!" ("Down with poverty!"), soon evolved into cries of "Aba Duvalier!" Well aware of the unbridled corruption that marked the Duvalier regimes, Haitians had for long placed the responsibility for their poverty on the dictatorship. Yet while some peasants could fall back on household production of a few garden crops—even if they still lived below the threshold of subsistence—the mushrooming lumpen of the towns, freshly born of that peasantry, had lost both their gardens and their sense of political isolation. Now that they were more conscious of a national life, they also paid more attention to the occupants of the National Palace.

THE PERCEPTION OF INDIFFERENCE

In the 1970s, Haitians had seen the young Duvalier as an indolent playboy who cared more about his cars, his girlfriends, and his music lessons than about the burdens of his office. Yet because of his youth, his style, and his reputation for being somewhat obtuse, and especially because he was visibly controlled by prominent figures of the Duvalierist old guard (including his mother and his sister Marie-Denise), Jean-Claude Duvalier enjoyed the indulgence of many otherwise disgruntled citizens. Criticism of his government in the press or on the streets during this "liberal" phase of his tenure often bypassed him personally.[1]

This perception changed sharply after Duvalier's marriage to Michèle Bennett in 1980. As he gradually removed the Duvalierist old guard from the centers of decision-making, he appeared increasingly responsible, if not for the unpopular decrees of his new appointees, at least for the fact of having appointed them. Further, and more important, his wife quickly came to symbolize his presidency in the eyes of the people.

The masses knew of the regime's indifference. Michèle Bennett worsened the regime's image with an exaggerated arrogance and a sense of wanton greed. The presidential couple and their new cronies of middle- and lower-middle-class origin tried to outdo in luxurious expenditures the traditional bourgeoisie with whom they now mixed. Nouveaux riches themselves, they spurned the nouveaux riches of the two preceding decades, whose position and insatiable consumption they had inherited. They chased out earlier Duvalierists, who looked too *classes moyennes* in their eyes. Led by the light-skinned First Lady, they systematically courted light-skinned individuals who had—or claimed—"bourgeois" connections.

The desire to act "bourgeois" overnight put the Bennett-Duvalier clan under a spotlight. Intimates of the presidential couple boasted of personal expenses covered by a Treasury increasingly dependent on consumption taxes and US support. Everyone who cared knew how much it cost to remodel the couple's residential quarters or to maintain the bar at their weekend retreat. Such expenditures, and the "creole pig" affair, came to symbolize the regime's indifference to the masses.[2] Ostentatious presidential parties, televised on presidential demand, showed officials and bourgeois alike flaunting expensive designer gowns, jewels, champagne, and caviar.[3] In the middle of still another food shortage, in 1985, Michèle Duvalier returned from a shopping spree in Paris accompanied by reports in the US media that she had spent $1.7 million in two weeks. Those and similar reports spread more rapidly than even Mme. Duvalier might have wished: with the new national roads and major improvements in telecommunications, Haiti had become a truly "national space." Words and images meant to impress certain segments of the population now reached unintended audiences. In the streets of the provincial towns, despair turned into anger, and anger into defiance.

DEFYING THE GUNS

That defiance paralleled what many people saw as the growing independence of two national institutions formerly subdued by the Duvalierist state: the Catholic church and the army. Cornered by grassroots Protestant missions, which had made large inroads among the lower classes during the 1970s and early 1980s, Catholic bishops had allowed—more or less reluctantly—the spread of socially oriented ministries, and activities so markedly different from traditional Catholic practice that Haitians soon dubbed them *ti-legliz*—the little churches. During the 1960s, François Duvalier's offensive against the national institutions and the "nationalization" of the Haitian clergy had led to changes in the class composition of that clergy. Up until then, Haitian priests constituted a minority within the church, and most of them came from traditionally intellectual or professional families, well-rooted in Port-au-Prince or the provincial towns. By 1980, a majority of the Catholic priests were Haitian, and a majority of these came from more modest backgrounds than their pre-Duvalier predecessors. They were at the forefront of the ti-legliz movement, increasingly steering Catholic discourse toward a message of social justice, a mild version of liberation theology adapted to the repressive character of the country. That message received an unexpected boost from Pope John Paul II during his 1983 visit. From then on, the Conférence Episcopale (the formal body that included all the bishops) joined the ti-legliz. Religious radio stations, especially the Port-au-Prince–based Radio Soleil, undertook a systematic if modest politicization of the populace, infusing a civic discourse within the "national space" newly created by increased centralization and improvements in transport and telecommunications.

At the same time, the higher echelons of the army appeared increasingly neutral. Rumors of open disobedience to presidential orders, and even of impending coups d'état by some of the higher brass, spread in 1984 and 1985. Such rumors may have been wishful thinking on the part of those who spread them. But they were believed in part because many officers—especially those of lower-middle-class origin who had risen from the rank-and-file during the first phase of Duvalierism—had lost their enthusiasm to defend at all costs a regime now symbolized by Michèle Bennett. Further, many among the higher ranks believed that the president's reactions to the early signs of disquiet only served to irritate the populace.

Indeed, Jean-Claude Duvalier, advised by his wife and his youngest and most ambitious ministers, at first chose to respond to the popular discontent only with increased repression. Soldiers and elite battalions of the militia shot point-blank at demonstrators and closed down radio stations, including Radio Soleil, which by then had become the key symbol of anti-Duvalierist resistance. This overreaction seemed counterproductive to both past and current allies. Some prominent colonels and some civilian members of the Duvalierist old guard, for instance, favored a two-pronged response that would include carefully hedged concessions to popular demands. Resident US officials in turn reacted so ambivalently to the new developments that they were associated with the new wave of repression in the popular perception. In Washington, however, the State Department tried to distance itself from its client's latest tactics. As demonstrations grew in size and intensity in 1985, so did Washington's public disapproval.

Pressured by allies and foes alike and surprised at the quiet withdrawal of many of his father's traditional collaborators, Jean-Claude Duvalier wavered. Momentum shifted irreversibly from the government to the demonstrators in the streets. Government measures were contradictory, shifting according to the fluctuating fortunes of individuals within the cabinet and the polyvalent reading of Washington's own contradictory signals. In early 1985, the government approved legislation allowing the existence of political parties, denied until then, and trumpeted the release of thirty-six political prisoners. Some press organs were allowed to function one week, and then closed down the next. In July 1985, mostly because of pressures from the US Congress to hold new elections, Duvalier conducted a mock referendum on the basis of which he claimed renewed legitimacy. Discontent failed to subside; so did repression.

Then, on November 27, the army shot four schoolchildren in the streets of Gonaïves. The murder not only exacerbated demonstrators there—Gonaïves had been the site of one of the earliest food riots—it fueled public protest throughout the country. The government's clumsy attempt on December 5 to stop the flow of information by once more shutting down the now legendary Radio Soleil misfired. As protests grew despite constant killings and beatings, what remained of the Duvalier team continued to waver. On December 31, 1985, Duvalier revamped the cabinet and, in early January, announced a 10 percent reduction in the price of basic commodities controlled by the state, notably flour, cooking oil, and diesel fuel. Demonstrations nevertheless continued unabated. On January 26, 1986, the government dissolved the "political police," the nucleus of a *makout* network that gathered information on dissidents and engineered many of the repressive tactics, and whose existence the regime had until then denied.

This was too little, too late. Roadblocks had sprung up all over the country. Some provincial towns held demonstrations daily, in spite of indiscriminate shootings and beatings by the armed forces. On January 27, the day after the official disbanding of the political police, the number of demonstrators reached a reported peak of 40,000 in the northern town of Cap-Haïtien (pop. 65,000). Three days later, US presidential spokesman Larry Speakes announced that the government of Haiti had collapsed and that the leadership, including Duvalier, had fled the country.

The Haitian president quickly denied the news and suggested, in a public message, that his regime was "as strong as a monkey's tail." In part to measure the depth of the dissent, in part to prove that he was still in control, on Monday, February 3, the president joined his wife in an impromptu tour of Port-au-Prince, the ultimate scene of all Haitian political struggle— and until then the only quiet urban area in the country. But a majority of the Port-au-Prince masses, emboldened by the false news of the government's collapse, had finally taken to the streets. On February 7, 1986, Jean-Claude Duvalier and his wife left Haiti with their immediate family and a small group of followers.

DUVALIERISM AFTER DUVALIER

Good news about Haiti has repeatedly been premature, beginning with Larry Speakes's curious announcement of January 1986. Duvalier was replaced by a National Council of Government (CNG), a military-controlled regime led by General Henri Namphy, the chief of the armed forces. Within a week, there were numerous announcements, notably by the US State Department, that the CNG would lead Haiti on the road to democracy. President Reagan promised increased US support "as this interim government moves forward to institute democracy." US support indeed came, but history proved the prognosis about democracy hasty. The Reagan administration granted $2.8 million in military aid for the CNG's first year. A joint letter from human rights organizations to then US Secretary of State George Schultz asserted later that the aid had only served "to strengthen the tendency of the CNG to violate the rights of the citizens." By April 1987, while signs of support from Washington increased, there were as many demonstrators in the streets of Port-au-Prince as there had been in the last days of Duvalier. By the end of its first year in office the CNG, generously helped by the US taxpayers' money, had openly gunned down more civilians than Jean-Claude Duvalier's government had done in fifteen years.

The state was not alone in its use of violence. Popular calls for a *dechoukaj* (uprooting) of the former ruling team were followed by summary judgments and executions of Duvalierists openly carried out by a civilian mob. The dechoukaj also included the removal from office, by force or by popular demand, of known Duvalierists. But many observers and participants came to realize that this brand of popular "justice," which started a few hours after Duvalier's departure and continued well into the hot months of July and August, touched only the small fry of the Duvalierist machine. Understandably, most of the vigilantes were from the urban slums; equally understandably, the most important supporters of the deposed president were not. The latter were protected from the former by the government or by relatives and friends. Reputed criminals were quietly allowed to take the road to exile; others felt so secure that they did not even bother to leave. Private "justice" continued to operate until at least the end of 1986, especially in the countryside, but it became increasingly clandestine. By February 1987, a year after Duvalier's departure, most citizens were disillusioned with the results of the transition (Chamberlain 1987; Hooper 1987).

Then, in March 1987, upon discovering that the new "liberal" Constitution drafted by a majority of CNG appointees drastically curtailed the power of the presidency and explicitly forbade a Duvalierist return to power, many Haitians thought that the tide had finally turned. The Constitution was overwhelmingly approved by referendum. Presidential candidates revamped their speeches, but they could not raise much enthusiasm among an electorate that revealed itself both suspicious of all politicians and more issue-oriented than in any previous presidential contest. However, state-sponsored violence returned with a vengeance in the summer of 1987: more than fifty demonstrators were shot between late June and late July. Progressive clergymen were attacked by "unknown" aggressors; the premises of the nongovernment radio stations were vandalized. In August, a presidential candidate was killed by an unidentified gang; another was shot in October, in front of the country's most important police station.

Hundreds of peasants were killed by retaliating Duvalierists. The renewed violence, and the perception that the new Constitution offered true safeguards, convinced an otherwise reluctant electorate that the presidential elections might lead to a political solution.

Thus, hope filtered back into the countryside as the elections neared. The rhetoric of the political parties, the large number of international observers, and the optimism of the press gave many Haitians a spurious sense of security. Alas, when the polls opened on November 29, 1987, Duvalierist thugs, often backed by uniformed soldiers, openly shot at lines of waiting voters. Estimates of the number of deaths ranged from 39 to 200. Hundreds of people who had committed no other crime than standing in line to exert their electoral rights for the first time in a generation were seriously wounded. Expectations were crushed once again, so much so, in fact, that very few citizens bothered to take part in the army-run "elections" of January 17, 1988, that led to the installation of Leslie François Manigat as president of Haiti.

This time, humbled by the turn of events, pundits were reluctant to prognosticate. The situation was also harder to read. On the one hand, Manigat's accession to power was clearly illegitimate, and pressure from abroad against the new regime mounted rapidly, notably in Canada and the United States. On the other hand, some saw in the forced "election" of a man whose background and qualifications were at least equal to those of his competitors a momentary relief, and perhaps an alternative to even worse cataclysms. But even muted expectations that the Manigat government could lead to a new era in Haitian politics were at the very least premature. As Namphy begot Manigat, so Namphy brought down Manigat: on June 20, 1988, the general resumed power alone and forced Manigat into exile.

But this was not the end of the series of coups and countercoups. Namphy was in turn brought down by an army coup, whose instigators again hinted at a clean sweep. Hope was rekindled once more. Lower rank soldiers, reported to have masterminded Namphy's ouster, ran the show for a few days, demoting many officers known for their Duvalierist ties. Street justice started anew, claiming to complete the dechoukaj that had begun in February 1986. By December 1988, however, when it appeared that the new president, General Prosper Avril, former head of Jean-Claude Duvalier's Presidential Guard and former member of the CNG, was (at least temporarily) in control, many knew that the clean sweep had not yet come.

If the last two-and-a-half years of Haitian politics look like a badly dubbed movie where the words and gestures do not always match, it is because something is wrong with the premises of the script that most observers chose to read. For different reasons, the US government, the CNG, the Haitian urban elites, political parties of all tendencies, and large chunks of the Haitian masses have fancied the assumption that Baby Doc's departure was a clear step on the march to democracy, an immediate and inevitable consequence of the disturbances and massive riots of 1984–85. To be sure, the riots were a necessary factor in the end of the Duvalier dynasty: had the Haitian masses not defied the army and militia with their bare hands during a month of daily encounters in which many unarmed citizens were injured and killed, chances are that Jean-Claude Duvalier would still be ruling the country. But if the riots were necessary for Duvalier to leave, they certainly were not a sufficient condition for him to depart the way he did. It took something else to orchestrate his departure at that particular time, under those specific circumstances, and with a no less specific aftermath.

Thus, the problem with the dominant version of Duvalier's downfall is not what it acknowledges but what it leaves out. Two series of events occurred on February 7, 1986: first, the departure of Duvalier; second, *the takeover of the state machinery by a group of apparently disparate individuals*: civilians and career army officers, Duvalierists and former opposition figures, past backers of repression and former human rights leaders. Missing from the dominant version, or at best viewed as secondary, are the negotiations—the tacit and explicit understandings between Haitian and US politicians, in Haiti and in the United States, local and foreign military and intelligence personnel, ambassadors, power brokers, and bureaucrats—that led to, and tied together, the two sets of events. For what Haitians witnessed on February 7, 1986, was not the disorderly escape of an "entire leadership" pushed out by popular pressure, as portrayed in Larry Speakes's untimely announcement, but a transmission of power, orchestrated with absolute order—albeit against the background of a popular uprising.

Before dawn on that Friday, February 7, Jean-Claude Duvalier drove his favorite BMW to the airport—hardly the behavior of a deported captive. Awaiting him was a US C-141 Starlifter cargo plane—dispatched, according to rumor, from South Carolina or from Guantanamo, but in any case presumably authorized at the highest levels of the US executive. The Duvaliers' belongings, and those of their companions, were already loaded onto the plane. Finally, while most Haitians did not know the time of the president's departure in advance—there had been no announcement—some diplomats and foreign reporters were waiting at the airport, cameras in hand, as if for an Oscar night. Some had arrived before the landing of the Starlifter. At 3:45 a.m. the plane left; so did the cameras.

Popular beliefs notwithstanding—and note that the masses were not at the airport—this was the most graceful exit of a dictator in Haitian history. No previous dictator, even one of the less hated ones, had left for exile in the midst of so much civility on the part of those who took him to his boat or plane. Fignolé, the last president removed by the army before François Duvalier took power, was handled rather roughly, according to one of the arresting officers (Pierre 1987). The two chiefs of state who left after Baby Doc, Henri Namphy and Leslie Manigat, were at least harassed by their captors, and some of Manigat's supporters were arrested the night he left. Yet three months after Duvalier's departure, not a single Duvalierist had been questioned by the "new" authorities.

The more time passes, the more the events surrounding Duvalier's departure appear at least partly staged. What accounts for Larry Speakes's "mistaken" announcement? Who tipped off so many journalists, and why? Who allowed Duvalier to take what Haitians report to be millions of dollars in cash from the Banque Centrale? Was that part of his compensation for leaving gracefully? Who decided on the composition of the team that replaced him? Yet the incongruities of the night soon vanished with the dictator. Soon after, under the cover of national jubilation, a new government was in place. Understandably happy with the end of the dynasty, few people in Haiti or abroad bothered to ask how the transition had been managed and what it was meant to hatch. Questions came later, in April and May 1986, but by then they were clouded by preparations for one more fruitless electoral campaign. Hence the events of February 7 continue to appear as an important landmark in an otherwise uninterrupted advance toward "democracy."

There is, however, a strong case for an alternative reading of the script, one that would see the supervision of Duvalier's departure and the constitution of the first CNG as a multinational exercise in "crisis management," a calculated break in the democratic path that the Haitian people had embarked upon. We may never learn the details of the negotiations, but negotiations there were. And we need not know these details, or fully investigate ex-US Marine Colonel Oliver North's claim to have brought an end to Haiti's nightmare, to be certain of one crucial fact: Jean-Claude Duvalier was brought down by a high-level coup d'état executed with international connivance.[4] Further, the management of his departure and of its aftermath effectively prevented the complete dechoukaj that most Haitians were calling for.

Interestingly, Duvalier was one of the first to question the dominant version of his departure. From his viewpoint, his resignation was part of a covenant among friends designed to avoid further bloodshed. His apparently genuine surprise at the news that he had fled the country to escape a popular uprising was attributed to his notoriously slow thinking. Thus most observers missed the significance of the fact that Duvalier did not direct his anger at his traditional enemies, or even at the demonstrators, but at the people who had replaced him, most of whom were close friends. Duvalier's main disagreement with his former allies was, strangely enough, not their account of his government's misdeeds but their account of its downfall.

More curious still, Duvalier's successors replied in kind. On February 17, ten days after Duvalier's demise, the CNG put out an official bulletin that seemed odd at the time and appears even more bizarre in retrospect. It read in part: "The National Council of Government insists upon reaffirming that the ex-president's resignation and departure for abroad have been provoked by popular pressure." Just in case the people doubted.

The dominant version of the end of the Duvalier saga has not been openly challenged in part because of the political rhetoric stimulated by the end of the dynasty. Most Haitians were eager for a drastic change. Few, especially among the urban poor, were willing to admit that their "revolution" had been tampered with. The economic and political elites gained the most from this confusion, and also recovered much quicker. Many promptly understood the need to muffle the street power that had speeded up the pace of the political process until Duvalier's departure. To be sure, the public denunciation of prominent Duvalierists continued, off and on, until early 1989. To be sure, most politicians and political parties used the relative freedom of expression of those three years to engage in vehement anti-Duvalierist posturing. To be sure, a tiny minority went against the current to address some of the most troubling long-term issues that the nation faced. But they found little echo among the candidates of 1986 or, later, among the most prominent opponents or backers of the successive Manigat, Namphy, and Avril governments.[5] Three years after Jean-Claude Duvalier's departure, in spite of an extraordinary period of free expression—at least by Haitian standards—the dominant political discourse has shown few signs of dynamism. Post-Duvalier Haiti seems to be drifting aimlessly.

This aimlessness stems from an implicit understanding among the Haitian elites that goes beyond the immediate bargains made, broken, and renewed just before Duvalier's departure. The months following clearly indicated to religious, business, and political leaders, Duvalierists and non-Duvalierists alike, that what Haitians called the "democratic steamroller" might not stop at *their* door if the dechoukaj continued. First, the list of individuals condemned by association kept growing despite the political gymnastics of many bourgeois and professionals, who suddenly claimed to be age-old opponents of the deposed dictator. More important, at many points mob violence threatened to go beyond political boundaries to associate perceived class positions and Duvalierism. Mobs of young people threatened the US consulate in Port-au-Prince at least three times. Never too seriously, perhaps—but on one occasion at least they were stopped only by Haitian soldiers from the nearby barracks. Expensive cars were ransacked repeatedly in Port-au-Prince. Truck drivers twice closed down the only road linking Port-au-Prince and the suburban areas of Fermathe and Thomassin, where prominent Duvalierists lived next door to merchants, diplomats, and foreign aid consultants. The road to suburbia had to be cleared with tanks from the army's elite battalions. Similarly, throughout 1986, crowds of peasants formed roadblocks on the national roads, exacting money from private motorists regardless of political identification.

In the midst of these alarming incidences of popular justice, many urbanites retreated to the time-honored leitmotif of the commercial bourgeoisie: the absurdity of Duvalierism. At times by design but more often because it was simply too convenient an excuse to forgo, middle-class political or religious leaders presented the Duvalier era as a monstrous phenomenon, a parenthesis after which Haitians could, presumably, pick up the reins of their history and proceed. On the basis of such an understanding, they endorsed an article of the Constitution that forbade known Duvalierists from running for office—as if a stroke of the pen could erase the Duvalierist nightmare and the crisis on which it fed. Yet only a distorted presentation of the Haitian past and present can sustain the illusion that the crisis will subside spontaneously if and when the dictatorship it nurtured disappears. The Duvalierist state has its roots deep in the organization of

Haitian society itself. Similar regimes will inevitably succeed each other unless the relation between state and civil society is reformulated.

EPILOGUE

If wishes alone sufficed, I would have ended on a more cheerful note. As things stand, my analysis (Trouillot 1990) is offered partly as a warning. For if the Duvalierists are understandably among the villains of the story, there is nevertheless no clear champion of the popular cause. To be sure, the founders of the Haitian state deserve great credit; theirs was the most visionary revolution of its times. To be sure, many nineteenth-century Haitian intellectuals lucidly addressed some of the most important issues facing their ostracized nation. Yet whenever they took part in the political process, their deeds consistently fell short of their stated intentions.

Throughout the twentieth century, and especially under the Duvalier dictatorships, the Haitian left, as well as many urban democratic or nationalist factions, endured death and injury at the hands of both foreign and local soldiers and thugs. No analyst has the right to disregard these deaths or the individual sacrifices they represent. But it would be equally dishonorable to use them as an excuse for the dogmatic analyses prevalent among Haitian progressives, or for the middle-class contempt that most urban liberals feel toward the common people of Haiti. Moreover, though Haitian activists willingly acknowledge the need to redistribute the country's resources more equitably, most are reluctant to face the complex problems created by declining agricultural productivity. We can understand the emphasis on economic justice in a country where drafting and enforcing a graduated income tax package might be the most revolutionary measure imaginable in the near future. But if corruption and unequal taxation are still at the forefront of Haiti's problems, their elimination can only set the stage for the creation of policies that will improve conditions in the rural world.

For better or worse, the size and social resilience of the peasantry are important aspects of the uniqueness of Haiti as an American nation. While Haitian peasants cannot be blamed for the institutions that regulate the state, or for the transfer of surplus out of the countryside, their inflexible attachment to a labor process that is unlikely to generate growth or increase productivity is certainly part of the Haitian dilemma. Ultimately, there is only one Haitian question: that of the peasantry. For it is in the contradictions of the peasantry that the resources, stakes, and predicaments of the nation intertwine. How to measure the limits and potential of this peasantry—whose diversity has barely been studied—against the economic, social, political, and cultural problems I have outlined (Trouillot 1990) is probably beyond the means of any one politician or scholar. But any solution to the Haitian crisis must face the peasant question. It must find its roots in the resources of that peasantry, the very same resources that have contributed to the fortunes of thousands of Haitians and foreigners during a century and a half of unbridled exploitation. And to do this, Haitians must create institutional channels through which *all* sectors within the peasantry can participate in a political debate from which they have been too long excluded. Both steps in turn require that intellectuals, politicians, and planners—foreign and Haitian alike—talk less about (or "for") the peasantry and begin listening more attentively to what its diverse subgroups have said in the past and have to say now about their own future. The long overdue reconciliation of state and nation requires the fundamental understanding that, in Haiti, the peasantry *is* the nation.

NOTES

Editors' Note: This chapter first appeared as "The Interrupted March to Democracy," chapter 8 of *Haiti: State against Nation; The Origins and Legacy of Duvalierism* (New York: Monthly Review Press, 1990), 217–30.

1. The "liberal" phase of Jean-Claudisme, which lasted from about 1975 to 1980, was part condition and part effect of the light industry strategy. In more immediate terms, it was also a positive result of the Carter administration's emphasis on human rights in the Americas—including the limited amnesty trumpeted by the regime in 1977 and the creation of the Haitian Human Rights League in 1978. That phase ended abruptly on November 20, 1980, with a wave of arrests, the expulsion of many journalists, and the closing down of independent press organs. We cannot help but notice that the change came six months after the president's wedding; but it is more important to point out that it occurred less than three weeks after the 1980 US elections. No matter who actually gave the orders, the new wave of repression expressed the Haitian government's reading of the implications of the Reagan landslide for human rights in Latin America and the Caribbean.

2. "After an outbreak of African swine fever in 1981, on advice from the US government, the regime ordered the slaughter of the entire population of native

Haitian pigs. Between 1982 and 1984, it killed more than one million animals belonging primarily to low-income peasants, for whom pigs have always been a major form of investment. Few peasants understood the need to kill the pigs, and, despite promises, few received compensation. Those who did received pinkish US pigs, soon baptized *kochon grimèl* ('light-skinned pigs') by the populace. The imported animals required imported food, which few peasants could afford, and they had none of the ritual value of the native black pig that they replaced. By 1984 pig-raising had become a bourgeois venture, and the price of all meat had increased greatly" (Trouillot 1990, 215).

3. The most publicized of these parties was a $500-a-plate dinner in which the *crème* of the bourgeoisie, the nouveaux riches of the regime, and many foreign officials and entrepreneurs took part. It was supposedly a fundraising event for a charitable foundation headed by the First Lady. Indeed, Michèle Bennett tried to counter rumors of her unscrupulous ambition with a philanthropic image. This worked for the first few months after her wedding, but the image later disintegrated, despite the public accolade Mother Theresa gave to the Haitian First Lady. By the time of the celebrated dinner, no one cared about the charitable pretext for the extravagant party.

4. Colonel North's Haitian connection received little attention in the US press. Nevertheless, according to the *Village Voice* (December 29, 1987), before the Iran-Contra affair became public, "In Washington, Duvalier's removal became yet another feather in the rakish cap of a mysterious marine colonel named Oliver North, abetted by his State Department sidekick, Elliott Abrams."

5. A good case in point is the issue of decentralization. That issue was born in the grassroots struggle at a time when, in contrast to the deafening silence from Port-au-Prince, the entire population of many provincial towns had clearly gambled with their lives by defying the regime. Had Duvalier survived, these provincials would have paid dearly for it. The 1964 Jérémie massacres showed how Duvalierism could punish an entire town. The provincial slum-dwellers also knew that, and by January 1986 it had become clear in places like Gonaïves and Cap-Haïtien that the entire community's survival depended on the government's fall. In the midst of Port-au-Prince's silence, the issue of decentralization found fertile ground in the provinces. After Duvalier's fall and up until April and May 1986, the provincials loudly denounced Port-au-Prince's unfair share of the national revenues. Yet the illusion of an undisturbed march toward democracy defused that particular issue until the drafting of the Constitution, when the problem was solved brilliantly by the bureaucrats—on paper at least. Yet the people hardly noticed, and the bureaucrats failed to remind them that numerous reports and dossiers had "solved" that problem many times in the past.

REFERENCES

Chamberlain, Greg. 1987. "Up by the Roots." NACLA *Report on the Americas* 21, no. 3: 14–23.

Hooper, Michael. 1987. "The Monkey's Tail Still Strong." NACLA *Report on the Americas* 21, no. 3: 24–31.

Pierre, Pressoir. 1987. *Témoignages: 1946–1976; L'espérance déçue*. Port-au-Prince: Imprimerie Henri Deschamps.

Trouillot, Michel-Rolph. 1990. *Haiti: State against Nation; The Origins and Legacy of Duvalierism*. New York: Monthly Review Press.

A Comprehensive
Bibliography of the Work
of Michel-Rolph Trouillot

This bibliography brings together works by and about Michel-Rolph Trouillot to showcase the range, importance, and reach of Trouillot's contributions to the fields of anthropology, history, Caribbean studies, and Haitian studies. Effort has been made to document the various reprints and translations of his texts in the interest of making his writings available to a broad audience. In addition to traditional scholarly works, the titles listed below also include nonacademic publications, government reports, newspaper articles, educational materials, and popular writings to highlight the variety of languages, registers, and forums in which Trouillot developed his arguments as well as the multiplicity of publics, communities, and sites of interventions that he traversed.

BOOKS AND MONOGRAPHS

n.d. *Ti difé boulé sou istoua Ayiti*. Vol. 2, *Ki mò k-touyé lanprè?*
[*Editors' Note:* There is no source for this other than a citation in Trouillot, *Les racines historiques de l'Etat duvaliérien* (1986).]
1977. *Ti difé boulé sou istoua Ayiti*. Brooklyn, NY: Kóleksion Lakansièl.
1984. "The Economic Integration of a Caribbean Peasantry: The Case of Dominica." PhD diss., Johns Hopkins University.

1985. *Nation, State, and Society in Haiti, 1804–1984*. Washington, DC: Woodrow Wilson International Center for Scholars.

1986. *Les racines historiques de l'État duvaliérien*. Port-au-Prince: Éditions Deschamps.

1988. *Peasants and Capital: Dominica in the World Economy*. Baltimore, MD: Johns Hopkins University Press.

1990. *Haiti: State against Nation; The Origins and Legacy of Duvalierism*. New York: Monthly Review Press.

1995. *Silencing the Past: Power and the Production of History*. Boston: Beacon Press.

2003. *Global Transformations: Anthropology and the Modern World*. New York: Palgrave Macmillan.

Reviews of Books and Monographs

Abadía Barrero, César Ernesto. 2012. Review of *Global Transformations*, by Michel-Rolph Trouillot. *Maguaré* 26, no. 1: 363–70.

Allen, Michael H. 1993. "Rethinking Political Economy and Praxis in the Caribbean." *Latin American Perspectives* 20, no. 2: 111–19.
        [Review of *Political Economy in Haiti*, by Simon M. Fass; *The Poor and Powerless*, by C. Y. Thomas; and *Peasants and Capital*, by Michel-Rolph Trouillot.]

Bellegarde-Smith, Patrick. 1992. Review of *Haiti: State against Nation*, by Michel-Rolph Trouillot. *The Americas* 48, no. 3: 438–39.

Bernard, Mergen. 1996. Review of *Silencing the Past*, by Michel-Rolph Trouillot. *American Studies International* 34, no. 1: 73–75.

Bonnicksen, Andrea. 1989. Review of *Haiti: State against Nation*, by Michel-Rolph Trouillot. *Library Journal* 114, no. 20: 147.

Brana-Shute, Gary. 1989. Review of *Peasants and Capital*, by Michel-Rolph Trouillot. *Hispanic American Historical Review* 69, no. 4: 799–800.

Dash, Michael. 1991. Review of *Haiti: State against Nation*, by Michel-Rolph Trouillot. *Social and Economic Studies* 40, no. 3: 199–202.

Donham, Donald L. 1997. Review of *Silencing the Past*, by Michel-Rolph Trouillot. *Journal of the Royal Anthropological Institute* 3, no. 2: 397–98.

Dupuy, Alex. 1988. "Conceptualizing the Duvalier Dictatorship." *Latin American Perspectives* 15, no. 4: 105–14.
        [Review of *Les racines historiques de l'État duvalierien*, by Michel-Rolph Trouillot.]

Gilderhus, Mark T. 1996. Review of *Silencing the Past*, by Michel-Rolph Trouillot. *The Americas* 53, no. 1: 190–91.

Gregg, Robert. 1998. Review of *Silencing the Past*, by Michel-Rolph Trouillot. *Social History* 23, no. 2: 223–25.

Grindle, Merilee S. 1993. "Agrarian Class Structures and State Policies: Past, Present, and Future." *Latin American Research Review* 28, no. 1: 174–87.
        [Review of *Agricultural Policy and Collective Self-Reliance in the Caribbean*, by W. Andrew Axline; *Peasants, Entrepreneurs, and Social Change*, by Lesley Gill;

Agrarian Reform Policy in the Dominican Republic, by Ana Teresa Gutierrez-San Martin; *Land Reform in Latin America*, by Carrie A. Meyer; *Our Daily Bread*, by Nola Reinhardt; *Peasants and Capital*, by Michel-Rolph Trouillot; *Coffee and Democracy in Modern Costa Rica*, by Anthony Winson; *The Death of Ramón González*, by Angus Wright; and *Rural Development and Survival Strategies in Central Paraguay*, by E. B. Zoomers.]

Gros, Jean-Germain. 2000. "Haiti: The Political Economy and Sociology of Decay and Renewal." *Latin American Research Review* 35, no. 3: 211–26.

[Review of *Haiti in the New World Order*, by Alex Dupuy; *Haitian Frustrations, Dilemmas for US Policy*, edited by Georges Fauriol; *Building Peace in Haiti*, by Chetan Kumar; *Haiti: Dangerous Crossroads*, edited by NACLA; *From Dessalines to Duvalier*, by David Nicholls; *Haiti Renewed*, by Robert Rotberg; *The Haitian Dilemma*, by Ernest Preg; and *Silencing the Past*, by Michel-Rolph Trouillot.]

Hay, Fred. 1992. Review of *Haiti: State against Nation*, by Michel-Rolph Trouillot. *Latin American Anthropology Review* 4, no. 2: 81–82.

Henfrey, June. 1989. Review of *Peasants and Capital*, by Michel-Rolph Trouillot. *Bulletin of Latin American Research* 8, no. 2: 329–30.

Knight, Franklin W. 1997. Review of *Silencing the Past*, by Michel-Rolph Trouillot. *Hispanic American Historical Review* 77, no. 3: 483–84.

Lawless, Robert. 1994. Review of *Haiti: State against Nation*, by Michel-Rolph Trouillot. *Journal of Third World Studies* 11: 473.

Mandle, Jay R. 1988. Review of *Peasants and Capital*, by Michel-Rolph Trouillot. *Journal of Economic History* 48, no. 4: 962–63.

Maxwell, Kenneth. 1996. Review of *Silencing the Past*, by Michel-Rolph Trouillot. *Foreign Affairs* 75, no. 4: 152.

Nichols, David. 1991. Review of *Haiti: The Breached Citadel*, by Patrick Bellegarde-Smith; *Haiti: State against Nation; The Origins and Legacy of Duvalierism*, by Michel-Rolph Trouillot; and *La Republique exterminatrice. Deuxieme partie: L'Etat vassal*, by Roger Gaillard. *Hispanic American Historical Review* 71, no. 3: 650–52.

Nichols, David. 1996. Review of *The Catholic Church in Haiti*, by Anne Greene; *Sociologie prospective d'Haïti*, by Claude Souffrant; *Silencing the Past*, by Michel-Rolph Trouillot; *Haitian Frustrations*, edited by Georges A. Fauriol; and *Haiti Briefing Papers Series*, by The Hopkins-Georgetown Haiti Project. *Journal of Latin American Studies* 28, no. 3: 721–24.

Nugent, David. 1989. Review of *Peasants and Capital*, by Michel-Rolph Trouillot. *American Ethnologist* 16, no. 2: 405–6.

Paquette, Robert L. 1997. Review of *Silencing the Past*, by Michel-Rolph Trouillot. *Journal of American History* 84, no. 1: 189–90.

Roseberry, William 1989. Review of *Peasants and Capital*, by Michel-Rolph Trouillot. *Nieuwe West-Indische Gids/New West Indian Guide* 62, nos. 3–4: 165–67.

Roseberry, William. 1997. "Review Essay: On Historical Consciousness." *Current Anthropology* 38, no. 5: 926–31.

[Review of *Performing Dreams*, by Laura R. Graham; *Neither Cargo nor Cult*, by Martha Kaplan; *Purity and Exile*, by Lisa H. Malkki; and *Silencing the Past*, by Michel-Rolph Trouillot.]

Silverman, Marilyn. 1989. Review of *Peasants and Capital*, by Michel-Rolph Trouillot. *American Anthropologist* 91, no. 1: 211.

Winichakul, Tongchai. 1997. Review of *Silencing the Past*, by Michel-Rolph Trouillot. *American Historical Review* 102, no. 2: 426–27.

Translations and Excerpts of Books and Monographs

2001. Trouillot, Michel-Rolph. "Looking for Columbus." In *The Butterfly's Way: Voices from the Haitian Dyaspora in the United States*, edited by Edwidge Danticat, 201–3. New York: Soho Press.

2002. Trouillot, Michel-Rolph. "Undenkbare Geschichte: Zur Bagatellisierung der haitischen Revolution." In *Jenseits des Eurozentrismus: Postkoloniale Perspektiven in den Geschichts und Kulturwissenschaften*, edited by Sebastian Conrad, Shalini Randeria, and Beate Sutterlüty, 84–115. Frankfurt am Main: Campus.

2011. Trouillot, Michel-Rolph. *Transformaciones globales: La antropología y el mundo moderno*. Translated by Cristóbal Gnecco. Popayán, Colombia: Editorial Universidad del Cauca.

2012. Trouillot, Michel-Rolph. "An Unthinkable History: The Haitian Revolution as a Non-Event." In *Haitian History: New Perspectives*, edited by Alyssa Goldstein Sepinwall, 33–54. New York: Routledge.

2013. Trouillot, Michel-Rolph. "From *Ti difé boulé sou istoua Ayiti*." Introduced and translated from Haitian Creole by Mariana Past and Benjamin Hebblethwaite. *Transition* 111: 74–89.

COMMISSIONED REPORTS

1996. *Open the Social Sciences: Report of the Gulbenkian Commission on the Restructuring of the Social Sciences*, by Immanuel Wallerstein, Calestous Juma, Evelyn Fox Keller, Jürgen Kocka, Dominique Lecourt, V. Y. Mudimbe, Kinhide Mushakoji, Ilya Prigogine, Peter J. Taylor, and Michel-Rolph Trouillot. Stanford, CA: Stanford University Press.

1996. "Rural Localities, National Reality: Issues in Haitian Development." In *Haiti Briefing Papers Series*, by the Hopkins-Georgetown Haiti Project. Baltimore, MD: Hopkins-Georgetown Haiti Project.

1997. *Democracy in Haiti: A Strategic Assessment*, by Michel-Rolph Trouillot, Michel Acacia, Gina Ulysse, Ira Lowenthal, and Malcolm Young. Submitted by Development Associates, Port-au-Prince. Washington, DC: USAID.

2000. "Exclusión social en el Caribe." In *Exclusión social y reducción de la robreza en America Latina y Caribe*, edited by Estanislao Carlos Sojo Gacitúa and Shelton H. Davis, 111–47. San José, Costa Rica: FLASCO, Banco Mundial.

2000. "Social Exclusion in the Caribbean." In *Social Exclusion and Poverty Reduction in Latin America and the Caribbean*, edited by Estanislao Gacitúa, Carlos Sojo, and Shelton H. Davis, 103–42. Washington, DC: World Bank.

JOURNAL ARTICLES

1982. "Motion in the System: Coffee, Color, and Slavery in Eighteenth-Century Saint-Domingue." *Review (Fernand Braudel Center)* 5, no. 3: 331–88.

1984. "Caribbean Peasantries and World Capitalism: An Approach to Micro-level Studies." *Nieuwe West-Indische Gids/New West Indian Guide* 58, no. 1–2: 37–59.

1984. "Labour and Emancipation in Dominica: Contribution to a Debate." *Caribbean Quarterly* 30, nos. 3–4: 73–84.

1989. "Discourses of Rule and the Acknowledgment of the Peasantry in Dominica, W.I., 1838–1928." *American Ethnologist* 16, no. 4: 704–18.

1990. "Contrapunto caribeño: El café en las Antillas (1734–1873)." *El Caribe* 6, nos. 16–17: 58–65.

1990. "Good Day, Columbus: Silences, Power, and Public History (1492–1892)." *Public Culture* 3, no. 1: 1–24.

1990. "The Odd and the Ordinary: Haiti, the Caribbean, and the World." *Cimarrón: New Perspectives on the Caribbean* 2, no. 3: 3–12.

1991. "Anthropology as Metaphor: The Savage's Legacy and the Postmodern World." *Review (Fernand Braudel Center)* 14, no. 1: 29–54.

1991. "From Planters' Journals to Academia: The Haitian Revolution as Unthinkable History." *Journal of Caribbean History* 25, nos. 1–2: 81–99.

1992. "The Caribbean Region: An Open Frontier in Anthropological Theory." *Annual Review of Anthropology* 21: 19–42.

1993. "Jeux de mots, jeux de classe: Les mouvances de l'Indigénisme." *Conjonction: Revue Franco-Haïtienne* 197 (January–March): 29–44.

1994. "Haiti's Nightmare and the Lessons of History." *NACLA Report on the Americas* 27, no. 4: 121–32.
> [Reprinted 1995 in *Haiti: Dangerous Crossroads*, edited by NACLA, 121–32. Boston: South End Press.]

1998. "Culture on the Edges: Creolization in the Plantation Context." *Plantation Society in the Americas* 5, no. 1: 8–28.
> [Reprinted 2002 in *From the Margins: Historical Anthropology and Its Futures*, edited by Brian Keith Axel, 189–210. Durham, NC: Duke University Press.]

1999. "Peuples des terres mêlées: Les républiques d' Hispaniola/Peoples of the Jumbled Lands: The Republic of Hispaniola." *Creole Connection* 5, no. 3: 1–9. Available at http://www.geocities.ws/CollegePark/Library/3954/.

2000. "Abortive Rituals: Historical Apologies in the Global Era." *Interventions: International Journal of Postcolonial Studies* 2, no. 2: 171–86.

    [Excerpt reprinted 2011 in *The Collective Memory Reader*, edited by Jeffrey K. Olick, Vered Vinitzky-Seroussi, and Daniel Levy, 458–64. New York: Oxford University Press.]

2001. "The Anthropology of the State: Close Encounters of a Deceptive Kind." *Current Anthropology* 42, no. 1: 125–38.

2002. "North Atlantic Universals: Analytical Fictions, 1492–1945." *South Atlantic Quarterly* 101, no. 4: 839–58.

    [Reprinted 2009 in *Enchantments of Modernity: Empire, Nation, Globalization*, edited by Saurabh Dube, 45–66. New Delhi: Routledge, Taylor and Francis.]

2011. "Universales nordatlánticos." In *El encantamiento del desencantamiento: Historias de la modernidad*, edited by Saurabh Dube, translated by José Raúl Vázquez de Lara Cisneros. Mexico City: El Colegio de México.

BOOK CHAPTERS IN EDITED COLLECTIONS

1981. "Peripheral Vibrations: The Case of Saint-Domingue's Coffee Revolution." In *Dynamics of World Development*, edited by Richard Rubinson, 27–41. Beverly Hills, CA: Sage.

1991. "Anthropology and the Savage Slot: The Poetics and Politics of Otherness." In *Recapturing Anthropology: Working in the Present*, edited by Richard G. Fox, 17–44. Santa Fe, NM: School of American Research Press.

1992. "The Inconvenience of Freedom: Free People of Color and the Political Aftermath of Slavery in Dominica and Saint-Domingue/Haiti." In *The Meaning of Freedom: Economics, Politics, and Culture after Slavery*, edited by Frank McGlynn and Seymour Drescher, 147–82. Pittsburgh, PA: University of Pittsburgh Press.

1993. "Coffee Planters and Coffee Slaves: From Saint-Domingue to Dominica." In *Cultivation and Culture: Labor and the Shaping of Slave Life in the Americas*, edited by Ira Berlin, 124–37. Charlottesville: University of Virginia Press.

1993. "État et Duvaliérisme." In *La république haïtienne: État des lieux et perspectives*, edited by Gérard Barthélemy and Christian Girault, 189–92. Paris: Karthala and AEDC.

1994. "Culture, Color, and Politics in Haiti." In *Race*, edited by Steven Gregory and Roger Sanjek, 146–74. New Brunswick, NJ: Rutgers University Press.

1995. With Sidney W. Mintz. "The Social History of Haitian Vodou." In *Sacred Arts of Haitian Vodou*, edited by Donald Cosentino, 123–47. Los Angeles: UCLA Fowler Museum of Cultural History.

1996. "Beyond and below the Merivale Paradigm: Dominica's First 100 Days of Freedom." In *The Lesser Antilles in the Age of European Expansion*, edited by

Robert L. Paquette and Stanley L. Engerman, 302–23. Gainsville: University Press of Florida.

1996. "Démocratie et société civile." In *Les transitions démocratiques: Actes du colloque international de Port-au-Prince*, edited by Laënnec Hurbon, 225–31. Paris: Syros.

1997. "Silencing the Past: Layers of Meaning in the Haitian Revolution." In *Between History and Histories: The Making of Silences and Commemorations*, edited by G. Sider and G. Smith, 31–61. Toronto: University of Toronto Press.

1997. "A Social Contract for Whom? Haitian History and Haiti's Future." In *Haiti Renewed: Political and Economic Prospects*, edited by Robert Rotberg, 47–59. Washington, DC: Brookings Institution Press.

1998. "Labour and Emancipation in Dominica: Contribution to a Debate." In *Apprenticeship and Emancipation*, edited by Rex M. Nettleford, 84–98. Kingston, Jamaica: University of the West Indies.

1999. "Historiography of Haiti." In *General History of the Caribbean*. Vol. 6, *Methodology and Historiography of the Caribbean*, edited by Barry W. Higman, 451–77. London: UNESCO.

2001. "Bodies and Souls: Madison Smartt Bell's *All Souls' Rising* and the Haitian Revolution." In *Novel History: Historians and Novelists Confront America's Past (and Each Other)*, edited by M. Carnes, 184–97. New York: Simon and Schuster.

2002. "Adieu, Culture: A New Duty Arises." In *Anthropology beyond Culture*, edited by Richard G. Fox and Barbara J. King, 37–60. Wenner-Gren International Symposium Series. Oxford: Berg.

2002. "The Otherwise Modern: Caribbean Lessons from the Savage Slot." In *Critically Modern: Alternatives, Alterities, Anthropologies*, edited by Bruce Knauft, 220–37. Bloomington: Indiana University Press.

    [Translated 2011 by Sonia Serna as "Moderno de otro modo: Lecciones caribeñas desde el lugar del salvaje." *Tabula Rasa* 14: 79–97.]

2002. "The Perspective of the World: Globalization Then and Now." In *Beyond Dichotomies: Histories, Identities, Cultures, and the Challenge of Globalization*, edited by Elisabeth Mudimbe-Boyi, 3–20. Albany: State University of New York Press.

2004. "The North Atlantic Universals." In *The Modern World-System in the Longue Durée*, edited by Immanuel Wallerstein, 229–38. Boulder, CO: Paradigm Press.

REVIEW ARTICLES AND NOTES

1980. Review of *Peasants and Poverty: A Study of Haiti*, by Mats Lundahl. *Journal of Peasant Studies* 8, no. 1: 112–16.

1982. Review of *The Haitian Maroons: Liberty or Death*, by Jean Fouchard. *Nieuwe West-Indische Gids/New West Indian Guide* 56, nos. 3–4: 180–82.

1983. "The Production of Spatial Configurations: A Caribbean Case." *Nieuwe West-Indische Gids/New West Indian Guide* 57, nos. 3–4: 215–29.

[Review of *Atlas critique d'Haïti*, by Georges Anglade; *Espace et liberté*, by Georges Anglade; *Hispaniola*, by G. Anglade, R. E. Yunén, and D. Audette; and *Le commerce du café en Haïti*, by Christian A. Girault.]

1984. Review of *Slave Populations of the British Caribbean, 1807–1834*, by B. W. Higman. *Caribbean Quarterly* 30, nos. 3–4: 131–33.

1985. Review of *Plantations Peasants and the State: A Study of the Mode of Sugar Production in Guyana*, by Clive Y. Thomas. *American Ethnologist* 12, no. 4: 799–800.

1986. "The Price of Indulgence." *Social Analysis* 19: 85–90.

[Comments on *Civilization and the Stolen Gift*, by J. M. Chevalier; and *The Devil and Commodity Fetishism in South America*, by M. Taussig.]

1986. Review of *So Spoke the Uncle*, by Jean Price-Mars. *Research in African Literatures* 17, no. 4: 596–97.

1989. Review of *Afro-Caribbean Villages in Historical Perspective*, by Charles V. Carnegie. *Social and Economic Studies* 38, no. 2: 321–25.

1989. "The Lost Continent of the Americas: Recent Works on Afro-America and the Caribbean." *Latin American Research Review* 24, no. 2: 246–52.

[Review of *After Africa*, by Roger D. Abrahams and John F. Szwed; *Urban Life in Kingston, Jamaica*, by Diane J. Austin; *Death Row*, by Mario Hector; *Africa in Latin America*, by Manuel Moreno Fraginals; and *Race, Class, and Political Symbols*, by Anita M. Waters.]

1991. Afterword to *Babouk: Voices of Resistance*, by Guy Endore. New York: Monthly Review Press.

1991. Review of *Voodoo and Politics in Haiti*, by Michel S. Laguerre. *American Ethnologist* 8, no. 2: 397–98.

1992. "The Vulgarity of Power." *Public Culture* 5, no. 1: 75–81. [*Editors' Note:* Reflections on the work of Achille Mbembe.]

1993. Review of *Dominican Sugar Plantations: Production and Foreign Labor Integration*, by Martin F. Murphy. *Hispanic American Historical Review* 73, no. 3: 535–36.

1993. Review of *Transitions et subordinations au capitalism*, by Maurice Godelier. *American Anthropologist* 95, no. 1: 193.

1994. Reply to "A Taste for 'the Other': Intellectual Complicity in Racializing Practices," by Virginia Dominguez. *Current Anthropology* 35, no. 4: 333–48.

1994. Review of *Mama Lola: A Vodou Priestess in Brooklyn*, by Karen McCarthy Brown. *American Ethnologist* 21, no. 3: 653–54.

ENCYCLOPEDIA ENTRIES

2001. "Caribbean: Sociocultural Aspects." In *International Encyclopedia of the Social and Behavioral Sciences*, edited by Neil J. Smelser and Paul B. Baltes, 1484–88. New York: Elsevier Science.

CLASSROOM MATERIALS

1991. "The Haitian Revolution and Its Impact on the Americas." In *Caribbean Connections Overview of Regional History*. Washington, DC: EPICA/NECA.

1992. "Beyond the Mountains." *Faces: The Magazine about People* 8, no. 6: 4–9.

1992. "October 12, 1492." In *Reading Culture: Contexts for Critical Reading and Writing*, edited by Diana George and John Trimbur, 452–57. New York: HarperCollins.

NEWSPAPER AND MAGAZINE ARTICLES

1990. "A Turning Point in Haiti?" *Miami Herald*, March 18.

1994. "Aristide's Challenge." In "Forum: Three Haitian Writers on What Is Aristide's Future." *New York Review of Books* 41, no. 18.

1994. "The Peanut Man Didn't Help the Coconut Man." *Newsday*, September 25.

1995. "Haiti's Only Hope Is More Hope." *New York Times*, December 16.

2000. "Esclavage et colonialisme: Des silences assourdissants. " *Le monde des débats*, November.

NEWSLETTER COLUMNS

1993. "Beyond the Hype." *Cross Currents: Newsletter of the Institute for Global Studies in Culture, Power, and History* 1, no. 1.

1994. "Discipline and Perish." *Cross Currents: Newsletter of the Institute for Global Studies in Culture, Power, and History* 1, no. 2.

1995. "Borderlines." *Cross Currents: Newsletter of the Institute for Global Studies in Culture, Power, and History* 2, nos. 1–2.

1995. "Modernizing Loyalties." *Cross Currents: Newsletter of the Institute for Global Studies in Culture, Power, and History* 3, no. 1.

1996. "Open the Social Sciences." *Cross Currents: Newsletter of the Institute for Global Studies in Culture, Power, and History* 3, no. 2.

1996. "Taking Stock." *Cross Currents: Newsletter of the Institute for Global Studies in Culture, Power, and History* 4, no. 1.

1996. "Theorizing a Global Perspective: A Conversation with Michel-Rolph Trouillot." *Cross Currents: Newsletter of the Institute for Global Studies in Culture, Power, and History* 4, no. 1.

1997. "Between the Cracks." *Cross Currents: Newsletter of the Institute for Global Studies in Culture, Power, and History* 4, no. 2.

Agard-Jones, Vanessa. 2013. "Bodies in the System." *Small Axe: A Caribbean Journal of Criticism* 17, no. 3 (42): 182–92.

Beckett, Greg. 2013a. "The Ontology of Freedom: The Unthinkable Miracle of Haiti." *Journal of Haitian Studies* 19, no. 2: 54–74.

Beckett, Greg. 2013b. "Thinking with Others: Savage Thoughts about Anthropology and the West." *Small Axe: A Caribbean Journal of Criticism* 17, no. 3 (42): 166–81.

Bellegarde-Smith, Patrick. 2013. "Reflections and Musings on a Life Well Lived!" *Journal of Haitian Studies* 19, no. 2: 168–70.

Bonilla, Yarimar. 2013a. "Burning Questions: The Life and Work of Michel-Rolph Trouillot, 1949–2012." NACLA *Report on the Americas* 46, no. 1: 82–84.

Bonilla, Yarimar. 2013b. "Ordinary Sovereignty." *Small Axe: A Caribbean Journal of Criticism* 17, no. 3 (42): 152–65.

Bonilla, Yarimar. 2014. "Remembering the Songwriter: The Life and Legacies of Michel-Rolph Trouillot." *Cultural Dynamics* 26, no. 2: 163–72.

Charles, Carolle. 2013. "New York 1967–71, Prelude to *Ti difé boulé*: An Encounter with Liberation Theology, Marxism, and the Black National Liberation Movement." *Journal of Haitian Studies* 19, no. 2: 152–59.

Dahomay, Josué. 2012. "Michel-Rolph Trouillot: Une citadelle contre les silences de l'histoire." *Le Nouvelliste*, August 1. https://lenouvelliste.com/article/107639/michel-rolph-trouillot-une-citadelle-contre-les-silences-de-lhistoire.

Dash, J. Michael. 2013. "Neither Magical nor Exceptional: The Idea of the Ordinary in Caribbean Studies." *Journal of Haitian Studies* 19, no. 2: 24–32.

Dayan, Colin. 2012. "Remembering Trouillot." *Boston Review*, July 18. https://bostonreview.net/books-ideas/remembering-trouillot-colin-dayan.

Dayan, Colin. 2013. "Remembering Trouillot." *Journal of Haitian Studies* 19, no. 2: 12–23.

Dayan, Colin. 2014. "And Then Came Culture." *Cultural Dynamics* 26, no. 2: 137–48.

Delné, Claudy. 2013. "*Silencing the Past* ou faire taire le passé dans la fiction: Un compte-rendu de thèse." *Journal of Haitian Studies* 19, no. 2: 127–50.

Dubois, Laurent. 2012. "Eloge pour Michel-Rolph Trouillot." *Transition* 109: 20–32.

Espinosa Arango, Monica L. 2008. "¿Cómo escribir una historia de la imposible? Michel-Rolph Trouillot y la interpretación de la Revolución Haitiana." *Memorias: Revista digital de historia y arquelogia desde el Caribe* 4, no. 8: 30–40.

Fatton, Robert. 2013. "Michel-Rolph Trouillot's *State against Nation*: A Critique of the Total Paradigm." *Small Axe: A Caribbean Journal of Criticism* 17, no. 3 (42): 203–12.

Fernando, Mayanthi L. 2014. "Ethnography and the Politics of Silence." *Cultural Dynamics* 26, no. 2: 235–44.

Hazard, Ethel. 2013. "Alterity and History: The Cross-Current Contributions of the Work of Michel-Rolph Trouillot." *Journal of Haitian Studies* 19, no. 2: 33–46.

Khan, Aisha. 2014a. "No Gates on the Frontier." *Cultural Dynamics* 26, no. 2: 131–35.

Khan, Aisha, ed. 2014b. "The Life and Work of Michel-Rolph Trouillot: An Interdisciplinary Homage." Special issue, *Cultural Dynamics* 26, no. 2.

Lambert, Laurie R. 2014. "The Sovereignty of the Imagination: Poetic Authority and the Fiction of North Atlantic Universals in Dionne Brand's *Chronicles of the Hostile Sun*." *Cultural Dynamics* 26, no. 2: 173–94.

Ménard, Guy-Gérald. 2013. "Tanbou Libète: Yon Eksperyans kiltirèl patriyotik." *Journal of Haitian Studies* 19, no. 2: 160–64.

Ménard, Nadève. 2013. "Adieu, Gérard." *Journal of Haitian Studies* 19, no. 2: 6–9.

Neptune, Harvey R. 2014. "Savaging Civilization: Michel-Rolph Trouillot and the Anthropology of the West." *Cultural Dynamics* 26, no. 2: 219–34.

Palmié, Stephan. 2013. "The Trouble with History." *Small Axe: A Caribbean Journal of Criticism* 17, no. 3 (42): 193–202.

Past, Mariana. 2004. "Toussaint on Trial in *Ti difé boulé sou istoua Ayiti*, or the People's Role in the Haitian Revolution." *Journal of Haitian Studies* 10, no. 1: 87–102.

Past, Mariana, and Benjamin Hebblethwaite. 2014. "*Ti difé boulé sou istoua Ayiti*: Considering the Stakes of Trouillot's Earliest Work." *Cultural Dynamics* 26, no. 2: 149–61.

Pierre, Jemima. 2013. "Haiti and the 'Savage Slot.'" *Journal of Haitian Studies* 19, no. 2: 110–16.

Pierre, Nathalie. 2014. "*Ti difé boulé sou istoua Ayiti* as Haitian Civic Education." *Cultural Dynamics* 26, no. 2: 209–17.

Price, Richard. 2013. "Michel-Rolph Trouillot (1949–2012)." *American Anthropologist* 115, no. 4: 717–20.

Quesada, Sarah. 2013. "Los ideales políticos-sociales de Michel-Rolph Trouillot y sus aportes crítico-históricos a la literatura." *Journal of Haitian Studies* 19, no. 2: 117–26.

Scott, David. 2012. "The Futures of Michel-Rolph Trouillot: In Memoriam." *Small Axe: A Caribbean Journal of Criticism* 16, no. 3 (39): vii–x.

Sepinwall, Alyssa Goldstein. 2013. "Still Unthinkable? The Haitian Revolution and the Reception of Michel-Rolph Trouillot's *Silencing the Past*." *Journal of Haitian Studies* 19, no. 2: 75–103.

Smith, Katherine. 2014. "Haiti, an Urban Nation? Revisiting Michel-Rolph Trouillot's *Haiti: State against Nation*." *Cultural Dynamics* 26, no. 2: 195–208.

Woodson, Drexel. 2008. "Trouillot, Michel-Rolph." In *The International Encyclopedia of Social Sciences*, edited by William A. Darity, 457–58. Detroit, MI: Macmillan Reference.

Woodson, Drexel G., and Brackette F. Williams. 2013. "Memoriam Dr. Michel-Rolph Trouillot (1949–2012)." *Caribbean Studies* 40, no. 1: 153–62.

principles, 90–91, 178, 323, 388; and utopias, 61–62

ethnic studies, 14, 228, 344–45

ethnography: autocritique/textual turn, 17, 80n15–16, 80n18; comparative, 9, 161; definitions of, 269n9–10; of diasporas, 250, 252–53, 269–70n15; "ethnographic authority," 74; "ethnographic trilogy," 29, 243, 250, 355; and historicizing, 23, 163, 177–78; as metaphor, 65, 73–77; multisited, 7, 250–51; and native voice, 33, 254–65; paraethnography, 59–62; "realist ethnography," 60, 75, 271n23; of the state, 252, 298, 300–301, 309–12, 313n1. *See also* anthropology; mediation; fieldwork; "Savage slot"

fact creation vs. fact assembling, 117n3

feminism, 73, 76, 80n16, 81n21, 170, 236, 315n18

Fénelon, François, 61

Fernando, Mayanthi L., 11, 35, 38, 42n16, 42n21–22

Fick, Carolyn, 334

fieldwork: changing access to, 77n2; critiques of, 29, 36, 245–68; different national approaches to, 181, 248, 355; fetishization of, 247–49, 355; and gender, 269n14; and language, 36, 180; and notion of cultures as isolated wholes, 167, 171, 247, 252, 355; reduction of ethnography to, 245–49; tension between public sphere and guild practices, 269n14. *See also* anthropology; ethnography; mediation

Firmin, Anténor, 90

Foucault, Michel, 81, 235, 237, 268n2, 341, 344

Fouchard, Jean, 152, 336n15

Fouché, Franck, 135, 141n20

1492, 59, 66–68, 103–106, 116, 117n2, 122n34, 161, 345

Franklin, James, 89

Geertz, Clifford, 9, 19, 35, 57, 166, 254, 256–59, 262, 265

Geggus, David, 334, 336n15–16

gender: and anthropology, 34, 73, 80n20, 236, 269n14, 370; and Caribbean studies, 92, 152, 167–71; Women in the Caribbean project, 179–80. *See also* matrifocality

Genovese, Eugene, 333

Ghani, Ashraf, 77, 78n8

Glissant, Édouard, 41n11, 41n14, 167, 181, 194, 200, 202, 210, 221; on West as project not place, 68, 144

global studies, 237; promises of, 344, 346; as replacement for area studies, 49–51; weaknesses of, 51–52

globalitarism, 309, 314n11, 345

globalization, 215–31; and anthropology, 9, 17, 296–316, 367; and area studies, 49–52; and essentialism, 226; and fragmented globality, 306, 345; how Caribbean societies trouble theories of, 8, 25, 27, 345; and North Atlantic Universals, 157n1; and silencing, 219, 230n1, 302, 400; and spatiality of capital, 145–46, 217–18, 302–304; and temporality, 219; wonder as response to, 222, 226–27. *See also* desire (global production of); silences

Gramsci, Antonio, 35, 171–72, 270n20, 300–301, 313n3, 314n11

Granada (importance of surrender of), 66, 103–5, 117n2. *See* Christendom

Grass, Günter, 393

Greene, Jack, 342

Guadeloupe, 38, 42n22, 93, 180, 210n1, 286

Guyana, 165, 170–71, 176, 178, 180, 287, 325

Habermas, Jürgen, 384n6, 392

Haiti: 1915–34 US occupation of, 5, 91, 93, 201; anti-Communist law of 1969, 91; and democracy, 22, 261, 406–19; as departure point for theorizing the West, 21; Griot school, 91, 94n4; Haitian diaspora, 2–5, 7, 15, 134, 341; Haitian exceptionalism, 20, 85–95, 180; Haitian Revolution, 5, 87, 90, 129, 140n7, 211n14, 319–36, 341; Haitian Revolution as unthinkable history, 20, 31, 38, 319–36. *See also* Duvalier, François; Duvalierism; Krèyol; peasantry; Saint-Domingue; silences; *Ti dife boule sou istwa Ayiti*

Haitian studies, 85–95, 166; need for comparative framework, 91–94

Harris, Marvin, 109, 119n14, 351

Harrison, Faye V., 33, 42n18, 170, 179–80

Hartog, François, 153

Harvey, David, 49, 57, 78n4, 199, 218–19, 229

Hedley, Max, 282, 291n4

Hegel, Georg, 148, 341

Heinl, Robert, and Nancy Heinl, 85, 88–89, 94n1

Here/Elsewhere dichotomy, 22, 59, 61, 79n12, 144, 147–48, 150, 244, 251, 308; in relation to utopias, 63, 68–70. *See* historicity; "Savage slot"; utopias

Herodotus, 78n9, 153

Herskovits, Melville J., 41n13, 79, 93, 94n4, 166, 173–74, 178, 369n4, 370n7

These original essays were edited for typographical and stylistic errors and updated for orthography and stylistic naming conventions.

PRELUDE: "Remembering the Songwriter: The Life and Legacies of Michel-Rolph Trouillot," by Yarimar Bonilla, first appeared in *Cultural Dynamics* 26, no. 2 (2014): 163–72. © 2014, Yarimar Bonilla. Republished by permission. DOI: 10.1177/0921374014526021.

INTERLUDE 1: "Between the Cracks," first appeared in *Crosscurrents in Culture, Power and History: A Newsletter of the Institute for Global Studies in Culture, Power, and History* (Johns Hopkins University) 4, no. 2 (1997).

CHAPTER 1: "Anthropology and the Savage Slot: The Poetics and Politics of Otherness," first appeared in *Recapturing Anthropology: Working in the Present*, edited by Richard G. Fox, 17–44 (Santa Fe, NM: School for Advanced Research Press, 1991). © 1991, School for Advanced Research, Santa Fe, New Mexico. All rights reserved. Republished by permission.

CHAPTER 2: "The Odd and the Ordinary: Haiti, the Caribbean, and the World," first appeared in *Cimarrón: New Perspectives on the Caribbean* 2, no. 3 (1990): 3–12.

CHAPTER 3: "The Vulgarity of Power," first appeared in *Public Culture* 5, no. 1 (1992): 75–81. © 1992, Duke University Press (by assignment).

CHAPTER 4: "Good Day, Columbus: Silences, Power, and Public History (1492–1892)," first appeared in *Public Culture* 3, no. 1 (1990): 1–24. © 1990, Duke University Press (by assignment).

INTERLUDE 2: This interview was transcribed and translated from the following source: "Michel-Rolph Trouillot sou *Ti difé boulé sou istoua Ayiti*. Entèvyou Richard Brisson," Radio Haiti Collection, David M. Rubenstein Rare Book and Manuscript Library, Duke University, https://repository.duke.edu/dc/radiohaiti/RL10059-RR-0094_02 and https://repository.duke.edu/dc/radiohaiti/RL10059-RR-0094_01.

CHAPTER 5: "The Otherwise Modern: Caribbean Lessons from the Savage Slot," first appeared in *Critically Modern: Alternatives, Alterities, Anthropologies*, edited by Bruce Knauft, 220–37 (Bloomington: Indiana University Press, 2002). © 2002, Indiana University Press, Bloomington. Reprinted with permission of Indiana University Press.

CHAPTER 6: "The Caribbean Region: An Open Frontier in Anthropological Theory," first appeared in *Annual Review of Anthropology* 21 (1992): 19–42. © 1992, Annual Reviews, Inc. Republished by permission.

CHAPTER 7: "Culture on the Edges: Creolization in the Plantation Context," reprinted in *From the Margins: Historical Anthropology and Its Futures*, edited by Brian Keith Axel, 189–210 (Durham, NC: Duke University Press, 2002). © 2002, Duke University Press (by assignment).

CHAPTER 8: "The Perspective of the World: Globalization Then and Now," first appeared in *Beyond Dichotomies: Histories, Identities, Cultures, and the Challenge of Globalization*, edited by Elisabeth Mudimbe-Boyi, 3–20 (Albany: State University of New York Press, 2002). © 2002, State University of New York Press. Republished by permission.

INTERLUDE 3: "Discipline and Perish," first appeared in *Crosscurrents in Culture, Power and History: A Newsletter of the Institute for Global Studies in Culture, Power, and History* (Johns Hopkins University) 1, no. 2 (1994).

CHAPTER 9: "Making Sense: The Fields in Which We Work," first appeared as chapter 6 of *Global Transformations: Anthropology and the Modern World*, 117–39 (New York: Palgrave Macmillan, 2003). © 2003, Palgrave Macmillan. Republished by permission.

CHAPTER 10: "Caribbean Peasantries and World Capitalism: An Approach to Micro-level Studies," first appeared in *Nieuwe West-Indische Gids/New West Indian Guide* 58, nos. 1–2 (1984): 37–59. © 1984, Brill Academic Publishers. Reprinted by permission.

CHAPTER 11: "The Anthropology of the State in the Age of Globalization: Close Encounters of the Deceptive Kind," first appeared in *Current Anthropology* 42, no. 1 (2001): 125–38. © 2001, University of Chicago Press. Republished by permission.

CHAPTER 12: "From Planters' Journals to Academia: The Haitian Revolution as Unthinkable History," first appeared in *Journal of Caribbean History* 25, nos. 1–2 (1991): 81–99. © 1991, The University of the West Indies Press, www.uwipress.com. Reproduced and distributed by permission.

INTERLUDE 4: "Theorizing a Global Perspective: A Conversation with Michel-Rolph Trouillot," first appeared in *Crosscurrents in Culture, Power and History: A Newsletter of the Institute for Global Studies in Culture, Power, and History* (Johns Hopkins University) 4, no.1 (1996)

CHAPTER 13: "Adieu, Culture: A New Duty Arises," first appeared in *Anthropology beyond Culture*, edited by Richard G. Fox and Barbara J. King (Westport, CT: Bergin and Garvey, 2002), 37–60. Wenner-Gren International Symposium Series. Oxford: Berg Publishers, an imprint of Bloomsbury Publishing Plc. © 2002 Richard G. Fox and Barbara J. King.

CHAPTER 14: "The Presence in the Past," first appeared as chapter 5 of *Silencing the Past: Power and the Production of History*, 141–53 (Boston: Beacon, 1995). © 1995, Beacon Press. Republished by permission.

CHAPTER 15: "Abortive Rituals: Historical Apologies in the Global Era," first appeared in *Interventions: International Journal of Postcolonial Studies* 2, no. 2 (2000): 171–86. © 2000, Taylor and Francis. Republished by permission.

CHAPTER 16: "The Interrupted March to Democracy," first appeared as chapter 8 of *Haiti: State against Nation; The Origins and Legacy of Duvalierism*, 217–30 (New York: Monthly Review Press, 1990). © 1990, Monthly Review Press. Republished by permission.

COMPREHENSIVE BIBLIOGRAPHY: Yarimar Bonilla, "Michel-Rolph Trouillot: A Comprehensive Bibliography," *Small Axe* 17, no. 3 (2013): 213–22.

www.ingramcontent.com/pod-product-compliance
Lightning Source LLC
Chambersburg PA
CBHW050329270326
41926CB00016B/3367